Implicit Contract Theory

The International Library of Critical Writings in Economics

Series Editor: Mark Blaug

Professor Emeritus, University of London
Professor Emeritus, University of Buckingham
Visiting Professor, University of Exeter

This series is an essential reference source for students, researchers and lecturers in economics. It presents by theme an authoritative selection of the most important articles across the entire spectrum of economics. Each volume has been prepared by a leading specialist who has written an authoritative introduction to the literature included.

A full list of published and future titles in this series is printed at the end of this volume.

Implicit Contract Theory

Edited by

Sherwin Rosen

Edwin A. and Betty L. Bergman Professor
Department of Economics
University of Chicago, US

An Elgar Reference Collection

© Sherwin Rosen 1994. For copyright of individual articles please refer to the Acknowledgements.

Published by
Edward Elgar Publishing Limited
Gower House
Croft Road
Aldershot
Hants GU11 3HR
England

Edward Elgar Publishing Company
Old Post Road
Brookfield
Vermont 05036
USA

British Library Cataloguing in Publication Data
Implicit Contract Theory. –
(International Library of Critical
Writings in Economics; No. 35)
I. Rosen, Sherwin II. Series
331.2

Library of Congress Cataloguing in Publication Data
Implicit contract theory / edited by Sherwin Rosen.
    p. cm. — (The International library of critical writings in
economics; 35)
1. Labor market. 2. Labor contract. 3. Unemployment. I. Rosen.
Sherwin. II. Series.
HD5707.I49 1994
331.1—dc20   93–39146
                                                                                            CIP

ISBN 1 85278 748 1

Printed in Great Britain by Galliard (Printers) Ltd, Great Yarmouth

Contents

Acknowledgements

The editor and publishers wish to thank the following who have kindly given permission for the use of copyright material.

American Economic Association for articles: Martin Feldstein (1978), 'The Effect of Unemployment Insurance on Temporary Layoff Unemployment', *American Economic Review*, **LXVIII** (5), December, 834–46; Ian M. McDonald and Robert M. Solow (1981), 'Wage Bargaining and Employment', *American Economic Review*, **71** (5), December, 896–908; Robert E. Hall (1982), 'The Importance of Lifetime Jobs in the U.S. Economy', *American Economic Review*, **72** (4), September, 716–24; Robert H. Topel (1983), 'On Layoffs and Unemployment Insurance', *American Economic Review*, **73** (4), September, 541–59; Carl Shapiro and Joseph E. Stiglitz (1984), 'Equilibrium Unemployment as a Worker Discipline Device', *American Economic Review*, **74** (3), June, 433–44; Sherwin Rosen (1985), 'Implicit Contracts: A Survey', *Journal of Economic Literature*, **XXIII** (3), September, 1144–75; Dennis W. Carlton (1986), 'The Rigidity of Prices', *American Economic Review*, **76** (4), September, 637–58; Assar Lindbeck and Dennis J. Snower (1988), 'Cooperation, Harassment, and Involuntary Unemployment: An Insider–Outsider Approach', *American Economic Review*, **78** (1), March, 167–88.

Basil Blackwell Ltd. for article: Robert J. Gordon (1982), 'Why U.S. Wage and Employment Behaviour Differs from that in Britain and Japan', *Economic Journal*, **92** (365), March, 13–44.

Brookings Institution for article: Martin S. Feldstein (1975), 'The Importance of Temporary Layoffs: An Empirical Analysis', *Brookings Papers on Economic Activity*, **3**, 725–45.

Elsevier Science Publishers B.V. for articles: David M. Lilien (1980), 'The Cyclical Pattern of Temporary Layoffs in United States Manufacturing', *Review of Economics and Statistics*, **LXII** (1), February, 24–31; Gary D. Hansen (1985), 'Indivisible Labor and the Business Cycle', *Journal of Monetary Economics*, **16** (3), November, 309–27; Richard Rogerson (1988), 'Indivisible Labor, Lotteries and Equilibrium', *Journal of Monetary Economics*, **21** (1), January, 3–16.

M.I.T. Press Journals for articles: V.V. Chari (1983), 'Involuntary Unemployment and Implicit Contracts', *Quarterly Journal of Economics*, **XCVIII** (3), Supplement, 107–22; Sanford J. Grossman and Oliver D. Hart (1983), 'Implicit Contracts under Asymmetric Information', *Quarterly Journal of Economics*, **XCVIII** (3), Supplement, 123–56; Jerry Green and Charles M. Kahn (1983), 'Wage–Employment Contracts', *Quarterly Journal of Economics*, **XCVIII** (3), Supplement, 173–87; Clive Bull (1987), 'The Existence of Self-Enforcing Implicit Contracts', *Quarterly Journal of Economics*, **CII** (1), February, 147–59.

Review of Economic Studies Ltd. for articles: Martin Neil Baily (1974), 'Wages and Employment under Uncertain Demand', *Review of Economic Studies*, **XLI** (1), January, 37–50; George A. Akerlof and Hajime Miyazaki (1980), 'The Implicit Contract Theory of Unemployment Meets the Wage Bill Argument', *Review of Economic Studies*, **XLVII** (2), January, 321–38; Oliver D. Hart (1983), 'Optimal Labour Contracts under Asymmetric Information: An Introduction', *Review of Economic Studies*, **L** (1), January, 3–35.

University of Chicago Press for articles: Costas Azariadis (1975), 'Implicit Contracts and Underemployment Equilibria', *Journal of Political Economy*, **83** (6), December, 1183–1202; Tomio Kinoshita (1987), 'Working Hours and Hedonic Wages in the Market Equilibrium', *Journal of Political Economy*, **95** (6), December, 1262–77.

Western Economic Association International for article: Donald F. Gordon (1974), 'A Neo-Classical Theory of Keynesian Unemployment', *Economic Inquiry*, **XII** (4), December, 431–59.

Every effort has been made to trace all the copyright holders but if any have been inadvertently overlooked the publishers will be pleased to make the necessary arrangement at the first opportunity.

In addition the publishers wish to thank the Library of the London School of Economics and Political Science and the Marshall Library of Economics, Cambridge University for their assistance in obtaining these articles.

Introduction

The theory of implicit contracts originated as part of the general development of the economics of information and contracts during the past 20 years. Its intellectual interest concerns the workings of the macro-labour market over business cycles. How can the unemployment levels and employment fluctuations that are observed during recessions be explained in terms of rational economic behaviour? Why don't wages fall to clear the market? The facts are well documented and hardly in dispute. They pose a problem for the logic of economic theory that has proven remarkably resistant to solution over the years.

The problem was first discussed by Keynes in *The General Theory*, but he finessed it by assuming nominal wage rigidity to focus on other matters. Intensive empirical studies also begun in the 1930s and continuing to the present day show that real wages do not exhibit systematic procyclical variation. In fact systematic cyclical wage patterns of any kind are difficult to discern in the data. At the microeconomic level, recessions are associated with layoffs and temporary plant closures. Most workers are unilaterally laid off by firms and are not given the opportunity to bargain instead for lower wages or shorter working hours. Furthermore, those who remain employed are largely unaffected by the state of the general labour market. For example, in England during the Great Depression, unemployment rates soared to a quarter of the labour force, yet those people who managed to remain employed worked 50 hours per week or more. Weekly working hours per worker are far shorter today, but still vary remarkably little over the business cycle.

In economics we usually expect similarly endowed agents to behave similarly. Market competition makes it so. For if one agent fares much differently than another, entry or exit will tend to equalize outcomes. Unemployment and layoffs seem to be exceptions to this rule. Here outcomes among measurably similar individuals can be sharply different, and the unemployed are not in a position to haggle over price. In fact often they do not have the opportunity to offer their employment services to many firms, who simply close their hiring windows during recessions.

The analogy of labour markets to an organized market exchange or bourse breaks down for these reasons. Does this mean that the laws of economics do not apply to labour markets, that wage and employment prospects do not influence entry into and exit from various occupations and industries, or that labour resources do not tend to flow to their highest valued uses? Of course not! What it does require is a nontrivial extension of the simple demand and supply framework to incorporate the *frictions* manifest in labour markets at business cycle frequencies. The theory of implicit contracts represents one interesting assault on these questions.

Needless to say, the practice of macroeconomics could hardly wait for an acceptable microeconomic solution to these logical difficulties. For years most macroeconomic economists implicitly adopted Keynes's assumption of wage rigidity and went about other business. However, in the 1960s, economists began to think seriously about what conceivable economic functions might be served by the unemployment of resources, and, if any could be found, what type of behaviour might be provoked by it. The newly emerging economics of information pointed directly toward the possible productive role of job search. The transactions costless bourse paradigm vanishes because job assignments cannot be delegated through a centralized, impersonal labour market exchange when transactions must be evaluated one at a time. The theory of equalizing differences explains why this is so. The net advantages of both wages and working conditions matter to workers and firms, not wages alone, because the worker has to deliver his own labour services and cannot disassociate himself with conditions at the work site. The more modern idea of firm- or relationship-specific human capital investments, also developed in the 1960s, reinforced these earlier thoughts, because firms would also care strongly about what kind of worker they hired under these circumstances.

The main point is that the efficient allocation of labour has many elements in common with a marriage problem. Workers and firms are optimally assigned to each other depending on their joint attributes and characteristics. In a world with imperfect information, these matches take time to find and must be actively sought out by all concerned. Periods of unemployment can be productive through the search process. Certainly no-one would argue that mass un-employment of the 1930s or the more normal unemployment associated with typical recessions is itself productive in this way (quite the contrary, since much investment in past search activities is irrevocably lost). These ideas on the costs and benefits of unemployment and search led to a more thorough-going economic analysis of the problem, and allowed economists to think about what had been previously unthinkable: what were the costs and *benefits* of unemployment? The paper by Donald F. Gordon, who is generally acknowledged, along with Martin N. Baily and Costas Azariadis, as one of the founders of implicit contract theory, is an early classic statement of basic ideas that is hard to improve upon.

Parallel empirical work made this line of thought worth pursuing. Martin Feldstein discovered that a very large fraction of layoffs in the US economy were temporary, and that many of these workers ultimately were recalled back to work by their previous firms. This finding was confirmed in an important paper by Lilien, also reprinted here, and by many others since then. With proper qualification for bankruptcy, it is widely accepted today as an important component of labour market dynamics in recessions. Extensive research in the 1970s and 1980s found that most job turnover occurs early in a worker's lifetime as a natural part of the search and matching process. Once a proper match has been found, it lasts for remarkably long periods of time, as shown by Hall on the importance of 'lifetime' jobs. These enduring relationships between workers and firms strengthened the empirical basis for modelling the theoretical contracting problem by Baily and by Azariadis.

The theory of implicit contracts is built upon the idea that long-term employment relationships break the linkages between current wage payments and current employment decisions. Longer term considerations are also at work. The search and firm-specific human capital investment activities associated with a successful job match make employment relationships similar to certain kinds of partnership contracts. The relation-specific bond of worker and firm lends credence to the analogy between employment and partnership contacts. Just as partners jointly contribute to the fortunes of the enterprise and share in its risks and rewards, earnings represent annual installment payments on accrued shared investments.

Labour contracts are said to be 'implicit' in the 'as if' sense commonly used by economists, because employment and partnership law are distinctly different in most countries. But if mutual employment obligations are analysed as if they were formal contracts, the theory would have no empirical content unless all agents agree to live by its implicit terms. It is one thing to agree to a contract with all its hypothetical contingencies *ex ante*. It is quite another matter also to agree with its conditions *ex post*, when the actual facts are on the table. Agreements that work both *ex ante* and *ex post* are said to be self-enforcing, and the paper by Clive Bull is one of the earliest and best treatments of the problem in this particular context.

Implicit contract theory basically augments the usual employment relation to include mutual insurance provisions between workers and their firms. It adds a kind of private unemployment insurance to the normal supply and demand problem. Viewed as an equalizing difference, unemployment risk requires that workers be paid more during periods when they are working, to allow them to accumulate funds necessary to sustain their consumption in slack periods when work is unavailable. Though widely recognized over the years, this Smithian idea seemed inapplicable to unemployment generated by business cycles. Kinoshita's paper shows that the theoretical apparatus needed to accommodate work scheduling and, by implication, risk shifting is rather different and more complicated (and interesting!) than is commonly recognized.

Implicit contract theory poses a plausible, operational mechanism for meaningful application by combining the logic of risk-compensation with modern notions of insurance and contracts. Observed wage and employment behaviour are seen as having both labour supply and insurance components. Gains from trade on the insurance margin arise because the principal source of wealth of workers is their own nondiversifiable human capital. Employers, are, in part, specialists in risk-bearing and can diversify risks more efficiently through the stock market and other asset markets. Some aspects of the apparent inconsistencies in the data may be explained when these insurance/savings components are added to the more conventional microeconomic analysis. The formal insurance analogy is strong and explicit in Baily's paper. Azariadis couches the analysis in more formal contract theory terms and paraphenalia.

The empirical relevance of these ideas is expressed in Robert J. Gordon's investigation of differences in wage and employment variability among three countries. Wage and hours variability are largest in Japan, but employment variability is smallest there. Wage variability is smallest, but employment variation is largest in the USA. The UK falls somewhere in between the other two. It is well known that worker turnover is lowest in Japan and highest in the USA, so the wage, hours and employment variation rankings suggest that greater employment security is linked to greater wage variability when the joint attachment of workers and firms is larger, as it is in Japan.

Dennis Carlton extends the investigation to price variability observed in goods markets, carefully documenting substantial differences among industries in the frequency and extent to which transactions prices of products change over time. This is also related to the common observation that variability in 'spot' market prices is greater than that in contract markets. Even for such homogeneous goods as metals and coal, where organized markets coexist with long-term, continuing forward contracts, buyer–seller understandings tend to smoothe transactions prices for many goods in the economy at large and to ration them in ways other than by pure price allocations.

Development of this theory was propelled by complementary economic analysis of public unemployment insurance systems. In a series of important papers, of which one is reprinted here, Martin Feldstein suggested that the financial structure of the USA unemployment insurance system created socially excessive unemployment. In a sense these studies and related work by others were among the first broad scale empirical studies of agency problems in economics. The distortion in the US system arises because insurance premiums paid by firms are not actuarially based on the risk exposure they impose on insurance system reserves. The problem is compounded by the fact that these firms, at least in part, control their layoff decisions and can shift part of their insurance costs to the public at large.

The American system is experience rated on each firm's prior unemployment layoff record after a certain point. However, unit tax rates rise with experience only up to a maximum limit. This implies that firms in highly cyclical industries, such as durable goods or construction, paying the limiting tax rate do not face the true social costs of their layoff decisions. At the margin they impose more costs on the system at large then they pay themselves. Low risk firms are in the opposite circumstances. These implicit subsidies of layoffs among high risk firms and implicit taxes for low risk firms cause excessive unemployment.

Robert Topel's empirical investigation provides convincing evidence that greater experience rating reduces the layoff rate for any given demand shock. The measured effect is quite large. Yet the US system is virtually the only one in the world that is experience rated to any extent. In most countries unemployment insurance is linked directly to the welfare system. Firms' costs are unrelated to experience, so they do not see *any* of the social costs of their actions. Why these schemes have been financed in such socially inefficient ways is a mystery of Political Economy that remains to be solved.

The theory of implicit contracts generated much academic interest in the 1970s and early 1980s because it provided an economic approach to an important problem that previously had defied rational analysis for years. However, flies inevitably appeared in the ointment. An implicit contract that acted as optimal private insurance would specify indemnity payments to workers in the laid-off (unemployed) state as well as in the employed state. The insurance payment follows from the optimizing condition that the marginal utility of income is constant across all possible realizations in the efficient contract. If, as most economists think is true, the marginal utility of consumption depends on leisure, it can be shown in a large class of cases that full contract workers are at least as well off when laid off as when they are employed. In other words, their unemployment could not be 'involuntary'.

Akerlof and Miyazaki were among the first to express this point. In the article reprinted here, they showed that Azariadis's principal result followed from his failure to allow indemnity payments in the adverse state. Had he done so, workers' welfare would be independent of state and business cycle employment risks would be completely insured. Some market failure in the provision of full insurance, still yet to be fully identified and analysed, is necessary for these models to produce involuntary unemployment. In spite of this theoretical problem, a more important question not yet fully resolved is the extent to which these models empirically can account for observed wage, employment and hours variations at business cycle frequencies.

A highly original extension of the contract apparatus appears in the papers by Gary Hansen and Richard Rogerson. They lay out an interesting economic rationale for layoffs. Employment decisions of firms having all-or-nothing elements due to fixed costs and indivisibilities creates nonconvexities that cannot be efficiently priced in the usual manner. Instead, randomization of layoffs among employees is required to convexify the firm's problem. Drawing layoffs by lot improves overall welfare in these circumstances. This analysis gives a neat economic interpretation of why identical agents in similar circumstances can be observed in much different employment status outcomes, which is one of the fundamental questions that motivated interest in the subject in the first place. Still, this work does not resolve the incomplete contracting problem. Even with random layoffs complete contracts would guarantee full insurance and no involuntary unemployment *ex post*.

Only one serious line of attack on contractual incompleteness has been vigorously pursued so far. It concerns incomplete (private) information. Firms are assumed to know the state of demand for their product, but their employees do not know it. In the general case, workers know the opportunity costs of layoff status and firms do not. The contract is necessarily incomplete. It must be specified in terms of observable actions of all parties, not in terms of the proximate causes of these actions, because agents have strong private incentives to misrepresent what they know to each other. Three papers on this topic are reprinted here. Grossman and Hart's article is probably the most complete and general mathematical treatment. The papers by V.V. Chari and by Jerry Green and Charles Kahn emphasize the contractual issues in somewhat less general, but simpler terms.

Contracts cannot be efficient when there is private information. A single instrument, the wage conditional on work status, is called upon to perform too many allocative functions. On the one hand wages must be smoothed to provide insurance and allow workers to maintain consumption in all states of the world. On the other hand, if wages are assured, workers have no incentive to work unless commanded to do so by the firm, and firms don't have proper *ex post* incentives to request efficient effort. Insurance must be incomplete to provide the necessary motivation to work in an incomplete contract.

The main theoretical question addressed to date is whether or not this compromise results in socially excessive unemployment. The conclusions are interesting and unexpected. Employment is found to be *excessive* if leisure and consumption are direct complements in workers' utility functions. Loosely speaking, the reason is as follows. Complementarity between leisure and consumption implies over-insurance of layoffs: it is efficient for workers to consume more when laid off than when employed because the marginal utility of consumption is larger when the person is not working. However, this is impossible in a private information equilibrium because no-one could care to work. Therefore the private information contract must underinsure consumption during layoffs and this promotes socially excessive work. The argument is reversed if consumption and leisure are direct substitutes instead of complements. Then private information contracts result in socially excessive layoffs. Labour economists believe that complementarity is the rule in standard labour supply problems. However, the evidence in this particular context, when household production can substitute for market goods when a person is laid-off, is not so clear nor straightforward.

The work on private information has taken implicit contract theory to its current theoretical limits. Many of its details are summarized, criticized and linked to classical labour supply and demand analysis in the papers by Oliver Hart and by myself. The fact that incomplete contracts produce involuntary unemployment, but socially excessive employment (under complementarity) has been taken as an unfortunate implication that limits its applicability for business cycle analysis. In addition, Hart shows that possible enforcement problems (in the sense discussed by Bull) arise in private information contracts: there are incentives *ex post* to renege on the *ex ante* contract terms once the private information is revealed by realizations and behaviour. Still, the empirical implications of wage, employment and hours variability have not been fully worked out and tested, and probably deserve a fairer hearing.

In the meantime work in this general area has moved in several different directions. Some very influential papers are reprinted in the final section. The one by Ian MacDonald and

Robert Solow stimulated a revival of interest in whether union-firm bargains are efficient in the sense of the bargaining-theory contract curve. An extensive empirical literature has emerged to investigate the question. This work assumes the existence of collective union preferences over wages and employment, and places (implicit) constraints on side payments among individual workers that are fully equivalent logically to the incomplete contract difficulty of implicit contracts.

There is also an extensive literature on efficiency wages, nicely exposited in the paper by Carl Shapiro and Joseph Stiglitz. This construct is also based on limitations of writing complete contracts due to private information. Again, a single wage has to perform too many functions to achieve full economic efficiency. In the version reprinted here, high wages and the threat of dismissal are needed to deter workers from shirking. Wages must be higher than opportunity costs to provide them a carrot for good behaviour and the threat of unemployment if shirking is detected provides the necessary stick in a market equilibrium. Like the others, this model also imposes arbitrary restrictions on contractual completeness. It does not allow up-front (bond) arrangements to operate and they would clear these markets without unemployment. Many economists feel that applying these ideas to business cycle unemployment is a bit of a stretch, but efficiency wage theory has strong and influential adherents and a lively and controversial empirical literature and debate has developed.

The paper by Assar Lindbeck and Dennis Snower is a highly original recent development that introduces elements of club theory and unusual forms of price and quantity discrimination into short-run employment and layoff decisions. Here the club members or 'insiders' are the existing workers. The 'outsiders' are the newcomers trying to get in. Insiders impose various barriers on outsiders to increase their own welfare at the expense of others. This is an interesting area of current research and its full implications are in the process of being worked out. However, it also imposes some arbitrary limitations on the completeness of contracts in not allowing all gains from trade between insiders and outsiders to be realized.

In conclusion, all current theories require unmodelled elements of contractual incompleteness to avoid unattractive empirical and theoretical implications. Surely incompleteness must be a necessary ingredient in understanding the costs and welfare losses of business cycle layoffs. Yet there is no professional consensus on how this might best be accomplished. Consequently matters of style, professional taste and aesthetics now play too large a role in choosing among alternative formulations, and these differences of opinion are irresolvable on reasonable scientific criteria. Contract theory has taken the original problem several steps further than it started with, but there is still a fairly long way to go. Further progress will be hastened by a fundamental breakthrough in our economic understanding of why some of these markets fail, but that is not obviously on the near horizon.

Part I
Basic Ideas

[1]

Implicit Contracts and Underemployment Equilibria

Costas Azariadis

Brown University

This paper studies an industry with demand uncertainty which prompts risk-neutral firms to act both as employers and as insurers of homogeneous, risk-averse laborers. The resulting contractual arrangements turn out, in their simplest form, to be more likely to specify full employment the more of the following conditions prevail: small variability in product price, above-average economy-wide labor demand, highly risk-averse workers, small unemployment compensation, and highly competitive product market. Otherwise, it may be optimal for firms to lay off, by random choice, part of the work force during low states of demand.

I. Introduction

Competitive wage theory predicts that firms will adjust to a contraction in product demand by lowering both employment and the real wage rate, in contradiction to the normal industrial practice of laying off unneeded workers and paying unchanged wages to the rest of the work force. This paradox,[1] which arises from the close relationship between competitive equilibria and Pareto optima in auction markets, spawned a

This paper is based on chapter 2 of a doctoral dissertation submitted to the School of Industrial Administration, Carnegie-Mellon University, January 1975. Earlier versions were presented at the European meeting of the Econometric Society, Oslo, August 1973, and at the University of Chicago Money and Banking Workshop, December 1973. I am indebted to Robert E. Lucas and Edward Prescott for innumerable discussions; to Robert Barro, David Cass, Herschel Grossman, John Kennan, Christopher Sims, and an anonymous referee for constructive criticism; and to the U.S. Department of Labor for financial support. All are absolved from any sins of omission or commission.

[1] To quote from Arrow (1972): "One of the mysterious things is why [the employers] do not cut wages. It may be that they really do not know what is going on in terms of the possible need to rehire labor in the future and are worried about the impact of any wage cuts on their ability to proceed in the labor market later."

[*Journal of Political Economy*, 1975, vol. 83, no. 6]

substantial corrective effort by economic theorists. One reaction, exemplified in the writings of Keynes (1936) and of a diverse group of epigones (Patinkin 1956; Clower 1966; Leijonhufvud 1968; Barro and Grossman 1971), has been to abandon short-run market clearing as a workable assumption and focus instead on quantity adjustments as the primary means of response to market disturbances.

A far less systematic, but intuitively more transparent, commentary[2] has appeared periodically in the literature, arguing in effect that deviations from Pareto optimality occur because continuous-auction models cannot do justice to certain attributes peculiar to the labor resource. Chief among these attributes are the limited mobility of the labor resource and the difficulty of diversifying human capital under uncertainty.

The relative immobility of labor over markets, especially those involving different industries or geographical locations, is fairly well documented.[3] However, the obvious fact bears repeating that no markets exist for the direct exchange of claims on future labor services;[4] the costs of monitoring and enforcement, and "moral hazard," are some reasons why such markets have not arisen.[5]

Nevertheless, at least part of the risk an uncertain labor income stream creates for its recipient can be shifted to third parties by employee intermediation, that is, by the tacit or open commitment of the firm to guarantee its personnel that their wage rates, hours worked, employment status, or a combination of all such factors, will be in some degree independent of the vicissitudes of the business cycle.[6] The risk is thereby transferred from wages to profits and, via the capital market, to the income streams of the firm's owners and creditors.

This process is subject to two limitations. First, assurances of the sort just described will not be handed out evenly to all personnel. In breadth and firmness of commitment, employers will discriminate in favor of persons in whose training substantial investment has been or is about to be made. Others who are thought to possess superior qualities of productivity, reliability, adaptability, etc., will be similarly favored. Second, a rational entrepreneur will not shield the terms of employment of even his most valuable group of employees against arbitrary demand fluctuations if doing so involves more than a token probability that the firm might go bankrupt.

Neither qualification should be a hindrance in the short-run, homo-

---

[2] For interesting early specimens, see Knight (1921, chap. 9) and Hicks (1932, chap. 3).

[3] Cf. the evidence in Parker and Burton (1971).

[4] Unions could conceivably serve that function were it not generally the case that incomes of the members of any single union are highly correlated.

[5] This discussion draws heavily on Brainard and Dolbear (1971); see also Tobin (1972) and Gordon (1974).

[6] It is in this sense that Knight (1921, pp. 271–72) characterizes wages as "contractual" income and profits as "residual" income.

UNDEREMPLOYMENT EQUILIBRIA 1185

geneous-labor problem that is studied in this paper; it is sufficient that, in the course of the relationship between employer and employees, enough scope exists for the former to unburden the latter of at least some of the variability that otherwise would accompany wage income. At first approximation, one need not worry whether risk shifting occurs merely because the firm's net worth far exceeds that of its average employee or because it is in the nature of hiring that "the confident and venturesome 'assume the risk' or 'insure' the doubtful and timid by guaranteeing to the latter a specified income in return for an assignment of the actual results" (Knight 1921, pp. 269–70).

The drift of the preceding arguments points to a more complex view of the labor market than is customary in conventional short-run analyses: in uncertainty, labor services are not auctioned off in quite the same way fresh fruit is. Rather, they are exchanged for some implicit set of commitments, hereinafter called an *implicit labor contract*, on the part of the firm to employ the owner of those labor services for a "reasonable" period of time and on terms mutually agreed upon in advance.

In such a market, job choice will depend on what subjective value prospective employees place on alternative contracts, and not on the value of *any one* contract component. After all available contracts have been compared, and before the state of demand in any industry is known, suppliers of labor services will each gravitate toward the highest attainable value. The initial distribution of the labor force thus achieved will be independent of the state of nature; it will also tend to have some permanence, as indicated by the large proportion of rehires in manufacturing accessions.

If contracts, then, are not easily abrogated, employers should possess considerable discretion over specific terms of employment. The possibility arises, for instance, that a job which requires the same technical skills as another will pay a different wage. The freedom to set specific components of contracts at a level above or below what prevails elsewhere is limited by the familiar property of any equilibrium distribution of the labor force over firms: no economic agent values the bargain he/she has actually agreed to less than any other feasible contract.[7]

A systematic study of these issues begins in Section II with a stochastic environment in which risk-neutral entrepreneurs and identical, risk-averse workers with indivisible leisure endowment exchange a particularly simple type of contract. Section III examines the conditions under which the wage schedules of labor contracts will be invariant to changes in relative product price. A necessary and sufficient condition for the suboptimality of full-employment contracts is developed and interpreted in Section IV. A complete characterization of the optimal contract follows

[7] Cf. Stiglitz (1974).

in Section V along with a comparison of its provisions with what would prevail in a labor acution market beset by identical stochastic disturbances. A summary and conclusions appear in Section VI.

II. Uniform Contracts

Suppose that the quantity of a perfectly homogeneous, nonstorable commodity demanded of an industry depends on the prevailing price, p, of the commodity relative to that of all other goods (the fixed, exogenous "price level"), on the state of nature, s, and, possibly, on a vector of nonrandom, nonprice variables over which the industry has no control. For simplicity, assume that the actual state is drawn randomly from a set of discrete states $S = \{s | s = s_1, s_2, \ldots, s_J\}$ according to a known probability distribution $q(s)$, for which

$$\sum_{s \in S} q(s) = 1. \tag{1}$$

The industry consists of a fixed number of identical, perfectly competitive, risk-neutral firms to which changes in s are revealed through shifts in the product price they can charge their customers. Let $p(s)$ be the (parametrically given) mapping of states into prices and, without loss of generality, suppose that, for any s_1, s_2 in S,

$$s_1 < s_2 \Leftrightarrow p(s_1) < p(s_2). \tag{2}$$

On the other side of the labor market there is an even larger number, M, of risk-averse workers who are identical[8] in tastes, endowments, and technical ability and who may or may not have alternatives outside this industry. Assume, for simplicity, that these workers command one indivisible unit of leisure and that their preferences over consumption, c, and leisure, l, are embodied in a monotone, bounded utility function $v(c, l)$, concave in c.[9]

Let the random variable y denote current labor income; the constants α and c_0 denote, respectively, current property income and the maximum level of consumption attainable when $y = 0$ and $l = 1$. That level may exceed α by the amount, if any, of unemployment compensation which accrues to the worker. Without loss of generality, we set

$$v(c_0, 0) = 0 \text{ and } v(c_0, 1) = K \tag{3}$$

---

[8] This assumption serves to keep down the dimensionality of the contract space. For instance, if workers differed systematically in preferences or in their endowment of human or nonhuman wealth, then contracts indexed on all of these characteristics would generally be appropriate.

[9] Observed labor preferences for lumpy leisure streams (long weekends, paid vacations, etc.) raise a strong suspicion that v is not concave in l for high enough values of leisure consumption. The implications for unemployment of preferences locally nonconvex in leisure are examined in Sec. IV.

and define an increasing, concave function $u(\cdot)$ from

$$u(y) \equiv v(\alpha + y, 0). \tag{4}$$

The range of contracts offered by each firm will depend partly on how varied its work force is in skill, attitude toward risk, and the like, and partly on the length and the administrative costs of striking, monitoring, and enforcing each agreement. The most important nonwage component of such agreements is probably "job security," which depends crucially on variations in employment.

Suppose, then, for simplicity, that all freely agreed upon contracts are strictly enforceable, perhaps because "cheaters" suffer a catastrophic loss in reputation; are of the same, institutionally fixed duration; and pay no direct compensation to unemployed workers. Since workers are, by assumption, absolutely identical, a *uniform* contract will likely be offered to all of them. This will be a random vector of the form

$$\delta = \{w(s), n(s)\}, \tag{5}$$

which reveals what wage (relative to the price level) and volume of employment the typical firm plans to offer in each state.

Valuation and Dominance

The valuation of a contractual offer by laborers is clearly contingent on the ultimate size, m, of the firm's work force. The larger the number of people who consent to a given contractual offer before the state of nature is known, the smaller the (equal for all) probability, $\rho(s)$, that any of them will end up employed in state s. In fact,

$$\rho(s) = \min\,[1, n(s)/m]. \tag{5a}$$

Let $V(\delta, m)$ be the expected utility from a contract δ which attracts m workers, where the expectation in V should be taken with respect to both s *and* employment status. Recall that the utility of working in s is $u[w(s)]$ and of not working is K. Hence,

$$V(\delta, m) = E_s[\rho u(w) + (1 - \rho)K]. \tag{5b}$$

From (5a) and (5b) it follows directly, as one might expect of a competitive labor market with mobile laborers of known quality, that all vacancies will be filled.[10] Hence,

$$\rho(s) = n(s)/m \qquad \forall s. \tag{5c}$$

[10] This is a statement about averages. It does not mean to deny that the firm could profitably use more than the contracted amount of labor services in a particularly favorable state of nature but, rather, that it cannot do so on the basis of information available at the time contracts are struck.

The actual value of m corresponding to any contract offer will depend, naturally, on market alternatives. Let $\lambda(K < \lambda)$ be the market valuation attached to such offers under an equilibrium distribution of the labor force. Then the right-hand side of (5b) must equal λ, and m is a function of both λ and the components w and n of the contract.

Some useful nomenclature follows. In *definition* 1, a contract $\delta = \{w(s),\ n(s)\}$ is called (i) *feasible* if $V(\delta,\ m) = \lambda$ for some positive m such that $n(s) \leq m$ for all s; (ii) *full employment* (underemployment) if $n(s) = m$ for all s $(< m$ for some $s)$; and (iii) *fixed wage* (variable wage) if w is (is not) independent of s. An example of an infeasible contract is $n(s) > 0$ for some s, $Eu(w) < K$. A Paretian criterion for comparing contracts follows. *Definition* 2: Let m be the size of the work force attracted and $\pi(\delta_1)$ be the expected profit accruing to a firm under a feasible contract, δ_1. Then δ_1 is said to (i) *dominate* $\delta_2(\delta_1 \gtrsim \delta_2)$ if δ_2 is feasible for m and $\pi(\delta_1) \geq \pi(\delta_2)$; and (ii) be *optimal* if it dominates all feasible contracts.

These definitions suggest that the optimum contract, δ^*, is simply the solution to a well-defined constrained maximum problem. The primary aim of this paper, however, is not to characterize δ^* fully (which is done in Sec. V) but, rather, to find out whether δ^* is a full-employment contract. In Section III I reduce the dimensionality of the firm's opportunity set by excluding contracts that are demonstrably inferior.

III. Wage Rigidity

Two sources of variability in wage income are present in the class of contracts set forth in (5): one arises from the stochastic nature of the wage schedule, the other from uncertainty over employment status. That under certain circumstances it is profitable (for both sides) to remove the former is shown in

Lemma 1: Given any feasible variable-wage contract $\delta_1 = \{w(s),\ n(s)\}$, there exists a feasible fixed-wage contract δ_2 that dominates δ_1, with strict dominance if $u(\cdot)$ is strictly concave.

Proof:[11] Let m satisfy $V(\delta_1,\ m) = \lambda$, and define $\delta_3 = \{\hat{w},\ n(s)\}$ where $\hat{w} = E(wn)/En$. The contract δ_3 produces the same expected labor income for workers and the same expected cost and expected revenue for firms as does δ_1. Note also that

$$\Delta \equiv V(\delta_3,\ m) - V(\delta_1,\ m) = \frac{1}{m} En[u(\hat{w}) - u(w)]$$

$$\geq (>)\ En(\hat{w} - w)\ u'(\hat{w}),\ \text{by concavity (strict concavity)},$$

$$= u'(\hat{w})(\hat{w}En - Ewn) = 0.$$

Since $V(\delta_3,\ m) \geq \lambda$, there exists a nonnegative (positive if u is strictly concave) constant ε such that the contract $\delta_2 = \{\hat{w} - \varepsilon,\ n(s)\}$ satisfies $V(\delta_2,\ m) = V(\delta_1,\ m)$ and $\pi(\delta_2) \geq \pi(\delta_1)$, QED.

[11] For a similar result in an intertemporal context, see Baily (1974).

A direct corollary of this result is that, in an expected-value sense, enforceable labor contracts dominate labor auctions. Let $w(s)$ be the (parametric) wage schedule associated with an auction market, $f(\cdot)$ be the production function of the typical firm, and $F(\cdot)$ be the inverse of the marginal product function. The outcome of the auction is then equivalent to the contract $\delta_a = \{w(s), F[w(s)/p(s)]\}$, which, for some nonnegative ε, is clearly dominated by the contract $\delta = \{Ew(s) - \varepsilon, F[w(s)/p(s)]\}$.

Two further points should be emphasized. First, workers who are neutral toward risk are indifferent between a variable-wage contract $\delta_1 = \{w(s), n(s)\}$ and a fixed-wage one $\delta_2 = \{Ew(s), n(s)\}$. Second, the primary use of lemma 1 is to reduce the complexity of the ensuing mathematics without affecting the ultimate results. A literal interpretation of it would be misplaced, for it is not robust to changes in assumptions about the indivisibility of leisure, the enforceability of contractual bargains, the nature of the random disturbance, and, possibly, the risk of ruin to the firm. With variable hours of work, for instance, wage income $w(1 - l)$ becomes state invariant if preferences are additive; if not, a more complicated function of income and leisure will still be non-stochastic.

Nor should one jump to the conclusion[12] that the real wage schedule is invariant to random disturbances in *aggregate* demand. In fact, theories of speculative labor supply[13] seem to argue against such invariance: when prices are higher than average, workers desire to accumulate assets faster than they normally do. To support a higher flow of savings, they will increase their "propensity" to save and accept a somewhat lower wage in terms of commodities, so that commodity producers have some incentive to hire a larger-than-normal amount of labor services.

In addition, few real-world agreements can prevent workers laid off in a temporarily depressed industry from auctioning off their services to the highest bidder in another industry. What effect these instances of imperfectly enforceable contracts will have on the wage schedule industry is not immediately obvious, but, as a brief argument in Section IV suggests, the outcome will likely be a softening of wage rigidity.

IV. Are Full-Employment Contracts Optimal?

Let $\Phi = \langle \delta_f \rangle$ be the class of all full-employment contracts that are feasible for the typical firm, and imagine that we isolated the dominant member, $\delta_f^* = \{w_f^*, m_f^*\}$, of that class. Consider now the class $D = \langle \delta \rangle$

---

[12] One might be tempted in that direction by the apparent failure of econometric work to find a significant correlation between trend-corrected average real compensation per man-hour (obviously a procyclically biased proxy for the real wage rate) and any price index. Cf. Bodkin (1969), who also reviews earlier efforts in that field.

[13] See Tobin (1947) and Lucas and Rapping (1969).

of all feasible contracts with the same labor force as δ_f^* which are formed from it by reducing employment below m_f^* in at least one state; that is, $\delta = \{w, n(s)\}$ where w is a nonstochastic parameter at least equal to w_f^* and

$$n(s) \leq m_f^* \text{ for all } s, \; < m_f^* \text{ for some } s. \tag{6}$$

To continue the process of whittling away at the firm's opportunity set, we ask now whether there is an underemployment contract in D which dominates δ_f^*. Note that full-employment agreements possess two desirable features, namely, zero variance in labor income and the lowest wage rate consistent with atomistic competition in the labor market. Against these advantages one must weigh the drawback of a state-invariant employment schedule which does not permit full-employment contracts to vary work force directly with the relative product price, that is, to use a larger amount of labor services in more profitable states of nature.

Every underemployment bargain in class D will pay a wage $w > w_f^*$ to compensate employees for the risk of temporary job loss. For small risks, the *average underemployment premium*, $w - w_f^*$, can be computed from the requirement that all members of D are feasible contracts. Thus, if $\bar{n} \equiv En$,

$$\lambda = (\bar{n}/m_f^*)\, u(w) + (1 - \bar{n}/m_f^*)K \Rightarrow m_f^*(\lambda - K) = \bar{n}[u(w) - K].$$

Note that $u(w_f^*) = \lambda$. Expanding $u(w)$ about w_f^* and neglecting terms of order higher than first, we obtain

$$m_f^*(\lambda - K) = \bar{n}[\lambda + (w - w_f^*)\, u'(w_f^*) - K], \tag{6a}$$

whence

$$(w - w_f^*)\bar{n} = (m_f^* - \bar{n})\,(\lambda - K)/u'(w_f^*). \tag{7}$$

The expected wage bill, $w\bar{n}$, of any δ in D may be thought of as consisting of two parts: a direct expected cost, $w_f^*\bar{n}$, equal to the minimum dollar outlay required to secure the average amount of labor used; and a premium expected cost $(w - w_f^*)\bar{n}$. Expected profit from contract δ is then

$$\pi(\delta) = E\big(p(s)f[n(s)] - w_f^*\, n(s) - [m_f^* - n(s)](\lambda - K)/u'(w_f^*)\big). \tag{8}$$

Now let

$$\phi(w_f^*) = (\lambda - K)/u'(w_f^*) = [u(w_f^*) - K]/u'(w_f^*) \tag{9}$$

denote the *marginal* underemployment premium, that is, the increment to premium cost required to compensate the labor force for the loss of one job in any state. The profit contribution of the nth laborer in state s is

$$p(s)\, f'(n) - w_f^* + \phi(w_f^*). \tag{10}$$

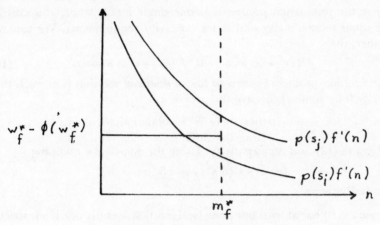

$$w_f^* - \phi'(w_f^*)$$

$$p(s_j)f'(n)$$

$$p(s_i)f'(n)$$

$$n$$

$$m_f^*$$

FIG. 1.—Inferiority of full-employment contracts

If there is a state $\hat{s}$ such that

$$p(\hat{s})f'(m_f^*) + \phi(w_f^*) < w_f^*, \tag{11}$$

it follows that, relative to δ_f^*, expected profit will be raised if workers are laid off in state $\hat{s}$. *For full-employment contracts to be suboptimal, it suffices, then, that there exist a state of nature in which the fully employed wage rate exceeds the sum of the marginal product value of fully employed labor plus the marginal underemployment premium.* The implication is (fig. 1) that, if s_i is the worst state, full-employment contracts will be suboptimal. It is not clear what type of contract is best when s_j is the lowest state—unless we are certain that (11) is both necessary and sufficient for the inferiority of full-employment agreements.[14] This is examined next.

The Maximum Problem

The fixed-wage feasible contract that firms offer will be the one that generates the highest expected profit. Given any $\delta = \{w, n(s)\}$ with $u(w) > K$ and a positive number m such that

$$\lambda = E[(n/m)u(w) + (1 - n/m)K] \Leftrightarrow m = (\lambda - K)^{-1}[u(w) - K]En,$$

feasibility is equivalent to $n \leq m$, or

$$n(s) \leq (\lambda - K)^{-1}[u(w) - K] \sum q(s)\, n(s) \qquad \forall s. \tag{12}$$

Expected profit is

$$\pi(\delta) = \sum q(s)\, (p(s)f[n(s)] - wn(s)), \tag{13}$$

---

[14] It might be, for instance, that when s_j is the worst state δ_f^* is dominated by an underemployment contract which does not belong to class D.

where the production process uses one single input, labor, and satisfies the usual monotonicity and strict concavity requirements. We assume, further, that

$$f'(n) \to \infty \text{ as } n \to 0, \; f'(n) \to 0 \text{ as } n \to \infty. \tag{14}$$

The decision problem is then to find a *nontrivial* solution [i.e., such that $n(s) > 0$ for some s] to solve the problem

$$(P) \max_{(\delta)} \pi(\delta)$$

subject to (12) and nonnegativity. Using the one-to-one mapping

$$(w, n) \to (t, n): t = n[u(w) - K],$$

one easily shows

Lemma 2: (P) has at least one nontrivial solution, exactly one if u is strictly concave.

Let $\mu(s)$ be the set of nonnegative multipliers corresponding to the set of inequalities in (12). It follows from lemma 2 and (14) that the unique solution to (P) is completely characterized by the (Kuhn-Tucker) conditions

$$-1 + u'(w) \sum \mu(s)/(\lambda - K) = 0, \tag{15}$$

$$q(s) \{ p(s) f'[n(s)] - w + (\lambda - K)^{-1}[u(w) - K] \sum \mu(s) \} = \mu(s) \qquad \forall s, \tag{16}$$

$$n(s) \le (\lambda - K)^{-1}[u(w) - K] \sum q(s) n(s), \; = \text{ if } \mu(s) > 0 \qquad \forall s. \tag{17}$$

Equation (15) confirms lemma 1 and is useful in eliminating $\sum \mu(s)$ from (16). Then

$$q[pf'(n) - z(w)] = \mu \qquad \forall s \tag{16a}$$

where the wage rate net of the marginal underemployment premium,

$$z(w) \equiv w - [u(w) - K]/u'(w), \tag{18}$$

represents the reduction in labor cost accomplished by eliminating one job in any state.

The Inferiority of Full-Employment Contracts: A Necessary and Sufficient Condition

Let h be the inverse function u^{-1}. From feasibility and equation (13), one readily obtains

Lemma 3: $w_f^* = h(\lambda); \; m_f^* = F[h(\lambda)/Ep]$.

We can now formalize the preceding argument in

Theorem 1: There exists an underemployment contract, δ^*, which dominates δ_f^* if and only if

$$p(s) f'(m_f^*) < z(w_f^*) \text{ for some } s \in S. \tag{19}$$

Proof: Sufficiency. Recall that $\mu(s) \geq 0$, $\forall s$. If (19) holds, then δ_f^* clearly violates (16a) for some state; neither it nor any other full-employment contract can then be optimal. Necessity. We will use a constructive proof of the contrapositive statement, that is, that

$$p(s)f'(m_f^*) \geq z(w_f^*) \qquad \forall s \in S \tag{20}$$

implies optimality of δ_f^*. Indeed, if (20) holds, then we can define nonnegative multipliers $\mu^*(s)$ such that

$$\mu^*(s) = q(s)[p(s)f'(m_f^*) - z(w_f^*)] \qquad \forall s. \tag{21}$$

Summing both sides of (21) over s, one obtains

$$\sum \mu^*(s) = f'(m_f^*)Ep - z(w_f^*) = (\lambda - K)/u'(w_f^*)$$

by (18) and lemma 3. It follows that the vector $[w_f^*, m_f^*, \mu^*(s)]$ satisfies conditions (15), (16a), and (17) and, therefore, (15), (16), and (17). If (20) is true, then δ_f^* is the optimal contract, QED.

This result is helpful in reducing the issue of underemployment ever being optimal, in an expected value sense, to one of whether or not a given inequality holds. What is it in labor force preferences of consumption versus leisure, in their attitude toward risk, and in material endowments and industry demand characteristics that makes (19) more likely, or less likely, to prevail?

It is useful to limit temporarily the range of attitudes toward risk under consideration by assuming that the *index of relative risk aversion*,

$$r \equiv -(\alpha + w)u''(w)/u'(w), \tag{22}$$

is independent of $\alpha + w$.[15] We can thus concentrate solely on preferences embodied in linear transformations of the following functions:[16]

$$u(w) = (\alpha + w)^{1-r} \qquad \text{if } r < 1 \tag{23a}$$

$$= \log (\alpha + w) \qquad \text{if } r = 1 \tag{23b}$$

$$= -(\alpha + w)^{-(r-1)} \qquad \text{if } r > 1. \tag{23c}$$

I summarize in the next two lemmas some useful bits of information. Both proofs are straightforward.

Lemma 4: Let $k \equiv u^{-1}(K)$ be the wage rate which makes workers indifferent between work and leisure. Then the function $z(w)$ is decreasing

[15] Recall that $u(w) = v(\alpha + w, 0)$, where the constant α is nonlabor income. Arrow (1971, pp. 96–97, 103–4) argues that r is weakly increasing in wealth partly on the basis of empirical findings that the wealth elasticity of money demand is at least 1 (which makes money a "luxury" good). The evidence, however, seems less than overwhelming that demand for cash balances has *significantly* higher than unitary elasticity (Meltzer 1963, pp. 236–38; Laidler 1969, pp. 98–102).

[16] See Pratt (1964, pp. 133–35) for details.

for all $w \geq k$, is invariant to linear transformations of the utility function v, and satisfies $z(k) = k$.

The lemma immediately below is based on the assumption that r is constant.

Lemma 5: The equation $z(w) = 0$ has a unique root, w_0, which satisfies (i) $w_0 = ke - \alpha$ if $r = 1$, $= kr^{1/(r-1)} - \alpha$ if $r \neq 1$, where e is the natural logarithm base; and (ii) w_0 is a decreasing function of r such that $w_0 \to \infty$ as $r \to 0$, $\to -\alpha$ as $r \to \infty$.

These lemmas point out two factors, the workers' opportunities outside the industry and their attitude toward risk, which bear on the optimality of full-employment contracts in an industry. For a large enough value of the index of relative risk aversion, w_0 will inevitably fall short of w_f^* and hence $z(w_f^*) \leq 0$, which rules out (19). Underemployment is more likely to occur, on the other hand, for values of r low enough to place $z(w_f^*)$ in the interval $(0, k]$. Similarly, the higher aggregate demand is (or whatever other exogenous parameter happens to define the economy-wide outlook for these workers), the more attractive working is relative to not working and the larger w_f^* becomes relative to w_0. This lowers the probability that (19) will hold.[17]

Other determinants of the likelihood of layoffs are readily apparent in (19). Layoffs should be more frequent in industries with relatively volatile (high variance in s) or relatively inelastic (p highly responsive to s) demand schedules, in markets with relatively little competition, and in cases of relatively high unemployment compensation (which boosts K and thereby depresses the marginal underemployment premium).[18]

Divisible Leisure

If one were interested in what statements a theory of labor contracts might make about, say, the behavior of hours worked over the cycle or about seniority claims on overtime, the obvious extension of the simple contract form is

$$\delta = \{w(s, t), x(s, t), n(s, t)\},$$

where $x(s, t) = 1 - l(s, t)$ is the amount of hours worked by each laborer if state s occurs in period t. As one might expect from Section III, such

[17] Since the constant k in lemmas 4 and 5 depends on α, it is not obvious in this model how the size of nonhuman wealth affects unemployment. For a *fixed* economy-wide full-employment wage rate, both working and not working become more attractive as nonlabor income rises. If, on the other hand, wealthier workers were able to hold out—as they might in a search-oriented model—for better opportunities than could their poorer colleagues, nonhuman wealth and the probability of accepting a uniform contract offer might be negatively correlated (see Danforth 1974).

[18] For additional factors affecting layoffs, see Gordon (1974).

augmented contracts will soften wage rigidity somewhat but affect little else. Of particular interest for this paper is whether these agreements will react to a decline in product demand by reducing, primarily, hours worked rather than employment and thereby prevent (19) from holding.

One reason we do not observe arbitrarily short work schedules[19] has to do with the well-known tendency of people to prefer lumpy leisure streams over entirely smooth ones, for example, long weekends, paid vacations, etc. Suppose, for instance, that labor preferences over alternative consumption and leisure streams are represented by monotone transformations of the additive function

$$v(c, l) = E\{\sum_{t=0}^{T} \beta^{t}[u(c) + k(l)]\}. \tag{24}$$

where the expectation is taken with respect to the joint distribution $q(s_0, s_1, \ldots, s_T)$ of states of nature over the (presumed exogenous) duration of the contract. Then the tastes for lumpy leisure streams would be reflected in the requirement that $k(l)$ be concave over some interval $(0, l_0)$ and convex over $(l_0, 1)$. And work schedules which consume nearly all or nearly none of the leisure available to workers will bear prohibitively high "overtime" or "undertime" costs. The latter type of premium simply reflects the fact that it takes a very high hourly wage to persuade people that they must abandon the comforts of home for 1 hour's work at the factory.

Is Contractual Unemployment Involuntary?

The rest of the conclusions drawn from theorem 1 are unexceptional, perhaps to the point of fomenting suspicion that they could be arrived at via the familiar auction model with some restrictions on labor mobility. Indeed, the perfect enforceability of contracts, an assumption uncomfortably close to indenture, does guarantee that whoever is laid off when (19) prevails will be unable to seek employment outside the industry. Furthermore, if interindustry labor mobility is low because of, say, moving costs or industry-specific skills, some (voluntary) unemployment will occur in states for which a condition reminiscent of (19) holds, that is,

$$p(s) f'(\mu) < k, \tag{25}$$

where μ = labor stock per firm.

On reflection, perfect bilateral enforceability of contracts does not seem to be as stringent a restriction as its name would imply. Suppose, for instance, that such agreements are one-sided bargains enforceable on the

---

[19] Setup costs in production is another obvious cause, one that has received much formal attention in inventory theory.

employer but not on the employee.[20] Persons whose contracted services are temporarily not in demand would be the ones most likely to prefer a job outside the industry in question over their current status of pure leisure consumption. Such temporary jobs, probably offered in auction, will materialize only if there exist industries with demand sufficiently strong to ensure full employment to their permanent labor force and to justify hiring *additional* help (filling "vacancies") at wages no smaller than k.

Idled workers will search actively if and only if temporary jobs outside their industry are available at wage rates sufficient to compensate them for the loss of leisure. In times of relatively slack aggregate demand, temporary vacancies will tend to fall relative to layoffs; hence, the probability of landing any temporary job (alternatively, the market-clearing auction wage) will fall and search will be discouraged. The converse will be true in periods of above-average aggregate demand. the auction wage will be high compared with the minimum working wage k, and searchers may well be able to secure employment at wages in excess of what prevails in the contractual labor market. This implies that firms which do not wish to have their production plans upset by a high quit rate cannot afford to maintain a rigid wage, at least not upward, against protracted fluctuations in aggregate demand.

V. Optimum Contracts—a Complete Characterization

Thus far we have derived a condition under which full-employment contracts are suboptimal. Recall the assumption that all contracts are strictly enforceable and have a parametrically given equilibrium value, λ. Without further loss of generality, suppose that the distribution of s is uniform in the interval $(0, 1)$. The optimal contract is then completely characterized by[21]

Theorem 2: If (19) holds for all $s \leq \hat{s}$ and some $\lambda \in (K, \infty)$, then there exist two continuous decreasing functions $M(\lambda)$ and $Y(\lambda)$ and a continuous increasing function $T(\lambda)$, all three unique and such that

(i) $w_f^* < T(\lambda) < w_0 \quad \forall \lambda \in (K, \infty)$;

(ii) $M(\lambda) \to \infty$ as $\lambda \to K$, $M(\lambda) \to 0$ as $\lambda \to \infty$;

(iii) $M(\lambda) > m_f^* \quad \forall \lambda \in (K, \infty)$;

(iv) $Y(\lambda) \to 1$ as $\lambda \to K$, $Y(\lambda) \to 0$ as $\lambda \to \infty$;

(v) $p[Y(\lambda)]f'[M(\lambda)] = z[T(\lambda)] \quad \forall \lambda \in (K, \infty)$.

---

[20] Casual empiricism reinforces this belief to the extent that it is easier, or less costly, to secure information on the reputation and past personnel policies of firms than on the employment record of not very highly paid employees.

[21] The proof, which essentially involves characterizing the solution of two simultaneous nonlinear equations in two unknowns, is available on request from the author.

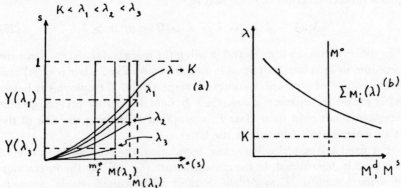

FIG. 2.—Employment schedules of optimal contracts

Furthermore, the optimal contract $\delta^* = \{w^*, n^*(s)\}$ satisfies

(vi) $Epf'(n^*) = w^* - \psi(w^*) < w^*$;

(vii) $w^* = T(\lambda)$;

(viii) $\psi(w^*) = [u(w^*) - \lambda]/u'(w^*) > 0$;

(ix) $n^*(s) = F[z(w^*)/p(s)]$ for $s < Y(\lambda)$

$\qquad = M(\lambda)$ for $s > Y(\lambda)$;

(x) $n^*(s)$ is continuous, nondecreasing in s, increasing in λ for $s < Y(\lambda)$, and decreasing in λ for $s > Y(\lambda)$; and

(xi) $n^*(s) = m_f^*$ at some $s \equiv s^* < \min\{\hat{s}, Y(\lambda)\}$.

This theorem argues that the wage associated with the underemployment contract exceeds its full-employment counterpart, and so does work force size. The first of these two departures from full-employment norms is necessary to compensate laborers for a positive probability of unemployment; the second one allows employers to shift output from relatively unprofitable to relatively profitable states of nature.

As λ rises relative to both the product price schedule, $p(s)$, and the value of leisure, it becomes more "expensive" for the firm to maintain a risky, that is, steeply sloped, employment schedule. Thus, the underemployment and full-employment portions of $n^*(s)$ shift to the right and left, respectively (fig. 2a), the critical state $Y(\lambda)$ declines in value, and $n^*(s)$ comes closer to a full-employment schedule.

Workers in active employment are paid a wage rate[22] which exceeds the expected value of labor's marginal product by a marginal underemployment premium $\psi(w^*)$. A comparison with equation (9) shows that

[22] There seems to be no relationship between the full-employment wage rate and the expected marginal product of labor under the optimal contract.

ψ is a smaller function than ϕ, that is,

$$\phi(w) - \psi(w) = \lambda - K > 0 \text{ for all } w \geq k. \tag{26}$$

The difference arises from ϕ and ψ being the marginal underemployment premium in the class D of feasible contracts with fixed labor pool m_f^* and in the class F of all feasible contracts, respectively. If employment below m_f^* is called for in some states, class D must inevitably present greater unemployment risks than class F: the option of varying the size of the labor force is available only in the latter.

For fixed tastes, technology, and population, the equilibrium value of contracts is determined, in the usual manner (fig. 2b), by the interaction of a fixed supply $M^s = M^0$ of workers with economy-wide demand, $M^d = \sum_i M_i(\lambda)$, for "work force," where i indexes industries.

Contracts versus Auction[23]

We return now to the issue of whether the employment (and output) pattern in a labor contracts economy is identical to, or varies systematically from, what would prevail if labor services were sold in instantaneous auction. With unlimited labor mobility, the latter type of market organization is Pareto efficient and, hence, must generate at least as high a volume of employment and output as a market for contractual bargains.

A less vacuous comparison would recognize that low mobility is one of the primary reasons long-term attachments arise between workers and firms. Reduced to its barest essentials, the issue is: given a labor stock of μ workers (in per firm terms) without job opportunities outside the industry, how does the outcome of an auction market compare with the terms of the optimal contract?

Let $w_a(s)$, $n^s(s)$, $n^d(s)$, and $n_a(s)$ be the wage, labor supply, labor demand, and employment schedules, respectively, in the auction market. Define s^0 from

$$p(s^0)f'(\mu) = k \tag{26a}$$

and note that $k = z(k)$. Next let the function $g(w, m)$ solve

$$p(g)f'(m) = z(w). \tag{27}$$

Now one can show[24]

Lemma 6: The function $g(w, m)$ is unique, continuously differentiable, decreasing in w, increasing in m, and bounded above by 1 and below by 0, and is such that (i) $s^0 = g(k, \mu)$ solves (26a); and (ii) $g(k, \mu) > Y(\lambda)$, where $Y(\lambda)$ is defined in theorem 2.

---

[23] I am indebted to Milton Friedman for provoking this section.
[24] N. 21 applies here, too.

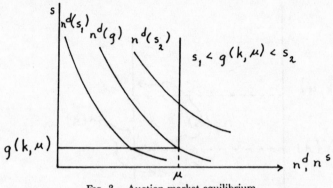

FIG. 3.—Auction market equilibrium

Now since

$$n^d(s) = F[w(s)/p(s)]; \; n^s(s) = \mu \text{ if } w_a(s) > k,$$
$$= 0 \text{ if } w_a(s) < k, \tag{28}$$

it follows from lemma 6 that

$$n_a(s) = F[k/p(s)], \; w_a(s) = k \text{ if } s < g(k, \mu)$$
$$= \mu \quad , \qquad = p(s)f'(\mu) \text{ if } s > g(k, \mu). \tag{29}$$

These relations are graphed in figure 3.

In the contractual market, assume that a full-employment contract paying the lowest possible wage is profitable on average, that is,

$$f'(\mu) \; Ep > k. \tag{30}$$

The optimal agreement will be of the form $\delta_f^* = \{f'(\mu)Ep, \mu\}$ if

$$p(s)f'(\mu) \geq z[f'(\mu)Ep] \qquad \forall s \tag{31}$$

holds; otherwise, theorem 2 is in force, with the additional proviso that

$$M(\lambda) = \mu. \tag{32}$$

Let w^*, $n^*(s)$, and $\bar{w}_c$ be the wage rate, employment schedule, and expected wage income under the optimal contract and let $\bar{w}_a$ be the expected wage income in an auction market. Note that

$$\bar{w}_a = z(k)g(k, \mu) + \int_{g(k,\mu)}^{1} f'(\mu)p(s)ds. \tag{33}$$

Now, if (31) is true, then $\bar{w}_c = w_f^* = f'(\mu)Ep$ and $n^*(s) = \mu$ for all s. Hence,

$$\bar{w}_c - \bar{w}_a = \int_0^g [f'(\mu)p(s) - z(k)]ds < 0 \tag{34a}$$

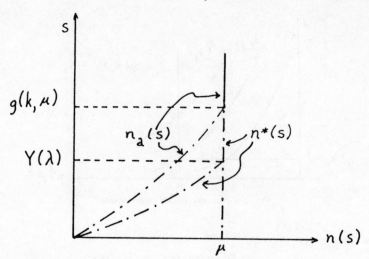

FIG. 4.—Comparative employment

and, from (29),

$$n^*(s) \geq n_a(s), \; > \text{ if } s < g(k, \mu). \tag{35}$$

If, on the other hand, (31) does not hold, then we know that $z(w^*) <$ k and $w^* \in (w_f^*, w_0)$; hence, part (ix) of theorem 2 suggests that (35) is equally true in this case also. Note, further, that in this case again

$$\bar{w}_c = w^* E n^*/\mu = w^*(\lambda - K)/[u(w^*) - K],$$

which is readily shown to be a decreasing function of w^* for all w^* in the relevant range (k, w_0) and all $\lambda > K$. Hence,

$$\bar{w}_c < w_f^*(\lambda - K)/[u(w_f^*) - K] = w_f^* = f'(\mu)Ep < \bar{w}_a. \tag{34b}$$

Observe also from theorem 2(v) and lemma 6 that

$$Y(\lambda) \equiv g[T(\lambda), M(\lambda)] = g(w^*, \mu) < g(k,\mu).$$

This completes the proof of

Theorem 3: (i) $\bar{w}_c < \bar{w}_a$; and (ii) $n_a(s) \leq n^*(s)$ $\quad \forall s, < \text{ for } s < g(k, \mu)$; where (iii) $g(k, \mu) > Y(\lambda)$.

As one might expect, labor markets generate riskier employment schedules (fig. 4) and larger expectations of wage income when they are organized as auctions rather than as contract exchanges.

VI. Summary and Conclusions

This paper examines a simple industry with demand uncertainty which motivates risk-neutral firms to act both as employers and as insurers of homogeneous, risk-averse laborers. The resulting contractual agreements turn out, in their simplest form, to be more likely to specify full employment the more of the following conditions prevail: small variability in product price, above-average economy-wide labor demand, highly risk-averse workers, small unemployment compensation, and highly competitive product market. Otherwise, it may be optimal to lay off, by random choice, part of the work force during low states of demand.

In such "underemployment" contracts it is profitable, under certain assumptions, to eliminate wage fluctuations, but not employment status, as a source contributing to wage income variability. If the labor force is industry specific, contractual organization of the labor market will result in the volume of employment being no lower in any state, and higher in some states, than that associated with a labor auction.

The employment path generated in a contractual labor market is not much different from the one which prevails in a spot auction market; because of rigid wages, however, reductions in employment appear as layoffs rather than as voluntary withdrawals of labor services.

Some extensions of the work reported in Sections II–V are worth contemplating. The first involves dropping the assumption of perfect homogeneity of the labor force and finding out what sort of wage distributions, layoff provisions, and participation rates are consistent with labor market equilibrium when different contracts are offered to persons of varying technical skills, tastes, asset positions, and home production opportunities. A related paper of mine (Azariadis 1975) examines the incidence of unemployment in a technology with two asymmetrically substitutable skill grades of labor. That paper finds that the trade-offs between wage income and the expected rate of unemployment embodied in optimal contracts clearly favor skilled workers over common laborers.

Another extension, passingly discussed in Section IV, is relaxing the restriction of contract enforceability, at least on employees. In a model with at least two industries whose product price ratio varies according to a well-defined stochastic process, unilaterally enforceable contracts may lead to a natural definition of (temporary) vacancies and, in all likelihood, to a softening of wage rigidity.

Perhaps the most interesting area of application for the class of models treated in this paper arises when the assumption of exogeneity in the price level is dropped. Perceived disturbances of the price level relative either to its average long-term value or to the price of commodities in informationally segmented markets are at the heart of modern treatments of the Phillips curve.[25] Whether we can model price movements of this sort to learn something about wage rigidity in the large and, more generally, optimal escalator clauses in money-wage contracts seems to me an issue worth pursuing.

[25] See Friedman (1968), Phelps (1968), and Mortensen (1970) on the role of movements in contemporaneous price ratios and Lucas and Rapping (1969) and Lucas (1972) on the role of movements in intertemporal ones.

References

Arrow, K. J. *Essays in the Theory of Risk-Bearing.* Chicago: Markham, 1971.
———. *New York Times* (November 26, 1972).
Azariadis, C. "On the Incidence of Unemployment." *Rev. Econ. Studies* (in press, 1975).
Baily, M. N. "Wages and Employment under Uncertain Demand." *Rev. Econ. Studies* 41 (January 1974): 37–50.
Barro, R. J., and Grossman, H. I. "A General Disequilibrium Model of Income and Employment." *A.E.R.* 61 (March 1971): 82–93.
Bodkin, R. G. "Real Wages and Cyclical Variations in Employment." *Canadian J. Econ.* 2 (August 1969): 353–74.
Brainard, W., and Dolbear, F. T. "Social Risk and Financial Markets." *A.E.R.* 61 (May 1971): 360–79.
Clower, R. "The Keynesian Counter-Revolution: A Theoretical Appraisal." In *The Theory of Interest Rates,* edited by F. H. Hahn and F. P. R. Brechling. London: Macmillan, 1966.
Danforth, J. P. "Expected Utility, Mandatory Retirement and Job Search." Working paper, Univ. Minnesota, 1974.
Friedman, M. "The Role of Monetary Policy." *A.E.R.* 58 (March 1968): 1–17.
Gordon, D. F. "A Neo-classical Theory of Keynesian Unemployment." *Econ. Inquiry* 12 (December 1974): 431–59.
Hicks, J. R. *The Theory of Wages.* London: Macmillan, 1932.
Keynes, J. M. *The General Theory of Employment, Interest and Money.* London: Macmillan, 1936.
Knight, F. H. *Risk, Uncertainty and Profit.* Boston: Houghton-Mifflin, 1921.
Laidler, D. E. W. *The Demand for Money: Theories and Evidence.* Scranton, Penn.: International Textbook, 1969.
Leijonhufvud, A. *On Keynesian Economics and the Economics of Keynes.* London: Oxford Univ. Press, 1968.
Lucas, R. E. "Expectations and the Neutrality of Money." *J. Econ. Theory* 4 (April 1972): 103–24.
Lucas, R. E., and Rapping, L. "Real Wages, Employment, and Inflation." *J.P.E.* 77, no. 5 (October 1969): 721–54.
Meltzer, A. H. "The Demand for Money: The Evidence from the Time Series." *J.P.E.* 71, no. 3 (June 1963): 219–46.
Mortensen, D. "A Theory of Wage and Employment Dynamics." In *Microeconomic Foundations of Employment and Inflation Theory,* edited by E. S. Phelps et al. New York: Norton, 1970.
Parker, J. E., and Burton, J. F., Jr. "Voluntary Labor Mobility in the U.S. Manufacturing Sector." In *Readings in Labor Market Analysis,* edited by J. F. Burton et al. New York: Holt, Rinehart & Winston, 1971.
Patinkin, D. *Money, Interest, and Prices.* New York: Harper & Row, 1956 (2d ed., 1965).
Phelps, E. S. "Money Wage Dynamics and Labor Market Equilibrium." *J.P.E.* 76, no. 4, pt. 2 (August 1968): 688–711.
Pratt, J. W. "Risk Aversion in the Small and in the Large." *Econometrica* 32 (January 1964): 122–36.
Stiglitz, J. "Incentives and Risk Sharing in Sharecropping." *Rev. Econ. Studies* 41 (April 1974): 219–56.
Tobin, J. "Money Wage Rates and Employment." In *The New Economics,* edited by S. E. Harris. New York: Knopf, 1947.
———. "Inflation and Unemployment." *A.E.R.* 62 (March 1972): 1–18.

[2]

Wages and Employment under Uncertain Demand [1,2]

MARTIN NEIL BAILY
Yale University

This paper examines some implications of two postulates for firms' wage and employment policies. The first is that firms, or stockholders, have easier access to capital markets at lower costs or higher returns than do small investors, such as workers. Second, there are important mobility and turnover costs incurred when a worker moves from one firm to another.

The existence of mobility costs means that the labour market is not a perfect market. Each firm is not restricted to taking as given some exogenous market wage, period by period, but has some amount of freedom about the wage strategy it sets. The firm cannot choose any wage-employment path it wishes, however, and I shall assume that in the long-run the firm must offer the same (expected) utility as that available elsewhere. In the short-run there is a constraint that the wage offer must never be so bad that all the firm's workers will quit and incur the mobility cost.

There are solid grounds for believing that great differences exist between stockholders and workers with regard to capital markets. The majority of stocks are held by very wealthy persons indeed, who also hold almost all the state and local bonds and large proportions of the property and other assets.[3] In addition, stockholders are frequently company executives or professionals with greater financial expertise and salaries many times that of the average industrial worker. The worker typically has a rather small net worth. His assets are durable goods and a rather small holding of money. He frequently has consumer credit liabilities outstanding.[4] He also has much less knowledge of financial assets and institutions.

A principal function of capital markets is to allow wealth-holders to diversify their holdings and so reduce the risk of their total portfolios. Stockholders, through their greater wealth and expertise, are much better able to bear risks than are workers.[5] The difference in ability to bear risk between the two groups immediately suggests an opportunity to trade. In deciding what wage-employment strategy to set, the firm will be willing to reduce worker risk. By doing so, the firm is offering a joint product, employment plus an insurance or financial intermediation service. The firm does not do this simply because workers prefer it. Risk-reducing policies are the cheapest and hence most profitable way of attracting any given work-force.

The choice of a risk-reducing policy by the firm will have an important impact on both the wage set and on employment variations—and hence the probability of unemployment. The firm will, in general, wish to reduce the uncertainty of the workers' incomes. An important feature of the model presented here is that the tendency of the firm to reduce risk has an asymmetrical effect on the wage strategy and on the employment strategy.

[1] *First version received February* 1973; *final version received May* 1973 (*Eds.*).
[2] I am indebted to Robert M. Solow, Franklin M. Fisher, Peter A. Diamond, the members of the theory workshop at MIT and a referee for many helpful comments and criticisms. I retain responsibility for error. Financial support from the Canada Council is acknowledged.
[3] Projector [8], Lampmann [4].
[4] Katona [2], Projector [8].
[5] In addition, one might feel that stockholders as a class are more willing to bear risk simply because of differences in aversion to risk.

Subject to the (somewhat restrictive) assumptions of the model, one can show that a pre-announced non-stochastic wage strategy will be set by the firm. This is true even though the future path of employment is stochastic and hence there is a positive probability of being laid off. An equivalent result is not true for the employment strategy. The firm will wish to vary the size of its work-force.

Workers dislike income uncertainty and dislike being laid off. The asymmetry between the wage and employment strategies arises because when a worker is laid off he receives a non-zero income. To attract workers, the firm must pay a higher wage if there is some positive probability of unemployment than it would if employment were guaranteed. As against this, the firm can save on its wage costs by cutting its work-force during periods of slack product demand. Provided workers have some alternative sources of income when they are laid off, the savings from employment variations will outweigh the higher wage necessary, even though workers are risk averse. The alternative sources of income are from unemployment compensation, from working outside the sector considered and from the income equivalent of avoiding the disutility of work. Workers dislike lay-offs; the question is how much do they dislike them relative to how much the firm saves on its wage bill.

One way of thinking about the alternatives facing the firm is to compare two possible policies, one which implies more employment variation and another which implies more wage variation. Such comparisons are an intuitively appealing approach, but it is not the one followed here, nor is it necessary to make comparisons of this type to prove the desired result. This is discussed further in Section IV (including footnote 2, p. 44).

The result, that a pre-announced non-stochastic wage is set by firms, is intended to provide an explanation of the phenomenon of sticky wages. In particular, it suggests an explanation for the fact that the real wage does not seem to adjust in the short-run to clear the labour market.

There is a question of what is meant by sticky wages. In the formal model presented there are a number of rather strong assumptions which allow a clear result. The wage rate is strictly non-stochastic, pre-announced. It does not respond at all to fluctuations in demand. To reach this conclusion firms are assumed to be risk neutral, maximizing the present value of expected profits. Workers are risk averse, and do not operate in capital markets. These assumptions are intended to reflect the asymmetry between workers and capitalists that I described, but clearly they are strong. In Sections VI and VII the consequences of changing these assumptions are discussed.

I. A SINGLE FIRM AND UNCERTAIN DEMAND

I shall discuss first the case of a single firm which has a stochastic demand for its product. The simplest assumption to make is that the firm is a perfect competitor in the product market. It is a price-taker and sets quantity as the decision variable.[1] I shall consider in this model a finite time-horizon of T periods.

Assumption 1. The price of the firm's product in period t, p_t, is a random variable. The p_t are jointly distributed and are bounded above and below. $p_t \in \Omega_t$ ($t = 1, ..., T$).

If the joint density function of the prices is $F(p_1, ..., p_T)$, then there is a prior or unconditional expectation of p_t defined by:

$$E(p_t) = \int_{\Omega_1}, ..., \int_{\Omega_T} p_t F(p_1, ..., p_T) dp_1, ..., dp_T. \qquad ...(1)$$

[1] I am not examining what determines price. One could assume a fluctuating world price. Also, the price-taker assumption is not essential. It is the easiest way to introduce uncertain demand but a monopolist with a fluctuating demand curve would serve as well.

BAILY   WAGES AND EMPLOYMENT   39

The unsubscripted expectations operator will be used to denote this expected value, i.e. when the state variables from 1, ..., T (the prices $p_1, ..., p_T$ in the above case) are unknown. The operator E_t will denote the expected value of a variable when state variables up to period t are known. It is the conditional expectation defined in the usual way.[1]

It is convenient to take the technology and capital equipment to be constant.[2] It is doubtful if any essential features of the results depend upon this, but a number of awkward problems are avoided.

Assumption 2. The firm's output in period t is x_t and is given by:

$$x_t = g(L_t) \qquad g' > 0, \ g'' < 0, \qquad\qquad ...(2)$$

where L_t is employment in period t.[3]

Let a worker's income in period t be y_t. The values $(y_1, ..., y_T)$, which depend upon the wage and employment prospects of the worker, will in general be stochastic variables. Each worker's decision function is of the form given by:

Assumption 3. A worker making a decision in $t-1$ which affects his path of income $y_t, ..., y_T$ will maximize V_{t-1} given by:

$$V_{t-1} = E_{t-1}\left\{ \sum_t^T U(y_t)(1+\rho)^{-\tau+t-1}\right\}, \qquad\qquad ...(3)$$

where $U' > 0$, $U'' < 0$ and ρ is a constant.

The assumption implies all workers are alike in their preferences. This makes life much easier, as I shall comment later, but obviously is pretty strong. The firm and industry are assumed small relative to the rest of the economy. The overall price level is constant, and wage and employment prospects in the rest of the economy are given exogenously. There may, in fact, be many choices open to a worker who is not employed with the firm we are analysing. But just as one assumes an equilibrium wage prevailing in the economy in the standard textbook theory, I shall assume a given (possibly stochastic) path of income available elsewhere.

Assumption 4. The path of income available to a worker elsewhere in the economy is $y_1^0, ..., y_T^0$. The y_t^0 are stochastic and may be jointly distributed.

Consider a worker who does join the firm we are analysing. If he is employed in period t, his income is simply the firm wage w_t. If there were no mobility or information costs in this economy the firm would have no real choice. It would pay $w_t = y_t^0$ in each period as a perfect competitor in the labour market. More realistically, however, although a firm may face a long-run horizontal supply of labour, this is not true period by period because of information and mobility costs.

The fact that mobility costs exist has been well recognized in the literature.[4] In actual practice the cost of changing jobs may be quite different from one worker to another. Some workers may have many jobs open to them in the same location and have a general skill needed in many industries. There would seem to be many workers, however, for whom changing jobs would involve considerable costs. These might be moving expenses, search expenses, income foregone and possible retraining. For almost all firms there are significant costs involved when a new worker joins the company. He may have to be

---

[1] Thus $E_t(p_t)$ is the expected value over the conditional density of p_t, defined as the ratio of the integral of F over $p_{t+1}, ..., p_T$ to the integral of F over $p_t, ..., p_T$.

[2] Inventory fluctuations are also excluded.

[3] The length of the period can be taken as the order of one month or one quarter. This paper is not intended as an analysis of very short-run fluctuations and overtime working. An interesting paper by Lucas [5] deals with such a framework and an incorporation of some of the ideas presented here with his analysis could be a fruitful area for further research.

[4] Stigler [9], Oi [6], Phelps *et al.* [7].

given some on-the-job training or equivalently his productivity may be lower during the first few periods after he is hired, as he learns by doing.

It is hard to do justice to the full complexity of the factors described, particularly differences between workers at different skill levels and different geographical locations. Instead, the following simple parametrization is used.

Assumption 5. If a worker leaves the firm where he has been seeking work and moves to another firm in period t he suffers a mobility cost in period τ given by $C_\tau^t \geqq 0$ $\tau \geqq t$.

The mobility cost experienced by the worker he pays directly. The firm's turnover cost is assumed to take the form of a reduced wage for the first few periods after the worker joins the firm.[1]

II. FIRM WAGE AND EMPLOYMENT STRATEGIES

Once we include mobility and information costs the single firm has a measure of freedom about the wage and employment policies it can set. To model this the distributions of the state variables are assumed known and the firm announces at time zero a strategy with respect to wages and employment. The strategy will consist of two decision rules conditional on the values of the state variables, which are the prices $p_1, ..., p_T$ and the incomes available elsewhere $y_1^0, ..., y_T^0$.[2] A particular (and not in fact very likely) strategy would be to choose a constant level of employment and let the wage always equal the marginal product times price in each period. The announced strategy can be defined by two sets of mappings from the state variables into employment and wages.

Assumption 6. The firm announces at time zero a strategy S defined by two sets of mappings $(a_1, ..., a_T)$ and $(b_1, ..., b_T)$ such that

$$L_t = a_t(p_1, ..., p_t, y_1^0, ..., y_t^0)$$
$$w_t = b_t(p_1, ..., p_t, y_1^0, ..., y_t^0). \qquad ...(4)$$

These mappings could be analytic functions or perhaps integral equations where L_t and w_t depend on some function of the expected values. This assumption is very weak in the sense that the class of possible strategies is very general. The announced strategy together with the known distribution of the variables mean that the worker can evaluate the expected utility of seeking work at the firm.

The knowledge requirements of this formulation are quite considerable but the stylized model makes the framework seem more unrealistic than it actually is. Workers clearly do not make complex calculations upon announced joint probability distributions. They are, however, concerned with the past behaviour of firms, how frequently lay-offs occur and what is the likely path of wages. Firms are concerned about their reputations as employers, suggesting that short-sighted decisions do not necessarily imply long-run profit maximization. In terms of the model, they stick to an implicit strategy since it is in their long run-interests to do so. In addition, the conclusions of this paper suggest that the wage strategy will be one of setting a non-stochastic pre-announced wage path; this is the strategy which reduces the knowledge requirements and simplifies the calculation of utility.

This section deals with an easy case. Employment variations are excluded so that the wage strategy is considered given a constant employment level. This keeps everything

---

[1] In practice, this latter cost may be reflected in the fact that a firm will hire workers who have been working for the firm in previous periods in preference to a new, unknown worker. Hence the cost experienced by the worker may be a queuing cost.

[2] As far as the firm is concerned, the product price and incomes available elsewhere have exogenously given densities.

very simple and gives the flavour of the more complex case where employment varies, which is handled subsequently.

Consider the properties then of two specific strategies.

↳ *Strategy S_1*: the firm pays a constant wage $\tilde{w}$ and employs a constant number of workers $\tilde{L}$.

Any worker taken on is guaranteed employment up to time T. He may, of course, quit if he wishes.

Strategy S_2: the firm employs a constant number of workers $\tilde{L}$ but the path of wages is unknown at time zero, i.e. $w_t = b_t(p_1, ..., p_t, y_1^0, ..., y_t^0)$ so that w_t is a stochastic variable.

In order for these strategies to be meaningful the level of wages set must be such that the firm actually can employ $\tilde{L}$ workers.

Definition. Strategies S_1 and S_2 are said to be *feasible* if the firm has at least $\tilde{L}$ workers available in each period $t = 1, ..., T$.

To model the assumption of a long-run horizontal labour supply, assume that at time zero all workers search for firms to find the best expected utility offer. A single firm can then ensure $\tilde{L}$ workers at the *beginning of period one* by offering the same expected utility as that available elsewhere.

Assumption 7. If the labour supply condition (5) is satisfied by strategies S_1 and S_2 then the firm will have $\tilde{L}$ workers available at the beginning of period one.

$$V^0 = E\left\{\sum_1^T U(y_t^0)(1+\rho)^{-t}\right\}$$

$$= \sum_1^T U(\tilde{w})(1+\rho)^{-t} \text{ for } S_1. \qquad ...(5)$$

$$= E\left\{\sum_1^T U(w_t)(1+\rho)^{-t}\right\} \text{ for } S_2.$$

The simple form of Assumption 7 depends upon the fact that workers were assumed to have identical preferences. If this assumption were changed the analysis would become a lot more complicated. It seems intuitively likely that if workers, *on the average*, are risk averse, then the risk-reducing strategy S_1 is going to turn out to be the cheapest way of attracting any given size of work-force. It might be tricky to prove, however.

Once workers have chosen to come to this firm they can re-evaluate their positions at any time. If they decide to move they incur the mobility costs C_τ^t. For S_1, consider the inequality:

$$\sum_t^T U(\tilde{w})(1+\rho)^{-\tau+(t-1)} \geqq E_{t-1}\left\{\sum_t^T U(y_\tau^0 - C_\tau^t)(1+\rho)^{-\tau+(t-1)}\right\}. \qquad ...(6)$$

If this inequality is satisfied for $t = 2, ..., T$ then a worker who leaves the firm operating S_1 will always be worse off. The firm will retain its workers and S_1 will be feasible. To interpret this condition consider a strategy S_1 which satisfies the labour supply condition (5). It is clear that if the variations of y^0 are large relative to mobility costs then the constant wage strategy will not be feasible. A large sustained increase in y^0 will force the firm to adjust its own wage upwards. The force of the inequality (6) is therefore that the constant wage strategy, that satisfies the labour supply condition, will be feasible provided mobility costs are sufficiently large relative to the short-run fluctuations in y^0 (the wage income available elsewhere in the economy).

Definition. The feasibility condition for S_1 will be said to be satisfied if mobility costs relative to fluctuations in the wage income available elsewhere in the economy are large enough so that a strategy S_1 which satisfies (5) will satisfy the inequality (6).

Strategy S_2 is really the class of strategies with stochastic wage paths which the firm may wish to choose. The set of these which is feasible must also satisfy a feasibility constraint as well as the labour supply condition. This is given by:

$$E_{t-1} \left\{ \sum_t^T U(w_t)(1+\rho)^{-t+(t-1)} \right\} \geqq \quad \text{the RHS of (6)}. \qquad \ldots(7)$$

The formulation has a slight musical chairs air to it, since everybody searches at once and then joins a firm when period one starts. This feature results from the synchronization of everyone's actions, rather as the exact consumption loan model does. Let me try and relate the model a little more closely to reality as follows.

Workers enter the labour force or retire at random. Some workers quit to look for better conditions and some others come from other firms. What I am trying to capture in the labour supply condition is that, provided the firm offers an expected utility over a period equal to that available elsewhere in the economy, it will find that it can balance quits and retirements with new entrants and hiring. The feasibility condition is a measure of the amount of period by period freedom open to the firm resulting from the mobility costs of the labour market.

The strategy S_1 is defined in terms of a constant wage. Constancy is stronger than certainty but it is the latter that is really the key feature of S_1. This model has ignored such factors as capital accumulation and technical change. In a more general model, or in thinking about the relevance of the results, one might plausibly generalize by allowing S_1 to include a trend rate of change of real wages. Wage stickiness then consists of smoothing fluctuations around the trend. I have commented (and will comment) on uncertain or stochastic strategies compared with pre-announced, non-stochastic wage strategies in the course of the general discussion since it is the wage certainty not the wage constancy that is important.

III. EXPECTED PROFITS AND ALTERNATIVE STRATEGIES

The firm will make a profit in period t given by: [1]

$$\Pi_t = p_t g(L_t) - w_t L_t. \qquad \ldots(8)$$

The present value of expected profits evaluated at the beginning of period one is given by:

$$E(\Pi) = \sum_1^T (1+r)^{-t} E\{p_t g(L_t) - w_t L_t\}, \qquad \ldots(9)$$

where r is the discount rate and the mappings (4) define the distributions of w_t and L_t. There is a minor complication introduced by the parameter ρ in the utility function and the discount rate r. I will set $r = \rho$ to keep things simple. [2] With the framework developed the following proposition can be shown.

Proposition 1. *Provided the feasibility constraint is satisfied, the strategy S_1 with constant wage and employment yields larger expected profits than S_2 with a stochastic wage.*

Notice that the worker's expected utility and the firm's expected profits are evaluated at the beginning of period one, when future values of the state variables are unknown. The expected values are, therefore, the prior or unconditional values. Developing the formal proof of the proposition for this case does not seem worth while. The result is

---

[1] Ignoring a constant capital cost term. This is important only for the long-run shutdown decision.
[2] This simplification would be unnecessary if S_1 was not defined in terms of wage constancy. If $r \neq \rho$ we could get effects familiar from Fisher interest theory but not central to the issues here.

BAILY   WAGES AND EMPLOYMENT   43

intuitively clear. Both strategies S_1 and S_2 have the same constant employment path. The difference in expected profits between the two is therefore given by:

$$E(\Pi \mid S_1) - E(\Pi \mid S_2) = \sum_{1}^{T} (1+r)^{-t} \{E(w_t) - \tilde{w}\}\tilde{L}, \qquad \ldots(10)$$

which is the difference in the present value of wage costs. The two strategies must both yield the same expected utility for workers from condition (5). Since workers are risk averse, the non-stochastic wage $\tilde{w}$ can be less than the expected value of the stochastic wage $E(w_t)$. The firms costs are, therefore, lower and its expected profits higher.

In the next section simultaneous employment and wage variations are dealt with, but in a somewhat different context. Instead of a single relative price changing, overall fluctuations in an economy are considered.

IV. WAGES UNDER UNCERTAIN AGGREGATE DEMAND

We now consider an economy where the price level and aggregate output fluctuate. The economy consists of M firms producing a single (composite) good with the same technology. Even though the general equilibrium framework (in which wages and profits feed back into aggregate demand) is not allowed for, the force of the result, it will be argued, does not depend upon this.

Workers and producers are assumed to be uncertain about the level of aggregate demand over the future period $t = 1, \ldots, T$. There is uncertainty about the actions of consumers or investors or the government or the foreign trade sector or some combination of these. Producers, in turn, will react to changes in aggregate demand—leading to price and output movements. There is no very satisfactory theory of price and output dynamics in response to overall fluctuations. As long as prices do not respond fully and instantaneously then output will certainly fluctuate. *Some breakdown in competition in the product market seems to occur,*[1] at least in the short-run. Each producer has to guess what demand will be and how other producers will respond. He then forms expectations about the movements of output and the price level. Based upon these expectations each producer, as before, sets a strategy for wages and employment. This will in general, be conditional on the values of output and price that actually occur. The strategy then defines the distributions of wages $(w_{i1}, \ldots, w_{iT})$ and employment $(L_{i1}, \ldots, L_{iT})$ for $i = 1, \ldots, M$.

All firms operate under the same conditions with the same technology. For the purposes here, they differ only in scale. Consider first the properties of *equilibria such that all firms adopt the same wage, employment and output strategy.*[2] The results do not necessarily mean that this economy would actually reach or remain at such a point under competitive conditions. This question is examined subsequently.

The labour force consists of N workers who seek work over the periods $t = 1, \ldots, T$. Each firm sets the same wage and employment strategy over the period so that workers distribute themselves between firms to equalize the probability of employment at each firm.[3]

Assumption 9.   The probability of finding employment in period t is the same in each firm and is, hence, equal to the overall probability of employment q_t given by:

$$q_t = \frac{L_t}{N}, \quad L_t = \sum_{1}^{M} L_{it}. \qquad \ldots(11)$$

[1] Hence we are dropping the assumption that each firm can sell all it wants at the going price.
[2] Apart from scale differences.
[3] Since the strategies are all the same, it does not matter here whether there are mobility costs and workers search only at time zero or whether there are no mobility costs and they can move freely in each period.

There is no money illusion in the economy. Workers are concerned about their real wage and producers about the real value of profits. The real wage in t is v_t. In any period when a worker is laid off he receives unemployment compensation and avoids the disutility of work. Realistically one might also allow him to do temporary work within the household sector, but this is not specifically modelled here. The worker's real income in any period when he is unemployed is v_u, a constant.[1]

Consider any strategy, S, set by all M firms which involves some uncertainty of future wages. The wage under S may respond to fluctuations in demand and employment. The strategy may also involve employment variations and hence a positive probability of a lay-off for each worker. I shall now show the following proposition:

Proposition 2. *There exists a strategy $\hat{S}$ with a non-stochastic wage, and the same path of employment and output as S, which has the following properties. (a) Each worker's expected utility under $\hat{S}$ is the same as under S. (b) The present value of expected real profits of the firms is higher under $\hat{S}$.*

We are comparing two economies, as it were, one where all firms adopt S and the other where all adopt $\hat{S}$. Notice that the proposition states that the profit-maximizing strategy (for all firms) involves a non-stochastic wage, whatever the path of employment. If you consider any strategy S with a stochastic wage path, there is always another that yields higher profits, for a given expected utility.[2] For those who find it natural to make comparisons between more employment uncertainty with less wage uncertainty versus less employment uncertainty with more wage uncertainty, the form of Proposition 2 may seem incomplete, since it compares strategies with the same employment path. This is not so. Compare two strategies: (i) S_α with a large degree of wage uncertainty but with a small or zero probability of unemployment and (ii) S_β with little or no wage uncertainty but a large probability of unemployment. It is not possible (without much more information) to say which of the two is preferred or yields larger profits. Proposition 2, however, tells us that there exists a strategy $\hat{S}_\alpha$ which gives higher expected profits than S_α. *This means that a strategy like S_α cannot be profit-maximizing even though it might possibly be better than S_β.*

There is, however, a much more fundamental, and much harder, question of the extent to which the existence of a market equilibrium involving a wage that does not adjust to fluctuations in demand is inefficient, and may exacerbate unemployment in the economy or sector as a whole. Proposition 2 says nothing about the social efficiency of alternative strategies. It is quite possible for a strategy like $\hat{S}$ to maximize expected profits and for an alternative strategy, with less unemployment to be more socially efficient. There are transactions (or mobility) costs and other market imperfections involved in the model.

A formal proof of Proposition 2 is desirable for this case, where employment can vary, since the result is less obvious. When employment varies, a worker's income is still somewhat uncertain even under a constant wage strategy. The proposition goes through because variations in L_t affect only the probability of being in each of the two states—employed or unemployed. The setting of a constant, non-stochastic, wage represents a partial reduction of risk for the worker. Income, in the event of being employed, is non-stochastic. The firms' expected profits under strategy S are given by:

$$E(\Pi \mid S) = \sum_1^T (1+r)^{-t} E\left\{ \sum_1^M g_i(L_{it}) - v_t L_t \right\} \qquad \ldots(12)$$

and under strategy $\hat{S}$ by:

$$E(\Pi \mid \hat{S}) = \sum_1^T (1+r)^{-t} E\left\{ \sum_1^M g_i(L_{it}) - \vartheta L_t \right\} \qquad \ldots(13)$$

[1] Two arguments of the utility function—income and leisure—are reduced into an income equivalent.
[2] In particular, if we knew the profit-maximizing employment strategy $\{L_t^*\}$ then we would know that the profit-maximizing wage strategy that went with it was non-stochastic. The strategy S *may* involve employment variation *but it need not*. If the profit-maximizing strategy were to offer an employment guarantee, then the profit-maximizing wage strategy would be to offer a non-stochastic wage in addition.

BAILY   WAGES AND EMPLOYMENT 45

where $\hat{v}$ is the non-stochastic wage under $\hat{S}$ and $g_i(L_{it})$ is the output of the ith firm. The difference between the two is given by:

$$E(\Pi \mid \hat{S}) - E(\Pi \mid S) = \sum_1^T (1+r)^{-t} E\{v_t L_t - \hat{v} L_t\}. \qquad \ldots(14)$$

In the economy under S the worker has an income v_t with probability q_t and an income v_u with probability $(1-q_t)$. His expected utility when he joins the firm is given by:

$$V = \sum_1^T (1+\rho)^{-t} E\{q_t U(v_t) + (1-q_t) U(v_u)\}. \qquad \ldots(15)$$

n the economy under $\hat{S}$ we have:

$$\hat{V} = \sum_1^T (1+\rho)^{-t} E\{q_t U(\hat{v}) + (1-q_t) U(v_u)\}. \qquad \ldots(16)$$

If we now choose $\hat{v}$ so that (15) and (16) are equal—as specified in the proposition—we have that: [1]

$$\sum_1^T (1+\rho)^{-t} E\{L_t U(v_t) - L_t U(\hat{v})\} = 0. \qquad \ldots(17)$$

$U(v_t)$ can be expanded in a Taylor series to give:

$$U(v_t) = U(\hat{v}) + U'(\hat{v})(v_t - \hat{v}) + \tfrac{1}{2} U''(\phi_t)(v_t - \hat{v})^2, \qquad \ldots(18)$$

where ϕ_t lies between v_t and $\hat{v}$. Multiply through by $L_t(1+\rho)^{-t}$, sum over t and take expected values. Substitution of the condition (17) then gives:

$$\sum_1^T (1+\rho)^{-t} E\{v_t L_t - \hat{v} L_t\} = \sum_1^T (1+\rho)^{-t} \frac{1}{2U'(\hat{v})} E[-U''(\phi_t) L_t (v_t - \hat{v})^2]. \qquad \ldots(19)$$

We know that $U'' < 0$, $U' > 0$, $L_t \geqq 0$ and $(v_t - \hat{v})^2 \geqq 0$ so that the left hand side of (19) is positive (strictly positive unless $v_t = \hat{v}$ for all $L_t > 0$). Since $r = \rho$ the left hand side of (19) is equal to (14), the difference in expected profits between the two strategies, so the proposition is proved. If we ignore U''' and higher order terms the expression in (19) for the profit difference can be simplified to:

$$E(\Pi \mid \hat{S}) - E(\Pi \mid S) = R_A \left[\sum_1^T (1+r)^{-t} \tfrac{1}{2} E\{L_t (v_t - \hat{v})^2\} \right], \qquad \ldots(20)$$

where R_A is the degree of absolute risk-aversion of workers. The more risk averse the workers, the greater is the return from the non-stochastic wage. [2]

Proposition 2 has shown that it is profitable for all firms together to set a constant wage. This does not show that it will be profit-maximizing for each firm taken singly. To show this requires introducing mobility costs once again.

We have not really considered mobility in this economy so far. Let us now apply essentially the same framework as that used in the previous section. Suppose that all firms in the economy follow a strategy S with a stochastic wage. Consider a single firm deciding on its wage strategy over the period. Let this firm decide to offer $\hat{S}$ instead. This implies the same employment path and the same expected utility for a worker joining the firm, so that the firm will expect the same number of workers to join it at time zero as it would have had under S. The firm's expected profits will be higher, provided it can ensure that it still has the same share of the work force over the time-period $t = 1, \ldots, T$ (or at least whenever

[1] We have multiplied by the constant N. Recall that $q_t = L_t/N$.
[2] There seems to be no terribly illuminating manipulation of the term in parenthesis. Clearly the greater the variation of v_t around $\hat{v}$ the greater is the difference in expected profits.

there is full employment). A sufficient condition for the firm to retain its workers is given by: [1]

$$E_{t-1}\left\{\sum_{t}^{T}(1+\rho)^{-\tau+(t-1)}(q_{\tau}U(\theta)+(1-q_{\tau})U(v_{u}))\right\}$$

$$\geqq E_{t-1}\left\{\sum_{t}^{T}(1+\rho)^{-\tau+(t-1)}(q_{\tau}U(v_{t}-C_{\tau}^{t})+(1-q_{\tau})U(v_{u}))\right\} \quad ...(21)$$

for $t = 2, ..., T$. Rearranging gives:

$$E_{t-1}\left\{\sum_{t}^{T}(1+\rho)^{-\tau+(t-1)}(U(\theta)-U(v_{t}-C_{t}^{t}))q_{\tau}\right\} \geqq 0. \quad ...(22)$$

This is the equivalent of the feasibility condition used earlier. If (22) is satisfied, the firm can retain its workers. $\hat{S}$ will then be feasible and will hence maximize expected profits for each firm separately.

There is a corresponding condition associated with a sustained fall in v_{t}. The effect of this is not to force a reduction in θ, but we might expect a reduction, as I shall describe. Consider the following condition:

$$E_{t-1}\left\{\sum_{t}^{T}(1+\rho)^{-\tau+(t-1)}(q_{\tau}U(\theta-C_{\tau}^{t})+(1-q_{\tau})U(v_{u}))\right\}$$

$$>E_{t-1}\left\{\sum_{t}^{T}(1-\rho)^{-\tau+(t-1)}(q_{\tau}U(v_{\tau})+(1-q_{\tau})U(v_{u}))\right\} \quad ...(23)$$

or rearranging:

$$E_{t-1}\left\{\sum_{t}^{T}(1+\rho)^{-\tau+(t-1)}q_{\tau}(U(\theta-C_{\tau}^{t})-U(v_{\tau}))\right\} > 0. \quad ...(24)$$

If this condition were violated by a fall in v_{t} then workers from other firms would come to this firm looking for work. This would mean the probability of employment for workers already at the firm would decline. The firm could adjust the wages downwards, increasing its profits, deterring new workers and leaving its current workers no worse off than they would have been had their probability of employment declined. There is not a perfect symmetry, however, between upward and downward wage rate adjustments and this would be accentuated if we allowed for the general practice of favouring existing workers when a firm reduces its work-force. This feature of the model, showing more definite downward stickiness of the wage strategy, seems not undesirable.

To summarize the results of this section, we have shown that the profit-maximizing strategy for all firms together is to set a pre-announced wage path that does not respond to period by period fluctuations in the state variables and hence to changes in aggregate demand, price or employment. This strategy will also be profit maximizing for each single firm, provided the fluctuations in demand are not too large. If there is a large sustained change in demand, particularly an increase in demand, then each firm will see gains from adjusting the wage path.

In comparing the two strategies S and $\hat{S}$ there may be general equilibrium effects on aggregate demand.[2] This does not affect the force of the results obtained because any single decision-making firm must surely ignore the impact of its own actions on aggregate demand.

V. EMPLOYMENT STRATEGIES

Employment strategies are much harder to analyse than wage strategies and I shall have a lot less to say about this topic. It is important to observe, however, that, while the firm

[1] The worker is shown in (21) as paying no mobility cost if he quits and is unemployed (apart from his loss of wage income of course). We could modify this. For example he might still incur search costs—some fraction of C_{t}^{t}.
[2] The difference between S and $\hat{S}$ in terms of these effects on demand is only distributional in any case.

may smooth employment fluctuations to some extent, setting a non-stochastic level of employment does not in general maximize expected profits.

Consider the M firm economy of Section IV and suppose we knew the profit-maximizing path of output for this economy. Now compare two strategies $\tilde{S}$ and $\hat{S}$. Strategy $\hat{S}$, as defined previously, has a constant wage path but variations in employment. Strategy $\tilde{S}$ has both wage and employment constant. In both cases let the firms produce the profit-maximizing path of output. Hence with $\tilde{S}$ the firm is hoarding labour beyond its instantaneous production needs. Expected utility with $\hat{S}$ is simply (16) which I restate:

$$\hat{V} = \sum_{t}^{T} (1+\rho)^{-t}E(q_t U(\hat{v}) + (1-q_t)U(v_u)). \qquad \qquad ...(27)$$

With strategy $\tilde{S}$ we have:

$$\tilde{V} = \sum_{t}^{T} (1+\rho)^{-t}U(\tilde{v}). \qquad \qquad ...(28)$$

Choose $\tilde{v}$ so that these two are equal.

$$\sum_{t}^{T} (1+\rho)^{-t}\{E(q_t)U(\hat{v}) + (1-E(q_t))U(v_u) - U(\tilde{v})\} = 0. \qquad \qquad ...(29)$$

The difference in the firm's expected profits between these two strategies is given by:

$$E(\Pi \mid \hat{S}) - E(\Pi \mid \tilde{S}) = \sum_{t}^{T} (1+r)^{-t}(\tilde{v} - \hat{v}E(q_t))N. \qquad \qquad ...(30)$$

The important parameters are the path of output, the value of v_u and the concavity of $U(v_t)$. If the profit-maximizing path of output were to keep output constant then clearly keeping employment constant would be profit-maximizing. There is no theory here of the determination of the optimal price-output strategy but observation suggests variations in output are the rule. The level of v_u is the value of workers' income and leisure in periods of unemployment. If $v_u > 0$ we can certainly find paths of L_t (and hence q_t), where $L_t < N$ for some t, which satisfy equation (29) and for which (30) is positive. This means that this model will certainly predict fluctuations in employment following fluctuations in aggregate output.

Although the optimal employment strategy would have to be determined simultaneously with the optimal price-output strategy we can still see how some of the parameters would be likely to influence the result. As v_u changes the cost of unemployment changes. Government policies have a considerable impact on this. The taxation of wage income and the payment of unemployment compensation operate to lower the cost of employment variations.[1] Even without the government, however, v_u would be non-zero. A worker might find work outside the sector we are considering, perhaps within the household sector. The utility of leisure is important, particularly when the length of lay-off is not too great. The value of leisure is not independent of income; if unemployment implies starvation, leisure is worth little. In a relatively affluent economy, however, the utility of avoiding forty hours on the production line is considerable.

Although it is clear that there will be a positive probability of unemployment implied in the strategy set by the firm, it is also likely that the firm does hoard labour beyond its immediate production needs. This would reduce the probability of lay-off and be consistent with the risk-reducing role of the firm. Labour hoarding is a phenomenon that has been noted and is consistent with the observation that productivity per man increases in an upturn despite the forces which one would expect to lead to decreasing returns.[2]

---

[1] In principle the government has realized the incentive effect of its policies and imposes a penalty, in terms of higher social insurance contributions, for firms that have a high variance of employment. The penalties are not very effective, however, and only somewhat offset the incentive to employment variation provided by the tax on earned income and subsidy to unemployment. Feldstein [1] discusses the incentive effects of such policies in some detail.

[2] The income-smoothing motive for hoarding labour would reinforce the factors discussed by Oi [6] to explain the same phenomenon.

48   REVIEW OF ECONOMIC STUDIES

VI. OPTIMAL WAGE STRATEGIES AND THE CAPITAL MARKET

It has been shown in the preceding sections how, subject to some conditions, the present value of expected profits would be maximized by a policy of a non-stochastic wage path. The assumptions made about the relative risk-bearing abilities of workers and firms were strong.

Consider now a situation where firms consider the present value of expected profits but, instead of workers considering expected utility, they also consider the present expected value of their incomes. If workers are to be indifferent between strategies $\hat{S}$ and S as before then we have that:

$$\sum_{t}^{T} (1+r)^{-t} E\{q_t v_t + (1-q_t)v_u\} = \sum_{t}^{T} (1+r)^{-t} E\{q_t \hat{v} + (1-q_t)v_u\} \qquad \dots(31)$$

or by rearranging and multiplying by N:

$$\sum_{t}^{T} (1+r)^{-t} E\{L_t v_t - L_t \hat{v}\} = 0. \qquad \dots(32)$$

This means—comparing (32) with (14)—that the firm is also indifferent between $\hat{S}$ and S. Hence the strategy of the pre-announced wage path does not become worse than the other. The firm becomes indifferent between the two. This is at least suggestive that, given the asymmetry between workers and stockholders that I described in the introduction, then $\hat{S}$, the pre-announced wage strategy, will still show superiority even if the strict risk neutrality versus risk aversion dichotomy were relaxed.

Even a rich stockholder will not be able to hold a portfolio which is perfectly diversified. The capital market itself contains a measure of aversion to risk. If we are willing to operate in mean-variance space, we can plot the worker's indifference curve superimposed on the standard portfolio theory diagram.[1] (Figure 1). The slope of the *RA* line measures the increase in expected value of returns the market requires for an increase in standard deviation of the return. If the worker's indifference curve is steeper than the *RA* line at the point *A* then the optimum firm strategy will involve a strictly non-stochastic wage.

A more formal analysis seems to be extremely difficult. Since strategies S and $\hat{S}$ may involve variations in employment each worker still faces uncertainty of income even when the wage is certain. It is easy enough to find the indifference curve in the space of mean and variance of the worker's income, but when employment varies profit space and workers' income space are related only in a very awkward way.

Ideally one should also allow workers some costly or limited access to capital markets explicitly. Allowing workers to borrow and lend subject to a budget constraint could modify the optimal strategy, although this ability clearly does not eliminate risk, even though it can smooth out the consumption path.[2] In general, if firms actually set a stochastic wage path then workers would want to operate in the market for uncertain assets. The picture of millions of workers continuously taking positions in different assets immediately suggests the possibility of financial intermediation. The savings in transactions and information costs would be immense. One can therefore think of a firm which is setting a pre-announced non-stochastic wage path as providing a joint product—employment and intermediation— for its workers. The difference in profits between the two strategies is the return to the intermediation. The stockholder is willing to provide the intermediation service since he can adjust his portfolio in response to the increased risk. The firm does not set a wage strategy which pushes workers into capital market operations because it is more efficient for the stockholders to operate in the capital market.

---

[1] See, for example, Tobin [10].
[2] It is possible to apply essentially the same approach that is used in Section IV to prove Proposition 2 when workers borrow and lend, provided stochastic independence of the random variables is assumed. The algebra becomes extremely burdensome, however. The result holds even with no divergence between borrowing and lending rates.

BAILY   WAGES AND EMPLOYMENT   49

There is the intriguing possibility that a third party—perhaps an agency or a labour union—might offer to provide the intermediation service instead of the firm. One may in fact observe examples of this where an agency contracts to supply labour and pays the workers a constant wage rate and receives a fluctuating margin from the firm actually using the workers in production. It would seem in most cases, however, that the firm is most advantageously placed to provide the intermediation. It will always have to have an administrative

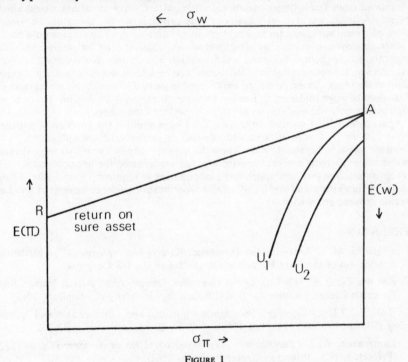

FIGURE 1

Market equilibrium with non-stochastic wage.

machinery to organize personnel matters. Its administrative costs are likely, in fact, to be minimized by a constant wage rate policy. A third party would incur the costs of an alternative administrative machinery to receive fluctuating wage payments from the firm and pay constant wage payments to workers. There is a return to the intermediation from the difference in expected profits between the alternative strategies but this does not necessarily mean that the firm has excess profits available to be bid away. If there are many competing firms then the strategy of paying a constant wage path will earn normal returns and any another strategy less than normal returns.

VII. CONCLUSIONS AND EXTENSIONS

It would be a mistake to overemphasise the strict results of Propositions 1 and 2. Changing some of the assumptions could easily modify the results. The important ideas are that firms set long-run wage and employment strategies, that these strategies embody a risk-reducing or insurance role for the firm and that employment fluctuations will be smoothed somewhat, but less than wage fluctuations. To specify clearly what sticky wages meant for the model a strictly non-stochastic (and in fact constant) wage strategy was used. A more general framework could lead to conclusions about smoothing of fluctuations, but this is harder to specify formally.[1] Even without a more general formal framework, it is hoped that the ideas presented here can provide some insight into the rather vague but pervasive view that wages are sticky.

There are many questions unanswered and directions to go in. I have made some attempt to incorporate monopoly elements on both sides of the labour market. In particular, the fact that unions impose seniority rules on the laying-off process means that a majority are insulated from employment variations. By contrast, wage variations would affect all workers. A union working on a majority vote principle would, therefore, be willing to trade employment variations for higher wages in its bargaining. This factor would reinforce the wage-employment asymmetry described above. Introducing bargaining and unions changes the whole picture, however, and I mention it here only as a direction for further work. A more obvious extension of this paper is to look for some direct empirical evidence to support the ideas. In particular, to look for evidence to distinguish this model from other explanations of wage stickiness.[2] It is not necessary for there to be only one factor at work, though presumably some influences are more important than others.

Apart from a brief mention in Section IV, I have avoided the question of whether or not one can say that wage stickiness has caused or exacerbated unemployment. I have avoided the question because I do not know the answer. My feeling is that wage stickiness, or rather the underlying market imperfection, has exacerbated the unemployment. These are deep waters, however, and much more information is required. Specifically, a general equilibrium framework and a price adjustment specification under conditions of fluctuating aggregate demand are needed.

REFERENCES

[1] Feldstein, M. " Lowering the Permanent Rate of Unemployment ", a forthcoming publication of the Joint Economic Committee of the US Congress.

[2] Katona, G. *et al.* 1968 *Survey of Consumer Finances* (Ann Arbor, Mich.: Survey Research Center, Institute for Social Research, University of Michigan, 1969).

[3] Kuh, E. " Unemployment, Production Functions and Effective Demand ", *Journal of Political Economy*, **74** (June 1966).

[4] Lampmann, R. J. *The Share of Top Wealth-Holders in National Wealth 1922-56* (Princeton, N.J., Princeton University Press, 1962).

[5] Lucas R. E. Jr. " Capacity, Overtime and Empirical Production Functions ", *American Economic Review, Papers and Proceedings*, **60**, no. 2 (May 1970).

[6] Oi, W. Y. " Labor as a Quasi-Fixed Factor of Production ", *Journal of Political Economy*, **70** (December 1962).

[7] Phelps, E. S. *et al.* *Microeconomic Foundations of Inflation and Employment Theory* (New York: W. W. Norton, 1970).

[8] Projector, D. *et al.* *Survey of Financial Characteristics of Consumers* (Washington, D.C.: Board of Governors of the Federal Reserve System, 1966).

[9] Stigler, G. J. " Inflation in the Labor Market ", *Journal of Political Economy*, *Supplement*, **5**, part 2 (October 1962).

[10] Tobin, J. " Liquidity Preference as Behavior Toward Risk ", *Review of Economic Studies*, **25** (February 1958).

[1] One might use reduction of variance as a criterion, but this is approximate at best and runs into awkward covariance problems when employment and wages vary.
[2] Notably the contributions in the Phelps volume [7]. Professor Alchian has told me that some UCLA students are collecting data which may help, although I think they are more concerned with price setting behaviour. Historical data on the real wage rate and a discussion of wage rigidity can be found in Kuh [3].

[3]

A NEO-CLASSICAL THEORY OF
KEYNESIAN UNEMPLOYMENT*

DONALD F. GORDON
The City University of New York

This paper could be described as another effort to find a microeconomic rationale, or more simply and better, an economic rationale, for the Phillips curve.[1] The latter is defined for convenience as the negative relationship, which is here presumed to be a fact of observation for sufficiently short periods, between the level of unemployment and the rate of change of money wages. More accurately, however, the interest here is to find an economic rationale for wage rigidity and involuntary unemployment which, it will be argued, given the fluctuations in aggregate nominal demand that we typically observe, produce the sets of data that have been termed Phillips curves.

The introductory section contains a brief comment on the significance of an economic explanation of the Phillips curve and a discussion of its historical interpretation in a somewhat different fashion than appears to be customary. Section II contains a brief sketch of two recently developed classes of economic explanations for the Phillips curve and of what I believe are serious empirical and logical omissions in these accounts. In Section III an additional theory is offered together with some empirical implications.

I. BACKGROUND

At the risk of laboring the obvious I would enter a plea for wider recognition of the fact that without an economic explanation of the Phillips curve we have no theory of employment and unemployment and of movements of aggregate output and the price level in the short run. Certainly the "old" or pre-Keynesian quantity theory had no explanation since, to use the most common (if inaccurate) phrase, it "assumed" full employ-

*This paper, in essentially its present form, was originally given at the Rochester Conference on the Phillips Curve in April 1973 and is to appear together with other papers and comments at the conference in *The Phillips Curve and Labor Markets* (K. Brunner, ed.), to be published by North Holland Press. I would like to thank the North Holland Press for permission to publish here.

1. The original stimulus for the paper I owe to John Young and George Freeman, Chairman and Commissioner, respectively, of the (Canadian) Prices and Incomes Commission, with whom I worked during the summer of 1971. Their skepticism regarding conventional explanations of unemployment persuaded me that a new approach was needed, and some aspects of the positive theory of this paper are contained in the Final Report of the Commission (1972). I have also benefited from conversations with and comments by many others, particularly, Armen Alchian, James Ferguson, John Floyd, Milton Friedman, Harry Gilman, J. Allen Hynes, Thomas Mayer, William Meckling, Ronald Schmidt, and the conferees at the Rochester conference on the Phillips curve, and my two critics.

ment. In other words, it postulated a vertical Phillips curve, thereby effectively denying the facts to be explained. The "new" quantity theory also
has no explanation. It purports to be only a theory of the demand for
money, and hence of aggregate nominal demand, and eschews any attempt
to explain the division of a change in nominal demand between changes in
quantities (and hence employment and unemployment) and changes in
prices.[2]

The "Keynesian model" as it has usually been interpreted is a simple
right-angled Phillips curve with the horizontal branch at the zero rate of
increase in money wages. (This is not inconsistent with the fact that at
various points Keynes himself considered situations where the wage unit
did in fact change.) While clearly accounting for short run fluctuations in
output and employment in response to fluctuations in aggregate demand,
it is not consistent with the fact that money wages rise substantially at
levels of unemployment far in excess of some irreducible minimum,
judged simply by past minima. And, of course, many if not most economists have been troubled by Keynes' attempt to give an economic explanation of this wage rigidity.

Thus a first interpretation of the Phillips curve is that it arose, or more
likely, that it became accepted, as a compromise between the right-angle
and vertical versions, being compatible with both sets of facts that were
inconsistent with one or the other of the previous models. But while the
Phillips curve accounts for these facts, it does not explain them unless the
curve itself can be shown to be explained by more fundamental forces
(leaving aside the question of its stability). Indeed one could argue, and I
believe correctly, that the Phillips curve is a contradiction of traditional
price theory as it has developed over some two centuries. For that theory
suggests that it is irrational for both workers and for employers to permit
extended periods of non-equilibrium money wages, even for periods as
brief and mild as, for example, the recession of 1969-71, let alone what we
observe in major recessions.

Perhaps some economists would argue that there is no contradiction
between Phillips curves and traditional price theory on the ground that
the latter deals only with comparative statics and says nothing concerning
rates of change to new equilibrium positions. They might contend that
dynamic analysis of prices in disequilibrium arose only after the enuncia-
tion of Samuelson's (1947) fundamental postulate for competitive markets

$$(1) \qquad dp/dt = F(D - S), \quad F' = 0 \text{ and } F(0) = 0,$$

2. Cf. Friedman (1966). In a significant sense the new quantity theory is a retreat. The words
"quantity theory" in the old sense were surely short for "the quantity theory of the value of
money" or the price level; the new quantity theory should have a new name.

where D and S are quantities demanded and supplied respectively. Thus a second interpretation of the Phillips curves is that it is merely the application of relationship (1) to labor markets in particular, with insignificant transformations of the variables to percentage changes.

However, this in itself simply transfers the need for an economic explanation of the special case of the Phillips curve to a need for an explanation of Samuelson's postulate. First, whether traditional price theory treats of dynamics or not, a relationship such as (1) would appear to be inconsistent with maximizing behavior, at least in markets for commodities which are in any degree storable or for labor which produces such commodities. If such relationships were to exist they would create opportunities for speculative buying and selling which would eliminate them. As the popular random walk theory of the stock market suggests, prices should *always* be in equilibrium, relative to current knowledge or belief, and these are already embodied in demand and supply curves.[3] Even apart from this logical difficulty, an economist, before accepting such an equation as an axiom, would naturally be curious concerning whose behavior is being described by the equation, particularly since it concerns competitive markets where buyers and sellers are usually assumed to regard price as parametric. He would be immediately inclined to search for a basis in maximizing behavior as in ordinary static demand, supply and cost schedules. The Phillips curve as an axiom is hardly a more satisfying explanation for unemployment than its predecessor, the rigid money wage.

Thus a future historian of economics might describe the rise of the Phillips curve as a natural theoretical advance growing out of the state of economic analysis and empirical evidence and produced by the logical requirements of two separate intellectual strands more or less simultaneously. One was the inconsistency between the facts and both the Keynesian and classical models; the other was Samuelson's development of disequilibrium price dynamics. *Such an historian would, I believe, be profoundly wrong.* Historically speaking, it would be more accurate to describe the Phillips curve as simply the embodiment in a differential equation of a loose set of impressionistic facts that have been observed by practical men for generations, if not centuries; that have been accepted and commented upon by many economists; and that were increasingly well known to be consistent with empirical evidence prior to the Keynesian era.

It would require a whole volume to track down and report on all the

---

3. Note that this objection applies to purely *disequilibrium* price movements described by (1), which Samuelson was discussing. It is not applicable to any relationship describable by a differential or difference equation in which prices move over time but are always in equilibrium (where demand equals supply) relative to current output and beliefs.

textual evidence bearing on this third interpretation; only a few examples will be given here. It has been a commonplace for centuries that "good times," i.e., rising output, have been associated with high or rising prices while recessions have been associated with the opposite. The most plausible interpretations of the scores of economic writers of the mercantilist and pre-mercantilist periods would emphasize their recognition of the connection between the quantity of money and demand and in turn its favorable effects upon output. Many of these writers likewise recognized the additional effect of money upon prices.

It is not clear, however, how many of the early writers saw that it was precisely because wages and prices were sticky that the demand created by money could stimulate output and employment. But Hume in the middle of the eighteenth century clearly saw the entire chain. An autonomous increase in the quantity of money enables employers "to employ more workmen than formerly, who never dream of demanding higher wages." (Hume, 1779, p. 304). Similarly, Henry Thornton, writing of recession rather than boom, contended that "A fall (in price) arising from temporary distress will be attended probably with no correspondent fall in the rate of wages" (Thornton, 1802, p. 82). In the late nineteenth and early twentieth centuries economists who studied the phenomenon of the "business cycle" found a correlation between rising output and wages, and their findings were later more thoroughly confirmed by the National Bureau of Economic Research. Even Irving Fisher in the twenties did a statistical study finding a negative correlation between unemployment and rising prices (Fisher, 1926). When the late Jacob Viner (1936) reviewed the *General Theory*, he suggested that most of Keynes' results were precisely the same as those of other economists who knew that sticky wages combined with fluctuations in velocity could create trouble.

A question might be raised whether it is proper to equate long held views about sticky wages with a belief in the Phillips curve. By "sticky" wages we presumably mean that they are slow moving relative to the movements of aggregate nominal demand. If, over a longish period, these fluctuations of nominal demand move back and forth around some average level, or rate of increase, we would observe a set of points which would be termed the Phillips curve for that period.

An economic explanation for the Phillips curve requires, therefore, no more (and no less) than an explanation for this long accepted relative rigidity of wages. Why are labor markets said to be so often in "disequilibrium"?[4] (This is a highly unfortunate expression since economic theory

4. Aggregate Phillips curves can of course be derived by postulating individual labor markets in disequilibrium and their individual Phillips curves. But this is restating the problem rather than providing a solution.

requires each employer or employee to be in equilibrium at all times, relative to his beliefs, costs and obligations, or he would be doing something else). Even if monetarists and Keynesians resolve their conflicts over the determinants of aggregate demand, economists would still have no explanation for cyclical unemployment until the rigidities on the supply side cease to be loose empirical generalizations and yield to an explanation in terms of wealth maximizing behavior.

This sketch of a third interpretation of the historical place of the Phillips curve contrasts sharply with the view that it is the "only significant contribution to emerge from post-Keynesian theorizing" (Johnson and Croome, 1970, p. 110). In my view, it is neither theorizing, nor post-Keynesian, nor an advance. It is an ancient empirical generalization, superficially at odds with economic theory; the theoretical basis for it is unclear or at least not widely accepted, and it has only attracted attention during the last decade. It far pre-dates Keynes, and far from being an advance, it is a retreat—to reality, albeit common sense reality—from the formal classical or Keynesian models.

II. TWO KINDS OF EXPLANATION

While we have argued that the Phillips curve merely embodies an ancient piece of casual empiricism, it is likely that its explicit formulation has stimulated considerable thinking on the theoretical basis for such a relationship, and during the past decade two kinds of explanations have emerged.[5] In this section, we will briefly sketch both of them and indicate the respects in which they appear unsatisfactory or incomplete in their account. In the following section, a new explanation is offered. Both existing classes of explanation ignore the existence of labor unions and minimum wage laws and we will do the same. Most of the labor force is not unionized, and more important, the phenomena represented by the Phillips curve appear to have existed over long periods when labor unions were virtually nonexistent. Moreover, we will imagine that we are dealing with an economy which over a long period of time has exhibited a steady trend rate of increase in money wages, say 5 per cent. But while this is the trend over the long period, there have been shorter spans characterized by greater and lesser inflation. The basic question is: What are the fundamental forces that associate booms and depressions with these periods of greater and lesser inflation?

5. Space precludes dealing with all popular alternative explanations. "Market Power" has properly, I think, been rejected by many economists as incompatible with rational maximizing. Cf. for example, Tobin (1972) or Friedman (1966). The Keynesian allegation of concern over relative wages seems to require a very peculiar utility function in which putative money wages dominate actual money wages.

The Auction Market Model

The first explanation associated recently with Milton Friedman (1968) and Lucas and Rapping (1970) treats the labor market much as a commodity market in an ordinary commodity exchange. It could be termed the continuous auction market theory. Labor is presumed to be sufficiently homogeneous within classes so that "the" level of wages for a particular class of labor or skill can be observed by all participants. It is presumed, therefore, to fluctuate much as commodity prices fluctuate in response to demand and supply. Potential employees can always find employment at this "going" wage or at a wage that is a trivial amount below it. If there are fluctuations around the long run rate of increase in money wages and prices, workers will wish to work more at times when money wages and commodity prices are relatively high, or above the trend level. For money earned at such times can be spent (after it has been kept at the interest rate reflecting the inflationary trend) at times when commodity prices are relatively low. Thus to the extent that workers can vary over their life-times the periods in which they work more or less, varying their "vacations" or "overtime" accordingly, they will work more in relatively inflationary periods. This may be particularly true for part-time workers such as married females, the fairly young or the fairly old. Output as a consequence should be higher in relatively inflationary periods and lower in relatively deflationary periods, and such fluctuations in output would, of course, moderate the fluctuations in price.

The above effects may be strengthened if the worker believes that the transitory rise in his wage relative to trend is not part of a general increase in inflation but an increase in his wage relative to other wages. This may be plausible, for he must only observe one price, his wage, to see the increased money demand for the item that he sells, while he must sample perhaps hundreds of prices before he can observe the general increase in inflation in the prices of the things that he buys. If this is the case, he may suspect that an increase has occurred not only in real wages measured in future (expected) prices, but in real wages measured in current prices.

It is fairly clear that under the conditions that we have postulated, the commodity market theory of the labor market would give rise to what has been called the Phillips curve. Relatively inflationary periods will draw workers into the labor force while relatively deflationary conditions will induce them to retire temporarily. It is perhaps equally clear that should this long run 5 per cent trend be replaced by a long run 10 per cent trend, say, then the relationship will break down. To begin with, output will be stimulated by the thought that the increased inflation is temporary. But when it becomes clear that the continually higher rate of money wage increases are associated with continual commensurate increases in commodity price increases the short run stimulus to output will falter. Henceforth, if the long run trend rate of money increases remains at the new 10 per cent level, only temporary fluctuations of more than 10 per cent will induce greater output, and increases of less than 10 per cent will now be associated with depressions in output (or perhaps depressions in the rate of increase of output). The Phillips curve will have shifted upwards.[6]

For many purposes the auction market theory of the labor market is a useful abstraction. Relative to the lifetime of the individual there is a continuous market in lawyer, carpenters, doctors, and so forth. The young person can observe the going price—current incomes in these occupations—and use this in choosing a vocation. Even for shorter periods there is no doubt that it provides part of the explanation for the association of boom periods and increased employment for certain types of casual labor—for the young and the old, and possibly for married females who are frequently in and out of the labor force—and for overtime and wartime increases in output.

Yet there are major respects in which it does not seem to coincide with widely known short period facts of employment and unemployment. It suggests that the downward phase of a recession is typically characterized by cuts in money wage increases and by workers quitting in response to such cuts. In fact, there is usually a decrease in quit rates during a recession. Secondly, while it explains unemployment of labor it is hard to see how it would explain the unemployment among non-human factors of production which does occur. In typical recessions, for example, rental residential housing suffers a significant increase in vacancies together with sticky prices. But the owners of such resources have no motive to withdraw them from the market, as with labor services, unless they cannot earn even their operating costs. They have no leisure alternative! Finally, a period of recession appears to be one in which laborers either search for jobs at "reasonable" wages, or in some cases, while they can observe the wage without search, they cannot get a job at that wage because of job rationing. They do not appear to observe an available job

---

6. It might be reasonably argued that while this model produces a positive association between employment and the rate of change of money wages, it does not produce a negative association between measured unemployment and the rate of change of money wages. In a strict sense this is true since in an auction market all unemployment is obviously voluntary. Nevertheless, if we can imagine inserting current methods of measuring unemployment into such a highly abstract model, measured unemployment need not necessarily be zero. If an unemployed worker were asked if he had looked for a job he might plausibly answer in the affirmative, even if his looking had consisted of no more than eliciting an unsatisfactory wage quotation over the telephone from his job broker.

Milton Friedman has pointed out to me that these effects do not require that the employer and employee have systematically asymmetric price and wage expectations—since the real wage that is relevant for the employer, the "product wage," is different from the real wage that is relevant for the employee, his "basket-of-goods wage."

(in their usual occupation) and then decide to retire temporarily from the labor force.

The Search Model

The second explanation of the Phillips curve starts from the observed fact that when workers are unemployed, normally or abnormally, they are frequently looking for jobs. It may be called the search model and differs sharply from the previously sketched auction model.[7] Potential employees cannot observe a quoted price for their talents as on a commodity exchange. They do not know where the jobs are, at what price, and with what characteristics. The lack of an organized market in jobs can be attributed to the vast heterogeneity of workers on the one hand with respect to skill, temperament, and so forth, and the equally vast variety of job openings with respect to wages, working conditions, and skill requirements on the other. On securities and commodity exchanges there is also, of course, a vast heterogeneity. But presumably on those markets the essential characteristics can be much more accurately standardized, quantified and summarized, and hence prices are quoted. The labor market is more akin to the market for individual family residences.

The unemployed worker must formulate a search strategy. In one form of the search model, for example, he forms an estimate of the probabilities of finding a reasonable job at various wages, and chooses a wage to hold out for (and hence a probability of success in any one period) that balances the costs of continuing search against the costs of setting too low a wage. He would then continue to search until either he revises his estimate or finds a job at his chosen wage.

The employer is also searching the labor market. He likewise cannot observe a given wage or a given static supply curve which enables him to hire any desired quantity of labor "instantaneously." In a finite period of time, only a finite number of applicants will apply and a mutually satisfactory determination be made of the worker and of the job. He has, therefore, an estimate of a dynamic stochastic supply curve giving the probability distribution of achieving a net accession rate (hires minus quits) at different levels of the money wage. His supply curve

$$(2) \qquad dN/dt = a = f(w, u)$$

where a is net acquisitions, w is the money wage, N is total employment and u is an error term, has the upward slope of a static monopsonistic supply curve even though in the long run he may be a purely competitive buyer.

---

7. Phelps *et. al.* (1970) provides a variety of search models.

There is an important difference between the imperfect information in the auction market model and in this search type model. In the auction market model the future is unknown, but the present is known.[8] In the search model the present as well as the future is unknown.

Unemployment would exist in search type labor markets even if there were no fluctuations in total demand tending to make wages rise and fall on the average. Unforeseen new tastes, new commodities, and new methods of production are continually appearing while older methods and older products fall into disuse. These forces created fluctuations in demand and supply for branches of the economy and for groups of workers even while overall demand is stable. These fluctuations require search on both sides of the labor market and this creates what might be called the normal or natural rate of unemployment. It might also be called frictional unemployment.

As in the case of the auction market model, the search model of the labor market gives rise, under the conditions that we have imagined, to a Phillips curve tradeoff between unemployment and rates of wage change. From a position of overall stability (in which employers are raising money wages at 5 per cent per year and are finding on average the desired change in the labor force) an increase in demand will first affect the employer's product. When he and all other employers raise their wage increases, workers who are searching for jobs will find higher wages available, and if they have previously formulated an optimum wage for which to search, unemployment will be reduced. The worker is "fooled" into taking more employment, since if he knew that there is a general increase in the rate of inflation proceeding he would revise upwards his acceptance wage (which already is rising, of course, at 5 per cent per year). Again, increases in employment will be associated with more rapidly rising wages and prices. The opposite will be true for decreases in the rate of increase of overall demand. (If the employer was not conscious that there was a general abnormal increase in demand he will be disappointed in the response to his wage increase, and after reformulating his estimate of the dynamic supply curve will raise his wage increase again.)

It is likewise true that the Phillips curve associated with a long run trend of 5 per cent money wage increases is replaced if this trend is changed to one of increasing money wages at 10 per cent. Temporarily, wage increases and output will both increase. But the expectations of both sides will eventually change. The worker looking for a job will adjust his estimates of the wages he can expect to get, while the employer will likewise adjust his estimates of what he expects to pay. Only when fluctua-

8 Save for the additional point elaborated on page 436 above, regarding the difficulty of knowing current consumer prices.

tions in the rate of increase in demand justify more than the expected 10 per cent will the employer be offering more than 10 per cent and the employee be fooled into accepting "too much" employment. Similarly, temporary recessions will occur even with rising money wages if demand is not increasing sufficiently to provide normal employment at wage estimates which will be rising at the expected rate of 10 per cent. In this case as in the commodity market model of the labor market, the Phillips curve will shift upward so that for each rate of unemployment the wage increase will be five per cent higher than before.

The search model no doubt accounts for a good deal of normal frictional unemployment and for some of the abnormal unemployment that appears in recessions. Contrary to the commodity market view, it is compatible with the impression that workers do search for jobs rather than simply make employment decisions on observed wages, and it predicts the unemployment of some forms of non-human capital such as residential housing.

But it has both logical and empirical difficulties.[9] A logical difficulty is the incompatibility between the decisions of prospective employees and the decisions of employers. A prospective employee can make an intelligent decision to accept or reject a job only if he has some idea, not only of the current wage, but of the future wage and employment at that wage. Most search models assume—sometimes implicitly—that the worker believes that each job being offered will continue indefinitely or that the wage will stay constant or both. (Some do allow for a constant probability of unemployment.) Otherwise he has a much more complicated decision problem involving presumably probability distributions of both future wages and unemployment periods. The assumption of stability, it will be argued in the following section, has a considerable element of validity, but until the reasons for this supposed stability are established the search model is both incomplete and contradictory. It is contradictory because such presumed stability is inconsistent with the presumed behavior of the employer. This latter is assumed to adjust more or less continually along a dynamic supply function which itself will be continually reformulated as he receives new data.

More important difficulties in the search model are empirical. It has no place for layoffs, it makes incorrect predictions about quits, and perhaps most vital it implies that all employers are always willing to hire in any

9. The present author has been fully guilty of the incompleteness and errors ascribed in the text to the search theories. See Gordon and Hynes (1970). The housing and rental market models developed in that paper avoid the difficulties in the labor market which are here criticized. But we had no justification for extending that analysis to the labor market without further elaboration and such elaboration would have been incompatible with the sketch of the demand side. Cf. p. 382. I believe the theory developed in III below clears up these problems.

job classification at any stage of the business cycle. With the onset of a recession an employer should gradually perceive the state of the labor market, lower money wage increases (perhaps making them negative) and experience decreased and very possibly negative accession rates. Symmetrical with boom conditions workers should be fooled into accepting too little employment by rejecting job offers and by increased quitting. In fact, quit rates decrease and presumably suitable job applicants rise. And surely it is true that a very large part of the time most firms are simply not hiring, or hiring only those quantities that they "need."

The facts concerning the quit rate, the fact of layoffs, and most important the fact that firms are frequently, or perhaps generally not hiring at their existing wage rates all point to the proposition that jobs are generally being rationed at existing money wages. The employer is typically off his dynamic supply curve (p. 438 above) setting a wage at which the supply of net accessions is greater than he wants to employ at that wage.[10] It is of some interest to note that if job rationing is prevalent, stickiness in money wages is produced by firms rather than workers. Keynes, his followers, and many of his critics have on the contrary supposed that rigid money wages are produced by the demands of the workers and their resistance to money wage cuts whether due to irrational money illusion or allegedly rational interest in relative wages. If jobs are rationed, workers do not get a chance to resist money wage cuts (except, of course, for the union sector).

Finally, some of the broad facts of economic history make the search model appear implausible. Even during the recent mild recession it seemed that unemployment was discussed *ad nauseam* in the media while money wages were rising substantially. Did employers really feel that such increases were necessary to maintain their employees?

If that recession is implausible on the basis of the search theory, the depression of the 1930's is incredible. Until 1933, money wages fell, although sluggishly. (They had fallen much more sharply in the recession of 1919-21 with substantially less stimulus from unemployment.) With about 24 per cent of the work force unemployed in 1933, real wages in manufacturing were higher than in 1929! After 1933, money wages rose annually despite massive unemployment.[11] The search theory requires us

---

10. In left wing literature, an important figure has been the heartless and avaricious employer who drives his workers to exhaustion by pointing out the window to the line of unemployed job applicants. What has to be explained is why such an employer is so generous.

11. Unemployment, money wages and real wages for manufacturing in the thirties are cited in Kuh (1966); employment, real wages and money wages are cited for particular periods in Rees (1951) for separate manufacturing industries.

442   ECONOMIC INQUIRY

to believe that a degree of misinformation concerning the state of the labor market that can only be described as fantastic persisted among employers for over a decade. It was not only during the 1970-71 recession that the "laws of economics" did not appear to work as expected.[12]

III. AN ECONOMIC RATIONALE FOR INVOLUNTARY UNEMPLOYMENT

In this section, a different model of the labor market is outlined, which attempts to account for rigidities in wages on the basis of a simple extension of neo-classical theory and its maximizing postulates. The discussion here is an informal first step in an attempt to develop the plausibility of the basic propositions and their empirical implications. No attempt will be made to derive formal general market solutions.

Two Basic Postulates

The basic idea is simply that job hirings can be typically viewed as implicit, and in some cases, explicit understandings—legally unenforceable contracts—promising that under reasonable and more or less understood conditions, employees have a certain security with respect to both wages and employment. We may term this model the quasi-contract model.[13] The quasi-contract model is suggested by fairly well-established economic propositions quite apart from the logical and empirical difficulties in the auction and search models which were discussed earlier. Some of the propositions are commonplaces of everyday life.

The simplest version of the theory is based upon two fundamental but simple propositions. The first is that in a continuous auction labor market discrepancies would arise between the marginal rates of substitution of risk for income between sellers of the services of human as compared to sellers of non-human capital and that for legal reasons and for transactions cost reasons these discrepancies cannot be removed by voluntary exchanges which are legally enforceable.

---

12. It is frequently alleged and plausibly so, that certain actions of government depressed the demand for labor and retarded the recovery. This in no way resolves our question, however, which is why money wages did not respond to this unemployment.

13. Since first formulating this "original" theory I have noticed a variety of forerunners. Hicks (1966, pp. 52, 55) hints at the desire for security on the part of employees and of the "social" aspects of labor markets as explaining rigidity of money wages. (But contrary to the theory of this paper he suggests that otherwise employees would leave during the recession.) Rees (1951) argues that it is employers rather than employees that hold wages rigid because, among other reasons, of a concern for future reputation as a "good employer." But he is skeptical of whether employers are optimistic enough during depressed periods to be much concerned for the future. Phelps (1970, p. 133) seizes upon the preference for security as a basis for rigidity but later appears to reject it (1972, p. 18). Finally, since this paper was completed I have learned that Martin Baily (1974) and Costas Azariadis (1973) have independently developed certain aspects of the same basic idea. The contribution of the present paper is primarily to provide a rationale for the asymmetric attitudes of employers and employees toward risk, and to draw some implications for rigid wages and other kinds of observed behavior.

For the vast majority of people, the bulk of their assets is in the form of prospective wage and salary income over a working life. Much of this human capital is fairly specialized and frequently cannot be transferred without loss in earnings to the production of a variety of commodities or services. Even if this were possible, it would be subject to cyclical variations. Thus, in a world of both micro and macro economic change and uncertainty, the owners of human capital might expect a considerable degree of risk.

Of course, the owners of non-human capital are also subject to risk, but this risk can be substantially reduced in two ways. In the first place, they can enter into long-term contracts or contingent contracts for the sale of the services or products of such assets at specified real or money prices. Such contracts, of course, can reduce risk to both seller and buyer. A particularly useful variant of this ability to commit the future services of non-human capital is the opportunity it creates for mortgaging those services, riding out downturns by borrowing, and hence diversifying over time. Secondly, holders of non-human capital can diversify by holding only a small fraction of their non-human wealth in any one asset.

It is widely recognized that human capital has important differences from other assets for institutional reasons. Because of the legal system, its services cannot be rented or sold under enforceable contracts for long periods of time, and even if they could, there would be important incentive costs since the productivity of human capital requires the cooperation of its owner in a manner that is not true of physical capital. It is likewise difficult to mortgage them. These forces create a second handicap in that one cannot diversify out of one form into many others. One cannot, for example, sell a piece of oneself if one is a lawyer in Cincinnati and buy a portion of a carpenter in San Diego. Thus, while human capital is not necessarily inherently more risky than physical capital, its owners cannot avoid risks in the same manner. At the same time, studies of financial markets suggest that the representative individual is risk averse, and so far as I know, where large portions of an individual's income and assets are concerned, there is general agreement that risk aversion is dominant. These forces, then, create the discrepancy in marginal rates of substitution between risk and return which is our first postulate.

The second fundamental proposition asserts the existence of quasi-contracts. A quasi-contract exists when an individual or firm, by behaving consistently in a particular manner, can induce another individual or firm to act to a large degree *as if* the former were legally constrained to act in that manner. This is no more than to say that people learn about the behavior of others, that they act upon that knowledge, and that such knowledge constrains the behavior of the first actors involved. Such constrained behavior covers the great mass of all "non-economic" behavior. But it also covers a wide variety of economic behavior.[14]

With these two postulates a mutual gain is available to employers and employees if we start from a world of purely auction labor markets. Employees will, to some degree, prefer a lower expected wage with a smaller variance to a larger more uncertain income. In the interest of getting cheaper labor, employers can enter into implicit long-term quasi-contracts with their employees by guaranteeing them some reasonable security.[15]

Since such guarantees will be unenforceable on the employer, he must somehow persuade the employee to accept the implied lower real wage. It seems clear that he can only do so by performance over a period of time which will create for him a reputation of being a "good employer." If, for example, wages fluctuate over a long period with a 5 per cent trend, such an employer will not take advantage of a slack market by lowering the rate of increase in money wages, or perhaps by not lowering real wages. On the other hand, the employee must be deterred from leaving to join other employers in boom times. He will be so constrained by the thought that his present employer will not be hiring during the next recession. His present employer will at that future time have redundant employees to whom he feels honor bound (or more accurately, profit bound) to maintain at reasonable (i.e., above market) wages.

Keynesian Unemployment

A first implication of this view of the labor market is that there will periodically be involuntary unemployment following the strict Keynesian definition. In a period of slump, the employer will have redundant labor because of a discrepancy between the current money wage and the current marginal revenue product, and hence he will be turning away new workers at that money wage. A general increase in demand will find a willing additional supply and a willing additional demand provided that the increase in demand is sufficient to eliminate redundancy among the previous employees. Since prices will rise, the employees will be working at a lower real wage. This is the Keynesian criterion:

> Men are involuntarily unemployed if, in the event of a small rise in the price of wage-goods relatively to the money wage, both the aggregate supply of labour willing to work for the current money-wage and the aggregate demand for it at that wage would be greater than the existing volume of employment (Keynes, 1936; p. 15).

14. See Alchian, A. and Demsetz, H. (1972, p. 778, note 2) and the literature there cited.

15. It should be noted that the insecurity which the worker avoids in this theory, to the extent that he avoids insecurity, does not simply consist of "set up" costs such as buying a home, making new associations, etc. It consists of all types of fluctuations in income whether cyclical or specific to a trade or occupation.

But in contrast to Keynes and many of his followers, the rigidity in this model is created by employer job rationing.[16] We do not have to resort to worker resistance either because of money illusion or because of peculiar utility functions with respect to relative wages; nor must we imagine that during slumps employers are so amazingly uninformed on the state of the labor market.

This implication may sound paradoxical. Why, it may be asked, would a wage and employment system evolve which created unemployment in the interest of *security*? Surely an employee is more secure in a system of fluctuating wages than in a system characterized by high wages in the boom and zero wages during recessions.

The resolution of this seeming paradox depends upon showing that these are not the relevant alternatives. First, we will show that a slightly formal but simple model will create Keynesian unemployment, but without the layoffs that are envisaged in the stated objection. Second, we will tackle the question of layoffs. Let Figure 1 depict a specific labor market of the auction type in which demand fluctuates according to a rectangular distribution between D_1 and D_2. To simplify further, suppose there are no fluctuations in aggregate demand and that a fixed supply curve may be assumed. Finally, let long-term contracts for labor be strictly enforceable and negotiable without legal or incentive costs.

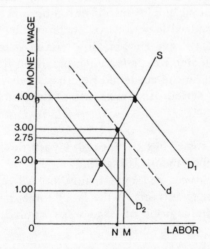

FIGURE 1

16. The job rationing in this model is to be distinguished from the "hoarding" of labor in order to have a buffer stock against both fluctuations in demand for the final product and in accession to the labor force. Our model asserts that whatever the buffer stock there will be times when it will be paid more than sufficient to maintain it, even after allowing for all risks of stochastic fluctuations.

Without contracts, the wage would fluctuate between $4.00 and $2.00 and if employers and employees were risk neutral, they would be indifferent between this and a long-term fixed wage of $3.00. But if employees are risk averse while employers are risk neutral, any one employer can go to that class among all workers who are still in this labor market at the wage of $2.00 and who are most risk averse and find takers at something less than $3.00. Say this figure is $2.75 and that his demand at this figure is less than the amount supplied.

Assume that he is a "representative" competitive employer so that his demand at all prices is proportional to total market demand, e.g. 1/1000 of total demand. Then, by change of scale, we may draw his demand curve as d. Notice that he hires OM rather than ON when he switches his employment policy for that is where his expected demand cuts the (to him) horizontal supply. Notice also, that at no demand below d would he be willing to hire "temporary" employees at the "going" market wage ($2.75) since his demand price, when he already has OM workers, is below that wage. (When the market wage is $2.00, his demand price for additional workers is $1.00.) Naturally in depressed periods, he also does not hire workers at his wage of $2.75. (This is not, of course, a market solution. Other employers will bid up the contractual wage so that the most risk averse employees will enjoy a rent.)

These simple numbers serve to illustrate the point. In this model what we may call the tenured employees do not choose between a system of high wages interspersed with periods of unemployment and a system of fluctuating wages. They have chosen "low" fixed wages and steady employment. This has created Keynesian unemployment for the non-tenured employees.[17] (No one in the academic field has surely ever imagined that academic tenure in a period of slow growth of demand is an advantage to those without it.)[18]

Layoffs

The model just discussed has no place for layoffs despite the possibility of involuntary unemployment. Using that model we might envisage a world where all employees had rigid tenure and all unemployment fell upon new entrants or re-entrants to the labor force; more plausibly perhaps we should imagine a group of fixed wage tenured employees plus a

17. It should be noted that this theory is not the ancient proposition to the effect that workers will be paid more in occupations with much unemployment. That proposition deals with industries and occupations rather than firms, and does not itself explain the unemployment.

18. Many readers will notice certain similarities between this model and the "lifetime security" said to be common in the Japanese economy. The argument of this paper is that the U.S. and other western economies are much more similar to the Japanese than is implied in auction models of the labor market.

group of non-tenured employees with flexible wages. In this latter case there may still be substantial involuntary unemployment in the Keynesian sense. In either case there would be no layoffs, and while layoffs are among the most commonplace facts, they pose awkward and obtrusive questions for economic theory which for the most part economists have somewhat shockingly managed to ignore.

The difficulties that economic theory has with the notorious fact of layoffs are illustrated in Figure 2. The firm is observed to cut back its employment from L_j to L_i, and economists from Keynes (1936) to Alchian (1970), using essentially an auction market model, have interpreted this to mean a drop in demand from D_1 to D_2 combined with a horizontal supply curve S. The layoff simply short circuits wages cuts plus voluntary quits. (For the moment we ignore the other lines in Figure 2.)

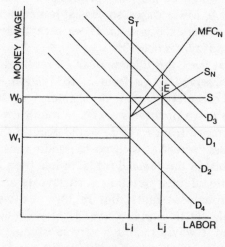

FIGURE 2

But this interpretation conflicts with the "common sense" belief that the short run supply curve at E typically has a positive finite slope. That this common sense impression can be consistent with rationality plus some information on the part of employees, is indicated by imagining the strained circumstances in which the short run supply curve would be perfectly elastic. If (a) there were no cyclical fluctuations of aggregate demands, (b) each drop in demand in a particular market were known to be permanent (or at least very long run) by all concerned, and (c) if each employer were small in the relevant labor market, then a completely elastic supply curve would indicate rational behavior (neglecting perhaps employees who are close to retirement). But if cyclical downturns are believed to be temporary on the basis of common experience and if one has some knowledge of the general state of the labor market, it would be foolish to quit at a slight drop in wages. And the fact that quits decline rather than rise, at *given* money wages, at the onset of a recession indicates that the requisite information is available. Further, if declines in demand occurred in specific labor markets, if their duration were initially unknown, and if some job search were required, it would again seem irrational to quit immediately.

To refute the impression that employees typically have short run supply curves with finite slopes economists have had to resort to money illusion, to emphasis on relative (hypothetical) money wages as opposed to unemployment, or to an astonishing lack of information, and they have had to ignore the facts concerning quit rates. They resort to these devices because it would seem that if the short run supply curve were rising through E it would be mutually profitable for employers and some employees to move to lower wages, somewhat less employment, and some quits, rather than experience layoffs. If we accept the rising short run supply curve, why do layoffs occur?[19]

For some cases at least this dilemma can be resolved by another interpretation of the observed move from L_j to L_i even in the context of rigidly tenured and completely non-tenured employees. If L_i workers were tenured the supply curve of these workers to the firm would be the vertical line L_iS_T. The move from L_j to L_i would occur if the supply curve of non-tenured workers were S_N with corresponding marginal factor cost MFC_N and if the shift in the demand for labor had been from D_3 to D_4.[20] As in the conventional interpretation such layoffs are a substitute for wages cuts and subsequent quits. But in this case we do not have to assume a completely elastic supply curve. The layoffs occur because after the drop in demand it would require a very substantial, not a trivial drop in wages to make it worthwhile to hire any of the non-tenured employees. And this is because the marginal revenue product of the tenured employees, W_1, is not an epsilon but far below the previous wage of the non-tenured employees. In this quasi-contract model the employer may know that the supply elasticity at the current wage for non-tenured workers is

19. Of course we are speaking of involuntary layoffs where the individual suffers a finite loss of expected income and/or utility. This loss approaches zero presumably where layoffs are predictable, e.g., weekends off. (Ch. Alchian (1970) pp. 39-40). But from this point of view layoffs associated with a horizontal supply curve would also approach the voluntary, and these are not layoffs in which we are interested. If only the probability of a layoff is known the extent of its involuntary nature depends, it would seem, on its effect on the employees' risk, i.e., on his ability to diversify, and on his risk aversion.

20. We are omitting the complexities arising from an employer's dynamic supply curve mentioned above.

not infinite: but this is irrelevant because a mutually profitable exchange cannot take place at a slightly lower wage.

In this model, for any given horizontal change in demand, layoffs as opposed to wage cuts will be more frequent the smaller the elasticity of derived demand and the higher the proportion of tenured workers. What would make the demand very inelastic? We might first suppose—as Stigler suggested long ago and as more recent putty-clay capital models assume—that the short run variability of factor proportions is very low, or in the limit, zero. Then we would expect that layoffs, as opposed to wage cuts, would vary with the other Marshallian factors determining the elasticity of demand—the proportion of labor cost in variable cost, the elasticity of the supply of the other variable factors, and the elasticity of demand for the final product. We would hence predict that, holding other relevant variables constant, for a given change in demand there would be more layoffs and less wage cuts in concentrated industries (where the demand for the final product is more inelastic) and in those with a low proportion of wage costs in variable costs. These, of course, are testable propositions.

A Third Postulate: More Layoffs

The above analysis is not satisfactory in as much as it does not cover cases of "small" changes in demand, as a glance at Figure 2 will show. In these instances conventional auction market models would expect the employer to slide down his marginal factor cost curve for non-tenured employees.[21] However, the principle involved—that layoffs will occur where the cut in wages required to employ profitably the workers involved is substantially rather than infinitesimally below the existing wage—can be more generally applied with the addition of a third postulate.

To this point, we have treated quasi-contracts in the labor market as if they shifted all risk from employee to employer, and we have envisaged only one type of quasi-contract which divides all employees into only two classes, tenured and non-tenured. But in some areas where the employer is subject to a great deal of "natural" risk, there may be more advantage to both parties in sharing this risk. Our third basic proposition, then, is that labor contracts will be similar to contracts in other markets in that they frequently exhibit risk sharing.

In security and other markets, there are virtually indefinite possibilities of varying the degree of riskiness of various instruments and providing for

---

21. It could also be argued that it is unsatisfactory because it predicts behavior for other variables during a recession that we do not observe. If a very large portion of labor costs were fixed costs, the resulting low level of variable costs should produce sharper price fluctuations in final products, smaller decreases in output, and more bankruptcies than would otherwise be the case. It might, however, be difficult to translate these qualitative predictions into quantitative assertions with which to confront actual price changes, quantity changes and bankruptcies.

unforeseen contingencies, and as a consequence, there exists a bewildering variety of securities and other contracts. In the labor market we would expect, in addition to a necessary additional vagueness, at least as much variety. Some firms, with highly uncertain demands, will choose to offer very little security. Others will offer year to year security with expected seasonal variations. Still others may offer expected cyclical variations in their package. At the other extreme, even the most secure employee is not to be envisaged as having an implicit contract that guarantees his income in the face of threatened bankruptcy of the firm or even in the presence of long periods of sustained losses. In the face of uncertainty, a labor market contract must be thought of as being more in the nature of a preferred share rather than as a debenture or mortgage.

Another way of stating these facts is to say that in a plane with expected income and variance as axes few employers or employees will be in equilibrium at a corner solution. Employees will not typically sacrifice so much expected income so as to have zero risk, while employers will not absorb all risk in order to minimize wages. In a perfect market, between any two classes of employers and employees, contracts will be such that they make the marginal rates of substitution between risk and expected income the same for both.[22]

In many organizations, particularly in large organizations, we would suppose that the labor contract will take the form of a fairly clearly structured labor relations and wage policy administered by specialists in wage and personnel management. Employees and employers alike will work within a multitude of defined rules governing such items as pensions, seniority, overtime, job rules and privileges, job classifications and grades, steps within grade, and provisions for periodic wage and salary review. It seems reasonable to suppose that the more structured and formal such a wage and salary program is, the smaller the degree of subjective uncertainty the potential employee will feel. For that reason, he can be hired for less. (It would seem that one of the functions that unions provide for employers is to create a similar feeling of security.)

Thus, there is no reason why, within the firm, there should not be different risk sharing quasi-contracts with different employees, just as one may imagine different legal contracts with different customers or suppliers of non-labor inputs. In particular, there is no reason why a firm may not find it advantageous to offer all employees some security but with different groups, even among otherwise homogeneous employees, having dif-

---

22. We should probably require that employers as well as employees cannot buy and sell contracts in the labor market so that the results of portfolio theory and other aspects of the modern theory of finance are not applicable.

ferent degrees of security.[23] If the firm were to experience a continuing decline in demand, or possibly if a given decline in demand were to continue for a long enough period, the continuing misfortunes would cause each class of employees to lose their security successively. Yet each time these undesirable outcomes triggered the loss of security for a particular group, that group may have a marginal revenue product far below (because of the number of still tenured employees) its contract wage and below its minimum supply price. If this were true, we would expect to see a succession of layoffs, of the nature analyzed earlier, rather than wage cuts.

Figure 3, a modification of Figure 2, illustrates some dimensions of a very simple risk-sharing contract which would produce rational layoffs and no wage flexibility. A group of employees, $(L_j - L_i)$, has been hired by this firm at wage W_0 with some degree of tenure, but with the least security of all employees. They are guaranteed "full" employment at the wage W_0 until profits, P, have declined to a particular level, P_i, after which there are no further guarantees. Suppose that given this package, the long run supply curve, S, to the firm of such employees is horizontal, beginning at H. (It may, of course, require search time to move out along this curve.)

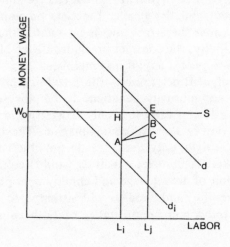

FIGURE 3

23. One criterion immediately suggests itself for choosing which employees to offer greater security—those with greater seniority. Security will be most valuable to those employees who are most risk averse and pay can be on average lower. Risk aversion cannot be directly observed, but one may guess that the class of employees who stayed through the last boom because of risk aversion ("loyalty to the firm"), are more likely to stay through the next boom than those who have just joined the firm and about whom one knows nothing. Therefore, if layoffs are necessary, the recent accessions would be the first to go.

The short run supply curve, here labeled AC, (with marginal factor cost AB) is somewhat special in these circumstances, and does not bear the normal relationship to S. It shows the wage at which various numbers of these employees (or others outside the firm) could be employed if the quasi-contract were broken; that is, if it became known that the firm was henceforth going to hire them at the lowest possible wage, because in fact the firm had commenced to operate in this manner. Except coincidentally this short run curve will not go through the point E since the short run wage and the long run wage carry different non-wage provisions. In a boom market the short run curve should be above E, but in a depressed market, it would be below.[24]

Under these conditions if a fall in demand to some level d_i reduces earnings of the firm to the level P_i the $(L_i - L_j)$ employees will be laid off. As before, the layoff occurs because a small cut in wages would be insufficient to permit mutually profitable employment despite the short run monoposonistic supply curve. If the demand were then to fall more, still more employees to the left of L_i would fall into a similar situation and we would observe a succession of layoffs. As in Figure 2, layoffs would be more likely for any given horizontal change in demand the more inelastic that demand and the smaller the class of employees with the least security. But under the arrangements postulated there would be no short run wage flexibility; the contract precludes the employer from using the short run supply curve for any of his employees.

While this kind of contract resolves the puzzle of layoffs, that, is, it explains why it is not mutually beneficial to employ some of the discharged workers at a lower wage, it is only illustrative, and is but one of an almost infinite variety that we could imagine. The theory does not require that wages be rigid, only that they do not fluctuate so as to clear the short run market. A complete analysis would require an extensive empirical investigation of actual wage and employment practices with the theoretical structure in mind, and would attempt to reconcile these practices with the tastes and opportunities of both employers and employees.[25]

---

24. One cannot casually extend this supply curve to the right beyond C, even if there were an outside auction type labor market. These employees have hitherto opted for this particular arrangement and they cannot be considered homogeneous with employees in the outside market. Search costs in this and other employments will also be a factor.

25. In our simple example we have avoided the question of the expected duration of the decline in demand which can be expected to play a role. In this connection it should be noted that if the employer has better information on the expected duration than the employee, he would be a "good employer" (giving up short run benefits for long run advantage) if, when he expected the decline in demand to be a long one, he laid off the employee rather than "exploit" him along the short run monoposonistic supply curve.

Our discussion of layoffs should indicate that the paradox indicated earlier—a security system of quasi-contracts that creates insecurity in the form of layoffs—is a false one. For society as a whole, continuous full employment and perfectly flexible wages and prices will have a higher expected output and less variance than one with any layoffs. But no individual in our theory chooses less income with greater variance. The $(L_i - L_j)$ employees in our example do not necessarily have more variance in their income (the usual measure of risk) than if their wages fluctuated continuously. And if they do we would expect a higher expected income as compensation. Presumably they could have guaranteed themselves against all unemployment but only at an unacceptable cost in terms of income. What is true in this risk sharing model as in the earlier rigid tenure model, and what is true in non-labor markets as in labor markets, is that for any given "objective" quantity of risk, the more security that is purchased by some individuals the less there is available for others. An employment system organized to create security for some at the expense of layoffs for others is no paradox; a similar phenomenon abounds in securities markets and creates the elementary distinction between stocks and bonds.

Naturally, when we allow employers and employees to share risk, we lay ourselves open to the charge that the model predicts that "anything can happen." Nevertheless, this third proposition makes specific predictions that diverge from received analysis. It predicts that among firms operating in the same labor market, those with higher profits at any point in time will grant larger wage increases. They are clearly not forced to do so by reason of scarcity; they do so because they are to some degree sharing the risk with their employees.

The Phillips Curve, or Why Wages are Sticky

Like the auction and search theories of the labor market, this theory predicts that we should observe a Phillips curve. Like them, it also predicts that in the long run this curve will shift up or down due to the effects of expectations, whenever the unemployment rate is different from its long run equilibrium or "natural" value.[26] But the manner in which expectations operate are sharply different in this model than in the other two, and may be expected to operate with a much longer lag.

Dealing first with the short run, the Phillips curve is a combination of wage rigidity and flexibility. Naturally, the wage rigidity is a consequence of the quasi-contracts. Even short run wage flexibility follows from two factors. The first is the fact that the labor market contains some non-tenured employees who are in search type or auction type markets. The second is the degree to which employees share risk with employers.

---

26. The distinction between movements along and movements of the Phillips curve seems non-operational; the data seem simply to suggest that wages are sticky but not wholly rigid.

454   ECONOMIC INQUIRY

Turning to the question of the long run shift in the Phillips curve, we must suppose that the quasi-contracts between employer and employee are free from money illusion and are in terms of real wages. But the employer can hardly be expected to predict every wiggle in the business cycle, and it is the essence of the theory that he can and will avoid adjustments to short run supply and demand considerations—to the extent that he believes them to be transitory—even when he is fully aware of them. (Sharing current prosperity or losses, due to risk sharing provisions, is not inconsistent with this.)

On the other hand, we must suppose that his long run expectations are not perfectly rigid. A particularly lengthy boom, with higher prices and a tighter labor market than had been expected, will shift, to some degree, his subjective probability that the economy is entering a secular inflation, or a higher rate of secular inflation. Presumably, the amount of the shift will depend in a Bayesian manner upon the strength of his prior convictions and upon the degree of divergence from the expected. He will then change the money terms of his quasi-contracts by an appropriate amount, i.e., what we may call his personal Phillips curve will have shifted upward (for wealth maximizing reasons).

In the contract model, the Phillips curve shifts more slowly than, for example, in the search model, because of the nature of the prediction problem. In the search model, the employer changes his wage increase when he concludes from a *current* net accession rate that the labor market is such that the wage increase is not optimal for current conditions. His problem is to predict the current excess supply from his limited observation of a stochastic variable. Having concluded that the current labor market situation has changed, he would fully adapt to that change. In the quasi-contract model, the employer also adapts when he can form a conclusion as to the current state of the market; but in this case, *only to the extent that this conclusion affects his long-term prediction of future wages and prices.* He does not adjust optimally to meet the current situation.[27]

How long would a long run adjustment take? It seems impossible to calculate a period of adjustment for a "rational" decision maker when that adjustment requires predicting the future. There is no "given" probability distribution with which to work, unless it be the whole of human history. There is no way to calculate a rational prior probability distribution, or a prior probability distribution of probability distributions, etc.

---

27. Given the difficulty of the prediction problem, one might suppose that the individual firm or industry would look to other firms or industries for clues as to the future. If wage increases in one industry or firm provoke wage increases in other industries and firms, this is almost to be expected. It does not have to be looked upon as indicating the importance of relative wages in the employees' utility functions. Similarly one could almost predict that the circumstances discussed in the text would give rise to a variety of cost-push and other non-maximizing theories of inflation.

However, we would expect subjective prior judgments formed on past experience to be particularly resistant to events that are virtually historically unique, e.g., the collapse of aggregate demand during the thirties or the unprecedented secular inflation of the postwar period. It is not surprising that full adjustment may be slow. If the effects of inflation on money interest rates can be lagged by decades, one might expect similar adjustment periods for the full adaptation of employment practices.[28]

Involuntary Unemployment at Full Employment

It is of some interest to note that, according to this explanation, Keynesian unemployment will be widespread under conditions of "full employment." Full employment equilibrium has the property that the rate of increase in nominal demand cannot be increased without eventually raising the average rate of price and wage increase until unemployment returns to its previous level. It has always been recognized that full employment is consistent with a positive level of search or frictional unemployment. This would be the only kind of unemployment in a full employment equilibrium if aggregate demand were always distributed among separate labor markets in accordance with supplies in those markets. If, however, aggregate demand fluctuates over separate markets, and if supply cannot adjust instantaneously, some markets will be experiencing excess supply and involuntary unemployment with wage increases below the average. These will be offset by other markets with excess demand and higher than average wage increases.

Some economists might prefer the term "structural" for the additional unemployment created by fluctuating demands. Terms are of little consequence. Yet it is important to notice that this is involuntary unemployment in the Keynesian sense and that it cannot be permanently lowered if the initial position is one of long run full employment equilibrium, i.e., it is one in which actual and expected wage and price increases are consistent with the rate of increase in nominal demand.

Certainly, an increase in the rate of growth of nominal demand will create additional employment at stable wage rates (or at least within stable individual wage and employment policies) since jobs were previously rationed in some industries, and this increased employment will be at lower real wage rates due to the more rapid rise in prices. But the increased pressure in the labor market and the higher rate of price increase will cause employers to revise (if only gradually) their long term expectations, and hence their quasi-contracts. The Phillips curves for all markets will rise until the level and rate of increase of wages again corresponds to

28. With this qualification the contract theory predicts a vertical Phillips curve, absence of money illusion and no "inflationary biases." The long delayed effects of long run periods of secular inflation may, however, easily create the illusion of inflationary biases.

nominal demand. Unemployment will rise to its original rate with its component of involuntary unemployment.

Other Implications

While the quasi-contract theory provides an alternative explanation for the Phillips curve, it also has a number of other testable implications. Perhaps its sharpest confrontation with the search and auction models arises from its prediction that quit-rates should fall in a recession and rise in a boom as they do. The other models predict the opposite. The contract model further predicts that hiring should be a lagging cyclical indicator and that (average) productivity should fluctuate pro-cyclically as it does.

Keynes, trained as a neo-classicist, predicted that real wages, and by implication productivity, should fluctuate contra-cyclically on the basis of diminishing marginal productivity. The quasi-contract theory cuts any necessary relationship between the *current* wage and *current* marginal productivity. If there is risk sharing between employer and employee, real wages will fluctuate pro-cyclically.

The theory also predicts that firms with relatively stable demands for their product over the cycle will have more stable and lower wages than do other firms. Such stable firms will find it cheaper to offer more security to more employees. This may not be a prediction which impresses the non-economist who will find it obvious that more stable firms "can afford" a reasonable wage increase even in recessions. But for an economist it should be a puzzle despite its common sense sound. Do cyclically stable firms pay more for gasoline during a recession than others do? Presumably not, unless on the basis of this stable demand they have negotiated a long term contract; and this is precisely what the theory asserts about the labor market.

Finally. the theory predicts that returns to equity holders should fluctuate more than wages and salaries and that self-employed workers should have higher incomes with a greater variance than employed workers. These facts are commonplace, but their explanation is not clear outside of the contract theory.

Concluding Comments

(a) The contract theory is not a denial of the search theory insofar as the latter deals with optimal job search on the part of the potential employee. On the contrary, it complements that theory of the supply side, and removes its inconsistency, in some models, with the employer's behavior. It complements the search theory by specifying something about the things for which the worker is searching, and creates consistency between this and what the employer is offering.

(b) The contract theory is in the tradition of Knight and Say which finds the firm or employer as the principal risk bearer. But it is not simply that the more risk averse become employees rather than employers. This may be true, but the essential element is that being an employee, or owner of non-human capital, creates a greater degree of (marginal) risk aversion.

(c) It seems that a complete articulation of Becker's [3] well known theory of specific human capital requires something like a contract theory of the labor market. In that theory, the employer and employee split the cost of creating specific human capital skills that can be used with only one employer and later split the difference between the lower outside marginal product of the worker and his higher inside product. What is to prevent the employer from later cheating the employee by paying him merely an epsilon over his outside wage?

In a similar vein the existence of non-vested pension plans is difficult to understand without a contract theory of the labor market. Presumably, this is a risk sharing arrangement. But what is to prevent the employer from similarly cheating the employees by regularly laying them off a week, say, before their pensions become vested?

A sensible answer to these questions, which would occur to virtually anyone, is that of course the employer cannot so cheat without losing his reputation and experiencing later difficulties in hiring. But if this is so obvious, it should also apply to job and wage security where employees are risk averse, and this, as we have seen, has powerful implications for the question of wage rigidities.[29]

(d) Despite the teachings of many generations of neo-classical economists it is clear that people do in fact regard the price of labor as somehow different from the prices of commodities. Labor is not a commodity! Such attitudes have been the despair of many economists. While wages make up the livelihood of human beings, so do the prices of commodities. Why should attitudes about fairness dominate discussions of wages to a greater

---

29. Cf. also Oi (1962). Becker suggests that non-vesting may be a method of retaining the employee and the firm's investment in his specific human capital. As noted this would appear to admit the contract theory as part of the theory of specific human capital. Once, however, the employee's benefits are not tied closely to his current productivity there is no reason that these should be limited to pensions. In particular seniority pay raises with no precise connection with current productivity may be part of a contract. If this were true there would be more than specific human capital and its current productivity to account for the observed rising age-earnings profiles of typical employees.

A "pure" specific human capital theory devoid of all quasi-contract considerations is, however, distinct from the theory of this paper. It explains the relative incidence of layoffs for given wages. But if the short run supply curve is upward sloping this is not the relevant question, for both the wage and the level of employment must be explained jointly. Further it would appear that for given wages the specific human capital theory implies that employees approaching retirement, in whom the firm has little remaining capital to retain, will be particularly susceptible to layoffs (and of course without induced retirement benefits). The quasi-contract theory has no such implication.

degree than discussions of prices? Any textbook on wage and salary administration will drive even a novitiate in economics to despair. Why can't personnel or human relations experts understand the simplest elements of demand and supply? Why is there a "social" element in wages in addition to an economic element, as J. R. Hicks (1966) argues? Is it all muddle-headedness?

This theory suggests an economic explanation for these attitudes. Even a tough-minded neo-classicist might admit that it is unfair to break negotiated and enforceable contracts (if one could get away with it) in the sense that it is socially undesirable. By reducing the value of property rights, such behavior reduces the social gains from voluntary exchange. But, in fact, there is only a continuum, not a sharp break between enforceable and non-enforceable contracts. The quasi-contract theory suggests that the same rationale lies behind non-contractual understandings.

The most frequent comment I have heard in discussing the rigidity of wages is the allegation that wage cuts would have a disastrous effect on morale and seriously damage productivity if not inducing outright sabotage. If this is true, it does not explain why sellers of farm commodities or corporate stock behave differently. Given that labor contracts do in fact exist, and that wage cuts are hence avoided save in drastic situations, it is very likely true that the effect on any one employer of an "unfair" wage cut might be as alleged. But this does not explain the original wage rigidity itself. It explains the serious consequences of deviating from the system once it is established and not the system itself.

(e) Wage controls have been defended on the grounds that they may be useful in breaking inflationary expectations, and the contract theory creates a much more powerful theoretical case for controls than does the search theory alone. According to both theories, a break in a long-term inflationary policy is going to produce an increase in unemployment until expectations are revised. But in the search theory, employers and employees must only correctly perceive the increased slack in the labor market in order to adjust their behavior. According to the contract theory, on the other hand, employers and employees must really believe that a new long-term era of price stability is at hand before wage increases are adjusted downward. Current excess supply is not sufficient. Thus wage and salary ceiling increases can, in principle, force the economy toward the long run equilibrium, given that the government is in fact going to maintain its rein on inflationary demand. Such controls on wage increases do not lower wages below an equilibrium and create shortages; they lower wages toward an equilibrium and eliminate surpluses. Naturally, with such wage controls there is no economic need for price controls.

I know of no instance in practice of such a control program, and it seems unlikely, if I may venture into a non-economic area, to be politically feasible.[30]

30. Another question of some interest is the extent to which employer provision of unemployment insurance has been reduced by public unemployment insurance. It would appear fairly obvious, because of adverse selection and moral hazard, that private insurance companies would find it difficult to enter this field.

REFERENCES

1. A. Alchian, "Information Costs, Pricing and Resource Unemployment," in Phelps, (1970).

2. _____, and H. Demsetz, "Production, Information Costs, and Economic Organization," *American Economic Review*, December, 1972.

3. C. Azariadis, "On the Incidence of Unemployment," paper read at Econometric Society Meetings, December, 1973.

4. M. N. Baily, "Wages and Employment under Uncertain Demand," *Review of Economic Studies*, January, 1974.

5. G. Becker, *Human Capital*. New York, 1964.

6. Canada, Prices and Incomes Commission; *Final Report: Inflation, Unemployment and Incomes Policy*.

7. Irving Fisher, "A Statistical Relation between Unemployment and Price Changes," *International Labour Review*, June, 1926.

8. M. Friedman, "What Price Guidelines," in G. Schultz and R. Aliber, eds., *Guidelines: Informal Controls and the Market Place*, Chicago, 1966.

9. _____, "The Role of Monetary Policy," *American Economic Review*, March, 1968.

10. _____, "A Theoretical Framework for Monetary Analysis," *Journal of Political Economy*, March/April, 1970.

11. D. F. Gordon and J. A. Hynes, "On the Theory of Price Dynamics," in Phelps (1970).

12. J. R. Hicks, *The Theory of Wages*. 2nd ad., New York, 1966.

13. D. Hume, *Essays and Treatises on Several Subjects*. Dublin, 1779.

14. H. Johnson and D. Croome, *Money in Britain, 1959-1969*. London, 1970.

15. J. M. Keynes, *The General Theory of Employment, Interest and Money*. New York, 1936.

16. E. Kuh, "Unemployment, Production Functions, and Effective Demands," *Journal of Political Economy*, June, 1966.

17. R. Lucas and L. Rapping, "Real Wages, Employment, and Inflation," in Phelps (1970).

18. Walter Oi, "Labor as a Quasi-Fixed Factor," *Journal of Political Economy*, December, 1962.

19. E. Phelps, ed., *Microeconomic Foundations of Employment and Inflation Theory*. New York, 1970.

20. _____, *Inflation Policy and Unemployment Theory*. New York, 1972.

21. A. Rees, "Wage Determination and Involuntary Unemployment," *Journal of Political Economy*, April, 1951.

22. P. Samuelson, *The Foundations of Economic Analysis*. Harvard, 1947.

23. H. Thornton, *An Enquiry into the Nature and Effects of the Paper Credit of Great Britain*. London, 1802.

24. J. Tobin, "Inflation and Unemployment," *American Economic Review*, March, 1972.

25. J. Viner, "Mr. Keynes on the Causes of Unemployment: A Review," *Quarterly Journal of Economics*, November, 1936.

[4]

THE EXISTENCE OF SELF-ENFORCING
IMPLICIT CONTRACTS*

CLIVE BULL

Implicit contracts are nontrivial Nash equilibria to the post-hiring trading game between a worker and the employer. These are supported by intrafirm, rather than labor market, reputations. The existence of an implicit contract that supports efficient trade is proved in a simple model.

INTRODUCTION: ENFORCEABILITY AND IMPLICIT CONTRACTS

This paper is an effort to explain, in part, an empirical paradox in the U. S. labor market. Many types of behavior in this market, notably layoff and real wage behavior, have proved inexplicable if the labor market is modeled as a sequence of spot auction markets. However, if we treat trade in this market as being mediated via long-term contracts, we gain a great deal of explanatory power. A particular example of this is the progress made by the "implicit" contract literature [Azariadis, 1975; Baily, 1974; Gordon, 1974]. There is, though, one major problem with explaining U. S. labor market behavior in terms of optimal contracts, and that is that explicit labor contracts are rare. Indeed, labor contracts are almost coterminous with the unionized sector of the labor market, which means that, at most, 20 percent of the U. S. labor market is governed by contracts.[1] Thus, we have a puzzle: much behavior in the labor market seems to be explicable only in terms of long-term labor contracts, and yet such contracts are rare.[2]

This puzzle can be sharpened into the following two distinct,

*I wish to thank Jess Benhabib, Benjamin Eden, Boyan Jovanovic, John Kennan, Lewis Kornhauser, Edward Lazear, Kevin Murphy, Roy Radner, Bruno Stein, Robert Topel, Charles Wilson, and an anonymous referee for their comments. As if that were not enough, I owe a special debt of thanks to Roman Frydman, Carolyn Pitchik, Peter Rappoport, and Andrew Schotter. All errors in the paper are mine alone. The research in this paper was financed by grants from the C. V. Starr Center for Applied Economics, New York University and the National Science Foundation (SES 8409276).

1. Even union contracts differ from the long-term contracts in the literature in being nonbinding on union members.
2. The lack of explicit labor contracts does not per se imply a lack of labor contracts. In the goods markets, for instance, there are truly implicit contracts [Calamari and Perillo, 1977, pp. 9–20]. It is the employment-at-will doctrine that rules out implied contractual clauses and so allows us to conclude from the lack of explicit contracts that no contracts exist. This situation may be changing as in some states the courts appear to be starting to circumscribe the employment-at-will doctrine, e.g., *Toussaint* [1980], and find implied contracts instead, as in the McGraw-Hill case [Lewin, 1983].

148   *QUARTERLY JOURNAL OF ECONOMICS*

but economically closely related, questions:

    (i) Given their lack of enforceability by the courts, why do so many agents in the labor market choose noncontractual agreements instead of contracts?

    (ii) Given their lack of enforceability, why are noncontractual agreements valuable?

An answer to the first of these questions based upon asymmetric information will be given in Section I. However, the bulk of the paper will concentrate on answering the second question. In doing so, it is important to note that an agreement can be broken in two distinct ways: either party can cease to trade with the other and trade instead with a third party, or either party can unilaterally change the terms of trade. The first form of breach will not occur if, after the worker has been hired, the transactions costs to both the firm and the worker of trading with a third party are prohibitive. Several sources of such transactions costs have been identified. On this see Hall [1980], Hall and Lazear [1984], Mayers and Thaler [1979], and Williamson et al. [1975]. Moreover, such costs can explain the observed job tenure data.[3] Thus, the assumption of prohibitive transactions costs of trading with third parties that is usual in the "implicit" contract literature[4] and that is adopted here may be a reasonable first approximation, at least for prime age males.

    Prohibitive transaction costs, however, do nothing to prevent the second form of breach—unilaterally changing the terms of trade. The only force that can prevent this is reputation. Holmstrom [1981] and Carmichael [1984] have tried to deal with this using market reputations. However, reputation effects are only as strong as the information flows that support them. Strong reputation effects require that accurate information about breach of the agreement flows rapidly to a large portion of the labor market. While in some labor markets, e.g., for economics professors, one might argue that information flows fulfill such requirements, it seems unlikely that they are fulfilled in most markets, e.g., unskilled or semi-skilled, blue-collar workers. In fact, it will be argued in Section I that it is precisely the very imperfect nature of information flows from the parties to the trade to third party enforcers that make contracts infeasible and force agents to choose

---

    3. In 1978, 43 percent of all U. S. workers were in jobs that had lasted, or were expected to last, ten years or more. Twenty-eight percent were in jobs that had lasted or were expected to last twenty years or more. Approximately half the male workers aged thirty-five or over were in jobs lasting twenty years or more [Hall, 1982].
    4. Bull [1983] is an exception to this.

noncontractual agreements in the first place. Certainly the importance of word-of-mouth information transmission [Granovetter,
1974; Datcher, 1983] indicates that information is likely to flow
slowly to the market. Accuracy of information is also a problem.
The reputation effect itself will give rise to incentives for strategic
information transmission; after a breach both parties have an
incentive to claim that the other side is at fault. This, of course,
compounds the inference problem of people in the market. For
these reasons, it is unlikely that market reputation effects will, in
many labor markets, be strong enough to support noncontractual
agreements.

While the market will not have timely, accurate information on
the outcomes of trades within the firm, the information flows within
the firm will be fast and accurate. Given that we have assumed that
upon hiring, the firm and the worker are locked into a finitely
repeated trading game, these intrafirm information flows give rise
to strong intrafirm reputation effects. It is these strong intrafirm
reputations that will support noncontractual agreements.

We can, then, summarize the analysis of the paper as follows.
Hiring is modeled as the firm and new hire entering into a finitely
repeated, bilateral trading game. Anticipation of this provides the
incentive for both sides to precommit to strategies via a long-term
labor contract. However, the third parties who would enforce the
contract cannot, unlike the firm and its workers, observe some of
the outcomes of the trading game, and so these aspects of the trade
cannot be written into the contract. Because of this problem, firms
and workers enter into noncontractual agreements concerning the
sequence of trades. As flows of information to third parties are very
imperfect, it is intrafirm reputations that will support such agreements. We then define an implicit contract as follows:

DEFINITION. An implicit contract is a noncontractual agreement
    that corresponds to a Nash equilibrium to the repeated,
    post-hiring, bilateral trading game other than the degenerate
    agreement consisting of a sequence of Nash equilibria to the
    one-shot trading game.[5]

The paper is organized as follows. Section I presents the simple
model of hiring in a labor market in which the rest of the analysis is
conducted. The optimal contract is derived, and it is shown how the

_____

5. If the hiring process together with the trading game were modeled as a game
of incomplete information, then this definition would have to be modified to require
the noncontractual agreement to be a sequential equilibrium.

informational asymmetry between the firm and workers on one hand and third parties on the other causes the contract to break down and so gives rise to incentives to form an implicit contract. Section II deals with the trading game and in particular the complications caused by the finite life of each worker and the infinite life of the firm. The existence of an implicit contract together with the corresponding intrafirm reputations is established. Section III contains some concluding comments.

I. TRADE WITH COMPLETE, EXPLICIT CONTRACTS

This section presents the simple model of hiring in a labor market within which the analysis of the paper will be conducted. It also shows the incentives to use a contract and how an information asymmetry can destroy the viability of some clauses in such a contract and force the parties to use a noncontractual agreement instead.

Every worker has a working life of finite length which, for ease of exposition, is assumed to be two periods long. Each worker is indexed by $s \in (-\infty, \infty)$, the period in which he entered the labor market. Apart from this index, all workers are identical. In particular, they all have the same utility function over the consumption good c and their level of work effort e. The lifetime utility U_L^s of an individual who enters the labor market at s is given by

(1) $$U_L^s = U(c_s^s, -e_s^s) + \beta U(c_{s+1}^s, -e_{s+1}^s).$$

Here, and throughout the paper, the superscript denotes the individual's index, while the subscript denotes the time period. The above function is assumed to be increasing in all its arguments, quasi-concave, and to fulfill the conditions,

$$\lim_{c \to 0} \frac{\partial U(.,.)}{\partial c} = \infty, \qquad \lim_{c \to \infty} \frac{\partial U(.,.)}{\partial c} = 0,$$

$$\lim_{e \to 0} \frac{\partial U(.,.)}{\partial e} = 0, \qquad \lim_{e \to \infty} \frac{\partial U(.,.)}{\partial e} = -\infty.$$

The following restrictions are imposed:

$$c_t^s \in [0, \infty), \forall t, e_t^s \in [0, \infty), \forall t, 0 < \beta \leq 1.$$

In the labor market a job consists of a sequence or vector of payments to the worker, $y^s = \{y_s^s, y_{s+1}^s\}$ together with a sequence of effort levels, $e^s = \{e_s^s, e_{s+1}^s\}$. For simplicity, we assume that all workers have access to a perfect capital market on which the real

SELF-ENFORCING CONTRACTS   151

rate of interest r is such that $(1 + r)^{-1} = \beta$. Define the discounted present value of a vector of payments, y^s, as $V(y^s)$. Access to this capital market is crucial for the existence of an efficient implicit contract as it leaves the time path of payments free to be adjusted to provide the required strategic incentives. In contrast, in the implicit contract literature, because of a lack of access by workers to capital markets, the time path of payments must try to fulfill both an incentive and an income smoothing role.[6]

Assume that in every period new entrants to the labor market can assure themselves of a lifetime utility U by working elsewhere. Further, assume that having joined the firm it is prohibitively costly to leave the firm during one's working life.

Firms, in contrast to workers, are assumed to be infinitely long-lived institutions. The current owners of the firm are assumed to try to maximize the net present value of the firm. Labor is the only variable input to the firm, and the firm is constrained to hire zero or one worker of each index. The profit from hiring a new worker at s to perform a job (y^s, e^s) is given by

$$(2) \qquad \Pi(-y^s, e^s) = \pi(-y^s_s, e^s_s) + (1 + r)^{-1} \pi(-y^s_{s+1}, e^s_{s+1}),$$

where $\pi(.,.)$ is increasing in its arguments, quasi-concave, and fulfills

$$\lim_{e^s_{s+t} \to 0} \frac{\partial \pi}{\partial e^s_{s+t}} = \infty,$$

and

$$\lim_{e^s_{s+t} \to \infty} \frac{\partial \pi}{\partial e^s_{s+t}} = 0, \qquad t = 0, 1.$$

Assume that having hired a worker, it is prohibitively costly to fire him.

The hiring decision in this environment will depend crucially on the prevailing institutions because both parties know that, ex post, they will be locked into a bilateral monopoly and consequently a post-hiring bargaining game. This prospect provides a strong incentive for both parties to precommit themselves to strategies at the time of hiring, most obviously by the use of a multiperiod contract. See Klein et al. [1978], Hashimoto and Yu [1980], Hall and Lazear [1984], and Crawford [1982]. Let us assume, then, that there is perfect, costless enforcement of labor contracts provided by a third party which shall simply be called the courts.

----

6. For a thorough analysis of the roles of capital markets and savings in implicit contracts, see Topel and Welch [1983].

Given this institutional setting, the firm's decision problem, because of the separability of the profit function across workers, is

(3)   max $\Pi(-y^s, e^s)$, $\forall s$, subject to

$$U_L^s \geq \overline{U}$$
$$e_{s+t}^s \geq 0, \qquad t = 0, 1$$
$$y_{s+t}^s \geq 0, \qquad t = 0, 1.$$

It is crucial to note that the form of this maximization assumes that the firm can physically observe the worker's level of effort. This assumption will be maintained throughout the rest of the paper. Let the set of pairs of vectors $(\hat{y}^s, \hat{e}^s)$ that solve (3) for each s be denoted by S. The assumptions about the profit and utility functions ensure that S is not empty and that e^s is unique and positive, while the stationarity of the problem ensures that $\hat{e}^s$ is the same for all generations of workers. This is, of course, not true for $\hat{y}^s$. Given that the workers have access to perfect capital markets, that $\beta = (1 + r)^{-1}$, and that the stream of payments is guaranteed by the threat of enforcement by the courts, (3) only determines a unique $V(\hat{y}^s) > 0$.

At present there is no incentive for either party to use a noncontractual agreement of any kind. Note especially that removing the workers' access to some capital markets, as in the implicit contract literature, would give rise to incentives for the firm to smooth the time path of wage payments but would not give rise to any incentives to use noncontractual agreements. Consider instead introducing an asymmetry of information between the trading partners and the third party enforcers of the contract.[7]

While it may be reasonable to assume that the courts can observe, i.e., find objective data on, whether worker A is in fact working for firm B and on whether firm B pays worker A the amount specified in the contract, it is less plausible that objective data are available to the courts concerning the work effort expended by worker A. Time cards and pay slips provide evidence on the former, while only the testimonies of the employer, the worker, and his coworkers are usually available on the latter. This informational asymmetry makes the enforceability of the effort clause of the contract dubious, thereby raising the probability that the worker will breach the contract. In the limit, as the data available to the courts become completely uninformative, the effort clause becomes

7. The importance of this asymmetry was mentioned by Holmstrom [1982, p. 330]. See also Klein [1984] and Eden [1985].

completely unenforceable and so redundant. In this limiting case it is clear that the effort sequence in the set of optimal contracts S will no longer be incentive compatible and the worker will provide zero effort. A trade involving zero effort is inefficient, and so there is a strong incentive for both parties to enter into a noncontractual agreement concerning worker effort to complement the wage contract. Of course, to be of use, the agreement must be self-enforcing. The existence and structure of a self-enforcing, noncontractual agreement that will allow an efficient trade to take place is dealt with in the next section.

II. TRADE WITH AN IMPLICIT CONTRACT

We are interested in establishing the existence of a noncontractual agreement that will support the efficient trade that would be carried out in the presence of complete, costless contracting. This can be done most easily if some necessary conditions on the form of such a noncontractual agreement are established. These necessary conditions arise from the finite life, and so sequence of trades, of the workers.[8]

Consider an agreement that is in some sense a minimal deviation from a complete labor contract. The worker promises to provide the sequence of levels of effort $\hat{e}^s$ and in return the firm contracts to pay the worker a sequence of payments $\hat{y}^s$. Although this combination of a promise and a contract constitutes a productively efficient trade, obviously it is not strategically viable as, having signed the wage contract and joined the firm, the worker has a clear incentive to provide zero effort.[9] In particular, in order to ensure that the worker provides the required level of effort in the last period of his career with the firm, the firm must offer some payment, $R_{s+1}^s > 0$, which will be paid to the worker if and only if $e_{s+1}^s \geq \hat{e}_{s+1}^s$. This type of payment, a form of severance pay or bonding, is analogous to a nonvested pension or retirement bonus. See Lazear [1981, 1983] and Abowd and Manaster [1983].

This fact that the firm must promise a payment R_{s+1}^s after the

8. This feature differentiates the post-hiring trading game from the infinitely repeated trading games dealt with in the oligopoly literature pioneered by Friedman [1971, 1977]. The approach used here of having the finitely lived players' information sets overlap has been used in Hammond [1975] and Berman and Schotter [1982].

9. The worker is assumed to ignore the risk of bankruptcy on the part of the firm. This would be correct if the firm's labor force were large and the workers behaved noncooperatively.

154   QUARTERLY JOURNAL OF ECONOMICS

completion of the worker's last period of work is important. Because the payment of $R_{s+1}^{\cdot}$ is conditional on the worker's effort, it cannot be enforced through the courts and so cannot be part of the explicit labor contract. Moreover, the payment occurs after the worker's last period of work; i.e., the firm (the infinitely lived player) has the last play in the game against the worker (the finitely lived player). Thus, although initially the lack of enforceability of the effort clause of the labor contract created the problem of how to make the workers keep their promises about effort, we see that in order for the productively efficient trade to take place, the firm must also be made to behave honestly.

In order to simplify the analysis, we restrict the firm's strategy set by the following two assumptions.[10]

A1. The only conditional payment the firm can agree to make is a single payment $R > 0$ after the last period of each worker's career with the firm.

A2. The firm must pay either all of R to the worker or none of R to the worker.

Both of these assumptions work against a successful noncontractual agreement by restricting the firm, if it wishes to break the agreement, to breaking the agreement totally and after the worker has completed his career.

One final assumption is needed before the post-hiring trading game can be analyzed. Define a payment scheme as a pair $(\hat{w}, R)$, where $\hat{w}$ is a nonnegative vector of contractual wage payments and R is a payment that the firm promises to make if and only if the worker provides $\hat{e}^{s}$. Let S be the set of payment schemes that would yield a firm which honestly followed the scheme nonnegative profits given that, at entry, each new worker planned to fulfill the agreement concerning effort. Let all potential employees have a common prior probability p^{H} on the honesty of each firm in the industry. For any given payment scheme, the expected utility from joining a firm and providing $\hat{e}^{s}$, denoted by $EU(p^{H}; w, R)$, is increasing in p^{H}. The expected utility from joining a firm and providing zero effort, denoted by $EU(\hat{w})$, is, however, independent of p^{H} and R. Thus, in order to have productively efficient trades take place, it is necessary that a firm can adopt a payment scheme that can attract workers, give them an incentive to provide $\hat{e}^{s}$ and that will, if adhered to by

10. In view of the stationarity of the problem, to simplify notation the sub- and superscripts on R are dropped.

SELF-ENFORCING CONTRACTS   155

the firm, yield the firm nonnegative profits. We therefore assume

A3. p^H is such that for at least one payment scheme in S,

$$EU(p^H;\hat{w},R) \geq \overline{U}$$

and

$$EU(p^H;\hat{w},R) \geq EU(\hat{w}).$$

Notice that this assumption is phrased as a restriction on the workers' prior beliefs. However, to the extent that these beliefs are a function of the true fraction of honest firms in the labor market, this is really an assumption concerning the existence of a certain type of labor market equilibrium. The question of the existence of a labor market equilibrium such that workers have rational expectations which fulfill A3 is discussed briefly at the end of this section.

The post-hiring trading game can now be examined. The asymmetry of information between third parties and the worker-firm combination means that unattached workers in the market have no information with which they can distinguish honest and dishonest firms. They will therefore, given A3, join a randomly chosen firm and in their first period of work there provide $\hat{e}_s^*$. At the end of this period, worker s observes whether worker $s - 1$ provided $\hat{e}^{s-1}$ and whether that worker receives R or not. On the basis of this observation worker s carries out the following strategy.

S1: (a) If $s - 1$ provided $\hat{e}$ and received (did not receive) R, then s goes on to provide $\hat{e}_{s+1}^*$ (zero effort).
    (b) If $s - 1$ did not provide $\hat{e}$, then s goes on to provide zero effort.

The rationale behind (a) stems from the workers' belief that firms in the industry follow a pure strategy of either fulfilling the noncontractual agreement—being honest—or of not fulfilling it—being dishonest. Given this belief, a Bayesian worker would conclude that he was with an honest (dishonest) firm if he observed R being paid (not paid) and so would choose to provide (not provide) effort in his last period with the firm. From the stationarity of the problem, if worker s observed that $s - 1$ did not provide $\hat{e}$, then he would conclude that he was with a dishonest firm and so should not provide effort in his last period.

For this strategy to be part of a Nash equilibrium that will support the efficient trade, the firm, when maximizing against this strategy, must choose a pure honesty strategy. Define

$$\Pi_t^H = \Pi(-w_t^t, e_t^t) + \beta(-\hat{w}_{t+1}^t - R, e_{t+1}^t) \qquad \text{and}$$

$$\Pi_t^D = \Pi(-w_t^t, e_t^t) + \beta(-\hat{w}_{t+1}^t, 0).$$

Then the efficient trade will constitute a Nash equilibrium under the conditions of the following proposition.

PROPOSITION 1. Given the utility and profit functions of the previous section and assumptions A1–A3, then strategy S1 by all workers and a pure honesty strategy by the firm constitutes a Nash equilibrium if, and only if, for all s

$$\Pi(-\hat{w}_{s+1}^s - R, \hat{e}_{s+1}^s) + \sum_{t-s+1}^{\infty} \beta^{t-(s+1)} \Pi_t^H$$

$$> \Pi(-\hat{w}_{s+1}^s, \hat{e}_{s+1}^s) + \sum_{t-s+1}^{\infty} \beta^{t-(s+1)} \Pi_t^D.$$

Proof of Proposition 1. See Appendix.

The condition contained in this proposition is intuitively appealing. The firm's "punishment" for dishonesty consists of reduced effort on the part of future workers, and so one would expect that if the firm had a discount rate of infinity ($\beta = 0$) or its profits did not depend upon effort, then the pure honesty strategy would not be optimal. This is, indeed, the case. With $\beta = 0$, the condition reduces to $\Pi(-\hat{w}_{s+1}^s - R, \hat{e}_{s+1}^s) > \Pi(-\hat{w}_{s+1}^s, \hat{e}_{s+1}^s)$ which is never fulfilled while if the firm's profit function is independent of effort $\Pi_t^H < \Pi_t^D$, for all t, and again the condition is violated. Similarly, as one would expect, the smaller is R, the smaller are the gains from cheating, i.e., not paying R, and so the easier it is to fullfill the condition in Proposition 1.

Given that the condition in Proposition 1 holds, we have seen that an implicit contract exists and, moreover, that one exists which will support the efficient trade that would have taken place under full, costless, explicit contracting. This does not mean that, from an efficiency point of view, the absence of explicit contracts is insignificant. In a market equilibrium, P^H, the unattached worker's prior belief that a randomly chosen firm will turn out to be honest, would reflect the actual proportion of honest firms in the market. In such an equilibrium, if it exists, unattached workers would bear a risk that would not be present if costless and complete explicit contracting were available. Moreover, the mix of honest and dishonest firms in market equilibrium will differ between explicit and implicit contracting equilibria which could have adverse effects from the point of view of productive efficiency. For an explicit example in which the existence and efficiency of such market equilibria are discussed, see Bull [1985].

III. CONCLUSIONS

The previous sections have given an answer to why implicit contracts are used to mediate a large proportion of all trades despite the fact that from an enforcement point of view they are worthless. In Section II it was shown that such "gentlemen's agreements" can bind parties ex post to trade and so fulfill the role of a legal, multiperiod contract.

Perhaps the most encouraging aspect of the paper is that it holds out the hope of understanding some of the "myths" and "traditions" surrounding the labor market rather than dismissing them as the attempts of economically beknighted participants to rationalize their actions.[11] The "image" or "reputation" of the industry to potential workers, p^H in the paper, is in fact an important restriction on the types of implicit contracts that can be arrived at. In the model of this paper, if the potential workers' perception of the industry is that it is populated by rogues who would break any promise, then no implicit contract could exist. In the same vein, the objection to myopic profit-maximizing behavior toward older employees is often that such behavior would be regarded as "unfair" by, and would result in a loss of "morale" among, the workforce. In the model of the previous sections, such myopic profit maximization would result in a discrete drop in the expected utility of the young workers, and presumably long faces around the plant, together with reduced labor effort, all of which could be described as an unprofitable drop in the morale of the workforce. Moreover, when asked why they were behaving in such a way, the young employees might well complain about the unfair breach of a promise on the part of the employer.

APPENDIX

Proof of Proposition 1. S1 is obviously an optimal response to firms playing pure honesty or pure dishonesty strategies. Consider any strategy by the firm that, with probability one, will involve not

---

11. The use of a repeated resource allocation game to explain customs and social institutions has been developed by Schotter [1981].

158 *QUARTERLY JOURNAL OF ECONOMICS*

paying R to a worker that has supplied $\hat{e}$. Denote the set of such strategies by Ω. The only feasible strategies not in Ω are the pure honesty strategy and mixed strategies that require the firm to be dishonest with probability zero. These latter strategies will be treated as the equivalent of pure strategies. Let the worker who is first dishonestly treated under strategy ω in Ω be s and so the period in which this occurs is $s + 1$. The firm's profits up to $s + 1$ are the same under ω as under the pure honesty strategy. Thus, for the latter to dominate the former it must generate higher discounted profits as of $s + 1$. These profits under a pure honesty strategy are

$$\Pi(-\hat{w}^s_{s+1} - R, \hat{e}^s_{s+1}) + \sum_{t-s+1}^{\infty} \beta^{t-(s+1)} \Pi^H_t.$$

Alternatively, if the firms does not pay R at $s + 1$, its discounted profits are

$$\Pi(-\hat{w}^s_{s+1}, \hat{e}^s_{s+1}) + \sum_{t-s+1}^{\infty} \beta^{t-(s+1)} \Pi^D_t.$$

Hence, the firm will only choose a pure honesty strategy over a strategy in Ω if the condition in Proposition 1 is fulfilled.

PAINEWEBBER, INC., AND NEW YORK UNIVERSITY

REFERENCES

Abowd, John M., and Steven Manaster, "A General Model of Employment Contracting: An Application of Option Theory," Salomon Brothers Center, Graduate School of Business Administration, New York University, Working Paper 288, March 1983.

Azariadis, Costas, "Implicit Contracts and Underemployment Equilibria," *Journal of Political Economy*, LXXXIII (1975), 1182–1202.

Baily, Martin N., "Wages and Employment Under Uncertain Demand," *Review of Economic Studies*, XXXXI (1974), 37–50.

Berman, Simeon, and Andrew Schotter, "A Duopoly Model with Endogenous Leader-Follower or Follower-Follower Equilibrium Conventions of Behavior," mimeo, December 1982.

Bull, Clive, "Implicit Contracts in the Absence of Enforcement and Risk Aversion," *American Economic Review*, LXXIII (1983), 658–71.

———, "The Existence of Self-Enforcing Implicit Contracts," New York University, mimeo, June 1985.

Calamari, John D., and Joseph M. Perillo, *Contracts* (St. Paul, MN: West Publishing, 1977).

Carmichael, H. Lorne, "Reputations in the Labor Market," *American Economic Review*, LXXIV (1984), 713–25.

Crawford, Vincent P., "Long-Term Relationships Governed by Short-Term Contracts," International Center for Economics and Related Disciplines, #59, 1982.

Datcher, Linda, "The Impact of Informal Networks on Quit Behavior," *Review of Economic Studies*, LXV (1983), 491–95.

Eden, Benjamin, "Labor Contracts, Enforcement and Aggregate Unemployment," University of Iowa, mimeo, 1985.

Friedman, James W., "A Non-cooperative Equilibrium for Supergames," *Review of Economic Studies*, XXVIII (1971), 1–12.

——, *Oligopoly and the Theory of Games* (Amsterdam: North-Holland, 1977).

Gordon, Donald F., "A Neoclassical Theory of Keynesian Unemployment," *Economic Inquiry*, XXII (1974), 431–59.

Granovetter, Mark, *Getting a Job: A Study of Contacts and Careers* (Cambridge, MA: Harvard University Press, 1974).

Hall, Robert E., "Employment Fluctuations and Wage Rigidity," *Brookings Papers on Economic Activity* (1980), 91–124.

——, "The Importance of Lifetime Jobs in the U. S. Economy," *American Economic Review*, LXXII (1982), 716–24.

——, and Edward P. Lazear, "The Excessive Sensitivity of Layoffs and Quits to Demand," *Journal of Labor Economics*, II (1984), 233–58.

Hammond, Peter, "Charity: Altruism or Cooperative Egotism?" in *Altruism, Morality, and Economic Theory*, Edmund S. Phelps, ed. (New York, NY: Russell Sage Foundation, 1975).

Hashimoto, Masanori, and Ben Yu, "Specific Capital, Employment Contracts and Wage Rigidity," *Bell Journal of Economics*, XI (1981), 536–49.

Holmstrom, Bengt, "Contractual Models of the Labor Market," *American Economic Review*, LXXI (1981), 308–13.

——, "Moral Hazard in Teams," *Bell Journal of Economics*, XIII (1982), 324–40.

Klein, Benjamin, "Contract Costs and Administered Prices: An Economic Theory of Rigid Wages," *American Economic Review*, LXXIV (1984), 332–38.

——, Robert G. Crawford, and Armen A. Alchian, "Vertical Integration, Appropriable Rents and the Competitive Contracting Process," *Journal of Law and Economics*, XXI (1978), 297–326.

Lazear, Edward P., "Agency, Earnings Profiles, Productivity and Hours Restrictions," *American Economic Review*, LXXI (1981), 606–20.

——, "Incentive Effects of Pensions," NBER Working Paper #1126, May 1983.

Lewin, Tamar, "Help for Workers Lacking Contracts," *New York Times*, 21 April 1983, D1.

Mayers, David, and Richard Thaler, "Sticky Wages and Implicit Contracts: A Transactional Approach," *Economic Inquiry*, XVII (1979), 559–74.

Schotter, Andrew, *The Economic Theory of Social Institutions* (New York, NY: Cambridge University Press, 1981).

Topel, Robert H., and Finis Welch, "Self-Insurance and Efficient Employment Contracts," mimeo, Graduate School of Business, University of Chicago, August 1983.

Toussaint v. Blue Cross Blue Shield of Michigan, 408 Mich. 579, 292 N.W. 2d 880 (1980).

Williamson, Oliver, M. Wachter, and J. Harris, "Understanding the Employment Relation: The Analysis of Idiosyncratic Exchange," *Bell Journal of Economics*, VI (1975), 250–78.

Part II
Empirical Background: Temporary Layoffs and Job Durations

[5]

MARTIN S. FELDSTEIN
Harvard University

The Importance of Temporary Layoffs: An Empirical Analysis

EVERY GOOD theoretical or econometric study must be based on a reasonably accurate empirical foundation. If the basic magnitudes of the subject are misperceived, the theoretical model or econometric specification will lead the research astray.

In recent years, research on the central macroeconomic questions of unemployment and wage inflation has been advanced by the empirical studies of Hall, Holt, Parnes, Perry, Wachter, and others. Meanwhile, the U.S. Bureau of Labor Statistics has benefited the profession by expanding the data base with detailed monthly summaries of household and establishment data and through the provision of complete data from the Current Population Survey.

All of this microeconomic evidence has greatly enriched understanding of the nature of unemployment. The traditional view, based on the experience of the depression, pictured the unemployed as an inactive pool of job losers who had to wait for a general business upturn before they could find new jobs. Modern research has shown that this picture is distorted. The majority of the unemployed do not become unemployed by losing their previous jobs; they quit voluntarily or are new entrants or reentrants into

Note: I am grateful to the National Science Foundation for financial support, to Alan Auerbach and Pamela Hannigan for research assistance, to Thomas F. Bradshaw of the Bureau of Labor Statistics for providing unpublished tabulations, and to Richard B. Freeman and members of the Harvard seminar in labor economics for useful discussions.

725

the labor force. Moreover, the typical duration of unemployment is very short; more than half of unemployment spells end in four weeks or less.

However, one very important aspect of unemployment has been largely ignored: temporary layoffs. In my 1972 study for the Joint Economic Committee, I noted that during 1971 manufacturing firms rehired about 85 percent of the same workers that they had laid off.[1] This remarkable statistic whetted my appetite for more information about temporary layoffs—that is, unemployment without job change. Since then I have examined a number of sources of unpublished data on the phenomenon and I am now convinced that it is of great importance and requires a major reevaluation of current theories of unemployment.

Despite their obvious importance, no data on temporary layoffs are currently published. My purpose in this paper is to present a range of new empirical information on temporary layoffs that can provide a foundation for future analytic and econometric research. The evidence is based on the analysis of unpublished data from the U.S. Manpower Administration's National Longitudinal Survey of work experience of older men, from the Current Population Survey of March 1974, and from special monthly tabulations of job seeking since 1970 made by the Bureau of Labor Statistics. The paper goes on to analyze the manufacturing turnover data that first aroused my interest in temporary layoffs. Finally, I will comment briefly on some of the implications of temporary layoffs for the theory of unemployment, wage rigidity, the Phillips curve, and unemployment insurance.[2]

Definitions of Unemployment

Because the official terminology of unemployment statistics is unfamiliar, some definitions are in order. Estimates of unemployment are based on a national household survey, the Current Population Survey. If an individual reports that he is not working but that he has looked for work in specified

1. Martin S. Feldstein, *Lowering the Permanent Rate of Unemployment*, A Study Prepared for the Use of the Joint Economic Committee, 93 Cong. 1 sess. (1973), p. 12.

2. For a first step toward an explicit theory of temporary layoffs, see my "Temporary Layoffs in the Theory of Unemployment," *Journal of Political Economy* (forthcoming, June 1976). That paper deals with some but not all of the issues raised in the concluding section below.

ways within the past four weeks, he is classified as unemployed.[3] The means of looking for work include checking newspaper ads and talking to friends as well as seeing employers or employment agencies.

However, looking for work is not the only criterion of unemployment. An individual who has a new job that he is planning to start within thirty days is classified as unemployed even if he has not looked for work within the past four weeks. Far more important, those who are on layoff from a job are counted as unemployed. Any individual who reports that he did not work at all during the week before the survey is asked, "Did you have a job (or business) from which you were temporarily absent or on layoff last week?" Those who answer "yes" are then asked, "Why were you absent from work last week?" Answers involving illness, weather conditions, and vacation are not considered unemployment. But an individual is regarded as unemployed if he reports that he is on layoff from his regular job and expects to be recalled. Thus, an individual can be unemployed even though he responds that he has a job. Moreover, these individuals are not even asked about their job-seeking activity in the past four weeks.

Individuals with a job but on layoff are classified into two groups. Someone with a definite date of expected recall within thirty days is classified as on "temporary layoff" while all others are classified as on "indefinite layoff." Since all layoffs are expected to be temporary in some sense, I will refer to the first group as "fixed-duration layoffs" and the second group as "indefinite-duration layoffs."

The term "layoff" is also used by the Bureau of Labor Statistics somewhat differently in describing manufacturing turnover on the basis of data reported by establishments rather than households. In that context, layoffs are defined as "suspensions without pay lasting or expected to last more than 7 consecutive calendar days, initiated by the employer without prejudice to the worker."[4] This definition of layoffs includes permanent separations as well as temporary layoffs, but excludes discharges "for cause" and compulsory retirements as well as separations initiated by the workers.

Persons designated as unemployed in the Current Population Survey are

3. A single adult in the household describes the employment and unemployment experience of everyone in the household. It would therefore be more accurate to say, "If it is reported that an individual is not working but. . . . " I will not bother to make this distinction in the remainder of the text.

4. *Employment and Earnings*, vol. 22 (November 1975), p. 135.

classified according to four "reasons" for unemployment: job losers, job leavers, new entrants, and reentrants. The definitions are complex and not always intuitively obvious. *Job losers* include individuals on layoff—of both fixed and indefinite duration—even though they state that they have a job from which they consider themselves to be absent without pay. Individuals who already have a new job at which they will begin work within thirty days are also classified as job losers if they lost their previous job rather than quitting or being new entrants or reentrants. Finally, a job loser can be anyone who actually lost his previous job without expectation of recall and has, in principle, been looking for work since then. In practice, looking within the past four weeks is the only job-seeking test for someone who says that he started looking when he lost his previous job.

A *job leaver* is one who quit his previous job and has been looking for work since then. A *new entrant* is one who never worked before at a full-time job lasting at least two weeks. *Reentrants* are essentially a residual category, including individuals who quit or lost their previous jobs but who have been out of the labor force before starting the current period of job seeking.

Unemployment without Job Change: The National Longitudinal Survey of Older Men

One of the four National Longitudinal Surveys that were conducted for the Department of Labor provides information on unemployment and job changes during the five years from 1966 to 1971 among men aged 45 to 59 in 1966.[5] Because these data cover the same group of men over five years, they permit study of the frequency of unemployment without job change (that is, change of employer) and of job change without unemployment.

The importance of temporary layoffs during the first year of the survey is shown by the first column of table 1. During the year, 9.4 percent of men

---

5. The survey was directed by Herbert Parnes and conducted by the Bureau of the Census; for a description, see U.S. Department of Labor, Manpower Administration, *The Pre-Retirement Years: A Longitudinal Study of the Labor Market Experience of Men*, Manpower Research Monograph 15, vol. 2 (1970). The four surveys covered only selected subgroups of the population: men aged 45–59, women aged 30–44, and young persons aged 14–24 of both sexes.

in this age group experienced some unemployment.[6] Even among men with
no job change during the year, 4.2 percent experienced unemployment.
Indeed, this group accounted for 40.5 percent of all weeks of unemployment and 49.5 percent of all unemployed persons. One reason why so much
of the unemployment occurs among those who do not change jobs is that
nearly two-thirds (65.8 percent) of those who do change jobs do so without
experiencing any unemployment. Finally, the mean number of weeks of
unemployment is much shorter for those who experience temporary layoffs
(8.2 weeks) than for those who are unemployed while changing jobs (11.8
weeks).

The data for the entire five-year period provide even stronger evidence
of the importance of temporary layoffs. In this longer period 21.2 percent
of those with no job change had at least one spell of unemployment and
61 percent of those experiencing unemployment did not change jobs.
Again, 40 percent of the weeks of unemployment were experienced by those
with no job change. Although 11 percent had changed jobs during one
year, only 21 percent changed jobs during the five-year period, which suggests that job changing is concentrated in a small group with multiple job
changes.

Even these figures understate the importance of temporary layoffs. Since
some of those who change jobs also experience temporary layoffs, the percentage of all weeks of unemployment accounted for by temporary layoffs
exceeds the 39.7 percent experienced by those with no job change.

Table 1 also compares the unemployment experience of the older men
in different industries in 1966–67 and 1966–71. The estimates for manufacturing for the single year are similar to those for all industries except
that a substantially higher percentage of weeks of unemployment is accounted for by those with no job change (54.8 percent) and a substantially
higher fraction of unemployment spells involves temporary layoffs (62.6
percent of persons experiencing unemployment have no job change).
Workers in wholesale and retail sales exhibited a quite different pattern in
1966–67, but the five-year evidence suggests that it was a highly atypical
year. The construction industry sustained a much higher unemployment
rate; nearly one-third of its employees in this age group were unemployed,

6. The survey data are weighted for the sampling fractions so that rates are representative of the relevant population. Unlike the practice in the Current Population Survey,
the interview was always with the man himself in this survey.

Table 1. Unemployment Experience among Men Aged 45–59 in 1966, Total and by Selected Industries, 1966–67 and 1966–71

Aspect of unemployment experience	All industries		Manufacturing		Wholesale and retail trade		Construction		Transportation	
	1966–67	1966–71	1966–67	1966–71	1966–67	1966–71	1966–67	1966–71	1966–67	1966–71
Unemployment rate in survey week[b] (percent)	2.1	...	2.0	...	1.7	...	5.8	...	1.5	...
Percent who experience unemployment[b]	9.4	31.9	9.2	33.3	4.5	27.6	31.6	57.4	6.7	31.1
Percent of those with no job change who experience unemployment	4.2	21.2	4.9	24.1	0.3	17.6	17.7	34.4	4.4	25.7
Percent changing job	11.0	20.6	8.0	15.1	10.2	21.9	29.7	45.9	5.5	13.2
Percent of job changers without unemployment	65.8	47.6	66.1	45.4	73.9	55.3	49.8	31.2	80.6	45.5
Weeks of unemployment among those with no job change as percent of all unemployment weeks	40.5	39.7	54.8	63.1	5.4	53.0	57.7	32.5	57.2	75.3
Those with unemployment and no job change as percent of all persons with unemployment	49.5	61.0	62.6	71.3	8.2	58.4	45.5	37.1	79.6	75.7
Mean weeks of unemployment per man with no job change and with unemployment	8.2	16.2	5.5	10.4	7.6	11.6	10.1	31.7	5.2	14.0
Mean weeks of unemployment per job changer with unemployment	11.8	38.6	7.6	15.0	11.9	14.5	6.2	38.8	15.1	14.3
Addendum										
Number in entire group (millions)[a]	13.0	10.1	3.9	3.0	2.0	1.6	1.3	0.9	1.3	1.0

Source: Unpublished data from the National Longitudinal Survey of Work Experience of Men 45–59 Years of Age, provided by the U.S. Manpower Administration. The survey is described in U.S. Department of Labor, Manpower Administration, *The Pre-Retirement Years: A Longitudinal Study of the Labor Market Experience of Men*, Manpower Research Monograph 15, vol. 2 (1970).

a. Data for the 1966–67 and 1966–71 periods are from the 1967 and 1971 surveys, respectively.

b. Includes those unemployed at the time of the survey who could not be classified as job changer or nonchanger. The analysis excludes everyone who was out of the labor force at the time of the survey.

but almost half of them and nearly 60 percent of the weeks of unemployment are accounted for by those with no job change. Temporary layoffs are even more important in transportation, as revealed in the table. The five-year experience by industry, presented in the second column for each industry in table 1, again shows that temporary layoffs are relatively most important in manufacturing and transportation.

In short, the National Longitudinal Survey shows that most older men who experience unemployment do so as the result of temporary layoffs and most who make job changes do not experience a spell of unemployment.

Layoffs without Job Loss: The Current Population Survey

The Current Population Survey, the source of the official estimates of unemployment, is a monthly survey of approximately 45,000 households. Although the CPS does not make it possible to follow an individual over a period of time, as does the National Longitudinal Survey, it has the advantage of a very large sample that is representative of the entire labor force. The survey also provides detailed information on the numbers of job losers and of temporary layoffs.

This section analyzes the March 1974 survey. The overall unemployment rate of 5.3 percent (5.1 percent seasonally adjusted) was only slightly above the postwar average, and marked the beginning of the continuous rise in the unemployment rate until the spring of 1975.[7] In March 1974, 49 percent of the unemployed were job losers; the remainder were new entrants into the labor force (11 percent), reentrants (25 percent), and those who had quit their previous jobs (15 percent). Young people accounted for a very large fraction of new entrants and reentrants, and women reentrants for a substantial fraction of the unemployment not associated with job loss. Among men aged 25 to 64, 73 percent of the unemployed were job losers.

Table 2 shows the distribution of job losers among those on layoff, permanently separated, and scheduled to start a new job within thirty days. Layoffs account for 37.4 percent of all job losers and 40.4 percent of men aged 25 to 64 who had lost their previous jobs. Thus, a high proportion of

7. The March survey in each year collects information on family and individual incomes during the previous year. I had acquired these data for a different study that requires such information. As far as I can tell, March 1974 is not very different from other periods before the recent recession.

732   *Brookings Papers on Economic Activity, 3:1975*

Table 2. Percentage of Job Losers on Layoff, with No Jobs, or with Jobs Starting Soon, and Duration of Unemployment, March 1974

| | *Job status* | | | | | |
| | *With job, on layoff* | | | | *New job* | *All* |
Group and characteristic	*Total*	*Fixed duration*	*Indefinite duration*	*No job*	*starting within 30 days*	*job losers*
All persons						
Percent of all job losers	37.4	10.1	27.3	61.4	1.2	100.0
Percent of all job losses[a]	56.1	32.2	23.9	42.4	1.4	100.0
Percent of job losers who search[b]	10.1	3.8	12.4	63.3	11.6	42.8
Mean duration (weeks)	8.5	2.9	10.6	13.4	7.8	11.5
Men aged 25–64						
Percent of all job losers	40.4	13.0	27.4	58.1	1.5	100.0
Percent of all job losses[a]	60.0	36.0	24.0	38.6	1.5	100.0
Percent of job losers who search[b]	11.9	4.6	15.4	81.4	0.0	52.1
Mean duration (weeks)	8.9	3.6	11.4	15.0	10.2	12.4

Source: Tabulated from unpublished data from the March 1974 Current Population Survey provided by the U.S. Bureau of Labor Statistics. Figures are rounded.

a. A job loss is a *new* spell of unemployment that creates a job loser. These relative frequencies of unemployment are estimated on the assumption that the mean duration of completed spells is proportional to the mean duration of uncompleted spells in the survey week for each of the four mutually exclusive types of unemployment reported here.

b. Percent of job losers who looked for work during the week before the survey.

"job losers" have actually reported that they "have a job from which [they were] temporarily absent" during the week examined by the survey.

Only 10 percent of those on layoff said they were looking for work when asked what they had been doing during the previous week; among men aged 25 to 64, only 12 percent were looking.[8] In contrast, among job losers with no job, 63 percent were looking for work; the proportion for men aged 25 to 64 was 81 percent. Unemployed workers on layoff clearly act as if they will be recalled.[9]

8. Recall that the report on the individual's activity may be made by some other household adult. Although those on layoff are not asked about their job seeking during the past four weeks, all of the unemployed are asked about their activities during the previous week.

9. Although looking for work is required as a condition of receiving unemployment insurance in many states, this requirement is often waived in practice for those on layoff who are expected to return to their original jobs. Individuals could, of course, satisfy such an unemployment-insurance requirement without regarding themselves as looking for work during the relevant week.

Laid-off personnel can also be divided into those with a fixed duration of less than thirty days and those with a variable or indefinite duration. The first group accounts for 27 percent of all layoffs (32 percent among prime-age men). Looking for work was very uncommon in both groups.

Even these very high proportions of the unemployed who are on layoff understate the *frequency* of new layoffs relative to new permanent separations. The unemployment rates understate this relative frequency because the mean duration of layoffs is substantially shorter than that of other job losses. Table 2 shows that the mean duration of unemployment until the time of the survey is 11.5 weeks for all job losers; but it is only 8.5 weeks for those on layoff while it is 13.4 weeks for those with no job. The relative frequency of the type of separation within the *flow* of new job losses can be estimated with the assumption that the mean completed durations of unemployment are proportional to the mean durations up to the date of the survey.[10] This implies that 56 percent of all "job losses" are actually temporary layoffs rather than permanent separations: for men of 25 to 64, layoffs account for 60 percent of all "job losses."

Table 3 compares the characteristics of job losers and job losses in four major industry groups. In manufacturing, temporary layoffs are especially important, accounting for 50.6 percent of job losers among men aged 25 to 64 and 79.9 percent of job losses.

Table 4 shows the actual duration of unemployment spells (up to the survey date) by type of job loser. While 31 percent of those with no job have been out of work for four weeks or less, among those on layoff the fraction is much higher—44 percent. Similarly, while 12.4 percent of those with no job have been out for more than twenty-six weeks, only 3.7 percent of those on layoff have been out that long.

Manufacturing Layoffs and Rehires

I turn now to the statistics on manufacturing turnover that first aroused my interest in temporary layoffs. Manufacturing establishments are re-

10. The mean duration of completed spells is less than the mean duration of spells to the date of the survey; see Hyman B. Kaitz, "Analyzing the Length of Spells of Unemployment," *Monthly Labor Review*, vol. 93 (November 1970), pp. 11–20. The assumption of proportionality is unlikely to introduce more than a second-order error but deserves more detailed examination. The calculation of the relative number of job losses uses the separate information on fixed-duration and indefinite-duration layoffs.

Table 3. Characteristics of Job Losers and Duration of Unemployment, by Selected Industries, Men Aged 25–64, March 1974[a]

		Industry			
Characteristic	*Manu-facturing*	*Wholesale and retail trade, finance, business and repair services*	*Con-struction*	*Trans-portation and public utilities*	*Total, all industries*
		Job losers (percent)			
With job, on layoff					
Fixed duration	21.5	5.4	10.4	15.8	13.0
Indefinite duration	29.1	13.4	36.0	34.0	27.4
No job	47.5	79.4	52.6	47.7	58.1
New job to start within 30 days	1.9	1.8	1.0	2.5	1.5
		Job losses (percent)			
With job, on layoff					
Fixed duration	58.4	27.6	18.2	48.8	36.0
Indefinite duration	21.5	9.3	32.0	21.4	24.0
No job	18.4	62.1	44.8	27.7	38.6
New job to start within 30 days	1.7	1.0	5.0	2.1	1.5
		Mean duration of unemployment (weeks)			
With job, on layoff					
Fixed duration	2.5	2.3	5.7	3.2	3.6
Indefinite duration	9.2	16.9	11.2	15.7	11.4
No job	17.5	15.0	11.7	17.0	15.0
New job to start within 30 days	7.6	20.7	2.0	12.0	10.2

Source: Same as table 2. Figures are rounded.
a. Average durations and job-loss percentages based on small percentages of job losers are subject to substantial sampling variation.

quired to report each month the number of separations, divided into quits, layoffs, and "other separations," and the number of accessions, divided into new hires and "other accessions," where accessions are defined as "the total number of permanent and temporary additions to the employment roll, including both new and rehired employees." Layoffs in this context include some permanent separations as well as temporary ones. More formally, layoffs are "suspensions without pay lasting or expected to last more than 7 consecutive calendar days, initiated by the employer without prejudice to the worker." Other separations not counted as layoffs include "terminations of employment because of discharge, permanent disability,

Table 4. Percentage Distribution of Duration of Unemployment among Job Losers, Men Aged 25–64, March 1974

Weeks of unemployment up to date of survey	Job status					
	With job, on layoff				New job starting within 30 days	Total job losers
	Total	Fixed duration	Indefinite duration	No job		
0–4	44.3	87.4	23.5	30.7	66.5	36.7
5–10	23.8	6.0	32.5	20.1	0.0	21.3
11–14	17.4	2.6	24.5	13.6	11.0	15.1
15–26	10.7	0.0	15.9	23.3	22.5	18.3
27–39	2.4	4.0	1.7	6.2	0.0	4.6
40 and over	1.3	0.0	2.0	6.2	0.0	4.1
Mean	8.9	3.6	11.4	15.0	10.2	12.4

Source: Same as table 2. Figures are rounded.

death, retirement, transfers to another establishment of the company, and entrance into the Armed Forces" for more than thirty days.[11]

Table 5 shows the very high turnover rate in manufacturing. Since 1960, manufacturing firms averaged 1.6 layoffs per 100 employees per month. During the same period, these firms were rehiring 1.3 persons per 100 employees per month. The rehire rate—that is, the ratio of rehires to layoffs—averaged 85 percent and did not drop below 70 percent in any year.[12] In short, the vast majority of those laid off in manufacturing are ultimately rehired by their original employers, although in some cases they take jobs elsewhere in the interim. This is further confirmation of the estimates based on household surveys reported in the preceding two sections.[13]

11. *Employment and Earnings*, vol. 22 (November 1975), p. 135.

12. Rehires are calculated as the difference between total accessions and new hires; they include a small number of persons arriving from intrafirm transfers who were not previously counted as layoffs. Although separate estimates of the numbers of rehires and transfers are not available, discussions with the Massachusetts Department of Employment Security confirmed that the number of transfers is small. Telephone interviews with the individuals who prepare the turnover report for each of the six largest manufacturing employers in the Boston metropolitan area disclosed that reported transfers were never greater than 5 percent of other accessions. Two firms did not regard transfers as separations or accessions and therefore did not count them as part of turnover.

13. When those who are laid off take other, temporary, jobs before being recalled, the CPS data classify them as employed. Thus, the existence of temporary jobs does not distort the statistics recording the importance of temporary layoffs among the unemployed.

736   *Brookings Papers on Economic Activity, 3:1975*

Table 5. Layoff and Rehire Rates in Manufacturing, 1960–75[a]

Per 100 employees; average of seasonally adjusted monthly rates

Year and quarter	Layoffs	Rehires	Ratio of rehires to layoffs
1960	2.4	1.6	0.7
1961	2.2	1.9	0.9
1962	2.0	1.6	0.8
1963	1.8	1.5	0.8
1964	1.7	1.4	0.8
1965	1.4	1.2	0.9
1966	1.2	1.2	1.0
1967	1.4	1.1	0.8
1968	1.2	1.1	0.9
1969	1.2	1.0	0.8
1970	1.8	1.2	0.7
1971	1.6	1.3	0.8
1972:1	1.2	1.3	1.1
2	1.2	1.2	1.0
3	1.1	1.1	1.0
4	0.9	1.0	1.1
1973:1	0.8	0.8	1.0
2	0.8	0.9	1.1
3	0.9	1.0	1.1
4	1.0	0.9	0.9
1974:1	1.3	0.9	0.7
2	1.1	1.1	1.0
3	1.2	1.0	0.8
4	2.4	1.1	0.5
1975:1	2.9	1.8	0.6
2	2.4	1.9	0.8
3	1.6	1.6	1.0

Sources: *Employment and Earnings*, vol. 22 (December 1975), and vol. 19 (April 1973), tables D-1 and D-3 in each.

a. *"Layoffs* are suspensions without pay lasting or expected to last more than 7 consecutive calendar days, initiated by the employer without prejudice to the worker." Other separations not included in layoffs are "terminations of employment because of discharge, permanent disability, death, retirement, transfers to another establishment of the company, and entrance into the Armed Forces" for more than thirty days; see *Employment and Earnings* (November 1975), p. 135. *Rehires* are calculated as the difference between total accessions and new hires; they include a small number of intrafirm transfers.

Cyclical Variations in Temporary Layoffs

Although the information on temporary layoffs that is collected by the CPS is not currently published, some indirect evidence has been available since 1973.[14] Each month *Employment and Earnings* reports the number of

14. See Thomas F. Bradshaw, "Jobseeking Methods Used by Unemployed Workers," *Monthly Labor Review*, vol. 96 (February 1973), pp. 35–40.

job losers who were seeking work during the past four weeks. Anyone who is officially classified as unemployed who has not sought work during the past four weeks is either on layoff or planning to start a new job within thirty days. Table 2 gave evidence that the latter group accounts for about 3 percent of those on layoff. The number of job losers who did not seek employment during the past four weeks (the "nonseekers") can therefore be used as a reasonably accurate measure of the number on layoff.[15]

Table 6 presents quarterly averages of the numbers of unemployed, of job losers, and of nonseekers since 1970.[16] The final column displays the substantial cyclical variation in the ratio of nonseekers to job losers. Layoffs accounted for only 24 percent of all job losers in the third quarter of 1973 (when the unemployment rate was a relatively low 4.8 percent) but 47 percent of all job losers in the first quarter of 1975, when the unemployment rate reached a peak of 9.1 percent (not seasonally adjusted). The average ratio for the period was 33 percent, close to the 37 percent for March 1974.

The column next to the last shows the *marginal* share of temporary layoffs among all job losers. On average over the period, temporary layoffs contributed 58 percent of the quarter-to-quarter change in job losers.[17] The important implication is that temporary layoffs constitute an even higher percentage of the *cyclical variation* in unemployment than they do in the static picture suggested in the section on the CPS.

Some Implications

I believe that the theory of unemployment and the analytic framework of econometric analyses must be revised to reflect the great importance of

15. The Current Population Survey does not ask anyone who is on layoff or about to start a new job about his job-seeking activities during the past four weeks. All of these persons are counted as nonseekers even if they have looked. All other unemployed must have done some job seeking to be counted as unemployed. This published information is separate from the question about search during the previous week that is asked of all the unemployed and reported in the section above on layoffs without job loss.

16. Data since 1973 are based on monthly figures published in *Employment and Earnings*; unpublished data were provided by the Bureau of Labor Statistics and are available only since January 1970. By focusing on nonseekers among job losers I can exclude those nonseekers who are about to start a new job but are new entrants, re-entrants, or persons who quit their previous job. The number of nonseeking job losers is the published figure that corresponds most closely to the number of persons on layoff.

17. This average excludes the three quarters in which the number of job losers changed too little (less than 5 percent) to permit a meaningful calculation.

Table 6. Cyclical Variation in Job Seeking by Job Losers, Quarterly, 1970–75

Not seasonally adjusted; numbers of persons in thousands[a]

Year and quarter	Total unemployed	Job losers	Job losers not seeking employment[b]	Ratio of incremental nonseekers to incremental job losers	Ratio of nonseekers to job losers
1970:1	3,644	1,737	736	...	0.42
2	3,867	1,582	554	1.17	0.35
3	4,340	1,762	653	0.55	0.37
4	4,501	2,142	831	0.47	0.39
1971:1	5,343	2,877	1,080	0.34	0.38
2	4,859	2,212	672	0.61	0.30
3	5,077	2,124	654	0.20[c]	0.31
4	4,692	2,112	693	−3.25[c]	0.33
1972:1	5,358	2,697	906	0.36	0.34
2	4,822	2,050	568	0.52	0.28
3	4,897	1,941	526	0.39	0.27
4	4,284	1,767	477	0.28	0.27
1973:1	4,677	2,156	709	0.60	0.33
2	4,274	1,571	436	0.47	0.28
3	4,308	1,444	349	0.69	0.24
4	3,959	1,520	417	0.89	0.27
1974:1	4,967	2,473	943	0.55	0.38
2	4,608	1,852	563	0.61	0.30
3	5,115	1,892	556	−0.18[c]	0.29
4	5,612	2,604	935	0.53	0.36
1975:1	8,283	5,029	2,341	0.58	0.47
2	8,004	4,491	1,781	1.04	0.40
3	7,809	4,045	1,397	0.86	0.35

Sources: *Employment and Earnings,* various issues, tables A-1, A-15, and unpublished tabulations from the U.S. Bureau of Labor Statistics. See text note 16 for additional information.

a. Quarterly average of monthly data for persons 16 years of age and over.

b. Nonseekers are those unemployed job losers who did not seek work within the past four weeks. An individual must be on layoff or planning to start a new job within thirty days in order to be counted as unemployed without job search.

c. Based on changes in job losers of less than 5 percent and therefore an unreliable statistic.

temporary layoffs. In this section I will sketch some of the other ways in which I believe the current view of unemployment should be altered.

SEARCH THEORY

During the past decade, the best of the modern work on unemployment has developed Stigler's analysis[18] of search behavior with a model in which

18. George J. Stigler, "The Economics of Information," *Journal of Political Economy,* vol. 69 (June 1961), pp. 213–25.

Martin S. Feldstein 739

the unemployed worker samples job offers until he finds one that exceeds his optimal reservation wage.[19] Like all good ideas, the application of search theory to unemployment is easily carried too far. In contrast to the earlier Keynesian view, later theories commonly equate unemployment with search and job change. The evidence in this paper shows that this equation does not hold for the substantial portion of unemployment that stems from layoffs that are temporary, end in recall, and involve no search.

Therefore, an explanation of why temporary layoffs are the norm, and what the implications are for the theory of wages and employment, is important. The question has two aspects. First, why does employment typically last so long even when demand varies enough to induce temporary layoffs? The answer involves a broad concept of firm-specific human capital that includes not only specific technological know-how but also such things as management's knowledge of the worker's ability and reliability; friendships within the workforce that make for greater productivity; and the employees' preference for stable employment, which implies a willingness to work for lower wages in order to reduce the prospect of involuntary job change. The effect of unemployment insurance on this decision also deserves attention. The independent role of unions and seniority systems must be separated from the unions' codification of an arrangement that would exist in any competitive labor market.

Second, given that some employees are in effect permanently associated with a firm, what determines the firm's response to a fall in demand? To what extent is it expressed in temporary layoffs, inventory accumulation, price reduction, and variation in hours? In the special case of a price-taking firm with no inventories, a powerful effect of unemployment insurance can be demonstrated. A more general analysis of a price-setting firm with inventories would be a useful extension.

19. This work includes Robert J. Gordon, "The Welfare Cost of Higher Unemployment," *BPEA, 1:1973*, pp. 133–95; Robert E. Hall, "Turnover in the Labor Force," *BPEA, 3:1972*, pp. 709–56; and Hall, "The Process of Inflation in the Labor Market," *BPEA, 2:1974*, pp. 343–93; Charles C. Holt, "How Can the Phillips Curve Be Moved to Reduce Both Inflation and Unemployment?" in Edmund S. Phelps and others, *Microeconomic Foundations of Employment and Inflation Theory* (Norton, 1970); J. J. McCall, "Economics of Information and Job Search," *Quarterly Journal of Economics*, vol. 84 (February 1970), pp. 113–26; Dale T. Mortensen, "Job Search, the Duration of Unemployment, and the Phillips Curve," *American Economic Review*, vol. 60 (December 1970), pp. 847–62; George L. Perry, "Unemployment Flows in the U.S. Labor Market," *BPEA*, 2:1972, pp. 245–78; and Edmund S. Phelps, *Inflation Policy and Unemployment Theory: The Cost-Benefit Approach to Monetary Planning* (Norton, 1972).

740   *Brookings Papers on Economic Activity, 3:1975*

VOLUNTARY VERSUS INVOLUNTARY UNEMPLOYMENT

Search theory implies that the ending of a spell of unemployment reflects a voluntary act by the unemployed worker, who has decided to stop searching. In contrast, a layoff that begins the spell of unemployment is involuntary—not chosen by the employee. The current emphasis on quasi-permanent employment and temporary layoffs requires a reconsideration of this distinction between voluntary and involuntary unemployment.

For those on layoff, the return to work results not from a voluntary decision by the employee but from recall by the employer. However, the decision rule that leads to layoffs and that governs their duration is chosen by the employees, either explicitly in collective bargaining or by the operation of a competitive labor market. Although any particular spell of unemployment may be involuntary, the rules for layoffs are part of the package of wages, hours, and work-sharing rules that employees choose or for which they bargain.

THE PHILLIPS CURVE

The Friedman-Phelps explanation of the short-run Phillips curve also requires reexamination. According to this now familiar story, the short-run statistical Phillips curve exists because the unemployed are induced to stop searching when an unanticipated general increase in the wage level tricks them into thinking that they have found a particularly good job. The natural rate of unemployment—the rate at which the long-run Phillips curve is vertical—depends (according to this theory) on the optimal duration of search of the unemployed.

This theory must be overhauled to reflect the fact that so much of the cyclical variation in unemployment reflects the temporarily laid off, who do not search, and that so much job change occurs without unemployment. Given these conditions, a statistical Phillips curve could easily be observed even if no job searchers were being tricked in the way that Friedman and Phelps suggest. An increase in demand for firms' products would reduce the rate of layoffs and therefore lower the rate of unemployment. Firms would also seek to hire new workers away from other firms and to prevent other firms from attracting away their own employees, and wages would rise as part of this process. Thus, periods of increased demand for output would witness a lower rate of unemployment and a higher rate of wage inflation—a statistical Phillips curve. Of course, these wage increases would be in addition to any resulting from anticipated inflation. Layoffs and job changes without unemployment thus provide an explanation of the observed short-run Phillips curve that does not rest on the misperceptions of the unemployed.

This explanation of the observed relation between unemployment and wage inflation is quite different from the theory originally suggested by Phillips. He interpreted the unemployment rate as a measure of the supply of labor, with a greater supply putting downward pressure on wage rates. Subsequent studies by Lipsey and others used the difference between the unemployment rate and the vacancy rate to measure *excess* supply.[20] In contrast, the vast majority of unemployed workers on layoff are not part of the supply of workers to other firms and should not be compared with the number of vacancies. Those on layoff have little effect on the supply conditions in the labor market but reflect the demand for labor by firms.

WAGE INFLEXIBILITY

The downward inflexibility of wages has long been a crucial puzzle in macroeconomics. For many Keynesians, it is simply a datum with important implications. Some have tried to explain it in terms of institutional constraints or government regulations. More recently, Baily and Gordon have suggested that wages are stable because workers are risk averse while firms are risk neutral.[21] However, the risk-avoidance logic of the Baily-Gordon model requires that firms stabilize *real* wages while the evidence is that many wages adjust slowly to changing prices and are rarely (if ever) fully indexed.

Temporary layoffs and quasi-permanent employment provide two new and important reasons for downward wage rigidity. First, if workers are associated with a firm quasi-permanently, wage rates are explicitly or implicitly a long-term arrangement. Since the workers and the firm stay to-

20. Richard G. Lipsey, "The Relation between Unemployment and the Rate of Change of Money Wage Rates in the United Kingdom, 1862–1957: A Further Analysis," *Economica*, n.s., vol. 27 (February 1960), pp. 1–31.

21. Martin N. Baily, "Wages and Employment under Uncertain Demand," *Review of Economic Studies*, vol. 41 (January 1974), pp. 37–50; Robert J. Gordon, "The Microeconomic Foundations of Wage Rigidity" (Northwestern University, 1974; processed).

gether, what matters is the average relation over the cycle between the wage rate and the marginal revenue product of labor. There is no reason to adjust wages continually.[22] The stability of the wage rate under these conditions of employment is reinforced by the difference between labor's and management's information about demand conditions and labor's justifiable suspicion of any management claim that wages must be cut because of weak demand. An explicit or implicit contract that requires layoffs (and the resulting loss of production) instead of wage cuts is a method of "keeping management honest" in this situation of unequal information.

Second, the fact that most of the cyclical variation in unemployment among job losers, and thus much of the cyclical variation in the unemployment of mature men, involves temporary layoffs is relevant to downward rigidity for a different reason. Because those who are on layoff so rarely take other permanent work, this source of variation in the number of unemployed represents only a tiny variation in available labor. Most of those who are on layoff do not force wage rates down by accepting new jobs with lower wages; and firms do not reduce their offers, because they do not observe a significantly greater availability of experienced workers. Because the mature men who are unemployed are primarily on layoff, much new hiring in this age and sex group must still be done by attracting those who are already employed.

UNEMPLOYMENT INSURANCE

The current analysis also sheds light on the role of unemployment insurance in the U.S. economy. Much of the discussion of the disincentive effect of unemployment insurance has focused on the duration of search. I have emphasized more generally that unemployment insurance affects not only this duration but also the frequency and duration of temporary layoffs and the relative importance of seasonal, cyclical, and temporary jobs.

This paper shows the potential significance of inducing more layoffs and extending their duration. The exact relation between unemployment insurance and temporary layoffs deserves careful study. A theoretical analysis indicates that the current poor method of experience rating and the exclusion of unemployment insurance benefits from taxable income imply a very

22. The overtime premium does cause some cyclical variation in the average wage rate and may enable management to increase hours in the short run.

Martin S. Feldstein 743

large subsidy to temporary layoffs. A careful econometric evaluation remains to be done.

The greater relative frequency of temporary layoffs among the insured unemployed than among the uninsured unemployed also affects the measurement of the impact of unemployment insurance on the duration of unemployment.[23] Since temporary layoffs tend to be substantially shorter than other types of unemployment,[24] if unemployment insurance had *no* real effect on the duration of unemployment, the average duration of insured unemployment would be *less* than the duration of uninsured unemployment. More generally, a comparison of the mean durations of the insured and uninsured unemployed tends to understate the extent to which unemployment insurance lengthens the average duration of each unemployment spell.[25] Moreover, to the extent that unemployment insurance induces additional temporary layoffs, it may lower the mean duration of unemployment while increasing total unemployment.

THE SOCIAL COST OF UNEMPLOYMENT

Hall has suggested that the social cost of unemployment may be substantially less than the value of the lost output.[26] However, his "inventory" approach to the optimal rate of unemployment assumes that the unemployed are a reserve available for other firms to hire. This premise is clearly false for the large number of workers who are on layoff. Most of this group does not engage in productive job search and is not available to other firms. The social cost of an unemployed worker on layoff is thus equal to the worker's lost output reduced only by his value of leisure.[27]

23. Almost all temporary layoffs will be insured while new entrants and many reentrants will be uninsured. Even among job losers, those on temporary layoff are most likely to have the required experience.

24. See the sections above on the National Longitudinal Survey and the Current Population Survey.

25. See Stephen T. Marston, "The Impact of Unemployment Insurance on Job Search," *BPEA, 1:1975*, pp. 13–48, and my discussion in the same issue, pp. 52–58.

26. Robert E. Hall, "Turnover in the Labor Force," *BPEA, 3:1972*, pp. 709–56, and "An Aspect of the Economic Role of Unemployment" (paper presented to the International Economic Association Conference on the Microeconomic Foundations of Macroeconomics, S'Agaro, Spain, April 1975; processed).

27. Gordon, in "Welfare Cost of Higher Unemployment," argued that unemployment has a high social cost, but his method understates that cost by assuming that the unemployed are job changers and use their unemployment for at least some job search.

CONCLUSION

These cursory remarks on the implications of temporary layoffs can only suggest a direction for research and for modifications of the current theory. I hope that this evidence of the empirical importance of temporary layoffs will convince others that these theoretical and empirical developments deserve prompt attention.

Discussion

A NUMBER of participants commented on the implications of Feldstein's statistics for the relevance and validity of the search theory of unemployment. Some argued that temporary layoffs did not fit the search model, but instead resembled the kind of unemployment that Keynesians had stressed in the thirties: people losing their jobs, recognizing without exhaustive search that no satisfactory substitutes were available, and hence waiting for recall. Feldstein responded that, in contrast to the "old" view of unemployment, according to which laid-off workers have long periods of joblessness and basically must await a general business upturn before regaining their jobs, many of those on temporary layoff have very short durations and are recalled even though the economy has not recovered. James Tobin was particularly impressed by the evidence in table 1 on the large number of job switches made with no intervening spell of unemployment, a phenomenon he regarded as devastating to any claim that search theory could serve as a general explanation of unemployment. Robert J. Gordon recalled his finding (*BPEA, 1:1973*) that the unemployed spend their time mainly in waiting rather than searching.

Robert Hall, on the other hand, argued that neither job shifts without unemployment nor temporary layoffs without search were inconsistent with search theory. In his view, search theory explains why jobless people *may* wait and not take the very first job that becomes available. It does not preclude their taking a job without waiting, and thus avoiding any spell of unemployment, if that job is good enough. Nor does it preclude their judgment that it doesn't pay to search actively if they believe the probability of prompt recall is high and the probability of finding a better job in the interim is very low. Feldstein responded that, while in a formal sense all nonsearching could be viewed as a special case of search, that interpretation did not help to explain the unemployment of the nonsearchers.

A number of distinctions between workers on temporary layoff and the other unemployed were discussed. George Perry noted that, when those on temporary layoff are taken separately, it becomes clear that the rest of the unemployed are much worse off in terms of duration and of weekly probability of finding a job than is implied by the averages for all unemployed people. Charles Holt reminded the group of earlier studies that had found marked differences in the job-seeking behavior and the duration of unemployment between those who had been laid off and the rest of the unemployed. Michael Wachter conjectured that the people waiting for recall were probably heavily concentrated in high-wage industries; he suspected that those who lose jobs in low-wage industries generally find a job elsewhere rather than waiting for recall. This hypothesis could be tested if the data identified the previous occupational and industrial affiliations of the temporarily laid-off workers.

Tobin cautioned against any inference that those on temporary layoff had no influence on the excess supply of labor during a recession. Even if they did not actively search, they created "negative vacancies" since they would be rehired before their employers generated any unfilled vacancies. Similarly, Arthur Okun cautioned against any inference that people who ultimately returned to their previous jobs had remained unemployed during the entire period of layoff. On the contrary, considerable evidence suggested that a substantial fraction found interim jobs elsewhere. First, the employment of prime-age men in service industries is countercyclical, indicating that those low-paying sectors provide a temporary refuge for workers laid off from cyclical industries. Second, the rise in the unemployment rate of manufacturing workers during the recent recession was considerably smaller than the cumulative excess of layoffs over rehires shown in table 5. Many of those who had escaped from the category of unemployed factory workers must have found other jobs. Okun also observed that, if the incentive to employers to make temporary layoffs had greatly increased over time as a result of unemployment insurance or any other consideration, declines in output during recessions should now generate more unemployment, and correspondingly less shortening of hours and reduction of productivity. Yet he saw no evidence that the relationship between reduced output and incremental unemployment had shifted.

[6]

THE CYCLICAL PATTERN OF TEMPORARY LAYOFFS IN UNITED STATES MANUFACTURING

David M. Lilien*

O NE important question arises out of current attempts to provide a microeconomic foundation for aggregate wage rigidity and unemployment. How mobile are unemployed workers? Recent theoretical models of unemployment can be divided into two basic categories: the "new microeconomic" search theories attribute unemployment to the job search and job changing behavior of workers who become permanently separated from their jobs. The newer microeconomic contract theories attribute unemployment to the periodic employment reductions (via temporary layoffs) that are necessary to accommodate demand fluctuations when workers remain indefinitely attached to specific firms. The relative importance of these two approaches in explaining cyclical unemployment hinges on the share of unemployment over the business cycles that is associated with real labor turnover. Unfortunately no data are currently collected on the fraction of unemployment with or without job change.

This paper derives estimates of temporary layoff unemployment for U.S. manufacturing from Bureau of Labor Statistics (BLS) establishment turnover data. After a brief discussion of current unemployment data, a time dependent distributed lag model of manufacturing rehires is developed. The model allows estimation of both the percentage of each month's layoffs that end in rehire and the average duration of unemployment before rehire. Together with the layoff rate, these two statistics determine an estimate of manufacturing unemployment without job change.

Cyclical Unemployment

Between 1974 and 1975, the U.S. unemployment rate went up by 2.9 points (see table 1).

Received for publication April 6, 1978. Revision accepted for publication March 8, 1979.

* University of California, San Diego.

This research was supported by the Sloan Foundation and the National Science Foundation. I would like to thank Robert Hall, Olivier Blanchard, James Medoff and Michael Piore for useful suggestions.

Involuntary job losers accounted for 79% of this increase. This compares with a 3% increase in unemployment due to voluntary job leavers (quits) and only an 18% increase due to labor force entrants. In manufacturing, this pattern was even more pronounced. Of the 5.2 point increase in experienced manufacturing unemployment, 92% was due to increased unemployment of involuntary job losers, 8% to entrants and a marginal decline was actually recorded for job leavers. These statistics clearly indicate the involuntary nature of cyclical unemployment. They do not, however, provide any information about the mobility of unemployed workers.

The BLS does separate involuntary unemployment into "job losers on layoff" and "other job losers." A job loser on layoff is one who has a job from which he is temporarily absent. Note that here the term layoff has a meaning that is quite different from the one used throughout this paper. The unemployment series definition of layoff includes only workers who consider themselves as having a job. That is, workers who are certain of being recalled. All other layoffs (involuntary separations without prejudice) are included in the other job loser category. While the BLS household survey suggests that the subjective probability of recall is less than unity for other job losers, it does not imply a zero probability of recall. Many workers classified as other job losers are eventually rehired into their old jobs.

Furthermore, the fact that recall is near certain for job losers on layoff does not imply that they fail to engage in job search. To the contrary, existing evidence suggests that the majority of workers on layoff actively search for new employment. Workers on layoff differ from other job seekers in that they have already acquired firm specific skills and seniority rights from one particular employment prospect, i.e., recall. In terms of the search vocabulary, laid-off workers may be thought of as having an increased reservation wage reflecting their seniority premium and the probability of recall to their old job.

Job search on the part of job losers is a neces-

LAYOFFS IN U.S. MANUFACTURING   25

TABLE 1.—UNEMPLOYMENT RATES

	Total Job Losers	Job Losers on Layoff	Job Leavers	Labor Force Entrants and Reentrants	Total
Total Private					
1974	2.4	0.8	.8	2.3	5.6
1975	4.7	1.9	.9	2.8	8.5
Change	+2.3	+1.1	+.1	+0.5	+2.9
Experienced Manufacturing					
1974	3.5	1.7	.8	1.2	5.5
1975	8.3	4.4	.8	1.6	10.7
Change	+4.8	+2.7	+.0	+0.4	+5.2

sary component of the search explanation of unemployment. However, the validity of current search models not only requires that workers on layoff search for new jobs but that they actually find them. If in fact most workers are recalled before finding an acceptable job prospect, the optimal search patterns of workers are largely irrelevant in determining the duration of unemployment spells. Rather, the duration of unemployment is determined largely by the firm's recall policy.

Turnover Data

Unfortunately, no data on unemployment without job change is currently collected for the United States. The BLS monthly establishment survey does, however, collect monthly labor turnover data from U.S. manufacturing firms. Turnover data are collected under five general headings:

Separations	Accessions
Quits	New Hires
Layoffs	Other Accessions
Other Separations	

Prior to 1959, other accessions included only rehires while other separations included retirements and discharges (involuntary terminations with cause). Since 1959, transfers of workers between establishments within the same firm have been included in the definition of both other separations and other accessions. While rehires cannot be directly separated from transfers, evidence[1] suggests that they make up a small frac-

tion of other accessions and are relatively constant over the business cycle. Layoffs are defined as "suspensions without pay, lasting or expected to last more than seven consecutive calendar days, initiated without prejudice to the worker." Thus, layoffs lasting less than one week and their subsequent rehires, are systematically excluded from the turnover data.

It is from these data that Feldstein (1975) makes the claim that 83% of all layoffs generate rehires. "During the last decade there were approximately 1.33 layoffs per 100 manufacturing employees. During the same period there were 1.11 rehires per 100 employees." Therefore, Feldstein concludes that 83% of layoffs end in recall. The Feldstein measure suffers from a significant upward bias. His measure of rehires includes not only recalls from layoffs, but also inter-establishment employee transfers. Further, this measure provides no information about the

---

variance in the monthly percentage of employment involved in transfers. Medoff (1976) estimates that retirements and discharges make up approximately 75% of other separations. This leaves a remainder of 25%, or approximately 0.2% of employment per month since 1959, which is attributable to transfers and separations due to disability. This compares with an average rehire plus transfer rate (other accessions) of 1.4% per month.

Further evidence comes from a comparison of pre- and post-1959 "other separations." If there was little structural change between these two periods, the difference in variance between pre- and post-1959 "other separations" can be used as an estimate of the variance of transfers.

Other Separations

	1951–1958	1959–1975
Mean	.60	.81
Standard Deviation	.20	.16

It should be noted that the difference between the means, of 0.21, is similar to the estimate implied by Medoff. This suggests that transfers are indeed relatively small as compared to rehires.

---

[1] While no direct measures of transfers exist before 1976, evidence suggests that: (1) there are relatively few transfers, as compared with rehires; and (2) there is relatively little

cyclical pattern of rehires or the duration of temporary spells of unemployment.

Measuring the Cyclical Pattern of Temporary Layoffs

Disregarding the transfer problem for the moment, the establishment turnover data give the monthly level of rehires and layoffs for manufacturing industries. What it does not reveal is the correspondence between each rehire and its generating layoff. If this information were known, both the percentage of layoffs each month that were temporary (i.e., resulted in rehire), and the level and the duration of unemployment spells associated with these temporary layoffs, could be derived easily.

This correspondence can be thought of in terms of a set of parameters θ_{it}, where θ_{it} is the percentage of layoffs in period $t - i$ that result in rehire in period t. Thus, by definition,

$$R_t \equiv \sum_{i=0}^{\infty} \theta_{it} L_{t-i}$$

where R_t is defined as the number of rehires in period t and L_t is the number of layoffs in period t.

With this definition of the θ's, the percentage of layoffs initiated in period t that result in recall, r_t, is

$$r_t = \sum_{i=0}^{\infty} \theta_{it+i}.$$

The mean duration of completed unemployment spells resulting from temporary layoffs initiated in period t, d_t, is

$$d_t = \frac{1}{r_t} \sum_{i=0}^{\infty} \theta_{it+i} \delta_i$$

where δ_i is the average duration of unemployment of workers who are rehired i periods after having been laid off.[2]

Finally, the average unemployment associated with temporary layoffs initiated in period t, u_t, is

$$u_t = d_t r_t L_t.$$

---

[2] δ_i is the duration of unemployment spells that end in rehire in the ith month after layoff. By BLS definition the minimum duration of layoffs in the establishment turnover series is one week, or 0.23 months. The longest possible duration of layoffs generating rehire in the same month is one month. Thus, in this paper, δ_0 is approximated as the average of these two extremes. The other δ's are similarly calculated as the average of the extreme possibilities that can generate a rehire in the ith month after layoff.

If there was no variation in the θ's over time (i.e., $\theta_{it} = \theta_{is}$), estimates could be derived easily by regressing the current level of rehires on past levels of layoffs. This assumption of constancy of the θ's is not consistent with an attempt to measure the cyclical patterns of rehires. Nevertheless, the basic approach is reasonable. If variations of θ_{it} from its average value can be parameterized in terms of some observable variables, X_t, i.e., $\theta_{it} = \bar{\theta}_i + \alpha_i X_t$, then the following equation could be estimated:

$$R_t = \Sigma \bar{\theta}_i L_{t-i} + \Sigma \alpha_i X_t L_{t-i}.$$

The X_t's must be capable of capturing the two major cyclical causes of variation of θ_{it}: that is, the speed at which job searchers find new jobs and the speed at which firms recall layoffs.

When aggregate labor markets are tight, there is a relative excess of high compensation jobs for the number of workers on layoff. Job searchers can find employment at a relatively rapid rate. Some workers who might otherwise have been recalled and returned to their old employer are now successful in finding new employment before being recalled. This results in fewer actual rehires than average. Obviously, the argument goes both ways. When aggregate labor markets are slack, the duration of unsuccessful job search increases. Under these conditions, some workers who might otherwise have found new jobs before being recalled are now recalled before finding new jobs.

On the other hand, if within a particular industry the level of voluntary turnover reduces, or the rate of desired employment increases, firms will increase the rate at which workers are recalled (and reduce the rate at which they are laid off). This, in turn, causes the rehiring of some workers who might otherwise have found new jobs. Similarly, a reduction in the hiring of particular industries causes some workers, who would normally be rehired, to find new jobs.

At the economy level of aggregation, the distinction between these two effects tends to be somewhat blurred. What allows distinction between these two effects is the level of aggregation at which they take place. Tight aggregate labor markets affect the search behavior of all workers regardless of the conditions in the firm from which they were laid off. In contrast, systematic increases in hiring affect only those workers on layoff from firms offering increased recalls. By

LAYOFFS IN U.S. MANUFACTURING 27

looking at the pattern of rehires at the industry level of aggregation, these two effects can be separated. This will be accomplished in this paper by estimating the θ_{it}'s at the two-digit industry level of aggregation and then reconstructing an aggregate measure of the θ_{it}'s.

The unemployment rate of prime aged males, those between ages 25 and 54, will be used as the measure of aggregate labor market conditions. This rate, rather than the total unemployment rate, is selected because it does not suffer from the compositional bias caused by the increased participation of women and teenagers over the last 15 years. Net industry hiring, defined as change in industry employment plus quits as a percentage of industry employment, will be used as the measure of recall potential.

One final factor needs consideration. If current hiring and aggregate labor market conditions affect the flow out of unemployment, they also affect the size of the pool of workers on layoff who are available to be recalled in future periods. Thus, current rehires may vary from the industry average, due to past fluctuations in hiring or unemployment. This does not seem to pose much of a problem in terms of the unemployment rate. Very little change in unemployment occurs in the period of time it takes most workers to be rehired. However, industry hiring does exhibit a fair amount of short-run fluctuations, making it necessary to include lagged values of industry hiring, H, in the specification of θ_{it}, although the expected sign of their coefficients is somewhat ambiguous. Given that the recent history of the industry is characterized by an unusually high level of hiring, there will be less workers available to be recalled, leading to a fall in θ_{it}. At the same time, there will be fewer workers being laid off, so that a smaller number of recalls will be necessary to yield the same value of θ_{it}. An industry with unusual expansion will have both of these quantities below their usual level with an uncertain effect on θ_{it}.

The unemployment and industry hiring variables are designed to capture cyclical effects in the pattern of rehires from layoff. It has been argued that expansion of the unemployment compensation system may have induced secular increases in the number of temporary layoffs. In order to capture any trends in the pattern of rehires from layoff, a simple time trend variable and an unemployment compensation variable

were included in the initial specification of the industry rehire equations. As the estimated coefficients of these secular variables were not significantly different from zero in any of the industry equations, they have been excluded from the specifications presented in this paper.

The actual parameterization of θ_{it} being used is then:

$$\theta_{it} = \bar{\theta}_i + \alpha_{1i}H_t + \alpha_{2i}\bar{H}_{t-1} + \alpha_{3i}\bar{H}_{t-2} + \alpha_{4i}U_t$$
$$\alpha_{1t} > 0; \; \alpha_{2t} \lesseqgtr 0; \; \alpha_{3t} \lesseqgtr 0; \; \alpha_{4t} > 0$$

where

$\bar{\theta}_i$ is a constant measuring the average value of θ_{it};

H_t is the monthly net hiring rate (at the two-digit SIC industry level) defined as the percentage change in industry employment plus voluntary quits;

$$\bar{H}_{t-1} = \frac{1}{3} \sum_{i=1}^{3} H_{t-i};$$

$$\bar{H}_{t-2} = \frac{1}{3} \sum_{i=4}^{6} H_{t-i};$$

U_t is the six month average of the aggregate unemployment rate of prime aged males (i.e., males 25 to 55).

The final specification of the equation to be estimated is

$$R_t = \alpha_0 + \sum_{i=0}^{k} \bar{\theta}_i L_{t-i} + \sum_{i=0}^{k} \alpha_{1i} H_t L_{t-i}$$
$$+ \sum_{i=0}^{k} \alpha_{2i} \bar{H}_{t-1} L_{t-i} + \sum_{i=0}^{k} \alpha_{3i} \bar{H}_{t-2} L_{t-i}$$
$$+ \sum_{i=0}^{k} \alpha_{4i} U_t L_{t-i}$$

where α_0 is a positive constant included to measure transfers[3] and the variables H_t, $\bar{H}_{t-1}$, $\bar{H}_{t-2}$

---

[3] Using a constant to proxy for transfers introduces no bias to the θ estimates so long as transfers are uncorrelated with the independent variables of equation (1). While this correlation cannot be currently measured, a small variance of transfers is a sufficient condition for any bias to be small. If, for example, transfers are perfectly correlated with layoffs, the θ estimates will exceed their true value by $\partial T/\partial L$. If the variance of transfers is small, it follows that $\partial T/\partial L$ must also be small. As existing evidence suggests that transfers are far less common than rehires and have a relatively small variance as compared with rehires, the assumption of constant transfers will not lead to significant bias of the θ estimates.

28   THE REVIEW OF ECONOMICS AND STATISTICS

and U_t enter the equation around their mean value over the period of estimation.

Estimation

The resulting equation is a series of five distributed lags in L_t, where the lag coefficients are themselves functions of observable variables. With sufficient observations, the lag distributions could be estimated directly. However, with five lag distributions if some temporary layoffs are of long duration, the number of independent variables required for the estimation is rather large. In actual estimation lag lengths of between four and seven months were used. Since all of the variables except U_t are related to employment conditions within the same industry, collinearity presents a serious problem in obtaining reasonably tight estimates of the θ's. Thus, polynomial distributed lags will be used in actual estimation for the usual reasons.

Table 2 gives summary regression statistics for the twenty-one industry regression estimated over the 1960–1974 period. The first five columns present the sum of the θ's where

$$\bar{\theta} = \Sigma \bar{\theta}_t$$
$$\alpha_1 = \Sigma \alpha_{1t}$$
$$\alpha_2 = \Sigma \alpha_{2t}$$
$$\alpha_3 = \Sigma \alpha_{3t}$$
$$\alpha_4 = \Sigma \alpha_{4t}.$$

As the hiring and unemployment variables were entered around their period mean the $\bar{\theta}$ coefficient may be loosely interpreted as the industry average rehire rate from layoff. The range of average rehire rates between industries is quite large. The extremes of 88% in Primary Metals, 27% in Petroleum and Coal, suggest that there are fundamental differences in the level of temporary layoffs between industries. These differences are explored by Medoff (1976) and Lilien (1977). When the $\bar{\theta}$'s are weighted by the average number of layoffs in their industry, an average recall rate for manufacturing of 68% is derived. For every percentage increase in the unemployment rate above the 3.2% period average (prime aged male unemployed rate), the manufacturing average rehire rate goes up approximately 4.3%.

The θ's also determine an estimate of the mean duration of temporary layoffs. The theoretical

effect of aggregate demand on d is somewhat ambiguous. d is a function both of firms' recall policies and the rate at which workers find alternative employment. In relatively slack labor markets, a greater percentage of layoffs are short duration, temporary layoffs, as opposed to indefinite layoffs resulting from permanent shifts of firm specific demand. However, the duration, as well as the frequency of periodic layoffs, may be used to accommodate temporary cyclical demand reduction. Thus, the effect of aggregate demand on the average layoff duration before recall is not clear. Furthermore, d measures only the duration of workers who are eventually rehired. Thus d does not reflect the mean interval between layoff and recall. Since d is estimated from only those workers who are rehired, it understates the mean interval before recall by sampling more heavily from workers on relatively short duration layoffs. As job changing is less likely in slack labor markets, d through the θ's will tend to be increasing in U independent of firms' recall policies.

Steady state estimates of d presented in column 7 of table 2 generally support these last two effects on d. In all but five industries, the steady state ($H = \bar{H}_{t-1} = \bar{H}_{t-2}$) values of d, evaluated at the mean of H and U over the 1960–1974 period, are increasing in U. It should be noted that these steady state durations considerably understate the true duration where the pattern of fluctuation in H leads to higher estimates of the true duration.

Temporary Layoffs Over the Last Decade

Table 3 presents estimates of the actual pattern of temporary layoffs for total manufacturing. The estimates reveal considerable cyclical variation in the rehire rate, with 78% of the layoffs in the recessionary year of 1975 generating rehires, as compared with 60% in 1970. The lowest rehire rates were in the three years immediately preceding large increases in unemployment: 1969, 1970, and 1974. The low rehire rates in these years reflect the reduced hiring that accompanied the unemployment increases. Similarly, the highest rehire rates, in 1972 and 1975, were for layoffs preceding the increase in hiring that contributed to the reduction of unemployment.

The duration of unemployment spells as-

LAYOFFS IN U.S. MANUFACTURING

TABLE 2.—REHIRE EQUATION RESULTS

	Sum of Lag Coefficients					Mean Duration		R^2
Industry	$\dfrac{r}{\theta}$ [a]	$\dfrac{H_t}{\alpha_1}$	$\dfrac{\bar{H}_{t-1}}{\alpha_2}$	$\dfrac{\bar{H}_{t-2}}{\alpha_3}$	$\dfrac{U_t}{\alpha_4}$	d [a]	$\dfrac{\partial d}{\partial U}$ [a]	S.E. of Reg.
Ordinance	.301 (.087)	.169 (.023)	−.072 (.025)	−.068 (.020)	.050 (.016)	1.36	−.25	.525 .178
Lumber & Wood	.553 (.046)	.116 (.007)	−.047 (.007)	−.039 (.007)	.020 (.009)	1.00	.24	.927 .153
Furniture	.408 (.072)	.099 (.010)	−.065 (.010)	−.010 (.015)	.017 (.015)	1.30	.18	.751 .157
Stone, Clay & Glass	.738 (.126)	.190 (.020)	−.009 (.018)	−.032 (.021)	.058 (.014)	0.97	.27	.806 .248
Primary Metals	.880 (.066)	.196 (.020)	−.023 (.016)	−.033 (.024)	.064 (.014)	1.89	.20	.862 .216
Fabricated Metals	.544 (.071)	.145 (.007)	−.034 (.007)	−.055 (.009)	.017 (.012)	1.99	−.66	.913 .158
Machinery	.679 (.056)	.218 (.007)	−.014 (.008)	−.050 (.008)	.060 (.017)	1.33	.42	.898 .161
Electrical Equipment	.592 (.069)	.211 (.015)	−.061 (.016)	−.042 (.021)	.068 (.010)	1.05	.25	.849 .122
Transportation Equipment	.643 (.042)	.131 (.004)	−.018 (.008)	−.024 (.008)	.068 (.008)	0.82	.04	.941 .281
Instruments	.716 (.113)	.240 (.028)	−.018 (.034)	−.029 (.041)	.033 (.016)	1.40	.38	.684 .130
Miscellaneous Mfg. Industries	.618 (.079)	.096 (.010)	−.016 (.010)	−.062 (.008)	.002 (.010)	1.12	−.06	.804 .096
Food	.712 (.061)	.091 (.005)	−.002 (.007)	−.029 (.005)	.035 (.006)	1.00	−.04	.917 .178
Tobacco	.571 (.122)	.104 (.008)	.013 (.015)	−.024 (.008)	.068 (.020)	1.82	.29	.744 1.087
Textile Mill Products	.468 (.073)	.196 (.017)	−.103 (.017)	−.010 (.012)	.027 (.014)	0.72	.76	.744 .097
Apparel	.594 (.045)	.124 (.008)	−.047 (.010)	.016 (.009)	.027 (.009)	0.74	.10	.814 .229
Paper Products	.654 (.033)	.231 (.014)	−.126 (.018)	−.071 (.013)	.003 (.010)	1.24	.10	.892 .089
Printing & Publishing	.360 (.075)	.185 (.018)	−.145 (.024)	−.058 (.018)	−.006 (.010)	0.76	−.06	.630 .070
Chemicals	.290 (.077)	.222 (.017)	−.158 (.021)	−.072 (.021)	.032 (.016)	1.84	.11	.757 .070
Petroleum & Coal Products	.277 (.100)	.289 (.029)	−.188 (.042)	−.160 (.024)	.002 (.020)	0.56	.75	.674 .100
Rubber & Plastic	.709 (.077)	.183 (.016)	−.031 (.017)	−.035 (.013)	.101 (.016)	1.11	.46	.807 .036
Leather Products	.614 (.075)	.140 (.010)	−.079 (.016)	−.005 (.013)	.029 (.013)	0.78	.24	.740 .225

[a] Evaluated at the mean of H, $\bar{H}_{t-1}$, $\bar{H}_{t-2}$, U.

sociated with temporary layoffs also shows significant cyclical variation. Layoffs in the recessionary year of 1975 that resulted in rehire generated mean unemployment spells of approximately two months, as compared with only about 1.5 months for the boom period of the late sixties. The average duration over the last de-

cade is estimated at 1.6 months. Figure 1 shows the estimated average rehire pattern of temporary layoffs from which the 1.6 month average duration estimate was calculated. Note that these duration estimates should not be confused with BLS household survey unemployment duration data, which measure the duration of incompleted

30   THE REVIEW OF ECONOMICS AND STATISTICS

TABLE 3.—THE PATTERN OF TEMPORARY LAYOFFS OVER THE LAST DECADE

					Involuntary Job	Experienced Manufacturing Unemployment		
Year	$\hat{r}_t$	$\hat{d}_t$	L_t	$\hat{u}_t$	Changers[a]	Total	Total Over 6 Months	Involuntary Job Losers
1965	.70	1.7	1.4	1.7	0.8	4.0	0.5	N/A
1966	.68	1.6	1.2	1.3	0.9	3.2	0.3	N/A
1967	.65	1.5	1.4	1.4	1.0	3.6	0.3	2.1
1968	.68	1.6	1.2	1.3	0.9	3.3	0.3	1.9
1969	.63	1.4	1.2	1.1	0.9	4.4	0.2	1.8
1970	.60	1.4	1.8	1.6	1.2	5.6	0.2	3.7
1971	.70	1.7	1.6	1.8	0.9	6.8	0.8	4.7
1972	.75	1.8	1.1	1.5	0.7	5.6	1.0	3.5
1973	.71	1.8	0.9	1.1	0.8	4.3	0.4	2.4
1974	.64	1.5	1.5	1.6	1.0	5.7	0.5	3.6
1975	.78	2.0	2.1	3.3	0.8	10.9	2.4	8.4
1976	.74	1.9	1.3	1.8	0.7	7.8	2.0	5.4

[a] Discharges plus layoffs not rehired.

unemployment spells and overstate the duration of completed spells of unemployment.[4]

The duration estimates, $\hat{d}_t$, are somewhat higher than might have been expected. Kaitz (1970) estimated the duration of completed unemployment spells for all unemployed workers from BLS household survey data. For the periods our estimates overlap, the Kaitz estimates exceed $\hat{d}_t$ by approximately 33%. This suggests that either non-manufacturing unemployment spells and the other sources of manufacturing unemployment, i.e., quits and discharges, are of significantly shorter duration than manufacturing temporary layoffs, or $\hat{d}_t$ may suffer from an upward bias.

A somewhat surprising aspect of the estimates presented in table 3 is the relatively low estimates of unemployment without job change, $\hat{u}_t$. Since 1965 $\hat{u}_t$ has averaged 30.0% of manufacturing unemployment or an average contribution of 1.6 percentage points to the manufacturing unemployment rate. Despite the fact that over 68% of layoffs generate rehires, $\hat{u}_t$ explains only 50% of the unemployment of involuntary job losers. Furthermore, the fraction of job loser unemployment not explained by $\hat{u}_t$ follows a strong cyclical pattern. In 1975, with 78% of layoffs generating rehires, $\hat{u}_t$ accounts for only 39% of job loser unemployment, while in 1969, with only 63% of layoffs generating rehire, $\hat{u}_t$ accounts for 67% of job loser unemployment.[5]

[4] The distinction between the duration of completed and uncompleted unemployment spells is discussed in Kaitz (1970).
[5] One characteristic of the establishment turnover data

While the estimates in table 3 imply that the majority of layoffs, particularly the increase in layoffs associated with slack labor markets, are temporary, they do not imply that temporary layoffs account for the bulk of cyclical unemployment. Between 1974 and 1975 the manufacturing layoff rate increased by 0.6% of employment per month. Layoffs ending in rehire increased by almost 0.7% of employment per month; implying an actual decline in the number of layoffs generating job changes between 1974

may account for some of the discrepancies between $\hat{u}_t$ and the BLS household survey unemployment series. The establishment survey systematically over-samples large establishments, which tend to have lower turnover rates than smaller establishments. See Hall and Lilien (1978). Thus the manufacturing layoff series understates the true incidence of involuntary manufacturing unemployment.

FIGURE 1.—AVERAGE PERCENT OF TEMPORARY LAYOFFS REHIRED IN THE ith MONTH AFTER LAYOFF

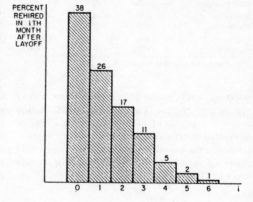

LAYOFFS IN U.S. MANUFACTURING   31

and 1975. Of the 4.8 point increase in the involuntary manufacturing unemployment rate only 1.7 points is accounted for by the increase in $\hat{u}_t$. That is, temporary layoffs accounted for only 35% of the increase in involuntary manufacturing unemployment between 1974 and 1975, even though they accounted for all of the increase in the layoff rate.

The relatively small increase of temporary layoff unemployment in 1975 suggests that the majority of cyclical unemployment is due to the longer unemployment spells of job changing job losers. This hypothesis is supported by the dramatic increase in long term unemployment in 1975 and 1976, as can be seen in table 3. Clearly, the traditional notion of the unemployed as people without jobs still applies to the majority of those who are unemployed during a recession.

Concluding Remarks

Clearly, temporary layoffs are an important labor market phenomenon. Many workers remain attached to a single firm through several spells of unemployment. Firm specific human capital, as well as efficient risk shifting, makes labor turnover relatively unprofitable for both workers and firms when demand reductions are thought to be temporary. Thus, on average, less than 30% of manufacturing workers on layoff actually change jobs. Further, the percentage of layoffs generating job change in recessionary periods is considerably less than 30%.

The overwhelming source of variation in the manufacturing layoff rate is variation in the frequency of temporary layoffs. Over the last decade the variance of the annual layoff rate with rehire has been well over three times the variance of the involuntary job changer separation rate. Despite this fact, temporary layoffs do not appear to be the overwhelming source of cyclical unemployment. Roughly 35% of the increase in job loser unemployment during the 1975 recession was due to temporary layoffs. Much of the remaining increase was due to longer unemployment spells for job changers.

REFERENCES

Feldstein, Martin S., "The Importance of Temporary Layoffs: An Empirical Analysis," *Brookings Papers on Economic Activity* 3 (1975), 725–745.

Hall, Robert E., and David M. Lilien, "The Measurement and Significance of Labor Turnover" (1978), forthcoming in volume of studies of the *National Commission on Employment and Unemployment Statistics.*

Kaitz, Hyman B., "Analyzing the Length of Spells of Unemployment," *Monthly Labor Review* 93 (Nov. 1970), 11–20.

Lilien, David M., *The Cyclical Pattern of Temporary Layoffs,* unpublished Ph.D. dissertation, M.I.T., 1977.

———, "Relative Demand Disturbances, Labor Turnover and Fluctuations of the Natural Rate," University of California, San Diego, Working Paper, Oct. 1978.

Medoff, James L., "Layoffs and Alternatives under Trade Unions in United States Manufacturing," mimeograph, Harvard University, December 1976.

[7]

The Importance of Lifetime Jobs in the U.S. Economy

By ROBERT E. HALL*

Though the U.S. labor market is justly notorious for high turnover and consequent high unemployment, it also provides stable, near-lifetime employment to an important fraction of the labor force. This paper investigates patterns of job duration by age, race, and sex, with the following major conclusions:

1) The typical worker today is holding a job which has lasted or will last about eight years. Over a quarter of all workers are holding jobs which will last twenty years or more. Sixty percent hold jobs which will last five years or more.

2) The jobs held by middle-aged workers with more than ten years of tenure are extremely stable. Over the span of a decade, only 20 to 30 percent come to an end.

3) Among workers aged 30 and above, about 40 percent are currently working in jobs which eventually will last twenty years or more. Three-quarters are in jobs which will last five years or more.

4) The duration of employment among blacks is just as long as among whites. Even though the jobs held by blacks are worse in almost every other dimension, they are no more unstable than those held by whites.

5) Women's jobs are substantially shorter than men's, on the average. Only about one-quarter of all women over the age of 30 are employed in jobs which will last over twenty years, whereas over half the men over 30 are holding these near-lifetime jobs.

These findings are highly relevant in the debate over the existence and nature of long-term employment contracts. I have elaborated this point elsewhere (1980) and have given extensive citations, which will not

*Hoover Institution, and department of economics, Stanford University; National Bureau of Economic Research. This research was supported by the National Science Foundation through a grant to the National Bureau of Economic Research, and is part of the NBER's research program on economic fluctuations. I am grateful to Jane Mather for exceptionally capable assistance. All opinions expressed are my own.

be repeated here. If most workers in the United States were holding relatively brief jobs, then theories of long-term employment arrangements would be off the point. The findings reported here of the considerable importance of lifetime work do not clinch the case in favor of any particular theory of long-term contracts. Even in markets for completely homogeneous products, where simple ideas of competitive spot markets work perfectly, it is conceivable that the typical buyer deals with the same seller year after year. But the finding of extensive long-term employment in the U.S. labor market does add to the interest in understanding long-term employment arrangements.

All of the results in this paper are derived from published tabulations of job tenure, that is, the length of time that workers have been employed to date in their jobs. Most of the results rest on projections of how much longer workers will remain on their current jobs. These projections are most important for workers in midcareer, where many have just started jobs which will ultimately last twenty or thirty years. The techniques used in this research were inspired by the related literature on the duration of unemployment, for example, the work of Hyman Kaitz. My concentration on the distribution of job duration across workers was suggested by the work of Kim Clark and Lawrence Summers on the distribution of the duration of unemployment across unemployed workers. This paper will not make any explicit use of a very different distribution, that of the duration across jobs. It is true, but not relevant for the points to be made here, that the typical job is extremely brief, lasting only a matter of months (see R. A. Jenness). Most workers hold very stable jobs, even though stable jobs are a small fraction of the flow of jobs filled each month. The relationship between the distribution of the lengths of jobs, sampled randomly from the universe of newly started jobs, and the distribution obtained by sampling randomly among workers, is explained in detail by Stephen Salant, and by George Akerlof and Brian Main. Everything in this paper is based on sampling workers.

The stability of jobs among middle-aged and older workers has been noted by a number of earlier authors, though the computation in this paper of additional time on the job is new, as far as I know. My own earlier work (1972) presented low estimates of separation rates from the National Longitudinal Survey of Work Experience for older men, but without any comment on the significance of the low rates. Martin Neil Baily cited the same source in defense of theories of long-term employment contracts. Kazuo Koike has compared data on tenure for the United States and Japan, and concluded that tenure of fifteen years or longer is actually more common in the United States, in spite of the celebrated *nenko* system of lifetime employment in Japan. Akerlof and Main present computations of the mean length of jobs held by workers in the United States, with results that are fully compatible with the complete distributions reported here. Main shows that jobs lasting twenty years or more are slightly more prevalent in Britain compared to the United States.

I. Data on Job Tenure

On six different occasions in the postwar period, the *Current Population Survey* has inquired about the starting date of the current job of each of the roughly 100,000 workers included in the survey.[1] A job is defined as continuous employment with the same employer, possibly in different occupations. Interruptions in jobs for vacation, illness, strikes, and layoffs of less than thirty days are not counted. For the self-employed and household service workers with multiple employers, the entire spell in the same line of work is counted as a single job.[2] Tenure is

[1]See Bureau of the Census and Bureau of Labor Statistics 1963, 1967, 1969, 1975, and 1979.
[2]Only 1.5 percent of workers are in household service, and, in any case, their distribution by tenure is very similar to the distribution for workers in general. The self-employed form 8.4 percent of all workers and have typically longer tenure (especially farmers). However, for most of the self-employed, the definition of a job used in the survey is probably quite reasonable.

defined as the number of years since the workers' current job began.

The data on tenure do not immediately suggest that lengthy employment is an important feature of the American labor market. The median job tenure among workers in general was only 3.6 years in 1978; 40 percent had tenure of less than two years and only 9.5 percent had been on the same job for twenty years or more. The distribution of all workers among the categories (years) of tenure was

Category	Percent
0–0.5	19.0
0.5–1.0	9.2
1–2	11.7
2–3	7.7
3–5	12.5
5–10	16.7
10–15	8.7
15–20	5.0
20–25	3.7
25–30	2.8
30–35	1.7
35+	1.3

The median was 3.6 years.

However, the labor force contains a large proportion of young workers who could not possibly have long tenure even if lifetime jobs were the general rule. A better way to diagnose long-term employment from data on tenure is among older workers. The percentages of workers who have had the same jobs for twenty or more years are

Age	Percent
35–39	1
40–44	7
45–49	17
50–54	25
55–59	30
60–64	33
65+	35

From these data, one might reasonably infer that lifetime employment is the exception in the U.S. labor market. Only about one-third of older workers are currently in jobs which have lasted a large fraction of their careers. But this inference is obscured by the failure to count large numbers of middle-aged workers who are now working in jobs which ultimately will last twenty or twenty-five years, but which have lasted less than twenty years to date. Among the 45 to 49-year-olds, for example, in addition to the 17 percent who are working in jobs which have lasted at least twenty years so far, another 44 percent are in jobs which have lasted five to twenty years, and, as I will demonstrate, there is a large probability that these jobs will last a good many more years. Over 40 percent of all 45 to 49-year-olds are in near-lifetime jobs. This inference is not inconsistent with the small fraction—again about one-third—of workers near retirement age who have twenty or more years of tenure. Ages of retirement vary widely; many of the workers in this age group are now holding new jobs after retiring from near-lifetime jobs in the recent past. There is no single age at which the fraction of workers with long tenure reveals the true importance of long-term jobs.

II. Inferring the Prospective Length of a Job

In order to get a clearer picture of the importance of long jobs, it is necessary to project the likely additional time a worker will spend in his current job. Then what I will call "eventual tenure" can be computed as the sum of actual reported tenure and the projected additional time on the job. The key element in the projection is the probability that a worker with a given age and tenure will retain his current job for one, ten, twenty years, and so on. In the work presented here, the retention probabilities are measured from the number of workers in one age-tenure category who move on to higher age-tenure categories. If the fraction is large, it means that there is considerable prospective additional time on the job for a worker in the first category. This kind of comparison can be made for widely separated categories; for example, to compute the probability that a worker aged 25 to 29 who has been on the job for five years will remain on the job for ten more years, I use the number of workers aged 35 to 39 with fifteen years of tenure divided by the number of workers aged 25 to 29 with five years of tenure.

The computation of job retention rates can be done historically by comparing the number of workers in an age-tenure category in one survey with the number in a later survey in correspondingly higher age and tenure categories. Job retention rates computed in this way appear in Table 1 for the ten-year period 1968–78. Alternatively, what I will call "contemporaneous" job retention rates can be computed by comparing two categories in the same survey. In this approach, an adjustment for differences in the population by age must be used. The effect of the adjustment is to compare the fraction of the population in an age group who have a specified amount of tenure with the fraction of the population in an older group with correspondingly higher tenure. The two methods of calculating job retention rates will give the same results if the distribution of tenure within age groups remains stable over time. Both are just estimates of future retention rates, and it is not clear as a theoretical matter which is better. At the practical level, the contemporaneous retention rates are the only ones that can be calculated for less than five-year spans because the survey has been taken only at five-year intervals in the past decade. Examples of the differences between the two rates appear in Table 1 for selected age-tenure groups. The only important discrepancy occurs among 40 to 44-year-olds with fifteen to twenty years of tenure. An unusually large fraction of this age group in 1968 took jobs in the immediate postwar period, 1948–53. As a result, the numerator in the contemporaneous retention rate, which contains the same group ten years later, is biased upward as an estimate of the likely fraction of 50 to 54-year-olds with twenty-five to thirty years of tenure in 1988. Biases of this kind are largely offsetting because the same high number appears in the denominator of other estimates of retention rates. The fact that the disturbance in job-taking patterns caused by World War II shows up clearly in the 1978 data on job tenure is an illustration in itself of the importance of long-term jobs.

The computation of retention rates in Table 1 takes account of all the major sources of departure from jobs—movements to other jobs and departures from the labor force through permanent retirement or temporary

TABLE 1—TEN-YEAR JOB RETENTION RATES

Age in 1968	Tenure in 1968 (years)	Percent of Age Group in this Category		Age in 1978	Tenure in 1978 (years)	Percent of Age Group in this Tenure Category 1978	Historical Retention Rate 1968–78 (percent)	Contemporaneous Retention Rate 1978 (percent)
		1968	1978					
20–24	0–5	50.76	58.83	30–34	10–15	7.36	14.5	12.5
30–34	0–5	39.24	45.27	40–44	10–15	10.83	27.6	23.9
	5–10	14.25	16.61		15–20	7.61	53.4	45.8
40–44	5–10	12.30	15.36	50–54	15–20	7.10	57.7	46.2
	15–20	9.24	7.61		25–30	6.02	65.2	79.1
	20–25	4.93	4.61		30–35	3.58	72.6	77.7
50–54	5–10	11.12	12.58	60–64	15–20	4.23	38.0	33.6
	20–25	7.25	6.42		30–35	3.40	46.9	53.0
55–59	20–25	6.54	5.45	65–69	30–35	1.09	16.7	20.0

Source: Computed from Bureau of Labor Statistics (1969, 1979).

withdrawal. This is achieved by taking the percent of the population in each age-tenure category, rather than the percent of workers (which is what is reported in the tabulations of the survey). Data on the civilian noninstitutional population were used to restate the data in this form; details on the computations and the resulting distribution are given in an appendix which is available from the author. Two other less important sources of departure from jobs are not counted in Table 1: death and emigration. An examination of data on deaths and on population changes within cohorts showed that neither flow has any perceptible effect on the calculation of retention rates. In the modern U.S. economy, almost nobody dies or emigrates while holding a job. Finally, the restriction to civilian employment and population means that military service is not included—the reported retention rates are correct estimates for nonmilitary jobs.

III. Computed Job Retention Rates and the Distribution of Eventual Tenure for the U.S. Labor Force

Table 1 shows that both measures of job retention rates agree that all but the youngest workers face a substantial probability of remaining on their current jobs for at least another ten years. Eventual tenure is far greater than tenure to date, especially for workers in their forties. About half of those aged 40 to 44 who have been on their current jobs for five to ten years so far will retain their jobs ten years from now. And for those in their forties who have spent most of their working lives in their current jobs, the great majority (65–79 percent) will remain in those jobs for the next ten years as well. Job retention rates are lower among younger workers, who are still in the process of finding good lifetime matches, and for older workers, who have substantial probabilities of retirement in the next ten years.

With a complete set of job retention rates, it is possible to calculate the distribution of additional years of work for workers in each observed age-tenure category. The results for 40 to 44-year-olds with eventual tenure of twenty-plus years are

Category	Percent
0–0.5	4.6
0.5–1	7.8
1–2	11.3
2–3	15.7
3–5	20.4
5–10	35.5
10–15	59.0
15–20	98.0
20+	100.0

For all tenure groups, the percent was 39.5.

Although the entire distribution can be inferred, all that is shown here is the fraction of workers whose additional years of work will be enough to give them eventual tenure of at least twenty years on the current job. As in every group in the labor force, those aged 40 to 44 who have just taken new jobs have only a small likelihood of remaining in those jobs for the next twenty years. But those who have been on their current jobs for five to ten years have a 35 percent chance of keeping their current jobs for the ten to fifteen additional years necessary to give them an eventual tenure of twenty years or more. Those who have already lasted ten to fifteen years have a 59 percent chance of lasting the additional five to ten years, and those with fifteen to twenty years on their current jobs are 98 percent likely to reach twenty years of eventual tenure. In the entire age group, just under 40 percent will have eventual tenure on their current jobs of twenty years or more. This should be compared to the much smaller figure—7.5 percent—who have already reached twenty years of tenure. Very long-term jobs are quantitatively important in this age group, but that fact is not apparent directly in the distribution of tenure. Computations of eventual tenure from job retention rates are needed to appraise the incidence of very long jobs.

The following is the distribution of eventual tenure across all age and tenure categories for all U.S. workers in 1978:

Years	Percent
0–0.5	9.8
0.5–1	6.7
1–2	7.0
2–3	5.0
3–5	13.5
5–10	14.8
10–15	10.4
15–20	4.7
20–25	4.7
25–30	6.2
30–35	10.0
35+	7.0

The median was 7.7 years; the percent with twenty-plus years was 28.0.

The typical worker is currently on a job which will last about eight years in all, counting the years it has already lasted. An important minority—about 28 percent—are currently employed in near-lifetime jobs lasting twenty years or more, and 17 percent are in jobs which will last thirty years or more.

An equally important minority are at work in what will turn out to be very brief jobs—about 23 percent will have eventual tenure of less than two years. A clear majority of workers—58 percent—are currently holding reasonably lorlg jobs, those which will last five years or more.

IV. The Process of Moving into Long-Term Work

The data on job tenure reveal a good deal about the probability process through which most workers eventually settle into near-lifetime jobs. The typical pattern is to hold a number of very brief jobs in the first few years after leaving school. Eventually one job turns out to be a good match and lasts several years. The probability that any given new job will become a lifetime job is extremely low for young workers and never rises above 6 percent in any age group. But after a job has lasted five years, the probability that it will eventually last twenty years or more in all rises to close to one-half among workers in their early thirties. As a general matter, the data suggest that most job changes occur in the first few years after a job begins, because the worker or the employer or both perceive that the worker and the job are poorly matched. Once this period of job shopping reaches a successful conclusion, workers have very low probabilities of losing or leaving jobs. Again, it is important to emphasize that good matches are not necessarily good jobs in any absolute sense—a worker who is placed above his competence will not last any longer than will a worker who realizes he would be happier in another job for which he is qualified.

At no age is the probability very high of a given new job becoming a lifetime job (the percent shown is the probability that a job will last twenty-plus years):

Age	Percent
16–17	0.4
18–19	0.3
20–24	2.2
25–29	4.8
30–34	5.3
35–39	5.7
40–44	4.6
45–49	1.8
50–54	1.0

TABLE 2—ASPECTS OF THE PROCESS OF MOVING INTO LONG-TERM JOBS, ALL WORKERS, 1978

Age	Percent Working in New Jobs (1)	Probability of Retaining Job to 5 Years (2)	Percent of All Workers 5 Years Older Who Have Reached Tenure of 5+ Years (3)	Percent of those Who Reach 5 Years of Tenure Who Go on to Reach Tenure of 20+ Years (4)
16–17	59.5	1.7	5.5	26.2
18–19	52.5	1.2	5.5	26.2
20–24	34.1	5.9	19.9	36.6
25–29	22.3	10.8	35.3	44.9
30–34	17.1	13.6	46.3	39.3
35–39	13.6	16.0	53.7	35.5
40–44	11.3	18.1	61.7	25.2
45–49	8.6	20.0	67.1	8.7
50–54	7.1	24.4	71.4	4.3
55–59	6.2	20.0	73.7	–
60–64	6.2	9.8	63.5	–
65–69	8.2	7.1	72.9	–

Note: Column (1) is the reported fraction of workers in the age group who have zero to six months of tenure. Column (2) is the contemporaneous five-year job retention rate from 0–6 months tenure to 5–10 years tenure. Column (3) is the reported fraction of workers in the age group with five or more years of tenure. Column (4) is the fifteen-year contemporaneous job retention rate from five to ten years tenure to twenty to twenty-five years tenure. Source for all data is Bureau of Labor Statistics (1979).

The very low chance of success in any given new job means that the typical worker has to take a number of different jobs in order to have a good chance of finding a lifetime match. The small probability in each new job presumably reflects the paucity of information available to workers about prospective jobs before they try them out, and the similar paucity of information available to employers about the talents of prospective workers before they can be observed at work. Even workers in their thirties and forties, who generally have substantial amounts of experience, face low chances of landing lifetime jobs on any given try.

Still, most workers do wind up in lifetime work, as earlier parts of this paper have shown. Table 2 illustrates how multiple tries eventually succeed. It uses the point of five years of tenure as an intermediate milestone in describing the process. Column (1) gives the fraction of workers who are in new jobs, that is, jobs which began in the six months before the survey. The fraction declines smoothly from a majority of teenagers to about 6 percent of workers aged 55 to 64; it rises slightly around retirement age. Column (2) gives the probability that a newly em-

ployed worker will reach the milestone of five years on the job. The chances are insignificant among teenagers, rise to a peak of about one in four among workers in their early fifties, and then fall back to low levels for workers near retirement age. The third column shows the fraction of all workers in each age group who have reached the five-year point on their current jobs. The fraction rises smoothly from close to zero for teenagers to about three-quarters for workers in their early sixties. At age 40, a majority of workers have passed the five-year milestone, generally after a number of trials. For example, if the chances are about 10 percent that any given job will last at least five years, and half of all workers have made it, then the typical worker has taken roughly five tries. Column (4) gives the prospects for a total duration of twenty years or more at the five-year point. The probability reaches a peak of nearly half among workers in their early thirties and then declines among older workers, who will probably retire within the next fifteen years.

The result of this process of moving into long-term jobs is the following fraction of workers with eventual tenure of at least twenty years on the job they currently hold:

Age	Percent
16–17	0.0
18–19	0.6
20–24	7.4
25–29	18.6
30–34	27.7
35–39	35.5
40–44	39.5
45–49	41.0
50–54	41.1
55–59	40.1
60–64	39.4
65–69	40.9

The fraction of workers rises until they are in their late thirties, as more and more find good job matches. The fraction then remains remarkably constant at about 40 percent until retirement age. However, these aggregate results conceal very important differences between men and women, a topic I will take up shortly.

Another way to express the movement of workers into stable jobs is by the number of jobs held by the average worker. The flow of new jobs is recorded directly in the tenure data in the form of the number of workers who have tenure of six months or less, though this measure understates the total flow of new jobs because some workers will have started two or more jobs in the six months before the survey. The annual number of new jobs started by the average person in an age group is roughly twice the fraction of the age group that is found in the zero to six-month tenure category. The average number of jobs held over a two-year span is twice the annual rate, and the average over a five-year span is five times the annual rate. These simple computations yield the results shown in Table 3 for the number of jobs held by the average worker (again, brief jobs are under-counted somewhat). Job shopping is most intense in the early twenties—by age 24, the average worker has held four jobs out of the ten he or she will hold in an entire career. The next fifteen years, from age 25 through 39, will contribute another four jobs. Then, during the ages when near-lifetime work is characteristic, less than three more jobs will be held on the average.

TABLE 3—NEW JOBS

Age Group	New Jobs per Year	New Jobs over the Age Interval	Cumulative Number of Jobs Held to this Age
16–17	.394	0.8	0.8
18–19	.534	1.1	1.9
20–24	.425	2.1	4.0
25–29	.309	1.5	5.5
30–34	.240	1.2	6.7
35–39	.192	1.0	7.7
40–44	.167	0.8	8.5
45–49	.126	0.6	9.1
50–54	.096	0.5	9.6
55–59	.076	0.4	10.0
60–64	.054	0.3	10.3
65–69	.032	0.2	10.4
70+	.010	0.1	10.5

V. Long-Term Jobs among Blacks and Women

Many accounts of the disadvantages facing blacks and women in the labor market emphasize their lack of success in finding and holding permanent jobs. The techniques of this paper reach a surprising conclusion in testing this view—it is upheld strongly for women, but not at all for blacks. Lifetime employment is almost as common among blacks as among whites, and long-term employment is actually more common.[3] (See Table 4.)

TABLE 4—COMPARISON OF BLACKS AND WHITES

1978	Percent with Eventual Tenure of	
	5+ Years	20+ Years
All Blacks	63.4	26.4
All Whites	57.3	28.7

The lower-paying jobs where blacks are concentrated are not systematically briefer than are the better jobs typically held by whites. Discrimination against blacks does

[3] The same conclusion is reached by Steven Director and Samuel Doctors using personnel data from three firms, and by Akerlof and Main.

not take the form of exclusion from lifetime jobs. Blacks are heavily represented in certain occupations with lower status and pay, but these are not occupations with systematically shorter jobs. Moreover, the vastly higher incidence of unemployment among blacks —generally double the white rate—is not at all the result of larger flows of workers out of jobs. Further investigation of the surprising finding of equal or higher job stability among blacks relative to whites cannot be done with the published data and will require tabulation of the survey itself.

On the other hand, the comparison between men and women confirms the general impression that men typically hold longer jobs than do women (see Table 5). Shorter job duration among women is almost unrelated to their concentration in certain occupations. For example, more than one-third of all employed women (34.9 percent) in 1978 were in clerical occupations, against 6.4 percent of men. Median tenure for women clerical workers was 2.6 years compared to 4.7 years for men. The gap between women and men in the total labor force was close to the same—median tenure was 2.6 years for women and 4.5 years for men. Similarly large sex differences in tenure are found in the other two major occupations employing women, professional-technical and service workers. It is not possible to compute the distribution of eventual tenure by occupation with the published data, but it seems likely that large differences in eventual tenure would be found within occupations as well.

Although lifetime work is much less common among women than among men, the typical number of jobs held over a lifetime is about the same for both sexes—about ten or eleven jobs. Longer periods spent out of the labor force by women almost exactly offset the shorter durations of the jobs they hold. In other words, although the time between starting one job and starting the next is the same for women and men, women spend a larger part of that time not working. This is roughly true within age groups as well as over the typical entire career (see Table 6). Women slip behind men by about 0.6 jobs during the period of most intense job shopping and then recover a little after age 35.

TABLE 5—COMPARISON OF WOMEN AND MEN

1978	Percent with Eventual Tenure of	
	5+ Years	20+ Years
Women	49.6	15.1
Men	63.8	37.3

TABLE 6—CUMULATIVE JOBS FOR WOMEN AND MEN

Age	Cumulative Number of Jobs Held	
	Women	Men
16–17	0.7	0.8
18–19	1.8	1.9
20–24	3.8	4.1
25–29	5.2	5.8
30–34	6.4	7.0
35–39	7.4	7.9
40–44	8.3	8.7
45–49	9.0	9.3
50–54	9.4	9.8
55–59	9.8	10.2
60–64	10.0	10.5
65–69	10.2	10.7
70+	10.2	10.8

VI. Further Results for Men

Because lifetime work is so much more common for men than for women, it seems worthwhile presenting some further detailed results for men alone. Actual and eventual tenure are shown in Table 7. Once past the

TABLE 7—TENURE AND EVENTUAL TENURE FOR MEN

Age	Percent Who had Worked 20+ Years to Date	Percent with Eventual Tenure of 20+ Years
16–17	0.0	0.3
18–19	0.0	1.2
20–24	0.0	11.5
25–29	0.0	27.0
30–34	0.1	38.4
35–39	1.7	47.0
40–44	10.2	51.1
45–49	24.4	52.6
50–54	33.4	51.0
55–59	39.3	49.5
60–65	41.4	48.0
65–69	38.9	50.2

TABLE 8—JOB RETENTION FOR MEN

| Age | Percent of Jobs Retained for 10 Years, Starting from Tenure of: | |
	10–15 Years	20–25 Years
30–35	73	–
35–39	81	–
40–44	64	79
45–49	66	61
50–54	47	59

years of job shopping, half of all men are in lifetime jobs.

The jobs held by middle-aged men are remarkably stable—ten-year job retention rates are shown in Table 8. Monthly separation rates, which are of the order of 3 percent for workers in general, are about 0.25 percent for middle-aged men with at least ten years on the job.

REFERENCES

Akerlof, George A. and Main, Brian G. M., "An Experience-Weighted Measure of Employment and Unemployment Durations," *American Economic Review*, December 1981, *71*, 1003–11.

Baily, Martin Neil, "Contract Theory and the Moderation of Inflation by Recession," *Brookings Papers on Economic Activity*, 3: 1976, 585–622.

Clark, Kim and Summers, Lawrence, "Labor Market Dynamics and Unemployment: A Reconsideration," *Brookings Papers on Economic Activity*, 1: 1979, 13–60.

Director, Steven M. and Doctors, Samuel I., "Racial Differences in Blue-Collar Turnover Rates," *Industrial Relations*, October 1976, *15*, 338–42.

Hall, Robert E., "Turnover in the Labor Force," *Brookings Papers on Economic Activity*, 3: 1972, 709–56.

_____, "Employment Fluctuations and Wage Rigidity," *Brookings Papers on Economic Activity*, 1: 1980, 91–124.

Jenness, R. A., "Taux de Roulement et Permanance de l'Emploi dans l'Industrie Canadienne," *l'Actualité Economique*, Avril–Juin 1974, *50*, 152–76.

Kaitz, Hyman B., "Analyzing the Length of Spells of Unemployment," *Monthly Labor Review*, November 1970, *93*, 11–20.

Koike, Kazuo, "Japan's Industrial Relations: Characteristics and Problems," *Japanese Economic Studies*, Fall 1978, *7*, 42–90.

Main, Brian G. M., "The Length of a Job in Great Britain," unpublished paper, University of Edinburgh, October 1980.

Salant, Stephen W., "Search Theory and Duration Data: A Theory of Sorts," *Quarterly Journal of Economics*, February 1977, *91*, 39–57.

U.S. Bureau of the Census, *Current Population Reports: Labor Force*, Series P–50, No. 36, November 5, 1951.

U.S. Bureau of Labor Statistics, Special Labor Force Report No. 36, *Job Tenure of American Workers, January 1963*, Washington: USGPO, 1963.

_____, Special Labor Force Report No. 77, *Job Tenure of Workers, January 1966*, Washington: USGPO, 1967.

_____, Special Labor Force Report No. 112, *Job Tenure of Workers, January 1968*, Washington: USGPO, 1969.

_____, Special Labor Force Report No. 172, *Job Tenure of Workers, January 1973*, Washington: USGPO, 1975.

_____, Special Labor Force Report No. 235, *Job Tenure Declines as Work Force Changes*, Washington: USGPO, 1979.

Part III
The Importance of Wage and Price Rigidity

[8]

The Economic Journal, 92 (*March* 1982), 13-44
Printed in Great Britain

WHY U.S. WAGE AND EMPLOYMENT BEHAVIOUR DIFFERS FROM THAT IN BRITAIN AND JAPAN*

Robert J. Gordon

If a poll were to be conducted among American academic economists to select 'The Most Mystifying Economic Phenomenon of Our Time,' surely the sticky nominal wage rate would emerge at or near the top of the list. The slow and partial response of the nominal wage rate to changes in aggregate nominal spending has been a central postulate of macroeconomic theory for the past 45 years, from Keynes' *General Theory*, down to the standard postwar textbook Keynesian paradigm, to the more modern fixed-wage-price models of Robert Barro and Herschel Grossman (1976), and Edmond Malinvaud (1977). Unwilling passively to accept nominal wage rigidity as an unexplained assumption, many labour-market theorists have followed the lead of Costas Azariadis (1975) and Martin Baily (1974) in building models to explain rigid wages and layoff unemployment as the rational outcome of a profit-maximising calculus.

As I pointed out in an early critique of the Azariadis-Baily model (1976a) their assumptions cannot explain cycles in employment, but rather why workers would want fixed *incomes*, i.e., a fixed wage rate and fixed employment. Soon thereafter, Barro (1977) went one step further and argued that contract theory is a 'facade' which cannot explain why workers would choose a rigid wage and variable employment in preference to the classical equilibrium quantity of employment that equates the marginal product of labour with the marginal value of time. Now an examination of the evidence has led me to the realisation that rigid wages cannot provide the underpinnings for a universally valid theory of the business cycle, simply because wages are not universally rigid. I document below with postwar quarterly data that the share of fluctuations in the manufacturing wage bill taking the form of nominal wage changes, as compared to changes in hours worked, is *five to ten times greater* in Britain and Japan than in the United States. I then argue that American economists, whose theoretical ingenuity is matched by their institutional chauvinism, have not succeeded in developing an adequate economic explanation of labour-market arrangements; their theories that purport to explain wage stickiness are mainly based on elements that do not differ across nations and thus have little potential for

* The author acknowledges the financial support of the National Science Foundation and the John Simon Guggenheim Memorial Foundation, as well as helpful discussions and correspondence with Costas Azariadis, William Branson, V. V. Chari, George Dalton, Martin Feldstein, Stanley Fischer, Walter Galenson, Margaret S. Gordon, Herschel Grossman, Robert E. Hall, Masanori Hashimoto, Edward Lazear, Dale Mortensen, Joel Mokyr, Franz Palm, Jeffrey Sachs, Kumiharu Shigehara, and Robert Solow. Any opinions expressed are those of the author and not those of the National Bureau of Economic Research. George Kahn provided invaluable aid in finding and processing the data.

explaining why the degree of wage flexibility is much greater in some places than in others.

It seems remarkable that the modern American literature on labour-market contracts contains no mention of cross-country differences in the extent of wage flexibility, much less any explanation of these differences.[1] This paper begins the difficult task of providing such an explanation, concentrating on just three countries to limit its scope. It seems obvious to include my country (the United States), and yours (the United Kingdom). The choice of the third country is also easy, because the recent Japanese achievement of flexibility in both nominal and real wage rates has made possible the remarkable 2 % rates of both inflation and unemployment experienced in 1979 and 1980, a 'second Japanese miracle' to accompany the first and more widely recognised productivity-quality-export miracle.[2] Like any attempt to explain either miracle, this study of Japanese wage-setting and employment determination must ultimately come to grips with the history of institutions and with culture, i.e., shared customs and habits. Can we duplicate Japanese performance through the manipulation of policy tools and incentives that we usually classify as 'economic,' or must we explore the less familiar terrain of collectively remoulding institutions and customs?

Barro's critique of contract theory argues that business cycles are due to 'easily correctible malfunctions' in private market arrangements (1979). But his approach represents a dead end, because it exhibits no recognition that private market arrangements differ across countries, nor any explanation of such differences. This inquiry into the source of institutional differences asks, in essence, whether a decentralised free-market economy possesses a servomechanism that automatically reforms institutions and customs that lead to an inefficient macroeconomic performance, or whether it can become stuck in an inefficient Akerlof-type equilibrium (1980). Institutional constraints together with decentralised decision-making may leave individual agents in a 'prisoners' dilemma,' unable without collective action to loosen the institutional constraints that bind them.

Any economist who dares to mention institutions as central determinants of macroeconomic performance had better tread carefully, lest he be branded a dangerous renegade or traitor. One only has to recall the British debate of a decade ago between cost-push and monetarist theories of inflation to recognise that an appeal to institutional or social differences is likely to be labelled a distressing resort to 'amateur sociology and politics' which can play 'no part

---

[1] The index of the late Arthur M. Okun's much-discussed final book (1981) on wage and price adjustment contains only one reference to a foreign country, the United Kingdom, and this is in connection with incomes policy rather than wage or price flexibility. In criticising theorists for their sins of omission, I do not mean to slight the comparative empirical papers that have called attention to cross-country differences in wage behaviour, especially Nordhaus (1972), Perry (1975), Gordon (1977), Sachs (1979), and Branson-Rotemberg (1980). Sachs (pp. 303-7) does a particularly good job of calling attention to labour market institutions as a source of differing dynamic wage behaviour.

[2] See also my recent cross-country analysis (1981b). As Walter Galenson has pointed out to me, the 2 % Japanese unemployment statistic is misleading, since the government subsidises firms to carry the unemployed on their payrolls.

whatsoever in the problem.'[1] In my view inflation is basically a monetary phenomenon, in the sense that a monetary expansion is necessary to propogate inflation, but institutions can influence the willingness of the central bank to print money.[2] For instance, *ceteris paribus* a central bank would be less willing to engineer a monetary deceleration if existing institutions were likely to prevent a rapid response of wages and prices, forcing output to take up the slack, than in an alternative society in which the same spending deceleration were likely to be rapidly absorbed by wages and prices with little output response. In this view inflation is the outcome of a genuine two-way interaction between the central bank and the wage-price adjustment process, in which both economic and non-economic aspects of the institutional environment determine the feasibility of slowing simultaneously the growth rates of money, wages, and prices.

The paper begins in Section I, which reviews a set of identities giving the conditions necessary for wage rigidity to imply fluctuations in employment, and then comments on the recent claims by Barro (1977) and Robert Hall (1980) that rigid wages do not imply or explain employment fluctuations. Section II displays and analyses data on the flexibility of wages, hours, and employment in the United Kingdom, United States, and Japan, including both postwar quarterly and annual historical data prior to 1940. Section III develops the notion of 'ideal' labour market institutions from the standpoint of macroeconomic efficiency, asking how wages, hours, and employment should be adjusted in response to nominal demand disturbances. Section IV then juxtaposes actual labour-market institutions in the United Kingdom, United States and Japan with the ideal world of economic theory. Are there economic factors that can explain the inter-country differences, or must we appeal at least in part to politics, and/or culture to complete the explanation? Section V summarises the conclusions.

This paper is complementary to the recent cross-country studies of Jeffrey Sachs (1979), and William Branson and Julio Rotemberg (1980), which document the contrast between nominal wage inertia in the postwar United States and real wage inertia in Europe and Japan, and examine the theoretical and policy implications of this contrast. Here I begin with another procedure for documenting the difference in nominal wage behaviour among the United Kingdom, United States and Japan, and then concentrate on explaining its causes rather than its consequences. Real wage inertia plays no role in my analysis, reflecting my finding that the real wage rate in quarterly postwar data for the United Kingdom and Japan displays more variability than in the United States.

The paper's scope is broader than most, in its attention to three countries and to non-economic factors, but nevertheless is carefully circumscribed. I am concerned with the dynamic response of the aggregate supply curve to nominal demand fluctuations that are taken to be exogenous. No attention is given to

---

[1] The quotes are from Harry Johnson (1972, pp. 310-1). He was attacking those, like Aubrey Jones (1973), who argued (p. 40) that 'a tightening of the money supply is not, therefore, a solution to the problem of rising prices.'

[2] This section summarises an argument that is developed in full in Gordon (1975).

cross-country differences in saving behaviour, openness to foreign trade, or other factors that might explain why demand fluctuations have been more severe in one place than another. Feedback from inflation to nominal demand (e.g. through Pigou and expectations effects) and to investment and productivity growth are ignored. Although the response of the inflation process to nominal demand swings depends both on the firm's price-setting decisions in product markets and its wage- and employment-setting decisions in labour markets, the paper concentrates on the latter and refers the reader to a recent companion piece on the product market (1981 a).

I. IS THERE A CONNECTION BETWEEN WAGE STICKINESS AND EMPLOYMENT FLUCTUATIONS?

Although most economists now accept as obvious the proposition that the sluggish adjustment of wages increases the variability of employment over the business cycle, nevertheless some have argued that wage stickiness is not a central issue. In this view the fixity of wages would not necessarily imply lay-offs or fluctuations in employment, since 'even in contracts that specify *ex ante* the value of nominal wages over some interval of time, it would be mutually advantageous for workers and firms to determine levels of employment in an efficient manner' (Barro, 1979, p. 54). There is, in short, a 'limited allocational role of the wage payment for employment' (Hall, 1980, p. 92).

Adopting the practice of designating proportional growth rates as lower case letters, we can write down an identity that displays the relationship of the growth rate of nominal GNP (y) to that of the nominal wage (w), hours per man per week (h), employee-weeks per year (e), and nominal non-labour income (n):

$$y \equiv \mu(w+h+e) + (1-\mu)\, n, \tag{1}$$

where μ is labour's income share. The cyclical behaviour of the variables in (1) can be examined if we purge both sides of the equation of the influence of trend growth in real output (q^*), hours (h^*), and employment (e^*):

$$y - q^* \equiv \mu[w - (q^* - h^* - e^*) + (h - h^*) + (e - e^*)] + (1-\mu)\,(n - q^*). \tag{2}$$

The simple truths contained in this expression become more obvious when we combine terms, using ω to designate trend productivity growth ($q^* - h^* - e^*$), h' for the deviation of hours growth from trend ($h - h^*$), e' for the deviation of employment growth from trend ($e - e^*$), and a 'hat' to designate the growth of nominal GNP and non-labour income relative to trend output ($\hat{y} = y - q^*$, $\hat{n} = n - q^*$):[1]

$$\hat{y} \equiv \mu(w - \omega + h' + e') + (1-\mu)\hat{n}. \tag{3}$$

In the long run, when the cyclical hours and employment deviations are zero ($e' = h' = 0$), (3) states simply that output-trend-adjusted nominal GNP

[1] Equation (3) and some of the accompanying discussion overlaps Gordon (1981a), p. 498.

growth must be a weighted average of trend unit labour cost $(w - \omega)$ and the growth of adjusted nominal non-labour income. But there are clearly no arithmetically necessary implications of nominal wage rigidity for the cyclical behaviour of employment, because fluctuations in nominal GNP growth on the left-hand side of (3) can be offset by changes in hours (h') or in non-labour income $(\hat{n})$ even if both wages and employment are fixed.

The Barro-Hall argument cited above states that in principle there is nothing to prevent the firm from offering each employee a contract that fixes labour income, i.e., the wage rate, hours per week, and weeks of employment, with profit fluctuations $(\hat{n})$ taking up the slack. However, this proposition is valid only for very special sorts of firms that are risk-neutral and face perfect capital markets that are equally unperturbed by profit instability. The downward pressure on profits that occurs when a drop in nominal GNP is accompanied by a fixed wage bill must have allocative consequences if it persists for any length of time, by altering the market's expectations of the future net worth of the firm, and consequently by raising its supply price of capital and re-allocating capital elsewhere. The firm is thus under pressure to shift some of the burden of the adjustment from profits to the wage bill. There is surely some drop in nominal income large enough, or of sufficiently long duration, to force firms to adopt some combination of wage cuts, 'work sharing' (reductions in hours per employee), or a reduction of employment.

We can go further and note that (3) contains some hints that might contribute to an economic explanation of cross-country differences in the stability of employment. First, profits will be able to absorb relatively more of a nominal GNP change, and thus the wage bill will be forced to absorb less, the larger is the normal profit share $(1 - \mu)$. The larger share of non-labour income in Japan than in Britain or the United States might help to explain how large Japanese firms can afford to offer their employees lifetime employment. Further, to the extent that the Japanese bonus system can be regarded as a form of profit sharing, as is argued by Masanori Hashimoto (1979), the effective share of profit-type income is increased, and there is a larger buffer to insulate the remainder of the wage bill. If the change in wages (w) consists of the change in the wage base (v) and in the bonus (b) with weights ψ and $(1 - \psi)$, and if the change in the bonus is a fixed fraction σ of the change in non-labour income $(b = \sigma n)$, then (3) becomes:

$$\hat{y} \equiv \mu(\psi v - \omega + h' + e') + [(1 - \mu) + \mu(1 - \psi)\,\sigma]\,\hat{n}. \qquad (4)$$

A final difference among countries suggested by (3) and (4) is the nature of the link between firms and capital markets. British and American firms, financed largely by equity, may be more sensitive to fluctuations in share values caused by profit instability, than debt-financed Japanese firms. The bankers who oversee loans to Japanese firms, with the Central Bank and Ministry of International Trade and Industry looking over their shoulder, may take a longer view than UK and US shareholders.[1] The converse proposition, that debt finance makes profits less stable, may not matter for Japanese firms if far-

[1] I owe this idea to V. V. Chari.

18   THE ECONOMIC JOURNAL   [MARCH

sighted bankers and government agencies allow firms to look beyond the short run.

II. SOME EVIDENCE ON THE RESPONSIVENESS OF WAGES, HOURS, AND EMPLOYMENT

II. 1 Postwar Quarterly Data for Manufacturing

This section analyses postwar quarterly data on the volatility of wages, hours, and employment in the United States, United Kingdom, and Japan. Comparable data across countries seem easiest to obtain if we limit our attention to manufacturing. The wage data include fringe benefits for the United States and bonuses for Japan. Two measures of volatility are examined, the standard deviation of rates of change, and the coefficient of response of each variable to changes in nominal GNP. The standard deviations in Table 1 are calculated for two periods, ending respectively in 1972 and 1980, in order to determine whether the results for the period ending in 1980 are dominated by special features of the two oil shocks that occurred after 1972. The starting date of 1963:Q1 is determined by the 1960 starting date of the UK and Japanese data in our source, and by unusual behaviour of the Japanese hours and employment series in 1961 and early 1962.[1] The computations are based on four-quarter overlapping rates of change, in order to minimise problems of seasonality and high-frequency quarter-to-quarter volatility. The procedure involves estimating a regression in which the only right-hand variable is a single constant for the period ending in 1972, and two constants (broken at 1972:Q4) for the period ending in 1980.

The qualitative differences among the three nations seem unaffected by the choice of the 1972 or 1980 termination date. The striking finding, presented in lines 2 to 5 of Table 1, is that a much larger fraction of the variability of the manufacturing wage bill takes the form of nominal wage changes relative to changes in hours worked $(h+e)$ or employment (e) in Britain and Japan than in the United States. The ratio exhibited in line 6 of wage variability relative to hours variability is only 0·35 in the United States, but is 4·7 times larger in Britain and 12·7 times larger in Japan for the 1963–80 period. For the shorter 1963–72 period, the ratio is 3·1 times larger in Britain and 7·6 times larger in Japan, indicating that part but by no means all of the cross-country differences are associated with the extreme volatility of wage changes experienced in Britain and Japan at the time of the first oil shock in 1973–5.

A surprising finding on line 5 is that employment in the United Kingdom is no less stable than in Japan. Line 7 exhibits the ratio of wage to employment variability, and for the full period this ratio is 0·42 for the United States, but is almost six times larger in both Britain and Japan. For the shorter period the British and Japanese ratios are 3·6 and 2·7 times larger, respectively. Why do these ratios differ more for Japan in line 6 than line 7, i.e., why is the volatility of hours worked $(h+e)$ so much less than either of the components, hours per

---

[1] During this period Japanese employment grew very rapidly but hours fell, creating a strong negative correlation between hours and employment growth, and leading to an even greater discrepancy between the $(h+e)$ and e results than appears in Table 1.

week (*h*) or employment (*e*)? The distributed lag analysis discussed below reveals that, more than in the other two nations, hours per week in Japan are a temporary buffer that absorbs part of the impact of a swing in nominal spending, but only for a single quarter. Then, over the next four or five quarters, employment begins to respond in the direction of the spending disturbance, while hours per week return to normal, thus creating a negative correlation between hours per week and employment changes during those quarters.

Table 1

Standard deviations of four-quarter percentage rates of change of manufacturing wage rates, hours, and employment

	1963:Q1–1980:Q3*			1962:Q1–1972:Q4		
	US (1)	UK (2)	Japan (3)	US (4)	UK (5)	Japan (6)
Variables						
(1) $w+h+e$	3·82	4·35	4·97	3·56	3·26	3·68
(2) w	1·69	5·29	4·84	1·66	3·40	2·83
(3) $h+e$	4·78	3·22	1·09	4·06	2·70	0·91
(4) h	1·09	1·74	1·98	1·06	1·37	1·17
(5) e	4·05	2·18	2·03	3·39	1·95	2·15
Addenda						
(6) Ratio of line 2 ÷ 3	0·35	1·64	4·44	0·41	1·26	3·11
(7) Ratio of line 2 ÷ 5	0·42	2·43	2·38	0·49	1·74	1·32
(8) Real wage $(w-p)$	1·46	3·86	2·78	0·82	1·74	2·50

* The full-period results include two constants defined respectively from the first observation to 1972:Q4, and from 1973:Q1 to the last observation.

A final addendum in line 8 of Table 1 presents figures on the volatility of the real wage in the three countries for the two periods. The results show quite consistently, for both the long and short period, that the volatility of both real and nominal wage rates is greater in Britain and Japan as compared to the United States. Here are the ratios of nominal and real wage variability relative to the United States for the other two countries:

	Nominal wage, from Table 1, line 2	Real wage, from Table 1, line 8
1963–80		
UK/US	3·1	2·6
Japan/US	2·9	1·9
1963–72		
UK/US	2·0	2·1
Japan/US	1·7	3·0

These simple calculations lead me to question the characterisation by Sachs (1979) and Branson-Rotemberg (1980) of the United States as having stable nominal wage growth and variable real wage growth, and other major industrialised nations as having the reverse. For both sample periods, real wage growth in the United Kingdom and Japan was between two and three times more variable than in the United States.

I recently presented evidence that the responsiveness of the aggregate US price deflator to changes in nominal GNP has varied widely over time. Because price changes have ranged from very sticky to very flexible over US history, I called attention to the absence of any explanation for this parameter shift in conventional macroeconomic theory (1981 *a*, pp. 500–2). Just as that analysis was based on a regression of quarterly changes in prices on a distributed lag of current and past changes in nominal GNP, so here in Table 2 I present a parallel characterisation of differences in the labour-market adjustment process in the three countries, by regressing various components of the wage bill on current and past changes in nominal GNP. In contrast to Table 1, where four-quarter overlapping changes are calculated, here the data are one-quarter changes, expressed at annual rates (i.e. multiplied by four). All lag distributions are constrained to lie along a fourth-degree polynomial, with a zero end-point constraint. As explained in the notes to Table 2, all regressions also include a constant and a trend term. The long-period results for all countries include a variable to represent the influence of changes in food and energy prices in the 1970s and all regressions for the United States also include dummy variables to capture the effects of the 1971–4 Nixon control programme.[1]

Of all the sums of coefficients in Table 2 showing the response of each variable to changes in nominal GNP in the current and preceding eight quarters, the two sets that stand out are those on lines 1, and 2. First, the responsiveness of the manufacturing wage bill to nominal GNP in the United Kingdom and Japan is only half that in the United States. Second, and more interesting for this investigation, nominal wages are much more responsive in the United Kingdom and Japan than in the United States for both sample periods. As shown on line 6, the ratio of the nominal wage rate response (line 2) to the wage bill response (line 1) is 10 % or less in the United States and between 57 and 128 % in Britain and Japan.

What accounts for the relatively high wage elasticities in Japan in the full period, and in Britain in the shorter period? The Japanese experience is dominated by the 1974 wage explosion, in which the four quarter change in wages reached 27 % in 1974:Q2 and 1974:Q3, and which was partly but not completely accommodated by nominal GNP growth (with peaks of 20·5 % in 1973: Q4 and 19·4 % in 1974:Q3). Nominal wages and GNP growth dropped precipitously in 1975 to respective troughs of 7·7 % (1975:Q2) and 8·0 % (1975:Q3). Partly because wages accelerated more than nominal GNP in 1974, the four-quarter growth rate of manufacturing hours worked $(h+e)$ fell from 1·6 % (1973:Q1) to −5·2 % (1975:Q1), and then rebounded to 1·2 % (1976:Q1). This decline in hours in 1974, while nominal GNP was rising

---

[1] The dummy variables are those that I used in my latest detailed analysis of US postwar inflation (1982). I experimented with dummy variables for UK incomes policies, but decided that the details of the procedure might aggravate my present audience and detract their attention from the more important points in the paper.

rapidly, accounts for the otherwise puzzling negative coefficients for Japan in column (3), line 3.[1] In the shorter 1963–72 sample period, the growth of hours worked (line 3) shows the expected positive response to nominal GNP changes. The large British wage response in the short sample period stems from the monetary accommodation of the 1970 wage explosion. Nominal wage growth, again calculated on a four-quarter change basis, accelerated from 5·0% (1969:Q2) to 12·5% (1971:Q1), and then jumped after a brief hiatus to 15·6% (1972:Q4). Nominal GNP growth displayed a similar pattern, increasing from 4·5% (1969:Q3) to 14·6% (1971:Q3), and then jumping after a short relapse to 18·4% (1973:Q1).

Table 2

Sums of coefficients when components of the change in the manufacturing wage bill are regressed on current and eight lagged changes in nominal GNP†

	1961:Q1–1980:Q3			1961:Q1–1972:Q4		
	US‡§ (1)	UK‡ (2)	Japan‡ (3)	US§ (4)	UK (5)	Japan (6)
Variables						
(1) $w+h+e$	2·16***	0·91**	0·95**	2·64***	0·84*	1·38***
(2) w	0·06	0·59*	1·22***	0·28	0·87**	0·80***
(3) $h+e$	2·10***	0·32	−0·28*	2·36***	−0·03	0·58***
(4) h	−0·19	0·20	−0·31**	−0·20	−0·04	−0·25*
(5) e	2·29***	0·12	0·03	2·57***	0·00	0·83***
(6) Ratio of line 2 to line 1	0·03	0·65	1·28	0·11	1·04	0·57

† All regressions include a constant and a trend term.
‡ All regressions also include changes in the difference between the growth rates of the US consumption deflator, respectively including and excluding expenditures on food and energy.
§ Regressions also include dummy variables for the impact of the Nixon controls. Asterisks designate significance levels of sums of coefficients, as follows: 10% (*), 5% (**), and 1% (***).

This chronology raises the issue of direction of causation. Did nominal GNP changes cause wage changes, or vice versa? If nominal GNP is at least partly endogenous, and responds quickly to wage changes, then the sums of coefficients in Table 2 may be contaminated by simultaneous equations bias, with an upward bias if the reverse feedback to nominal GNP is positive, and a downward bias if the reverse feedback is negative. A method introduced by Clive Granger (1969) can be used to test for exogeneity in a two-way relationship. A variable, say y_t (nominal GNP change) is regressed on a constant, a time trend, its own lagged values, and lagged values of the other variable of interest, say, w_t (wage change):

$$y_t = \alpha_0 + \alpha_1 t + \sum_{i=1}^{M} \beta_i y_{t-i} + \sum_{j=1}^{N} \gamma_j w_{t-j} + \epsilon_t. \tag{5}$$

[1] Illustrating the greater volatility of growth in US manufacturing hours worked, the corresponding peak-trough-peak figures are 6·3% (1973:Q1), −12·8% (1974:Q2), and 6·3% (1976:Q2). Because nominal GNP growth slowed down from 1973 to 1974, rather than staying high as in Japan, the US coefficients exhibit the expected positive response of hours worked and employment to nominal GNP changes.

Now the variable y is exogenous with respect to w if the lagged w's fail to make a significant contribution to the explanation of y over and above the serial correlation process captured by the lagged values of y. A symmetric test for the exogeneity of w with respect to y is available with the y's and w's in (5) reversed. Such a test for the exogeneity of wage change amounts to running the regressions of Table 2 with the current nominal GNP change omitted but the lagged values included.

The results of the Granger tests are exhibited in Table 3. Line A shows the sums of coefficients (γ_j) on lagged wage changes in the equations for nominal GNP change. The sums of coefficients are negative in both sample periods for the United States, positive for the United Kingdom, and mixed for Japan. Only in the short sample period for the United States, however, does the significance level reach 5 %. One would expect the negative feedback from wage to nominal GNP changes for the United States to cause the coefficients in Table 2 to be biased downward, and indeed the US coefficients in line B of Table 3 are modestly higher. Nevertheless, the conclusion still emerges that the responsiveness of wage change to past nominal GNP changes is several times higher in Britain and Japan than in the United States.

Table 3

The two-way relation between quarterly changes in nominal GNP and manufacturing wage rates

	1962:Q2–1980:Q3			1962:Q2–1972:Q4		
	US (1)	UK (2)	Japan (3)	US (4)	UK (5)	Japan (6)
(A) Nominal GNP equations, sum of coefficients on lagged wages	−0·56	0·58*	0·07	−1·11**	0·91*	−1·48*
(B) Wage change equations sum of coefficients of lagged nominal GNP	0·11	0·70**	0·78	0·39	0·79**	1·25**
(C) F ratios for inclusion of: (1) Wages in nominal GNP equation	0·31	0·83	0·76	1·18	5·89***	1·05
(2) Nominal GNP in wage equation	0·92	2·21**	0·53	0·97	1·98*	1·47

Asterisks designate significance levels of sums of coefficients, as follows: 10 % (*), 5 % (**), and 1 % (***).

For this paper, however, the main issue is the unique nature of the sluggish wage response in the United States. Is this a phenomenon that economic theory can help to explain, or must economists throw up their hands in despair, turning the question over to the speculations of historians and sociologists? Because the most obvious institutional feature of the US manufacturing labour market is the three-year staggered wage contract, we proceed in the next section to examine differences between American, British, and Japanese wage responsiveness before 1940, that is, prior to the introduction of the three-year US union wage contract.

II. 2 Pre-1940 Data on Wage Rates and GNP Deflators

Prior to World War II comparable data on key labour market variables are harder to obtain than for the most recent two decades. I have simplified my task by concentrating on the response of wage changes to nominal GNP, in order to learn whether sums of coefficients analogous to those in Table 2, line 2, differ as much among the three countries before World War II as afterwards. It is possible to find annual nominal wage rate and GNP data going back to 1870 in the United Kingdom, 1878 in Japan, and 1889 in the United States. Allowing for first-differencing and lags, I have estimated response coefficients of wage rates to nominal GNP changes for sample periods ending in 1940 for each country, and beginning in 1873 for the United Kingdom, 1881 for Japan, and 1892 for the United States. And, although the main focus of the paper is on wages rather than prices, I also present analogous results for the response of the GNP deflator to changes in nominal GNP – in order to display for the United Kingdom and Japan results analogous to those discussed for the United States in two recent papers of mine (1980, 1981 a).

Since the data are unfamiliar, sample means and standard deviations for three sub-periods are presented, as a basic introduction, in Table 4. The period of World War I and its aftermath is singled out for special attention, as a result of my finding (1981 a) that US prices were much more responsive to spending changes during that interval than before or afterwards. The UK and Japan data also share this feature of a much higher mean and standard deviation of wage and price change during 1914–22 than either before or after. Another finding is that Japanese spending growth was the most volatile before 1914, with the United States most volatile after 1922, and the British achieving the most stable demand growth in each period. But perhaps the most interesting conclusion to be drawn from Table 4 is that, in stark contrast to Table 1 for the postwar years, there was no tendency for US wage changes to be more stable than in Britain and Japan. In fact the standard deviation of the year-to-year change in US wage growth ranks first among the three nations before 1914 and after 1922, and is tied for second place during the world War I era. The GNP deflator generally mirrors the behaviour of wages, with a tendency for prices in the United States to be less volatile relative to wages, whereas in the other two countries prices are either as variable or more variable than wages.

A more interesting set of results is presented in Table 5, which is analogous to Table 2. The top half of the table displays coefficients of response of annual wage changes to current and two lagged changes in nominal GNP. All regression equations also contain a constant term, and, to maintain consistency with my other papers, two dummy variables for the United States. The first captures the impact of price controls during the last year of World War I, and the second captures the marked but temporary impact of the National Recovery Act in raising wages and prices in 1933 and 1934. The dummy variables are defined in a special form that imposes the restriction that the termination of each programme of government intervention completely reversed its effect on the price or wage level.[1]

Table 4

Means and standard deviations of historical percentage growth rates, 1873–1940

	Starting Date*		
	–1913 (1)	1914–1922 (2)	1923–1940 (3)
Means			
Nominal GNP (y)			
US	4·71	6·96	1·65
UK	2·39	6·12	2·19
Japan	6·68	12·23	4·71
Wage rate (w)			
US	1·79	7·94	2·22
UK	0·48	7·59	0·25
Japan	4·63	12·27	0·73
GNP Deflator (p)			
US	0·93	5·64	−0·73
UK	0·52	7·89	−0·16
Japan	3·79	7·85	1·09
Standard Deviations			
Nominal GNP (y)			
US	6·77	15·58	11·65
UK	3·08	14·07	5·30
Japan	10·53	16·33	8·51
Wage rate (w)			
US	4·46	13·21	6·71
UK	1·63	15·12	4·08
Japan	3·98	13·28	5·20
GNP Deflator (p)			
US	2·87	12·36	4·20
UK	1·76	14·16	3·53
Japan	4·99	13·97	7·15

* Starting dates are: US 1892; UK 1873; Japan 1881. Source: See data appendix.

The most important conclusion in Table 5 can be gleaned from column (4), which shows the sums of coefficients on current and two lagged values of nominal GNP. Here the three countries display roughly similar degrees of wage responsiveness, whereas, in Table 2 for the postwar period, the United States is a definite outlier. In Table 5, the smallest value for wages in column (4) is achieved by Japan during 1881–1913; this may reflect measurement error rather than a substantive difference (note the much higher responsiveness of

[1] Through an error of omission, the World War I variable was not included in my paper using annual data (1980), but was included in the quarterly study (1981a). Here it is defined as +1 for 1918 and −1 for 1920. The *NRA* variable, following (1980), is defined as follows: 1933, +0·35; 1934, +0·75; 1935, −0·75; 1936, −0·25. For a justification of the use of dummy variables in the study of government intervention programmes, see Frye and Gordon (1981).

the GNP deflator in Japan for this period in the bottom part of the table).[1] The other main patterns for wages are the uniform increase across countries in the degree of responsiveness during World War I, and the evidence of a substantial decline in responsiveness in the United States after 1922 as compared to pre-1914.

Table 5

Regressions of changes in wage rates and the GNP deflator on current and lagged changes in nominal GNP, 1873–1940

	Coefficient on			Sum of Coefficients (4)	Dummy Variable (5)	R^2 (6)	S.E.E. (7)
	y_t (1)	y_{t-1} (2)	y_{t-2} (3)				
Wage Changes							
Starting Date† – 1913							
US	0·376**	0·413**	−0·047	0·742	—	0·589	3·08
UK	0·246**	0·191**	0·159**	0·596	—	0·635	1·14
Japan	0·101**	−0·037	0·114**	0·252	—	0·223	3·87
1913–1922							
US	0·628**	0·388**	0·103	1·119	0·0	0·962	3·65
UK	0·376**	0·764**	0·442*	1·582	—	0·911	5·71
Japan	0·230	0·468**	0·242	0·940	—	0·879	5·82
1923–1940							
US	0·296**	0·283**	−0·111**	0·468	12·2**	0·844	3·02
UK	0·376**	0·215*	0·153*	0·744	—	0·686	2·51
Japan	0·314**	0·124	0·231**	0·669	—	0·820	3·35
Price Changes							
Starting Date† – 1913							
US	0·275**	0·193**	0·032	0·498	—	0·501	2·19
UK	0·346**	0·118	0·113	0·577	—	0·421	1·75
Japan	0·475**	0·124*	0·213**	0·812	—	0·573	5·78
1913–1922							
US	0·644**	0·374**	−0·147	0·871	−8·1**	0·959	3·52
UK	0·742**	0·262**	0·439**	1·443	—	0·940	4·36
Japan	0·774**	0·097	−0·033	0·838	—	0·812	2·48
1923–1940							
US	0·267**	0·110**	−0·019	0·358	4·9**	0·886	1·62
UK	0·326**	0·226**	0·122*	0·674	—	0·754	1·93
Japan	0·530**	0·352**	−0·070	0·812	—	0·820	3·35

† Starting dates are the same as in Table 4.
Asterisks designate significance levels of sums of coefficients, as follows: 10% (*) and 5% (**).

The results for the GNP deflator, displayed in the bottom half of the table, seem generally consistent with those for wages. In all countries price responsiveness increased during World War I, a phenomenon I have explained by formulating a theory in which people use common information on the variance of aggregate demand shocks to guess what will happen to their costs of purchased

[1] There also seems to be a negative correlation between wage and nominal GNP changes during 1904–7, perhaps reflecting some programme of government intervention, with which I am not familiar, during or after the Russo-Japanese war.

inputs (1981 *a*, pp. 519–25). This theoretical explanation is also roughly consistent with the Japanese results, which show a large but fairly stable price response in the three periods, since Table 4 reveals that the variance of Japanese nominal GNP growth was relatively high in all three sub-periods.

In a recent study of the Great Depression (with James Wilcox, 1981), I called attention to the greater flexibility of prices in Europe than in the United States as a partial explanation for the relatively milder and shorter Depression in Europe. Table 5 for the 1923–40 sub-period confirms that US wages and prices, while sufficiently flexible to absorb (after a one-year lag) roughly half of the nominal spending change in the case of wages, and about one-third in the case of prices, nevertheless were less flexible than in Britain and Japan. It would thus appear that the phenomenon of sluggish wage and price responsiveness had begun to emerge in the United States before World War II, prior to the invention of the three-year staggered wage contrast in 1948.

III. THE ORGANISATION OF LABOUR MARKETS

The empirical results in the preceding section establish, at least for the postwar period, that changes in the manufacturing wage bill were accompanied by greater changes in hours worked, and by lesser changes in nominal wages, in the United States than in Britain or Japan. Among the institutional arrangements that might help to explain these empirical phenomena are the postwar US system of three-year staggered, overlapping, and imperfectly escalated wage contracts, the absence in Britain of written wage agreements, and the Japanese institutions of lifetime employment and bonus payments. To determine what elements economic theory can contribute to an explanation of these international differences, this section identifies a set of ideal institutions dictated by purely economic considerations. Then Section IV compares these to real-world practices in the three nations. Is an important element of inefficiency introduced because real-world labour-market institutions were invented spontaneously by decentralised and uncoordinated actions of economic agents, rather than by the firm hand of an up-to-date economic theorist?

The organisation of the analysis corresponds to the central distinction between real shocks, i.e., innovations or oil cartels, and nominal shocks, i.e., changes in the supply of money. The recent theory of labour markets is amenable to a corresponding division between purely real factors that foster income stability and long-term attachments between firms and workers, and the interaction of real and nominal factors that determine the extent to which indexation will insulate the real economy from nominal disturbances.

III. 1 *Long-term Worker-Firm Attachments in the Face of Real Shocks*

In the simple labour-market model of the elementary textbook, there are neither institutions nor long-term attachments. Supply equals demand, and there is a three-way equality between the real wage, the marginal product of labour, and the marginal value of time (or disutility of work). If the schedules have the usual shapes, a negative productivity shock reduces labour input and the real wage, but a shift in nominal demand has no effect on either real variable. There is no need to introduce formal indexation, since the freely adjusting wage automatically mimics the movements of the freely adjusting price. Two separate lines of intellectual development have emerged to explain long-term attachments between firms and workers. The first treats workers as homogeneous and was stimulated by the original models of Azariadis (1975), Baily (1974), and Donald F. Gordon (1974), each of which independently introduced the assumption that workers are more averse to risk than firms. The second introduces a training cost or 'toll' that differentiates among members of the labour force, was invented by Gary Becker (1962), and has been the subject of innumerable papers, including the recent formal analysis of Mortensen (1979) and extended verbal treatment by Okun (1981).

The Quest for Real Income Insurance. The Azariadis-Baily-Gordon (A-B-G) model explains why firms would offer real income insurance to risk-averse workers. Seeking income stability, workers are willing to accept a smaller mean income over the cycle from a firm offering a stable income than from one offering a variable income, and competition forces all firms to match the stable-income offer. Firms 'sell' real income insurance to workers, accepting greater instability in profits and, in conditions of a sharp leftward shift in the real demand for labour, stand ready to finance losses on the perfect capital market. Although initially heralded in corridor conversation as providing a microeconomic foundation of the Keynesian phenomena of rigid nominal wages and involuntary layoff unemployment, the A-B-G model – it soon became apparent – could explain neither.

Consider the standard version of the A-B-G model with risk-averse workers, risk-neutral firms, a known distribution of states of nature, an atemporal setting in which present choices have no future consequences, a prohibition on mobility of workers between firms after the invisible handshake, and a symmetric access by workers and firms to information about the state of nature that has actually occurred. Since all the elements of the model are stated in real terms, there is no impact of a purely nominal disturbance, which can be absorbed by a fully escalated nominal wage.

The effects of shifts in the real demand schedule depend on which of several assumptions are made about the preferences of workers and the nature of unemployment compensation, if any. With a utility function for workers that is separable in consumption and leisure, and with no unemployment compensation, firms offer a fixed income. A leftward shift in real labour demand causes firms to eliminate those hours each day or week which yield a marginal product below the value of time. Because all workers are identical, hours reductions are shared equally, and no worker is fully unemployed.

Now we add an additional assumption, which in the theoretical jargon is called 'a lump-sum reward for unemployment.' This must be funded by some source besides the firm itself, e.g., a general tax. Now firms can offer workers a larger compensation package if they lay off individual workers to make them eligible for the lump-sum reward, instead of imposing an evenly shared reduction in hours. The individuals receiving the layoff notice are not at all unhappy about their lot, because the firm continues to provide them with a stable income by paying laid-off workers the difference between the wage of employed workers and the sum of (*a*) the unemployment reward and (*b*) the value of leisure. Thus the A-B-G model can explain layoffs only through the intervention of a special kind of outside-financed unemployment compensation system, and the resulting unemployment is not involuntary. Involuntary unemployment in this model requires the unsupported and arbitrary assumption that firms cut the pay packet of inactive workers (including leisure and the outside reward) below the packet of active workers.

When the assumption of symmetric information is dropped, then firms may be able to determine the true state of nature and to conceal it from workers. Once workers have agreed to work any required amount for a fixed income, firms have an obvious incentive to overstate labour demand and ask workers to supply (implicitly forever) an above-normal number of hours. Recognising the incentive of firms to cheat, workers will insist on an arrangement that allows a change in hours to occur only if income responds positively. Guillermo Calvo and Edmund S. Phelps (1977), Robert E. Hall and David Lilien (1979), and Sanford Grossman and Oliver Hart (1980), have all shown that income and hours worked will vary in the same direction when information is asymmetric. Phelps (1977) was the first to capture the irony that in this context the A-B-G model yields just the same result as the old-fashioned textbook model: 'It is just as we always thought – prior to the advent of state-contingent contract theory!' (1977, p. 153).

Income variability can also be deduced with symmetric information, when the assumption of completely risk-neutral firms is dropped. Firms may not be able to absorb unlimited losses. While local supply shocks may be diversifiable, some risks are economy-wide and nondiversifiable. Herschel Grossman (1977) shows that there is some level of the marginal product of labour sufficiently low to prevent firms from absorbing all risk. A further and more complex analysis with the A-B-G model introduces dynamics. Firms attempt to assess the likelihood that employees may quit in good times to obtain a wage higher than the fixed income level. Dynamic analysis also erodes the significance of the asymmetric information assumption; firms are unlikely to cheat when they know that workers may soon learn the true outcome and shun them forever.

What, then, does the A-B-G model contribute to an understanding of international differences in labour-market arrangements? It cannot explain differences in nominal wage responsiveness, since it is stated entirely in real terms. It can explain the greater reliance on layoffs in the United States than in Britain and Japan as a result of differences in unemployment compensation systems, but the role of unemployment insurance can be discussed independently of the A-B-G model and assumptions. Finally, the A-B-G model does not explain long-term attachments between firms and workers, but rather assumes this outcome by basing its analysis on an atemporal world with no *ex post* mobility. Its main positive contribution within the context of this paper is to stress the potential role of firms as intermediaries providing real income insurance; the ability and willingness of firms to stabilise incomes in a particular country, i.e.,

Japan, may depend on size of firms, diversification, attitudes toward risk in financial markets, debt-equity ratios, and other factors related to the A-B-G analysis.[1]

Firm Specific Human Capital and Seniority Rules. A more fruitful approach to the explanation of long-term worker-firm attachments was introduced by Becker (1962), who argued that the costs and returns from investments in firm-specific capital would be shared by the firm and its workers. For the firm to capture all of the return would leave the employee with nothing to 'glue' him to the firm and would lead to excessive quits; for the worker to capture all of the return would leave the firm with no incentive to train him. In Okun's (1981) terminology the initial training and hiring investment can be likened to a 'toll', collected at the beginning of the worker's attachment, the incidence of which must be divided between worker and firm. The resulting relationship, in which each party has an investment, is Okun's 'career labour market.' Since nothing in the career labour-market model prevents the resulting wage from being fully escalated to the price level, the Becker-Okun analysis should not be viewed as providing an explanation of business cycles, but rather of institutions like separation procedures and penalties, seniority rules, age-earnings profiles, compulsory overtime, and mandatory retirement.

Hashimoto (1979), Mortensen (1979), and Lorne Carmichael (1980) have analysed the consequences for the human capital model of imperfect but symmetric information; the realised surplus available to be divided depends on productivity, which the firm knows more about, and job satisfaction, which the worker knows more about. Each party has an incentive to influence the division of the surplus by cheating, with firms understanding productivity and workers understating job satisfaction. An optimal arrangement would appear to involve separation penalties. A worker who is dissatisfied may quit, but must pay a separation penalty equal to the firm's lost training investment; a firm dissatisfied with a low-productivity worker can fire him, but must offer a severance payment.

The fact that these 'symmetric separation penalty' contracts are not observed is attributed by Carmichael to moral hazard introduced by the need to distinguish between a quit and a fire in order to administer the separation penalties. Firms have an incentive to make workers unhappy and get them to quit, so that the 'firing' penalty will be saved, and workers have an incentive to slack off until they get fired, thus earning the 'firing' penalty. From this observation Carmichael proceeds to show that seniority rules for layoffs and promotions can reproduce the turnover incentives of the penalty contracts without the same exposure to moral hazard. Seniority rules allow inter-worker transfers, with junior workers 'collecting' from senior workers who quit, in the form of promotion and protection from layoffs. The moral hazard problem disappears,

---

[1] A question may be raised as to the justification for a discussion of the A-B-G model in the previous section, in light of its minor usefulness for students of macroeconomic fluctuations. In light of the substantial interest in this approach among economic theorists, I think it important to provide an overall evaluation of its relation to macroeconomics, just as I have previously done (1976*b*, pp. 205–7) for the search/island model of Alchian, Phelps, Mortensen, Holt, and others.

because the junior worker moves up the ladder regardless of whether the separation is a quit or a fire.

The possibility that workers may featherbed on the job has an impact on the form of labour-market institutions. In a pair of papers, Edward Lazear (1979; 1981) has shown that it is possible to explain important features of existing institutions, particularly mandatory retirement and a positively sloped age earnings profile, as optimal in a competitive labour market. A steep age-earnings relation alters a worker's incentives to perform efficiently on the job. The productivity of each hour spent working is increased when the bulk of wage payments is delayed until relatively late in life, since the worker is more anxious to please the firm in order to avoid a job termination. Thus the wage schedule may rise with experience, even if productivity does not, a phenomenon that is consistent not just with the Japanese lifetime employment system, but also with recent findings by James Medoff and Katherine Abraham (1980) in a study of several US firms.

An undesirable side effect of the steep age-earnings profile is that, if hours are freely chosen, young workers work too little and older workers work too much. Since there is only one degree of freedom, the wage rate adjusts the effort margin and quantity constraints (compulsory overtime; mandatory retirement) determine hours. Hence it is not surprising that we observe complaints by younger workers about compulsory overtime (which they may try to fight with absenteeism), while older workers complain about being prevented from working as much as they would like. Mandatory retirement goes hand-in-glove with a steep age-earnings profile, since the firm cannot afford to expose itself to a period of unpredictable length during which the worker receives more than his marginal product. This approach relies on the fact that it is easier to monitor the number of hours worked than the amount of effort expended, and for this reason belongs in the class of human capital models that incorporate imperfect information.

III. 2 Contract Length and Indexation

In Arthur Okun's words, 'there are more reasons than we need to explain why real-world employers care about retaining experienced workers' (1981, p. 48). Risk aversion, monitoring costs, and training costs, can lead to long-term attachments between firms and workers. But now, to explain why real variables are not completely insulated from nominal disturbances, we must determine which contingencies, if any, should be included in the written or unwritten contracts binding workers and firms.

A basic idea that runs through the literature, e.g., Azariadis (1981), is that the choice of contract form can be posed as an economic tradeoff. 'Naive' contracts that predetermine prices or wages without new information are cheap to write but expose agents to inefficient outcomes when unpredictable events occur. Contingent contracts that incorporate new information are more costly to write but can minimise or eliminate risk. The tradeoff is easiest to understand in Jo Anna Gray's (1978) analysis of optimal contract length.[1] If a fixed

---
[1] See also the explicitly dynamic analysis provided by Ronald Dye (1979).

cost is incurred each time a contract is renegotiated, then amortisation of the fixed cost calls for a long contract duration. But if the contract does not eliminate all conceivable risks, then a long contract duration exposes agents to a larger potential efficiency loss than a short duration. Thus contract length depends inversely on the expected level of uncertainty. If contracts can be written to eliminate all real consequences of purely nominal disturbances, then the variance of nominal aggregate demand is irrelevant for choosing the contract length, and only uncertainty about potential real supply shocks matters. The US postwar three-year wage contract, as contrasted to shorter contract lengths in Britain and Japan, would be explained within the Gray framework as the consequence of relatively high perceived renegotiation costs and a relatively low level of uncertainty in the United States.

What range of possible contingencies will be written into contracts? Asymmetric information mitigates against contracts contingent on 'local' variables specific to the firm, e.g., firm sales, product price, or worker productivity. As in the Grossman–Hart and Hall–Lilien models, any informational advantage on the part of the employer leads to a moral hazard problem, that the firm has an incentive to understate the realisation of the variable on which the wage is contingent, in order to minimise wage cost. Contracts are thus more likely to be contingent on aggregate nominal variables, i.e., the consumer price index and/or the money supply. But, as Gray's paper shows, indexation to a consumer price index rigidifies real wage growth over the life of the contract. While this is an optimal outcome if all disturbances are nominal, and the growth of productivity is perfectly predictable, full consumer-price indexation imposes an efficiency loss when an unpredictable supply shock (e.g. OPEC) changes the equilibrium real wage.

Since full indexation to the consumer price index has the fatal defect that it rigidifies the real wage, an appealing alternative is indexation to nominal GNP, since this allows the real wage to adjust automatically to unexpected changes in productivity growth (the advantages and disadvantages of indexation to a nominal monetary aggregate are treated below in paragraph (4)). Adopting the notation in section I above, with changes in nominal GNP, prices, actual real GNP, and equilibrium real GNP designated respectively as y, p, q and q^*, we have the identity:

$$y - q^* \equiv p + q - q^*. \tag{6}$$

Let us assume for convenience that equilibrium labour input is constant, so labour productivity growth in equilibrium is the same as equilibrium real GNP growth (q^*). Then indexation of the wage rate to nominal GNP ($w = y$) implies, when substituted into (6):

$$w - p \equiv q^* + (q - q^*). \tag{7}$$

Thus growth in the real wage ($w - p$) automatically reflects equilibrium productivity growth (q^*) as long as there are no fluctuations in real output relative to its equilibrium value ($q - q^* = 0$).

No matter how superficially attractive, nominal GNP indexing of wage contracts has never been observed. This occurs, I suggest, because four sets of barriers prevent agents from making the comfortable assumption that real business cycles have been vanquished ($q - q^* = 0$) and therefore in (7) that the growth of the real wage mimics the growth of productivity. The barriers are (1) pre-set prices and wages, (2) foreign trade, (3) information imperfections and delays, and (4) velocity shifts.

(1) *Pre-set prices and wages.* I have recently argued (1981 *a*) that firms have a legitimate reason to fear that nominal GNP fluctuations will, at least initially, take the form of real GNP fluctuations. First, in many markets it is efficient for prices to be pre-set rather than established in auction markets, to save on the time and transportation costs that centralised auctions impose. Second, prices that are preset for even a short interval imply that firms will initially experience a nominal fluctuation as a real event – a decline in real purchases at the initially preset price. Their expectation that the real demand shock will soon be eliminated depends on the speed with which costs of inputs purchased from other firms mimic the movement in nominal demand. If information on the nominal stock is imperfect, firms may, at least initially, interpret it as local rather than aggregate in nature and may believe that there is no reason for their input costs to move in proportion to the demand shift. Once it is admitted that individual product prices, and hence the aggregate price level, may adjust gradually to changes in nominal GNP, then workers will fear the consequences of nominal-indexed wage contracts. Consider a 20 % decline in nominal GNP, accompanied initially by only a 10 % decline in the aggregate price level. Workers having a wage contract indexed to nominal GNP would experience a decline in their real wage of 10 %. Eventually prices would adjust fully in proportion to the nominal GNP change, but workers, particularly if they are risk averse, would object to the instability of real wages implied by nominal-GNP indexation in a world of gradual price adjustment.

The preceding paragraph is unconventional in that it deduces nominal wage stickiness from price stickiness, while it is more common to do the reverse. But in fact the argument works both ways. If nominal wages do not adjust instantly, then firms face nominal marginal costs that are less than unit elastic with respect to nominal GNP changes. The problem is properly treated as dynamic rather than static, in which several sources of resistance to full nominal indexation interact and reinforce each other.

(2) *Foreign trade.* When firms observe an increase or decrease in their real sales at the initially pre-set price, their choice of a new price depends on a guess about the fraction of the demand shift representing a nominal aggregate shock, as opposed to a real aggregate or real local shock, and, a guess about the extent to which suppliers of inputs recognise the aggregate component of the shock. As will be recognised by economists in Britain, Japan, and other open economies, the perceived stickiness of marginal cost is a rational response when agents recognise that a substantial fraction of their inputs are imported from abroad, where suppliers may have been unaffected by an aggregate nominal demand shock that is national rather than international in origin. Full insulation of real sales from a perceived nominal *national* disturbance would require that each

agent (*a*) assumes his national suppliers immediately perceive the same shock and (*b*) ignores the fact that suppliers of imports are unaffected by a national demand shock. Both (*a*) and (*b*) surely strain credulity.

(3) *Information imperfections and delays*. Prior to the postwar development of monetary aggregates and national income accounts, timely measures of nominal aggregates did not exist, as good a reason as any to explain why nominal aggregate indexation has never occurred. Even today, nominal GNP indexation would require a two-month average delay in the United States (data for the second quarter, centred on May 15, become available in the third week of July). Lags are considerably longer in some other countries. Wage contracts indexed to nominal GNP thus cannot prevent a short-run reduction in hours worked in situations when nominal GNP growth suddenly decelerates, as in the United States in 1980:Q2 and 1981:Q2. Profit-maximising firms naturally resist the implications of nominal GNP indexation that, because of information lags in situations of temporary fluctuations of nominal GNP growth, they reduce prices just when the economy is recovering and raise prices just when it is collapsing.

(4) *Velocity shifts*. Information on monetary aggregates is available fairly promptly, but indexation to a particular monetary aggregate cannot insulate real variables even if information is contemporaneous. Stochastic disturbances in commodity and money demand functions, which may be serially correlated, lead to serially correlated fluctuations in the velocity of money. A price-setting agent choosing to index his product price to M1 in the United States would find that a slump in real sales would occur in any week or month in which velocity grows more slowly than the average written into the indexation formula.

III. 3 *Conclusions Regarding Optimal Labour-Market Arrangements*

Contractual arrangements cannot obviate fluctuations of hours worked in response to fluctuations in real supply or in nominal demand. Firms and workers are both unwilling to accept the risk implied by a contract that is fully indexed to nominal spending or money. If it is impossible to eliminate fluctuations in nominal demand, then labour-market contracts should be of relatively short duration. Frequent contract renewals can partially substitute for the absence of nominal GNP indexation, by allowing the latest information on both real and nominal shocks to be incorporated into wage-setting and price-setting decisions.

Firms are not entirely indifferent about the extent of fluctuations in their profits. This being the case, contracts should not only be of short duration, but in addition should expire simultaneously across all firms. Simultaneous contract renegotiation is preferable to staggered contracts, because workers are more likely to accept a slower rate of wage growth in response to a nominal GNP slump if they are in the same boat, than if one group of workers is asked to accept a sacrifice that was not required of another group whose contract was settled a month or two earlier.

Short contract durations, while minimising allocational losses in the face of uncertainty, impose extra fixed costs of renegotiation. There is a shortage of degrees of freedom. Contract duration, a single institution, cannot perform two

2

different functions – the achievement of macroeconomic efficiency and the resolution of conflicts over income shares. Efficiency requires short contracts, while the minimisation of negotiation and strike costs requires long contracts. Thus an economic theorist designing institutions must simply decree that the initial income distribution is just, and is not to be the subject of disputes at contract renegotiation time, if he wants contract duration to be chosen to maximise macroeconomic efficiency.

Efficient labour-market institutions to achieve microeconomic efficiency would seem to involve an age-earnings profile that is steeper than the age-productivity profile, together with mandatory retirement, in order to induce efficient performance and avoid featherbedding by younger workers. Seniority rules should be instituted for promotions and hours reductions. Unemployment compensation should be paid proportional to hours of time lost, rather than days of full-time work lost, in order to encourage work-sharing. To the extent that it is actually necessary for firms to lay workers off, seniority rules should be adopted that concentrate job layoffs on junior workers, in whom there is likely to be a smaller cumulative training investment.

IV. ORIGINS OF LABOUR-MARKET INSTITUTIONS IN JAPAN, THE UNITED KINGDOM, AND THE UNITED STATES

Many of the labour-market arrangements selected by the economic theorist to achieve macroeconomic efficiency and high productivity appear to correspond rather closely to well-known features of the Japanese labour market. Long-term attachments between workers and firms are formalised in the lifetime employment system, with wage flexibility encouraged through a semi-annual variable bonus. The seniority wage, or nenkō, system, in its purest form relates earnings solely to length of service and not to work performance. Wage renegotiations take place annually and are roughly simultaneous during the 'spring wage offensive.'

If Japanese labour-market institutions are more compatible with macroeconomic efficiency than those in the United Kingdom and United Sates, we may naturally wonder whether the Japanese achievement occurred by design or historical accident. And, by comparing the historical background, we may try to identify those basic forces that inhibit change in the other two countries. My central theme is the differing role of labour-management and class conflict in the three nations, forcing labour-market institutions in the United Kingdom and United States to be geared mainly to the resolution of disputes rather than the achievement of macroeconomic efficiency, This theme parallels the theorist's demonstration that wage contracts cannot perform two functions at once, and that social conflict would simply have to be abolished by decree in order to allow contract renegotiations to concentrate on macroeconomic efficiency. In stressing the role of social conflict as an indirect explanation for cross-country differences in macroeconomic performance, I have been influenced by Albert Hirschman's parallel finding that in Latin America:

'...Various groups maintain and prize an attitude and phraseology of un-
bending opposition and hostility...The Chilean situation appears to be
weighted more heavily with the avoidance of agreement, with the maintenance of a militant stance on the part of all contending groups. In a sense,
this stance is the desired benefit and inflation is its cost' (1973, pp. 208–9).

IV. 1 *The Japanese System*

Underlying Japanese institutions is a stratification system, based on non-
occupational criteria, that is deeply rooted in social relations. This tradition
'suggests that vertical, that is, hierarchical, social relations rather than those
based upon egalitarian norms represent the ideal' (Kazuo Okochi *et al.* 1974,
p. 485). Analysts dating back to Thorstein Veblen have attributed the high
degree of respect for authority to the rapidity of Japan's forced-draft transition
from a feudal to an industrial society. 'It is in this unique combination of a
high-wrought spirit of feudalistic fealty and chivalric honour with the material
efficiency given by the modern technology that the strength of the Japanese
nation lies' (Veblen, 1915, p. 251–2).[1]

The lifetime employment system apparently developed after World War I
with the introduction of belt conveyors and assembly lines. Previously Japanese
skilled workers had been mobile and independent, but the new production processes required workers with narrow skills on particular machines rather than
broad, easily transferable skills. This transition seems compatible with Becker's
distinction between general and firm-specific human capital, and implies that
firms moved to the lifetime employment system in order to amortise their
specific training investment. Worker loyalty was cemented by the seniority
wage structure, combined (as in Lazear's model) with the rule of mandatory
retirement at the age of fifty-five.

Since British and American factories had introduced similar production techniques earlier, the existence of firm-specific human capital is clearly insufficient
to explain the unique features of the Japanese lifetime employment system.
Walter Galenson and Konosuke Odaka argue that another necessary ingredient
is homogeneity of the work force, since heterogeneity in worker ability makes it
inefficient to base wage payments exclusively on seniority. While there is no
doubt that the massive immigration into the United States during the main
period of industrialisation made American workers less homogeneous than the
Japanese, this consideration does not seem to have much payoff in explaining
differences between the Japanese and British systems.[2]

---

[1] Space does not permit a more extended quote from Veblen's fascinating piece, which is perceptive
in its comparisons of Germany and England to Japan, although wrong in predicting that the distinctive
characteristics of the Japanese system would soon be eroded by industrialisation. Veblen explains the
absence of feudal habits of thought in England as a result of its much slower transition to industrialisation: '...the consequently changing state of the industrial arts among them [the English] had time
and scope concomitantly to work out its effect upon the habits of thought of the community, and so to
bring about a state of the institutional conventions answering to the altered state of the industrial arts'
(1915, p. 154).

[2] Koji Taira (1970, pp. 97–127) argues that the nenkō system was management's response to high
labour turnover and absenteeism during the period of industrialisation. See also Dore (1973, Chapter
13).

Differences in the degree of long-term attachment between workers and firms across the three nations should not be exaggerated. The Japanese lifetime employment system is mainly concentrated in large firms, ends at age 55, and does not apply to women or employees of numerous subcontractors and other satellites that act as a buffer during economic downturns. In the United States, as Hall (1980) has shown, a surprisingly large fraction of US workers hold what are essentially lifetime jobs (although not to the extent prevalent in Japan).[1] Thus what is unique about the Japanese system is not so much the average duration of the worker-firm attachment, but rather the role of seniority rather than ability in determining payment. Galenson and Odaka consider the nenkō payment system an important way in which grievances are minimised in the Japanese system, and this fits in with our theme of conflict-minimisation:

'All employees, once hired, are entitled equally to all the rights and privileges of the organisation to which they belong. There may be variations in individual talent, but it is assumed that everyone is doing his best to serve the company in his own way; no one should be discriminated against.'[2]

Another ingredient in the Japanese system is the integration of economic and social life within the large firm. William Ouchi's discussion implies that this custom, which he attributes to the 'historical accident' that Japan 'rushed' from feudalism to a modern industrial society, plays a large role in conflict avoidance:

'Intimacy of this sort discourages selfish or dishonest action in the group, since abused relationships cannot be left behind. People who live in a company dormitory, play on a company baseball team, work together on five different committees, and know the situation will continue for the rest of their lives develop a unique relationship. Values and beliefs become mutually compatible over a wide range of work-related and non-work-related issues.'[3]

At the heart of conflict avoidance in the Japanese system is a greater degree of equality, with less influence of social class, so that there is less to fight about. Nathan Glazer (1976, pp. 887–8), states flatly, 'The Japanese factory or company is at present perhaps the most egalitarian in the world, outside China...Clearly, class is relatively less evident than in England, and even relatively less evident than in the United States.' Glazier's summary of in-plant sociological studies cites the absence of any distinction of dress between white-collar and manual workers; the informal familiar level of speech used within the factory contrasted with the formal level of address used with those on the outside; the lack of distinction between annual salaries and hourly pay; the

[1] In 1966, 56% of males aged 35–39 had more than ten year's seniority in Japan, against only 34% of the same group in the United States, according to Robert E. Cole (1972, p. 618).

[2] Galenson and Odaka, p. 610. The authors point out that economic pressures, including problems of dealing with low-quality workers, and the growing burden of high-cost older workers, have led to a modest degree of shifting toward an ability basis for pay.

[3] William Ouchi, 'Individualism and intimacy in an industrial society.' *Technology Review*, July 1981, p. 36.

one-class company cafeteria (no executive dining room); and communality of access to sick pay, sports clubs, and vacation resorts.[1] It may seem paradoxical that the Japanese combine a greater respect for hierarchy with greater equality in the perquisites of managers and workers, but this seems to be explained by the non-occupational nature of Japanese attitudes toward hierarchy.[2]

I have stressed conflict avoidance, because I believe that this helps to explain why the Japanese have one-year wage contracts and why the United States has three-year wage contracts. But there are two other important features of the Japanese system that foster macroeconomic efficiency, the simultaneity of contract expiration dates in the spring wage negotiations, and the prevalence of flexible wages in the form of bonus payments. The spring wage offensive, or Shuntō, developed in 1955 at the initiative of the largest of the Japanese labour federations. Despite the fact that the actual bargaining takes place between management and the enterprise union at each firm, the institution of the simultaneous offensive seems to have brought about some standardisation of wage increases across firms (Galenson and Okada, pp. 644–5). The simultaneity of the offensive may be partially explained as an attempt by the Japanese trade union movement to compensate for its basic weakness and fragmentation.[3] The greater power and strike-proneness of American labour may help to explain the persistence of staggered contract expiration dates, in spite of its macro-economic inefficiency, since government and management may have reason to fear that a simultaneous expiration date would make possible a nationwide general strike.

The bonus system is interpreted by Hashimoto as a form of profit sharing, which in turn makes another contribution to conflict avoidance. The practice developed along with the nenkō compensation system in order to 'enhance the loyalty and commitment of employees to their firms' (1979, p. 1090). By studying cross-section differences among Japanese firms, Hashimoto concludes that high profitability and 'the low costs of reaching agreements, that is, low transactions costs,' help to explain the widespread use of bonusses. All the major elements of the Japanese system seem to interact together, acting as a 'virtuous circle' from the standpoint of macroeconomic efficiency. Paternalism and relative equality encourage conflict avoidance, which in turn allows firms to maintain high profitability, while sharing part of the profits with workers in the form of cyclically sensitive bonus payments.

IV. 2 The British System

The chief institutional features of British labour market institutions are class consciousness, class conflict, labour militancy, and weak management. These help to cause a low level and growth rate of productivity which, in turn, has

---

[1] Numerous qualifications can be made to this sentence without altering its validity as a statement about comparative equality across the three countries. For instance, both Glaser's text and Galenson in correspondence with me mention the fact that most of the benefits of the 'expense account society' (limosines, meals, nights out on the town) go to management. Glazer also points out that education is beginning to play a larger role in determining status in the factory.

[2] For more on the relative avoidance of conflict, see Galenson and Odaka, pp. 638–42.

[3] Galenson and Odaka, while stressing the complexity of the background, provide a brief explanation of the weak union movement: '...the initial hothouse growth of unionism under the American occupation, the immediate factionalism along prewar lines, and the purge of communists in 1950 imparted an internal instability that has proved impossible to overcome' (1976, p. 629).

both aggravated the struggle over income shares and has fostered a macro-economic policy that in the 1970s aggravated inflation through monetary accommodation.

The greater importance of class distinctions in Britain was cited above in Glazer's analysis of social equality in Japan. Dore (1973, p. 140) stresses the contrast between the refusal of British workers and management to accept the legitimacy of the power which the other enjoys, in contrast to Japan where 'both sides look forward to an indefinite future in which their relations will not be very different from what they are now. Britain's is an Arab-Israeli situation with shifting frontiers which only constant vigilance can defend. Japan's is a Franco–German situation; there are memories of monumental disputes over Alsace and the Saar, but now the border is not an issue.'

The sources of class consciousness go deep into British history, stemming partly from the unparalleled historical continuity of the political and legal system and the absence of external conquest. In Mancur Olson's (1977) analysis, common-interest organisations like labour unions are difficult to form spontaneously, because they provide collective goods for their members and are subject to a free-rider problem, and once formed are difficult to change. He stresses the contrast between Britain, with its history of victory in war and entrenched institutions, and both Germany and Japan in which dictatorships and wartime defeat destroyed or weakened common-interest groups. Two other historical events helping to explain the minor role of class distinctions in Japan are the much more recent feudal period of relative cultural homogeneity, and the fact that at the end of the feudal period Japan created an almost completely universal school system in which 'bureaucrats' sons and fishmongers' sons absorbed a uniform curriculum in the same schools' (Dore, p. 284). In contrast the British three-way distinction between 'public' (i.e. private), 'grammar' (i.e. academic), and vocational secondary schools divided the population not just by intellectual level, but also by accent and culture. Finally, the class system fostered executive dining rooms and other barriers to shopfloor communication, which in turn caused class distinctions and working class distrust to become more firmly entrenched.

Lloyd Ulman (1968, pp. 331–2) notes that British workers tend not only to be class conscious, but suspicious of progress and to have 'an atavistic opposition to redundancy' that is compounded of 'an unfading memory of prewar unemployment and a deep-seated distrust of employer motives and capability.' But management is not free of blame, failing to control overmanning as a result of 'hereditary nepotism in family-owned concerns and backwardness in employing modern techniques for identifying the profitability of investment opportunities' (p. 335). To union 'bloodymindedness' Ulman joins management 'sleepyheadedness.' 'Labour efficiency readily becomes a casualty in a prolonged encounter between a management which is understaffed and inexpert in industrial relations and members of a plant work force who find little reason to discard their fathers' suspicion of class along with their fathers' ideology' (p. 338).

In the early postwar years British labour relations were relatively quiescent, and days lost from strikes were comparable to those in Japan and far less than in the United States. But in the late 1960s labour militancy increased, and there was a substantial increase in the annual average days lost from strikes per 1,000 employed (Smith, p. 109):

	1964-6	1967-71	1972-6
Japan	240	194	294
UK	190	608	968
US	870	1,644	1,054

The increase in labour militancy manifested itself not only in more strikes, but in an acceleration in the growth of nominal wage rates that has been identified by Perry (1975) and myself (1977) as having an autonomous component rather than being entirely induced by prior episodes of monetary expansion or incomes policy. David Soskice (1978, p. 245) traces the rise in militancy in Britain to the interaction of the 1967 devaluation and incomes policies.

Ulman and Richard Caves (1980) both attribute low British productivity and slow economic growth in part to labour militancy and the industrial relations system. But what is the relationship of the system to the subject of this paper, the responsiveness of wages and employment to nominal demand disturbances? The empirical evidence in section II above exhibits variability and responsiveness coefficients for British wages that are almost identical to those for Japanese wages, and a standard deviation of employment changes that is about half of the American experience. I believe that, in light of this evidence of wage responsiveness in Britain, the well-known problems of inflation through the decade of the 1970s and the difficulties of adjustment in 1979-81 are the result of perverse government policy rather than an innately rigid wage adjustment system.

Class conflict and labour militancy, together with the historical fact that British party lines coincide with class divisions, help to explain why British governments have propogated inflation through monetary accommodation of wage push. The Labour party is naturally averse to the temporary increase in unemployment that would be required by a failure to accommodate, and Conservative governments have often been in the position of trying to buy off the unions in the hope that they will be able to push through reforms in trade union law. The long history of accommodation of wage explosions by the Bank of England, at least before 1979, stems partly from its lack of political independence, but may partly be the result of a fear of confrontation between bankers and the unemployed that dates back to the interwar years and the General Strike of 1926.

Table 3 above documents the significant positive feedback from wage changes to nominal GNP changes that has existed in Britain (but not in Japan or the United States) as a result of monetary accommodation. The two-way feedback between wages and nominal GNP evident in Table 3, together with relatively high response coefficients, makes the British inflation process particularly unstable. And, as Smith emphasises, an additional element in the vicious circle has been feedback from inflation to trade union militancy itself.

IV. 3 The American System

The central empirical result of this paper is the contrast between sluggish wage adjustment in the United States and a high degree of wage responsiveness in Britain and Japan. The historical evidence supports the interpretation that the invention of the US three-year staggered wage contract in the late 1940s accounts for the inertia-bound character of the US postwar wage behaviour. Thus our remaining task is to explain why these contracts developed in the United States, but not in Japan or Britain.

The 1948 contract between the United Auto Workers and General Motors established two key features of US wage bargains, the multi-year agreement, and the inclusion of a cost-of-living escalator. Jo Anna Gray's analysis provides the key hint in understanding this development, since it was the high cost of negotiation, as perceived by managers besieged during 1946–8 with annual strikes or threats of strikes in core industries, that led to the 1948 General Motors contract. Charles E. Wilson, GM President, had the idea of buying a long-term contract by offering unions cost-of-living protection. In 1950 the auto companies and the union signed a five-year contract, reopened in 1953, and since 1953 there have been nine three-year agreements.

In explaining why the United States developed three-year contracts, but the Japanese did not, differences in the perceived importance of industrial conflict must have played the major role. In Gray's model a higher degree of uncertainty leads to shorter contracts, but the United States had more unstable demand than Japan in the 1923–40 period, suggesting that negotiating costs are the dominant factor. The more interesting question seems to be why the British developed no such long-term contracts, since both the United States and United Kingdom have similar histories of labour strife. First, the United States unionised in a hurry, after the 1935 Wagner Act turned Washington's previous red light to green. Partly because unionisation took the form of large industrial unions in key industries, especially coal, steel, and autos, there was a widespread perception that strikes were more costly in the United States than in Britain. And in fact strikes were much more widespread in the United States, at least until the 1970s. Second, the United States has a legal tradition dating back to its written Constitution. Partially because it is a more heterogeneous society than Britain, there has been a tendency to put everything into written agreements and to establish an enormous legal profession to interpret and argue about the nuances of written contracts. The aversion to written agreements in Britain is attributed by Dore (1973, p. 145) to deep-seated tradition: 'Another factor contributing to this situation is doubtless the ineffable British faith in the superior virtue of relying on ancestral wisdom and the accumulation of "custom and practice", rather than on the written constitutions which lesser breeds need as a crutch to help them manage their affairs.' Third, firms in Britain did not have the same opportunity to buy off the unions in return for industrial peace, because they dealt with small craft unions rather than large industrial unions, and because negotiations tended to occur at the local plant level rather than at the national firm level. So the British had less strife to induce a three-year contract, less of a legal tradition to warrant a written contract as an escape from strife, and a less centralised union structure with whom to negotiate such an agreement.

V. CONCLUSION

The basic argument of this paper comes down to three main points:

(1) Macroeconomic instability in the United States has been aggravated by the unusually sluggish behaviour of nominal wages during the postwar era. Whether measured as the standard deviation of wages relative to hours worked, or the ratio of the respective response coefficients of wages and hours worked to changes in nominal GNP, wages in Britain and Japan are five to ten times more responsive than in the United States. Thus, of any given fluctuation in aggregate nominal demand, a larger fraction takes the form of a change in real output and employment in the United States than in the United Kingdom or Japan.

(2) The drastic decline of American wage responsiveness in the postwar period as compared to the years between 1892 and 1940, together with the 1948 invention of the three-year staggered wage contract in the American unionised industrial sector, seems to be more than coincidental. It is not only the long duration of US contracts, but also their staggered nature, that makes wage changes relatively unresponsive to expansions or contractions in nominal GNP growth.

(3) Japanese labour market institutions look much more like those suggested as optimal by recent economic theory than do American institutions. Economic theory predicts that long-duration contracts are more likely to emerge when the perceived cost of renegotiation is high, but we must appeal to history and cultural differences in order to explain why conflict avoidance has played a much greater role in the development of Japanese labour market institutions than in the American case. In this comparison Britain is the odd-man-out, with well-publicised industrial strife, together with short contract durations. I appeal to history, the different legal tradition, and the nature of British unions themselves to explain why the three-year contract became established in America but not in Britain.

American economists for too long have sought purely economic explanations of wage inertia, without recognising the much greater degree of wage responsiveness exhibited by Japan, Britain, and some other nations. They have been too narrowly concerned with monetary explanations of inflation, as if money were an autonomous variable, and have insufficiently understood that the dynamics of inflation emerge from a two-way interaction between, on the one hand, the monetary and fiscal institutions of government, and, on the other hand, society's wage- and price-setting institutions. The economic theory of contracts has performed a useful service in showing how the variance of nominal and real shocks interacts with costs of negotiation in determining contract form and length, but economists must defer to sociologists and historians (or unblushingly don the hat of amateur sociologist and historian) to learn why one society has a higher perceived cost of negotiation and conflict resolution than another. I hope that this fledgling exercise in comparative macroeconomic history will stimulate future investigators to tackle the many puzzles and unanswered questions that remain.[1]

Northwestern University
Date of receipt of final typescript: *September 1981*

REFERENCES

Akerlof, G. A. (1978). 'A Theory of social custom, of which unemployment may be one consequence.' *Quarterly Journal of Economics*, vol. 94, no. 4, pp. 749–76.
Azariadis, C. (1975). 'Implicit contracts and underemployment equilibria.' *Journal of Political Economy*, vol. 83, pp. 1183–202.
—— (1981). 'Implicit contracts and related topics: A survey.' *Economics of the Labour Market* (ed. Z. Hornstein, J. Grice and A. Webb), pp. 221–48. HMSO.
Baily, M. N. (1974). 'Wages and employment under uncertain demand.' *Review of Economic Studies*, vol. 41 (1), no. 125, pp. 37–50.
Barro, R. J. (1977). 'Long-term contracting, sticky prices, and monetary policy'. *Journal of Monetary Economics*, vol. 2, no. 1, pp. 1–32.
—— (1979). 'Second thoughts on Keynesian economics.' *American Economic Review*, vol. 69, no. 2, pp. 54–9.
—— and Grossman, H. I. (1976). *Money, Employment, and Inflation*. Cambridge: Cambridge University Press.
Becker, G. (1962). *Human Capital*. New York: Columbia University Press.
Branson, W. and Rotemberg, J. (1980). 'International adjustment with wage rigidity.' *European Economic Review*, vol. 13, no. 3, pp. 309–32.
Calvo, G. and Phelps, E. S. (1977). 'Employment-contingent wage contracts.' *Stabilization of the Domestic and International Economy* (ed. K. Brunner and A. Meltzer), *Carnegie-Rochester Conference Series on Public Policy*, vol. 5, pp. 160–8. Amsterdam: North-Holland.
Carmichael, L. (1980). 'Firm specific human capital and seniority rules.' Queens University working paper, October.
Caves, R. E. (1980). 'Productivity differences among industries.' *Britain's Economic Performance* (ed. R. E. Caves and L. B. Krause), pp. 135–92. Washington: Brookings.
Cole, R. E. (1972). 'Permanent employment in Japan: Facts and fantasies.' *Industrial and Labor Relations Review*, vol. 26, no. 1, pp. 615–30.
Dore, R. (1973). *British Factory, Japanese Factory*. Berkeley: University of California Press.
Dye, R. A. (1979). 'Optimal contract length.' Carnegie-Mellon working paper, October.
Feinstein, C. H. (1972). *National Income, Expenditure and Output of the United Kingdom, 1855–1965*. Cambridge: Cambridge University Press.
Frye, J. F. and Gordon, R. J. (1981). 'Government intervention in the inflation process: The econometrics of self-inflicted wounds.' *American Economic Review*, vol. 71, pp. 288–94.
Galenson, W. and Okada, K. (1976). 'The Japanese labor market'. *Asia's New Giant: How the Japanese Economy Works* (ed. H. Patrick and H. Rosovsky), pp. 588–671. Washington: Brookings Institution.
Glazer, N. (1976). 'Social and cultural factors in Japanese economic growth.' *Asia's New Giant: How the Japanese Economy Works* (ed. H. Patrick and H. Rosovsky), pp. 813–96. Washington: Brookings Institution.
Gordon, D. F. (1974). 'A neo-classical theory of Keynesian unemployment.' *Economic Inquiry*, vol. 12, pp. 431–59.
Gordon, R. J. (1975). 'The demand for and supply of inflation.' *Journal of Law and Economics*, vol. 18, pp. 807–36.
—— (1976a). 'Aspects of the theory of involuntary unemployment.' *The Phillips Curve and Labor Markets* (ed. K. Brunner and A. Meltzer), pp. 98–119, a supplementary series to the *Journal of Monetary Economics*, vol. 1. Amsterdam: North-Holland.
—— (1976b). 'Recent developments in the theory of inflation and unemployment.' *Journal of Monetary Economics*, vol. 2, no. 2, pp. 185–220.
—— (1977). 'World inflation and monetary accommodation in eight countries.' *Brookings Papers on Economic Activity*, vol. 8, pp. 409–77.
—— (1980). 'A consistent characterization of a near-century of US price behavior.' *American Economic Review*, vol. 70, pp. 243–9.

[1] In particular I do not understand the high level of British unemployment in the 1920s in light of the suggestion of Table 5's high responsiveness coefficients that British wages should have adjusted promptly to the return to gold in 1925. Also, the decline in the U.S. wage and price responsiveness coefficients between the pre-1914 and 1923–40 period, as well as other shifts in coefficients identified elsewhere (1980), remain as tantalising mysteries.

—— (1981a). 'Output fluctuations and gradual price adjustment'. *Journal of Economic Literature*, vol. 19, pp. 493–530.

—— (1981b). 'Why stopping inflation may be costly: Evidence from fourteen historical episodes.' NBER Conference Paper 108.

—— (1982). 'Inflation, flexible exchange rates, and the natural rate of unemployment.' Forthcoming in *Workers, Jobs and Inflation*. (ed. M. N. Baily), Washington: Brookings Institution.

—— and Wilcox, J. A. (1981). 'Monetarist interpretations of the great depression: Evaluation and critique.' *The Great Depression Revisited* (ed. K. Brunner), pp. 49–107. Boston: Martinus Nijhoff.

Granger, C. W. J. (1969). 'Investigating causal relations by econometric methods and cross-spectral methods.' *Econometrica*, vol. 37, no. 3, pp. 424–38.

Gray, J. A. (1978). 'On indexation and contract length.' *Journal of Political Economy*, vol. 86, pp. 1–18.

Grossman, H. I. (1977). 'Risk shifting and reliability in labor markets'. *Scandinavian Journal of Economics*, vol. 79, no. 2, pp. 187–209.

Grossman, S. and Hart, O. D. (1980). 'Implicit contracts, moral hazard, and unemployment.' Economic Theory Discussion Paper no. 37, University of Cambridge.

Hall, R. E. (1980). 'Employment fluctuations and wage rigidity.' *Brookings Papers on Economic Activity*, vol. 11, no. 1, pp. 91–123.

—— and Lilian, D. (1979). 'Efficient wage bargains under uncertain supply and demand.' *American Economic Review*, vol. 69, no. 5, pp. 868–79.

Hashimoto, M. (1979). 'Bonus payments, on-the-job training and lifetime employment in Japan.' *Journal of Political Economy*, vol. 87, no. 5, pt. 1, pp. 1086–104.

Hirschman, A. O. (1973). *Journeys Toward Progress: Studies in Economic Policymaking in Latin America*. New York: Norton.

Johnson, H. G. (1972). 'Panel discussion: World inflation.' *Stabilization Policies in Interdependent Economies* (ed. E. Classen and P. Salin), pp. 310–1. Amsterdam: North Holland.

Jones, A. (1973). *The New Inflation: The Politics of Prices and Incomes*. Baltimore: Penguin.

Lazear, E. P. (1979). 'Why is there mandatory retirement?' *Journal of Political Economy*, vol. 87, no. 6, pp. 1261–84.

—— (1981). 'Agency, earnings profiles, productivity and layoffs.' *American Economic Review*, vol. 71, no. 4, pp. 606–20.

Levitan, S. A. and Belous, R. S. (1977). 'Worksharing initiatives at home and abroad.' *Monthly Labor Review*, vol. 100, no. 9, pp. 16–20.

Malinvaud, E. (1977). *The Theory of Unemployment Reconsidered*. Oxford: Basil Blackwell.

Medoff, J. L. and Abraham, K. G. (1980). 'Experience, performance and earnings.' *Quarterly Journal of Economics*, vol. 95, no. 4, pp. 703–36.

Mortensen, D. (1979). 'The matching process as a non-cooperative bargaining game.' Center for Mathematical Studies in Economics and Management Science, Northwestern University, Working Paper no. 384.

Nordhaus, W. D. (1972). 'The worldwide wage explosion.' *Brookings Papers on Economic Activity*, vol. 3, no. 2, pp. 431–64.

Ohkawa, K. (1957). *The Growth Rate of the Japanese Economy Since 1878*. Tokyo: Kinokuniya University.

—— and Rosovsky, H. (1973). *Japanese Economic Growth*. Stanford: Stanford University Press.

Okochi, K., Karsh, B. and Levine, S. B. (1974). *Workers and Employers in Japan*. Princeton University Press and University of Tokyo Press.

Okun, A. M. (1981). *Prices and Quantities: A Macroeconomic Analysis*. Washington: Brookings Institution.

Olson, M. (1977). 'The political economy of comparative growth rates.' College Park, Maryland: University of Maryland, processed.

Perry, G. L. (1975). 'Determinants of wage inflation around the world.' *Brookings Papers on Economic Activity*, vol. 6, no. 2, pp. 403–35.

Phelps, E. S. (1977). 'Indexation issues.' *Stabilization of the Domestic Economy* (ed. K. Brunner and A. Meltzer), pp. 149–59. Carnegie-Rochester Conference Series on Public Policy, vol. 5. Amsterdam: North-Holland.

Sachs, J. (1979). 'Wages, profits, and macroeconomic adjustment: A comparative study.' *Brookings Papers on Economic Activity*, vol. 2, pp. 269–319.

Smith, D. C. (1980). 'Trade union growth and industrial disputes.' *Britain's Economic Performance* (ed. R. E. Caves and L. B. Krause), pp. 81–134. Washington: Brookings.

Soskice, D. (1978). 'Strike waves and wages explosions, 1968–1970: An economic interpretation.' *The Resurgence of Class Conflict in Western Europe Since 1968* (ed. C. Crouch and A. Pizzorno), pp. 221–46. London: Macmillan.

Taira, K. (1970). *Economic Development and the Labor Market in Japan*. New York: Columbia University Press.

Ulman, L. I. (1968). 'Collective bargaining and industrial efficiency.' (ed. R. E. Caves and Associates), *Britain's Economic Prospects*, pp. 324–80. Washington: Brookings.

US Department of Commerce (1973). *Long Term Economic Growth: 1860–1970*. Washington: Government Printing Office.

Veblen, T. (1915). 'The opportunity of Japan.' *Journal of Race Development*, vol. 6, no. 3. Reprinted in *Essays in Our Changing Order*. New York: Viking Press, 1934, pp. 248–66.

DATA APPENDIX
Sources of Data Prior to World War II

US

All data come from US Department of Commerce (1973).

Nominal GNP: Series A7, linked in 1909 to Series A8.

GNP deflator: Calculated as the ratio of nominal to real GNP, where the latter is series A1 linked in 1909 to Series A2.

Wage rate: 'Total compensation per hour of work in manufacturing, production workers, in 1967 dollars', Series B70 times 'Consumer Price Index' series B69.

UK

All data come from Feinstein (1972).

Nominal GNP: table 1, col. (11).

GNP deflator at factor cost: table 61, col. (7).

Wage rate: 'Average full-time weekly rate', table 65, col. (1).

Japan

Nominal GNP: Ohkawa (1957), table 3, col. (1), linked in 1905 to Ohkawa and Rosovsky (1973), table 1, col. (6).

GNP deflator: Ohkawa (1957), table 3, col. (1), divided by table 4, col. (1), linked in 1905 to Ohkawa and Rosovsky (1973), table 14, col. (3).

Wage rate: 'Wage Index', Ohkawa (1957), table 1, col. (1).

Sources of Data After World War II

US

Nominal GNP: Unpublished revised Department of Commerce data obtained in January 1981.

All other data refer to the manufacturing sector and come from a computer print-out supplied by the Division of Productivity Research, Office of Productivity and Technology, Bureau of Labor Statistics, February 1981:

'Hourly compensation including fringe benefits.'

'Hours of all persons.'

'Employment.'

UK

All data come from the following sources:

1957:1 to 1978:2: OECD, *Main Economic Indicators: Historical Statistics*, 1957–66 and 1960–79.

1978:3 to 1980:3: OECD, *Main Economic Indicators*, February 1981:

'GDP at factor cost.'

'Hourly rates in manufacturing.'

'Weekly hours of work in manufacturing for Great Britain.'

'Employment in manufacturing, all employees.'

Japan

Data sources are the same as those for the UK:

'GNP at current market prices, billion yen.'

'Monthly earnings (including bonuses) in manufacturing by regular workers.'

'Monthly hours of work in manufacturing by regular workers.'

'Employment in manufacturing of regular workers.'

[9]

The Rigidity of Prices

By DENNIS W. CARLTON*

For many transactions, prices remain rigid for periods exceeding one year. Price rigidity is positively correlated with industry concentration. For several products, the correlation of price changes across buyers is low. The paper also investigates the relationship between price rigidity, price change, and the length of time a buyer and seller have been doing business. The evidence emphasizes the importance of nonprice rationing and the inadequacy of models in which price movements alone clear markets.

Economists focus on price as a mechanism to allocate resources efficiently. It is well recognized that inefficient resource allocation could occur if prices are not free to adjust. Much of macroeconomics relies on some, usually unexplained, source of price rigidity to generate inefficient unemployment. And in industrial organization there is a large literature on "administered" prices which fail to respond to the forces of supply and demand. Recently, there have been several attempts to explain price rigidity (see, for example, Arthur Okun (1981) and Oliver Williamson (1975)) and to develop a theory to explain why efficient resource allocation requires price to be unchanging or "rigid" (see, for example, my forthcoming paper and Robert Hall, 1984). Whether or not price rigidity is efficient, one common conclusion emerging from models with price rigidity is that markets with rigid prices behave very differently than markets with flexible prices. Therefore, an important unanswered question is, just how rigid are prices? Despite the

great interest in this question, there have been virtually no attempts to answer it with data on individual transaction prices.

The purpose of this paper is to present evidence on the amount of price rigidity that exists in individual transaction prices. Previous studies of price rigidity have relied almost exclusively on an examination of aggregate price indices collected by the Bureau of Labor Statistics (BLS).[1] The use of BLS data has been strongly criticized on the grounds that the BLS data are inaccurate measures of transaction prices. George Stigler and James Kindahl sought to remedy this deficiency by collecting price data on actual transactions. Stigler and Kindahl then showed that price indices of average transaction prices were more flexible than the BLS price indices.

The difficulty with using indices is that they can mask the behavior of individual transaction prices. For example, suppose that two people buy varying amounts of commodity A monthly for many years. Suppose that each buyer pays a constant price on each transaction for a period of several years, that when the price to one buyer changes, the price to the other buyer is unaffected and that the price rigidity that exists is more pronounced for a downward price movement. All of these facts could be perfectly consistent with a flexible aggregate price in-

*Graduate School of Business, University of Chicago, 1101 East 58th Street, Chicago, IL 60637 and National Bureau of Economic Research. I thank the NSF and the Law and Economics Program at the University of Chicago for support. I thank Frederic Miller, Virginia France, Larry Harris, Deborah Lucas, and Steven Oi for research assistance. I also thank Claire Friedland and George Stigler for making these data available to me and for assisting me in their use. I thank Edward Lazear, Sam Peltzman, George Stigler, two anonymous referees, and participants at seminars at the NBER, Stanford, the universities of Chicago, Montreal, Pennsylvania, and Virginia for helpful comments.

[1] Research on prices includes the early and important work of Frederick Mills (1926), Gardiner Means (1935), and more recently, George Stigler and James Kindahl (1970).

dex as long as the amount purchased by each buyer varies from month to month. Yet the implication that many draw from a flexible price index, namely that price is allocating resources efficiently, could be completely inappropriate. Moreover, there are several interesting questions that cannot be answered by examining aggregate price indices. For example, how long do prices to a buyer remain unchanged, what is the relationship between contract length and price rigidity, and how closely together do the prices to different buyers move?

Using the Stigler-Kindahl data, I have examined the behavior of individual buyers' prices for certain products used in manufacturing. My main conclusions are:

1) The degree of price rigidity in many industries is significant. It is not unusual in some industries for prices to individual buyers to remain unchanged for several years.

2) Even for what appear to be homogeneous commodities, the correlation of price changes across buyers is very low.

3) There is a (weak) negative correlation between price rigidity and length of buyer-seller association. The more rigid are prices, the shorter the length of association.

4) There is a positive correlation between price rigidity and average absolute price change. The more rigid are prices, the greater is the price change when prices do change.

5) There is a negative correlation between length of buyer-seller association and average absolute price change. The longer a buyer and seller deal with each other, the smaller is the average price change when prices do change.

6) There is no evidence that there is an asymmetry in price rigidity. In particular, prices are not rigid downward.

7) The fixed costs of changing price at least to some buyers may be small. There are plenty of instances where small price changes occur. It appears that, for any particular product, the fixed cost of changing price varies across firms and buyers.

8) There is at best very weak evidence that buyers have systematic preferences across products for unchanging prices.

9) The level of industry concentration is strongly correlated with rigid prices. The more concentrated the industry, the longer is the average spell of price rigidity.

The most startling finding to me is that for many products, the correlation of price changes across buyers is low. Some of the theories referred to earlier explain why this is likely to occur, especially for specialized goods. The fact that it occurs for what most economists (though not necessarily businessmen) would regard as a homogeneous product emphasizes how erroneous it is to focus attention on price as the exclusive mechanism to allocate resources. Nonprice rationing is not a fiction, it is a reality of business and may be the efficient response to economic uncertainty and the cost of using the price system. (See my forthcoming paper.)

Two general caveats deserve mention. First, a rigid price, by itself, does not necessarily imply an inefficiency. If supply and demand are unchanging, prices will be rigid. Moreover, even in a changing market, a fixed-price contract for a fixed quantity creates no economic inefficiency in the standard competitive model. If prices change subsequent to the signing of the contract, the buyer incurs a capital gain or loss, but his marginal price remains the same as every other buyer as long as the product can be readily bought and sold. However, if either the buyer cannot readily resell his product, or if the buyer does not have a fixed quantity contract, then a fixed price may well lead to buyers facing different marginal prices. My understanding of the data I use is that the contracts typically leave the quantity unspecified, so that different buyers paying different prices do indeed face different marginal prices. Although this is inefficient in the standard competitive model, it need not be under more realistic assumptions that recognize the cost of making a market. (See my forthcoming paper. See also my 1978, 1979, 1982, 1983 papers for analyses reconciling observed price behavior with market equilibrium.) But the finding of different prices and price movements to different buyers does emphasize the inadequacy of the simple market-clearing model.

Second, the time period I examine is one with relatively low levels of inflation and therefore I have made no adjustment for it. However, even if inflation were rampant and all prices indexed so that no (nominal) price rigidity existed, the main conclusion of the paper would stand as long as some of the other empirical findings (such as the low correlation of price movements across buyers) continue to hold. The conclusion is that price alone is not allocating goods and that new theories are required to justify what looks like non-market-clearing behavior.

This paper is organized as follows. Section I describes the Stigler-Kindahl data and discusses measures of price rigidity. Section II analyzes the characteristics of price rigidity found in several general product groupings. Section III investigates the relationship between price rigidity, price change, and length of buyer-seller associations. Section IV examines whether buyers have systematic preferences for price stability across different products. One criticism of using broadly defined product groups as the unit of analysis is that there is so much heterogeneity of products within a single product grouping that results can be biased. Therefore, in Section V, I redo the analysis for a select group of narrowly defined products. Section VI shows how to measure whether the prices to different buyers move in concert and classifies the various products according to how similar are price changes to different buyers. Section VII examines some specific implications the results have for the prediction of price behavior. Section VIII examines whether there is any relationship of the various characteristics of price movements to the industry's structural characteristics.

I. The Stigler-Kindahl Data

Stigler and Kindahl collected data mainly from buyers on actual transaction prices paid for a variety of products. They tried to correct for any explicit or implicit discounting and for any changes in the specifications of the product. Although there is undoubtedly some misreporting of prices, and some unrecorded product changes (for example, physical characteristics, point of delivery, time of delivery), it is the most accurate and comprehensive data I know of on individual transaction prices.

The buyers who report prices are typically firms in the *Fortune* 500. The identity of the seller is not known.[2] Typically, there is only scant information on quantity purchased, though it is believed that during the course of the reporting buyers were using the product regularly. Ideally, actual transaction prices are reported monthly. However, in several instances, prices are reported less frequently. A decision on how (or whether) to interpolate prices had to be made.

If the price is unchanged between reportings, I assume that the intervening price is also unchanged. If the price is not the same, then I create two different series. One method assumes a change in each unobserved month. The other assumes only one change over the entire period. For example, suppose that for January, the price is $10, and for April, it is $20 with missing reports for February and March. The first interpolation approach assumes that the price was $13.33 in February and $16.67 in March (i.e., linear interpolation), while the second interpolation approach assumes that the price changed to $20 in either February, March, or April. (It turns out that the results on length of rigidity are unaffected by which particular month is assumed for the price change in this second approach.)

The period of observation is January 1, 1957 through December 31, 1966. Few associations between buyers and seller last for

---

[2] The form in which the data exist do not allow conclusive determination that the buyer is dealing with only one seller. However, it is believed that only one seller is involved when the buyer is reporting prices pursuant to a contract. Furthermore, when prices remain unchanged or when the specification of the good remains unchanged from observation to observation, the buyer is also likely to be dealing with only one seller. I thank Claire Friedland, who helped collect the original data, for helpful discussions on this matter. For expositional ease, I will regard each price series as arising from a transaction between one buyer and one seller. I will point out when this assumption would substantially alter the interpretation of the results.

the entire ten-year period, a point which I analyze later on. Transactions often take place under "contract" and the length of the contract (for example, semiannual, annual) is indicated. The Appendix provides additional information on each type of transaction. Many contracts specify neither a price nor quantity. They seem not to be binding legal documents, but rather more like agreements to agree.

The commodities chosen for study were preselected by Stigler and Kindahl to contain many that others had claimed were characterized by inflexible prices. The commodities are intermediate products used in manufacturing. Within broad commodity classes, finer product distinctions are made. So, for example, one can examine the general category of steel or a specific product category like carbon steel pipe less than 3 inches in diameter. Even within fine product specifications, the individual transactions will probably not involve perfectly homogeneous goods. Therefore, I never compare absolute price levels across products, but instead look only at percentage changes in price and compare movements in percentage changes in price across buyers.

There are a few instances where price series are believed to be list prices, and those prices have been excluded from the analysis. Also excluded are price series that contain inconsistent information. For example, a series is excluded if the reporter claims to produce prices through 1965, but instead prices only through 1960 appear. For several transactions, the product undergoes a specification change. When this occurs, I treat the prices under the new specification change as a new transaction.

II. Analysis of Product Groups

Table 1 describes the price rigidity present in the individual transaction prices by product group. The first column in Table 1 lists the type of product purchased. Column 2 lists the number of buyer-seller pairings that are observed for goods of unchanged specification. (One pairing could last anywhere from 1 month to 10 years.) Column 3 lists the average duration of price rigidity. This

last figure is computed as the average length of spell for which price remains unchanged. For example, if the observations on monthly price were $5, $5, $5, $6, $6, $7, $7, $7, $7, the average rigidity would be three months. The procedure for calculating an average rigidity actually involves an underestimate since the price before the period of observation may have been $5 and the price after the period of observation may have been $7. Calculations including and excluding the beginning and ending spells were done with no material change in the substantive interpretation of the results. The calculations in Table 1 are based on the second method of interpolation of prices (only one price change between missing observations—see Section I) and include the beginning and the end of each price series. Column 4 reports the standard deviation in the rigidity of prices. Column 5 reports the same estimate of price rigidity as in column 3, except that only "monthly" contract series are used. These series have fewer missing observations than the other types of transactions, hence much less interpolation is needed. (In fact, the results on rigidity for monthly contracts are similar for the two methods of interpolation.) If the implication of the numbers in column 3 across commodities differ greatly from those in column 5, one might be suspicious of the interpolation used in column 3. I expect price flexibility of monthly contracts to exceed that of all other contract types, so column 5 really puts a lower bound on column 3.

To avoid misinterpretation of the results, it may be helpful to review a standard issue in duration analysis. Imagine that there are two observed transactions, each lasting for a one-year period and each involving the same size of monthly purchase. The first transaction involves a different price each month, while the second involves the same price each month. There are 13 spells of rigidity, 12 of which last one month and one of which lasts twelve months. Based on spells, the average rigidity is $24 \div 13$ or 1.8 months with 92 percent of the spells lasting one month and 8 percent lasting twelve months. Conditional on a price change just having occurred, the average time to the next price

TABLE 1—PRICE RIGIDITY BY PRODUCT GROUP

Product Group (1)	Number of Buyer-Seller Pairings[a] (2)	Average Duration of Price Rigidity (Spells) (Months) (3)	Standard Deviation of Duration (Spells) (Months) (4)	Average Duration of Price Rigidity Monthly Contracts (Spells) (Months) (5)	Average Duration of Price Rigidity (Transactions) (Months) (6)
Steel	348	13.0	18.3	9.4	17.9
Nonferrous Metals	209	4.3	6.1	2.8	7.5
Petroleum	245	5.9	5.3	2.5	8.3
Rubber Tires	123	8.1	12.0	7.8	11.5
Paper	128	8.7	14.0	8.8	11.8
Chemicals	658	12.8	10.7	9.6	19.2
Cement	40	13.2	14.7	5.6	17.2
Glass	22	10.2	12.1	8.5	13.3
Truck Motors	59	5.4	6.3	3.7	8.3
Plywood	46	4.7	7.7	1.2	7.5
Household Appliances	14	3.6	3.6	2.5	5.9

[a]A "pairing" means a transaction over time for a good of constant specification.

change is 1.8 months. Yet, one-half of all goods sold involve a rigid price over the entire period. In other words, holding monthly purchases constant, the analysis based on spells underestimates the fraction of goods sold with rigid prices. The results in columns 3 and 5 utilize spells data. Therefore, even though I have no quantity information, I expect that these results underestimate the fraction of goods sold at rigid prices.

In column 6, I calculate price rigidity using a transaction as the unit of analysis, not a "spell." For each transaction, I calculate the average price rigidity, and then take an average (with each transaction weighted according to its length) over all transactions. Return to the earlier example of two transactions, each lasting one year, but one involving 12 price changes and the other no price changes. An analysis based on *transactions* (not spells) would calculate average rigidity to be $(1+12)/2$ or 6.5 months. It is that type of calculation that is reported in column 6.

Several interesting facts emerge from Table 1. In several industries, prices are on average unchanged over periods exceeding one year. The degree of price inflexibility varies enormously across products groups. Steel, chemicals, and cement have average rigidities exceeding one year while household

appliances, plywood, and nonferrous metals have average price rigidities of less than five months. For any one product group the standard deviation of rigidity is quite high. In fact, the standard deviation tends to rise as the average duration of rigidity rises. The simple correlation and the Spearman Rank Correlation between the standard deviation and the average duration (cols. 3 and 4) are both above .80. This suggests (though does not prove) either that each product group presented in Table 1 contains heterogeneous products which differ widely in their price flexibility or that for even a homogeneous product a great heterogeneity in price flexibility is present.[3]

Column 5 shows that using monthly contracts rather than all contracts does not change the basic implications of column 3 regarding price rigidity across groups. Column 6 shows that, as expected, the average of price rigidity rises when the unit of analysis is a transaction. Indeed, the results of

[3]An alternative explanation is that price movements for the same product are similar across different transactions at any one instant but not across time. As we will see in Section VI, this explanation will turn out to be incorrect.

TABLE 2—FREQUENCY OF DURATION OF PRICE RIGIDITY FOR VARIOUS TYPES OF
TRANSACTIONS BASED ON SPELLS OF PRICE RIGIDITY[a]

Product	Type of Transaction	Percent of all Trans-actions	Number of Pair-ings[b]	0–3 Months	4 Mo.– 1 Year	1–2 Years	2–4 Years	Over 4 Years
Steel	Annual	3	11	.11	.41	.24	.22	.03
	Quarterly	53	185	.34	.26	.18	.12	.09
	Monthly	32	111	.48	.27	.15	.07	.04
Nonferrous Metals	Annual	4	8	.16	.69	.12	.03	0
	Quarterly	19	40	.61	.29	.08	.02	.02
	Monthly	42	87	.78	.20	.02	.01	0
Petroleum	Annual	27	66	.20	.69	.07	.04	0
	Quarterly	15	37	.74	.23	.02	.00	–
	Monthly	7	16	.83	.15	.02	0	–
Rubber Tires	Annual	26	32	.19	.72	.07	.01	.01
	Quarterly	37	45	.34	.48	.11	.04	.04
	Monthly	20	24	.44	.44	.07	.01	.06
Paper	Annual	17	22	.04	.69	.18	.08	.01
	Quarterly	2	3	.17	.42	.29	.08	.04
	Monthly	28	36	.46	.36	.12	.04	.02
Chemicals	Annual	43	286	.11	.58	.17	.09	.06
	Quarterly	11	72	.37	.30	.12	.16	.04
	Monthly	20	134	.53	.27	.09	.06	.04
Cement	Annual	20	8	.04	.78	.13	.04	0
	Quarterly	50	20	.19	.27	.23	.14	.05
	Monthly	10	4	.64	.29	.02	.04	.02
Glass	Annual	36	8	0	.87	.10	.03	0
	Quarterly	9	2	.25	.50	.19	0	.06
	Monthly	41	9	.51	.22	.18	.09	0
Truck Motors	Annual	14	8	.05	.86	.09	0	0
	Quarterly	2	1	.21	.57	.21	0	0
	Monthly	58	34	.69	.26	.04	.01	0
Plywood	Annual	0	0	0	0	0	0	0
	Quarterly	96	44	.64	.29	.04	.02	.01
	Monthly	4	2	.99	.02	0	0	0
Household Appliances	Annual	21	3	0	.82	.18	0	0
	Quarterly	0	0	0	0	0	0	0
	Monthly	57	8	.78	.22	0	0	0

[a] The numbers in the rows of the table may not add to one because of rounding.
[b] The "Number of Pairings" is not the number of spells of price rigidity in all contracts. See the discussion preceding Table 1, and the footnote to Table 1.

column 6 are striking in that they show that every product group has an average rigidity in excess of roughly six months, and that 6 of the 11 product groups have average rigidities of roughly one year or more.

In Table 2, more detailed evidence is provided on the time pattern of price rigidity by product group for three types of transactions. The three transaction types are monthly, in which case the transaction occurred monthly (with no necessary future commitment), quarterly monthly in which case the

transaction was monthly but was observed quarterly, and annual in which case the transaction was pursuant to an annual contract. For most product groups, these three types of transactions account for well over 60 percent of all transactions. (See the Appendix for a description of the various types of transactions that comprise the sample.) One important point to note about these transactions is that an annual "contract" rarely means a price change every twelve months, nor does a monthly contract mean a price change every month. Although annual contracts do involve more rigidity than monthly ones, it is incorrect to think of contracts as inflexible price rules set at specified intervals. A more appropriate view is that they are flexible agreements that can be renegotiated when and if the need arises.

The results in Table 2 show that, as one would expect from Table 1, the pattern of rigidity across product groups is highly varied. As a general rule, all product groups for each of the three transaction types in Table 2 are characterized by spells of price rigidity that in the majority of cases last less than one year. Some commodities like non-ferrous metals and plywood are characterized by very flexible prices with over 60 percent of all spells in the monthly and quarterly monthly category lasting less than three months. On the other hand, there are definitely a substantial number of transactions involving very inflexible prices. For example, in steel, over 39 percent of the spells of rigid prices in the annual and quarterly monthly category (which comprises over half of all the transactions in steel) last more than one year. Other commodities with important transaction types showing fairly inflexible prices include paper, chemicals, cement and glass. In fact, a histogram analysis based on transactions (not spells) shows that 50 percent or more of all transactions involving steel, cement, chemicals, or glass, have average rigidities of one year or more for frequently used contract types.

As one would expect, the annual category involves less price flexibility than the quarterly category which itself exhibits less flexibility than the monthly category. It is also interesting to note that even within a particular product group and transaction type, there is a high degree of heterogeneity in price flexibility. For example, for chemicals monthly, over 50 percent of spells of rigidity are less than three months, but still a significant fraction (10 percent) involve spells of rigidity in excess of two years. This suggests that within any one product grouping, either the products sold are different, or the buyer-seller pairings have different properties, or the method chosen to allocate (i.e., price vs.

nonprice) across different pairings of buyers and sellers is simply different.[4]

One issue frequently raised in discussions of price flexibility is the cost of making a price change (see, for example, Robert Barro, 1972). There are many types of costs associated with a price change. New price sheets have to be constructed, price information must be conveyed to buyers, buyers may find planning more difficult, buyers may distrust sellers if prices change often, search costs are higher if prices change often, and so on. The real question is how important are these costs. One way to address this question is to see how important small price changes are. Table 3 reports the percent of all price changes that are less than 1/4, 1/2, 1, and 2 percent, in absolute value for the same product groups and transaction types reported in Table 2.

Table 3 makes two points. First, very small price changes occur more often in monthly than in quarterly monthly or in annual transaction types. Second, and most important, there are a significant number of price changes that one would consider small (i.e., less than 1 percent) for most commodities and transaction types. This finding presents a bit of a puzzle if buyers are homogeneous. Either the cost of changing price is small or the costs of being at the "wrong" price—even one off by 1 percent—are very high.[5] Yet these explanations have difficulty explaining how it can be that some transactions seem to involve prices that do not change over long periods. Another explanation is that perhaps price does not need to

---

[4]Alternatively, the heterogeneity in spells could arise because supply and demand are changing over time. This last explanation turns out not to provide the full answer, as we shall see in Section VI. Moreover, a table analogous to Table 2, based on transactions, not spells, confirms the heterogeneity across transactions.

[5]Even if the fixed cost of changing price is small, one cannot necessarily rule out large welfare effects caused by this fixed cost. In a model with distortions, even small fixed costs can lead to large welfare losses. See, for example, N. Gregory Mankiw (1985) and George Akerlof and Janet Yellen (1985). Furthermore, the presence of even small fixed costs might affect the time-series properties of economic variables. See, for example, Julio Rotemberg (1982) and Olivier Blanchard (1982).

TABLE 3—FREQUENCY OF SMALL PRICE CHANGES BY PRODUCT GROUP
BY CONTRACT TYPE

	Percent of Price Changes less than				Average Absolute Price Change (Percent)
Product	1/4 Percent	1/2 Percent	1 Percent	2 Percent	
Steel:					
Annual	4	8	11	27	3.3
Quarterly	5	11	17	24	4.2
Monthly	9	20	36	52	2.5
Nonferrous Metals:					
Annual	2	5	9	27	7.0
Quarterly	2	5	12	25	5.0
Monthly	8	15	28	49	2.9
Petroleum:					
Annual	0	0	8	24	5.3
Quarterly	0	0	2	17	5.4
Monthly	1	5	19	47	2.9
Rubber Tires:					
Annual	12	21	30	44	3.0
Quarterly	7	11	18	34	4.5
Monthly	13	23	38	63	2.3
Paper:					
Annual	4	9	8	27	6.3
Quarterly	0	19	24	33	3.6
Monthly	13	23	43	62	2.0
Chemicals:					
Annual	4	8	13	24	7.7
Quarterly	0	5	11	24	7.3
Monthly	5	14	30	42	5.0
Cement:					
Annual	14	22	32	46	3.3
Quarterly	0	0	1	19	4.1
Monthly	71	75	85	94	5.0
Glass:					
Annual	0	0	7	19	6.5
Quarterly	0	0	20	40	6.2
Monthly	3	20	45	67	2.1
Trucks, Motors:					
Annual	3	3	12	20	3.9
Quarterly	0	0	0	8	7.2
Monthly	12	27	50	75	1.7
Plywood:					
Annual	–	–	–	–	–
Quarterly	1	2	6	19	6.1
Monthly	19	38	54	72	1.9
Household Appliances:					
Annual	0	0	0	25	4.3
Quarterly	–	–	–	–	–
Monthly	22	44	70	95	.8

change in those transactions for which prices are unchanging (i.e., neither supply nor demand curves are shifting). This explanation runs into the problem that, as is suggested from Table 2 (and as will be confirmed later on), within the same product grouping there are likely to be changing prices for one transaction at the same time that there are constant prices for another. The only possible explanations consistent with efficiency seem to be either that firms differ in their allocation ability with some firms relying on price more than others, or, alternatively, that every firm must rely more on price when dealing with certain buyers than with others.[6]

The foregoing analysis can also shed light on the question of whether there is an asymmetry in price movements. For example, are prices rigid downward? If prices are rigid downward, then one can think of the fixed cost of changing price as being higher for price declines than price increases. If so, the minimum positive price change should be less than the minimum negative price change. In fact, an analysis of minimum positive and negative price changes reveals no such pattern.

III. Relationship Between Price Rigidity, Price Change, and Length of Buyer-Seller Association

If within a particular product group, there is a wide degree of heterogeneity in price rigidity across buyers, are there any predictable correlations that emerge between price rigidity, price change, and length of buyer-seller association?[7] There are several different theories of price rigidity and the theories often have different implications for these correlations. I now investigate three questions.

First, is there a positive correlation between length of association and price rigidity across transactions for the same product?[8]

---

[6]I recognize the possibility that nonefficiency explanations may help explain some pricing behavior (for example, Akerlof-Yellen and Daniel Kahneman, Jack Knetsch, and Richard Thaler, 1986), but feel that the efficiency explanations have not yet been fully explored (see my forthcoming paper).

[7]Length of association is measured as the total time the buyer and seller have engaged in a transaction for a product whose specifications may change over the time of the association. This measure is a noisy one, because the buyer and seller may be engaged in other transactions which affect their knowledge of each other, and may have been dealing with each other prior to the beginning of the data set. Moreover, to the extent that a buyer reported prices from several suppliers, rather than one, for each reported price series, the measure of length of association is flawed. (See fn. 2.)

[8]See Table A1 for data by product group on average length of association and average price change. Table 1 reports average duration of price rigidity. Correlation of these three variables across product groups is not as

That is, if buyer A has been dealing with his seller for ten years, while buyer B is beginning a new relationship, are buyer A's prices more rigid? One rationale for this relationship would be that if buyers and sellers deal with each other over long time periods, they set one average price and thereby save on the transaction cost of changing price constantly. However, it is quite possible to justify the reverse relationship. The impediment to changing price may be that the buyer or seller may feel the other side is taking advantage of him (see, for example, Williamson). If buyers and sellers have been dealing with each other for a long period of time, it will be in their interest not to take advantage of the other in the short run for fear of damaging the ongoing relationship (see, for example, Lester Telser, 1980). If buyers and sellers know each other well, because of their long-standing relationship, this fear of being taken advantage of in the short run will be reduced. In such a case, flexible prices may emerge.

Second, is there an inverse correlation between the size of price change and duration of price rigidity across transactions within the same product group? That is, if buyer A purchases steel on a contract in which price changes frequently, while buyer B has a contract in which price changes infrequently, are the price changes (when they occur) of buyer A larger (in absolute value) than those of buyer B? This relationship would make sense if prices are rigid on some transactions because there is a cost to changing price. If so, one would expect that those transactions with the most rigid prices (those to buyer B) have the highest costs of changing price and therefore only large price changes will be observed on those contracts. An alternative prediction would be that some prices are rigid because buyers (or sellers) want price stability for insurance-type reasons. In such a case, price changes on the more rigid con-

---

good a way of uncovering systematic relationships among these three variables as is correlation of the three variables across transactions for the same product, because many factors differ between product groups.

tract could well be smaller than on the flexible price contract since the function of insurance is to smooth out price fluctuations.

The third question is whether there is a negative association between length of association and the size of price change. If buyers' and sellers' distrust of or lack of knowledge about each other explains rigid prices, then the longer the association, the lower the cost of changing price, and hence the more flexible should be price and the smaller the observed price changes. The opposite prediction could emerge from a theory in which buyers and sellers who deal with each other over long periods care about getting only the average price right. In such a case, one would expect to see rigid prices that infrequently change. When they do change, they will change by larger amounts than prices in less rigid contracts.[9]

Table 4 reports the correlations between length of association, price change (absolute value), and rigidity for each product group, and indicates when the correlations are statistically significant at the 10 percent level, 5 percent level, and 1 percent level.[10] A strong positive association between length of association and rigidity exists only for chemicals, while a strong negative association exists for petroleum, household appliances, and truck motors. To the extent any general relationship exists between length of association and rigidity, it is a *negative* one. The second column of Table 4 indicates that there is a *positive* association between price change and rigidity. All but one correlation is positive, and all seven statistically significant correlations are positive. The third column suggests that there is a *negative* correlation between length of association and price change. All but two correlations are negative, and all five statistically significant correlations are negative.

TABLE 4—CORRELATIONS OF
CONTRACT CHARACTERISTICS

	Correlation Between:		
Product	Length of Association and Rigidity	Rigidity and Average Absolute Percent Price Change	Length of Association and Average Absolute Percent Price Change
Cement	.28	.17	.24
Chemicals	.16^c	.10^a	−.12^b
Glass	−.11	.69^c	−.24
Household Appliances^d	−.87^c	.71^b	−.66^b
Nonferrous Metals	.12	.12	−.15^b
Paper	.03	.20	−.25^a
Petroleum	−.25^c	−.06	−.09
Plywood	.10	.54^c	−.11
Rubber Tires	−.08	.43^c	−.27^b
Steel	.03	.14^b	.01
Trucks, Motors	−.56^c	.60^a	−.23

^{a}Statistical significance at the 10 percent level.
^{b}Statistical significance at the 5 percent level.
^{c}Statistical significance at the 1 percent level.
^{d}Based on only 11 observations.

In short, the evidence in Table 4 is *consistent* with the following explanation. Buyers and sellers who do not have long associations are more likely to use fixed price contracts because they don't trust or know each other. The "cost" of changing price on such a contract is to risk creation of mutual distrust. Prices change on these contracts only for substantial price movements. Buyers and sellers who have long associations aren't as worried about mutual distrust. Hence, price changes are more frequent (i.e., less rigid prices) and on average smaller.[11]

One common explanation for price (or wage) rigidity has to do with insurance. I have not incorporated that explanation into the one just given for several reasons. First, recent work (Sherwin Rosen, 1985) casts doubt on the theoretical underpinnings of an

---

[9]This assumes that price changes are motivated by changes in the permanent price component whose changes are assumed larger than the transitory component. The reverse relation between permanent and transitory would flip the prediction.

[10]My 1986 working paper reports data on average rigidity, average price change, and average length of association by product by type of contract.

[11]A model that would generate such results would be one where costs are undergoing a random walk, production is constant returns to scale, and the cost of changing price is negatively related to length of association.

insurance explanation. Second, large firms should be able to diversify such risks, and hence not need insurance.[12] Third, as we will see in the next section, the insurance explanation does not seem supported by the data.

IV. Relationship Among Types of Transactions

Do some buyers seek out stable pricing arrangements in which the price changes infrequently? If so, one would expect to see a correlation in the rigidity of pricing across transactions of different commodities. For example, if the transactions of a particular buyer who purchased steel involved price changing much less frequently than the industry average, will it also be the case that the buyer's transactions involving paper have prices that change less frequently than the industry average?

For the product categories of Table 1, I have calculated for each buyer a vector of the average price rigidity for each of the commodities he purchases. I then examine pairs of products to see if there is a correlation across firms in these rigidities, (i.e., does a firm buying steel with overly rigid prices buy paper with overly rigid prices?) There are 227 buyer firms in my sample. There are many fewer (around 60) who purchase any two commodities. The pairwise correlations were primarily positive, but in most cases the correlations were not statistically significant, and were often sensitive to the interpolation method used to calculate price rigidity. The most stable and statistically significant results were the (positive) correlations between price rigidity for contracts in steel and rubber, metals and plywood, and rubber and cement.[13] Because of the instability of the results, these results should be regarded as at best weak support that buyers may have certain preferences across transaction types for different products.

V. Analysis of Specific Products

One drawback to the analysis of the previous sections is that the product groups may be so broad that a heterogeneity appears in the results which is caused only by the heterogeneous nature of the products in any one commodity group. To remedy this problem, I analyzed 32 specific products. These 32 products were chosen primarily because there were numerous data on them. The products analyzed are listed in Table 5 along with information similar to that presented in Table 1.

The results are similar to those of Table 1 in several respects. As in Table 1, there is wide variation across products in the rigidity of price. Even within a single detailed product specification, there still exists a great deal of heterogeneity in durations of spells of rigidity. The standard deviation of duration rises with the average duration.[14] One is struck by the rigidity of some prices. Even for monthly contracts, there are many products (for example, chlorine liquid, steel plate) where the average length of a spell of price rigidity is well over one year. And, column 6 indicates that, using transactions as the unit of analysis, most commodities have average durations of price in excess of eight months.

In Table 6, I present the histograms of spells of price rigidity by commodity for a frequently used contract specification. The pattern that emerges is similar to that in Table 2. Even within detailed product specification for a particular contract type, there is considerable heterogeneity in length of spells of price rigidity. This suggests that the price of a good is changing for some transactions but not for others.[15] Table 6 reveals that although most prices do not remain in effect for over one year, for many products (for example, steel plate, hot rolled bars and rods, oxygen) a significant number of spells (over 20 percent) of rigid prices remain in effect for over two years.

---

[12] This must be qualified by agency theories of monitoring.

[13] One curious finding is that price rigidity is negatively correlated at a statistically significant level for truck and steel contracts.

[14] The simple and rank correlations of average duration and the standard deviation of duration exceed .9.

[15] Histograms like Table 6 based on a transaction (not spell) as the unit of analysis confirm this.

TABLE 5—PRICE RIGIDITY FOR DETAILED PRODUCT SPECIFICATIONS[a]

Product (1)	Number of Buyer-Seller Pairings (2)	Average Duration Price Rigidity (Spells) (Months) (3)	Standard Deviation of Duration (Spells) (Months) (4)	Aver. Duration of Price Rigidity Monthly Contracts (Spells) (Months) (5)	Average Duration of Price Rigidity (Transactions) (Months) (6)
Steel plates	28	18.5	19.4	21.6	20.3
Hot rolled bars and rods	33	15.1	17.6	10.6	17.5
Steel pipe and tubing (3" or less in diameter)	33	12.1	16.4	12.7	15.9
Copper wire and cable (bare)	26	3.8	5.4	2.6	4.1
Gasoline (regular)	66	6.2	5.7	2.7	8.9
Diesel oil #2	75	4.7	4.3	1.4	6.9
Fuel oil #2	41	7.3	4.9	4.6	8.3
Residual fuel oil #6	59	6.5	6.4	2.9	9.2
Container board, fiberboard	28	11.6	8.0	11.5	12.6
Caustic soda (liquid)	33	16.2	22.9	27.6	21.3
Chlorine liquid	28	19.9	18.7	60.0	27.1
Oxygen, cylinders	30	16.8	14.6	36.3	21.5
Acetylene	22	16.0	16.2	26.4	21.9
Portland cement (sack)	28	16.4	16.8	–	19.0
Steel sheet and strip, hot rolled	25	18.6	18.5	–	19.1
New rail (RR)	20	22.1	31.4	17.1	23.2
Tie plates (RR)	18	21.9	33.0	20.0	23.0
Steel wheels "one wear" (RR)	25	21.4	22.6	24.0	24.9
Track bolts (RR)	18	14.5	17.4	4.4	17.2
Zinc slab ingots	9	5.1	5.4	4.4	5.6
Coal (RR)	20	6.8	12.2	1.4	15.9
Kraft wrapping paper	12	7.5	6.0	5.7	9.2
Paper bags	16	9.4	5.3	20.0	10.3
Sulfuric acid, bulk	15	14.1	18.7	22.3	20.9
Sulfuric acid	19	11.0	17.1	5.1	19.5
Methyl alcohol	18	12.3	12.9	17.4	17.8
Phthalic anhydride	10	7.2	6.1	6.8	8.3
Succinate antibiotic	16	34.4	52.1	57.0	25.4
Kapseals antibiotic	16	56.1	66.7	40.0	44.0
Meprobanate tablets	16	13.8	12.0	18.7	15.5
Librium	13	19.1	23.1	56.0	20.9
Plywood	25	3.7	4.8	1.1	6.2

[a] See Table 1. The dashes in col. 5 indicate no data available.

In Table 7, I present the fraction of price changes that are less than 1/4, 1/2, 1, and 2 percent in absolute value in order to assess the importance of the fixed costs of changing price. Table 7 corroborates the message of Table 3. For most products, there are numerous (over 10 percent) instances of small price changes (below 1 percent). This fact reinforces my earlier conclusion that theories that postulate rigid prices solely because of a common high fixed cost of changing price to each buyer are not supported by the evidence. (See the discussion of the results of Table 3.) The most reasonable explanation is that firms and buyers must differ in their need to rely on the price system to achieve

TABLE 6—HISTOGRAMS OF DURATIONS OF RIGIDITY BY DETAILED
PRODUCT SPECIFICATION BASED ON SPELLS OF RIGIDITY

Product	0–3 Mo.	3 Mo.– 1 Yr	1–2 Yrs	2–4 Yrs	Over 4 Yrs
Steel plate	.24	.24	.23	.18	.11
Hot rolled bars and rods	.36	.21	.21	.16	.07
Steel pipe and tubing (less than 3″ diameter)	.39	.31	.16	.10	.05
Copper wire and cable (bare)	.67	.30	.02	0	.01
Gasoline (regular)(A)	.33	.59	.05	.03	0
Diesel oil #2	.79	.22	0	0	0
Fuel oil #2 (A)	.03	.88	.08	.02	0
Residual fuel oil #6 (A)	.22	.64	.07	.06	0
Container board, fiberboard (A)	0	.73	.19	.06	0
Caustic soda (liquid)(A)	.10	.64	.14	.06	.06
Chlorine liquid (A)	0	.69	.14	.10	.06
Oxygen, cylinders	.32	.27	.14	.26	.01
Acetylene	.37	.24	.15	.21	.01
Portland cement (bag or sack)	.19	.32	.24	.14	.05
Steel sheet and strip, hot rolled	.25	.27	.19	.21	.08
New rail	.53	.07	.16	.06	.18
Tie plates	.53	.08	.17	.06	.16
Steel wheels "one wear"	.13	.35	.22	.22	.09
Track bolts	.27	.34	.23	.06	.11
Zinc slab ingots	.44	.44	.09	.03	0
Coal, for RR	.60	.23	.11	.03	.03
Kraft wrapping paper	0	.40	.40	.20	0
Paper bags	.17	0	.67	.17	0
Sulfuric acid, bulk	.68	.18	.08	0	.05
Sulfuric acid (A)	.13	.56	.20	.05	.05
Methyl alcohol (A)	.38	.38	.15	.07	.01
Phthalic anhydride	.47	.41	.09	.03	0
Succinate antibiotic	0	.30	0	.50	.20
Kapseals antibiotic	0	.08	.08	.31	.54
Meprobanate tablets (A)	.14	.67	.11	.06	.03
Librium (A)	.13	.39	.22	.17	.09
Plywood	.73	.23	.03	.01	.01

Note: All contracts are monthly or quarterly monthly, unless followed by (A) which indicates annual. The numbers in rows may not add to one because of rounding.

allocative efficiency and that the fixed costs of changing price varies across buyers and across firms.

An analysis of the minimum positive and negative price changes reveals no tendency for one to exceed the other. Just as in the earlier analysis, there appears to be no evidence to support asymmetric price changes.

In Table 8, I present information, comparable to Table 4, on the relationship between price rigidity, length of association, and average price change for transactions in the same product.[16] (Table A2 in the Appendix presents information by product on average absolute price change and average length of association.) The results mirror those of Table 4. There may be a weak negative correlation between rigidity and length of association. Of the 18 correlations,

[16] Most correlations involve between 20 to 30 observations, with 15 being the minimum number of observations required in order to be reported.

TABLE 7—FREQUENCY OF SMALL PRICE CHANGES BY
DETAILED PRODUCT SPECIFICATION

	Percent of Price Changes less than			
Product	1/4 Percent	1/2 Percent	1 Percent	2 Percent
Steel plate	0	1	11	16
Hot rolled bars and rods	1	8	13	28
Steel pipe and tubing (less than 3″ diameter)	4	6	14	27
Copper wire and cable (bare)	3	5	8	19
Gasoline (regular)(A)	0	1	13	27
Diesel oil #2	0	0	2	19
Fuel oil #2 (A)	0	0	7	22
Residual fuel oil #6 (A)	0	0	2	25
Container board, fiberboard (A)	4	4	4	12
Caustic soda (liquid)(A)	2	5	11	15
Chlorine liquid (A)	6	13	17	31
Oxygen, cylinders	0	0	3	14
Acetylene	0	10	18	23
Portland cement (bag or sack)	0	0	1	19
Steel sheet and strip, hot rolled	0	2	7	13
New rail	1	3	6	10
Tie plates	3	5	5	9
Steel wheels "one wear"	4	4	10	16
Track bolts	1	3	14	16
Zinc slab ingots	6	6	11	20
Coal (RR)	3	8	18	37
Kraft wrapping paper	3	8	20	53
Paper bags	0	20	20	60
Sulfuric acid, bulk	3	12	34	54
Sulfuric acid	1	1	57	76
Methyl alcohol (A)	0	15	24	32
Phthalic anhydride	0	0	0	0
Succinate antibiotic	0	0	0	0
Kapseals antibiotic (A)	0	0	0	50
Meprobanate tablets (A)	0	0	0	27
Librium (A)	0	0	0	14
Plywood	1	3	7	18

Note: See Table 6.

only 4 were statistically significant. Two negative correlations were significant at the 1 percent level, while the positive correlations were significant at the 5 and 10 percent levels. (However, the number of positive correlations exceeded the number of negative ones.) The evidence on the correlation between price change and rigidity is clearer. Of the 9 significant correlations, 8 were positive. The number of positive correlations exceeded the number of negative ones. The evidence on the correlation between price

change and length of association suggests a negative correlation. Of the 5 significant coefficients, all were negative. (However, the number of negative correlations equalled the number of positives.)

VI. The Heterogeneity of Price Movements Across Buyers

The previous evidence reveals that price movements across different transaction types for the same commodity may be very differ-

TABLE 8—CORRELATIONS OF CONTRACT
CHARACTERISTICS

Product	Length of Association and Rigidity	Correlation Between: Rigidity and Average Absolute Percent Price Change	Length of Association and Average Absolute Percent Price Change
Steel sheet and strip, hot rolled	–	– .40[a]	–
Steel plate	.07	– .11	.27
Hot rolled bars and rods	– .00	.32[a]	.26
Steel pipe and tubing (3″ or less in diameter)	– .21	.19	– .32[a]
Plywood	.10	.04	– .34[a]
New rail	.14	.41[a]	– .64[b]
Tie plates	–	.47[b]	–
Steel wheels "One wear"	.07	– .33	– .14
Track bolts	–	.54[b]	–
Copper wire and cable, bare	– .06	.76[c]	– .20
Coal, for RR	–	– .14	–
Gasoline	.02	.08	– .02
Diesel oil #2	– .74[c]	– .22	.27
Fuel oil #6	– .12	– .02	– .14
Sulfuric acid, bulk	.51[b]	– .06	– .45[b]
Sulfuric acid	– .52[c]	.15	.10
Caustic soda, liquid	.35	.58[c]	.22
Chlorine, liquid	.40[a]	– .00	– .56[b]
Oxygen cylinders	.10	– .17	.07
Acetylene	.04	.50[b]	.12
Methyl alcohol	.21	.53[c]	.02
Portland cement, in bag or sack	.34	.19	.33

[a] Significance at the 10 percent level.
[b] Significance at the 5 percent level.
[c] Significance at the 1 percent level.

ent. In this section, I investigate in more detail the heterogeneity of price movements for the same commodity. By limiting the analysis to transactions of the same type, I have automatically screened out considerable heterogeneity. Despite this, I still find a startling amount of heterogeneity. I limit the analysis to annual contracts or quarterly monthly and monthly contracts, depending on the available data. I group price movements from quarterly monthly and monthly together on the grounds that they both represent price series whose prices are not nec-

essarily expected to remain in force for more than one month.

I use two methods to describe how heterogeneous price movements are. The first method measures the difference in the stochastic structure of each price change series while the second attempts to measure correlation in price movements across different transactions.

The first method computes for each individual price series the variance in the percent changes in price (actually the first difference of the log of the price series). A variance σ is computed for each transaction price series. If all the price series have the same stochastic structure, this variance should be the same across different price series for the same commodity. For each of 30 commodities, I present the mean variance (i.e., the mean of σ^2), the variance of σ^2 (i.e., a measure of how σ^2 varies across transactions), and the coefficient of variation (square root of variance of σ^2 divided by the mean).[17]

Table 9 shows that, in general, the individual price series within any one commodity and transaction type seems to be quite different from one another. The commodities that seem to have the least homogeneous transactions are steel pipe, oxygen, sheet steel, steel railway wheels, and coal.

Another method of characterizing the degree of heterogeneity among price series is to look at the correlation of contemporaneous price changes. A slight extension of this method is to examine the correlation of filtered price series. An example will illustrate.

Suppose two monthly price series are

```
    10 10 10  10  5  5  5   5  7.5 7.5 7.5 7.5,
and 10 10 10   5  5  5  5  7.5 7.5 7.5 7.5 7.5
```

One might be especially interested in seeing how closely the percent changes in the price series are correlated. The two derived series of percent price changes are

```
–  0  0   0  –50%  0  0   0  50%  0  0  0
–  0  0 –50%    0   0  0  50%   0  0  0  0
```

---

[17] Some products from Table 5 were dropped because of data incompleteness.

TABLE 9—MEASURES OF HETEROGENEITY AMONG PRICE SERIES

Product	Mean Variance of Individual Price Change	Variances of Individual Price Change	Coefficient of Variation
Steel plate	1.33 (10-6)	1.56 (10-9)	29.7
Hot rolled bars and rods	1.73 (10-6)	3.64 (10-9)	34.9
Steel pipe and tubing (3″ or less in diameter)	3.31 (10-6)	2.27 (10-8)	45.5
Copper wire and cable, bare	1.45 (10-5)	4.36 (10-8)	14.4
Gasoline	6.22 (10-5)	1.03 (10-6)	16.3
Diesel #2	1.59 (10-5)	6.50 (10-8)	16.0
Fuel oil #2 (A)	2.93 (10-5)	1.02 (10-7)	10.9
Fuel oil #6	2.57 (10-5)	4.54 (10-7)	26.2
Container board, fiberboard	2.94 (10-5)	5.62 (10-9)	2.5
Caustic soda, liquid	5.26 (10-5)	4.89 (10-8)	4.2
Liquid chlorine (A)	8.48 (10-6)	6.57 (10-8)	30.2
Oxygen, cylinders	3.07 (10-5)	2.49 (10-6)	51.4
Acetylene	6.66 (10-6)	4.63 (10-8)	32.3
Portland cement	1.97 (10-6)	4.79 (10-9)	35.1
Sheet steel and strip (hot rolled)	4.64 (10-6)	1.63 (10-7)	87.0
New rails	9.95 (10-7)	1.44 (10-10)	12.1
Tie plates	1.55 (10-6)	1.43 (10-10)	7.7
Steel railway wheels	9.51 (10-7)	8.08 (10-9)	94.5
Railroad track bolts	2.87 (10-6)	4.93 (10-9)	24.5
Zinc slab, ingot	6.21 (10-5)	7.09 (10-8)	4.3
Coal (RR)	9.15 (10-6)	1.60 (10-7)	43.7
Sulfuric acid, bulk (A)	5.92 (10-5)	1.91 (10-6)	23.3
Sulfuric acid (A)	5.54 (10-5)	9.05 (10-7)	17.2
Methyl alcohol (A)	7.24 (10-5)	1.55 (10-7)	5.4
Phthalic anhydride	2.78 (10-4)	1.52 (10-6)	4.4
Succinate (A)	5.42 (10-6)	3.13 (10-8)	32.6
Kapseals (A)	2.52 (10-6)	2.77 (10-9)	20.9
Meprobanate tablets (A)	2.59 (10-4)	3.83 (10-6)	7.6
Librium (A)	6.39 (10-5)	5.40 (10-7)	11.5
Plywood	2.08 (10-5)	1.43 (10-7)	18.2

Note: See Table 6.

It appears that the two series have no correlation in percent changes. But that conclusion is misleading. Both series change within one month of each other. Suppose that one constructs a new series that takes the arithmetic average of the last two monthly percent changes in prices. Then one obtains two series that look like

```
- - 0    0   -25% -25% 0  0   25% 25% 0 0
- - 0 -25% -25%    0  0 25% 25%    0 0 0
```

The correlation between the two new series will be positive and will equal .5. If one uses a three-month filter (i.e., average over the last three monthly percent changes in price), the correlation rises to .67. In general, one initially expects correlation to rise as the period of averaging increases.

Before presenting tabulations of correlations by product for different filter sizes, it will be helpful first to decide what is a "high" or "low" correlation. In other words, we must develop some underlying standard as to how closely two very related series should move. Suppose we adopt the position that two price series that change by identical amounts within, say, three months of each other are "highly" correlated. Let $\rho(F)$ be the contemporaneous correlation of the two price series when averaging over F periods is performed. Suppose that the two series representing percent price changes are identical, are displaced from each other by three months, and that price changes are independent of the preceding price change. Then, it is easy to show that

$$\rho(1) = \rho(2) = 0$$

$$\rho(F) = 1 - 3/F \qquad F > 3.$$

This means that for a filter of size 6, the correlation between our two series is .5, and rises to .75 for filters of one year. In general, one should expect that very high correlations (above .7) will probably be unusual for filters below twelve months, even for "well-behaved" price series.

Each of 30 products was analyzed separately. For each product, and for each contract type an average correlation for a particular filter size was computed. For example, suppose that there are 10 individual contract transactions for steel plates, each lasting ten years. The monthly percent change in price (differences in log of price) was calculated for each series for each month. The simple correlation was computed for every combination of contracts (i.e., 45 pairs) and an average correlation over the 45 pairs was then computed. If the average correlation is high, it says that on average the price series move together. If the average correlation is low, it suggests that price movements for the same good are only very loosely related to each other. If the low correlation persists as the filter increases to say two years, it says that knowing how person A's price has changed over a two-year period doesn't help much in predicting how person B's price will change (averaged over the two-year period).

In Table 10, I present measures of average correlation for filters of one month and twelve months for each of the 30 commodities for selected contract types.[18] As ex-

TABLE 10—HETEROGENEITY MEASURES: CORRELATIONS AMONG PRICE SERIES

Product[a]	$\rho(1)$[b]	$\rho(12)$[b]
Steel plate (M)	.42	.61
Hot rolled bars and rods (M)	.42	.60
Steel pipe and tubing (M)		
(3″ or less in diameter)	.16	.25
Copper wire and cable (M)	.53	.78
Gasoline (A)	.02	.07
(M)	.04	.30
Diesel fuel #2 (A)	.00	.06
(M)	.53	.69
Fuel oil #2 (A)	.01	−.03
Fuel oil #6 (A)	.02	.11
(M)	.26	.49
Container board,		
fiberboard (A)	.14	−.03
(M)	.06	.16
Caustic soda, liquid (A)	.07	.07
(M)	.04	.36
Liquid chlorine (A)	.05	.08
Oxygen, cylinders (A)	.03	.17
(M)	.28	.40
Acetylene (M)	.30	.54
Portland cement (M)	.15	.21
Steel sheet and strip, (M)		
hot rolled	.40	.44
Rails (M)	.81	.94
Tie plates (M)	.78	.88
Steel railway wheels	.37	.54
Railroad track bolts	.47	.62
Zinc slab ingots (M)	.52	.90
Coal (RR) (M)	.14	.17
Phthalic anhydride (M)	.27	.68
Sulfuric acid, bulk (A)	.13	.32
Sulfuric acid (A)	.10	.07
Methyl alcohol (A)	.22	.46
Succinate (A)	0.0[c]	0.0[c]
Kapseals (A)	0.0[c]	0.0[c]
Meprobanate tablets (A)	.03	−.07
Librium (A)	−.02	−.06
Plywood (M)	.16	.21

[a] Contracts are either quarterly monthly or monthly (indicated by M) or annual (indicated by A).

[b] $\rho(i)$: Correlations of price changes averaged over i months.

[c] No price movement in most contracts.

pected, $\rho(12)$ usually exceeds $\rho(1)$. If we use the criterion that correlations on the order of .5 and above represent price series that move pretty closely together, we see that for several

---

[18] Filters of 2 years produced results similar to those for filters of 1 year. Correlations were also calculated on

the timing of price changes (i.e., 0 or ±1 indicating whether or not a price change occurred and its direction) and the same low correlations persisted.

products, there is a homogeneity of price movements. On the other hand, there are several products like cement, container board, plywood, and several chemical products that have very low (sometimes even negative) correlations even for twelve-month averaging. In fact, it is startling to find so many products where it is clear that some mechanism other than only price is allocating resources.[19] It is noteworthy that container board exhibits low correlations of price, since I understand that quantity rationing is sometimes used in the paper industry in place of price rationing.[20]

It is interesting to see whether there is any agreement between the two methods of characterizing heterogeneity in Tables 9 and 10. In fact, there is a low degree of agreement. The simple correlation between the measures of heterogeneity in Tables 9 and 10 is below .1 and is not statistically significant. On the other hand, there is a high degree of statistically significant (negative) correlation between $\rho(1)$ (or $\rho(12)$) and other measures of heterogeneity such as the coefficients of variation for rigidity, price change, and length of association.[21] This may imply that the measure in Table 9 is capturing an aspect of price different from the other measures or, alternatively, that the measure in Table 9 is not a useful one.

VII. Implications for Price Behavior

Tables 1 through 10 can form the foundation for several predictions. For example, one could predict the following:

1) The products with high correlations for $\rho(12)$ in Table 10 should tend to have more serial correlation in their *WPI* component than products with low correlations;

2) Industrywide price adjustment for products with high values for $\rho(1)$ in Table 10 should tend to be swift;

3) Price controls on products with long spells of rigid prices (Table 1) are less likely to have harmful efficiency effects than controls on products with short spells of rigidity because nonprice methods are probably already used for products with very rigid prices to allocate resources.

I have not systematically investigated these three claims for each of the products listed in Table 10. However, I have done some work to corroborate at least some of the claims for some products. For example, from Table 10 copper wire and cable has a $\rho(12)$ of .78 while gasoline (monthly) has a $\rho(12)$ of only .30. The correlation between the monthly *WPI* and the monthly *WPI* lagged once (1957–66) for copper wire and cable is .99 which, as expected, exceeds that same measure (.88) for gasoline.[22]

Michael Bordo (1980) has estimated adjustment lags in prices for some of the commodity groups well represented in Table 10, such as metals and metal products, chemicals, and fuel. Based on the size of $\rho(1)$ in Table 10, I would predict the speed of adjustment to be fastest in metals and metal products, and the speed of adjustment in fuels and chemicals to be much slower and roughly equal to each other. In fact, Bordo (p. 1105) finds the mean lag of price adjustment for metals and metal products to 3.66 months, while the lag for fuels and chemicals are 6.64 and 6.20 months, respectively.

Finally, the only evidence I could find on the difficulty of price controls is John Kenneth Galbraith's *A Theory of Price Control* (1952) which is an account of his experience in controlling prices during World War II when he headed the Office of Price Administration (OPA). Although he does not deal explicitly with all the products in Tables 1–10, he does talk about steel products, which from Table 1 have a high degree of price rigidity. Galbraith states: "The Office of Price Administration controlled the price of all steel mill products with far less manpower and trouble than was required for

---

[19] My 1979 article presents a theory on buyer heterogeneity, which shows how prices to different buyers can exhibit low (or negative) correlations.

[20] Based on personal discussions with industry members.

[21] Table A3 in the Appendix reports these correlations.

[22] The source for *WPI* data was Stigler and Kindahl (Appendix C).

a far smaller volume of steel scrap...it is relatively easy to fix prices that are already fixed" (p. 17).

Although bits of evidence corroborate the predictions for some types of commodities, they obviously are far from conclusive. They do, however, show the value of evidence like that in Tables 1 through 10.

VIII. Structural Determinants of Price Behavior

Is there any correlation between industry characteristics and any of the measures of heterogeneity such as those in Tables 9 and 10? Using 30 products, I correlated the measures of heterogeneity in price movements of Tables 9 and 10 with the following variables: 1) mean absolute growth and variability of price (the higher is this number the higher the expected correlation of price movements); 2) measures of competitiveness (a) four-firm concentration ratio and (b) fraction of shipments beyond 500 miles; 3) growth and variability of total industry shipments; 4) length of buyer-seller association. Simple correlations never emerged statistically significant (with the exception of the variance of the growth rate in price), though the correlations were generally in the positive direction. However, since no more than 30 observations were available, it would be premature to conclude that these structural characteristics do not influence price heterogeneity in the industry.

Is there any correlation between concentration and duration of price rigidity or length of association or average price change? The only significant correlation was between concentration (four firms) and duration of price rigidity. That correlation was statistically significant at the 5 percent level. The correlation implies that for every 10 point increase in the four-firm concentration ratio, prices remain rigid for an extra 1.6 months.[23] This finding is particularly inter-

[23] The *OLS* equation is (standard errors in parentheses)

$$Av. \; Duration = \underset{(3.12)}{4.97} + \underset{(6.08)}{16.12} \; CR\,4 \quad \begin{matrix} R^2 = .22 \\ SEE = 4.9 \end{matrix}$$

where *Av. Duration* is the average length of a spell of

esting because it suggests that allocations are performed differently in concentrated and unconcentrated markets. I believe it is premature to draw the conclusions, implicit in the work of Means, Arthur Burns (1936), Galbraith, and others, that the markets have stopped working when they become concentrated. Instead, an alternative interpretation is that as firms become large they supplant the market's exclusive reliance on price as an allocation device and resort to other methods. In a world filled with transaction costs, exclusive reliance on a market-generated price to allocate goods could well be inferior to other nonprice allocation methods. It is the case, however, that markets that use nonprice allocation will respond to market shocks much differently than markets that exclusively use price to allocate. See my forthcoming paper for a fuller development of this theory.

IX. Conclusions

Since this paper began with a summary of the empirical results, I will not repeat them here. The main conclusion is that several of the empirical results are sufficiently startling that we should reexamine the central, often exclusive, role assigned to the price mechanism in theories of efficient resource allocation. It is not necessarily that the price mechanism has failed, but rather that alternative allocation mechanisms are used in addition to the price mechanism to achieve efficiency.

price rigidity and *CR 4* is the four-firm concentration ratio. This equation is based on 27 observations. The *CR 4* variable is the 1963 four-firm concentration ratio for the 5-digit SIC code that seems to correspond to the product. This correspondence is not exact and, for that reason together with the small number of observations, the results should be regarded with some caution. Another interesting finding involving concentration is that concentrated industries have a greater frequency of small price changes.

TABLE A1—CHARACTERISTICS OF CONTRACTS BY PRODUCT

Product	Average Length of Association Between Buyer and Seller (Months)	Average Size of Absolute Value of Percent Price Change	Product	Average Length of Association Between Buyer and Seller (Months)	Average Size of Absolute Value of Percent Price Change
Steel	105	3.5	Cement	103	3.0
Nonferrous Metals	86	4.0	Glass	91	4.2
Petroleum	87	4.4	Truck Motors	82	2.7
Rubber Tires	98	3.9	Plywood	114	5.0
Paper	91	3.4	Household		
Chemicals	81	7.0	Appliances	75	1.0

TABLE A2—CHARACTERISTICS OF CONTRACTS BY PRODUCT

Product	Average Length of Association Between Buyer/Seller (Months)	Average Size of Absolute Value of Percent Price Change	Product	Average Length of Association Between Buyer/Seller (Months)	Average Size of Absolute Value of Percent Price Change
Steel plates	108	3.8	New rail (RR)	116	3.9
Hot rolled bars and rods	109	3.7	Tiel plates (RR)	119	4.5
Steel pipe and tubing			Steel wheels "one wear"		
(3" or less in diameter)	114	4.6	(RR)	119	3.8
Copper wire and cable			Track bolts (RR)	119	4.2
(bare)	68	4.4	Zinc slab ingots	104	4.8
Gasoline (regular)	91	3.3	Coal (RR)	119	3.7
Diesel oil #2	94	4.3	Kraft wrapping paper	94	4.3
Fuel oil #2	89	4.6	Paper bags	88	4.8
Residual fuel oil #6	73	5.8	Sulfuric acid, bulk	96	4.8
Container board,			Sulfuric acid	103	3.5
fiberboard	78	5.2	Methyl alcohol	91	7.1
Caustic soda (liquid)	84	7.8	Phthalic anhydride	93	11.7
Chlorine liquid	89	5.0	Succinate antibiotic	58	8.3
Oxygen, cylinders	109	11.5	Kapseals antibiotic	70	14.9
Acetylene	116	6.9	Meprobanate tablets	64	12.1
Portland cement			Librium	48	8.6
(by sack)	104	3.7	Plywood	110	5.2
Steel sheet and strip,					
hot rolled	120	5.9			

TABLE A3—CORRELATIONS AMONG MEASURES OF HETEROGENEITY

	CV DUR	CV DP	CV ASSOC	CV VAR	$\rho(1)$	$\rho(12)$
CV DUR	1	.88[a]	.41[a]	−.03	−.63[a]	−.60[a]
CV DP		1	.35[a]	.39[a]	−.57[a]	−.66[a]
CV ASSOC.			1	−.58[a]	−.47[a]	−.30
CV VAR				1	.08	−.01
$\rho(1)$					1	.91[a]
$\rho(12)$						1

Notes: CV DUR = coefficient of variation of duration; CV DP = coefficient of variation of the absolute value of price change (log difference); CV ASSOC = coefficient of variation of the length of association; CV VAR = coefficient of variation of the actual price changes counting no change as zero change; $\rho(1), \rho(12)$ = correlations of price changes averaged over i months.
[a]Significant at 5 percent level.

APPENDIX

Transactions were classified into one of ten categories by Stigler and Kindahl. The most important classifications include:

Annual contract: contract in force for one year.
Annual average: average of transaction prices during the year.
Annual monthly: annual observations of a transaction that occurs monthly.
Semiannual contract: contract in force for six months.
Semiannual average: average of transaction prices during six months.
Quarterly contract: contract in force for three months.
Quarterly average: average of transaction prices during the quarter.
Quarterly monthly: quarterly observation of a transaction that occurs monthly.
Irregular: irregular.
Monthly: monthly observations of a transaction that occurs monthly.

Tables 1A and 2A of my 1986 working paper report the importance of each classification by product group and for individual products.

REFERENCES

Akerlof, George A. and Yellen, Janet L., "Can Small Deviations from Rationality Make Significant Differences to Economic Equilibrium?," *American Economic Review*, September 1985, *75*, 708–20.

Barro, Robert, "A Theory of Monopolistic Price Adjustment," *Review of Economic Studies*, January 1972, *39*, 17–26.

Blanchard, Olivier J., "Price Desynchronization and Price Level Inertia," NBER Working Paper 900, 1982.

Bordo, Michael, "The Effects of Monetary Change on Relative Commodity Prices and the Role of Long-Term Contracts," *Journal of Political Economy*, December 1980, *88*, 1088–109.

Burns, Arthur, *The Decline of Competition*, New York: McGraw-Hill, 1936.

Carlton, Dennis W., The Rigidity of Prices, NBER Working Paper 1813, 1986.

_____, "The Theory and The Facts of How Markets Clear: Is Industrial Organization Valuable for Understanding Macroeconomics?," in R. Schmalensee and R. Willig, eds., *Handbook of Industrial Organization*, Amsterdam: North-Holland, forthcoming.

_____, "Equilibrium Fluctuations When Price and Delivery Lags Clear the Market," *Bell Journal of Economics*, Autumn 1983, *14*, 562–72.

_____, "The Disruptive Effect of Inflation on the Organization of Markets," in R. E. Hall, ed., *Inflation*, Chicago: University of Chicago Press, 1982.

_____, "Contracts, Price Rigidity, and Market Equilibrium," *Journal of Political Economy*, October 1979, *87*, 1034–62.

_____, "Market Behavior with Demand Uncertainty and Price Inflexibility," *American Economic Review*, September 1978, *68*, 571–87.

Galbraith, J. K., *A Theory of Price Control*, Cambridge: Harvard University Press, 1952.

Hall, Robert E., "The Apparent Rigidity of Prices," NBER Working Paper 1347, 1984.

Kahneman, Daniel, Knetch, Jack L. and Thaler, Richard, "Fairness as a Constraint on Profit Seeking: Entitlements in the Market," *American Economic Review*, September 1986, *76*, 728–41.

Mankiw, N. Gregory, "Small Menu Costs and Large Business Cycles: A Macroeconomic Model of Monopoly," *Quarterly Journal of Economics*, May 1985, *100*, 529–38.

Means, Gardiner C., "Industrial Prices and Their Relative Inflexibility," U.S. Senate Document 13, 74th Congress, 1st Session, Washington 1935.

Mills, Frederick C., *The Behavior of Prices*, NBER General Series, No. 11, New York: Arno Press, 1927.

Okun, Arthur, *Prices and Quantities: A Macroeconomic Analysis*, Washington: The Brookings Institution, 1981.

Rosen, Sherwin, "Implicit Contracts: A Survey," *Journal of Economic Literature*, September 1985, *23*, 1144–75.

Rotemberg, Julio "Monopolistic Price Adjust-

658   THE AMERICAN ECONOMIC REVIEW   SEPTEMBER 1986

ment and Aggregate Output," *Review of Economic Studies*, October 1982, *49*, 517–31.

Stigler, George and Kindahl, James, *The Behavior of Industrial Prices*, NBER General Series, No. 90, New York: Columbia University Press, 1970.

Telser, Lester, "A Theory of Self-Enforcing Agreements," *Journal of Business*, January 1980, *53*, 27–44.

Williamson, Oliver, *Markets & Hierarchies Analysis and Antitrust Implications: A Study in the Economies of Internal Organization*, New York: Free Press, 1975.

Part IV
Unemployment Compensation

[10]

The Effect of Unemployment Insurance on Temporary Layoff Unemployment

By MARTIN FELDSTEIN*

Economists are now beginning to recognize that an understanding of temporary layoffs is crucial for a proper analysis of unemployment. In manufacturing, about 75 percent of those who are laid off return to their original employers. More generally, among all persons classified as "unemployed job losers," temporary layoffs account for about 50 percent of all unemployment spells. Temporary layoffs are an even larger fraction of cyclical changes in the number of job losers. While this group includes some seasonally unemployed, most temporary layoffs are induced by short random or cyclical fluctuations in demand. The conventional model of search unemployment is inappropriate for those on temporary layoff and the modern theory of the Phillips curve requires substantial modification because of the size and cyclical variation of temporary layoff unemployment.[1]

In a previous paper (1976), I showed analytically that our current system of unemployment insurance (*UI*) provides a substantial incentive for increased temporary layoff unemployment.[2] The present paper provides micro-economic evidence that *UI* actually has such a powerful effect. The estimates imply that the incentive provided by the current average level of *UI* benefits is responsible for approximately one-half of temporary layoff unemployment.

It is important to note that the current study shows that *UI* increases the *amount* of temporary layoff unemployment, but does not deal with the *mean duration* per spell. This distinction deserves emphasis because nearly all previous empirical work focused on the potential effect of *UI* on duration. This focus on duration is both unfortunate and surprising since *UI* can actually increase total unemployment while decreasing the mean duration per spell. While *UI* increases the duration of any *given* spell of unemployment, it may also induce more very short spells of unemployment. This possibility of reduced mean duration is clear in my 1976 theoretical analysis. An additional practical

*Professor of economics, Harvard University. I am grateful to the National Science Foundation for support of this research, to David Ellwood and Joseph Kahan for assistance with the statistical calculations, and to Richard Freeman, Zvi Griliches, Daniel Hamermesh, James Medoff, Melvin Reder, and Jeffrey Sachs for discussions and comments. Earlier versions of this paper were presented at seminars at Chicago, Harvard, and Yale universities.

[1] In my 1975 paper, pp. 737–42, I discuss the implications of temporary layoffs for the theory of search unemployment, the Phillips curve, and wage inflexibility. Although the standard criterion of unemployment is active job seeking within the past four weeks, individuals are officially classified as unemployed without any inquiry about recent job-seeking activity if they state that they are "on layoff awaiting recall by their employers." Some of those on layoff look for temporary jobs or alternative permanent employment, but the vast majority do return to their original employers. Readers should not be confused by the two quite separate meanings of the term "layoff" in the Department of Labor's lexicon. In manufacturing establishment data, a layoff is a separation initiated by the employer (not a quit) and may be permanent or

temporary. In the *Current Population Survey* (*CPS*), an individual is on layoff if he is not working but "has a job" to which he is expecting to be recalled by his employer. To emphasize that I am dealing with those layoffs expected to terminate in recall, I use the adjective "temporary." Unfortunately, the *CPS* uses the word temporary in a different and quite confusing way: persons on layoff are divided into an "indefinite duration" group (in which the individual does not have an expected date of recall within thirty days) and a "temporary" group (when such a date is known). When it is useful to distinguish these groups, I use the terms "indefinite duration" and "fixed duration"; in my usage, the term temporary layoff includes both groups.

[2] My 1976 paper is really an explicit proof of arguments made more informally in my earlier study for the Joint Economic Committee (1973). For a similar development, see Martin Baily.

matter reinforces this tendency. In the absence of *UI*, firms might be reluctant to lay off workers for short periods in response to random demand fluctuations, for fear of losing these workers to other firms, or at least of creating costly ill will; *UI* eliminates these problems and facilitates short-duration layoffs. In contrast, firms might have no choice but to lay off employees for long spells during the less frequent, but more protracted, spells of low demand. Unemployment insurance thus increases the number of spells of temporary layoff unemployment with a relatively greater increase for short spells. Since the duration should increase for any given spell, while the mix should change to add short spells that would otherwise not exist, the net effect of *UI* on duration is indeterminate. The existing estimates of the effect of *UI* on the mean duration of unemployment spells should therefore be regarded as an understatement—and, possibly, an extreme understatement—of the effect of *UI* on total unemployment.[3]

Although the presence of a labor union is not necessary to obtain the effects on temporary layoffs indicated by the theoretical analysis of *UI*, these predicted effects are likely to be magnified if the employees are unionized.[4] The basic reason is that employers are more willing to lay off workers when they are confident that they will return when recalled, while employees are more willing to be laid off if they can be confident that they will be recalled. Both conditions are more likely to be met in unionized firms where workers often receive compensation that exceeds their market al-

ternative, and have seniority privileges and pensions that are not portable. More directly, union contracts often guarantee that previous workers will be recalled before any new employees are hired (see U.S. Bureau of Labor Statistics, 1972). Finally, unionized firms may have more layoff unemployment because, as Freeman has suggested, unions provide an effective mechanism for expressing workers' collective preferences to management. All of this implies that temporary layoff unemployment should be higher for union members and suggests that the response of temporary layoff unemployment to *UI* benefits may also be greater.

The first section of this paper discusses the data and methods used in the present study. The econometric estimates are presented in Section II. The brief concluding section suggests some directions for future analysis and comments on the implications of the research for the optimal redesign of social insurance.

I. Data and Method

The current study uses a sample of nearly 25,000 individual observations collected by the *Current Population Survey* (*CPS*) to measure the effect of unemployment insurance benefits on temporary layoff unemployment. The estimated regression equations presented in the next section relate each individual's temporary layoff unemployment status (a binary variable equal to 1 if the individual is on temporary layoff) to three kinds of variables: 1) his potential *UI* benefit as a percentage of lost net wages; 2) his basic demographic characteristics; and 3) the basic characteristics of his employment. This section begins by discussing the *CPS* sample and the method of calculating the potential *UI* benefit "replacement ratio" for each individual. The measurement of demographic and employment characteristics is then discussed.

A. *The CPS Sample*

The *CPS* is the government household survey used by the Department of Labor to calculate official monthly unemployment

---

[3] This criticism applies more generally to those (like Stephen Marston) who measure the effect of *UI* on the average duration of all types of unemployment. Since *UI* is expected to induce additional temporary layoffs and the mean duration of temporary layoff unemployment spells is substantially less than that of other types of unemployment (see the author, 1975), *UI* may actually reduce the overall mean duration while increasing both total unemployment and the duration of every spell that would have existed without unemployment insurance.

[4] This paragraph reflects discussion with my colleagues Richard Freeman and James Medoff; see Medoff.

rates. About 60,000 households are interviewed each month about the employment activities of their members during the week prior to the survey. The March survey of each year also obtains information about labor force participation, employment, and earnings during the previous year. The current study uses the survey for March 1971, a period of relatively high unemployment.[5]

For this analysis, individuals were eliminated from this *CPS* sample if they were not in the experienced labor force, were reentrants to the labor force, or were self-employed; none of these groups is at risk of being laid off. Also eliminated because of the atypical character of their employment were employees in the public sector and in agriculture.[6] To avoid the problems associated with those who combine school and work, and with those on the verge of retirement, the sample was restricted to individuals between the ages of 25 and 55. Finally, a few observations were excluded, because data were missing on the individual's age, sex, color, marital status, industry and occupation of employment, union membership, or previous year's work experience. The sampling weights indicate that the resulting sample of 24,545 represents a population of 34.2 million persons.[7]

B. *Calculation of Potential UI Benefits*

The unemployment compensation benefits for which an individual is eligible depend on his previous earnings up to a ceiling of maximum benefits received by about half of all *UI* benefit recipients. Because unemployment insurance is actually a series of state programs that operate as part of a general federal system, the formulae relating benefits to past earnings and the maximum benefits differ among the states. In addition, dependents' benefits are also available in states with approximately one-third of covered workers.

The *CPS* collects no information about the unemployment insurance benefits received by the currently unemployed or the potential benefits of the employed.[8] A special computer program was therefore prepared to evaluate the potential *UI* benefits for each of the 24,545 individuals in the final *CPS* sample. The algorithm uses the particular rules for each individual's state of residence and incorporates information on his industry of employment, previous year's earnings and work experience, and number of eligible dependents.[9] As a rough test of the accuracy of this method, the program was used to determine the benefit eligibility and to calculate the benefits for *all* unemployed persons in the full *CPS* sample (and not the final subsample of 24,545 observations). The implied total benefits for March 1971 was $540 million; this is reasonably close to the total amount actually paid as reported by the individual state *UI* agencies, $630 million. The accuracy is likely to be greater for temporary layoffs for whom the reporting of previous year's income is much more reliable.

---

[5] The seasonally adjusted unemployment rate in March 1971 was 6.0 percent and had been stable during the previous three months. The March 1971 survey was not "selected," but was the first *CPS* tape that became publicly available. The use of that sample indicates the slow gestation of this project.

[6] Barry Chiswick presents evidence that the recent extension of unemployment insurance to agriculture has substantially increased the seasonality of employment and unemployment in agriculture. It will be important to see if that result is confirmed by data after the 1975 recession year.

[7] In 1971 there were 50.8 million persons in the labor force between the ages of 25 and 55. The difference between 50.8 million and 34.2 million represents primarily government employees, agricultural workers, and the self-employed.

[8] Individuals are asked about the total annual value of benefits received during the previous year, but these twelve-month recall data are notoriously bad and, in the aggregate, represent a 50 percent understatement of the amounts paid by the *UI* program.

[9] There is no information on "benefit exhaustion," i.e., on whether an individual has already been unemployed so long that his number of weeks of eligibility for benefits has been exhausted. However, for all types of unemployment, only about 20 percent of spells exhaust available benefits while, for those on temporary layoff, the percentage should be very much lower: in March 1974, only 4 percent of "job losers on layoff" were unemployed for more than twenty-six weeks, while 12 percent of "job losers with no job" were unemployed for that long (see the author, 1975, Table 4).

The central variable of interest is the ratio of the individual's potential unemployment insurance benefit to his foregone earnings net of marginal income and payroll taxes. This *UI* "benefit replacement ratio" measures the proportion of lost net-of-tax earnings that would be replaced by *UI* benefits. A 60 percent *UI* benefit replacement ratio implies that the unemployed individual would lose only 40 percent of his previous net-of-tax wage income. Stated differently, the benefit replacement ratio is analogous to a rate of tax levied on earnings when the alternative is insured unemployment; a 60 percent benefit replacement ratio implies that the individual, by working instead of collecting *UI*, receives additional income equal to only 40 percent of his total net wage. The computer program evaluated the benefit replacement ratio for each individual, using the federal income tax schedules, to evaluate a marginal tax rate for someone with the individual's family income and dependents who used the standard deduction. The relevant marginal social security tax rate and state income tax rate were added to the federal marginal tax rate.

Although theory predicts that the probability of being on temporary layoff is an increasing function of the benefit replacement ratio, there is no presumption of linearity. A movement in the benefit replacement ratio from 0.70 to 0.80 may increase unemployment by more than a movement from 0.30 to 0.40. To eliminate the restriction of a linear specification, equations are reported in the next section in which the continuous benefit replacement ratio variable (*BEN*) is replaced by a set of binary variables that classify individuals by their benefit replacement ratios: $BEN = 0$ (for those not eligible for benefits); $0 < BEN \leq 0.30$; $0.30 < BEN \leq 0.50$; $0.50 < BEN \leq 0.70$; $0.70 < BEN \leq 0.85$; and $0.85 < BEN$. This method has the further advantage that it can clearly separate those who are ineligible for benefits ($BEN = 0$) from the remaining variation in *BEN*.

Although I believe that this represents the best method of evaluating the benefit

replacement ratio with the available data, there are several problems that should be borne in mind in evaluating the results. First, there is no information on the extent of experience rating that is relevant for each individual's employer. If the extent of experience rating is uncorrelated with the benefit replacement ratio, ignoring experience rating does not bias inferences about the effect of the benefit replacement ratio on temporary layoff unemployment.[10] Second, there are three omissions that are likely to cause an overestimate of the impact of unemployment insurance on temporary layoff unemployment: cash and in-kind transfers that may be available to individuals on temporary layoff, the value of fringe benefits that are lost during unemployment, and the work expenses (transportation, meals, etc.) that are avoided during unemployment. None of these omissions is likely to be large for the quite short duration of unemployment that are relevant here. Moreover, to the extent that a higher probability of layoff is compensated by a higher gross wage (as implied by the firm's budget constraint), there will be an offsetting underestimate of the impact of *UI* on temporary layoff unemployment. It is difficult to assess the net effect of these countervailing influences, but the resulting bias is likely to be small.

It is much more important to understand that the regression coefficient of the benefit replacement ratio measures the effect of *interindividual differences* in unemployment benefits and that the effect of such differences is less than the effect of a *general* change in everyone's benefit replacement

---

[10]The regression of the unemployment variable on the benefit replacement ratio does, however, understate the effect on unemployment of differences in the net *UI subsidy*. The net *UI* subsidy is the difference between the benefits and the additional experience-rated tax payments induced by those benefits. In the notation of my 1976 paper, the net subsidy is $[1 - e(1 - t_y)]b$ where e is the ratio of induced employer tax to incremental benefits (i.e., the extent of experience rating), by the marginal personal income tax rate, and b is the weekly benefit. If $e(1 - t_y)$ were constant, the regression coefficient of b would understate the effect of changes in the net subsidy by a factor of $[1 - e(1 - t_y)]^{-1}$.

ratio. As a general rule, it is the employer who makes the decision to lay off and recall a worker, while the employee himself is essentially passive.[11] An employer can respond to his employees' benefit replacement ratios only as an average for the group whose layoff he is considering and not individually for each member in the group. It is because the relevant group of employees within a firm has similar benefit replacement ratios[12] that the individual benefit replacement information is relevant for understanding what is essentially an employer or employer-employee group decision. Since the benefit replacement ratios are not identical for the relevant group of the firm's employees, some part of the variation of *BEN* in the sample will not affect layoff unemployment. The effect of this is to make the estimated regression coefficient an underestimate of the effect of a *general* increase or decrease in all benefits.[13]

C. *Demographic and Employment Characteristics*

The demographic characteristics included in the analysis are the standard list of age,

sex, marital status, and race.[14] As I indicated above, separate equations are also estimated for men only. The sample is limited to individuals between the ages of 25 and 55. To avoid any assumption about the form of the relation between age and temporary layoffs, individuals are divided into four separate age groups and binary variables are used in the regression equation. The age groups included are 25–29, 30–39, and 40–49; the coefficient for persons 50–55 is implicitly zero. The other demographic variables are self-explanatory.

The potential role of unions was discussed briefly in the introduction. In the final *CPS* sample of 24,545, 6,845 individuals (or 27 percent of the sample) indicated that they were members of labor unions. There is no indication whether the individual's current employment is in a union job. This suggests that the estimated coefficient of the union variable may underestimate the full effect of unionization.

Individuals were classified according to industry group and occupation category and the corresponding binary variables were included in the regression to control for inherent "technological" differences among them in the likelihood of layoffs.[15] This procedure entails a danger of "overcontrolling" for the exogenous aspect of these variables. Individuals with high potential benefit replacement rates (for example, with low wage rates or high spouse income, or large families in states where dependents' allowances are paid) may seek employment in industries and occupations with high technological probabilities of layoff unemployment. To the extent that this is important, the regression coefficients will overstate the importance of the industry and occupation variables and will understate the impact of the benefit replacement ratio. Although it is not possible to model

---

[11]I say "as a general rule" because workers do frequently have "inverse seniority" privileges that permit more senior workers to *choose* to be laid off before or instead of others. See U.S. Bureau of Labor Statistics (1972) for a description of these privileges.

[12]The benefit replacement ratios are similar to the extent that members of the group have similar wages and, being located in the same state, have similar unemployment benefit schedules and state tax rates.

[13]This can be stated differently by noting that a firm can only perceive and respond to the mean *BEN* value for the relevant group of its employees and essentially ignores the *within-group variance*. A general change in all *UI* benefits shifts this mean while part of the sample variation includes the within-group variance. In still different language, the coefficient of *BEN* is biased down but the size of the bias is limited to the extent that the between-group variance is large relative to the within-group variance. This bias can be thought of as a classical "errors-in-variables" bias: the "true" value of *BEN required by the model* is the *mean* of the individual *BEN* values for the relevant employee group, while the *actual* individual *BEN* values may be regarded as equal to the "true" value plus an error. This errors-in-variables interpretation also indicates that there is a downward bias that is an increasing function of the within-group variance relative to the between-groups variance.

[14]It might be interesting to extend this list to other attributes that reflect differences in tastes for leisure, for example, education, home ownership, age of children of married women, etc. See, however, fn. 13.

[15]The twelve industry groups were combinations of two-digit industries. Recall that agricultural workers, the self-employed, and public employees were omitted from the sample. The nine occupation groups were combinations of more detailed two-digit classifications.

this simultaneous relationship, separate results will be presented with and without the industry and occupation variables.

The final variable considered in the analysis is the individual's wage rate. Temporary layoff unemployment is likely to be related to the individual wage in several quite different ways. First, for any given benefit replacement ratio, a higher wage implies both a higher absolute benefit and a greater absolute cost of unemployment; the sign of this effect is therefore indeterminate. Second, if a high wage reflects better pay relative to the individual's market opportunity,[16] the employer will be more likely to lay off workers with a confidence that they will return when recalled; this implies a positive coefficient for the wage variable. Third, a higher wage may *ceteris paribus* imply greater seniority; greater seniority means fewer involuntary layoffs relative to other employees within the firm, but a group with more seniority on average may have more temporary layoffs because workers are more likely to await recall.

Related to this seniority aspect is the possibility that more senior workers who are laid off perceive themselves (correctly) as only on temporary layoff, while their more junior coworkers who are laid off may regard the separation as permanent because their probability of recall is substantially lower. Finally, jobs with more layoffs may pay higher wage rates *ceteris paribus* than other jobs, implying that the gross wage is endogenous and positively related to the unemployment probability. While this source of wage variation is likely to be small relative to the wage variation reflecting individual skill differences, etc., some equations without this variable have been estimated to assess the effect of erring in the direction of its omission.

II. The Econometric Evidence

All of the equations that I have estimated imply that the current level of unemploy-

ment insurance benefits causes a substantial fraction of the observed temporary layoff unemployment. More specifically, the econometric evidence indicates that the temporary layoff unemployment rates would be reduced by approximately one-half if the adverse incentive provided by the current unemployment insurance were eliminated. This conclusion is not sensitive to the exclusion of questionable regressions or to the restriction of the sample to particular subsamples.[17]

Before looking at the estimated regression coefficients, it is helpful to examine the basic data on temporary layoff unemployment rates and *UI* benefit replacement ratios. In March 1971 the temporary layoff unemployment rate was 1.6 percent in the population corresponding to the final *CPS* sample of 24,545 employees; that is, on average, the corresponding population had a probability of 0.016 of being unemployed and on layoff during the sample week in 1971. The mean value of the benefit replacement ratio for this population was 0.55. Only 3 percent of the population was found to be ineligible for benefits[18] while 60 percent of the sample had benefit replacement rates above one-half and 30 percent had benefit replacement rates about 70 percent.[19]

Table 1 shows the temporary layoff unemployment rates corresponding to six levels of the benefit replacement ratio. This unemployment rate rises monotonically from 0.50 percent among the ineligibles ($BEN = 0$) to 2.17 percent in the highest benefit group ($BEN > 0.85$). Taken at face value, these unemployment rates imply that

[16] Recall that we are "holding constant" the effect of age, sex, color, unionization, industry, and occupation. It might be interesting to add education and other variables.

[17] The reader should remember the caveats and potential biases discussed in Section I; they will not be repeated here.

[18] Recall that the sample is restricted to eliminate many groups with no *UI* benefits, such as new entrants and the self-employed.

[19] The distribution of benefit replacement ratios for the population should not be confused with the distribution for the unemployed subgroup. The mean benefit replacement ratio of the unemployed was 0.59; if those with zero benefits are excluded, the mean benefit replacement rate for the eligible unemployed exceeds 0.60. This is consistent with the calculation that I presented for a range of hypothetical employees in my 1974 paper.

TABLE 1—UNEMPLOYMENT INSURANCE AND
TEMPORARY LAYOFF UNEMPLOYMENT[a]

UI Benefit Replacement Ratio (*BEN*) (1)	Percentage of Population (2)	Temporary Layoff Unemployment Rate (3)
0	3.3	0.50 (0.25)
$0 < BEN \leq 0.30$	8.4	1.26 (0.25)
$0.30 < BEN \leq 0.50$	27.9	1.30 (0.14)
$0.50 < BEN \leq 0.70$	30.0	1.80 (0.15)
$0.70 < BEN \leq 0.85$	23.4	1.83 (0.18)
$BEN > 0.85$	7.0	2.17 (0.35)
All Persons	100.0	1.60 (0.08)

[a] Based on the March 1971 *Current Population Survey* of 24,545 individuals. See text for definition of *BEN*. The figures in colums (2) and (3) are estimates of population rates based on *CPS* sampling weights. Approximate standard errors of the temporary layoff unemployment rates are shown in parentheses in column (3). (Note that these estimates are independent tabulations and not regression coefficients.)

reducing *BEN* to a maximum of 0.40 would lower the temporary layoff unemployment rate from 1.60 to 1.26, a reduction of 0.34 percentage points. It must, however, be borne in mind that this relation between benefits and temporary layoff unemployment rates is not adjusted for demographic or economic characteristics. We turn therefore to the multiple regression equations.

Table 2 presents the estimated coefficients of four basic regression equations. The dependent variable is binary, taking the value of 1 if the individual is unemployed and on layoff, and the value of 0 otherwise. The regression coefficients have all been multiplied by 100, converting the predicted dependent variable from a probability to a percentage unemployment rate. The sample means and proportions of the explanatory variables are shown in the first column.

Consider first the estimated coefficient of the benefit replacement ratio in equation (1).[20] The coefficient of 1.345 implies that

[20] Note that equation (1) includes all of the variables discussed in Section I; the coefficients of the twenty-seven industry and occupation variables are not shown since they are not of interest in themselves, and would require much extra space in the table.

the mean *BEN* value of 0.55 raises the mean temporary layoff unemployment rate by 1.345 x (0.55) = 0.74. Since the temporary layoff unemployment rate is 1.60, this equation implies that *BEN* is responsible for 46 percent of the observed temporary layoff unemployment rate. Because the industry and occupation variables may overcorrect for the truly exogenous effects of these variables, the basic specification is repeated without them as equation (2). The coefficient of the benefit replacement ratio rises slightly (to 1.545), implying that the mean benefit replacement ratio of 0.55 is responsible for 53 percent of the observed temporary layoff unemployment rate.[21]

The coefficient of the binary union variable in equations (1) and (2) provides strong evidence that union members are much more likely to experience temporary

[21] Omitting the other potentially endogenous economic characteristic variables (the gross wage rate and unionization) only lowers this coefficient to 1.515. (This equation is not shown in the table.) Other variants cluster around 1.3, rising as high as 1.7 and falling as low as 1.0. Replacing the gross wage rate by a set of six classification variables in gross wages has essentially no effect on the other coefficients.

TABLE 2—DETERMINANTS OF TEMPORARY LAYOFF UNEMPLOYMENT

Variable	Sample Means and Proportions	Regression Coefficients			
		(1)	(2)	(3)	(4)
BEN	0.55	1.345 (0.426)	1.545 (0.420)		
BEN = 0	0.03			−1.230 (0.539)	−1.484 (0.534)
0 < BEN ≤ 0.30	0.08			−1.552 (0.518)	−0.399 (0.516)
0.30 < BEN ≤ 0.50	0.28			−1.531 (0.391)	−1.343 (0.389)
0.50 < BEN ≤ 0.70	0.30			−1.074 (0.355)	−0.812 (0.356)
0.70 < BEN ≤ 0.85	0.24			−0.657 (0.344)	−0.490 (0.346)
Union	0.28	1.154 (0.204)	2.236 (0.183)	1.169 (0.204)	2.249 (0.183)
Age: 25–29	0.18	0.686 (0.270)	0.675 (0.270)	0.699 (0.270)	0.680 (0.270)
Age: 30–39	0.31	0.220 (0.238)	0.235 (0.239)	0.229 (0.238)	0.241 (0.239)
Age: 40–49	0.33	−0.196 (0.234)	−0.172 (0.235)	0.194 (0.234)	−0.168 (0.235)
Male	0.65	−1.460 (0.226)	−0.309 (0.195)	−1.279 (0.238)	0.189 (0.214)
Married	0.91	−0.267 (0.289)	−0.062 (0.289)	−0.243 (0.290)	−0.364 (0.291)
White	0.89	−0.068 (0.269)	−0.332 (0.261)	−0.068 (0.270)	−0.311 (0.262)
Gross Wage ($100)	1.64	0.202 (0.080)	0.127 (0.077)	.228 (0.094)	0.141 (0.092)
Industry-Occupation	−	a	−	a	−
Constant	−	2.025	0.333	3.687	1.931
Mean of Dependent Variable		1.601	1.601	1.601	1.601
N		24,545	24,545	24,545	24,545

Notes: All coefficients have been multiplied by 100, converting the dependent variable from a probability to a percentage unemployment rate. Standard errors are shown in parentheses. See text for description of sample and definitions of variables.

a Indicates that the twenty-seven industry and occupation variables were included in the equation.

layoff unemployment than nonunion members. The temporary layoff unemployment rate is 1.15 percentage points higher than the rate for nonmembers even after adjusting for this industry-occupation mix. Without that adjustment, the differential is 2.24 percentage points. I will return below to the evidence that the layoff unemployment rate of union members is also more sensitive to *UI* benefits.

The coefficients of the other variables are interesting but involve no important economic insights. There is clear evidence that the frequency of temporary layoff unemployment falls quite sharply with age,

a reflection of the powerful seniority system. There is no statistically significant difference between either whites and non-whites or marrieds and singles. Males appear to have a significantly lower temporary layoff unemployment rate when (but only when) the industry and occupation effects are included separately.[22]

[22] The sex differential is large and surprising to me. It may be an artifact of overadjustment for industry and occupation or it may reflect a real difference between the sexes. Women may be more likely to take seasonal work (within broad industry-occupation groups) or to have relatively long spells of temporary layoff. Nothing is known about these fascinating issues

Equations (3) and (4) replace the continuous benefit replacement ratio variable by a set of six binary classification variables. In each equation, an increase in the benefit replacement ratio always implies an increase in the predicted temporary layoff unemployment rates.[23] Both equations suggest that variations in the benefit replacement ratio below the 30 to 50 percent range have little effect on unemployment but higher benefit replacement ratios have a substantial adverse effect. The coefficients of the *BEN* variables in equation (3) imply that lowering *BEN* for everyone to 0.40 (with an implicit coefficient of −1.53) would reduce the temporary layoff unemployment rate to 0.46 percentage points.[24] With equation (4), the same calculation implies a reduction of the temporary layoff unemployment rate of 0.49 percentage points (with an implicit baseline coefficient of −1.40). It is not clear how much weight should be given to the implications of this more elaborate specification. On purely statistical grounds, there is little basis for choice; the reduction in the residual sum of squares in going from equation (1) to equation (3) is not quite significant at the 5 percent level, while going from equation (2) to equation (4) is not even significant at the 10 percent level.[25] The pattern of the coefficients does correspond to the a priori expectation that variations in benefit replacement ratios will have a weaker effect when *UI* benefits are "too small to bother taking into account" than when those benefits replace a substantial fraction of lost net wage income. However, the apparently weak effect at low benefit levels may reflect only the small fraction of the sample in this range; since only 11 percent of the sample had *BEN* values below 0.30, it is difficult to make any inferences about the effects of variations in benefits within the range below 0.30 or between this range and the next higher interval. It is probably best to remain agnostic on this question until more data become available.[26]

Table 3 confirms that union members have a substantially higher temporary layoff unemployment rate and are more sensitive to unemployment insurance benefits than are nonunionized workers. For the sample of 6,845 union members, the temporary layoff unemployment rate was 3.14 percent, twice the rate for the entire sample and thus three times the rate for nonunion members.[27] The coefficient of the benefit replacement ratio variable in equation (1) is 2.72, also about twice the corresponding coefficient for the entire sample.[28] A coefficient of 2.72 implies that the mean benefit replacement ratio of 0.54 (for union members) induces a 1.47 percent temporary lay-

---

and an adequate analysis would go beyond the proper focus of this paper.

[23] In equation (3) the step from "ineligible for benefits" to "eligible" appears to reduce temporary layoff unemployment. This implication should be given very little weight since the ineligible group is very small in the sample and the individuals who fall into that category are likely to have other special but unrecorded characteristics.

[24] There would be an additional long-run reduction in the temporary layoff unemployment rate as production and employment shift out of the industries and occupations with high rates of temporary layoff that are currently subsidized by unemployment insurance.

[25] This F-test is only appropriate as an approximation since the continuous *BEN* variable is only approximately a linear combination of the binary *BEN* variables. Henri Theil's $\bar{R}^2$ criterion also indicates only the slightest possible preference for the more complex specifications. All of the R^2 values are extremely low, approximately 0.02; this is common for household survey data with a low probability binary dependent variable.

[26] The coefficients of the *BEN* variables in equations (3) and (4) correspond quite closely to the conditional unemployment rates presented in Table 1; for example, an increase in *BEN* from 0.40 to 0.60 reduces the predicted temporary layoff unemployment rate by 0.50 percentage points in both the multiple regression equation and the unadjusted values of Table 1. It is clear from this comparison that replacing equations (3) and (4) by logit regression instead of ordinary least squares would be very unlikely to change any of the conclusions of the current analysis.

[27] The total rate of 1.601 is a weighted average of the union rate of 3.141 for 27.9 percent of the sample and 1.005 for the remaining 72.1 percent of nonunion members.

[28] The specification of equation (1) in Table 2 is exactly the same as equation (1) in Table 1 except that the union variable is now omitted. The coefficients of the other variables are not shown in order to save space.

TABLE 3—COEFFICIENTS OF BENEFIT REPLACEMENT RATIO VARIABLES FOR
UNION MEMBER SUBSAMPLE AND MALE SUBSAMPLE[a]

Variable	Subsample Means and Proportions	Union Members Only				Subsample Means and Proportions	Men Only			
		(1)	(2)	(3)	(4)		(5)	(6)	(7)	(8)
BEN	0.54	2.723 (1.499)	2.287 (1.495)				1.419 (0.708)	1.584 (0.696)		
BEN = 0	0.01			-2.460 (2.468)	-2.968 (2.471)	0.01			-2.349 (1.316)	-2.544 (1.319)
0 < BEN ≤ 0.30	0.07			-4.382 (1.518)	-3.755 (1.516)	0.12			-1.564 (0.869)	-1.491 (0.867)
0.30 < BEN ≤ 0.50	0.36			-3.876 (1.193)	-3297 (1.192)	0.40			-1.470 (0.795)	-1.367 (0.794)
0.50 < BEN ≤ 0.70	0.33			-2.834 (1.126)	-2.394 (1.128)	0.33			-0.985 (0.787)	-0.811 (0.788)
0.70 < BEN ≤ 0.85	0.19			-2.508 (1.106)	-2.296 (1.110)	0.12			-0.759 (0.816)	-0.680 (0.818)
Includes Industry-Occupation Variables?	–	Yes	No	Yes	No		Yes	No	Yes	No
Mean of Dependent Variable	3.141	3.141	3.141	3.141	3.141		1.600	1.600	1.600	1.600
Sample Size	6,845	6,845	6,845	6,845	6,845		15,873	15,873	15,873	15,873

[a]Each equation also contains age, sex, color, marital status, and wage variables and a constant term (as in Table 1); their coefficients are not shown to save space. The Men Only equations also contain a union variable. The table indicates when industry and occupation variables are included. The omitted BEN category corresponds to BEN > 0.85 and has an implicit coefficient of zero.

off unemployment rate, or 47 percent of the overall 3.14 percent rate.[29]

Although the mean benefit replacement ratio for union members is almost exactly the same as for the entire sample, the distributions of benefit replacement ratios differ noticeably. The replacement ratios for union members are clustered more closely around the average; 69 percent of union members have *BEN* values between 0.30 and 0.70, while 58 percent of the entire sample is in this range. Almost no union members appear to be ineligible for benefits. The coefficients of equations (3) and (4) also show that the temporary layoff unemployment rate varies inversely with the benefit replacement ratio. Both equations imply that increasing the benefit replacement ratio from 0.40 to 0.60 raises the tem-

porary layoff unemployment rate by about an entire percentage point.[30]

The results for the "men only" sample (presented in columns 5–8 of Table 3) are very similar to the estimates for the entire sample and need no detailed comment. The temporary layoff unemployment rate of 1.600 is almost identical to the rate for the entire sample (1.601). The regression coefficients differ substantially from the corresponding numbers of Table 1 only for the *BEN* = 0 subcategory; since only 0.01 percent of the men and 0.03 percent of the entire population are in this group, the comparison of the regression coefficients is without real substance.

Equations similar to those of Table 1 were also estimated with the "duration of

[29] Excluding the twenty-seven industry and occupation variables (as in equation (2)) reduces the coefficient slightly but leaves these conclusions essentially unchanged. The industry and occupation variables are themselves statistically significant so that equation (1) would be the clearly preferable specification except for the possible simultaneity problem noted in the text.

[30] The 1 percent of union members who are ineligible for benefits (*BEN* = 0) appear to have an unusually high layoff rate. This anomalous behavior also contributes to the relatively high standard error of the *BEN* variable in equations (1) and (2). The very small sample with *BEN* = 0 and correspondingly high standard error imply that no weight should be given to this group. For *BEN* > 0, equations (3) and (4) show a strong monotonic relation.

unemployment to date of survey" as the dependent variable. There was no significant relation between *BEN* and duration, implying that the effect of *UI* in inducing more short-duration spells of unemployment offset the effect of *UI* in lengthening the duration of spells that would otherwise have occurred.

Although I am tempted to compare the estimates presented in this section with the results of other recent studies, I believe that research is too dissimilar to warrant such comparison. There have been no previous econometric studies of the effect of unemployment insurance on temporary layoff unemployment. The recent econometric research has focused on the duration of unemployment spells or on the total unemployment rates for state aggregates.[31] There are several fascinating problems in the interpretation of these data, but their discussion belongs elsewhere.

III. Conclusion

The evidence presented in this paper implies that unemployment insurance has a powerful effect on temporary layoff unemployment. The average *UI* benefit replacement ratio implied by the current law can account for about half of temporary layoff unemployment. An increase in the *UI* benefit replacement ratio from 0.4 to 0.6 raises the predicted temporary layoff unemployment rate by about 0.5 percentage points, or one-third of the current average temporary layoff unemployment rate of 1.6 percent. Temporary layoff unemployment is more than twice as frequent among union members as among others between the ages of 25 and 55 who are in the experienced labor force. Unemployment insurance also has a correspondingly greater effect on that

unemployment rate among union members: an increase in the *UI* benefit replacement ratio from 0.4 to 0.6 raises the predicted temporary layoff unemployment rate of union members by a full percentage point.

These estimates must be understood as subject to the biases and caveats discussed in Section I. It would clearly be desirable to repeat this research with *CPS* data for a more recent year. A reanalysis with data from the National Longitudinal Survey would be useful because the temporary layoff character of the unemployment spell could be defined *ex post*. It would be particularly valuable to extend the current data to include information on the experience rated tax of each individual's employer. More generally, it would be useful to reexamine the effect of *UI* on temporary layoffs by studying data on a sample of individual firms in a variety of states.

I have refrained throughout this paper from making any normative judgments about the effect of unemployment insurance on layoff unemployment. It is clear, however, that our current *UI* program does impose an efficiency loss by distorting the behavior of firms to lay off too many workers when demand falls rather than cutting prices or building inventories. The substantial rate of temporary layoff unemployment suggests that this efficiency loss may be quite large.

The redesign of unemployment insurance is a difficult problem because the unemployed include the job losers who must find new jobs as well as those on temporary layoff. For those who are changing jobs, the optimal insurance must balance providing protection from financial loss against the distortion to socially inefficient search.[32] For those who are on temporary layoff, it is sufficient to eliminate the *subsidy* element in *UI* by making each firm repay in taxes the full value of the benefits paid its employees and by making *UI* benefits subject to the same taxation as other compensa-

---

[31] These studies include Kathleen Classen; Ronald Ehrenberg and Ronald Oaxaca; Herbert Grubel and Dennis Maki; Arlene Holen and Stanley Horowitz; Charles Lininger; Marston. It should be clear that the only reliable studies of duration effects *exclude* temporary layoffs and combine data for individuals in different states or years. See Daniel Hamermesh and Finis Welch for discussions of this research.

[32] This point is discussed in more detail in my 1973 paper. Baily provides an excellent formal solution of this optimization problem.

tion.[33] The difficult problem arises because the full experience rating that is optimal for temporary layoffs is not optimal for permanent layoffs: it would inappropriately discourage new hiring and desirable layoffs.[34] The problem cannot be solved by a lower tax for those layoffs who are not rehired since that would distort the rehire decision and waste job-specific human capital. The optimum balancing of these considerations is a complex problem that requires more information than is currently available. A formal analysis of the problem would be valuable because it would indicate more precisely the type of information required and might provide new insights about the optimal design even before that information is collected.

As a practical solution, I believe that much could be gained by having full employer experience rating for the benefits paid during the first month of each spell of unemployment (or some other moderately short period). It would also be important to tax individuals on *UI* benefits in the same way as other compensation is taxed. This combination of reforms would eliminate most of the subsidy currently provided for short spells of temporary layoff unemployment without unduly discouraging either new hiring or permanent separations.[35]

[33] See the author (1976).

[34] Firms can often assess a worker's quality only after he has worked for the firm for a period of time. If layoffs of unsuitable workers are made very expensive by experience rating, firms will be reluctant to hire new workers and, when they make a hiring mistake, to discharge those who were inappropriately hired.

[35] The bias against new hiring could be reduced further by making the "one-month experience rating" provision apply only to workers with a minimum of, say, six months of experience with the firm.

REFERENCES

M. N. Baily, "Unemployment Insurance as Insurance for Workers," *Econometrica*, July 1977, *45*, 1043–63.

Joseph Becker, *Experience Rating in Unemployment Insurance*, Baltimore 1972.

B. R. Chiswick, "The Effect of Unemployment Compensation on a Seasonal Industry: Agriculture," mimeo., Hoover Instit., Stanford Univ. 1975.

K. Classen, "The Effects of Unemployment Insurance: Evidence from Pennsylvania," mimeo., Center for Naval Analysis, Washington 1975.

R. G. Ehrenberg and R. L. Oaxaca, "Unemployment Insurance, Duration of Unemployment, and Subsequent Wage Gain," *Amer. Econ. Rev.*, Dec. 1976, *66*, 754–66.

M. Feldstein, "Lowering the Permanent Rate of Unemployment," Study for the Joint Economic Comm., 93d Cong., 1st sess. 1973.

_____, "Unemployment Compensation: Adverse Incentives and Distributional Anomalies," *Nat. Tax J.*, June 1974, *27*, 231–44.

_____, "The Importance of Temporary Layoffs: An Empirical Analysis," *Brookings Papers*, Washington 1975, *3*, 725–45.

_____, "Temporary Layoffs in the Theory of Unemployment," *J. Polit. Econ.*, Oct. 1976, *84*, 937–57.

R. B. Freeman, "Individual Mobility and Union Voice in the Labor Market," *Amer. Econ. Rev. Proc.*, May 1976, *66*, 361–77.

H. G. Grubel and D. R. Maki, "The Effect of Unemployment Benefits on U.S. Unemployment Rates," *Weltwirtsch. Arch.*, submitted for publication.

D. Hamermesh, "Unemployment Insurance and Unemployment in the United States," mimeo., Univ. Illinois 1976.

A. Holen and S. Horowitz, "The Effect of Unemployment Insurance and Eligibility Enforcement on Unemployment," *J. Law Econ.*, Oct. 1974, *17*, 403–32.

Charles A. Lininger, Jr., *Unemployment Benefits and Duration*, Ann Arbor 1963.

S. T. Marston, "The Impact of Unemployment Insurance on Job Search," *Brooking Papers*, Washington 1975, *1*, 13–48.

J. L. Medoff, "Layoffs and Alternatives under Trade Unions in U.S. Manufacturing," mimeo., Harvard Univ. 1976.

Henri Theil, *Economic Forecasts and Policy*, Amsterdam 1961.

F. Welch, "What Have We Learned from

Empirical Studies of Unemployment Insurance?," mimeo., Univ. California-Los Angeles 1977.

U.S. **Bureau of Labor Statistics,** *Layoff, Recall, and Worksharing Procedures*, Bull. 1425-13, Washington 1972.

_____, *Jobseeking Methods Used by American Workers*, Bull. 1886, Washington 1975.

_____, *Current Population Survey (CPS)*, data reported in *Manpower Report of the President*, Washington, Mar. 1971.

[11]

On Layoffs and Unemployment Insurance

By ROBERT H. TOPEL*

The problem studied in this paper is how current systems of providing and financing unemployment insurance (*UI*) affect the private decisions that generate unemployment. It is widely recognized that the provision of *UI* affects the search strategies of jobless individuals by raising reservation wages, thus increasing the average duration of unemployment spells.[1] In various forms, almost all empirical work on the impact of *UI* has studied this incentive. More recently, the focus of theoretical research has shifted to the role of *UI* in affecting the joint decisions of workers and firms that generate transitions *to* unemployment. Here the emphasis is on current methods of financing benefits—via partially "experience rated" payroll taxes on individual employers—and the incentives that these methods provide toward increasing the incidence of temporary layoff unemployment.[2] In terms of what is known about magnitudes of effects, this role of experience rating is probably the most important unresolved empirical issue in *UI* research. It is the main concern in this paper.

*Department of economics, University of Chicago, 1126 E. 59th Street, Chicago, IL 60637. I acknowledge support from the Center for the Study of the Economy and the State at the University of Chicago, and the U.S. Department of Labor. I have benefited from the comments of David Coppock, Joe Hotz, Sherwin Rosen, George Stigler, and Finis Welch, and of seminar participants at Chicago, Rochester, SUNY-Stony Brook, University of California-Los Angeles, and Yale University. Joe Tracy provided excellent research assistance.

[1] The empirical literature on duration effects of *UI* is large and continues to grow. For useful surveys of empirical estimates, see Finis Welch (1977) or Daniel Hamermesh (1979). Relatively recent contributions are Nicholas Kiefer and George Neumann (1979) and Steven Nickell (1979).

[2] The main reference is Martin Feldstein (1976). See also the discussions in Martin Baily (1976), and my article with Welch (1980). Temporary layoffs may account for as much as 50 percent of unemployment spells among workers who have separated from their previous jobs (quits, discharges, and layoffs). This share is strongly countercyclical, and is larger in manufacturing than elsewhere. See the discussion in Feldstein (1975), and my (1982a) article.

That current methods of financing unemployment insurance subsidize unemployment is undeniable; as it turns out, experience rating in determining employer taxes is normally incomplete, so that in almost all cases, the value of benefits received by unemployed workers exceeds their incremental cost to firms. The empirical magnitude of this wedge, which often equals or even exceeds the total money value of benefits paid out, can provide a powerful incentive toward increased layoffs. Despite this fact, however, previous research has been severely limited by the absence of any reliable measure of the experience rating subsidy to unemployment that is both relevant for individual workers, and that can be used in empirical analysis.[3]

My point of departure in this paper is in measuring the extent of subsidization that is implied by the structures of *UI* financing systems in the United States. Differences in these structures across states provide the empirical leverage needed to identify the incentive effects of the *UI* subsidy. The estimates reported below, based on a large sample of individuals from the 1975 Annual Demographic File of the *Current Population Survey* (*CPS*), indicate that incomplete experience rating may account for as much as 30 percent of all spells of temporary layoff unemployment. Additionally, most of the impact of *UI* on layoffs is accounted for by this subsidy; nonsubsidized benefits are found to have an insignificant impact on layoff decisions.

Appealing to the theory of job search, the duration of unemployment spells has played a prominent role in previous empirical research on the effects of *UI*. The incentives

[3] For example, Feldstein (1978) measures *UI* incentives by the ratio of available benefits to disposable weekly earnings. Nothing can be inferred from this variable about the role of experience rating and *UI* subsidization in affecting unemployment. Only Frank Brechling (1981) has attempted to tie experience rating attributes of states to measures of labor turnover.

that operate in the present context are quite different, however, and theory indicates that *UI* will affect *both* the probabilities that individuals enter unemployment (the frequency of spells, via layoff decisions) and that they leave unemployment (the duration of spells, via search and rehire decisions). The empirical methodology developed below estimates the effects of *UI*, and other variables, on each of these transitions. Consistent with theory, the estimates indicate that the *UI* subsidy increases unemployment by changing both the frequency and the expected duration of layoff spells. It is important to note that this methodology adjusts for the fact that *UI* may induce a greater number of short spells, which could actually reduce the mean duration of unemployment in any sample.

The paper is organized as follows. The first section develops the empirical foundation for the problem analyzed here, focusing on the structure of *UI* systems and methods of financing in the United States, and on the incentives implied for the joint employment decisions of workers and firms. Section II describes the data and the empirical strategy used to estimate *UI* effects on unemployment, and Section III reports the econometric evidence.

I. The Institutional Setting

Among unemployed individuals who have separated from their previous jobs (i.e., excluding entrants to the labor force), temporary layoffs and discharges consistently dominate quits, accounting for nearly 90 percent of this category in an average year.[4] Since quits are the major reason for *UI* ineligibility under state laws, it is clear that the large majority of passages to unemployment are, in principle, compensable by the *UI* system. In fact, tabulations of a special questionnaire administered with the May 1976 *CPS* indicate that 75 percent of all

temporary layoffs and 70 percent of discharges were either receiving *UI* benefits or had an application to receive them pending. In short, most "involuntary" transitions into unemployment involve the receipt of *UI* benefits for at least some portion of time spent unemployed.

Despite this important connection, not all individuals who may experience unemployment are equally "insured" by the *UI* system. Subject to several qualifying restrictions, a typical state program may pay weekly benefits to an unemployed worker that are equal to half of foregone, before-tax weekly earnings, up to a maximum for a stipulated period. Variations on this basic algorithm are numerous, however, and the proportion of spendable earnings that are replaced by *UI* benefits—the so-called "replacement ratio" —can differ across individuals both within and between state programs. To illustrate the range of these differences, Table 1 shows calculated values of the replacement ratio for hypothetical individuals in several state programs in 1975. Thus, for example, a married worker in Michigan with two dependents and a weekly wage of $100 would have experienced only a 4 percent decline in disposable income had he become unemployed,[5] while a layoff would have reduced the same worker's income by more than 40 percent in California or Florida. Similar differences can be generated within state programs: a tripling of the weekly wage to $300 in Texas implies a 34 percentage point decline in the replacement ratio, while the same experiment in Wisconsin—with a more liberal benefit ceiling and progressive state income taxes— would reduce the replacement ratio only slightly.

With experience-rated *UI* financing, the effects of these differences on the incidence of unemployment, and especially on layoff decisions, are theoretically ambiguous.[6] Con-

---

[4] These estimates are based on tabulations of the *CPS* data for the twelve years, 1968–79. Temporary layoffs are defined here to include individuals who have a definite recall date within thirty days of the survey, plus those whose layoff is of indefinite duration. Discharges are unemployed workers who do not anticipate rehire by their former firms.

[5] Though not shown in the table, a worker in Michigan with three or more dependents would experience a significant *increase* in disposable income during an unemployment spell.

[6] These points are developed formally in the expanded version of this paper, which examines the demand for insurance by workers and the feedback effects of workers' search strategies on the layoff and rehire decisions of firms. See my (1982a) article.

TABLE 1—BENEFIT REPLACEMENT RATIOS FOR
QUALIFIED WORKERS IN SELECTED STATE
UNEMPLOYMENT INSURANCE PROGRAMS, 1975

| | Weekly Wage | | | |
| | Single | | Married, 2 Dependents | |
State	$100	$300	$100	$300
California	.63	.50	.59	.45
Florida	.62	.38	.59	.35
Massachusetts	.70	.45	.81	.46
Michigan	.76	.45	.96	.50
New York	.65	.46	.69	.42
Ohio	.62	.40	.73	.41
Texas	.64	.29	.61	.27
Wisconsin	.67	.63	.63	.57

Note: Replacement ratio is calculated as potential benefit amount under state qualifying provisions as a proportion of after-tax weekly earnings. Marginal tax rates are based on standard deductions under federal and state income tax laws for the indicated family structure. Benefit amounts reflect dependency allowances where applicable.

sider, for example, the case where wages and benefits do not substitute perfectly in worker preferences (workers are risk averse), so that there is a private demand for *UI* as insurance for workers. In the absence of a *UI* system, optimal employment agreements between workers and firms would provide for some form of private unemployment compensation that mitigates workers' income risks. In this context, the incentive effects of publicly administered *UI* depend on 1) who pays for the benefits that workers receive, and 2) the level of required benefit payments relative to what would have existed privately. In general, if *UI* is a binding constraint on employment agreements, so firms must pay benefits above the privately optimal level, then higher benefits will increase the cost of laying off workers and the incidence of unemployment will decline.[7] In contrast, if firms are not liable for any increase in benefits, then *UI* subsidizes unemployment and the incidence

of layoffs will increase. Our current systems of financing benefit payments result in a diverse mixture of these offsetting extremes, with firms usually being only partially liable for the benefits their workers receive. Thus, the size and even the sign of *UI*'s effect on unemployment depend on the degree of subsidization that is relevant in any particular case.

The size of this subsidy can be quite important. In the United States, as in no other country, *UI* benefits are financed by taxes on employer payrolls that are related to their individual histories of generating unemployment. As already noted, this system of experience rating is highly imperfect. Yet some employers are more heavily subsidized by imperfect rating than others. To focus on these differences, and to highlight the main empirical issues, Table 2 reports some characteristics of the distribution of insured unemployment and tax liabilities for six major state systems in 1967 and 1978.[8]

An important feature of state programs is that assigned employer tax rates are bounded, so that firms with relatively high average unemployment, who pay the maximum rate, may consistently accumulate deficits of tax liabilities relative to benefit payments. For these employers and their workers, the marginal cost of benefits is zero since an increase in insured unemployment can cause no incremental taxes. The empirical importance of this fact is illustrated in row A of the table, which shows for each state the estimated proportion of total employment that occurred in firms whose accumulated past tax contributions were smaller than benefit withdrawals. Especially in 1967, this proportion is fairly small (averaging about 10 percent of covered employment), yet row B shows that roughly *half* of all *UI* benefits were received by employees of these firms. Evidently, firms that entered these years with negative balances due to high past unemployment had higher than normal unemployment during 1967 and 1978 as well. In fact, rows C and D show that estimated unemployment rates for deficit employers in 1967

---

[7]The same argument implies that firms would have a greater incentive to rehire a worker on layoff in order to avoid the costs of continued benefits. Thus, the duration of spells would be shorter as well. Of course, for workers who are discharged from their previous jobs, so there is no possibility of recall, only search incentives are relevant and average duration of spells would increase.

[8]The data used in these calculations were collected and compiled by Joseph Becker (1972, 1981). Complete data for other states and years are not available.

TABLE 2—SUMMARY STATISTICS FOR SELECTED STATE PROGRAMS: THE DISTRIBUTION OF INSURED UNEMPLOYMENT
FOR POSITIVE AND NEGATIVE BALANCE FIRMS, 1967 AND 1978

	California		Massachusetts		Michigan		New York		Ohio		Wisconsin	
	1967	1978	1967	1978	1967	1978	1967	1978	1967	1978	1967	1978
A. Proportion of Total Taxable Wages Paid by Negative Balance Firms[a]	14.2	14.3	11.8	13.1	3.6	28.0	13.8	28.4	4.4	29.9	8.5	14.4
B. Proportion of Total Charged Benefits Charged to Negative Balance Firms[a]	51.8	52.5	55.3	46.0	34.8	68.1	61.6	72.7	34.2	58.1	60.8	26.9
C. State Insured Unemployment Rate[b]	3.9	3.3	2.9	3.1	2.6	3.6	2.9	3.8	1.6	2.1	2.1	2.5
D. Estimated Insured Unemployment Rate for Negative Balance Firms[c]	14.2	12.1	13.6	10.9	25.1	8.7	12.9	9.6	12.4	4.0	15.0	4.7

[a]*Source*: Becker (1972, p. 112; 1981, p. 83).
[b]Average weekly insured unemployment. *Source*: U.S. Department of Labor, *Handbook of Unemployment Insurance Financial Data* (1978). Data for 1978 are unpublished, and were obtained directly from the Labor Department.
[c](Row B ÷ Row A)×Row C.

averaged about five times the implied means for positive balance employers, but this difference sharply narrowed as greater numbers of firms achieved deficits by 1978.[9] Thus, the data indicate extensive cross subsidization within self-financing state systems. And since most firms with negative balances pay the maximum allowable tax rates, it follows that the marginal cost of benefits that is relevant for a major portion of insured unemployment is also heavily subsidized.

While these facts document an important degree of cross subsidization in the current *UI* system, nothing is implied by them about the empirical role of *UI* financing in affecting unemployment, since workers in high unemployment sectors are, by construction, subject to larger subsidies. For example, the insured unemployment rate for workers in the construction industry is typically about 10 percent, which is sufficiently high to guarantee that employers in this industry pay

the maximum rate and face a full marginal subsidy on benefits. It is clearly not legitimate to infer from this fact that large subsidies cause above-average unemployment in this industry. This type of reverse causality presents a serious inference problem in isolating independent effects of the subsidy, and methodology for dealing with it is developed below. In addition, while these data indicate that a significant portion of unemployment is subject to zero experience rating, they say nothing about the costs and incentives implied for the majority of firms who pay tax rates between the state minima and maxima, and who are experience rated to some degree.[10] This *degree* of rating, which is implied by the structure of state systems, plays an important role in the empirical analysis. Here, I outline the essential features of measuring the degree of experience rating, and relegate technical details to the Appendix. More detailed descriptions of particular experience rating methods appear in my article with Welch.

[9]*Ceteris paribus*, this shift implies that a larger proportion of covered employment is subject to zero experience rating. For details and causes of these trends, see my article with Welch (1980).

[10]For the states listed in Table 2, about 75 percent of employment fell in this category. For further evidence, see Becker (1981, Table 24, pp. 164–67).

A. The Degree of Experience Rating in Current Financing Systems

Under federal legislation, states may design their own schemes of benefit financing and payroll taxation so long as assigned tax rates can be justified on the basis of an employer's unemployment history.[11] As with Social Security, these taxes are paid on a taxable wage base per employee that may be chosen by the states.[12] Federal requirements on the form of state systems are quite loose, and as a result there is considerable heterogeneity both in the type of system chosen and, for a given system, in the particular parameters that affect incentives. In this paper, I focus on two general methods of experience rating accounting, the reserve-ratio and benefit-ratio methods, because they are the most common and because their incentives can be parsimoniously summarized for empirical research. Together, these methods apply to more than 80 percent of insured employment in the United States.

I define the degree of experience rating e as the value of marginal tax liabilities paid by employers per dollar of benefits received by workers. Thus, an employer faces incomplete experience rating ($e < 1$) if an additional layoff spell generates benefits that have a greater present value than the associated increase in taxes. Empirically, there are two common features of financing systems that assure incomplete rating for most employers. First, as noted above, assigned tax rates are bounded above and below so that taxes are completely insensitive to changes in layoff behavior in some sectors. In these cases, $e = 0$. Second, even for rated firms whose tax rates fall between the minimum and maximum in a state, where taxes are sensitive to layoffs, incremental tax liabilities are spread through time. Interest is not charged on these liabilities, so the degree of rating depends on the time profile of tax changes. Thus, even in cases where the full nominal value of benefits is eventually repaid, which turns out to

be common, the *timing* of taxes yields an interest-free loan for which $0 < e < 1$.

The derivations required to completely characterize these dimensions of experience rating are contained in the Appendix. The results of this analysis may be summarized as follows. In a steady state, any employer's history of generating *UI* payments to workers is completely determined by his long-run equilibrium rate of insured unemployment, which I denote by μ. If the employer's tax contributions per worker are to balance the flow of benefits generated by μ, there must exist a tax rate, τ, such that $\tau W = \mu B$, where W is the taxable wage base per employee and B is *UI* benefits expressed as an annual rate. Therefore, in order that μ be sustainable in this sense, τ must lie between the minimum and maximum rates charged in the employer's state. Letting $\rho = W/B$, this requirement can be expressed in terms of a pair of bounds on the equilibrium unemployment rate μ:

$$(1) \qquad \rho \tau_{min} \leqslant \mu \leqslant \rho \tau_{max}.$$

If μ lies outside the range given in (1), the employer pays τ_{min} or τ_{max} independently of his layoff behavior, and so $e = 0$. Therefore, the bounds defined by (1) determine the *range* of equilibrium unemployment rates that are subject to experience rating within state systems.[13] The relation of these bounds to the data in Table 2 on negative balance firms is obvious.

If μ lies within the range given in (1), tax dynamics in response to changes in an employer's layoff behavior determine the degree of experience rating. These dynamics are nontrivial, and they differ substantially across state systems, but their implications can be summarized by the shape of the cost function shown in Figure 1. In the illustrated case, which depicts experience rating in a typical state in 1975, rated firms paid about 80 cents in future taxes for each incremental dollar of benefits received by their workers. Nonrated firms with unemployment rates greater than μ_{max} or smaller than μ_{min} paid

---

[11] For a summary of these laws, see Becker (1972) and U.S. Department of Labor (1979).

[12] The wage base chosen may not fall below a federally mandated level, which now stands at $6,000.

[13] Equation (1) applies exactly in reserve-ratio systems, but it requires slight modification for benefit-ratio accounting. See the Appendix.

546   *THE AMERICAN ECONOMIC REVIEW*   *SEPTEMBER 1983*

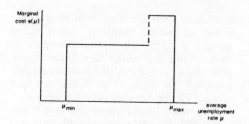

FIGURE 1. MARGINAL COST OF A LAYOFF
RELATIVE TO CHARGED BENEFITS, RESERVE-RATIO,
AND BENEFIT-RATIO STATES

TABLE 3—EXPERIENCE RATING PARAMETERS FOR
ILLUSTRATIVE STATE PROGRAMS, 1975

	Experience Rating Method	μ_{min}	$e(\mu)$	μ_{max}
California	RR	0.9	.58	3.8
Florida	BR	0.0	.99	6.2
Massachusetts	RR	3.2	.90	4.6
Michigan	RR	0.1	.86	7.0
New York	RR	1.5	.71	5.3
Ohio	RR	0.2	.75	4.0
Texas	BR	1.5	1.14	6.5
Wisconsin	RR	0.0	.81	4.5

Notes: μ_{min} and μ_{max} are calculated using maximum and minimum tax rates in effect and the state ratio of average weekly benefits to average weekly taxable wages. The data are from *Handbook of Unemployment Insurance Financial Data* (1978), *Comparisons of State Unemployment Insurance Laws*, and unpublished U.S. Department of Labor data. *RR* denotes reserve ratio accounting, and *BR* denotes benefit ratio.

nothing. In some states, depending on the speed with which taxes are adjusted, this marginal cost to rated firms may actually exceed $1 ($e > 1$) and, as shown, e need not be constant throughout the rated range.

Estimates of the bounds in (1) that are relevant for different state systems may be calculated from information on maximum and minimum tax rates, and on the levels of benefits and taxable wages in each state. Estimates of the degree of experience rating in each state can be similarly derived from the formulae used by each state to calculate taxes.[14] Some values for both margins of experience rating are shown in Table 3 for illustrative state programs. These data show that both the range of unemployment over which experience rating is relevant and the degree of rating within that range differ substantially across state systems. Thus, for example, in 1975, experience rating for firms and their workers in Michigan was truncated above at an insured unemployment rate of 7 percent, while this upper bound occurred at only 3.8 percent in California. This means that for employers with equilibrium rates of, say, 6 percent, *UI* would increase the value of unemployment relative to employment in California by the full amount of available benefits, while 86 percent of *UI* would be repaid in Michigan. In terms of magnitudes of incentives, at a typical 1975 weekly benefit amount of $90, that is a difference in costs of $77 per week.[15] Even within the

range where the marginal cost of benefits is positive, a California firm would repay only 58 cents of each dollar received by an additional unemployed worker. At the other extreme, an identically situated firm in Texas would repay *more* than the value of benefits that workers receive, so that layoffs are actually taxed for rated employers.

By any standard, these differences in layoff incentives offered to otherwise identical firms are large. It is this type of variation in the two relevant margins of experience rating —its range and degree—that may be exploited in the cross section to estimate the impact of these incentives on layoff decisions.[16] I turn to the empirical methodology for identifying these effects.

II. The Data and an Empirical Strategy

A. *The CPS Data and the Basic Model*

To estimate the impact of these differences in incentives on layoff unemployment, I utilize a sample of more than 8,000 individuals selected from the March 1975 file of the

---

[14]Described in the Appendix.
[15]These calculations ignore the additional effect on the subsidy caused by the tax-exempt nature of most *UI* payments. This omission is corrected in the econometric analysis.

[16]For purposes of empirical analysis, I treat these differences in costs as exogenous and do not speculate on the political forces that may support them.

Current Population Survey.[17] Simply stated, the empirical strategy links to each observation in the *CPS* information on the level of available *UI* benefits and the characteristics of experience rating that apply in an individual's state and industry. Using straightforward econometric techniques, it is then possible to decompose the effect of these variables on the probability that an individual is on layoff into component probabilities of transiting to and from layoff unemployment. The particular virtue of the March *CPS* file for this purpose is its wealth of information on the personal characteristics and employment status of individuals, which includes retrospective information on earnings and employment during the calendar year that preceded the survey. This retrospective data is essential, since it is used to establish the level of *UI* benefits for which each individual qualifies. The relative incidence of temporary layoff unemployment was fairly high in 1975, which facilitates an analysis of the factors that influence layoff and rehire decisions. Hence my choice of that year.

To minimize the influence of vagaries in individual labor force participation decisions on the results, the sample includes only persons who were between the ages of 20 and 65, and who were full-time, full-year labor force participants during the previous year. In addition, to focus on persons who were subjective to layoff risks, I selected privately employed, nonprofessional workers who were not self-employed and who did not work in the agricultural sector.[18] A final selection criterion was imposed by the data: the *CPS* reports "state" of residence for each observation, but smaller states are aggregated into larger geographic units to protect the confidentiality of responses. Since the identification of *UI* effects depends crucially on differences among states in methods of financing and liberality of benefits, I consider

only individuals for whom state of residence could be exactly identified. The resulting sample of 8,280 individuals represented 19 reserve-ratio and benefit-ratio financing systems and 29 two-digit (SIC) industry classifications.[19] Of these, 555 individuals (6.7 percent of the sample) were on temporary layoff. Since the economywide layoff rate was slightly above 3 percent in this year, it is clear that this sample faces greater layoff risk than the general population. No attempt is made here to extend the results to other, more heterogeneous populations or to those with weaker labor force attachment.

The estimation strategy uses two distinct pieces of information on an individual's labor market status to estimate the effects of *UI*, and other variables, on transitions to and from layoff unemployment: current status (for example, on temporary layoff) and, for unemployed workers, the duration of the current spell in progress. To use this information, certain assumptions on the processes that generate transitions are required. I assume that the underlying processes are stationary, and that the per period probabilities of entering and leaving layoff unemployment are constant, independent of time spent employed or unemployed. Denote these constant "hazards" by λ^{el} and λ^{le} for transitions from employment to layoff, and from layoff to employment, respectively.[20] With this structure, the Appendix establishes that in a sample of individuals who are employed or on layoff, the contribution to the sample likelihood by individual j who is on layoff at the survey date is

$$(2) \qquad L_j = \frac{\lambda_j^{el}\lambda_j^{le}\exp\left[-T_j\lambda_j^{le}\right]}{\lambda_j^{le} + \lambda_j^{el}},$$

---

[17]The *CPS* is a monthly survey from which the government's employment and unemployment statistics are compiled. The survey is slightly different in each month, and only the March file contains information on employment and earnings during the previous year.

[18]A complete listing of selection criteria and sample characteristics may be obtained from the author.

[19]These included all manufacturing industries, plus construction, mining, wholesale trade, retail trade, and transportation industries.

[20]The stationarity and constant hazards assumptions imply that transitions are first-order Markov. Thus, the probability that a person is on layoff at the sample date is simply the proportion of time that an infinitely lived person in such an environment would spend unemployed. Formally, the hazard is the conditional probability of passage given duration T. Constancy implies that this probability is independent of T, and so the distribution of completed spell lengths is negative exponential. Further details are appended.

where T_j is the duration of the layoff spell in progress. Equation (2) is simply the joint probability of observing an individual on layoff *and* in the Tth week of his spell. In contrast, if the individual is employed then duration in employment is not observed, and so the contribution to the likelihood is simply

$$(3) \qquad L_j = \lambda_j^{le} \Big/ \Big[\lambda_j^{el} + \lambda_j^{le} \Big].$$

The transition rates λ^{el} and λ^{le} are the basic elements that we seek to identify in the estimation procedure. Intuitively, under the stated assumptions the probabilities that a randomly selected individual is employed or on layoff depend on *both* these transition rates, as in (3). The single piece of information given by the empirical frequency of layoff spells in the sample would then be inadequate to identify each of λ^{el} and λ^{le}.[21] However, the information given by the empirical distribution of durations, T, among unemployed workers allows us to estimate λ^{le} —the rate at which individuals leave unemployment—separately. This estimate may then be used, via (3), to identify λ^{el}. Estimating the two transition rates jointly from the full sample of individuals who are both employed and on layoff enhances efficiency.

To close the empirical model, I specify the dependence of λ^{le} on a vector of explanatory variables, X_j, for the jth individual as

$$(4) \qquad \lambda_j^{le} = \exp\big\{ X_j \beta^{le} \big\},$$

and λ^{el}, the transition rate from employment, is written conformably. Equation (4) is nonnegative, as required, for all values of the vectors β, which are to be estimated. The number of individual parameters to be estimated is twice the number of regressors in **X**. Thus, for example, β^{el} measures the impact of exogenous variables on the probability of *entering* unemployment, while (3) implies that the total impact of **X** on the probability of unemployment (the unemployment rate) is

measured by the difference $\beta^{el} - \beta^{le}$.[22] The likelihood defined by equations (2), (3), and (4) is globally concave, and so standard techniques are effective in maximizing it. Summary statistics for the variables included in **X** are reported in Appendix Table A1, and are discussed below.

B. *Specifying and Identifying the Effects of UI*

In estimating this model, I focus on two *UI* variables as determinants of transitions, and thus of employment status at a point in time. These are the benefit-replacement ratio and the amount of benefits that are subsidized by methods of financing. The former variable is common in empirical work on the effects of *UI*, and in this specification it captures incentive effects that do not depend on imperfections in experience rating or the *UI* subsidy. Potential benefits were imputed for each observation from available personal information and from the qualifying provisions of each state's *UI* law,[23] while the relevant marginal tax rates were calculated from state and federal tax tables based on family structure and on earnings during the previous calendar year. As Table A1 indicates, for the typical individual in this sample, available *UI* benefits would have replaced 56 percent of spendable weekly earnings during a spell of unemployment. Sources of variance in this variable both within and between state programs were illustrated in Table 1 above.

Imputation of the *UI* subsidy that is relevant for each individual is based directly on the cost functions described above. The subsidy to unemployment occurs both because of imperfect experience rating and because *UI* benefits are not normally subject to in-

---

[21] With knowledge of only the relative frequency of spells, the ratio $\lambda^{le}/\lambda^{el}$ could be identified from (3).

[22] Equations (3) and (4) imply that the unemployment probability is determined by a logistic distribution. Thus $\beta = \beta^{el} - \beta^{le}$ is the coefficient on x in a standard logit model of unemployment incidence.

[23] The required information included weeks worked during the previous year, weekly earnings, and family structure (to calculate dependent's allowances). Given heterogeneity in state laws, the computer program for this imputation is fairly complex. It is available on request from the author.

come taxation. Thus, even with full experience rating ($e(\mu) = 1$), unemployment would be subsidized by the different tax treatments of earnings and benefits. Combining these two incentives, the change in the value of unemployment induced by a weekly benefit amount of $b is simply

$$(5) \qquad b((1/1-t) - e(\mu)),$$

where t is the individual's marginal tax rate on earned income.[24] The crucial element of (5) is $e(\mu)$, so that precise imputation of the subsidy requires information on μ for each individual's employer. Such detailed information on unemployment histories is clearly unavailable. In its place, I utilize time-series data on insured unemployment rates at the two-digit SIC level of aggregation,[25] and corresponding *CPS* information on the industry classification of each observation's most recent employer. I assume that in each industry the equilibrium insured unemployment rate is equal to the actual insured rate over the period 1971–74. Calling this rate in industry i, $\bar{\mu}_i$, the simplest imputation method would assign $e_s(\bar{\mu}_i)$ for individuals in state s. With slight modification to account for within-industry variation in equilibrium rates among employers, this method was used to impute the degree of experience rating in the 551 state-industry cells.

The modification simply recognizes that, within any industry, equilibrium rates will be distributed about the industry mean. Consequently, even in industries where $\bar{\mu}_i$ lies outside a state's experience rated range defined in (1), experience rating may affect layoff decisions for some firms and conversely for industries where $\bar{\mu}_i$ is within the rated interval. There is no information on the form of these distributions, and so any allowance for

this type of effect must be somewhat crude. Thus, since the potential for within-industry variance is larger in industries with high average unemployment, I assume an industry density for μ, $f_i(\mu)$, that is triangular with the range of variation in μ proportional to the mean.[26] The factor of proportionality γ is the same in all industries, and so the assumed range of μ is equal to $\bar{\mu}_i \pm \gamma\bar{\mu}_i$ in the ith industry. The *expected* degree of experience rating for person j in industry i may then be imputed using the density $f_i(\mu)$ and the cost function $e(\mu)$ in each state program. The parameter γ may be chosen on the basis of the model's overall fit, and a value of $\gamma > 0$ indicates effects of experience rating even where $\bar{\mu}_i > \mu_{max}$. Of course, because of the form of $f(\mu)$, this effect is constrained to die out the farther is $\bar{\mu}_i$ from the experience rated range.

The fact remains that industries with extremely high or low average unemployment will have less imputed experience rating—since a larger proportion of $f_i(\mu)$ would lie outside the range defined in (1)—and this may seriously bias the results in favor of powerful experience rating effects.[27] This source of bias may be purged by estimating the model with vectors of fixed industry effects in the specifications of both λ^{el} and λ^{le}. That is, I assume

$$(6) \qquad \mathbf{x}_j\beta^{el} = \alpha_i^{el} + \mathbf{Z}_j\theta^{el},$$

and

$$\mathbf{x}_j\beta^{le} = \alpha_i^{le} + \mathbf{Z}_j\theta^{le},$$

[24] Currently, workers who earn more than $18,000 annually are subject to federal income taxation on their *UI* benefits. This is a recent development, however, and in 1975 all benefits were tax exempt.

[25] These are nationwide unemployment rates for each industry. They appear in various issues of *Unemployment Insurance Statistics*. Some series were unpublished, but they may be obtained from the Department of Labor.

[26] The density is of the form

$$f_i(\mu) = \begin{cases} (1 + (\mu - \bar{\mu}_i))/(\gamma\bar{\mu}_i)^2 & \mu < \bar{\mu}_i; \\ (1 - (\mu - \mu_i))/(\gamma\mu_i)^2 & \mu > \mu_i. \end{cases}$$

[27] Table 5, below, makes this especially clear. Industries such as Apparel and Miscellaneous Manufacturing have relatively high values of $\bar{\mu}_i$, high sample layoff rates, and large imputed subsidies. Even if the subsidy did not affect layoffs, this relationship would almost surely yield a positive estimated effect of the subsidy on unemployment. The strategy indicated in the text simply subtracts these cross-industry effects, and concentrates solely on variation in the subsidy within industries.

where the α_i represent industry-specific shifters of the transition rates.[28] In this specification, differences in levels of exogenous variables across industries are captured by the α_i, so only *within-industry* variation in Z_j is used in estimating θ^{el} and θ^{le}.

Since $\bar{\mu}_i$ is the same for all persons in industry i, within-industry variation in the degree of experience rating is caused only by differences between states in the location and height of the cost function, $e(\mu)$. Therefore, any estimated impact of the *UI* subsidy reflects only the within-industry experiment of changing the function $e(\mu)$, while differences between industries in average levels of the subsidy and unemployment do not affect the results.

III. The Evidence

All of the specifications that I have estimated show strong effects of unemployment insurance on layoff unemployment. More importantly, the evidence is that most of *UI*'s impact on layoffs is caused by current methods of experience rating. In this sample, the layoff unemployment rate would have been about 30 percent lower if the subsidy to unemployment caused by the current *UI* system had been eliminated. In contrast, simple changes in the level of *UI* benefits that leave the subsidy constant would have only minor effects on layoffs.

Table 4 summarizes the main results for the determinants of temporary layoff unemployment. In the table, I report two specifications of the model, the first of which ignores any information on experience rating. Thus, all *UI* effects in this specification are captured by the replacement ratio, and the impact of this variable will reflect the average degree of *UI* subsidization in addition to any independent effects of changing the level of available *UI*. The estimates in the

first specification show a strong positive impact of *UI* on unemployment, and the dominant share of this effect is due to a statistically significant increase in the probability of experiencing a layoff, rather than to increased duration of spells. To fix ideas on the magnitudes of these effects, evaluating the model at sample means yields an estimated monthly probability of entering unemployment of .029. At means, the point estimate of the ratio's impact on this transition implies that the per period layoff probability is unit elastic with respect to benefits $(1.82 \times .56 = 1.02)$, so a 10 percent across-the-board reduction in the level of *UI* (about \$8 per week) would reduce the monthly probability of entering layoff by about 0.3 percentage points. At the other margin, however, there is no significant effect of the replacement ratio on the probability of leaving layoff.

Overall, the point estimate of *UI*'s total effect in the third column (1.70) implies that a 10 percent reduction in the level of benefits would eliminate about 8.8 percent of all layoff spells in this sample.[29] I have experimented with various nonlinear forms for the effects of the ratio (for example, splines and quadratics), but these findings were not affected by such changes in specification. In short, the estimates in the first specification indicate that the incidence of temporary layoff unemployment is quite sensitive to the availability of unemployment insurance, and that transitions *into* layoff unemployment play a prominent role in explaining this relationship.

The effects of other exogenous variables in model A are largely self-explanatory. Recall that the specification controls for differences caused by the characteristics of particular industries, so the estimates reflect within-industry changes in exogenous variables. For example, since the usual statistical determinants of earnings are controlled for in the

[28]Since there are 29 industries represented in the data, the model estimates 58 industry coefficients in addition to the other parameters of the model. In practice, this brought to 78 the number of parameters in the estimated models. The procedure for estimating the fixed effects in a nonlinear model like this one is considerably more complicated than simply subtracting out industry means and it is expensive to compute.

[29]This total impact of *UI* is similar to that of Feldstein (1978), who regressed layoff unemployment on the replacement ratio. Feldstein's data were for a different year (1971) and a more heterogeneous sample, which makes comparisons difficult. Note that Feldstein's *OLS* method of estimating the probability of a layoff is not capable of identifying separate effects on transitions.

TABLE 4—UNEMPLOYMENT INSURANCE AND LAYOFF UNEMPLOYMENT

Exogenous Variables: Z_j	Specification A				Specification B			
	Entering Layoff[a]	Leaving Layoff[b]	Total Effect[c]	Marginal Probability[d]	Entering Layoff	Leaving Layoff	Total Effect	Marginal Probability
Subsidy					.683 (1.35)	−.402 (−1.05)	1.09 (3.29)	.072
Replacement Ratio	1.82 (2.66)	.117 (.241)	1.70 (3.54)	.112	1.01 (1.24)	.414 (.729)	.603 (1.02)	.040
Weekly Wage ÷ 100	.047 (.404)	.065 (.794)	−.018 (−.217)	−.001	−.023 (−.193)	.061 (.730)	−.084 (−.967)	−.005
Age	−.058 (−1.52)	.034 (1.27)	−.092 (−3.38)	−.006	−.058 (−1.50)	.036 (1.29)	−.094 (−3.45)	−.006
Age² ÷ 100	.036 (.761)	−.047 (−1.39)	.083 (2.51)	.005	.036 (.752)	−.048 (−1.39)	.084 (2.49)	.005
Age = 25[e]	−.040 (−2.67)	.011 (1.03)	−.051 (−4.85)	−.003	−.040 (−2.63)	.011 (1.01)	−.051 (−4.82)	−.003
Age = 40[e]	−.029 (−5.25)	−.003 (−.829)	−.026 (−6.23)	−.002	−.029 (−5.20)	−.003 (−.819)	−.026 (−6.20)	−.002
Education	−.050 (−.428)	−.068 (−.890)	.018 (.204)	.001	−.046 (−.389)	−.072 (−.930)	.026 (.299)	−.002
Education² ÷ 100	−.066 (−.119)	.405 (1.08)	−.471 (−.732)	−.031	−.086 (−.154)	.432 (1.15)	−.519 (−1.24)	−.034
Education = 12[e]	−.066 (−1.96)	.027 (1.15)	−.093 (−3.88)	−.006	−.066 (−1.96)	.031 (1.32)	−.097 (4.05)	−.006
Race (White)	−.092 (−4.91)	.044 (.388)	−.136 (−1.00)	−.009	−.107 (−.563)	.050 (.385)	−.157 (−1.14)	.010
Sex (Male)	.177 (1.00)	.224 (1.79)	−.047 (−3.75)	−.003	.199 (1.22)	.226 (1.79)	−.027 (−.219)	−.002
Industry Effects	Yes	Yes	Yes		Yes	Yes	Yes	
ln £	−3636.5				−3631.2			
Proportion Unemployed	.071							

Note: Asymptotic normal statistics in parentheses.
[a] Estimate of θ^{el}.
[b] Estimate of θ^{le}.
[c] Estimate of $\theta^{el} - \theta^{le}$.
[d] Derivative of unemployment probability at sample mean.
[e] Age and education quadratics evaluated at the indicated level.

specification, the coefficient on the weekly wage might be interpreted as the effect of unobserved components of individual or job-specific productivity. There is no evidence in these data that unemployed workers are materially different in this respect than their employed counterparts, nor are the individual transition rates significantly affected by earnings capacity. This is not too surprising, since most workers on layoff will end up returning to their old jobs. The effects of age and education, however, are strong. On average, a 25-year old is about 50 percent more likely to be unemployed than a 40-year old (wage constant), and an extra year of schooling reduces unemployment by over half a point. The age profile of unemployment probabilities is nonlinear, becoming flatter at older ages. As with the impact of the replacement ratio, these effects are concentrated on the probability of entering layoff.[30] Finally, there are no significant effects of race or sex on layoff unemployment rates, although men have slightly shorter spells than women. These results are not sensitive to changes in the specification of *UI* effects, and so they will not be referred to further below.[31]

The imputed *UI* subsidy to unemployment is controlled for in specification B. It turned out that the dispersion parameter γ was quite costly to estimate directly in the maximum likelihood procedure, though in experiments with the imputation the data preferred a value of $\gamma = 0.25$. This value implies a within-industry standard deviation in μ of only about 15 percent of the mean, and the results are not statistically different from those obtained when $\gamma = 0$. Thus, there is little evidence that within-industry dispersion of μ is an important consideration in evaluating the incentive effects of experience rating. The direct impact of imputed experience rating on layoff unemployment, however, is both statistically and numerically significant.

In the specification, I have entered the subsidy as a proportion of weekly earnings so that the imputed degree of rating, $e(\mu)$, is the only source of independent variation in the subsidy relative to the replacement ratio.[32] In light of the powerful effect of the replacement ratio estimated in the first model, this restriction offers a strong test of the role of experience rating in affecting

layoff decisions, and serves to divide the total impact of *UI* between its subsidized and nonsubsidized components. Thus, note that when the subsidy is controlled for the estimated impact of the replacement ratio falls by over 60 percent relative to model A, and it is no longer significant by standard criteria. At means, the new point estimate of .603 implies that a 10 percent change in the benefit level that holds the subsidy constant would change the layoff probability by two-tenths of a percentage point.[33] In contrast, the *UI* subsidy has a powerful and statistically significant effect on the layoff unemployment rate. Since the average subsidy is equal to 31 percent of the weekly wage, the point estimate in the last column implies that the subsidy accounts for (approximately) $.072 \times .31/.071 = 31$ percent of the sample's layoffs. In other words, if the incentives toward increased unemployment offered by current methods of experience rating and income taxation were entirely eliminated, the average layoff unemployment rate in this sample would decline by more than one fourth.

The data and discussion of Section I imply that current methods of financing *UI* will have a larger impact on layoffs in high unemployment industries, where the subsidy to unemployment is larger and experience rating less relevant to layoff decisions. Table 5 illustrates this distributional effect, showing the predicted amount of the layoff unemployment rate that is accounted for by the subsidy in selected industries. Thus, for example, in the high unemployment Apparel industry ($\bar{\mu} = 7.65$ percent), the subsidy is equal to about 56 percent of weekly earnings, on average, and so it accounts for over 6.7 points of the industry layoff rate in this year. In contrast, in Primary Metals, average un-

---

[30] This finding is consistent with that of Robert Hall (1972) and others, who found that differences in the duration of unemployment across groups are of minor significance in explaining differences in unemployment rates. That this also holds for temporary layoffs is somewhat more surprising, given the symmetry of layoff and rehire decisions.

[31] Note that the worker's union status is not an explanatory variable. This is because union membership is not reported in the March file (except in 1971). However, any differences across industries in unionization rates are captured by the industry effects, α_i. It is therefore highly doubtful that the omission of union status could strongly affect the results.

[32] Since the replacement ratio is $b/w(1-t)$, the subsidy as a proportion of weekly earnings multiplies the ratio by the quantity $1 - e(\mu)(1-t)$. This is an interaction term, and the results imply that most of the effect of *UI* comes through this interaction with experience rating.

[33] The point estimate of 1.01 in the transition to layoff is still numerically large, but it is imprecisely estimated and is partially offset by a *positive* and insignificant estimated effect on transitions from layoff. Note that at the mean of the subsidy (.31), the effect of the same 10 percent change in benefits is also about .2 points ($.072 \times .31 \times .1 = .0022$), so that the total effect is almost evenly divided. When local market conditions are controlled for in Table 6, however, the share of this effect shifts strongly to the subsidy.

TABLE 5—ESTIMATED EFFECTS OF THE UNEMPLOYMENT INSURANCE SUBSIDY,
BY INDUSTRY, 1975

	$\bar{\mu}_i{}^a$	Subsidy/ Weekly Wage	Layoff Unemployment Rate^b	Total Effect of Subsidy (percent)^c
Wholesale Trade	1.82	.33	1.86	0.65
Machinery	1.92	.32	4.44	1.47
Chemicals	1.96	.32	1.78	0.60
Retail Trade	1.99	.27	1.98	0.58
Primary Metals	2.43	.23	7.34	1.70
Electrical Machinery	3.10	.29	8.38	2.46
Fabricated Metals	3.31	.27	11.72	3.04
Food	4.73	.36	5.10	1.88
Misc. Manufacturing	6.77	.61	9.82	5.86
Apparel	7.65	.57	12.54	6.76
Construction	8.33	.42	14.15	5.56
Total	3.75	.31	7.1	2.22

^{a}Calculated from average monthly *UI* compensated unemployment rates, by industry, 1972–74. *Source*: U.S. Department of Labor, *Handbook of Unemployment Insurance Financial Data*, various issues.

^{b}Workers on layoff as a proportion of workers employed and on layoff.

^{c}Approximate effect of eliminating the imputed *UI* subsidy. The formula is total effect $= 1.09 \times (\bar{p}_i) \times (1 - \bar{p}_i) \times$ subsidy, using model (2)–(4), where $\bar{p}_i$ is the industry layoff rate.

employment is much lower ($\bar{\mu} = 2.43$ percent) and experience rating more extensive, so the mean imputed subsidy accounts for only 1.7 points of total layoff unemployment.

The decomposition of the total impact of the subsidy into its component effects on probabilities of entering and leaving layoff also shows the expected signs, though the point estimates are only moderately larger than their standard errors. Using the point estimates, 62 percent of the total effect on unemployment is due to increased transitions from employment to layoff (the layoff probability is 20 percent higher), while the point estimate of $-.402$ in layoff transitions implies that the mean level of the subsidy increases the average duration of layoffs by about 1.3 weeks. Thus, though the estimates from the decomposition are imprecise, there is evidence in these data that the significant impact of the subsidy on layoff unemployment is due to both more frequent and longer layoff spells. And as in Table 5, these effects will be nonneutral across industries, being larger in poorly experience rated sectors.

Changes in the reported specification that excluded various combinations of demo-graphic characteristics did not materially affect the results, nor did restrictions of the sample to men only, or to white men only. However, one change in the basic specification does affect the estimated impact of unemployment insurance. Recall that the results shown in Table 4 rely heavily on between-state differences in the liberality of benefits, and the extent of experience rating to estimate incentive effects of *UI*. Thus, to the extent that there are important differences across states in "local" market conditions affecting layoff, rehire, and search decisions, these results may be biased.[34] For example, rapidly growing states such as Texas and Florida are reputed to be "strong" local markets, and the data of Tables 1 and 3 reveal relatively low benefit levels and strong experience rating in those states. To control for these long-term differences among areas, I have reestimated the model in Table 5 including as an explanatory variable the imputed growth rates of private, nonagricultural employment in each individual's state. These rates were estimated from quadratic trend regressions for each state, and the re-

[34]I am indebted to Bob King for raising this issue.

TABLE 6—ESTIMATED EFFECTS OF UNEMPLOYMENT INSURANCE AND STATE GROWTH OF LAYOFF UNEMPLOYMENT

Exogenous Variables: Z_j	Specification A			Specification B		
	Entering Layoff[a]	Leaving Layoff[b]	Total Effect[c]	Entering Layoff[a]	Leaving Layoff[b]	Total Effect[c]
Subsidy	.612 (1.21)	−.396 (−1.04)	1.007 (3.01)	.874 (1.98)	−.219 (.649)	1.093 (3.82)
Replacement Ratio	.861 (1.01)	.559 (.949)	.302 (.491)	—	—	—
Growth Rate	−.426 (−1.18)	.205 (.874)	−.631 (−2.28)	−.519 (−1.50)	.141 (0.32)	−.660 (−2.45)
ln £	−3926.2			−3627.9		

Note: Asymptotic normal statistics in parentheses. Other explanatory variables are as in Table 4.
  [a] Estimate of θ^{el}.
  [b] Estimate of θ^{le}.
  [c] Estimate of $\theta^{el} - \theta^{le}$.

sults of including them are summarized in Table 6.[35]

Even after controlling for industry composition, rapidly growing states have fewer layoffs, and the majority of this effect is again attributable to the probability of entering unemployment. At means, a one percentage point increase in long-term growth (less than a standard deviation) reduces the layoff rate by about .5 points. Most importantly, however, controlling for local growth reduces the impact of the replacement ratio by about 50 percent from the estimate in Table 4. In fact, the impact of the ratio is now negligible: a 10 percent change in the benefit level that leaves the subsidy constant would change the layoff unemployment rate by only one-tenth of a point, though the standard error on this estimate is large.[36] The effects of the unemployment insurance subsidy, however, are not materially different than in Table 4, and its total effect

on unemployment remains highly significant. For completeness, I also report in the table the estimated effect of the *UI* subsidy when the replacement ratio is excluded. Again, the results are not highly sensitive to this exclusion, though the impact on transitions into unemployment is somewhat larger in this case. I conclude from this evidence that the impact of *UI* is overstated when local market conditions are ignored, but this bias falls most on the replacement ratio. Methods of financing *UI*, in contrast, continue to have strong and stable effects on layoffs that are consistent with theory.

IV. Summary and Concluding Remarks

The vast majority of employer-initiated spells of unemployment involve the payment of unemployment insurance benefits. This empirical connection between layoff decisions and the *UI* system may affect observed unemployment rates for two reasons. First, the legislated level of benefits that must be paid to laid off workers can change the relative costs of unemployment to both workers and their employers, and this alone may influence layoff, rehire, and search decisions. Second—and this has been the main focus of this paper—current systems of *UI* financing clearly subsidize the occurrence of unemployment, since most employers are only partially liable for the benefits that their

---

[35] The data for these auxiliary regressions are taken from the U.S. Department of Labor, *Employment and Earnings, States and Areas*, various issues.

[36] The total effect of a 10 percent change in benefits that *includes* the effect of experience rating is, at means, .32 percentage points. Two thirds of this effect is accounted for by the subsidy. This total effect can also be decomposed into effects on entering and leaving unemployment, and it is clear from the point estimates that passages to layoff unemployment are more strongly affected by *UI*.

workers receive. Largely for lack of suitable measures of the incentives offered to firms, however, these effects of unemployment insurance on the decisions that generate unemployment have been previously untested.

The empirical evidence presented in this paper indicates that both the extent and the effect of *UI* subsidization are important. Examination of the structures of state financing laws shows that even experience-rated firms often face significant unemployment subsidies, and an important portion of aggregate employment is not subject to experience rating at all. The econometric analysis showed that the impact of the unemployment insurance subsidy on layoff unemployment is powerful—the imputed subsidy accounts for more than a quarter of all layoffs in the data —and the effects on the probabilities of entering and leaving unemployment are in accord with theory. For workers who are subject to temporary layoff, *UI* appears to have a more important effect on transitions *into* unemployment than on the more commonly studied duration of spells. Taken together, these findings offer strong support for the hypothesis, originally proposed by Feldstein (1973), that methods of financing unemployment insurance can have important effects on the incidence of unemployment.

These results imply that, *without changing benefit levels available to unemployed workers,* a significant reduction in layoff unemployment could be achieved by changing the incentives offered by current *UI* laws. It is tempting to conclude from these findings that subsidies to unemployment should be eliminated via complete experience rating of *UI* taxes (full employer liability) and the symmetric tax treatment of benefits and earned income. My analysis does not justify that conclusion, however, since very little is known about the optimal structure of *UI* financing systems. For example, under circumstances where labor turnover may be viewed as a public good (see Hall, 1979, and Peter Diamond, 1981), firms (and workers) will undervalue separations and so complete experience rating of *UI* may inefficiently discourage permanent layoffs. These arguments are far less applicable for temporary layoffs, however, and they cannot be used to justify

the current structure of experience rating where many layoff-prone employers face no marginal cost of benefits at all. On these grounds, the empirical effects identified in this paper can be viewed as costs of the current organization of unemployment insurance financing in the United States.

Appendix

A. *Calculating the Degree of Experience Rating*

1. *Benefit-Ratio Systems.* In benefit-ratio systems, an employer's tax rate depends on the ratio of total benefits charged to the employer's account over the past T years to total taxable wages for the same period. This is the benefit ratio:

$$BR = \sum_{j=1}^{T} B\mu_{t-j}N_{t-j} \Big/ \sum_{j=1}^{T} WN_{t-j},$$

or $\quad BR = \rho \sum_{j=1}^{T} n_{t-j}\mu_{t-j},$

where $\rho = B/W$ and $n_{t-j} = N_{t-j}/\Sigma N_{t-k}$ is the share of year $t - j$ employment in total employment over the past T years. Thus, the benefit ratio is just a share-weighted average of past unemployment rates times the "charge rate," ρ. In some benefit-ratio states, the firm's tax rate is just $\tau_t = BR_t$, but, in others, BR_t is multiplied by a factor of proportionality, λ, equal to the ratio of total state benefit payments to those which are charged to firm accounts. Thus $\tau_t = \lambda BR_t$ with $\lambda \geqslant 1$. The present value of taxes caused by a transitory change in μ relative to benefits received may then be calculated to be

$$e = \lambda\big(1 - (1+i)^{-T}\big)\Big/T_i,$$

where i is the rate of interest. This marginal cost of benefits is less than unity (for $\lambda = 1$) and is declining in T because the implicit interest-free loan is repaid over a longer period when T rises. In most states, $T = 3$ years, while the currently operating system in Michigan sets $T = 5$ years. Thus, with $T = 3$ and $i = .1$, $e = .828\lambda$ while with $T = 5e = .758\lambda$.

2. *Reserve-Ratio Systems.* Under this method of accounting, each employer's tax rate, τ, depends on the ratio of total funds in its account to its total taxable payroll—the reserve ratio. If R_t is total reserves credited to the employer's account in year t, W the taxable wage base per employee, and N the total number of employees, then the reserve ratio is $r_t = R_t/WN$. Assuming WN_t is approximately constant (most state programs use weighted averages over several years), r_t follows $r_t = r_{t-1} + \tau_t - \rho\mu_t$, where $\rho = B/W$.

Between the maximum and minimum rates, τ_t is defined as a step function of r_t. When these steps are small, the function may be treated as approximately linear: $\tau = \eta_0 - \eta_1 r$. Then taxes follow the difference equation

$$\tau_{t+1}W = \bar{\tau}_{t+1} = (1-\eta_1)\bar{\tau}_t + \eta_1 B\mu_t.$$

Using this equation, a current increment to μ_t generates future taxes worth $B\eta_1/(\eta_1 + i)$ where i is the rate of interest. Thus, dividing by the value of benefits received, $e = \eta_1/(\eta_1 + i)$. In a typical system, $\eta_1 = .3$ so with $i = .1$, $e = .75$.

For a large step in the tax function at ratio $\hat{r}$, the linear approximation is less appropriate. In general, the step may be characterized as $\tau = \tau_1$ for $r < \hat{r}$ and $\tau = \tau_0$ for $r > \hat{r}$. The tax rate that would support a steady-state value of μ is $\tau^* = \rho\mu = \tau_0 + \phi(\tau_1 - \tau_0)$ where $0 < \phi < 1$. Thus, when $\tau = \tau_0$, reserves decline at rate

$$r_t - r_{t-1} = \tau_0 - \rho\mu_t = -\phi(\tau_1 - \tau_0) = -\phi\Delta\tau.$$

Conversely, if $\tau = \tau_1$, reserves accumulate at rate

$$r_t - r_{t-1} = \tau_1 - \rho\mu_t = (1-\phi)\Delta\tau.$$

Now the tax authority sets τ on the basis of r at annual evaluations. A firm with $\tau_0 < \tau^* < \tau_1$ will find that its taxes alternate between τ_0 and τ_1 as its reserve ratio is above or below $\hat{r}$ at the evaluation dates. Define the beginning of such a cycle, $\hat{t}$, as the first instant where r_t crosses $\hat{r}$ from above, and let α be the proportion of a year remaining from $\hat{t}$ to an evaluation. Assuming $\phi < .5$ (derivations for $\phi > .5$ are symmetrical), reserves

decline to $\hat{r} - \Delta\tau\phi\alpha$ at the first evaluation, they rise for one year to $\hat{r} + \Delta\tau(1 - \phi(1+\alpha))$, and then decline to $\hat{r}$ after $\phi^{-1} - (1 + \alpha)$ periods. Thus, the length of a cycle is ϕ^{-1}, of which $\phi^{-1} - 1$ periods have a tax of τ_0 and one has a tax of τ_1. As of the first evaluation, the present value of the surcharge $\Delta\tau$ for one period is $\Delta\tau(1 - e^{-i})/i$. Assuming that α is uniformly distributed on the unit interval, the expected present value of the tax surcharge as of the period $\hat{t}$ is

$$\int_0^1 \Delta\tau \frac{(1-e^{-i})}{i} e^{-i\alpha}\,d\alpha = \Delta\tau\left(\frac{1-e^{-i}}{i}\right)^2.$$

Since this surcharge occurs every ϕ^{-1} periods, the present value of the firm's future tax rate is

$$\frac{\tau_0}{i} + \Delta\tau\left(\frac{1-e^{-i}}{i}\right)^2 + \Delta\tau\left(\frac{1-e^{-i}}{i}\right)\frac{e^{-i/\phi}}{1-e^{-i/\phi}}$$

Now consider a change in unemployment that lasts exactly one period and generates change in reserves $dr = -\rho\,d\mu$. This change implies that the end of the cycle occurs $dr/\phi\Delta\tau$ periods sooner, and so the change in the present value of taxes as measured from the point where the cycle would have ended is

$$\beta = \Delta\tau\left(\frac{1-e^{-i}}{i}\right)^2\left(\frac{(\exp(i\,dr/\phi\Delta\tau)-1)}{1-e^{i\phi-1}}\right).$$

Discounting this value to the period t_0, where the shock commences, and assuming that t_0 is uniformly distributed on $(0, \phi^{-1})$, that is, that layoffs can begin at any time, yields an expected present value of the tax increment of

$$(A1) \qquad \beta\int_0^{\phi^{-1}} \phi e^{-i(\phi^{-1}-t_0)}\,dt_0$$

$$= \left(\frac{1-e^{-i}}{i}\right)^2 (\exp(i\,dr/\phi\Delta\tau)-1)\frac{\phi\Delta\tau}{i}.$$

The change in benefits received per unit of taxable payroll is just dr, so dividing (A1) by dr and letting $x = (\phi\Delta\tau/i\,dr)^{-1}$, we have an expected marginal cost of benefits of $((1 - e^{-i})/i)^2(e^x - 1)/x$. Now $x \to 0$ as $dr \to 0$, and so as increments to unemployment become small this marginal cost approaches

$((1 - e^{-i})/i)^2 \approx 1/(1 + i)$. Therefore, the reserve-ratio system generates approximately a one-year interest-free loan for *UI* payments made by firms located in large steps of the tax function. Consequently, the marginal cost of benefits in reserve-ratio states jumps from $\eta_1/(\eta_1 + i)$ to $1/(1 + i)$ for equilibrium unemployment rates in the range $(\tau_0/\rho, \tau_1/\rho)$.

B. *The Likelihood Function*

In a sample of full-time full-year participants, individuals may be categorized among three labor force "states" as of the sample period, t. These are employment (e), on temporary layoff (l), and unemployed without prospect of rehire (d). Over time, individuals move among these states, and I assume that in a stationary environment the cumulative distribution of *completed* spell lengths τ in state i is $F^i(\tau)$. The conditional density of *incomplete* spell lengths among workers in state i at the survey date is then

$$(A2) \quad h^i(T) = \frac{v^i(t-T)}{V^i(t)}\{1 - F^i(T)\},$$

where $v^i(t - T)$ is the probability that a spell

commenced at $t - T$ and $V^i(t)$ is the probability of observing an individual in i. The probability of observing the Tth week of a spell of type i is then simply $h^i(T)V^i(t)$.

Now if transitions are first-order Markov, a well known result from renewal theory (D. R. Cox, 1962) states that the distribution functions $F^i(\tau)$ must be exponential. (For a more general analysis, see Chris Flinn and James Heckman, 1980.) The conditional exit-time densities given elapsed time in the state—the hazard functions—are constants given by $f^i(\tau)/(1 - F^i(\tau))$. Denote these transition rates by λ^{el}, λ^{ed}, λ^{le}, and λ^{de}. I assume that $\lambda^{dl} = \lambda^{ed} = 0$, so that permanent layoffs cannot become temporary and conversely.

Straightforward calculation shows that the steady-state probability of observing randomly selected individual a in state e, employment, is simply

$$(A3) \quad \phi^e(t) = \frac{\lambda^{le}}{\lambda^{el} + \lambda^{le} + \lambda^{ed}\lambda^{le}/\lambda^{de}},$$

which is independent of t. Using this, we have, for example, $v^l(t - \tau) = \lambda^{el}\phi^e(t)$. Therefore, the probabilities of observing the

---

TABLE A1—VARIABLE DEFINITIONS AND SUMMARY STATISTICS, MARCH 1975 *CPS* SAMPLE

Variable	Definition	Mean	Standard Deviation
Subsidy	Total *UI* subsidy as proportion of weekly earnings (imputed)	.31	.19
Replacement Ratio	Potential *UI* benefits as proportion of weekly after-tax earnings (imputed)	.56	.15
Growth Rate[a]	Predicted rate of growth of state, private, non-agricultural employment from auxiliary regressions	1.27	1.86
Weekly Wage	Annual earnings ÷ weeks worked last year	202.49	98.02
Age	Age in years	39.50	12.60
Education	Years of completed schooling	12.20	2.50
Sex	= 1 if individual is male, = 0 otherwise	.73	.45
Race	= 1 if individual is white, = 0 otherwise	.90	.31
T	Duration of a temporary layoff spell in progress (weeks)	10.50	7.50
Layoffs[a]	= 1 if worker on temporary layoff, = 0 otherwise	7.11	25.70
Observations		7,806	

Note: Original sample included 8,280 observations. The estimation procedure conditions on the sample of workers who are on layoff or employed, so discharges (435) and quits (39) are deleted from the final sample.

[a]Growth Rate and Layoffs are shown in percent.

*T*th week of a layoff and discharge spell are, respectively,

$$(A4) \quad \phi^l(t, T) = \phi^e(t)\lambda^{el}\exp\{-T\lambda^{el}\},$$

$$(A5) \quad \phi^d(t, T) = \phi^e(t)\lambda^{ed}\exp\{-T\lambda^{ed}\}.$$

These depend on all four hazards, and so estimation of the full model involves a number of parameters equal to four times the number of regressors. We may economize to analyze passages to and from temporary layoff, however, by conditioning the sample on those individuals who are not in state *d*. Using (A3) and (A4) this reduces the number of unknowns to λ^{le} and λ^{el}, and results in equations (2) and (3) of the text. This sample restriction reduced the sample size to 7,806 from 8,280.

Summary statistics for these data used in estimating this model are shown in Table A1.

REFERENCES

Baily, Martin Neil, "On the Theory of Layoffs and Unemployment," *Econometrica*, July 1976, *44*, 1043–63.

Becker, Joseph, *Experience Rating in Unemployment Insurance: An Experiment in Competitive Socialism*, Baltimore and London: Johns Hopkins University Press, 1972.

——, *Unemployment Insurance Financing*, Washington: American Enterprise Institute, 1981.

Brechling, Frank, "Layoffs and Unemployment Insurance," in S. Rosen, ed., *Studies in Labor Markets*, Chicago: University of Chicago Press, 1981.

Cox, D. R., *Renewal Theory*, London: Methuen and Co., 1962.

Diamond, Peter, "Mobility Costs, Frictional Unemployment, and Efficiency," *Journal of Political Economy*, August 1981, *89*, 798–812.

Feldstein, Martin, "The Importance of Temporary Layoffs: An Empirical Analysis," *Brookings Papers on Economic Activity*, 3: 1975, 725–44.

——, "Temporary Layoffs in the Theory of Unemployment," *Journal of Political Economy*, August 1976, *84*, 937–57.

——, "The Effect of Unemployment Insurance on Temporary Layoff Unemployment," *American Economic Review*, December 1978, *68*, 834–46.

——, "The Economics of the New Unemployment," *Public Interest*, Fall 1973, *33*, 3–42.

Flinn, Chris and Heckman, James, "Models for the Analysis of Labor Force Dynamics," Working Paper, National Opinion Research Center, Chicago, 1980.

Hall, Robert, "Turnover in the Labor Force," *Brookings Papers on Economic Activity*, 3: 1972, 709–56.

——, "A Theory of the Natural Unemployment Rate and the Duration of Unemployment," *Journal of Monetary Economics*, April 1979, *5*, 153–69.

Hamermesh, Daniel, *Jobless Pay and the Economy*, Baltimore: Johns Hopkins University Press, 1979.

Kiefer, Nicholas and Neumann, George, "An Empirical Job-Search Model, with a Test of the Constant Reservation-Wage Hypothesis," *Journal of Political Economy*, February 1979, *87*, 89–107.

Nickell, Steven, "Estimating the Probability of Leaving Unemployment," *Econometrica*, September 1979, *47*, 1249–66.

Salant, Steven, "Search Theory and Duration Data: A Theory of Sorts," *Quarterly Journal of Economics*, February 1977, *91*, 39–57.

Topel, Robert, (1982a) "Inventories, Layoffs, and the Short-Run Demand for Labor," *American Economic Review*, September 1982, *92*, 769–87.

——, (1982b) "Unemployment Insurance, Experience Rating, and the Occurrence of Unemployment," unpublished paper, University of Chicago, January 1982.

—— and Welch, Finis, "Unemployment Insurance: Survey and Extensions," *Economica*, August 1980, *47*, 351–79.

Welch, Finis, "What Have We Learned from Empirical Studies on Unemployment Insurance?," *Industrial and Labor Relations Review*, July 1977, *30*, 451–61.

U.S. Department of Labor, Bureau of Labor Statistics, *Employment and Earnings, States and Areas*, Washington: USGPO, 1909–75.

_____, *Current Population Survey*, March File (computer tape), 1975.

_____, *Unemployment Insurance Statistics*, Washington, 1979.

_____, **Bureau of Employment Security**, *Significant Provisions of State Unemployment Insurance Laws*, Washington, January

1979.

_____, **Employment and Training Administration**, *Handbook of Unemployment Insurance Financial Data [1938–76]*, Washington, 1978.

_____, **Unemployment Insurance Service**, *Handbook of Unemployment Insurance Financial Data [1938–1980]*, Washington 1971.

Part V
Critique and Extensions

[12]

Review of Economic Studies (1980) XLVII, 321–338
© 1980 The Society for Economic Analysis Limited

0034-6527/80/00160321 $02.00

The Implicit Contract Theory of Unemployment meets the Wage Bill Argument

GEORGE A. AKERLOF
London School of Economics

and

HAJIME MIYAZAKI
Stanford University

1. INTRODUCTION

In recent papers by Baily (1974), D. F. Gordon (1974) and Azariadis (1975) it has been proposed that labour market transactions can be viewed as typically (implicit) contractual arrangements between risk averse employees and less risk averse employers. Their contributions suggest that the employers, in these contracts, "insure" their employees by paying them wage rates with small variations over the states of nature; in return, the employers are compensated for their "gamble" by premia in the form of lower average wages (the average being taken over states of nature) which workers are implicitly willing to pay for such wage insurance. Although both Azariadis and Baily have been cautious about drawing macro-economic implications from sticky wages in their models, subsequent proponents of indexed labour contracts argue that the risk-shifting aspects of implicit contracts may successfully account for the non-neutrality of monetary policies on aggregate output and employment. (See for example Gray (1976), (1978), Poole (1976) and Fischer (1977).) Because unemployment in many Keynesian macro-models is caused by rigid wages, by a parallel argument it has been held that the smoothing of wages caused by implicit contracts results in non-Walrasian fluctuations in employment. The present paper questions this last claim on unemployment; for it is demonstrated here, if workers can (implicitly) make contracts with the firm, they can also readily insure against employment variations (i.e. layoffs) and, as a result, implicit contracts even with sticky wages will lead to full employment, in most instances, rather than to unemployment.

To outline our logic, suppose that there is an implicit contract whereby in a state of the world s a firm employs n_1 workers at a wage w but lays off n_2 workers, each worker randomly being laid off with the same probability $n_2/(n_1+n_2)$. First observe that a risk averse employee would prefer, *ex ante*, a contract which guaranteed him employment in state s at the wage $wn_1/(n_1+n_2)$ to the lottery of receiving w with probability $n_1/(n_1+n_2)$ and 0 with probability $n_2/(n_1+n_2)$. Secondly, note that the firm would be indifferent between this employment-guaranteeing contract and the layoff contract since its wage bill is unchanged at wn_1. These two observations (together with the assumed continuity of the worker's preferences) imply the existence of a wage rate w^* such that (i) $w^* < w_1n_1/(n_1+n_2)$ and (ii) the worker strictly prefers guaranteed employment at w^*. Likewise a profit-maximizing firm would be willing to offer a full employment guarantee at w^* because it can reduce its wage bill from wn_1 to $w^*(n_1+n_2)$ without sacrificing its output. Because

321

both firms and workers prefer full-employment to layoffs in any given state, it follows that unemployment cannot occur in an equilibrium with rationally negotiated contracts.

We call the argument just given the *Wage Bill Argument*. It says that both the firm and the worker prefer a wage with guaranteed employment to a contract in which the worker gambles on being employed only with probability less than one, albeit at a higher wage rate. It is called the Wage Bill Argument because the rationale behind full employment lies solely in the firm's ability to minimize its average wage bill in the market for labour contracts more or less irrespective of specific conditions in output markets. This paper concerns itself with the extent to which the Wage Bill Argument invalidates the use of implicit contract theory to account for layoffs and unemployment. In so doing it adds to the growing critical literature on implicit contract theory, which includes papers by R. J. Gordon (1976a), Negishi (1976), Sargent (1976), Varian (1976), Barro (1977), Grossman (1977), (1978a), Mortensen (1978), Polemarchakis and Weiss (1978) amongst others.

Section 2 of this paper presents the workings of the labour contract economy a bit more formally. The paper adopts the basic model of Azariadis, Baily and D. F. Gordon. The purpose of such formal modelling is dual: first, to elucidate the underlying (Nash) concept of competitive equilibrium in the labour market, and second to point out the critical assumption of ex-post immobile labour and its role in the basic Azariadis–Baily formulations. In Section 3, we use the Wage Bill Argument to show that with this immobility assumption there cannot be an equilibrium with less than full employment in any state. Further, we interpret and extend the logic of the Wage Bill Argument as various assumptions are relaxed, but always pay special attention to the macro-economic unemployment and wage-variation issues. It is equally important to investigate circumstances wherein the Wage Bill Argument may fail. Section 4 shows that the basic Azariadis–Baily contract model falls short of explaining unemployment beyond what has already been accounted for within the neoclassical framework of " spot " labour auctions; hence the contribution of implicit contract theory in this context is nugatory.

The failure of implicit contract theory to yield layoff unemployment in the basic Azariadis–Baily model, however, need not *ipso facto* lead to a rejection of the usefulness of the theory in all situations, notably for the real economy, of which the Azariadis–Baily model offers in many respects too simplistic a description. For that reason this paper further examines in Section 5 the possibility of unemployment, where a worker is *ex post* mobile and free to accept a job at a firm other than that of his initial contract. There we construct a simple economy to elucidate the cyclical nature of any unemployment due to ex-post labour mobility. In particular, this example of unemployment gives little reason to believe that implicit contracts are an explanation for a phenomenon so common as involuntary unemployment. More fundamentally, removal of the labour immobility assumption has important implications for the determination of the individual firm's labour pool, which is key to the meaning of contract models. Discussion of these implications is contained in Section 6, with the necessity of a richer institutional context for labour contracts being re-emphasized.

2. THE ECONOMY

2.1. *The Basic Azariadis–Baily Model*

We shall adopt the Azariadis formulation of a two-period steady-state economy that consists of a large number of identical firms and an even larger but fixed number of homogeneous workers. Such a formulation accords well with Baily's model and parallels D. F. Gordon's framework. The first period is an ex-ante situation wherein workers join the firm by agreeing on labour contracts before the occurrence of a specific state of the world. In the second period, a specific state is realized and the economy adjusts *ex post* to this reality within the limits of the flexibility permitted by the binding terms of ex-ante contracts. The set of firms is partitioned into industries,[1] each of which latter produces exactly one kind of uniform output using capital and labour. The capital is malleable *ex ante*, but becomes fixed and industry-specific *ex post*. To keep the model simple, we postulate that the firm rents only one unit of capital at the ex-ante market-clearing rental price r, which thus becomes a fixed cost to be paid in any ex-post state. The firm's production function is described as $f(n)$, which is strictly concave and increasing in the labour input n.

It is assumed that there are no contingent deliveries of outputs, and that each output market is always cleared by Walrasian auction in the competitive ex-post spot markets, in which the firm acts as a price-taker. Output prices, however, fluctuate depending on the state of the world. The occurrence of a particular state s is revealed to an agent *via* an economy-wide output price vector $[p_j]$ whose dimension equals the number of industries.[2] We assume that these states, or for that matter the random price vectors, $[p_j(s)]$, have a known stationary probability distribution $q(s) > 0$ and $\Sigma_s q(s) = 1$, $s = 1, ..., S$. We will then denote by $p_j(s)$ the output price the jth firm faces in state s. The interpretation of the random price vector is that the economy experiences stochastic inter-industry shifts in demand, as well as macro-economic fluctuations in the level of aggregate demand.

Even though each agent is interested in relative prices and real wages, a competitive agent in the specific market set-up of the Azariadis–Baily model takes as given the price level defined for each state. Thus, all prices p_j and wage rates w throughout the paper will represent real terms, meaning that they are all deflated by a well-defined general price index for each state (see Azariadis, Negishi, and Varian for this convention). It should be noted here, however, that the model is not cast as a complete general equilibrium framework, since any explicit feedback between prices and wages *via* profit disbursement and workers' income is ignored. In this paper, we do not pursue the cause of aggregate fluctuations in output demand. Instead, within the realm of partial equilibrium analysis, we ask a meaningful question, " What will be the individual firm's response in its wage–employment policies when it faces a fluctuating demand for its output? " From this viewpoint, a high output price is interpreted as the manifestation of a strong demand for the firm's output, and conversely, low demand for output is signalled *via* low output prices.[3]

2.2. *The Labour Market*

The model postulates that any labour contract must be concluded in the ex-ante period, and that the terms of a contract cannot be changed in the ex-post period. Since workers are identical by assumption, the firm first offers a uniform contract to all workers, and secondly, if the firm lays off workers, then it does so by random choice among the initial signers of the contract. We make additional simplifications by assuming that (i) the worker's income consists only of earned wages, (ii) there is an institutionally defined workday, and (iii) the worker chooses only one labour contract.[4]

The worker's preferences are represented by a von Neumann–Morgenstern utility function U defined on non-negative wage rates w. This U is assumed to be strictly concave, increasing and bounded on $[0, \infty)$; the condition $U(0) = 0$ is imposed for computational simplicity.[5] These assumptions on U mean that the worker is willing to work the whole day at any positive w, and chooses a whole day of pure leisure only at a zero wage. In terms of labour contracts, a zero wage rate is equivalent to the status of being laid off; thus, in any ex-post state, the worker either works the whole day at a positive wage rate, or does not work at all, thereby receiving no income.

The firm is an expected profit maximizer. A labour contract C_j offered by the jth firm specifies a pair $(w_j(s), n_j(s))$ where $w_j(s)$ is the wage rate promised and $n_j(s)$ the employment level planned by the jth firm in state s. Since the rental price r is a fixed cost to be paid in any state, the firm maximizes its mean return after payment of its wage bill. It is then convenient to define the expected profit of the jth firm offering the contract C_j as

$$E\Pi_j(C_j) = \Sigma_s q(s)\Pi_j(s)$$

where

$$\Pi_j(s) = p_j(s)f(n_j(s)) - w_j(s)n_j(s).$$

On the other hand, a worker cannot evaluate the expected utility of a given contract C_j unless he is also informed of the size of the firm's labour pool—the number of workers who join the firm under the given contract. Let λ_j represent the size of this labour pool. Then, the contingent probability of employment within the jth firm's labour pool is $\min(1, n_j(s)/\lambda_j)$.

2.3. *Critical Assumptions*

We now state the usually implicit, yet very critical, Assumption (A), without which the basis of equilibrium analysis in this and other existing contract models is profoundly affected. This assumption amounts to saying that labour is "economically" immobile in the ex-post period.

Assumption (A). The worker does not have an ex-post employment opportunity outside the firm of his ex-ante contract.

For the use and justification of such an assumption, the reader is invited to consult the discussion on "bilateral enforceability" by Azariadis and on "mobility costs" by Baily. This assumption not only is designed to simplify otherwise complex analysis, but represents also, it will be later argued, a proposition which is indispensable to the model's consistency in both the theoretical and institutional spheres: reappraisal of the theory consequent on the removal of (A) will be deferred until Sections 5 and 6. For the present our task is limited to an analysis of the questions of interest while keeping as close as possible to the content of the basic Azariadis–Baily model.

Two immediate simplifications are available as a result of the ex-post immobility assumption. First, under (A), the firm is able to secure its actual labour force only from its own labour pool; consequently, the expected utility value of a contract C_j with λ_j is simply

$$EU(C_j, \lambda_j) = \Sigma_s q(s)(n_j(s)/\lambda_j)U(w_j(s)).$$

Secondly, the ex-post lack of job opportunities outside the initial firm, say the jth, means effectively that contractual terms must be made contingent solely on the firm's own output price p_j.

Let EU^* be the level of expected utility available to workers through accepting contracts elsewhere in the economy. In this formulation, competitive bidding in the contract market means that the firm maximizes its expected profits subject to the constraint that it promises an expected utility level at least equal to EU^*, whose equilibrium value is determined in the market. Formally stated, the firm has to solve the constrained expected profit-maximization problem described below.

Maximize $E\Pi_j(C_j)$ subject to the constraints

$$n_j(s) \leq \lambda_j \quad \text{for all } s \text{ (labour pool constraint)}$$

$$EU(C_j, \lambda_j) \geq EU^* \text{ (expected utility constraint)}.$$

Several economic considerations ensure that this problem will have an interior solution, with $n_j(s) > 0$, $w_j(s) > 0$, and $\lambda_j > 0$. If $w_j(s)$ happens to be zero, then no worker will work for this firm, thereby precluding it from earning a positive profit in state s. A zero wage and zero labour input are clearly suboptimal for the firm. This is a direct implication of the assumption that U is concave on all non-negative wage rates. Because the worker has no alternative ex-post employment opportunity, the firm can secure any size of work force within λ_j by paying any positive wage rate. The firm can always find some positive wage rate to make a positive profit by employing some workers. Therefore, within the labour pool constraint, both $n_j(s) > 0$ and $w_j(s) > 0$ must hold for a profit-maximizing solution.

Without affecting the qualitative results we can make the innocuous assumption that the value of r appearing in the model is consistent with the given level of expected profit that characterizes a market equilibrium. In particular, we may impose a (long-run) zero expected profit condition $(E\Pi = r)$. The market valuation of EU^* should decrease if there are workers who are unable to sign up for contracts. If some firms cannot sign up enough workers to fill its planned $E\Pi$-maximizing labour pool, then EU^* will increase. In competitive equilibrium in the contract market, the firm perceives a horizontal supply curve of labour at EU^*, and all workers join firms through contracts in the ex-ante labour market; EU^* serves the role of a market-clearing price of contracts in the ex-ante labour market.

3. FULL-EMPLOYMENT EQUILIBRIUM

We present here an intuitive proof, *via* the Wage Bill Argument, that equilibrium is, in fact, characterized by a fixed-wage-*cum*-full-employment equilibrium.[6] Despite the simplicity of the logic involved in the Wage Bill Argument, it will prove to be a powerful aid in the derivation of extensive implications of contract theory. A few of these, to be found at the end of this section, should be unsettling to those users of the contract approach who so cheerfully advance their analyses under the presupposition that implicit contract models ineluctably generate layoff unemployment.

Theorem. *Under the immobility Assumption* (A), *equilibrium entails a set of fixed-wage-cum-full-employment contracts such that for each j,*

$$\lambda_j = n_j(s) \quad \text{for all } s, \qquad \qquad \text{...(T.1)}$$

$$w^* = w_j(s) \quad \text{for all } s, \qquad \qquad \text{...(T.2)}$$

and

$$f'(\lambda_j) = w^*/Ep_j, \quad \text{where } Ep_j = \Sigma_s q(s) p_j(s) \qquad \text{...(T.3)}$$

Proof of Theorem. The proof of the full-employment property (T.1) is based on the Wage Bill Argument. Suppose in an equilibrium there exists a state s in which some firms would lay off their workers. Let j be such a firm so that $0 < n_j(s) < \lambda_j$ with a positive wage rate $w_j(s)$.[7] We claim that this jth firm can raise its expected profit by lowering $w_j(s)$, without reducing its output level, while at the same time maintaining the expected utility level it guarantees to its workers. The existence of such a wage–employment policy is indicated by the inequality: $U(w_j(s)n_j(s)/\lambda_j) > (n_j(s)/\lambda_j)U(w_j(s))$ where $n_j(s) < \lambda_j$ by assumption. This means that there exists a $w'_j(s)$ strictly less than $w_j(s)n_j(s)/\lambda_j$ such that $U(w'_j(s)) \geqq (n_j(s)/\lambda_j)U(w_j(s))$. The firm can offer a contract that promises to employ all λ_j workers in state s at the wage rate $w'_j(s)$. Consequently, its wage bill $w'_j(s)\lambda_j$ is lower than $w_j(s)n_j(s)$, while the worker's utility level in that state remains the same. Even at the lower wage rate of $w'_j(s)$, the firm has no difficulty in securing λ_j workers since the λ_j workers have no employment opportunities outside this firm under (A). Therefore, the contract with $(w'_j(s), \lambda_j)$ replacing $(w_j(s), n_j(s))$ for the state s is feasible *ceteris paribus*, and improves the firm's expected profit. Hence, the contract specifying $n_j(s) < \lambda_j$ cannot be a profit-maximizing contract for the jth firm, contradicting the assumption that the market was in equilibrium. It has thus been shown that in an equilibrium all firms adopt the full-employment policy $n_j(s) = \lambda_j$ for all s. The expected utility of such a full-employment contract is $\Sigma_s q(s)U(w_j(s))$, where $[w_j(s)]$ now denotes the accompanying wage-policy.

We next prove the fixed-wage property (T.2). Once again by the use of an inequality on the strictly concave U, we can find a constant wage $w_j^* = w_j(s)$ such that

$$U(\Sigma_s q(s)w_j(s)) > U(w_j^*) > \Sigma_s q(s)U(w_j(s)).$$

The worker's expected utility is thus increased by the constant wage contract. Such a fixed wage policy is also preferred by the firm because the average wage bill is reduced from $\Sigma_s q(s) w_j(s) \lambda_j$ to $w_j^* \lambda_j$. Since expected profit is now expressed as

$$E\Pi_j = (Ep_j)f(\lambda_j) - w_j^* \lambda_j,$$

the profit maximizing labour pool is given by the familiar marginal condition

$$(Ep_j)f'(\lambda_j) - w_j^* = 0.$$

In equilibrium with homogeneous labour $EU^* = U(w_j^*)$ and all firms pay the uniformly fixed wage rate $w^* = w_j^*$. Competitive forces in contract bidding would gravitate the market toward satisfying the equilibrium conditions jointly determining EU^*.[8] ∥

The interpretation and generality of our full-employment theorem requires some further elaboration and comments. We have collected five remarks in the remainder of this section, which, it is hoped, will further elucidate the nature of contracts, and will emphasize the critical importance of the labour immobility Assumption (A), upon which the basic model of Azariadis–Baily, and its variants, are based. In the following remarks, the firm index j will be suppressed unless confusion might result.

Remark 1. *Concave Utility*

In considering the full-employment outcome, one might be tempted to suggest that our result depends upon the assumed " $U(0) = 0$ " and the assumption of zero income to the laid-off worker. In fact, under the proviso of concave utility, the Wage Bill Argument requires neither assumption in asserting the fixed-wage-*cum*-full-employment outcome.

Thus, let the firm pay its own compensation $c(s)$ per day to each of the $\lambda - n(s)$ workers that were laid-off, and the wage rate $w(s)$ to the worker retained on the job. Then, the worker's anticipated utility in the state s would be equal to

$$[n(s)/\lambda] U(w(s)) + [1 - n(s)/\lambda] U(c(s)).$$

Under the assumed concavity of U, the worker's expected utility will be raised if the firm agrees to promise an employment guarantee at the average wage rate

$$[n(s)/\lambda] w(s) + [1 - (n(s)/\lambda)] c(s).$$

The profit-conscious firm can be induced to offer such a full-employment provision because its total wage bill in this state is unchanged at $n(s)w(s) + [\lambda - n(s)]c(s)$. Consequently, the Wage Bill Argument is directly applicable and gives the full employment outcome.

In so far as the worker's utility is concave and bounded for non-negative wage rates, it is innocuous to normalize $U(0) = 0$ and to assume $c(s) = 0$. It is important, however, to examine plausible causes which render U locally non-concave. In the next section we shall see some of the qualifications that a non-concave U necessitates in the interpretation of our full-employment outcome. For the moment we limit our attention to considering implications of the Wage Bill Argument under a concave U.[9]

Remark 2. *Labour Hoarding*

The logic of the Wage Bill Argument has not had any recourse to the assumed competitiveness of the output markets, suggesting that our *Theorem* holds for a broad class of output markets. Even when the firm faces a non-Walrasian situation in the output market, it can always attain higher profits by reducing its wage bill *via* an employment guarantee in the given state. Specifically, let us consider the output market to include a so-called "disequilibrium" case, *aux* Barro–Grossman and Negishi. In a disequilibrial output market, in addition to the price signal $p(s)$, the firm faces a sales constraint $\bar{y}(s)$ beyond which it may perceive a downward sloping demand curve. The firm's subjective equilibrium in the output market is attained when the actual sales constraint becomes consistent with its perceived demand curve. So long as labour is cleared through ex-ante contracts, the Wage Bill Argument remains valid (cf. Negishi); in some states it will be the case that $f(\lambda) > \bar{y}(s)$, illustrating the firm's labour hoarding in s.

Thus, non-Walrasian output markets are helpful in understanding the labour hoarding behind our full-employment *Theorem* (cf. Varian); nonetheless, once the point of this interpretation is made, competitive spot auction in the output markets is perhaps a convenient simplification. Indeed, a strong proponent of contract theory would go further and say that the competitiveness of output markets is the assumption which underscores the purpose and intent of the implicit contract model;[10] we are thus led to the following remark.

Remark 3. *Macro-Indexation of Contracts*

In most Keynesian literature, the existence of unemployment depends on sticky wages, a base to which choice-theoretic micro-foundations have given only a grudging and partial support. Implicit contract theory can be seen as an attempt to explain wage determination as an aspect of equilibrium based on individuals' maximization behaviour. Given this, some macro-economists have invoked the contract approach to sticky wages in order to argue that monetary disturbances can cause non-Walrasian fluctuations in aggregate output and employment even in an environment characterized by rational expectations (e.g. Gray (1976), Poole (1976) and Fischer (1977)).

In the one-sector economy analysed by both Gray and Fischer, $P(s)$ is the nominal output price, $W(s)$ the nominal wage rate and $W(s)/P(s)$ the real wage rate in state s. The degree of wage indexation is said to be full if $W(s)/P(s)$ is constant, and to be zero if $W(s)$ remains constant for all s. By identifying monetary disturbances with random prices, and real disturbances with noise in the production function, their formal analyses try to show that the optimal degree of wage indexation in contracts is not full, but is only " partial " with respect to the output price. The Wage Bill Argument applied to the Gray–Fischer model demonstrates that the " optimal " degree of indexation in the model is full with respect to either type of disturbance. These disturbances are neutral, having little significance for the full-employment property of equilibrium contracts. This is because, once the firm and its own workers agree to use the firm's own output prices as their basis of wage indexation, it becomes immaterial what causes the fluctuations in $Pf(n)$. In any demand state with observable and given $P(s)$, the firm can always reduce its wage bill by paying the employment-guaranteeing lower wage rate to all its workers!

Since the Gray–Fischer analysis is concerned with disturbances of the firm's labour demand schedule and not with the worker's labour supply schedule, their framework is essentially that of our *Theorem*. Nevertheless, they derive their non-neutrality conclusion because their contracts specify only the wage policy without providing the firm's accompanying employment policy. The Wage Bill Argument emphasizes the *simultaneous* determination of wage and employment policies, leading to full employment and sticky real wages in the competitive equilibrium of the labour contract model (cf. Barro (1977)).

Remark 4. *Imperfect Information*

There has also been some speculation that imperfect information coupled with contractual arrangements may successfully explain the alleged macro-economic non-neutrality of short-run monetary policy (see Barro (1977) and Grossman (1978)). Notice that under the present assumption of ex-post immobility, all contingencies are written almost solely in terms of the firm's own output prices; this structure suggests that the full-employment result will continue to hold even when either the worker or the firm is uncertain of the general price level P, in so far as the agent's inference on P is conditioned on the firm's own output price. A possible story here is that neither the individual firm, say the jth, nor its workers, typically have complete information about the prices of a consumption bundle, and that they must therefore estimate the macro-state of P through their own micro signal

328   REVIEW OF ECONOMIC STUDIES

of the nominal output price P_j to the jth firm. Let $W(P_j)$ be the nominal wage rate contingent on P_j. Note that both $W(P_j)$ and $n(P_j)$ are determined and only P remains random for the given demand state of P_j. Then worker's average utility in a typical demand state is given by $E_j(n(P_j)/\lambda)U[W(P_j)/P]$, which is less than $E_jU[W(P_j)n(P_j)/\lambda P]$, where E_j denotes the expectation of a worker in the jth firm, taken over P, conditional on P_j. Hence by the Wage Bill Argument applied to this state, both the worker and the firm are made better off by agreeing on an appropriate wage with guaranteed employment. Observe further that, since the firm and its workers share the same information partitions *via* P_j signals, the Wage Bill Argument is unaffected even when the firm and worker differ in their respective conditional probability assessments of P given the signal P_j.

The point is that with ex-post immobile labour there is not much uncertainty under the shared information partition. However, even under such a simple information structure, the possibility of ex-post mobile labour allows an interesting, but rather specific, example of unemployment. (See the first paragraph of Section 7.)

Remark 5. *Firm's Risk Aversion*

Finally, we must question the role of different degrees in risk aversion between firms and workers in explaining the existence and rationale of labour contracts. Suppose, as is often argued, that the firm is also risk averse, having a von Neumann–Morgenstern utility V which is concave and increasing in its profits. Application of the Wage Bill Argument to this case shows that the firm can always exploit the worker's risk aversion in order to reduce the total wage bill without sacrificing its output. Thus, regardless of the firm's degree of risk aversion in V, both the firm and the worker will prefer a full employment contract as long as the worker is risk averse. The information on the firm's risk aversion is needed only to draw some conclusions about the variation of wage rates across the states. The less risk-averse V is relative to U, the stickier the equilibrium wage variation will be; unless V is linear there will be some wage fluctuations in equilibrium.

The foregoing observation suggests that the essential rationale for the existence of " implicit " contracts need not be, and may indeed be quite apart from, risk-shifting between firms and workers. The reason for contractual arrangements could be technological (on-the-job training), organizational (internal labour markets) or as a response to informational impactedness (cf. Williamson (1975)). Whatever its rationale might be, once the employer and the workers agree on the feasibility of labour contracts, the risk-averse worker then will obtain a full-employment contract in the equilibrium of a competitive labour market.

4. QUALIFICATIONS

Of equal importance is an examination of situations wherein the Wage Bill Argument fails even under the assumed ex-post immobility of labour. This will serve to delineate the role of everywhere concave utility in ensuring the full-employment outcome. Under the assumed institutional indivisibility of the workday, and given some underlying leisure–labour trade-offs, there will be a positive reservation wage rate $\underline{w}$ below which the worker prefers to withdraw entirely from labour service and spend the whole day in pursuit of pure leisure.[11] The effective reservation wage rate will be even higher than this utility-determined $\underline{w}$ when the unemployed worker is entitled to collect an unemployment dole paid by the government *independently* of his firm's own labour contract. Let $k(s)$ represent the aggregate of all exogenously-paid unemployment compensation the worker receives in state s upon separation from the firm. Let u be the worker's concave utility defined on the $(w, \text{leisure})$-space with the usual derivative conditions. Leisure takes the value of either 1 or 0 by our institutional assumption. Then, the effective reservation wage rate $v(s)$ in state s is given by $u(k(s), 1) = \underline{U}(s) = u(v(s), 0)$. Then,

$$U(w) = \max\left[\underline{U}(s), u(w(s), 0)\right] \geqq \underline{U}(s).$$

AKERLOF & MIYAZAKI   UNEMPLOYMENT THEORY   329

That is, $U(w(s)) = u(w(s), 0)$ for $w(s) > v(s)$, and $U(w(s)) = \underline{U}(s)$ whenever $w(s) \leqq v(s)$, in which latter case the worker chooses a zero wage and pure leisure for the whole day. Thus the worker's utility function U is non-concave in the neighbourhood of $v(s)$. The Wage Bill Argument could then be blocked if the full-employment wage rate w^* in the Wage Bill Argument were to fall below $v(s)$ in some state, then the profit-maximizing firm would either lay off all workers or retain only some fraction of the initial labour force at a wage rate above $v(s)$. To ensure that the firm's constrained profit maximization entails a positive $n(s)$, a boundary condition such as $f'(0) = \infty$ must be imposed (cf. Azariadis). The possibility of layoffs due to the non-concave U notwithstanding, we emphasize that the basic model of contract theory is a model of full employment rather than of unemployment in the following qualified sense. Our claim is that the incidence of layoffs in the contractual equilibrium will be less than that predicted by the neoclassical model of spot labour auctions wherein ex-post labour transactions are cleared instantaneously by the auctioneer in the absence of ex-ante contracts.

To illustrate this point, suppose that the firm employs only $n(s)$ workers under the wage rate $w(s)$ above $v(s)$, and the discharged workers receive $k(s)$, say from the government, in state s. Then, in order for the Wage Bill Argument to fail, the firm's profit must be reduced if it employs all λ workers at a wage rate equal to $[n(s)/\lambda]w(s) + [1 - (n(s)/\lambda)]v(s)$. Such a reduction in profits, in turn, can be stated as

$$p(s)f(n(s)) - w(s)n(s) > p(s)f(\lambda) - w(s)n(s) - [\lambda - n(s)]v(s),$$

rearrangement of which gives the condition $[f(\lambda) - f(n(s))]/[\lambda - n(s)] < v(s)/p(s)$. However, the LHS of this inequality is larger than $f'(\lambda)$ because of the strictly concave f. We thus obtain the condition

$$p(s)f'(\lambda) < v(s).$$

That is, the necessary conditions for layoffs is that the value of the marginal productivity of labour at the full-employment level must be less than the worker's " effective " *reservation wage* $v(s)$. This is the only unemployment that can occur in the basic Azariadis–Baily model.

Now, without recourse to the nexus of implicit contracts, it is already well known that reservation wages and exogenously available unemployment compensation can cause such " unemployment ". In the neoclassical regime without contracts, the labour market operates as an ex-post spot labour auction. Such a market will fail to clear if $p(s)f'(\lambda) < v(s)$. Thus, the set of unemployment states so generated in the labour contract regime is a *subset* of unemployment states of the corresponding neoclassical regime of labour auctions provided that the distribution of output prices and $v(s)$ are the same in each case.[12] In any event, such unemployment is purely voluntary: a worker values leisure with unemployment compensation more highly than working for a wage rate lower than $v(s)$.

In yet another variant of the labour contract model, it is possible to have layoffs if the firm incurs a training cost for each worker on the job. However, such layoffs are, in a well defined sense, not specific to the labour contract model. To demonstrate, we will have recourse to the contrapositive of the Wage Bill Argument as we did above. If the layoff of $\lambda - n(s)$ workers is to occur at the wage rate $w(s)$, then the firm's profit in state s must decrease when it retains all λ workers at a wage rate equal to $w(s)n(s)/\lambda$. Letting $t(n)$ be the training cost of " n " workers in real terms, this profit condition can be expressed as $p(s)[f(\lambda) - f(n(s))] < t(\lambda) - t(n(s))$, so that the net revenue product inclusive of the training costs of the extra $\lambda - n(s)$ workers in negative. In this case however, labour sold on a competitive spot market would have unemployment at any non-negative wage rate. And thus, unemployment will occur in the model with implicit contracts and training costs *only if* it also occurs in a corresponding neoclassical model of labour auctions with training costs; in this way training costs rather than implicit contracting cause the unemployment.

To sum up, consider a given industry with ex-post immobile labour, and imagine that the labour market of this industry is organized in two alternative ways; one is the neo-classical regime of ex-post spot auctions, and the other the ex-ante labour contract regime. In either case, the industry faces the same demand uncertainty. Then, it can be shown that the incidence of layoffs, due either to training costs or to reservation wage properties of U, is both more frequent and of greater magnitude under the neoclassical labour auction regime than under the labour contract regime.[13] In this regard, the explanatory power of the contract model in accounting for layoffs beyond what is already covered in the neo-classical story is nugatory. Since the neoclassical auction model of unemployment is seldom invoked to explain unemployment so persistent and prevalent as to cause the Keynesian social concern, the relative paucity of layoffs in the contract model can hardly prompt us to believe that this model adequately serves as a theory accounting for the importance of layoffs and unemployment. It is in this qualified sense that we regard the theoretical possibility of layoffs in the basic Azariadis–Baily model under immobile labour as being too limited to explain any aspects of the layoff process that were not well under-stood by the standard neoclassical paradigm (cf. Barro).[14]

In closing this section, we emphasize that the full-employment interpretation obtained above and in the *Theorem* depends heavily on the ex-post immobility assumption (A). It is this assumption that enables the firm to lower the wage rate in exploiting fully the worker's aversion to uncertainty without risking loss of some of them to rival firms. In turn, it was in the worker's interest to accept a steady employment path at a lower average wage in so far as he was unable to find jobs elsewhere *ex post*. Two important issues arise upon removal of (A). In the next section, it will be argued that ex-post mobile labour may result in a situation wherein the worker behaves as if unemployment compensation is provided by other firms. On the other side of the coin, the possibility of a worker's ex-post defection to other firms may cause the firm not to guarantee full employment to all of its own workers in order to maximize expected profits subject to the expected utility constraint. Hence, *if* an equilibrium exists in the presence of ex-post mobile labour, then there *may* be layoff unemployment in some states. To underscore the fact that layoff unemployment due to ex-post mobile labour is new and particular to the contract model, we shall continue to assume the restrictive conditions on U, namely, U is concave on all non-negative w and $U(0) = 0$ and also no training cost. If layoffs occur in such a set-up, we are thereby assured that they do not arise from those same causes which are familiar in the neoclassical story of labour auctions. A more fundamental issue to be dealt with in Section 6, however, is that removal of (A) results in non-negligible ramifications for the existence and proper concept of equilibrium to be applied in the labour-contract market.

5. EX-POST MOBILITY ADDED TO THE MODEL

The implausibility of the immobility Assumption (A) in the context of the Azariadis–Baily model will be argued on theoretical as well as legal grounds, especially under the assumed homogeneity of the labour force. In the full employment *Theorem*, the expected marginal-productivity condition (T.3) implies that there exists a state in which $p_j(s)f'(\lambda_j) > w^*$ since the economy under consideration is multi-sectoral and stochastic. Whenever the marginal value product of labour exceeds the wage rate, the firm can increase its profits by recruiting additional workers beyond λ_j in that state.[15] When there are such firms with an incentive to hire additional workers in the ex-post period, a worker then has employment oppor-tunities forthcoming from firms other than that of his initial contract. As to the legal basis of contracts, we observe in reality that a contract is " enforceable " only on firms but not on workers;[16] the bondage and discipline of labour is not licit. Of course the pecuniary and intangible cost of moving *ex post* from one firm to another could plausibly be argued to be greater than the cost involved in the ex-ante choice of firms. Neverthe-less, as we have ignored transaction costs in the ex-ante contracting process, the theory must not take ex-post cost too seriously either; the real world obviously lies somewhere

AKERLOF & MIYAZAKI   UNEMPLOYMENT THEORY   331

between the extremes of complete immobility and free mobility. Without affecting the ultimate implications of ex-post mobile labour, we shall consider the latter in theoretically polar opposition to the former, on which the existing contract theory is based.[17] Let us thus say that under any contract the worker is free to leave his initial firm and may seek employment at other firms that are recruiting in the ex-post period.

Once labour becomes freely mobile in the ex-post period, the worker's ex-ante evaluation of joining a firm must include both the contingent wage rates and the probabilities of employment by this and other firms in each state. Similarly, the firm must take into consideration the actual availability of labour in the ex-post period; if the wage rate is too low, then it may not be able to retain a viable work-force due to the recruitment drive of rival firms. Summing up, the evaluation of expected profits and utility both require a knowledge of $\{C_j\}$, the distribution of the set of all contracts offered in the economy. The information on $\{C_j\}$ is a sufficient statistic because, given the enforceability assumption, such ex-post labour reshuffles will be expected to take place only within the wage–employment configurations promised by the pre-existing set of labour contracts concluded in the ex-ante period.[18]

Economically, ex-post labour mobility allows the worker to seek an outside job, which if forthcoming plays the role of unemployment insurance to the worker in the case of layoffs by his initial firm. Furthermore, even if the worker is assured of employment by the firm, he will always search for employment at a higher-wage firm, and will stay at his initial firm only when no better opportunity materializes. Simply put, any lowering of a firm's wage rate induces more workers to quit the firm and accept *ex post* a better offer. This suggests that when the individual firm maximizes its profits subject to the expected utility constraint, it may not be in a position to lower its wage rate to accommodate a full-employment contract for its own workers. The Wage Bill Argument may thus fail and the possibility of unemployment equilibrium exists: We must, however, be careful about this logic because, unlike the government's payment of unemployment benefits, the opportunities of outside employment must be " endogeneously " generated as an equilibrium outcome of the contract market. In fact, we will demonstrate that the Wage Bill Argument is sufficiently powerful to cause any equilibrium with unemployment to be at least a trifle " odd ", in the sense which will be described presently.

When the economy is more or less uniformly in recession, outside employment opportunities are unlikely to be forthcoming, virtually eliminating the economic significance of labour mobility. In turn, the Wage Bill Argument becomes especially applicable to an economy in a general recession, which facilitates full-employment (labour hoarding) at low wage rates. On the other hand, when demand is relatively high across industries, the usual competitive mechanism operating to bid away ex-post mobile workers tends to bring forth a full employment state. Consequently, within the model of labour contracts with ex-post mobility, unemployment is most likely to occur, if ever, not in the recession but in an intermediate state between the peak and the trough, when some sectors absorb workers laid off by other sectors. In short, if ex-post labour mobility causes lay-offs, then such equilibrium may entail an unrealistic cyclical pattern of unemployment. We can pursue this unrealism even further and show that any such unemployment equilibrium requires a peculiar interpretation, namely, that the low demand sectors are paying higher wage rates than the sectors with higher demand. To illustrate this odd feature of unemployment, we construct below a simple example of a stochastic economy consisting of two symmetric industries.

The set of firms is partitioned into two industries, 1 and 2, of equal size; these two industries are assumed to be completely symmetric in regard to both market structure and the effects of uncertainty. There are four states of the world, labelled $s = s_0, s_1, s_2, s_3$, and a symmetric distribution of prices is summarized in Table I. Stochastic symmetry requires $q_1 = q_2$. Also, $p^+ > p^-$ is assumed, so that s_0 corresponds to the peak of a business cycle, s_3 the trough and s_1, s_2 are transition states between them.

TABLE I

		Industries	
Probabilities	States	1	2
q_0	s_0	$p+$	$p+'$
q_1	s_1	$p+$	$p-$
q_2	s_2	$p-$	$p+$
q_3	s_3	$p-$	$p-$

Given the symmetric structure of the economy, and the assumed homogeneity of agents, we may limit our discussion on contract equilibrium to the *symmetric equilibrium*, in which all firms adopt the same contract *strategies*, conditional upon their own output prices and the structure of the economy-wide price vector. The firm knows *ex hypothesi* the entire economy-wide price vector signal, not just its own output price. In particular, the equilibrium size of the initial labour pool λ is identical for all firms, and the state-dependent contingent terms constitute a mirror image between the two industries. (See Table II for a summary.) Thus, without ambiguity or confusion, we may use the subscript j ($j = 1, 2$) to denote both the industry and any member firm. We also arbitrarily choose a firm in industry 1 as the representative firm for our subsequent analysis of this economy; i.e. the economy is viewed in terms of this industry 1 firm.

TABLE II

A symmetric labour contract strategy

$$(w_1(s_0), n_1(s_0)) = (w_2(s_0), n_2(s_0))$$
$$(w_1(s_1), n_1(s_1)) = (w_2(s_2), n_2(s_2))$$
$$(w_1(s_2), n_1(s_2)) = (w_2(s_1), n_2(s_1))$$
$$(w_1(s_3), n_1(s_3)) = (w_2(s_3), n_2(s_3)).$$

To identify candidates for unemployment states in this two-industry equilibrium, first observe the following: if both industries adopt layoff policies for a given state, then *via* the Wage Bill Argument any firm will succeed in increasing its profit by offering a dominant full-employment policy for that state. We can immediately verify that a symmetric equilibrium entails full employment in both the boom state s_0 and the trough state s_3, so that unemployment, if it exists, will occur only in the transition states s_1 and s_2.

Without loss of generality we can henceforth limit our unemployment analysis to a state s wherein industry 1 lays off $\lambda - n_1$ workers at a wage rate w_1 while industry-2 firms recruit additional workers beyond λ at a wage rate $\bar{w}_2$. (s is either s_1 or s_2.) $Q(\bar{w}_2)$ shall denote the recruitment probability of the industry-1 worker who is seeking employment in industry 2. We are interested in the case where $0 < Q(\bar{w}_2) < 1$, so that we can characterize the necessary conditions of a symmetric equilibrium with ex-post unemployment. We do this first by proposing an alleged equilibrium wherein industry 1 lays off workers in some state. Then, we examine whether an individual industry-1 firm under Nash perception can increase its expected profits by deviating from the proposed equilibrium contract (w_1, n_1) which all other firms in industry 1 have adopted, given the industry-2 firm's contract ($\bar{w}_2$, $\bar{n}_2$), and $Q(\bar{w}_2)$. Because of the structural symmetry, the conditions that entail a symmetric equilibrium with unemployment are exhaustively specified in this way.

Let us examine the unemployment possibility by first supposing that $w_1 \leq \bar{w}_2$ in the alleged equilibrium with layoffs in industry 1. The worker in industry 1 first searches for employment in industry 2, and stays at his own firm only if he is unlucky enough not to be recruited into industry 2, but is lucky enough to be retained by his own firm. On the

AKERLOF & MIYAZAKI   UNEMPLOYMENT THEORY   333

average, of λ workers in the industry-1 firm, only $Q(\bar{w}_2)\lambda$ obtain jobs in industry 2. Hence, his valuation of utility in s is given by $(n_1/\lambda)U(w_1) + Q(\bar{w}_2)U(\bar{w}_2)$. Without loss of generality we may assume that $n_1 + \lambda Q(\bar{w}_2) < \lambda$.[19] Then by virtue of the Wage Bill Argument we can assert that any layoff configuration (w_1, n_1) with $n_1 < \lambda$, given $w_1 \leqq \bar{w}_2$, will be dominated by a full-employment configuration (w_1^*, λ) such that

$$w_1^* < n_1 w_1/\lambda(1 - Q(\bar{w}_2)) \quad \text{and} \quad (1 - Q(\bar{w}_2))U(w_1^*) > (n_1/\lambda)U(w_1).$$

Consequently, if an equilibrium entails $w_1 \leqq \bar{w}_2$, then it must be accompanied by full employment. Thus, a layoff equilibrium, if it exists, must entail $w_1 > \bar{w}_2$.

Now suppose that $w_1 > \bar{w}_2$, wherein the industry-1 worker looks for industry-2 employment only if he is laid off by the industry-1 firm.[20] Here, evaluation of the industry-1 worker's utility requires

$$V_1 = (n_1/\lambda)U(w_1) + [1 - (n_1/\lambda)]Q(\bar{w}_2)U(\bar{w}_2).$$

Now, depending on the values of $Q(\bar{w}_2)$ and $\bar{w}_2$, the Wage Bill Argument could fail in the sense that an employment-guaranteeing wage rate $(n_1/\lambda)w_1$ might adversely decrease the value of V_1.[21] Nevertheless, further inspection shows that the industry-1 firm, *under the proviso of* $p_1 > p_2$, can raise its profits by offering a policy which pays

$$w_1(n_1/\lambda) + (1 - (n_1/\lambda))Q(\bar{w}_2)\bar{w}_2$$

as a wage rate to its own λ workers. This follows from the following observation. The extra profit gained by employing λ workers at the wage rate $w_1(n_1/\lambda) + (1 - (n_1/\lambda))Q(\bar{w}_2)\bar{w}_2$ instead of n_1 workers at w_1 is

$$\Delta\Pi = p_1[f(\lambda) - f(n_1)] - (\lambda - n_1)Q(\bar{w}_2)\bar{w}_2$$

which is larger than $p_1(\lambda - n_1)[f'(\lambda) - Q(\bar{w}_2^{\frac{1}{2}})(\bar{w}_2/p_1)]$. Note that $f'(\lambda) > \bar{w}_2/p_2$ must hold in order for the industry-2 firm to hire additional workers beyond λ. Since $Q(\bar{w}_2) < 1$, $p_1 > p_2$ implies $\Delta\Pi > 0$ whenever $\lambda > n_1$. Such a wage rate and employment guarantee also raises the worker's expected utility. Thus, as a result of this modified Wage Bill Argument, we see that no unemployment layoffs occur in industry 1 under the provisos of $p_1 \geqq p_2$ and $w_1 > \bar{w}_2$. Consequently, the industry-1 firm's profit-maximizing solution entails a layoff contract only if $p_1 < p_2$.

Summing up, in a symmetric equilibrium, unemployment due to industry-1 layoffs occurs only if $w_1 > \bar{w}_2$ and $p_1 < p_2$ holds simultaneously. This last condition on the inter-industry price configuration makes intuitive sense; it means that industry 1 with a lower output price (hence a weak output demand) is dismissing workers, while industry 2 facing a higher demand (signalled *via* a higher output price) recruits additional workers. However, the existence of unemployment also implies that industry 1 with a lower output price pays a higher wage rate than industry 2 which has a higher output price.[22] This situation may be regarded as pathological, especially when a low output price signals weak demand for that industry. Nevertheless, such a peculiarity cannot be taken *ipso facto* as an indication of theoretical contradiction within the model. For, by the very nature of contractual arrangements across states, the usual unicursal link between the marginal productivity of labour and the actual wage rate paid in a given state is considerably weakened. However, such a peculiar combination of wages and prices does indicate a lack of realism on the part of the implicit contract model in explaining cyclical fluctuations in aggregate output and employment of the type we observe in most industrial economies. It is unrealistic because in equilibrium the firm is setting its own wage policy counter-cyclically in response to the fluctuation of demand states for its own output. We believe that such odd aspects of unemployment equilibrium persists in more complex settings of the labour contract model. In summary, with ex-post mobile labour there may be a contract equilibrium with layoffs, which was not previously accounted for by other models. Yet, the Wage Bill Argument is sufficiently powerful to insure that such a layoff equilibrium be odd and unrealistic, even though it is not sufficiently general to prevent the existence of such an equilibrium.

6. EQUILIBRIUM WITH MOBILE LABOUR

Competition in the labour market involves not only wages but also security (or probability) of employment status. Firms offer differentiated contracts as close substitutes in the labour market, and each worker chooses only one. It is then natural to adopt a Nash concept to characterize a " competitive " equilibrium of the labour market for contracts. That is, each agent computes the expected value of a contract taking the economy-wide distribution of contracts as given. The presence of uncertainty in the states of nature gives a rationale for state-contingent contracts. Additionally, the theory of implicit labour contracts emphasizes the importance of the firm's labour pool; it is this ex-ante labour pool that defines the worker's " attachment " to the firm, gives credence to the risk of layoffs, and finally, identifies the firm as being more than just a neoclassical production function. As a result, in order for the implicit contract model to make sense, it must have a Nash equilibrium with non-degenerate values of the firm's labour pool λ. That such a Nash notion underlies the Azariadis–Baily model is indicated by their formulations of the firm's constrained expected profit-maximization problem; allowing ex-post labour mobility serves to bring this point to the fore.

However, once the immobility assumption is removed, care must be taken in this extended Nash paradigm, for the economy under our specifications *might* have neither uniqueness nor even the existence of Nash equilibrium. This situation mainly arises because the Nash behaviour of the firm obscures the notion of λ_j, the firm's initial labour pool, which has been used as a central notion in defining the firm as an entity. Under the immobility assumption (A), profit maximization requires the firm to create a reasonably large labour pool within which the firm secures a viable supply of labour for all states. Once (A) is removed, λ_j becomes less crucial than heretofore as one of the firm's decision variables, but $w_j(s)$ becomes correspondingly more important as a means of both retaining and acquiring workers in the ex-post period.

To put it more dramatically, due to the ex-post availability of additional workers, in many circumstances the firm under Nash perception has a strong incentive to *reduce* the size of its initial labour pool in order to gain leverage in raising the expected utility guaranteed to its own contract workers, and thus to obtain additional increases in its expected profits. Nash equilibrium with non-degenerate labour pools may not obtain once the firm's choice variable λ is combined with the fact of ex-post mobile workers. It is perhaps possible to save the existence of equilibrium with well-defined labour pools by adopting a notion different from that of Nash. However, Nash equilibrium being one of the most plausible notions to describe the (non-cooperative) nature of large markets, one more attractive option here is to identify institutional and technological features which mitigate an individual firm's motive to reduce the size of its initial labour pool.

For instance, firm-specific human capital and skill acquisition on the job could necessitate the creation and maintenance of a labour pool in order for the worker to engage in life-cycle planning. Also, as a response to information impactedness and incentive problems, the firm may have to organize an internal labour market for efficient production. To this technological requirement, we can apply methods similar to Mortensen's search model, but allow the worker to move sluggishly due to either moving costs or imperfect information. In such an economy, the worker would feel a need to join the firm's labour pool without being completely deprived of ex-post mobility. Specifically, senior workers are likely to become attached to the firm's internal labour market as they accumulate firm-specific human capital; younger and more malleable workers, on the other hand, would tend to accept more readily attractive spot-job alternatives. Such a division between tenured senior workers and unproven younger entrants in the labour market seems a natural way to model labour turnover covering finitely many

AKERLOF & MIYAZAKI   UNEMPLOYMENT THEORY   335

periods (cf. D. F. Gordon and Grossman). Even though contract equilibrium with non-degenerate labour pools may be well-defined under appropriate regularity conditions, the anomalies associated with equilibrium unemployment would persist, for the reasons discussed in Section 5, on the worker who perceives *ex post* opportunities to default on his contract in favour of alternative " spot " employment.

7. CONCLUSIONS

The preceding sections have used the Wage Bill Argument to examine the implicit contract theory of unemployment. Many of the known results have depended critically on the assumption of ex-post labour immobility; yet, without mobility, there can be no ex-post layoffs whose causes the conventional neoclassical stories have previously failed to disclose. With mobility there can be layoffs, but such an equilibrium exhibits an unrealistic pattern of price–wage variations. One might perhaps wonder whether the effects of imperfect information (i.e. the type of imperfection discussed in Remark 4 in Section 3) on mobile labour would restore some needed relevance and realism to the contract theory of layoffs. We have presented elsewhere (1975), (1977), (1978), an example of a layoff equilibrium under these circumstances.[23] Nevertheless, we consider such a layoff equilibrium to be no more than an artifact of the model because it depends upon a peculiar specification of states which resembles a business cycle without a peak. Our view is that in a more realistic construct i.e. a state-of-the-world analogue of a complete business cycle, a full-employment rather than unemployment equilibrium would obtain. In sum, neither this type of imperfect information nor ex-post labour mobility provides a cogent argument for an equilibrium with a state of unemployment.

This paper has been hinting that in the type of contract models described implicit contract theory is inadequate in providing an explanation for layoffs that are frequent and persistent. Nevertheless, it remains important to extend the model to a general equilibrium framework, so that we may investigate the extent to which our results would survive endogenously generated demand uncertainty. For example, once the wage–profit circular flow of income is made endogenous, the output price distributions could differ as between a regime of implicit labour contracts and neoclassical spot labour auctions. It would no longer be valid to claim that unemployment states of the contract regime constitute a subset of the corresponding neoclassical unemployment states. We conjecture, however, that even in the extended model the contractual arrangement serves as a force toward smoothing the employment path rather than as a mechanism tending to exacerbate fluctuations in employment.

In some fundamental way, the weakness of the implicit labour contract theory in explaining layoff unemployment seems to lie in its reliance on risk aversion as sole *explanans* for the existence of labour contracts. Risk aversion is obviously *one theoretical* reason for the use of contracts. However, if the implicit labour contract theory is to explain non-neoclassical aspects of labour transactions, then perhaps we should also search for a rationale for labour contracts that incorporates the (implicit!) institutional content of labour markets. That such an institutional rationale is needed is indicated by the theoretical difficulties encountered in Section 6 either in justifying or removing the Assumption (A) of ex-post labour immobility.

First version received June 1976; *final version accepted March* 1979 (*Eds.*).

The authors would like to thank Steven Goldman and Hugh Neary for valuable discussions. They would also like to express their thanks to anonymous referees, Peter Hammond, Peter Howitt, Edward Prescott, and participants of Macro-Seminars at Berkeley and Davis (spring 1977), Stanford Sloan Workshop (fall 1977) and the UCLA Human Resources Workshop (winter 1978). The authors alone are responsible for any remaining errors. Financial support given by the National Science Foundation grant SOC75–23076 is gratefully acknowledged. Also, the use of research facilities were kindly extended by Stanford Center for Research in Economic Growth and by Governors of the Federal Reserve System.

336   REVIEW OF ECONOMIC STUDIES

NOTES

1. A multi-industry economy will be an appropriate set-up when the model is later extended to allow inter-industry labour reallocation in the ex-post period.

2. We are assuming that the price-space is isomorphic to the signal space, which makes an information partition of the state-space. The economic meaning of this assumption is that the state itself is unobservable and is identifiable only through a price signal. Azariadis adopts a similar view. Note that $p_j(s) = p_i(s)$ for all s if both firms j and i belong to the same industry.

3. All existing contributions to contract theory agree on this methodology. For an explicit statement of such a viewpoint, see Grossman (1977), (1978a) who also provides a descriptive essay on the general–equilibrial interactions in the contract economy.

4. See Azariadis and D. F. Gordon for the rationale and justification of such a contractual arrangement.

5. Provided that U is concave on R_+, $U(0)$ need not be zero. See Remark 1 of Section 3 and Section 4 for a fuller discussion on the worker's utility.

6. The full-employment property was indicated by R. J. Gordon, and was independently argued by Negishi and Varian in a different fashion; Varian credits an earlier proof to Sargent.

7. See the previous section for verification that both n_j and w_j must be positive for a profit-maximizing contract.

8. Given the distribution of output prices, the maximization conditions (T1, 2, 3) coupled with ex-ante market clearance in contracts are sufficient to determine the endogenous values (w_j^*, λ_j^*). To ensure a unique market equilibrium, however, an additional constraint such as the zero expected profit condition must be introduced.

9. One way to extend the Wage Bill Argument is explicitly to recognize the worker's consumption-leisure trade-offs in utility, and also to incorporate into the production function the distinction between the number of workers and the work hours of each worker on the job. However, this direction of generalization is undertaken by Mortensen and thus will not be a focus of this paper.

10. We concur with H. I. Grossman's opinion (1977), (1978a) that the implicit contract theory should be viewed as an attempt at modelling an alternative choice-theoretic framework for disequilibrium macro-economics.

11. This reservation wage is determined in the same way as we derive below the " effective " reservation wage in case the worker receives unemployment dole upon separation from the firm. Replace $k(s)$ by 0, and ψ will be determined in the equations below.

12. The marginal productivity condition is only a " necessary " condition for unemployment in the contract model. " Sufficiency " is not warranted because the contract may specify the retention of the worker at " w " despite his low marginal productivity. Also, see Section 7 for some general–equilibrial revision of this claim.

13. The demonstration of this claim regarding the magnitude of layoffs depends only on the fact that U remains concave on the $(v(s), \infty)$ interval if the training cost is ignored. In the presence of training costs, an additional assumption that the training cost function $t(n)$ is convex and increasing in " n " is needed. The proof utilizes the Kuhn–Tucker conditions implied by the firm's constrained expected profit maximization and is available upon request from the authors. See also Azariadis (1975).

14. We do recognize that the micro aspect of wage determination implied by the Azariadis–Baily model yields insight into the economics of pay and work hours. But, the layoffs in the model almost carry the flavour of planned layoffs at the full-employment level, or the natural rate of unemployment.

15. Since the wage rate w^* is uniform among firms in our *Theorem*, the firm can succeed in profitably expanding its labour force by bidding the wage rate only slightly above w^* for its entire work force. Note, if the firm perceives either a maximal sales constraint or discreteness in the wage distribution, then it may not have an incentive to expand its work force. However, we will confine our analysis to output markets under Walrasian auction for the reason stated in Note 10.

16. Despite the allegorical ex-ante/ex-post distinction, everything happens at once in theoretical time. Hence, no seniority rule is assumed; the following assumptions need to be explicated.

(i) Since workers are assumed to be perfectly homogeneous, the firm provides a uniform wage rate $w_j(s)$ to all workers without discriminating between ex-ante-contract workers and the ex-post recruits.

(ii) Random lay-offs and contract enforceability mean that the contracted workers cannot be fired, simply to be replaced by ex-post recruits. However, it means neither protection against layoffs nor priority in worker recalls.

17. Other authors have touched upon the ex-post mobile labour only casually, generally relegating it to an obscure " future topic of extension ". Ioannides and Chan (1978) and Grossman (1978b) consider the workers defecting to other firms *ex post*, without specifying the underlying inter-industry demand state. Unless they can first justify the equilibrium coexistence of auction and contractual firms, the theoretical ramifications to be unfolded here are all applicable to their models. Mortensen (1978) extends the basic model to include worker search in the ex-post state; however, his worker is searching for an alternative " contract " and no so much for outside jobs in the ex-post " spot job " auctions. Thus, in a

AKERLOF & MIYAZAKI   UNEMPLOYMENT THEORY   337

strict economic sense, Mortensen's worker conforms to (A); hence, Mortensen obtains the extended full-employment theorem once again.

18. Involved here are theoretical issues about the existence of contractual equilibrium in a model with ex-post labour mobility. However, our primary goal in this section is to investigate the possibility of the economy attaining full employment in the presumed equilibrium.

19. If $n_1 + Q(\bar{w}_2)\lambda = \lambda$, then full employment prevails across the two industries. Next, consider the case of $n_1 + Q(\bar{w}_2)\lambda > \lambda$. Given $w_1 \leqq \bar{w}_2$, this means that the industry-1 firm is constrained from obtaining the desired n_1 workers. Now, imágine that a firm is a very small entity *vis-à-vis* the industry; if a significant pool of the unemployed exists, then the firm can obtain n_1 workers at w_1. If the unemployed constitute a small pool, then the individual Nash firm will offer a slightly higher contract wage $w_1 + \varepsilon$ to gain workers from elsewhere in the industry. Since all firms have symmetric Nash incentives, in the proposed equilibrium we would have $n_1 + Q(\bar{w}_2)\lambda \leqq \lambda$.

20. We can further restrict the domain of (w_1, n_1) by assuming that

$$\max \{V_1 \mid w_1 \geqq \bar{w}_2\} \geqq \max \{(n_1/\lambda)U(w_1) + Q(\bar{w}_2)U(\bar{w}_2) \mid w_1 \leqq \bar{w}_2\}$$

where V_1 is defined below.

21. For a numerical example to indicate failure of the Wage Bill Argument, take

$$U(w) = \sqrt{w}, \; n_1/\lambda = 0\cdot8, \; 1 - (n_1/\lambda) = 0\cdot2, \; Q(\bar{w}_2) = 0\cdot8, \; w_1 = 100, \; \bar{w}_2 = 70.$$

Then

$$U(w_1 n_1/\lambda) = \sqrt{80} < (0\cdot8)\sqrt{100} + (0\cdot2)(0\cdot8)\sqrt{70} = V_1.$$

22. In emphasizing the peculiarity of this wage–price combination, we need to justify carefully why the firm in our model does not hire ex-post recruits at a differential wage rate that is lower than that promised to the regular contract workers. Since the workers are homogenous, the firm, if allowed, would fire all initially contracted workers, only to replace them by new spot recruits at a lower wage rate. Such ex-post availability of new recruits first puts downward pressure on the contingent wage rate in the process of ex-ante contracting, and thus narrows a gap that might otherwise be significant between the contract and spot wages. Secondly, because of its ability to acquire new workers *ex post*, the firm would have a strong incentive to reduce the size of its initial labour pool; this latter incentive, as we will show in the next section, makes the question of equilibrium somewhat nebulous. To give credence to the meaning of contracts with a non-degenerate labour pool, the model postulates two conditions spelled out in Note 16.

23. In previous papers (1975), (1978), we analysed the case of fair contracts. However, the definition of wage–employment fairness was identical to the imperfect information requirement that the firms and workers negotiate contractual terms based only on the observed value of the firm's own output price.

REFERENCES

AKERLOF, G. A. and MIYAZAKI, H. (1975), " A New Theory of Unemployment ", (Research Paper No. 7518, Federal Reserve Bank of New York).
AKERLOF, G. A. and MIYAZAKI, H. (1978), " The Implicit Contract Theory of Unemployment Meets the Wage Bill Argument ", (Memorandum No. 217, Center for Research in Economic Growth, Stanford University).
AZARIADIS, C. (1975), " Implicit Contracts and Underemployment Equilibria ", *Journal of Political Economy*, 83 (6), 1183–1202.
BAILY, M. N. (1974), " Wages and Unemployment Under Uncertain Demand ", *Review of Economic Studies*, 41, No. 125.
BARRO, R. J. (1977), " Long-term Contracting, Sticky Prices, and Monetary Policy ", *Journal of Monetary Economics*, 3, 305–316.
BARRO, R. J. and GROSSMAN, H. I. (1971), " A General Disequilibrium Model of Income and Employment ", *American Economic Review*, 61.
FISCHER, S. (1977), " Long-term Contracts, Rational Expectations and the Optimal Money Supply Rule ", *Journal of Political Economy*, 85, 191–205.
GORDON, D. F. (1974), " A Neo-Classical Theory of Keynesian Unemployment ", *Economic Inquiry*. (Also reprinted in *The Phillips Curve and Labor Market* Brunner and Meltzer (eds.) (Amsterdam: North-Holland, 1976).
GORDON, R. J. (1976a), " Aspects of Theory of Involuntary Unemployment ", *The Phillips Curve and Labor Market* Brunner and Meltzer (eds.), (Amsterdam: North-Holland).
GORDON, R. J. (1976b), " Recent Development in the Theory of Inflation and Unemployment ", *Journal of Monetary Economics*, 2, 185–219.
GRAY, J. A. (1976), " Wage Indexation: A Macroeconomic Approach ", *Journal of Monetary Economics*, 2.
GRAY, J. A. (1978), " On Indexation and Contract Length ", *Journal of Political Economy*, 86 (1).
GROSSMAN, H. I. (1977), " Employment Fluctuations and the Mitigation of Risk ", (Working Paper No. 77-21, Brown University).
GROSSMAN, H. I. (1978a), " Why Does Aggregate Employment Fluctuate? " (Working Paper No. 78-17, Brown University).

338   REVIEW OF ECONOMIC STUDIES

GROSSMAN, H. I. (1978b), " Risk Shifting, Layoffs, and Seniority ", *Journal of Monetary Economics*, **4**.
IOANNIDES, Y. M. and CHAN, K. S. (1978), " Unemployment and the Implicit Threat of Dismissal ", (Working Paper No. 78-2, Department of Economics, Brown University).
MIYAZAKI, H. (1977), " A Re-examination of Implicit Contract Theory ", (Essay 1, Ph.D. dissertation, University of California, Berkeley).
MORTENSEN, D. (1978), " On the Theory of Layoffs ", (Discussion Paper No. 322, The Center for Mathematical Studies in Economics and Management Science, Northwestern University).
NEGISHI, T. (1976), " Labor Contracts and Full Employment Equilibrium " (mimeo).
POLEMARCHAKIS, H. M. and WEISS, L. (1978), " Fixed Wages, Layoffs, Unemployment Compensation, and Welfare ", *American Economic Review*, **68**, 909–917.
POOLE, W. (1976), " Rational Expectations in the Macro Model ", *Brookings Papers on Economic Activity*, **2**, 463–514.
SARGENT, T. (1976), " Notes on Macroeconomic Theory " (University of Minnesota, mimeo).
VARIAN, H. R. (1976), " Keynesian Models of Unemployment ", (M.I.T. Working Paper).
WILLIAMSON, O. E. (1975) *Markets and Hierarchies: Analysis and Antitrust Implications: A Study of the Economics of Internal Organizations* (New York: The Free Press).

[13]

Working Hours and Hedonic Wages in the Market Equilibrium

Tomio Kinoshita

Musashi University

In the conventional model of labor supply, working hours are implicitly assumed to be divisible goods, which is an obviously unrealistic assumption. The purpose of this paper is to analyze working hours as indivisible goods. When working hours are indivisible, labors are differentiated in the market by their length, and wages will be a function of working hours. The main conclusions are that (1) in the market equilibrium, the elasticity of the hedonic wage curve with respect to hourly wage rates must be positive or less than -1, and (2) generally data will reveal neither demand nor supply structures.

I. Introduction

In labor economics, the supply curve of working hours is explained from laborers' utility-maximizing behavior. It is usually regarded that the elasticities of the supply curve with respect to hourly wage rates are negative because of the dominance of the income effect on the substitution effect (fig. 1). But the results of many empirical works are conflicting. Finegan (1962) and many others support negative elasticity. But Feldstein (1968), Rosen (1969), and Metcalf, Nickell, and Richardson (1976) showed the possibility of positive elasticity.[1]

I am very grateful to an anonymous referee for his valuable comments; to James Heckman, Mark Jewel, John Pencavel, Sherwin Rosen, and Yoko Sano for their suggestions and encouragement; and to Hiroyuki Chuma, Yoshio Higuchi, Kazuo Kuroiwa, Takaharu Masuda, Kazuo Nishimura, Shiro Yabushita, Takashi Yokokura, and the participants of workshops at Keio University and Tokyo Center of Economic Research for their helpful comments. Remaining errors are all my own responsibility.

[1] See Killingsworth (1983) for a comparison of these estimated results.

[*Journal of Political Economy*, 1987, vol. 95, no. 6]

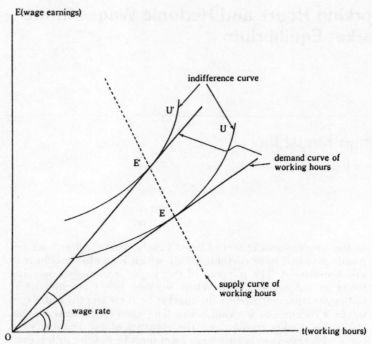

FIG. 1.—Conventional model of supply of working hours

In the conventional model of labor supply, it is implicitly assumed that working hours are divisible goods, which is obviously unrealistic.[2] The purpose of this paper is to analyze working hours as indivisible goods and to present a model in which I show the structure of working hours and wages in the market equilibrium. When working hours are indivisible goods, labors are differentiated in the market by an attribute (or the length of working hours), and hourly wage rates will be a function of working hours. This is a special case of hedonic prices as analyzed by Rosen (1974) and others.

Although this is developed independently, the idea is very similar to that of Lewis (1969). The common characteristic is that working hours and hourly wage rates are determined jointly. Lewis did not have any conclusions about the elasticity of the market-equalizing wage curve (the hedonic wage curve in my model) with respect to wage rates. But in this paper I show that it is positive or less than − 1, and a positive value is more probable than a negative one. Furthermore, it is a very interesting coincidence that the market equilibrium in this model is a special case of Rosen (1974), which is in turn said to derive its idea from Lewis (1969).

[2] I show later that the conventional model implicitly assumes the divisibility of working hours.

In Section II, I explain laborers' supply behavior with respect to working hours. In Section III, the demand behavior of firms for working hours and employment is shown. In Section IV, market equilibrium and the hedonic wage curve are shown. Finally in Section V, brief concluding remarks are given.

II. Supply of Working Hours

In this section, the supply behavior of working hours by laborers is explained.

Assumptions.—(1) The demand curve of working hours (the hedonic wage curve or the market-equalizing wage curve, which is explained below in Sec. IV) is $\Phi(t)$, where t is working hours. This means that the wage earnings for t hours' work is $\Phi(t)$. It is assumed that $d\Phi(t)/dt > 0$. (2) An employee has a utility function $U(E, t)$, where E is his wage earnings. The utility function is quasi-concave, and $U_E > 0$ and $U_t < 0$. (3) Working hours are indivisible, and multiple job holding is prohibited.

The equilibrium working hours are determined from a maximization problem such as

$$\text{maximize } U(E, t) \quad \text{subject to } E = \Phi(t).$$

Then the Lagrangian function is

$$R(E, t, \lambda) = U(E, t) - \lambda[E - \Phi(t)], \tag{1}$$

where λ is a Lagrangian multiplier. The first-order conditions are

$$\frac{\partial R}{\partial E} = \frac{\partial U}{\partial E} - \lambda = 0, \tag{2}$$

$$\frac{\partial R}{\partial t} = \frac{\partial U}{\partial t} + \frac{\lambda d\Phi(t)}{dt} = 0, \tag{3}$$

and

$$\frac{\partial R}{\partial \lambda} = -E + \Phi(t) = 0. \tag{4}$$

From these equations, we have

$$-\frac{\partial U/\partial t}{\partial U/\partial E} = \frac{d\Phi(t)}{dt}. \tag{5}$$

The result is shown in figure 2, where Q is the equilibrium point and OH and HQ are equilibrium working hours and equilibrium wage earnings, respectively.[3]

---

[3] I assume that second-order conditions are satisfied. As it is assumed only that $d\Phi(t)/dt > 0$, the equilibrium may not be unique. But for simplicity, I assume that uniqueness is also satisfied.

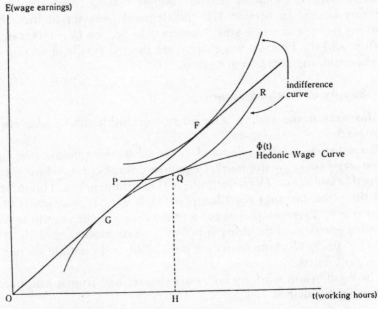

FIG. 2.—Offer wage curve

The solution of the partial differential equation that is obtained by replacing $\Phi(t)$ with $E(t)$ in (5)—$dE/dt = -(\partial U/\partial t)/(\partial U/\partial E)$—will give the relation between the working hours that the laborer supplies and the corresponding wage earnings that he will require because (5) is the equilibrium condition. The solution is obviously an indifference curve $U(E, t) = k$, where k is a constant. In equilibrium it will pass over the equilibrium point and becomes the indifference curve PQR in figure 2. Lewis (1969) termed the indifference curves of employees "employee-equalizing wage curves," for they are indifferent about the combination of working hours and wage earnings on an indifference curve. He showed that the equilibrium of an employee was given by the tangent point between an employee-equalizing wage curve and the market-equalizing wage curve, which is exactly the same idea as that in this section. Following Rosen (1974), I call the indifference curve in equilibrium (the curve PQR in fig. 2) the "offer wage curve."[4]

---

[4] Deardorff and Stafford (1976) used a similar model in the explanation of the supply behavior of working hours. They called the offer wage curve in my model "wage functions." Here it should be noted that working hours are assumed to be indivisible. If they are divisible for a laborer, the Lagrangian function should be $R(E, t, n, \lambda) = U(nE, nt) - \lambda[E - \Phi(t)]$, where n is the laborer's number of jobs and is an integer. If it is optimal for him when $n = 2$, the equilibrium point will be F in fig. 2, where $OG = FG$. If n is large enough to be approximately differentiated, the equilibrium conditions are $\partial R/\partial E = nU_Y - \lambda = 0$, $\partial R/\partial t = nU_T + [\lambda d\Phi(t)/dt] = 0$, $\partial R/\partial n = EU_Y + tU_T = 0$, and $\partial R/\partial \lambda = E - \Phi(t) = 0$, where $Y = nE$ (total earnings) and $T = nt$ (total working hours).

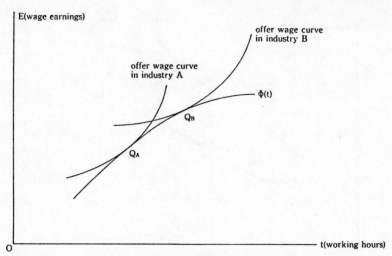

Fig. 3.—Heterogeneous offer wage curves

If the utility functions of employees are different among industries, then their equilibria are as in figure 3, where two different industries' offer wage curves are shown and Q_A and Q_B are the equilibrium points of each industry, respectively. Here the hedonic wage curve becomes the envelope of each offer wage curve.

Nonlabor incomes will make a different offer wage curve even if utility functions are the same. In figure 4, if nonlabor income is NI for an employee, then his budget constraint is $\Phi(t) + NI$, and his equilibrium point is Q_1, where working hours, wage earnings, and total incomes are t_1, $\Phi(t_1)$, and $\Phi(t_1) + NI$, respectively. On the indifference curve $P_1Q_1R_1$, he is indifferent about the combination of total incomes, $\Phi(t) + NI$, and working hours, t, so he will be indifferent about the combination of wage earnings and working hours on the curve $P_1'Q_1'R_1'$, which is obtained by shifting $P_1Q_1R_1$ downward by the amount of nonlabor income, NI. So his offer wage curve becomes the curve $P_1'Q_1'R_1'$. If leisure is a normal good, the offer wage curve will move leftward along the hedonic wage curve as in figure 4.

III. Demand for Working Hours and Employees

In this section, equilibrium working hours and employees of a firm that acts to maximize profits are analyzed.

The offer wage curve is the solution of the differential equation that is obtained substituting $E(t)$ for $\Phi(t)$ in the equations above. We get $dE/dt = E/t$ and the solution is $E = ct$, where c is a constant. It is obvious that the solution is the straight line OGF in fig. 2.

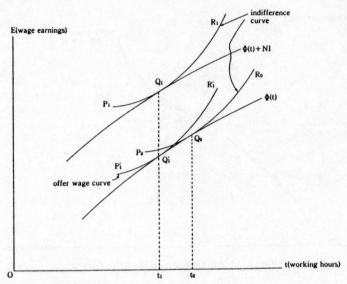

FIG. 4.—Nonlabor incomes and offer wage curve

Assumptions of the model.—(1) The production function of a firm is $Y = F(L, t)$, where Y is output, L is the number of employees, and t is working hours. Working hours are indivisible for the firm, and laborers are homogeneous in their quality. The production function is twice continuously differentiable, and $F_t > 0$, $F_L > 0$, and $F_{LL} < 0$. (2) The firm pays $E(t)$ for t hours' work per employee. Fixed employment costs per employee are C, which are independent of his working hours t. When the price of output is unity, the profit of the firm is $\Pi = F(L, t) - L[E(t) + C]$. (3) The supply curve of working hours (the hedonic wage curve or the market-equalizing wage curve, which is explained below in Sec. IV) is $\Phi(t)$. This means that the firm can choose any number of working hours and employees under the constraint $E(t) = \Phi(t)$ in a competitive labor market. It is assumed that $d\Phi(t)/dt > 0$ and $\Phi(0) > 0$.[5]

The equilibrium working hours and employees are determined from a maximizing problem such as

$$\max F(L, t) - L[E(t) + C] \tag{6}$$

$$\text{subject to } E(t) = \Phi(t). \tag{7}$$

Inserting (7) into (6), we get

$$\Pi = F(L, t) - L[\Phi(t) + C]. \tag{8}$$

---

[5] The term $\Phi(0)$ is a reservation wage and will be positive.

As the firm can control L and t, the equilibrium conditions are

$$\frac{\partial \Pi}{\partial L} = F_L - [\Phi(t) + C] = 0, \tag{9}$$

$$\frac{\partial \Pi}{\partial t} = F_t - \frac{Ld\Phi(t)}{dt} = 0. \tag{10}$$

Equilibrium working hours and employees are determined from equations (9) and (10) simultaneously. I assume that second-order conditions are satisfied, or

$$F_{LL} < 0, F_{tt} - \frac{Ld^2\Phi}{dt^2} < 0, \tag{11}$$

$$\Delta = \begin{vmatrix} F_{LL} & F_{Lt} - \dfrac{d\Phi}{dt} \\ F_{tL} - \dfrac{d\Phi}{dt} & F_{tt} - \dfrac{Ld^2\Phi}{dt^2} \end{vmatrix} > 0. \tag{12}$$

The result is shown in figure 5, where F and G are the equilibrium points of the firm, and t^* and L^* are equilibrium working hours and employees, respectively.[6]

The equilibrium point F is considered the tangent point between an isoprofit curve and the hedonic wage curve. The isoprofit curves are obtained as the solution $E(t)$ of the differential equations that are obtained by replacing $\Phi(t)$ with $E(t)$ in (9) and (10), or

$$E(t) = F_L - C, \tag{13}$$

$$\frac{dE(t)}{dt} = \left(\frac{1}{L}\right)F_t. \tag{14}$$

From (14), it is obvious that the isoprofit curves are increasing functions of working hours. Lewis (1969) termed the isoprofit curves of a firm employer-equalizing wage curves.[7] He showed that the equilib-

---

[6] The curve AFB in fig. 5 is obtained by shifting $(1/L^*)F(L^*, t)$ downward by a constant K^* until it is tangent to the hedonic wage curve. The equilibrium might not be unique, for I assume nothing about the signs of second derivatives of the production function and the hedonic wage curve with respect to working hours. But hereinafter, for simplicity I assume the uniqueness of the equilibrium.

[7] The definition of employer-equalizing wage curves in Lewis (1969) is "isocost curves for unit labor input." It must satisfy $(d/dt)\{L[E(t) + C]/Lt\} = 0$ or $[tdE(t)/dt] - [E(t) + C] = 0$. If the isoprofit curves derived from (13) and (14) are equivalent to employer-equalizing wage curves, then substituting (13) and (14) into the equation above, we get $tF_t = LF_L$. The solution of this partial differential equation is $F = F(Lt)$ (see Kreyszig 1962, chap. 7). This means that if the production function is not a function of man-hours (Lt), the equilibrium conditions of profit maximization are no longer equivalent to the condition of unit labor cost minimization. In other words, the minimization of unit labor cost does not yield an equilibrium condition of a firm.

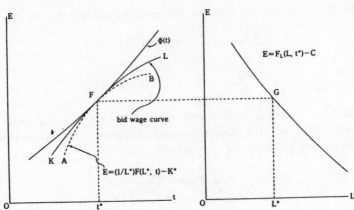

Fig. 5.—Bid wage curve and demand for employees

rium of a firm (or an employer) was given by the tangent point between an employer-equalizing wage curve and a market-equalizing wage curve (the hedonic wage curve in this model). It is the same idea as that in this section. Following Rosen (1974), I call the isoprofit curve that passes over the equilibrium point (the curve *KFL* in fig. 5) the "bid wage curve." It will show the relation between the wage earnings the employer pays and the corresponding working hours that he will require in equilibrium.[8]

If the production technologies are different among industries, then their equilibria are different as shown in figure 6, where two different industries' bid wage curves are shown, and F_A and F_B are their equilibrium points, respectively. Here the hedonic wage curve becomes the envelope of each bid wage curve.

Fixed employment costs (C)[9] and elasticities of output with respect to working hours (η_t) and employees (η_L) will show the production

[8] If working hours are divisible for a firm, then $F(nL_0, t_0/n) = F(L_0, t_0)$ for any L_0, t_0, and n, where n is an integer and is considered to be the number of the shift. If n is large enough so that the production function is approximately differentiated with respect to n, then $L_0 F_L + (t_0 F_t/-n^2) = 0$. Using the relation $L = nL_0$ and $t = t_0/n$, we get $LF_L = tF_t$, and the solution of this equation is $F = F(Lt)$. Conversely if $F = F(Lt)$, this means that working hours are divisible for a firm because $F(Lt) = F(nL \cdot (t/n))$ for any L, t, and n. So it is a necessary and sufficient condition for the divisibility of working hours that the production function be a function of man-hours. If working hours are divisible for a firm or $F = F(Lt)$, then from (13) and (14) the bid wage curve is the solution of $t dE/dt = E + C$. This is a straight line $E(t) = kt - C$, where k is a constant. If $C = 0$, this is the same equation as the demand curve of working hours in the conventional model. In other words, the conventional model assumes the divisibility of working hours.

[9] These costs include investment costs for human capital and the costs for on-the-job training that are stressed by Oi (1962), Becker (1964), and others. Lewis (1969) suggests that the investment effects of these costs should be taken into account. But I neglect these effects for simplicity.

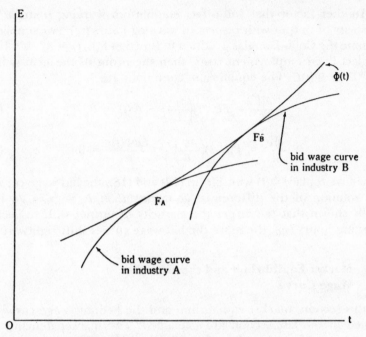

FIG. 6.—Heterogeneous bid wage curves

technologies, the differences of which cause the shift of bid wage curves and move the equilibrium points along the hedonic wage curve. Differentiating (9) and (10) with respect to C, we get

$$
\begin{bmatrix}
F_{LL} & F_{Lt} - \dfrac{d\Phi}{dt} \\[2ex]
F_{tL} - \dfrac{d\Phi}{dt} & F_{tt} - \dfrac{Ld^2\Phi}{dt^2}
\end{bmatrix}
\begin{bmatrix}
\dfrac{dL}{dC} \\[2ex]
\dfrac{dt}{dC}
\end{bmatrix}
=
\begin{bmatrix}
1 \\[2ex]
0
\end{bmatrix}.
$$

Then we have

$$
\frac{dL}{dC} = \left(\frac{1}{\Delta}\right)\left(F_{tt} - \frac{Ld^2\Phi}{dt^2}\right), \tag{15}
$$

$$
\frac{dt}{dC} = \left(-\frac{1}{\Delta}\right)\left(F_{tL} - \frac{d\Phi}{dt}\right). \tag{16}
$$

From (11) and (12), dL/dC is negative. But the sign of dt/dC is ambiguous. It depends on the sign of $F_{tL} - (d\Phi/dt)$.[10]

---

[10] Lewis (1969) asserted that dt/dC is positive. As stated in n. 6, his model of unit labor cost minimization assumes the special production function $F = F(Lt)$. In this case, $F_{tL} - (d\Phi/dt) = F_{tL} - (1/L)F_t = HF_{HH} < 0$, where $H = Lt$, and so dt/dC is positive. But generally this result will not hold.

Another factor that will affect equilibrium working hours is the elasticity of output with respect to working hours (η_t). For simplicity, assume the Cobb-Douglas production function $F(L, t) = AL^{\eta_L}t^{\eta_t}$. If we neglect fixed employment costs, then the profit of the firm is $\Pi = AL^{\eta_L}t^{\eta_t} - \Phi(t)L$. The equilibrium conditions are

$$\frac{\partial\Pi}{\partial L} = F(L, t)\left(\frac{\eta_L}{L}\right) - \Phi(t) = 0, \tag{17}$$

$$\frac{\partial\Pi}{\partial t} = F(L, t)\left(\frac{\eta_t}{t}\right) - \frac{Ld\Phi(t)}{dt} = 0. \tag{18}$$

When we replace $\Phi(t)$ with $E(t)$ in (17) and (18), the bid wage curve is the solution of the differential equation $(dE/dt)/E = (\eta_t/\eta_L)/t$. It is easily shown that the larger the elasticity of output with respect to working hours (η_t), the more the bid wage curves shift rightward.[11]

IV. Market Equilibrium and the Hedonic Wage Curve

In this section, market equilibrium and the hedonic wage curve assumed in the last section are explained. The market demand for employees with working hours t is $L^D(t)$, and $L^S(t)$ is the market supply of employees with working hours t. Then the hedonic wage curve is defined as a function $E = \Phi(t)$ such that $L^D(t) = L^S(t)$ for all t, and all employees and employers are in equilibrium under the hedonic wage curve as described in Sections II and III.[12]

As in Rosen (1974), the hedonic wage curve will be determined by the distribution of both laborers' preferences and firms' production technologies. If all laborers have the same preference and firms have different production technologies, then the hedonic wage curve will be an offer wage curve. Conversely, if all firms have the same technology and laborers have different preferences, then the hedonic wage curve will become a bid wage curve. If all firms have the same technology and all laborers have the same preference, then the hedonic wage curve will be a point. But generally, every firm's technology and laborer's preference, will be different from each other. Then the market equilibrium is as in figure 7, where the hedonic wage curve is the joint envelope of offer wage curves and bid wage curves. In this case, as in Rosen (1974, p. 50), the hedonic wage curve reveals neither supply nor demand structures. In other words, cross-section data will have little information on supply or demand functions.[13]

[11] The proof is almost the same as in the case of fixed employment costs.

[12] The idea of a hedonic model was used in Tinbergen (1951, 1956) in the explanation of income distribution.

[13] For both firms and laborers, if working hours are divisible and there are no fixed employment costs, then every bid wage curve and offer wage curve becomes a straight

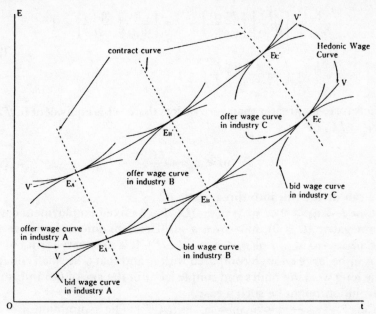

FIG. 7.—Hedonic wage curve

It is beyond the scope of this paper to solve the equation of the hedonic wage curve.[14] But it is evident that $d\Phi(t)/dt > 0$ because offer wage curves and bid wage curves are both increasing functions of working hours and the hedonic wage curve is their envelope. Then

$$\frac{d\Phi(t)}{dt} = \frac{d[tW(t)]}{dt}$$

$$= W(t)\left(1 + \frac{1}{\eta_\Phi}\right) > 0, \tag{19}$$

where $W(t)$ is the hourly wage rate—$W(t) = E(t)/t$—and η_Φ ($= [W/t] \times [dt/dW]$) is the working hours elasticity of the hedonic wage curve with respect to the hourly wage rate. From (19), it is evident that η_Φ is positive or less than -1. Furthermore, from (19), (9), and (10),

---

line that passes through the origin. They coincide with each other, and this is of course the hedonic wage curve. So the working hours of laborers in a firm are indeterminate. In other words, the contractual feature of the working hours decision disappears and the model degenerates to the conventional auction model. The offer wage curve and bid wage curve in the model degenerate to, so to speak, the wage rate in the conventional model.

[14] For an example of solving the equation, see Tinbergen (1951, 1956) and Rosen (1974).

$$\frac{1}{\eta_\Phi} = \left[\frac{1}{W(t)}\right]\left[\frac{d\Phi(t)}{dt}\right] - 1 = \left[\frac{t}{\Phi(t)}\right]\left[\frac{d\Phi(t)}{dt}\right] - 1$$

$$= \left(\frac{t}{F_L - C}\right)\left(\frac{F_t}{L}\right) - 1.$$

(20)

Therefore, η_Φ greater than zero or less than -1 is equivalent to $tF_t \gtrless LF_L - LC$, or

$$\eta_t \gtrless \eta_L - \frac{LC}{F}.$$

(21)

We can divide this into three cases.

Case 1.—$\eta_\Phi > 0$ or $\eta_t > \eta_L - (LC/F)$. As fixed employment cost is nonnegative ($C \geqq 0$), $\eta_t > \eta_L$ is a sufficient condition of positive η_Φ.

Case 2.—$\eta_\Phi < -1$ or $\eta_t < \eta_L - (LC/F)$. It is necessary for $\eta_\Phi < -1$ that η_L be large enough compared with η_t and that C be small enough. The long working hours and simple labor in the age of the Industrial Revolution might be such a case.

Case 3.—$\eta_\Phi \to \pm\infty$ or $\eta_t = \eta_L - (LC/F)$. The assumption $\eta_t = \eta_L$ —or $F = F(Lt)$—and $C = 0$ is a special case of this, which is often used in the illustration of the conventional model (fig. 1). But this means that $\eta_\Phi \to \pm\infty$, which is quite far from the empirical results.

Although hypothetical, I suppose it is probable that $\eta_t \geqq \eta_L$ and $C > 0$. Then I can conclude that η_Φ is positive.[15]

On the other hand, if the results of estimations are $0 > \eta_\Phi > -1$ or $d\Phi(t)/dt < 0$, this means that the data are gathered from different labor markets. For example, let the equilibria of industries B and B' be E_B and $E_{B'}$, respectively (fig. 7). Then an employer in industry B' pays more wages for shorter working hours compared with industry B. This cannot occur if they are in the same labor market.

So far I have explained the market equilibrium or cross-sectional implications of the model. Next I explain the time-series implications of the model. In figure 7, let VV be the hedonic wage curve in a year and E_A, E_B, and E_C be the equilibrium points of industries A, B, and C, respectively. The next year, the hedonic wage curve shifts from VV to $V'V'$ according to the growth of labor productivity and so on. Then the equilibria will move to $E_{A'}$, $E_{B'}$, and $E_{C'}$, respectively. From time-

---

[15] In the specification of the aggregate production function, Feldstein (1967) and Craine (1973) stress the difference between η_t and η_L. But Leslie and Wise (1980) support the opposite position. Although I cannot refer to empirical works on the interindustry difference between η_t and η_L, it is very probable that the characteristics of each industry (the possibility of shift work, inventory policy, and so on) make them disperse.

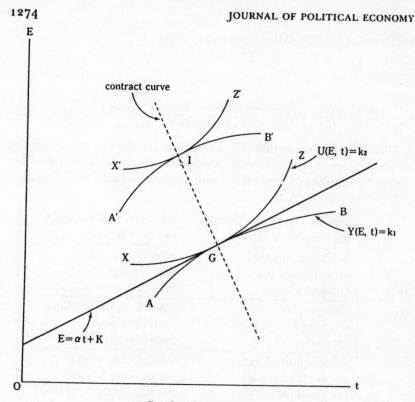

FIG. 8.—Contract curve

series data, the curve $E_A E_{A'}$, $E_B E_{B'}$, and $E_C E_{C'}$ will be estimated, each of which is a kind of contract curve, for they are the loci of the tangent points between isoprofit curves and indifference curves. Hereinafter I call these curves "contract curves."[16]

The contract curves will be determined bilaterally between a firm and its employees, being affected by other members in the labor market. Sometimes they might change their partners. But here I will consider a simple case in which there is no such switch. Let $Y(E, t) = k_1$ and $U(E, t) = k_2$ be a bid wage curve (a firm's isoprofit curve) and an offer wage curve (laborers' indifference curve), respectively (fig. 8), where k_1 and k_2 are parameters that indicate the level of profits and utility, respectively. Then the contract curve will be described as

$$\frac{U_t}{U_E} = \frac{Y_t}{Y_E}. \tag{22}$$

---

[16] If working hours are divisible, the contract curves in the model will degenerate to the supply curve of working hours in the conventional model.

Differentiating (22) with respect to t, we get

$$\frac{dE}{dt} = \frac{-U_t}{U_E}$$

$$\times \left\{ \frac{(-1/U_t)[(U_t U_{Et}/U_E) - U_{tt}] - (-1/Y_t)[(Y_t Y_{Et}/Y_E) - Y_{tt}]}{(1/U_E)[(-U_t U_{EE}/U_E) + U_{tE}] - (1/Y_E)[(-Y_t Y_{EE}/Y_E) + Y_{tE}]} \right\}. \quad (23)$$

It will be verified easily that (23) is composed of the ratios between the employees' income effects and substitution effects and the ratios between the employer's cost effects and substitution effects.[17] Equation (23) can be rewritten as

$$\frac{dE}{dt} = \alpha \begin{bmatrix} \dfrac{\begin{array}{l}\text{income effect on earnings} \\ \text{for employee } (I_U^E)\end{array}}{\begin{array}{l}\text{substitution effect} \\ \text{on earnings for} \\ \text{employee } (S_U^E)\end{array}} - \dfrac{\begin{array}{l}\text{cost effect on earnings} \\ \text{for firm (employer) } (C_Y^E)\end{array}}{\begin{array}{l}\text{substitution effect} \\ \text{on earnings for} \\ \text{firm (employer) } (S_Y^E)\end{array}} \\[2em] \dfrac{\begin{array}{l}\text{income effect on} \\ \text{working hours for} \\ \text{employee } (I_U^t)\end{array}}{\begin{array}{l}\text{substitution effect} \\ \text{on working hours} \\ \text{for employee } (S_U^t)\end{array}} - \dfrac{\begin{array}{l}\text{cost effect on working} \\ \text{hours for firm} \\ \text{(employer) } (C_Y^t)\end{array}}{\begin{array}{l}\text{substitution effect} \\ \text{on working hours} \\ \text{for firm (employer) } (S_Y^t)\end{array}} \end{bmatrix}.$$

[17] The equilibrium condition of an employee (a laborer) is obtained from such a maximizing problem: max $U(E, t)$ subject to $E = \alpha t + K$, where the constraint is the line tangent to both the offer wage curve and the bid wage curve at the equilibrium point G (fig. 8). Then the Lagrangian function is $R(E, t, \lambda) = U(E, t) + \lambda(E - \alpha t - K)$, and the equilibrium conditions are $U_E + \lambda = 0$, $U_t - \lambda\alpha = 0$, and $E - \alpha t - K = 0$. From these equilibrium conditions we have the familiar income effects and substitution effects:

$$I_U^E = \left(\frac{\partial E}{\partial K}\right)_{\alpha = \text{constant}} = \left(\frac{1}{\Delta_U}\right)\left(\frac{U_t U_{Et}}{U_E} - U_{tt}\right),$$

$$I_U^t = \left(\frac{\partial t}{\partial K}\right)_{\alpha = \text{constant}} = \left(\frac{1}{\Delta_U}\right)\left(\frac{-U_t U_{EE}}{U_E} + U_{tE}\right),$$

$$S_U^E = \left(\frac{\partial E}{\partial \alpha}\right)_{U = \text{constant}} = \left(\frac{1}{\Delta_U}\right)(-U_t),$$

$$S_U^t = \left(\frac{\partial t}{\partial \alpha}\right)_{U = \text{constant}} = \left(\frac{1}{\Delta_U}\right)(U_E),$$

where Δ_U is the bordered Hessian:

$$\begin{vmatrix} 0 & 1 & -\alpha \\ 1 & U_{EE} & U_{Et} \\ -\alpha & U_{tE} & U_{tt} \end{vmatrix}.$$

For the employer (or the firm), it is completely symmetric and sufficient to change the symbol from U to Y. We call the counterpart of income effects "cost effects." Equation (16) shows cost effects in another expression, where the sign of the cost effect is ambiguous.

From the quasi concavity of the utility functions, $S_U^E > 0$ and $S_U^l > 0$. If leisure and wage earnings are normal goods, $I_U^E > 0$ and $I_U^l < 0$. But the isoprofit curves are either quasi-concave or quasi-convex, so the signs of S_Y^E and S_Y^l are indeterminate. Also, the signs of cost effects (C_Y^E, C_Y^l) are indeterminate. So theoretically the signs of the slopes of contract curves are indeterminate.

V. Concluding Remarks

In this paper, the structure of working hours and wages in the market equilibrium is explained under the assumption that working hours are indivisible. There is one kind of hedonic price, and I termed it the hedonic wage curve. The equilibrium point of each firm or laborer is on this curve, where its bid wage curve and offer wage curve are tangent to the hedonic wage curve. In other words, the hedonic wage curve is the envelope of these curves. Generally the hedonic wage curve reveals neither supply nor demand structures of any industry. The elasticities of the hedonic wage curve with respect to wage rates must be positive or less than -1. Furthermore, for firms, if the elasticity of output with respect to working hours is larger than that with respect to employees, the elasticity of the hedonic wage curve must be positive. If the estimated results from cross-section data are not in these regions, this means that the data are gathered from different labor markets. If there are different labor markets, each labor market will have its own hedonic wage curve. Then the problem of identifying the hedonic wage curve will arise. On the other hand, the time-series data will show one kind of contract curve, which is determined bilaterally between an employer and his employees, being affected by other members in the labor market. The slopes of contract curves depend on the income effects and substitution effects of both employer and employee. The signs of the slopes could be either positive or negative.

References

Becker, Gary S. *Human Capital: A Theoretical and Empirical Analysis, with Special Reference to Education.* New York: Columbia Univ. Press (for NBER), 1964.

Craine, Roger. "On the Service Flow from Labour." *Rev. Econ. Studies* 40 (January 1973): 39–46.

Deardorff, Alan V., and Stafford, Frank P. "Compensation of Cooperating Factors." *Econometrica* 44 (July 1976): 671–84.

Feldstein, Martin S. "Specification of the Labour Input in the Aggregate Production Function." *Rev. Econ. Studies* 34 (October 1967): 375–86.

———. "Estimating the Supply Curve of Working Hours." *Oxford Econ. Papers* 20 (March 1968): 74–80.

Finegan, Thomas A. "Hours of Work in the United States: A Cross-sectional Analysis." *J.P.E.* 70 (October 1962): 452–70.

Killingsworth, Mark R. *Labor Supply.* Cambridge: Cambridge Univ. Press, 1983.

Kreyszig, Erwin. *Advanced Engineering Mathematics.* New York: Wiley, 1962.

Leslie, Derek G., and Wise, John. "The Productivity of Hours in U.K. Manufacturing and Production Industries." *Econ. J.* 90 (March 1980): 74–84.

Lewis, H. Gregg. "Employer Interests in Employee Hours of Work." Mimeographed. Santiago: Catholic Univ. Chile, 1969.

Metcalf, David; Nickell, Stephen J.; and Richardson, Ray. "The Structure of Hours and Earnings in the British Manufacturing Industry." *Oxford Econ. Papers* 28 (July 1976): 284–303.

Oi, Walter Y. "Labor as a Quasi-fixed Factor." *J.P.E.* 70 (December 1962): 538–55.

Rosen, Sherwin. "On the Interindustry Wage and Hours Structure." *J.P.E.* 77 (March/April 1969): 249–73.

———. "Hedonic Prices and Implicit Markets: Product Differentiation in Pure Competition." *J.P.E.* 82 (January/February 1974): 34–55.

Tinbergen, Jan. "Some Remarks on the Distribution of Labour Incomes." *Internat. Econ. Papers,* no. 1 (1951), pp. 195–207.

———. "On the Theory of Income Distribution." *Weltwirtschaftliches Archiv* 77, no. 2 (1956): 155–73.

[14]

Journal of Monetary Economics 21 (1988) 3–16. North-Holland

INDIVISIBLE LABOR, LOTTERIES AND EQUILIBRIUM

Richard ROGERSON*

University of Rochester, Rochester, NY 14627, USA

Received January 1987, final version received June 1987

This paper considers an economy where labor is indivisible and agents are identical. Although the discontinuity in labor supply at the individual level disappears as a result of aggregation, it is shown that indivisible labor has strong consequences for the aggregate behavior of the economy. It is also shown that optimal allocations involve lotteries over employment and consumption.

1. Introduction

During the last decade general equilibrium theory has become an increasingly common framework in which to study the aggregate properties of economies [see, e.g., Lucas (1981)]. In its original form [see Debreu (1959)] general equilibrium theory was developed in the context of convex economic environments, but has since been extended to non-convex environments [see Aumann (1966) and Mas-Colell (1977)]. The concern of these authors was the existence of equilibrium. They show that if there is a continuum of agents, then equilibrium exists even with non-convexities at the individual level. Their analysis left unanswered the question of whether or not these non-convexities had an important effect on the nature of equilibrium. The conclusion of this paper is that they may have major implications for the aggregate response of an economy to shocks. This claim is demonstrated in the context of an economy in which labor supply is indivisible. In particular it is shown that such an economy composed of identical agents behaves as if populated by a single agent whose preferences do not match the preferences of any individual in the economy. Furthermore the economy will display much larger fluctuations in hours of work in response to a given shock to technology.

The analysis also shows that attaining optimal allocations in such economies may involve holding lotteries over employment to determine which agents

*I am indebted to Ed Prescott for his guidance. I have benefited from conversations with John Geaneakoplos, Vittorio Grilli, Robert King, Glenn MacDonald, Rodolfo Manuelli, Walter Oi, and the comments of an anonymous referee. Financial support from the Social Sciences and Humanities Research Council of Canada and NSF Grant No. SES-8510861 is gratefully acknowledged.

supply labor. It is demonstrated how these lotteries may be decentralized through markets and how the use of lotteries facilitates computation of equilibria. Prescott and Townsend (1984,1985) found similar properties in economies with private information.

Although this paper only considers the case of indivisible labor, there are many other situations of practical importance where similar non-convexities may play an important role. Markets for durables such as houses or cars involve an element of indivisibility that may play an important role in understanding aggregate fluctuations in these markets. Decisions about mobility, marriage, fertility and occupational choice also involve a choice which is essentially a zero–one choice, and hence, the same types of considerations studied in this paper will be of interest in analysing those problems. Becker (1985) shows how human capital accumulation may lead to non-convexities.

2. The environment *E*

In this and the next three sections the problem to be studied is considered in its simplest form.

The economy consists of a continuum of identical agents with names in the interval [0,1]. There are three commodities: labor, capital and output (although, as will become clear later, capital only serves the role of allowing for a constant returns to scale technology together with a diminishing marginal product of labor). All activity takes place in a single time period. Capital (K) and labor (N) are used to produce output according to the concave constant returns to scale technology $f(K, N)$, which is assumed to be strictly increasing and twice continuously differentiable in both arguments with $f_{11}(K, N)$ and $f_{22}(K, N)$ strictly negative.

Each agent (or worker) is endowed with one unit of time and one unit of capital. Time is indivisible: either the entire unit is supplied as labor or none of it is supplied as labor. All workers have an identical utility function specified by

$$u(c) - v(n),$$

where $c \geq 0$ is consumption and $n \in \{0,1\}$ is supply of labor. It is assumed that u is twice continuously differentiable, increasing and strictly concave. If labor were perfectly divisible it would be natural to assume that $v(n)$ is convex, increasing and twice continuously differentiable. With labor assumed to be indivisible, the only values of $v(n)$ that matter are $v(0)$ and $v(1)$. It is assumed that $v(0) = 0$ and $v(1) = m$, where m is a strictly positive constant. For future reference it will be useful to define the consumption set X for each worker. According to the above specification,

$$X = \left\{ (c, n, k) \in R^3 : c \geq 0, \, n \in \{0,1\}, \, 0 \leq k \leq 1 \right\}.$$

It is of particular interest that the set X is non-convex. The above description will be referred to as the economy E.

3. Equilibrium and optimality in E

This section presents the standard notion of competitive equilibrium for E and displays some anomalies. First we define an allocation.

Definition. An allocation for E is a list $(c(t), n(t), k(t), K, N)$, where for each $t \in [0,1]$, $(c(t), n(t), k(t)) \in X$ and $K, N \geq 0$.

Definition. A competitive equilibrium for E is a list $(c(t), n(t), k(t), K, N, w, r)$ such that:

(i) For each $t \in [0,1]$, $(c(t), n(t), k(t))$ is a solution to

$$\max_{c, n, k} u(c) - mn,$$

subject to

$$c \leq nw + rk, \quad c \geq 0, \quad n \in \{0,1\}, \quad 0 \leq k \leq 1.$$

(ii) N and K are a solution to

$$\max_{N, K} f(K, N) - rK - wN,$$

subject to

$$K \geq 0, \quad N \geq 0.$$

(iii)

$$K = \int_0^1 k(t) \, dt,$$

$$N = \int_0^1 n(t) \, dt,$$

$$f(K, N) = \int_0^1 c(t) \, dt.$$

The above definition is standard. Conditions (i)–(iii) are, respectively, utility maximization, profit maximization and market clearing.

It is possible to show that a competitive equilibrium exists for E, however this is not central to the discussion here. The interesting feature of E that

6   *R. Rogerson, Indivisible labor, lotteries and equilibrium*

distinguishes it from purely neoclassical economies is the indivisibility in labor supply. One of the implications of this feature is that it is possible for identical agents to receive different allocations in equilibrium. If consumption and technology sets are convex and preferences are strictly convex, then in equilibrium identical agents always receive identical allocations. This result follows from the fact that budget sets are convex and hence if two distinct points each in the budget set give equal utilities then there necessarily exists a third point also in the budget set providing a greater level of utility. In the economy E being considered here the consumption set X is not convex and hence this argument no longer holds. As the following example demonstrates, neither does the result that identical agents receive identical bundles.

Example 1.   Consider the following specification for E:

$$f(K, N) = K^\alpha N^{1-\alpha}, \qquad \alpha = 0.5,$$

$$u(c) = \ln C,$$

$$m = \ln 2.5.$$

The only variable to be solved for is N: all capital will necessarily be supplied, the consumption of those supplying labor will be $(w + r)$ and of those not supplying labor it will be r; also, w is the MPL and r is the MPK. All workers must receive the same utility even if they receive different allocations. So solving the following equation will determine the equilibrium:

$$u(MPL + MPK) - m = u(MPK),$$

which, if $K = 1$, is simply an equation in N. For the given functional forms this becomes

$$\ln\left[\alpha N^{1-\alpha} + (1 - \alpha)N^{-\alpha}\right] - m = \ln\left[\alpha N^{1-\alpha}\right].$$

Solving this equation gives

$$N = \frac{1-\alpha}{\alpha} \frac{1}{e^m - 1}.$$

The equilibrium for the above specification is

$$(c(t), n(t), k(t)) = (1.1067972, 1, 1), \qquad t \in [0, 0.4],$$

$$= (0.3162278, 0, 1), \qquad t \in [0.4, 1],$$

$$(w, r) = (0.7905694, 0.3162278).$$

One of the surprising features of this equilibrium is that identical agents are receiving different allocations. Another surprising feature is that there are allocations which Pareto-dominate the above allocation. In particular, consider the following allocation rule. Give every individual a consumption of

$$c = 0.6324555,$$

(which is the average consumption in the previous example) but hold a lottery to randomly choose a fraction 0.4 of workers to supply labor. The utility obtained by an individual in the equilibrium allocation is given by

$$V = 0.5623413,$$

whereas the expected utility of the alternative allocation described above is

$$\bar{V} = 0.5993895.$$

At first this result seems to be troubling. As commonly stated [see, e.g., Debreu (1959, ch. 6)] the first welfare theorem applies to the economy E. The solution to this apparent logical inconsistency is that the alternative allocation described above does not belong to the set X and hence is outside the scope of the set of allocations considered by the first welfare theorem. Recall that the standard method of proof for the first welfare theorem involves an argument that if individuals prefer an allocation to their individual allocation then it must cost too much relative to their budget or else they would have purchased it. This argument does not hold here because the allocation involving lotteries is not viewed as a feasible one by consumers with consumption set X. However, the result is still troubling because it suggests that not all gains to trade are being realized even though apparently all markets are in operation. In the remainder of this paper it is shown how the consumption set X can be modified so that allocations like the one described above can be obtained as a competitive allocation.

4. Equilibrium with lotteries

In this section the consumption set is expanded by introducing a specific class of lotteries. All objects will remain the same except for the consumption sets and preferences. Define:

$$X_1 = \{(c, n, k) \in X: n = 1\},$$

$$X_2 = \{(c, n, k) \in X: n = 0\},$$

$$\bar{X} = X_1 \times X_2 \times [0, 1].$$

$\overline{X}$ will be the new consumption set for the workers. The set X_1 represents allocations where the individual is supplying labor and the set X_2 represents allocations where the individual is not supplying labor. Motivated by example one and the discussion that followed, it is desirable to allow workers to randomize the labor supply decision. Hence the third element, a number in the interval $[0,1]$ represents the probability that the X_1 allocation is realized, whereas one minus this number is the probability that the X_2 allocation is realized. Note that the set $\overline{X}$ is convex. An element of $\overline{X}$ will be written $((c_1,1,k_1), (c_2,0,k_2), \phi)$. Preferences must be defined over this set and the natural extension is to compute the expected utility of the lottery, i.e., the utility obtained from receiving the above allocation is

$$\phi[u(c_1) - m] + (1 - \phi)[u(c_2)].$$

The economy produced by making these changes will be denoted by $\overline{E}$ and a competitive equilibrium for $\overline{E}$ is defined by:

Definition. A competitive equilibrium for $\overline{E}$ is a list $(c_1(t),\ k_1(t),\ c_2(t),\ k_2(t),\ \phi(t),\ K, N, w, r)$ such that:

(i) For each $t \in [0,1]$, $(c_1(t),\ k_1(t),\ c_2(t),\ k_2(t),\ \phi(t))$ is a solution to

$$\max_{c_1, c_2, k_1, k_2, \phi} \phi[u(c_1) - m] + (1 - \phi)[u(c_2)],$$

subject to

$$\phi c_1 + (1 - \phi)c_2 \le w\phi + r[\phi k_1 + (1 - \phi)k_2],$$

$$c_i \ge 0, \quad 0 \le k_i \le 1, \quad i = 1, 2,$$

$$0 \le \phi \le 1.$$

(ii) K and N are a solution to

$$\max_{K, N} f(K, N) - rK - wN,$$

subject to

$$K \ge 0, \qquad N \ge 0.$$

(iii)

$$K = \int_0^1 (\phi(t)k_1(t) + (1 - \phi(t))k_2(t))\,dt,$$

$$N = \int_0^1 (\phi(t))\,dt,$$

$$f(K, N) = \int_0^1 (\phi(t)c_1(t) + (1 - \phi(t))c_2(t))\,dt.$$

Although the nature of the above three conditions is standard there is a non-standard element imbedded in them. This arises because individuals are buying and selling commodities contingent upon the outcome of an individual specific lottery. It is worthwhile to discuss possible institutional descriptions corresponding to the formal notion of equilibrium described above. A description of a fully decentralized equilibrium is as follows. The prices of output, labor, and capital are given by 1, w, and r, respectively. An individual chooses a lottery where with probability ϕ they work and supply k_1 units of capital and with probability $(1 - \phi)$ they don't work and supply k_2 units of capital. Hence, with probability ϕ they will receive income $w + k_1 r$, and with probability $(1 - \phi)$ they will receive income $k_2 r$. It is assumed that the individual can purchase insurance in the face of this income uncertainty. In particular, the individual can purchase consumption contingent upon the outcome of the lottery. Assuming a zero profit condition for the firm offering this insurance implies that relative prices between the work and don't work outcomes will be given by $(\phi/(1 - \phi))$. Hence the budget constraint is simply given by that which appears in condition (i) of the definition.

It is also worth noting that it is implicitly assumed that the wage rate that an individual faces is independent of the probability ϕ of working that is chosen. This occurs because there is a continuum of agents and each individual is choosing an individual specific random variable. Under these conditions a given agent's decision has no impact on the distribution of total labor supplied. In particular there is no difference between the case where all workers supply labor with probability one-half and the case where half the workers supply labor with probability one and the other half supply labor with probability zero. This is not the case with a finite number of workers: the two situations provide the same expected value of labor supply but the variance is different. In this case we might expect that the wage rate will depend on the value of ϕ chosen. With a continuum of agents the above mentioned variance is always zero.[1]

Call the maximization problem in condition (i) of equilibrium problem (P-1).

Lemma 1. If $(c_1, c_2, k_1, k_2, \phi)$ is a solution to (P-1) and $\phi \in (0,1)$, then $c_1 = c_2$.

Proof. The first-order conditions for this problem are

$$\phi u'(c_1) = \phi \theta \quad \text{and} \quad (1 - \phi) u'(c_2) = (1 - \phi)\theta,$$

---

[1] The case of a continuum of i.i.d. random variables can cause some problems. See Judd (1985) for a treatment of this problem.

where θ is the multiplier on the budget constraint. If ϕ is not zero or one then the result follows immediately. ∎

Note that if $\phi \notin (0,1)$, there is no harm in requiring that $c_1 = c_2$. We can also assume that $k_1 = k_2 = 1$. Then problem (P-1) becomes

$$\text{(P-2)} \quad \max_{c,\phi} u(c) - \phi m,$$

subject to

$$c = w\phi + r, \quad \cdot \quad c \geq 0, \quad 0 \leq \phi \leq 1.$$

Note that by the strict concavity of $u(\cdot)$ this problem has a unique solution. Since all agents are identical it follows that c and ϕ are independent of t. Hence, finding an equilibrium now reduces to finding a list (c, ϕ, K, N, r, w) such that

(i) (c, ϕ) solves problem (P-2).
(ii) (K, N) solves profit maximization problem.
(iii) $\phi = N, K = 1, c = F(K, N)$.

This is identical to the equilibrium one would obtain for an economy with technology $f(K, N)$, with one agent whose utility is specified by $u(c) - mn$ with consumption set

$$X = \left\{ (c, n, k) \in R^3 \colon c \geq 0, 0 \leq n \leq 1, 0 \leq k \leq 1 \right\}.$$

This economy is entirely neoclassical; in particular it has no non-convexity. Define the problem

$$\text{(P-3)} \quad \max_{c,\phi} u(c) - m\phi,$$

subject to

$$c \leq f(1, \phi), \quad c \geq 0, \quad 0 \leq \phi \leq 1.$$

This is the social planning problem for $\overline{E}$ which maximizes utility. Because this economy now appears identical to one without any non-convexities, the standard results on equivalence of competitive and optimal allocations can be applied [see, e.g., Negishi (1960)].

Proposition 1. If $(c^*, \phi^*, K^*, N^*, w^*, r^*)$ *is a competitive equilibrium for* $\overline{E}$, *then* (c^*, ϕ^*) *is the solution to problem* (P-3).

Proposition 2. If (c^*, ϕ^*) is the solution to problem $(P-3)$, then there exists $K^*, N^*, w^*,$ and r^* such that $(c^*, \phi^*, K^*, N^*, w^*, r^*)$ is a competitive equilibrium for $\bar{E}$.

Since (P-3) is a strictly concave programming problem, the above two results imply the existence of a unique equilibrium.

One of the reasons for adding lotteries to the consumption set was the potential gain in welfare. In essence, making labor indivisible creates a barrier to trade and the introduction of lotteries is one way to overcome part of this barrier. It should be noted that adding lotteries of the type considered here to an environment similar to E but without the indivisibility in labor would have no effect on equilibrium. Finally, in Example 1 it was demonstrated that an allocation involving lotteries Pareto-dominated the equilibrium allocation for E. That this result is general should be clear, but a formal statement is:

Proposition 3. If $(c^*(t), n^*(t), k^*(t), K^*, N^*)$ is an equilibrium allocation for E and $(\bar{c}_1(t), \bar{k}_1(t), \bar{c}_2(t), \bar{k}_2(t), \bar{\phi}(t), \bar{K}, \bar{N})$ is an equilibrium allocation for $\bar{E}$, then

$$u(c(t)) - n(t)m \le \bar{\phi}(t)\left[u(\bar{c}_1(t)) - m\right] + (1 - \bar{\phi}(t))u(\bar{c}_2(t)),$$

for all t, with strict inequality if $n(t)$ is not constant for all t.

Proof. Define

$$\bar{\phi} = \int_0^1 n^*(t)\,\mathrm{d}t \quad \text{and} \quad \bar{c} = \int_0^1 c^*(t)\,\mathrm{d}t.$$

Define an allocation for $\bar{E}$ as follows:

$$c_1(t) = c_2(t) = \bar{c}, \quad \text{all } t,$$

$$\phi(t) = \bar{\phi}, \quad \text{all } t,$$

$$k_1(t) = k_2(t) = 1, \quad \text{all } t,$$

$$K = K^*, \quad N = N^*.$$

This allocation is clearly feasible, and by definition of an equilibrium for E

$$u(c^*(t)) - n^*(t)m = \int_0^1 (u(c^*(t)) - n^*(t)m)\,\mathrm{d}t$$

$$\le u\left(\int_0^1 c^*(t)\,\mathrm{d}t\right) - m\int_0^1 n^*(t)\,\mathrm{d}t = u(\bar{c}) - \bar{\phi}m,$$

where the inequality follows from Jensen's inequality and is strict if $c(t)$ is not constant. Note that the right-hand side is simply the utility resulting from one particular feasible allocation in $\bar{E}$. By Proposition 1, the equilibrium for $\bar{E}$ must result in utility at least this large. ∎

5. Stochastic environments and computation

The previous analysis continues to hold for stochastic environments. Suppose that there is a random variable s taking values in a finite subset S of R^N. Let s_i index the realizations of s and p_i be the probability that $s = s_i$. In state i assume that preferences are given by

$$u(c, s_i) - m(s_i)n,$$

and technology is given by

$$f(K, N, s_i),$$

where these functions are assumed to have the same properties as before for each value of s_i. If lotteries are introduced then optimal allocations and equilibrium allocations are given by:

$$\max_{c_i, \phi_i} \sum_i p_i \big(u(c_i, s_i) - m(s_i)\phi_i \big),$$

subject to

$$0 \le c_i \le f(1, \phi_i, s_i), \qquad 0 \le \phi_i \le 1.$$

Note that this is equivalent to solving the following problem separately for each value of i:

$$\max u(c_i, s_i) - m(s_i)\phi_i,$$

subject to

$$0 \le c_i \le f(1, \phi_i, s_i), \qquad 0 \le \phi_i \le 1.$$

This property generally applies to all static models with homogeneous agents in convex environments but will not hold for the case of indivisible labor in the absence of lotteries.

To see this assume that S contains two elements. Computing separate equilibria for the two realizations produces vectors (c_w^i, c_n^i, ϕ^i), where c_w^i is consumption for individuals who work in state i, c_n^i is consumption for individuals who don't work in state i, and ϕ^i is the fraction of individuals who work in state i. In equilibrium it must be that

$$u\left(c_w^i, s_i\right) - m(s_i)n = u\left(c_n^i, s_i\right).$$

Take two individuals, one who works in state 1 but not state 2 and one who works in state 2 but not in state 1. (There is always an equilibrium of this form.) These two individuals will have uneven consumption streams across states of nature. In state 1 the first individual consumes relatively more and in state 2 the second individual consumes relatively more. Because utility is concave in consumption these individuals can become better off by trading claims for state i consumption. Hence the above cannot be an equilibrium. If there are M states of nature, this implies that there are $2M$ markets which need to be operated, one each for labor and output in each state. And because of the discrete choice in labor supply the aggregate demands will generally be correspondence, not functions. It appears that even simple stochastic versions of the indivisible labor economy will be excessively demanding computationally in the absence of lotteries.

This is not to imply that models which are easier to compute are inherently better. Rather, the point being made is that the preceding analysis suggests that our understanding of non-convexities will be facilitated by assumptions like this that facilitate computation even if ultimately a more refined or sophisticated notion of equilibrium is to be adopted for non-convex environments.

6. Implications for aggregate fluctuations

A recurring problem in attempts to produce equilibrium models of aggregate fluctuations has been the inability of these models to account for observed relative magnitudes of fluctuations in total labor supply and real wages. [For example, see Altonji and Ashenfelter (1980), Kydland and Prescott (1982).] In particular, the estimates of the elasticity of labor supply found using micro data are much smaller than that required to reconcile aggregate fluctuations with equilibrium theory. This paper demonstrates that non-convexities may be of substantial interest for this problem.

Consider the alternative specification of preferences for E:

$$u(c) - v(n), \quad c \geq 0, \quad n \in \{1,0\}, \quad v(0) = 0.$$

From problem (P-3) we have the result that if labor is indivisible this economy behaves as though there is a single agent with preferences given by

$$u(c) - m \cdot n.$$

Hence there is a discrepancy between the true preferences of agents and the preferences of the hypothetical representative consumer generating aggregate fluctuations. In particular, the second of these has preferences linear in n, indicating a higher elasticity of labor supply.

Hansen (1985) has shown that this feature has implications which are empirically relevant. Whereas many other individuals have found that movements in aggregate hours are too small relative to movements in real wages of productivity, Hansen's indivisible labor economy delivers too much movement in aggregate hours relative to real wages and productivity. It is important to know that the results of this paper do not depend critically upon the assumption of identical agents. It may be thought that having all agents simultaneously being indifferent between working and not working is what causes the large response in employment relative to productivity. A parametric example is offered to illustrate that heterogeneity need not affect the results of this paper. The important feature of the example is that each agent has a different reservation wage. Consider the following specification: there is a continuum of agents with total mass equal to one. Each agent has a utility function of the form

$$C^{\alpha} - m_i l^{\beta},$$

where C is consumption, l is labor supply, $0 < \alpha < 1$, $\beta > 1$, and m_i is an individual specific parameter. The values of m are uniformly distributed on an interval $[\underline{m}, \overline{m}]$. If the wage rate is W and labor is divisible, then individual labor supply is given by

$$l_i = \left(\frac{W^{\alpha} \cdot \alpha}{m_i \beta} \right)^{1/\beta - \alpha}.$$

Integrating over $[\underline{m}, \overline{m}]$ to obtain aggregate labor supply gives

$$l = \left(\frac{W^{\alpha} \cdot \alpha}{\beta} \right)^{1/\beta - \alpha} \cdot \frac{1}{\gamma} \left(\frac{\overline{m}^{\gamma} - \underline{m}^{\gamma}}{\overline{m} - \underline{m}} \right),$$

where

$$\gamma = 1 - (1/\beta - \alpha).$$

In logs this gives

$$\ln l = \frac{\alpha}{\beta - \alpha} \ln W + \text{constant}.$$

If it is assumed that labor is indivisible and agents trade lotteries as outlined in section 4, then the labor supply of individual i is given by

$$\phi_i = \left(\frac{W^\alpha \alpha}{m_i} \right)^{1/1-\alpha} .$$

Integrating gives

$$\phi = (W^\alpha \alpha)^{1/1-\alpha} \cdot \frac{1}{\gamma} \left(\frac{\overline{m}^\gamma - \underline{m}^\gamma}{\overline{m} - \underline{m}} \right),$$

where

$$\gamma = \frac{1}{1-\alpha} + 1.$$

In logs this gives

$$\ln \phi = \frac{\alpha}{1-\alpha} \ln W + \text{constant}.$$

As can be seen by comparison of these two expressions, the case where labor supply is indivisible produces a slope which is larger. In fact, in this example the heterogeneity has no impact on the elasticity of labor supply. Note that the elasticity in the indivisible case is found by setting β equal to one in the corresponding expression for the divisible labor case. Hence, the same result concerning linearity holds in this case.

Care should be taken not to misinterpret this result. It is derived in the context of a static deterministic environment. Computing equilibrium allocations for dynamic stochastic environments (like that of Hansen) is ultimately the object of interest, but is too difficult a task to be undertaken here for the case of heterogeneous consumers.

If there were no lotteries in the economy with indivisible labor, then each agent simply decides whether or not to work. Because the m_i's differ across agents, this decision will differ across agents. In particular, an agent supplies labor if $W^\alpha - m_i > 0$ and doesn't supply labor if $W^\alpha - m_i < 0$. When equality holds the individual is indifferent. In this economy each individual has a different reservation wage which causes them to enter the market, given by $\overline{w}_i = m_i^{1/\alpha}$. Note that in the economy with lotteries individuals always have the choice of $\phi_i = 1$ or $\phi_i = 0$, so implicitly it follows that lotteries are improving welfare.

16   *R. Rogerson, Indivisible labor, lotteries and equilibrium*

7. Conclusion

This paper has analyzed the problem of indivisible labor in an economy with identical individuals.

The main conclusion of this paper is that non-convexities at the individual level may have important aggregate effects even if there are a large number of individuals. In the case studied here, the aggregate economy behaves as if there were no non-convexities but all individuals have preferences which are linear in leisure even though no individual in the economy has such preferences.

References

Altonji, J. and O. Ashenfelter, 1980, Wage movements and the labor market equilibrium hypothesis, Economica 47, 217–245.
Aumann, R., 1964, Markets with a continuum of traders, Econometrica 32, 39–50.
Becker, G., 1985, Human capital, effort, and the sexual division of labor, Journal of Labor Economics 3, S33–58.
Debreu, G., 1959, Theory of value (Wiley, New York).
Hansen, G., 1985, Indivisible labor and the business cycle, Journal of Monetary Economics 16, 309–328.
Judd, K., 1985, The law of large numbers with a continuum of iid random variables, Journal of Economic Theory 35, 19–25.
Kydland, F. and E. Prescott, 1982, Time to build and aggregate fluctuations, Econometrica 50, 1345–1370.
Mas-Colell, A., 1977, Indivisible commodities and general equilibrium, Journal of Economic Theory 16, 443–456.
Negishi, T., 1960, Welfare economics and the existence of an equilibrium for a competitive economy, Metroeconomica 12, 92–97.
Prescott, E. and R. Townsend, 1984, General competitive analysis with private information, International Economic Review 25, 1–20.
Prescott, E. and R. Townsend, 1984, Pareto optimum and competitive equilibria with adverse selection and moral hazard, Econometrica 52, 21–46.

[15]

Journal of Monetary Economics 16 (1985) 309–327. North-Holland

INDIVISIBLE LABOR AND THE BUSINESS CYCLE

Gary D. HANSEN*

University of California, Santa Barbara, CA 93106, USA

A growth model with shocks to technology is studied. Labor is indivisible, so all variability in hours worked is due to fluctuations in the number employed. We find that, unlike previous equilibrium models of the business cycle, this economy displays large fluctuations in hours worked and relatively small fluctuations in productivity. This finding is independent of individuals' willingness to substitute leisure across time. This and other findings are the result of studying and comparing summary statistics describing this economy, an economy with divisible labor, and post-war U.S. time series.

1. Introduction

Equilibrium theories of the business cycle, such as Kydland and Prescott (1982) or Lucas (1977), have been criticized for failing to account for some important labor market phenomena. These include the existence of unemployed workers, fluctuations in the rate of unemployment, and the observation that fluctuations in hours worked are large relative to productivity fluctuations. Equilibrium models have also been criticized for depending too heavily on the willingness of individuals to substitute leisure across time in response to wage or interest rate changes when accounting for the last observation. This criticism is based at least partially on the fact that micro studies using panel data on hours worked by individuals have not detected the intertemporal substitution necessary to explain the large aggregate fluctuations in hours worked [see Ashenfelter (1984)].

In this paper, a simple one-sector stochastic growth model with shocks to technology is constructed in which there is high variability in the number employed and total hours worked even though individuals are relatively unwilling to substitute leisure across time. The model differs from similar models, such as Kydland and Prescott (1982), in that a non-convexity (indivisible labor) is introduced. Indivisible labor is modeled by assuming that individ-

*This paper is part of my doctoral dissertation written while a student at the University of Minnesota. I have benefited from conversations with many people including Robert King, Thomas Sargent, Christopher Sims, Neil Wallace, Sumru Altug, Patrick Kehoe, Ramon Marimon, Ian Bain, and Rody Manuelli. I owe my greatest debt, however, to my advisor, Edward Prescott. I wish to also acknowledge the Federal Reserve Bank of Minneapolis which has provided support for this research. All errors, of course, are mine.

0304-3923/85/$3.30©1985, Elsevier Science Publishers B.V. (North-Holland)

uals can either work some given positive number of hours or not at all – they are unable to work an intermediate number of hours. This assumption is motivated by the observation that most people either work full time or not at all. Therefore, in my model, fluctuations in aggregate hours are the result of individuals entering and leaving employment rather than continuously employed individuals adjusting the number of hours worked, as in previous equilibrium models. This is consistent with an important feature of U.S. post-war data: most fluctuation in aggregate hours worked is due to fluctuation in the number employed as opposed to fluctuation in hours per employed worker. This is a fact that previous equilibrium theories have not tried to account for.[1]

Existing equilibrium models have also failed to account for large fluctuations in hours worked along with relatively small fluctuations in productivity (or the real wage). Prescott (1983), for example, finds that for quarterly U.S. time series, hours worked fluctuates about twice as much (in percentage terms) as productivity. In this paper it is shown that an economy with indivisible labor exhibits very large fluctuations in hours worked relative to productivity. This stands in marked contrast to an otherwise identical economy that lacks this non-convexity. In this economy hours worked fluctuates about the same amount as productivity.[2]

Equilibrium theories of the business cycle have typically depended heavily on intertemporal substitution of leisure to account for aggregate fluctuations in hours worked.[3] The willingness of individuals to substitute intertemporally is measured by the elasticity of substitution between leisure in different time periods implied by an individual's utility function. However, the theory developed here is able to account for large aggregate fluctuations in hours worked relative to productivity without requiring that this elasticity be large. This follows because the utility function of the 'representative agent' in our model implies an elasticity of substitution between leisure in different periods that is infinite.[4] This result does not depend on the elasticity of substitution implied by the preferences of the individuals who populate the economy. Thus, the theory presented here is in principle consistent with the low estimates of this elasticity found from studying panel data [see Altonji (1984) or MaCurdy (1981)].

---

[1] The fact that existing equilibrium models are inconsistent with this observation has been stressed by Heckman (1983) and Coleman (1984).

[2] Kydland and Prescott (1982) attempt to explain the above fact by including past leisure as an argument in the individual's utility function so as to enhance the intertemporal substitution response to a productivity shock. However, even after introducing this feature, Kydland and Prescott were still unable to account for this observation.

[3] This is true for the technology shock theories, such as Kydland and Prescott's (1982), as well as the monetary shock theories of Lucas and Barro [see Lucas (1977)].

[4] In this model there is a crucial distinction between the utility function of the 'representative agent' and the utility function of an individual or household.

The paper is divided as follows: The next section provides a more detailed explanation and motivation of the indivisible labor assumption. In section 3 the artificial economies to be studied are constructed. The first is a standard stochastic growth model where labor is divisible, and the second introduces indivisible labor to that economy. The second economy is a stochastic growth version of a static general equilibrium model developed by Rogerson (1984). Lotteries are added to the consumption set (following Rogerson) which makes it possible to study a competitive equilibrium by solving a representative agent problem, as in Lucas and Prescott (1971). The addition of the lotteries also implies that the firm is providing full unemployment insurance to the workers.

The fourth section explains how the equilibrium decision rules and laws of motion are calculated, as well as how the parameter values used when simulating the model were chosen. Since the representative agent's problem is not one for which a closed form solution is available, in order to calculate decision rules a quadratic approximation of this problem is derived using the method described in Kydland and Prescott (1982). These equilibrium decision rules are a set of stochastic difference equations from which the statistical properties of the time series generated by the artificial economies can be determined. The statistics studied are a set of standard deviations and correlations discussed in section 5. In this section, the statistics computed using the artificial time series are compared to the same statistics computed using U.S. time series. Some concluding remarks are contained in section 6.

2. Motivation

Existing equilibrium theories of the business cycle analyze individuals who are free to adjust continuously the number of hours worked (the 'intensive margin') and who are always employed. There are no individuals entering or leaving employment (the 'extensive margin'). However, the extensive margin seems important for explaining some aspects of labor supply at both the micro and macro levels. Heckman and MaCurdy (1980), for example, discuss the importance of the extensive margin for explaining female labor supply. At the aggregate level, over half of the variation in total hours worked is due to variation in the number of individuals employed rather than variation in average hours worked by those employed. Consider the following decomposition of variance involving quarterly data:

$$\text{var}(\log H_t) = \text{var}(\log h_t) + \text{var}(\log N_t) + 2\,\text{cov}(\log h_t, \log N_t),$$

where H_t is total hours worked, h_t is average hours worked, and N_t is the number of individuals at work, where all variables are deviations from trend.[5]

[5] The data used for this analysis is available from the Bureau of Labor Statistics' Labstat data tape. The series I used were collected from households using the *Current Population Survey*. For a description of the detrending method, see footnote 18.

Using this decomposition, 55% of the variance of H_t is due to variation in N_t, while only 20% of this variance can be directly attributed to h_t. The remainder is due to the covariance term.[6]

Most people either work full time or not at all. This might be ascribed to the presence of non-convexities either in individual preferences for leisure or in the technology. For example, the technology may be such that the marginal productivity of an individual's work effort is increasing during the first part of the workday or workweek, and then decreasing later on. That is, the individual faces a production function which is convex at first and then becomes concave. This could be due to individuals requiring a certain amount of 'warm up' time before becoming fully productive. Such a technology could induce individuals to work a lot or not at all.

Another possibility is that the non-convexity is a property of individuals' preferences. If the utility function exhibited decreasing marginal utility of leisure at low levels of leisure and increasing marginal utility at higher levels, individuals would tend to choose a low level of leisure (work a lot) or use their entire time endowment as leisure (not work at all). These preferences may be interpreted as 'indirect' preferences which reflect costs associated with working each period, such as driving a long distance to work or enduring the hassle of putting on a suit and tie. Bearing these fixed costs makes an individual less likely to choose to work only half a day.

In this paper the non-convexity is assumed to be a property of preferences.[7] However, to make the model tractable, the non-convexity introduced – indivisible labor – is an extreme version of the non-convexity described above. Individuals are assumed to have preferences that are defined only at two levels of leisure – one level corresponding to working full time and the other corresponding to not working at all. This is modeled by assuming that the consumption possibilities set consists of only two levels of leisure. This assumption implies that an individual can only adjust along the extensive margin.

Of course fluctuations along both the extensive and intensive margins are observed in the actual economy, as the above evidence indicates. However, by studying two economies – one that exhibits fluctuations only along the intensive margin and another with fluctuations only along the extensive margin – we can determine the importance of non-convexities for explaining labor variability in business cycles. If it turns out that both economies exhibit the same cyclical behavior, then it seems likely that a model that incorporated both margins would also exhibit similar behavior. In fact, non-convexities of this

---

[6] Coleman (1984) comes to a similar conclusion using establishment data.

[7] One advantage of modeling the non-convexity as a feature of the technology is that it would likely explain why part-time workers are paid less than full-time workers, in addition to accounting for features of the data discussed in this paper.

sort could probably be safely abstracted from when studying business cycle phenomena. However, it happens that the two models have very different implications and that the non-convexity improves our ability to account for U.S. aggregate time series data.

3. Two economies

3.1. A one-sector stochastic growth model with divisible labor

The economy to be studied is populated by a continuum of identical infinitely lived households with names on the closed interval $[0, 1]$. There is a single firm with access to a technology described by a standard Cobb–Douglas production function of the form

$$f(\lambda_t, k_t, h_t) = \lambda_t k_t^{\theta} h_t^{1-\theta}, \tag{1}$$

where labor (h_t) and accumulated capital (k_t) are the inputs and λ_t is a random shock which follows a stochastic process to be described below. Agents are assumed to observe λ_t before making any period t decisions. The assumption of one firm is made for convenience. Since the technology displays constant returns to scale – implying that firms make zero profit in equilibrium – the economy would behave the same if there were many firms.

Output, which is produced by the firm and sold to the households, can either be consumed (c_t) or invested (i_t), so the following constraint must be satisfied:

$$c_t + i_t \le f(\lambda_t, k_t, h_t). \tag{2}$$

The law of motion for the capital stock is given by

$$k_{t+1} = (1 - \delta)k_t + i_t, \qquad 0 \le \delta \le 1, \tag{3}$$

where δ is the rate of capital depreciation. The stock of capital is owned by the households who sell capital services to the firm.

The technology shock is assumed to follow a first-order Markov process. In particular, λ_t obeys the following law of motion:

$$\lambda_{t+1} = \gamma \lambda_t + \varepsilon_{t+1}, \tag{4}$$

where the ε_t's are iid with distribution function F. This distribution is assumed to have a positive support with a finite upper bound, which guarantees that output will always be positive. By requiring F to have mean $1 - \gamma$, the unconditional mean of λ_t is equal to 1.

This technology shock is motivated by the fact that in post-war U.S. time series there are changes in output (GNP) that can not be accounted for by changes in the inputs (capital and labor). We follow Solow (1957) and Kydland and Prescott (1982) in interpreting this residual as reflecting shocks to technology.

Households in this economy maximize the expected value of $\sum_{t=0}^{\infty}\beta^t u(c_t, l_t)$, where $0 < \beta < 1$ is the discount factor and c_t and l_t are consumption and leisure in period t, respectively. The endowment of time is normalized to be one, so $l_t = 1 - h_t$. Utility in period t is given by the function

$$u(c_t, l_t) = \log c_t + A \log l_t, \qquad A > 0. \tag{5}$$

We now have a complete specification of the preferences, technology, and stochastic structure of a simple economy where individuals are able to supply any level of employment in the interval $[0, 1]$. Each period three commodities are traded: the composite output commodity, labor, and capital services. It is possible to consider only this sequence of spot markets since there is no demand for intertemporal risk sharing which might exist if households were heterogeneous.

Households solve the following problem, where w_t is the wage rate at time t and r_t is the rental rate of capital:

$$\max \mathrm{E} \sum_{t=0}^{\infty} \beta^t u(c_t, 1 - h_t), \text{ given } k_0 \text{ and } \lambda_0, \tag{6}$$

subject to

$$c_t + i_t \le w_t h_t + r_t k_t \quad \text{and} \quad (3).$$

Agents are assumed to make period t decisions based on all information available at time t (which includes r_t and w_t). They have rational expectations in that their forecasts of future wages and rental rates are the same as those implied by the equilibrium laws of motion. The first-order conditions for the firm's profit maximization problem imply that the wage and rental rate each period are equal to the marginal productivity of labor and capital, respectively.

Since there are no externalities or other distortions present in this economy, the equal-weight Pareto optimum can be supported as a competitive equilibrium. Since agents are homogeneous, the equal-weight Pareto optimum is the solution to the problem of maximizing the expected welfare of the representative agent subject to technology constraints. This problem is the following:

$$\max \mathrm{E} \sum_{t=0}^{\infty} \beta^t u(c_t, 1 - h_t), \quad \text{given } k_0 \text{ and } \lambda_0, \tag{7}$$

subject to

$$(1)\text{–}(4) \quad \text{and} \quad \varepsilon_t \sim \text{c.d.f. } F.$$

The state of the economy in period t is described by k_t and λ_t. The decision variables are h_t, c_t, and i_t.

This problem can be solved using dynamic programming techniques.[8] This requires finding the unique continuous function $V: S \to \mathbb{R}$ (where S is the state space) that satisfies Bellman's equation (primes denote next period values)

$$V(k, \lambda) = \max\{u(c, 1 - h) + \beta E[V(k', \lambda')|\lambda]\}, \tag{8}$$

where the maximization is over c and h and is subject to the same constraints as (7). The value function, $V(k, \lambda)$, is the maximum obtainable expected return over all feasible plans. It turns out that since the utility function is concave and the constraint set convex, the value function is also concave. This implies that the problem (8) is a standard finite-dimensional concave programming problem.

Unfortunately, this problem is not one which can be solved analytically. There is no known explicit functional form for the value function, V. In principle this problem could be solved using numerical methods [see Bertsekas (1976)], but a cheaper method – which does enable one to solve for closed form decision rules – is to approximate this problem by one which consists of a quadratic objective and linear constraints, as in Kydland and Prescott (1982). This method will be explained briefly in section 4.

3.2. An economy with indivisible labor

The assumption of indivisible labor will now be added to the above stochastic growth model. This will give rise to an economy where all variation in the labor input reflects adjustment along the extensive margin. This differs from the economy described above where all variation in the labor input reflects adjustment along the intensive margin. In addition, the utility function of the 'representative agent' for this economy will imply an elasticity of substitution between leisure in different periods that is infinite and independent of the elasticity implied by the utility function of the individual households.

Indivisibility of labor is modeled by restricting the consumption possibilities set so that individuals can either work full time, denoted by h_0, or not at all.[9]

---

[8] For a detailed presentation of dynamic programming methods, see Lucas, Prescott and Stokey (1984).

[9] This is consistent with the interpretation given in section 2. An alternative interpretation of indivisible labor assumes that households can work one of two possible (non-zero) number of hours, h_1 or h_2. This interpretation is consistent with an environment where each household consists of two individuals, at least one of whom works at all times. When only one member works, the household is working h_1 hours, and when both members work the household is working h_2 hours.

In order to guarantee [using Theorem 2 of Debreu (1954)] that the solution of the representative agent's problem can be supported as a competitive equilibrium, it is necessary that the consumption possibilities set be convex. However, if one of the commodities traded is hours worked (as in the above model), the consumption possibilities set will be non-convex. To circumvent this problem, we convexify the consumption possibilities set by requiring individuals to choose lotteries rather than hours worked, following Rogerson (1984).[10] Thus, each period, instead of choosing manhours, households choose a probability of working, α_t.[11] A lottery then determines whether or not the household actually works. After changing the economy in this manner, we make it possible for the competitive equilibrium to be derived by solving a concave programming problem, just as for the economy with divisible labor.

The new commodity being introduced is a contract between the firm and a household that commits the household to work h_0 hours with probability α_t. The contract itself is being traded, so the household gets paid whether it works or not. Therefore, the firm is providing complete unemployment insurance to the workers. Since all households are identical, all will choose the same contract – that is, the same α_t. However, although households are ex ante identical, they will differ ex post depending on the outcome of the lottery: a fraction α_t of the continuum of households will work and the rest will not.[12]

Using (5), expected utility in period t is given by $\alpha_t(\log c_t + A \log(1 - h_0)) + (1 - \alpha_t)(\log c_t + A \log 1)$.[13] This simplifies to the following function $U: \mathbb{R}_+ \times [0,1] \to \mathbb{R}$,

$$U(c_t, \alpha_t) = \log c_t + A\alpha_t \log(1 - h_0). \tag{9}$$

---

[10] In Rogerson's paper, a static economy with indivisible labor is studied and lotteries are introduced to solve the problem introduced by this non-convexity. Readers may wish to consult Rogerson's paper for a rigorous general equilibrium formulation of this type of model.

[11] Adding lotteries to the consumption set increases the choices available to households when labor is indivisible. If lotteries were not available, households would only be able to choose to not work (corresponding to $\alpha = 0$) or to work h_0 (corresponding to $\alpha = 1$). Therefore, adding lotteries can only make individuals better off.

[12] The lottery involves drawing a realization of a random variable z_t from the uniform distribution on $[0,1]$. Each individual $i \in [0,1]$ is now 'renamed' according to the following rule:

$$x_t(i,z) \equiv i + z_t \quad \text{if} \quad i + z_t \leq 1,$$
$$\equiv i + z_t - 1 \quad \text{otherwise.}$$

The amount worked by agent x in period t is equal to

$$h_t(x) = 0 \quad \text{if} \quad x_t(i,z) \leq 1 - \alpha_t,$$
$$= h_0 \quad \text{if} \quad x_t(i,z) > 1 - \alpha_t.$$

This provides a mechanism for dividing the continuum of agents into two subsets, one where each individual works zero hours and another where individuals work h_0. The first will have measure $(1 - \alpha_t)$ and the other measure α_t. This follows from the easily verified fact that $\text{Prob}[x_t(i,z) \leq 1 - \alpha_t]$ is equal to $1 - \alpha_t$ for each i.

[13] This uses the fact that, since preferences are separable in consumption and leisure, the consumption level chosen in equilibrium is independent of whether the individual works or not.

Since a fraction α_t of households will work h_0 and the rest will work zero, per capita hours worked in period t is given by

$$h_t = \alpha_t h_0. \tag{10}$$

The other features of this economy are exactly the same as for the economy with divisible labor. These include the technology and the description of the stochastic process for the technology shock. These features are described by eqs. (1) through (4).

Firms in the economy, as in the previous economy, will want to employ labor up to the point where $f_h(\lambda_t, k_t, h_t) = w_t$. However, due to the fact that lottery contracts are being traded, households are not paid for the time they actually spend working, but are instead paid for the *expected* amount of time spent working. This implies that each worker is paid as if he worked h_t [as defined in (10)] rather than for the amount he actually does work. Therefore, the budget constraint of a typical household differs from the budget constraint for the economy where labor is divisible (6) and is given by

$$c_t + i_t \le w_t \alpha_t h_0 + r_t k_t. \tag{11}$$

Thus, the problem solved by a typical household is

$$\max \mathrm{E} \sum_{t=0}^{\infty} \beta^t U(c_t, \alpha_t), \quad \text{given } k_0 \text{ and } \lambda_0, \tag{12}$$

subject to

(11) and (3).

This problem is equivalent to the problem solved by households in a slightly different economy where agents trade man-hours and actuarially fair insurance contracts, rather than the type of contracts traded in the economy studied here. In this alternative economy, which is described in more detail in the appendix, households only get paid for the time they actually spend working. However, if a household has purchased unemployment insurance, it will receive compensation if the lottery determines that the household does not work. In the appendix it is shown that households will choose to insure themselves fully. Therefore, in equilibrium, the households will have full unemployment insurance, just like the households populating the economy described in this section. This implies that the equilibrium allocations for these two economies are the same.

The following is the representative agent's problem that must be solved to derive the equilibrium decision rules and laws of motion:

$$\max E \sum_{t=0}^{\infty} \beta^t U(c_t, \alpha_t), \quad \text{given } k_0 \text{ and } \lambda_0, \tag{13}$$

subject to

$$(1)-(4), (10) \quad \text{and} \quad \varepsilon_t \sim \text{c.d.f. } F.$$

Like problem (7), this is a standard concave discounted dynamic programming problem. The state of the economy in period t is described by k_t and λ_t. The decision variables are α_t, c_t, and i_t.

A key property of this economy is that the elasticity of substitution between leisure in different periods for the 'representative agent' is infinite. To understand this result, first substitute $h_t = 1 - l_t$ into (10) and solve for α_t. After substituting this expression for α_t into (9) one obtains the following utility function for the representative agent (ignoring the constant term):

$$U(c_t, l_t) = \log c_t + B l_t, \tag{14}$$

where $B = -A(\log(1 - h_0))/h_0$. Since this utility function is linear in leisure it implies an infinite elasticity of substitution between leisure in different periods. This follows no matter how small this elasticity is for the individuals populating the economy. Therefore, the elasticity of substitution between leisure in different periods for the *aggregate* economy is infinite and independent of the willingness of individuals to substitute leisure across time.[14]

4. Solution method and calibration

The problems (7) and (13) are not in the class of problems for which it is possible to solve analytically for decision rules. This special class of problems includes those with quadratic objectives and linear constraints, as well as some other structures. For this reason, approximate economies are studied for which the representative agent's problem is linear-quadratic [see Kydland and Prescott (1982)]. It is then possible to obtain explicit decision rules for these approximate economies.

By making appropriate substitutions, one can express problems (7) and (13) as dynamic optimization problems with decision variables i_t and h_t and state variables λ_t and k_t. The constraints for these problems are linear although the

---

[14] The fact that in this type of model the representative agent's utility function is linear in leisure was originally shown by Rogerson (1984) for his model. This result depends, however, on the utility function being additively separable across time.

objective functions are non-linear. For each of these problems, Kydland and Prescott's procedure is used to construct a quadratic approximation of the objective function to be accurate in a neighborhood of the steady state for the appropriate model after the technology shock has been set equal to its unconditional mean of one.[15] The reader may consult Kydland and Prescott (1982) for details on the algorithm used for forming these approximations.[16]

To actually compute these quadratic approximations, solve for an equilibrium, and generate artificial time series, it is necessary to choose a distribution function, F, and specific parameter values for θ, δ, β, A, γ, and h_0. Kydland and Prescott (1982, 1984) follow a methodology for choosing parameter values based on evidence from growth observations and micro studies. This methodology will also be followed here. In fact, since they study a similar economy, some of the above parameters (θ, δ, β) also appear in their model. This enables me to draw on their work in selecting values for these parameters, thereby making it easier to compare the results of the two studies.

The parameter θ corresponds to capital's share in production. This has been calculated using U.S. time series data by Kydland and Prescott (1982, 1984) and was found to be approximately 0.36. The rate of depreciation of capital, δ, is set equal to 0.025 which implies an annual rate of depreciation of 10 percent. Kydland and Prescott found this to be a good compromise given that different types of capital depreciate at different rates. The discount factor, β, is set equal to 0.99, which implies a steady state annual real rate of interest of four percent.

The parameter A in the utility function (5) is set equal to 2. This implies that hours worked in the steady state for the model with divisible labor is close to $1/3$. This more or less matches the observation that individuals spend $1/3$ of

---

[15] Let the steady states for the certainty version of these models be denoted by the variable's symbol without any subscript. Eq. (3) implies that investment in the steady state is given by $i = \delta k$. Expressions for k and h can be determined by deriving the Euler equations for the appropriate representative agent problem and setting $h_t = h$, $k_t = k$, and $i_t = i = \delta k$ for all t. For both economies, the steady state capital stock is given by

$$k = [(\rho + \delta)/\theta]^{1/(\theta - 1)}h \quad \text{where} \quad \rho = (1/\beta) - 1.$$

Hours worked in the steady state for the economy with divisible labor is given by $h = (1 - \theta) \times (\rho + \delta)/[3(\rho + \delta) - \theta(\rho + 3\delta)]$; and for the economy with indivisible labor, $h = (1 - \theta)(\rho + \delta)/[\psi(\rho + \delta - \theta\delta)]$ where $\psi = -A[\log(1 - h_0)]/h_0$.

[16] Kydland and Prescott's method for approximating this problem requires choosing a vector of average deviations, $z \in \mathbf{R}^4$, which determines the size of the neighborhood around the steady state within which the approximation is accurate. The four components of z are average deviations from trend of the four variables, $x_t = (\lambda_t, k_t, i_t, h_t)$, as found in U.S. time series data. This implies that along those dimensions where there is more variability, the approximation will be accurate in a larger neighborhood around the steady state $(\bar{x})$. For the exercise carried out in this paper $\{z_i/\bar{x}_i\}_{i=1}^4 = (0.012, 0.006, 0.08, 0.017)$, reflecting the average standard deviations of these series as reported in the next section. Although attention was paid to specifying this vector in a reasonable way, it turns out that the results are not altered when the z_i components are decreased by a factor of ten.

their time engaged in market activities and 2/3 of their time in non-market activities.

To determine the parameter h_0, I set the expressions for hours of work in the steady state for the two models equal to each other. Since steady state hours worked in the model with divisible labor is fully determined by the parameters θ, δ, A, and β for which values have already been assigned (see footnote 15), it is possible to solve for h_0. This implies a value for h_0 of 0.53.

The distribution function F along with the parameter γ determine the properties of the technology shock, λ_t. The distribution of ε_t is assumed to be log normal with mean $(1 - \gamma)$, which implies that the unconditional mean of λ_t is 1. The parameter γ is set equal to 0.95 which is consistent with the statistical properties of the production function residual.[17] The standard deviation of ε_t, σ_ε, is difficult to measure from available data since this number is significantly affected by measurement error. A data analysis suggests that σ_ε could reasonably be expected to lie in the interval $[0.007, 0.01]$. A value of 0.007, for example, would imply that a little over half of the variability in ε_t is being attributed to measurement error, which is probably not unreasonable. The actual value used for the simulations in this paper is 0.00712. This particular value was chosen because it implies that the mean standard deviation of output for the economy with indivisible labor is equal to the standard deviation of GNP for the U.S. economy (see next section).

All parameters of the two models have now been determined. We are now ready to study and compare the statistical properties of the time series generated by these two models.

5. Results

For the purposes of this study, the statistical properties of the economies studied are summarized by a set of standard deviations and correlations with output that are reported in table 1.

The statistics for the U.S. economy are reported in the first two columns of the table. Before these statistics were calculated, the time series were logged and deviations from trend were computed. Detrending was necessary because the models studied abstract from growth. The data were logged so that standard deviations can be interpreted as mean percentage deviations from

---

[17]The production function residual is measured, using U.S. time series, by

$$\log \lambda_t = \log y_t - \theta \log k_t - (1 - \theta)\log h_t,$$

where data on GNP, capital stock (nonresidential equipment and structures), and hours worked is obtained from a standard econometric data base. The first-order autocorrelation coefficient for λ_t is about 0.95, indicating high serial correlation in this series. The parameter θ was assumed to be equal to 0.36 for calculating this residual. A more detailed study of the statistical properties of this technology shock is planned but has not yet been carried out.

Table 1

Standard deviations in percent (a) and correlations with output (b) for U.S. and artificial economies.

Series	Quarterly U.S. time series[a] (55,3–84,1)		Economy with divisible labor[b]		Economy with indivisible labor[b]	
	(a)	(b)	(a)	(b)	(a)	(b)
Output	1.76	1.00	1.35 (0.16)	1.00 (0.00)	1.76 (0.21)	1.00 (0.00)
Consumption	1.29	0.85	0.42 (0.06)	0.89 (0.03)	0.51 (0.08)	0.87 (0.04)
Investment	8.60	0.92	4.24 (0.51)	0.99 (0.00)	5.71 (0.70)	0.99 (0.00)
Capital stock	0.63	0.04	0.36 (0.07)	0.06 (0.07)	0.47 (0.10)	0.05 (0.07)
Hours	1.66	0.76	0.70 (0.08)	0.98 (0.01)	1.35 (0.16)	0.98 (0.01)
Productivity	1.18	0.42	0.68 (0.08)	0.98 (0.01)	0.50 (0.07)	0.87 (0.03)

[a] The U.S. time series used are real GNP, total consumption expenditures, and gross private domestic investment (all in 1972 dollars). The capital stock series includes nonresidential equipment and structures. The hours series includes total hours for persons at work in non-agricultural industries as derived from the *Current Population Survey*. Productivity is output divided by hours. All series are seasonally adjusted, logged and detrended.

[b] The standard deviations and correlations with output are sample means of statistics computed for each of 100 simulations. Each simulation consists of 115 periods, which is the same number of periods as the U.S. sample. The numbers in parentheses are sample standard deviations of these statistics. Before computing any statistics each simulated time series was logged and detrended using the same procedure used for the U.S. time series.

trend. The 'detrending' procedure used is the method employed by Hodrick and Prescott (1980).[18]

Since much of the discussion in this section centers on the variability of hours worked and productivity (output divided by hours worked), some discussion of the hours series is appropriate. The time series for hours worked used in constructing these statistics is derived from the *Current Population Survey*, which is a survey of households. This series was chosen in preference to the other available hours series which is derived from the establishment survey. The hours series based on the household survey is more comprehensive than

[18] This method involves choosing smoothed values $\{s_t\}_{t-1}^T$ for the series $\{x_t\}_{t-1}^T$ which solve the following problem:

$$\min\left\{(1/T)\sum_{t-1}^{T}(x_t - s_t)^2 + (\lambda/T)\sum_{t=2}^{T-1}[(s_{t+1} - s_t) - (s_t - s_{t-1})]^2\right\},$$

where $\lambda > 0$ is the penalty on variation, where variation is measured by the average squared second difference. A larger value of λ implies that the resulting $\{s_t\}$ series is smoother. Following Prescott (1983), I choose $\lambda = 1600$. Deviations from the smooth series are formed by taking $d_t = x_t - s_t$.

This method is used in order to filter out low frequency fluctuations. Although other methods (spectral techniques, for example) are available, this method was chosen because of its simplicity and the fact that other methods lead to basically the same results [see Prescott (1983)].

the establishment series since self-employed workers and unpaid workers in family-operated enterprises are included. Another advantage is that the household series takes into account only hours actually worked rather than all hours paid for. That is, it doesn't include items such as paid sick leave. A disadvantage is that the houschold series begins in the third quarter of 1955, which prevented me from using data over the entire post-war period.

Sample distributions of the summary statistics describing the behavior of the artificial economies were derived using Monte Carlo methods. The model was simulated repeatedly to obtain many samples of artificially generated time series. Each sample generated had the same number of periods (115) as the U.S. time series used in the study. Before any statistics were computed, the data were logged and the same filtering procedure applied to the U.S. data was applied to these time series. One hundred simulations were performed and sample statistics were calculated for each data set generated. The sample means and standard deviations of these summary statistics are reported in the last four columns of table 1.

When comparing the statistics describing the two artificial economies, one discovers that the economy with indivisible labor displays significantly larger fluctuations than the economy with divisible labor. This shows that indivisible labor increases the volatility of the stochastic growth model for a given stochastic process for the technology shock. In fact, it is necessary to increase σ_e by 30 percent (from 0.00712 to 0.00929) in order to increase the standard deviation of output for the divisible labor economy so that it is equal to the standard deviation of GNP for the actual economy, which is 1.76. It is still the case that 0.00929 is in the interval suggested by the data (see paragraph on measuring σ_e in the previous section). However, since it is likely that there is significant measurement error in our empirical estimate of the production function residual, one should prefer the lower value of σ_e.

Another conclusion drawn from studying this table is that the fluctuations in most variables are larger for the actual economy than for the indivisible labor economy. It is my view that most of this additional fluctuation (except in the case of the consumption series) is due to measurement error. Work in progress by the author attempts to correct for measurement error in the hours series (and hence some of the measurement error in the productivity series).[19] Preliminary findings seem to suggest that the above hypothesis is correct. In addition, the fact that the consumption series fluctuates much more in the actual economy than in the artificial economy can probably be explained by the fact that nothing corresponding to consumer durables is modeled in the economies studied here.

---

[19] The work referred to is a chapter of my dissertation. Copies will soon be available upon request.

Perhaps the most significant discovery made by examining table 1 is that the amount of variability in hours worked relative to variability in productivity is very different for the two model economies. This relative variability can be measured by the ratio of the standard deviation in hours worked to the standard deviation in productivity. For the economy with indivisible labor, this ratio is 2.7, and for the economy without this feature the ratio is not significantly above 1.[20] For the U.S. economy the ratio is equal to 1.4, which is between these two values.

As explained in the introduction, accounting for the large variability in hours worked relative to productivity has been an open problem in equilibrium business cycle theory. Kydland and Prescott (1982) study a version of the stochastic growth model where labor is divisible and the utility function of individuals is non-time-separable with respect to leisure. This non-time-separability property is introduced to make leisure in different periods better substitutes. However, this feature enables these authors to report a value for this ratio of only 1.17, which is still much too low to account for the fluctuations found in U.S. data.

On the other hand, the economy with indivisible labor studied here has exactly the opposite problem Kyland and Prescott's model has. The ratio implied by this model is much larger than the ratio implied by the data. However, this should not be surprising. In fact, it would be bothersome if this were *not* the case. After all, we do observe some adjustment along the intensive margin in the real world. Examples include workers who work overtime in some periods and not in others or salesmen who work a different number of hours each day. Since indivisible labor implies that *all* fluctuations are along the extensive margin, one would expect – even without looking at statistics calculated from the data – that the ratio discussed above should be somewhere between the one implied by an indivisible labor economy and a divisible labor economy.

6. Conclusion

A dynamic competitive equilibrium economy with indivisible labor has been constructed with the aim of accounting for standard deviations and correlations with output found in aggregate economic time series. Individuals in this economy are forced to enter and exit the labor force in response to technology shocks rather than simply adjusting the number of hours worked while remaining continuously employed. Therefore, this is an equilibrium model which exhibits unemployment (or employment) fluctuations in response to aggregate shocks. Fluctuations in employment seem important for fluctuations

---

[20] This ratio is still not significantly different from one even when σ_ϵ is increased to 0.00929.

in hours worked over the business cycle since most of the variability in total hours is unambiguously due to variation in the number employed rather than hours per employed worker.

An important aspect of this economy is that the elasticity of substitution between leisure in different periods for the aggregate economy is infinite and independent of the elasticity of substitution implied by the individuals' utility function. This distinguishes this model, or any Rogerson (1984) style economy, from one without indivisible labor. These include the model presented in section 3.1 and the economy studied by Kydland and Prescott (1982). In these divisible labor models, the elasticity of substitution for the aggregate economy is the same as that for individuals.

This feature enables the indivisible labor economy to exhibit large fluctuations in hours worked relative to fluctuations in productivity. Previous equilibrium models of the business cycle, which have all assumed divisible labor, have been unsuccessful in accounting for this feature of U.S. time series. This is illustrated in this paper by showing that a model with divisible labor fails to exhibit large fluctuations in hours worked relative to productivity while the model with indivisible labor displays fluctuations in hours relative to productivity which are much larger than what is observed. This seems to indicate that a model which allowed for adjustment along both the extensive margin as well as the intensive margin would have a good chance for successfully confronting the data.

In conclusion, this study demonstrates that non-convexities such as indivisible labor may be important for explaining the volatility of hours relative to productivity even when individuals are relatively unwilling to substitute leisure across time. They are also useful for increasing the size of the standard deviations of all variables relative to the standard deviation of the technology shock. Therefore, a smaller size shock is sufficient for explaining business cycle fluctuations than was true for previous models such as Kydland and Prescott's (1982). In addition, these non-convexities make it possible for an equilibrium model of the business cycle to exhibit fluctuations in employment. Therefore, non-convexities will inevitably play an important role in future equilibrium models of the cycle.

Appendix: A market for unemployment insurance

The purpose of this appendix is to show that the equilibrium of the economy presented in section 3.2 is equivalent to the equilibrium of an economy where labor is still indivisible but households are able to purchase any amount of unemployment insurance they choose. In the original economy, agents are assumed to buy and sell contracts which specify a probability of working in a given period as opposed to buying and selling hours of work. A lottery determines which households must work and which do not. A household is paid according to the probability that it works, not according to the work it actually does. In other words, the firm is automatically providing full unemployment insurance to the households.

In this appendix, households choose a probability of working each period and a lottery is held to determine which households must work, just as in the original economy. Also, preferences, technology, and the stochastic structure are exactly the same as for the original model. However, this economy is different in that households only get paid for the work they actually do – unemployed individuals get paid nothing by the firm. But, the household does have access to an insurance market which preserves the complete markets aspect of the original model. It is shown below that the equilibrium of this economy is equivalent to that of the original economy since individuals will choose to be fully insured in equilibrium. This is shown by proving that the problem solved by households is the same as the problem solved by households (12) in the original model.

The problem solved by the households can be described as follows: Each period, households choose a probability of working, α_t, a level of unemployment compensation, y_t, and consumption and investment contingent on whether the household works or not, c_{st} and i_{st} ($s = 1, 2$). These are chosen to solve the following dynamic programming problem (primes denote next period values):

$$\max V(\lambda, K, k) = \alpha\{u(c_1) + \nu(1 - h_0) + \beta\, EV(\lambda', K', k_1')\}$$

$$+ (1 - \alpha)\{u(c_2) + \nu(1) + \beta\, EV(\lambda', K', k_2')\},$$

$$(A.1)$$

subject to

$$c_1 + i_1 \le w(\lambda, K)h_0 + r(\lambda, K)k - p(\alpha)y, \qquad (A.2)$$

$$c_2 + i_2 \le y + r(\lambda, K)k - p(\alpha)y, \qquad (A.3)$$

$$k_s' = (1 - \delta)k + i_s, \qquad s = 1, 2. \qquad (A.4)$$

The function $V(\lambda, K, k)$ is the value function which depends on the household's state. The state vector includes the capital owned by the household, plus the economy wide state variables λ and K, where K is the per capita capital stock.[21] The functions $w(\lambda, K)$ and $r(\lambda, K)$ are the wage rate and rental rate

[21]Since we are allowing households to choose any level of unemployment insurance they wish, we have to allow for the heterogeneity that may come about because different households will have different income streams. This is why the distinction is made between the per capita capital stock, K, and the households accumulated capital stock, k. However, this heterogeneity will disappear in equilibrium since all households will choose full insurance, so $K = k$ in equilibrium.

of capital respectively, and $p(\alpha)$ is the price of insurance, which is a function of the probability that the household works. Also, since individuals' preferences are the same as for the original model, $u(c) = \log c$ and $v(l) = A \log l$.

The insurance company in this economy maximizes expected profits which are given by $p(\alpha)y - (1 - \alpha)y$. That is, the firm collects revenue $p(\alpha)y$ and pays y with probability $1 - \alpha$. To guarantee that profits are bounded, $p(\alpha) = (1 - \alpha)$. Therefore, the price the household must pay for insurance equals the probability that the household will collect on the insurance.

One can now substitute this expression for p into constraints (A.2) and (A.3). After eliminating the constraints by substituting out i_s and c_s ($s = 1, 2$), one can write the following first-order necessary conditions for k'_s and y:

$$u'(c_s) = \beta \, \mathrm{E} V_{k'}(\lambda', K', k'_s), \qquad s = 1, 2, \tag{A.5}$$

$$u'(c_1) = u'(c_2). \tag{A.6}$$

Eq. (A.6) implies, given the strict concavity of u, that $c_1 = c_2$. This plus eq. (A.5) imply that $k'_1 = k'_2$. This, in turn, implies that $i_1 = i_2$. Therefore, the left-hand sides of eqs. (A.2) and (A.3) are identical. Since these constraints will be binding in equilibrium, y will be chosen so that the right-hand sides are equal as well. This means that $y = wh_0$ in equilibrium. That is, households will choose to insure themselves fully. This has the implication that all households will choose the same sequence of capital stocks, so $K = k$.

Substituting these results into the household's optimization problem (A.1) yields the following problem: Households choose c, i, k', and α to

$$\max V(\lambda, k) = u(c) + \alpha v(1 - h_0) + (1 - \alpha)v(1) + \beta \, \mathrm{E} V(\lambda', k'),$$

$$\tag{A.7}$$

subject to

$$c + i \leq \alpha w(\lambda, k)h_0 + r(\lambda, k)k,$$

$$k' = (1 - \delta)k + i.$$

This problem is identical to problem (12). Therefore, the equilibrium allocation for the original economy, where the firm provides full unemployment insurance to workers by assumption, is equivalent to the equilibrium allocation for an economy where households get paid by the firm only for work done but have access to a risk-neutral insurance market. This result, of course, depends crucially on the probability α being publicly observable and the contract being enforceable. That is, it must be the case that the agent announces the same α to both the firm and the insurance company, and if the agent loses the lottery (that is, has to work) this is known by all parties. For example, this result would not hold if α depended on some underlying choice variable like effort that was not directly observed by the insurance company. In this case a difficult moral hazard problem would arise.

References

Altonji, J.G., 1984, Intertemporal substitution in labor supply: Evidence from micro data, Unpublished manuscript (Columbia University, New York).

Ashenfelter, O., 1984, Macroeconomic analyses and microeconomic analyses of labor supply, Carnegie–Rochester Conference Series on Public Policy 21, 117–156.

Bertsekas, D.P., 1976, Dynamic programming and stochastic control (Academic Press, New York).

Coleman, T.S., 1984, Essays on aggregate labor market business cycle fluctuations, Unpublished manuscript (University of Chicago, Chicago, IL).

Debreu, G., 1954, Valuation equilibrium and Pareto optimum, Proceedings of the National Academy of Sciences 40, 588–592.

Heckman, J.J., 1984, Comments on the Ashenfelter and Kydland papers, Carnegie–Rochester Conference Series on Public Policy 21, 209–224.

Heckman, J.J. and T.E. MaCurdy, 1980, A life cycle model of female labor supply, Review of Economic Studies 47, 47–74.

Hodrick, R.J. and E.C. Prescott, 1980, Post-war U.S. business cycles: An empirical investigation, Working paper (Carnegie-Mellon University, Pittsburgh, PA).

Kydland, F.E. and E.C. Prescott, 1982, Time to build and aggregate fluctuations, Econometrica 50, 1345–1370.

Kydland, F.E. and E.C. Prescott, 1984, The workweek of capital and labor, Unpublished manuscript (Federal Reserve Bank of Minneapolis, Minneapolis, MN).

Lucas, R.E., Jr., 1977, Understanding business cycles, Carnegie–Rochester Conference Series on Public Policy 5, 7–29.

Lucas, R.E., Jr. and E.C. Prescott, 1971, Investment under uncertainty, Econometrica 39, 659–681.

Lucas, R.E., Jr., E.C. Prescott and N.L. Stokey, 1984, Recursive methods for economic dynamics, Unpublished manuscript (University of Minnesota, Minneapolis, MN).

MaCurdy, T.E., An empirical model of labor supply in a life-cycle setting, Journal of Political Economy 89, 1059–1085.

Rogerson, R., Indivisible labour, lotteries and equilibrium, Unpublished manuscript (University of Rochester, Rochester, NY).

Prescott, E.C., Can the cycle be reconciled with a consistent theory of expectations? or a progress report on business cycle theory, Unpublished manuscript (Federal Reserve Bank of Minneapolis, Minneapolis, MN).

Solow, R.M., Technical change and the aggregate production function, The Review of Economics and Statistics 39, 312–320.

Part VI
Private Information

[16]

INVOLUNTARY UNEMPLOYMENT AND IMPLICIT CONTRACTS*

V. V. CHARI

This paper provides an explanation of involuntary umemployment arising as a consequence of asymmetric information between firms and workers. Involuntary unemployment is defined as a situation where ex post gains to trade exist. A model of labor contracts is developed where the allocations are not ex post optimal. It is shown that inferiority of leisure is a necessary and sufficient condition for the existence of involuntary unemployment.

I. INTRODUCTION

The fundamental theorems of welfare economics argue that in the presence of complete markets, a competitive equilibrium is Pareto optimal. Markets do not exist for the direct exchange of claims on future labor services; moral hazard and the abolition of slavery make it questionable that they ever can. Consequently, the risk inherent in an uncertain stream of labor income cannot be shifted entirely onto the capital markets, and the resulting allocation is, in general, not Pareto optimal. Recent developments in the theory of implicit contracts[1] suggest that at least part of the risk can be transferred to the capital markets through the institution of an employing firm that is assumed to be less risk-averse than its employees. Inevitably, this diversification of risk is accompanied by a pattern of employment quite different from what might occur in an otherwise identical auction market. In the extreme case when the mediating firm is risk-neutral and the utility functions of employees are separable in consumption and leisure, the firm absorbs all the risk, guaranteeing a constant wage to workers and reallocating employment from less to more favorable states of nature. If workers are endowed with indivisible units of leisure, then the contract may involve the practice of "laying-off" workers in some states, It is also possible in some (though not all) versions of these models that the resulting underemployment equilibria may contain the feature that the laid-off workers would prefer to work at the wage rate paid the rest of the labor force rather

---

* I am deeply indebted to Edward C. Prescott for his help, guidance, and encouragement. All errors are mine.

1. The original work is due to Azariadis [1975], Baily [1974], and Gordon [1974]. Drèze [1979] puts the implicit contract theory within a broader framework dealing with problems of bearing the risk associated with human capital. Holmström [1983] considers generalizations of Azariadis's model.

CCC 0033-5533/83/030107-16$02.60

108   *QUARTERLY JOURNAL OF ECONOMICS*

than stay out of work. In this sense, it has been argued that implicit contract theory explains "involuntary" employment.

Arguments have appeared in a quite unrelated strand of the literature that involuntary unemployment is best understood within the confines of disequilibrium theory.[2] Rejecting the proposition that wages and prices clear markets,[3] the protagonists argue that "what looks like involuntary unemployment is involuntary unemployment" [Solow, 1980]. Work in this area has in large part been motivated by the observation that prices and wages move "slowly" to clear markets. As a first approximation, prices are exogenously fixed [Malinvaud, 1977, or Barro and Grossman, 1971]. This is, of course, a serious shortcoming (though there are disequilibrium models [Hahn, 1978] that attempt to incorporate price-setting behavior). This paper attempts to forge a link between disequilibrium theory and the theory of implicit contracts.

I shall define involuntary unemployment to arise when the marginal rate of substitution between consumption and labor is less than the marginal rate of transformation between production and the labor input, and it is feasible to increase labor supplied. In such a situation there exist obvious gains to trade. The worker gains by supplying additional labor services, *and* the firm profits by accepting them. The difference between this formulation and that traditionally used by implicit contract theorists lies in the fact that in those formulations when the worker desires to supply his labor services at the wage rate his colleagues are receiving, the firm has no incentive to hire him.

A basic partial-equilibrium model is presented in Section II. A central assumption is that firms are better informed than workers about the true "state of nature." Since there are no markets in human capital in the model, the firm and the workers must negotiate a contract prior to the revelation of the state of nature that attempts to reconcile the potentially conflicting objectives of risk-sharing and information relevation.

The optimal contract is characterized in Section III and is found to yield a compensation schedule that is convex in the level of employment, i.e., the marginal wage rate increases with the number of hours worked. This is a consequence of the incentive compatibility constraints and is independent of the worker's preferences. Unlike the pure risk-sharing contract, compensation is not independent of

2. Drazen [1980] provides an excellent survey of recent work.
3. It is not clear whether the proposition that markets clear is testable. Lucas and Sargent [1979] argue forcefully that it is not.

INVOLUNTARY UNEMPLOYMENT, IMPLICIT CONTRACTS 109

the state of nature. Necessary conditions for the existence of involuntary unemployment are studied in this section.

Section IV compares the allocations obtained above with a contract where there are no asymmetries in information and argues that involuntary unemployment is impossible in such an environment. Section V concludes the paper.

II. THE MODEL

There are two types of agents in the economy: workers and firms. The firms are in an industry that produces a single homogeneous good at a constant price which is normalized to equal 1. The technology for producing the good is affected by a productivity shock.[4] Firms draw their productivity shocks independently from a known fixed distribution. For simplicity, assume that productivity shocks θ are drawn from a set of discrete states: $\Theta = \{\theta \mid \theta = \theta_1, \theta_2, \ldots, \theta_N\}$ according to a probability distribution Q; and $Q = \{q \mid q = q_1, q_2, \ldots, q_N; \Sigma_{i=1}^{N} q_i = 1\}$. The probability that $\theta = \theta_i$ is q_i. Then, without loss of generality, order productivity shocks so that $\theta_1 < \theta_2 < \cdots < \theta_N$. Workers know the probability distribution. One interpretation of this scenario is that there are a larger number of firms so that q_i is the fraction of firms that have labor productivity θ_i.

The only input into the production process is labor services offered by workers. The technology is constant returns to scale in the labor input and is additive across the number of workers employed by a firm:

$$(2.1) \qquad y_i = \theta_i \sum_{j=1}^{J} n_j,$$

where

y_i is the output of firm i;

n_j is the labor supplied by worker j;

J is the number of workers hired by the firm;

θ_i is the productivity of firm i.

The preferences of each worker is represented by an identical utility function, $U(c,n)$, where

c is consumption;

n is labor supplied;

4. The same analysis would go through if the element of private information was the price of the good produced by the firm. It must be noted, however, that then the price of any firm's product is highly correlated across the industry, and we need to impose the additional assumption that workers of different firms cannot communicate with one another.

$U(c,n)$: $R^+ \times [0,\bar{n}] \to R$ is bounded, twice differentiable in
both arguments, and strictly concave;
$U_c > 0$, $U_n < 0$, $U_{cc} < 0$, $U_{nn} < 0$, $U_{cc}U_{nn} - (U_{cn})^2 > 0$;
$\bar{n}$ is the maximum amount of labor that can be supplied.

Prior to the firm's observing its productivity shock, firms and workers enter into a "contract" specifying a compensation-employment schedule. Once workers and firms have signed their private contracts and the state of nature has been realized, workers cannot move to another firm. This assumption (which is uncomfortably close to involuntary servitude) can to some extent be justified by costs of moving from one location to another. Empirical evidence [Feldstein, 1975] suggests that about 70 percent of laid-off workers return to their old jobs. The lack of markets to diversify the risk in labor incomes ensures that it will, in general, be optimal for workers and firms to agree to a contract rather than resort to auction markets to organize production.

The information structure of the model is that each firm observes its productivity shock, while other agents in the economy do not. The objective function of firms is assumed to be maximization of expected profits, while workers seek to maximize expected utility. At the time of signing the contract, each worker has an alternative source of income that yields a utility of z. Thus, no worker will accept a contract, unless he is guaranteed at least z units of expected utility.

The additive separability of technology ensures that each firm will seek to maximize expected profits from each contract offered to each worker. We may safely therefore consider only contracts between a single firm and a single worker. All other contracts will be identical to this one. The contract specifies the total compensation c_i and the labor to be supplied n_i in each state of nature θ_i, $i = 1,2, \ldots, N$.

The contract is thus a pair of functions,

(2.2) $\{c(\theta),n(\theta)\}$:$\Theta \times \Theta \to R^+ \times [0,\bar{n}]$.

It will be noted that we have used the true value of θ as an argument of the functions. It is straightforward to show that any contract between the worker and the firm can be represented as shown above [Myerson, 1979; Harris and Townsend, 1977]. Suppose that the firm were to lie about the true value of θ. At the time of negotiating the contract, the worker knows that the firm will lie if it has an incentive to do so. The contract designed between the firm and worker will therefore be such that the firm will not have an incentive to lie. The optimal contract must therefore satisfy incentive compatibility or self-selection constraints,[5] which are of the form,

$$(2.3) \qquad \theta_i n_i - c_i \geqq \theta_i n_j - c_j \quad \text{all } i, j = 1, 2, \dots, N.$$

The firm's profits, if it reports the true value of θ, are at least as large as if it lies.

The optimal contract is chosen by solving the following program:[6]

$$(2.4) \qquad \max_{\overline{n} \geqq n \geqq 0} \sum_{i=1}^{N} q_i [\theta_i n_i - c_i]$$

subject to

$$(2.5) \qquad \sum_{i=1}^{N} q_i [U(c_i, n_i)] \geqq z$$

and

$$(2.6) \qquad \theta_i n_i - c_i \geqq \theta_i n_j - c_j \qquad \text{all } i, j = 1, 2, \dots, N.$$

The only novelty in this problem that distinguishes it from the standard risk-sharing problem is the incentive compatibility constraints (2.6).

III. CHARACTERIZATION OF THE OPTIMAL CONTRACT

The preliminary steps in characterizing the optimal contract are to note certain results that follow immediately from the incentive compatibility constraints.

PROPOSITION 1. c and n are nondecreasing in θ. Furthermore, the compensation-employment schedule is convex (see Figure I), and profits are nondecreasing in θ.

Proof. From equation (2.6), we have

$$\theta_i n_i - c_i \geqq \theta_i n_j - c_j \quad \text{and} \quad \theta_j n_j - c_j \geqq \theta_j n_i - c_i$$

or

$$\theta_i (n_i - n_j) \geqq c_i - c_j \geqq \theta_j (n_i - n_j).$$

5. See Harris and Townsend [1977] or Myerson [1979].

6. It is obvious from the programming problem that the assumption of constant returns to scale is not a serious restriction. Suppose that the production function is concave: $y = f(n)$. Then replace the labor term in the utility function by $f^{-1}(y)$, which is convex and the same analysis holds.

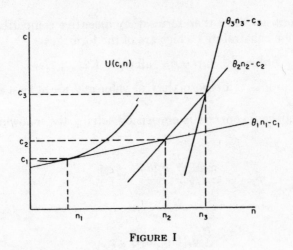

FIGURE I

It follows that

$$n_i \gtreqless n_j \text{ and } c_i \gtreqless c_j \qquad \text{iff } \theta_i \gtreqless \theta_j.$$

Thus, $n_1 \leq n_2 \leq \cdots \leq n_N$ and $c_1 \leq c_2 \leq \cdots \leq c_N$. Profits are nondecreasing, since

$$(3.1) \qquad \theta_i n_i - c_i \geq \theta_i n_j - c_j \geq \theta_j n_j - c_j \qquad \text{if } \theta_i \geq \theta_j.$$

Furthermore,

$$\theta_1 \leq \frac{c_2 - c_1}{n_2 - n_1} \leq \theta_2 \leq \frac{c_3 - c_2}{n_2 - n_1} \cdots \leq \theta_N.$$

Convexity in this discrete state case is simply the statement that the line passing through (c_{i+2}, n_{i+2}) and (c_i, n_i) does not lie below the line passing through (c_i, n_i) and (c_{i+1}, n_{i+1}) or the line joining (c_{i+1}, n_{i+1}) and (c_{i+2}, n_{i+2}).

Q.E.D.

It is to be noted that these conclusions are independent of any special assumptions about the preferences of workers and arise purely from the informational asymmetry in the model. In particular, convexity of the contract implies that the marginal wage rate required to induce additional units of employment is increasing as employment increases. This provides one justification for institutions such as overtime pay, incentive payments, bonuses, etc., quite independently.

INVOLUNTARY UNEMPLOYMENT, IMPLICIT CONTRACTS 113

of what workers' preferences are. This unusual feature does not occur in the pure risk-sharing contracts.[7]

Further investigation of the incentive-compatibility constraints yields useful results.[8] First, we need consider only sequential pairwise constraints; i.e.,

$$\theta_i n_i - c_i \geqq \theta_i n_{i+1} - c_{i+1} \qquad i = 1, \ldots, N - 2$$

and

$$\theta_{i+1} n_{i+1} - c_{i+1} \geqq \theta_{i+1} n_{i+2} - c_{i+2}$$

together imply that

$$\theta_i n_i - c_i \geqq \theta_i n_{i+1} - c_{i+2}.$$

The proof is immediate. We have (recalling that $\theta_1 < \theta_2 < \cdots < \theta_N$)

$$c_{i+2} - c_{i+1} \geqq \theta_{i+1}(n_{i+2} - n_{i+1}) \geqq \theta_i(n_{i+2} - n_{i+1}).$$

Hence,

$$\theta_i n_{i+1} - c_{i+1} \geqq \theta_i n_{i+2} - c_{i+2}.$$

But

$$\theta_i n_i - c_i \geqq \theta_i n_{i+1} - c_{i+1}.$$

Hence

$$\theta_i n_i - c_i \geqq \theta_i n_{i+2} - c_{i+2}.$$

Similar results hold when comparing allocations for higher values of θ with those for lower values of θ.

We may therefore rewrite the programming problem as

(3.2) $$\max_{0 \leqq n_i \leqq \bar{n}} \sum_{i=1}^{N} q_i [\theta_i n_i - c_i],$$

subject to

$$\sum_{i=1}^{N} q_i [U(c_i, n_i)] \geqq z$$

7. Constant returns to scale play an important, though not crucial, role in this result.

8. Many of these results are similar to those obtained by Spatt [1980] and indicate that for a broad variety of models with asymmetric information we should expect such results.

QUARTERLY JOURNAL OF ECONOMICS

and

$$\theta_i n_i - c_i \geqq \theta_{i+1} - c_{i+1} \qquad i = 1,2,\ldots,N-1$$

$$\theta_i n_i - c_i \geqq \theta_i n_{i-1} - c_{i-1} \qquad i = 2,\ldots,N.$$

PROPOSITION 2. The programming problem (3.2) has a unique solution.

Proof. The constraint set is clearly convex. We may restrict consideration of the optimum to a compact set. Define $\bar{c}$ by $U(\bar{c},0) = z$. Thus,

$$\sum_{i=1}^{N} q_i [\theta_i n_i - c_i] \geqq -\bar{c}.$$

Since

$$0 \leqq n_i \leqq \bar{n} \qquad \text{and} \qquad 0 \leqq c_i,$$

it is clear that c is bounded from above. The maximand is a continuous function and thus attains its maximum. Uniqueness follows from the fact that the worker's constraint must be binding (if not, reduce all c_i, thus increasing profits without violating incentive compatibility) and the fact that the worker's utility function is strictly concave.

Q.E.D.

What makes the model interesting is, of course, the possibility of involuntary unemployment. Within the context of this model, involuntary unemployment (or more precisely, involuntary underemployment) is defined in

DEFINITION 1. The worker is said to be involuntarily underemployed in state i if

(3.3) $- U_n/U_c < \theta_i \qquad \text{and} \qquad n_i < \bar{n}.$

The requirement is simply that the marginal rate of substitution be less than the marginal rate of transformation. The worker is involuntarily unemployed if (3.3) holds and $n_i = 0$.

The gains to trade in such a situation are evident. Both the firm and the worker would like to see a larger value of n for increased c.

To see the possibilities of involuntary unemployment, recast the programming problem in Lagrangian form,

$$L = \max_{0 \leqq n_i \leqq \bar{n}} \sum_{i=1}^{N} q_i [\theta_i n_i - c_i + \lambda U(c_i,n_i) - \lambda z] \qquad 0 \leqq c_i$$

$$+ \sum_{i=1}^{N-1} \mu_i [\theta_i n_i - c_i - \theta_i n_{i+1} + c_{i+1}]$$

INVOLUNTARY UNEMPLOYMENT, IMPLICIT CONTRACTS   115

$$+ \sum_{i=2}^{N} \gamma_i [\theta_i n_i - c_i - \theta_i n_{i-1} + c_{i-1}].$$

This yields

(3.4) $- q_i [1 - \lambda U_c(c_i, n_i)] + [\mu_{i-1} - \mu_j] + [\gamma_{i+1} - \gamma_i] \leqq 0$

with strict equality if $c_i > 0$;

(3.5) $q_i [\theta_i + \lambda U_n(c_i, n_i)] + [\mu_i \theta_i - \mu_{i-1} \theta_{i-1}] + [\gamma_i \theta_i - \gamma_{i-1} \theta_{i+1}]$
$$\leqq 0 \text{ if } n_i < \bar{n}, \quad \geqq 0 \text{ if } n_i = \bar{n}; i = 1, 2, \ldots, N$$

with the convention that $\mu_0 = 0$ and $\gamma_{N+1} = 0$.

To consider the possibility that the worker may be involuntarily underemployed, suppose that for some i, $c_i > 0$ and $0 < n_i < \bar{n}$. Then, by multiplying equation (3.4) by θ_i and adding equation (3.5), we have

(3.6) $q_i \lambda [\theta_i U_c(c_i, n_i) + U_n(c_i, n_i)] + \mu_{i-1}(\theta_i - \theta_{i-1})$
$$+ \gamma_{i+1}(\theta_i - \theta_{i+1}) = 0.$$

Thus, involuntary underemployment is possible if

$$\theta_{i+1} n_{i+1} - c_{i+1} = \theta_{i+1} n_i - c_i$$

and

$$\theta_{i-1} n_{i-1} - c_{i-1} > \theta_{i-1} n_i - c_i,$$

for then $\gamma_{i+1} \geqq 0$ and $\mu_{i-1} = 0$.

It is instructive to note that along with the possibility of involuntary underemployment goes the possibility of involuntary overemployment which is defined symmetrically.

Certain facts about the nature of the optimal contract and the occurrence of involuntary unemployment are also obvious from the first-order conditions. There can be no involuntary unemployment in the highest possible state; i.e., when $\theta = \theta_N$. If $0 < n_N < \bar{n}$, then equation (3.6) can be rearranged to read

$$- \frac{U_n(c_N, n_N)}{U_c(c_N, n_N)} = \frac{\mu_{N-1}(\theta_N - \theta_{N-1})}{q_N \lambda U_c(c_N, n_N)} + \theta_N \geqq \theta_N.$$

The marginal rate of substitution between leisure and consumption is at least as large as the marginal rate of transformation (recall that the productivity shocks are ranked in increasing order).

The economic rationalization for the existence of ex ante optimal contracts that involve involuntary unemployment ex post is straightforward. Against the gains to trade from increased employment in some states must be balanced incentives for the firm to tell the truth in the next higher state of productivity. In particular, if the next higher state is vastly more productive, it may be necessary to "take the lumps" in the form of involuntary unemployment to induce the firm to tell the truth when times are good.

We now establish necessary and sufficient conditions for the existence of involuntary unemployment in this model. It turns out that inferiority of leisure is crucial for the existence of involuntary unemployment. The implications of this proposition are explored in Section IV.

Before proving the theorem, we establish a useful lemma: Define

$$X_j(\theta) \equiv \left\{ c, n \mid \theta n - c = \theta n_j - c_j, n \geq n_j, c \geq c_j, -\frac{U_n(c,n)}{U_c(cn)} \leq \theta \right\}.$$

$X_j(\theta)$ is the set of allocations along a line with slope θ as we move northwest of (c_j, n_j). Note that $X_j(\theta)$ is nonempty if and only if $-U_n(c_j, n_j)/U_c(c_j, n_j) \leq \theta$. This follows from the strict concavity of the utility function.

LEMMA. If consumption and leisure are normal goods, then $U_c(c,n) < U_c(c_j, n_j)$ for all $(c,n) \in X_j(\theta)$ (if $X_j(\theta)$ is nonempty) for any choice of (c_j, n_j).

Proof. Consider the change in the marginal utility of the consumption as we move along the line with slope θ from (c_j, n_j):

$$\left. \frac{dU_c(c,n)}{dn} \right|_{\theta n - c = \theta n_j - c_j} = U_{cc}\theta + U_{cn}.$$

By assumption

$$-U_n(c,n)/U_c(c,n) \leq \theta.$$

Hence, the expression above reduces to

$$\frac{dU_c(c,n)}{dn} \leq U_{cc}\left(-\frac{U_n}{U_c}\right) + U_{cn} < 0.$$

The last inequality follows from the assumption of normality of consumption and leisure.

Hence, the marginal utility of consumption is decreasing along $X_j\theta)$.

Q.E.D.

We are thus led to

INVOLUNTARY UNEMPLOYMENT, IMPLICIT CONTRACTS   117

THEOREM. If consumption and leisure are normal goods, then there cannot be involuntary unemployment.

Proof. Suppose that for some state i the worker was involuntarily unemployed. Then a study of equation (3.6) reveals that necessarily $\gamma_{i+1} > 0$ or

$$\theta_{i+1}n_{i+1} - c_{i+1} = \theta_{i+1}n_i - c_i.$$

Consider the set $K(j,k)$ defined so that there is involuntary unemployment in the states between j and k, and there is no involuntary unemployment[9] at $j - 1$ or $k + 1$:

$$K(j,k) \equiv \{i \mid j \leqslant i \leqslant k, \theta_{i+1}n_{i+1} - c_{i+1} = \theta_{i+1}n_i - c_i, \theta_j n_j - c_j$$
$$> \theta_j n_{j-1} - c_{j-1}, \theta_j n_j - c_j > \theta_j n_{j+1} - c_{j+1}, \theta_{k+2}n_{k+2}$$
$$- c_{k+2} > \theta_{k+2}n_{k+1} - c_{k+1}, \theta_k n_k - c_k > \theta_k n_{k+1} - c_{k+1}\}.$$

Applying equation (3.4) to j and $k + 1$, we see that (assuming an interior solution)

$$(3.7) \quad 1 - \lambda U_c(c_j,n_j) - \frac{[\mu_{j-1} - \mu_j]}{q_j} - \frac{[\gamma_{j+1} - \gamma_j]}{q_j}$$

$$= 1 - \lambda U_c(c_{k+1},n_{k+1}) - \frac{[\mu_k - \mu_{k-1}]}{q_{k+1}} - \frac{[\gamma_{k+2} - \gamma_{k+1}]}{q_{k+1}}.$$

However, from the definition of $K(j,k)$ it follows that

$$\mu_j = 0$$
$$\gamma_j = 0$$
$$\mu_k = 0$$
$$\gamma_{k+2} = 0.$$

Consequently, it follows from equation (3.7) that

$$U_c(c_j,n_j) \leqslant U_c(c_{k+1},n_{k+1}).$$

However, note that (c_j,n_j) and (c_{k+1},n_{k+1}) lie on a line with a slope at least as steep as θ_j and $- U_n(c_j,n_j)/U_c(c_j,n_j) < \theta_j$. Consequently, from the lemma, $U_c(c_j,n_j) > U_c(c_{k+1},n_{k+1})$, which yields the desired contradiction.

Q.E.D.

This result establishes that leisure must be an inferior good for involuntary unemployment to occur.

9. It is possible that there is incomplete separation in the sense that the same allocation (c_j,n_j) may prevail for a number of states. In this case, choose the lowest state in this set and the highest in the set corresponding to (c_k,n_k).

It may seem at first sight that the perfect enforceability of ex ante (but *not* ex post) contracts is an unduly stringent restriction. Indeed, there seems no cause for either party to call in an enforcing authority (such as the government) when there are evident gains to trade[10] that they can exercise themselves. One rationalization is to suppose that the firm negotiates with *different*[11] workers in subsequent periods and that deviations from ex ante optimality will become known to workers in the future. Then, the firm would be unable to hire workers in the future and would have an incentive to stick to the ex ante optimal contract.[12]

IV. A COMPARISON WITH THE PURE RISK-SHARING CONTRACT

The model discussed in the preceding sections is not quite so specialized as may seem at first glance. In fact, a model such as that of Azariadis [1975] is mathematically very similar to the model of Section II.

Suppose that a firm, such as the one in Section II, has a production function $y = f(x)$, where x is the number of employees who work for the firm. There are J employees in a labor pool who are available to work for the firm. All workers are identical and have preferences described by

$$V(w,l) = U(w) + K \qquad \text{if } l = 1$$

$$= U(w) \qquad\qquad l = 0.$$

l is leisure. All workers are endowed with one indivisible unit of leisure. w is wages. Let x_i be the probability that a given worker will work in state i. The programming problem that the optimal contract must solve is

$$1 \geq \max_{x_i \geq 0} \sum_{i=1}^{n} q_i [\theta_i f(x_i J) - x_i w_i^1 - (1 - x_i) w_i^2], \quad w_i \geq 0$$

---

10. This, perhaps, is one reason why overtime pay is often legislatively fixed rather than a subject of bargaining.

11. This qualification is necessary to avoid the messy problem of multiperiod contracts.

12. These statements are conjectural. Selten's chain-store paradox shows that if the firm is in operation only for a finite number of periods, it will not build a reputation for honesty. The reasoning is simple. In the last period, there will be deviation from ex ante optimality. Then, in the second last period, the firm does not lose by an ex post trade. By induction, the firm will always make ex post trades. See Milgrom and Roberts [1980] for a way out of the paradox.

INVOLUNTARY UNEMPLOYMENT, IMPLICIT CONTRACTS 119

subject to

$$\sum_{i=1}^{N} q_i [x_i U(w_i^1) + (J - x_i) U(w_i^2) + (1 - x_i)K] \geqq z$$

and

$$\theta_i f(x_i J) - x_i w_i^1 - (1 - x_i)w_i^2 \geqq \theta_i f(x_j J) - x_j w_j^1 - (1 - w_j)w_j^2,$$
$$i, j = 1, 2, \ldots,$$

where w_i^1 is the wage paid to a worker, and w_i^2 is the wage paid to those laid off.

The convexity of the constraint set and strict concavity of the utility function ensure that $w_i^1 = w_i^2 = w_i$ (to see this, let $\hat{w}_i = x_i w_i^1 + (1 - x_i)w_i^2$). The firm is indifferent between the options. The worker strictly prefers the allocation marked with a caret.

Let

$$n_i = f(x_i J)$$

$$g(n_i) = x_i K = (K/J)f^{-1}(n_i)$$

and

$$c_i = w_i.$$

Then, it is immediate that the problems are formally similar.

Of course, in this formulation of the risk-sharing model, in the absence of informational asymmetries and with severance pay, there can be no involuntary unemployment in the sense implicitly used by contract theorists. No worker wishes to work at the wage rate offered his coworkers. In fact, every worker desires to be laid off. With a different formulation of the utility function of workers (see footnote 13), involuntary unemployment in this sense is possible.

It is trivial to verify that involuntary unemployment, as defined in Section III, is impossible in the absence of informational asymmetries. It might be conjectured that with informational asymmetries involuntary unemployment as defined here involving layoffs instead of reductions in work hours might be possible. The theorem, however, assures us that the separability induced by the 0-1 leisure decision

13. In Azariadis's formulation, preferences were

$$V(c,l) = K \qquad \text{if } l = 1$$
$$= U(c) \qquad \text{if } l = 0.$$

The firm could not pay laid-off workers. This seems to me to be an entirely arbitrary restriction.

which implies that leisure is a normal good also precludes the possibility of involuntary unemployment. Thus, for the particular structure studied here, though there are layoffs in equilibrium, there is never unemployment. Indeed, whenever there are gains to trade, there is overemployment: the marginal rate of substitution exceeds the marginal rate of transformation. In the original contract-theoretic formulation of the labor market, the absence of severance pay played a central role in the rationalization of involuntary unemployment. This lack of payment was never explained. The implicit idea was that unemployment benefits and other job opportunities made severance pay a costly luxury for the firm and workers. Risk sharing, however, implies that (with separable utility functions) the pie available for consumption will be evenly distributed, but workers in productive industries will have to work more than those in less productive industries. To put it differently, risk sharing implies a separation between contribution to the social product (through labor supply) and consumption or receipts from the social product. The marginal utility of consumption is kept constant, while the marginal disutility from labor supplied varies widely. Informational asymmetries allow the explanation of involuntary underemployment without arbitrary restrictions on severance pay. As the theorem cautions, however, informational asymmetries are *not* sufficient to explain the existence of involuntary unemployment.

Thus far, we have considered two extremes. One, where all variation occurs in hours of work and involuntary underemployment is possible, and another, where all variations occur as layoffs and unemployment is never involuntary. By relaxing the strong assumption of additive separability in the number of workers employed that was made in Section II and by introducing diminishing returns to the number of workers employed, it is possible to allow for layoffs as well as for changes in the workweek. It may then be possible to observe involuntary unemployment manifest itself as layoffs. In any of these formulations it seems essential that the marginal utility of consumption be an increasing function of labor supplied for involuntary unemployment to be possible.

V. CONCLUSIONS

Hall and Lilien [1979] and Calvo and Phelps [1977] in analyses similar to the one carried out here arrive at quite different conclusions. They contend that equilibrium contracts must involve ex post profit maximization. It is evident that an incentive-compatible contract that

INVOLUNTARY UNEMPLOYMENT, IMPLICIT CONTRACTS 121

also involves ex post profit maximization can be dominated *on average* by one that does not. Unfortunately, this involves possible dissatisfaction on both sides. Employees are laid off who are quite sincere when they respond to the government's unemployment survey that they wish to work. The *apparent* observation is that markets are not cleared. Yet the paradox disappears when viewed as an ex ante optimal contract. A casual observer of the economy described in this paper would observe the firm unilaterally deciding upon employment and compensation. He would observe workers sincerely declaring their desire to work. He would observe firms that seemingly have plenty of job-seekers at offered wage rates but apparently rationing by quantity.

Several issues remain unexplored in this analysis. Among them are contract length (see Dye [1979]), the lack of full indexing (see Chari [1980] and Gray [1978]) of contracts and questions such as the nature of the optimal contract when both layoffs and changes in the workweek are possible methods of altering labor supply. The last is particularly interesting, since what we do seem to observe is that a worker's compensation does not seem to depend upon the labor supplied by others in the firm but is strongly dependent upon the number of hours he works. I conjecture that layoffs are a signal to workers that demand in future periods is anticipated to be low but wages are not cut, since that would violate incentive-compatibility. For example, if θ_i contained a permanent and a transitory component, the incentive compatible contract that would allow workers to distinguish between the components may well involve layoffs when there is a drop in the permanent component and workweek changes when the transitory component is affected.

NORTHWESTERN UNIVERSITY

REFERENCES

Azariadis, C., "Implicit Contracts and Underemployment Equilibria," *Journal of Political Economy*, LXXXIII (Dec. 1975), 1183–1202.

Baily, M. N., "Wages and Unemployment Under Uncertain Demand," *Review of Economic Studies*, XLI (Jan. 1974), 37–50.

Barro, R. J., and H. I. Grossman, "A General Disequilibrium Model of Income and Employment," *American Economic Review*, LXI (1971), 82–93.

Calvo, G. A., and E. S. Phelps, "Employment Contingent Wage Contracts," in Karl Brunner and Allan Meltzer, eds., *Stabilization of the Domestic and International Economy*, Vol. 5., Carnegie-Rochester Conference Series on Public Policy #5 (Amsterdam: North-Holland, 1977).

Chari, V. V., "Equilibrium Contracts in a Monetary Economy," Discussion Paper No. 460, Center for Mathematical Studies in Economics and Management Science, Northwestern University, 1980.

Drazen, A., "Recent Developments in Macroeconomic Disequilibrium Theory," *Econometrica*, XLVIII (March 1980), 283–306.

Drèze, J., "Human Capital and Risk Bearing," The General Papers, #12, 1979.

Dye, R., "Optimal Contract Length," working paper, Carnegie-Mellon University, 1979.

Feldstein, M., "The Importance of Temporary Layoffs: An Empirical Analysis," *Brookings Papers, 3* (1975), 725–44.

Gordon, D. F., "A Neoclassical Theory of Keynesian Unemployment," *Economic Inquiry*, XII (Dec. 1974), 431–59.

Gray, J., "On Indexation and Contract Length," *Journal of Political Economy*, LXXXVI (Feb. 1978), 1–18.

Hahn, F., "On Non-Walrasian Equilibria," *Review of Economic Studies*, XLV (1978), 1–17.

Hall, R. E., and D. M. Lilien, "Efficient Wage Bargains Under Uncertain Supply and Demand," *American Economic Review*, LXIX (Dec. 1979), 868–79.

Harris, M., and R. Townsend, "Resource Allocation Under Asymmetric Information," Carnegie-Mellon University working paper, 1977.

Holmström, B., "Equilibrium Long-Term Labor Contracts," this *Journal, Supplement*, XCVIII (1983), 23–54.

Lucas, R. E., Jr., and T. J. Sargent, "After Keynesian Macroeconomics," University of Chicago, 1979.

Malinvaud, E., *The Theory of Unemployment Reconsidered* (Oxford: Basil Blackwell, 1977).

Milgrom, P., and J. Roberts, "Predation, Reputation and Entry Deterrence," Northwestern University discussion paper, 1980.

Myerson, R., "Incentive Compatibility and the Bargaining Problem," *Econometrica*, XLVII (Jan. 1979), 61–74.

Solow, R., "On Theories of Unemployment," *American Economic Review*, LXX (March 1980), 1–11.

Spatt, C., "Imperfect Price Discrimination, Variety and the Internal Structure of the Firm," working paper, Carnegie-Mellon University, 1980.

[17]

WAGE-EMPLOYMENT CONTRACTS*

Jerry Green and Charles M. Kahn

This paper studies the efficient agreements about the dependence of workers' earnings on employment, when the employment level is controlled by firms. The firms' superior information about profitability conditions is responsible for this form of contract governance. Under plausible assumptions, such agreements will cause employment to diverge from efficiency as a byproduct of their attempt to mitigate risk. It is shown that, if leisure is a normal good and firms are risk-neutral, employment is *always above* the efficient level. Such a one-period implicit contracting model cannot, therefore, be used to "explain" unemployment as a rational byproduct of risk sharing between workers and a risk-neutral firm under conditions of asymmetric information.

I. Introduction

Most labor agreements specify the relationship between total compensation and level of employment, but leave the latter under the firm's control. Such a provision for contract governance may be necessary because information about the value of the firm's short-run production is not easily perceived and verified by labor. This asymmetry sets up a potential conflict between the goals of risk-sharing and productive efficiency. In this paper we attempt to analyze the solution to this problem by looking at some properties of the labor contracts that are optimal in a model where the firm will choose the employment level after it ascertains some relevant random parameters.

The results can be roughly characterized as follows, subject of course to assumptions whose innocence and plausibility we shall later espouse:

1. There is more employment fluctuation under the optimal contract than would be observed if employment were chosen to maximize profits subject to the constraint that worker's utility be held constant in all situations. There is less income fluctuation.

2. There is less employment fluctuation and more income fluctuation than in the contract that would be implemented if all information could be directly verified by both parties.

3. The level of employment realized is in all cases one of "involuntary overtime." If workers could recontract with the firm ex post under conditions of symmetric information, the level of employment

* This research was supported by NSF Grant No. SOC78-06162. It was completed while the first author was a fellow of the Center for Advanced Study in the Behavioral Sciences, Stanford University. We would like to thank Olivier Blanchard, Eric Maskin, and Robert Solow for comments at several stages.

The Quarterly Journal of Economics, Vol. 98, Supplement, 1983
CCC 0033-5533/83/030173-15$02.50

would be lower. In other words, the value of the marginal product of labor is always less than workers' marginal valuation of their leisure.

4. Finally, although levels of employment are higher and firms are more profitable in states in which labor is more productive, workers' utility will be monotonically decreasing in the firm's profitability. "Good times" are not shared by all.

These results show that the asymmetry of information that has been suggested as a source of suboptimal employment policies results in the *opposite* bias. It cannot be used as a foundation for a theory of involuntary unemployment.

Risk sharing between firm and worker has been a central focus of the literature on implicit contracts.[1] In addition to a random profitability of firms, other features treated in various papers include private rather than common knowledge of this random fluctuation, risk aversion by firms as well as by workers, income effects in the demand for leisure, and random parameters in workers' utility functions as well as in firms' profit functions. The maintained assumptions of this paper are as follows:

1. Workers are risk-averse, and firms are risk-neutral.

2. Firms have complete control of employment, ex post, because the information about their profitability is not publicly available.

3. The worker's welfare is represented by a single collective utility function, as if a union with well-specified risk preferences were to strike the bargaining agreement. The actual implementation of the agreements within the group of workers—for example, seniority rules and the wage structure for different categories of workers—is not addressed.

4. The preferences of labor are assumed nonstochastic over the life of the contract. The relevant uncertainty affects only the value of the firm's output.

5. Finally, the form of feasible contracts is highly simplified. Compensation can be made to depend only upon the firm's contemporaneous choice of employment. More complicated arrangements in which compensation is allowed to depend upon the duration of unemployment, for example, are not considered.

These assumptions characterize the structure of the model. The qualitative result of overemployment will be the byproduct of the positive income effect on leisure.

---

1. We cannot attempt any reasonable summary of this interesting and rapidly expanding literature here. The papers most closely related to this one are Phelps-Calvo [1977] and Hall-Lilien [1979]. Their results are discussed below. An excellent survey of the research on implicit contracts is Azariadis [1979]. He mentions the problem treated here on pp. 28–30.

WAGE-EMPLOYMENT CONTRACTS   175

The model is presented in Section II. The main results are derived in Section III. In Section IV we offer some intuitive remarks and compare our results to those obtained under different specifications. We also briefly examine the relation of this problem to models from the principal-agent and the optimal-taxation literatures.

II. THE MODEL

The relevant uncertainty is parameterized by θ, and affects only the value of the firm's output. If l is the employment level, then $f(l,\theta)$ is this value. The contract specifies the wage paid $w(l)$ as a function of employment. The net payoff to the firm is thus $f(l,\theta) - lw(l)$. With the relevant uncertainty present in this general form, it is hard to derive specific results. Therefore, we shall treat the special case of *multiplicative uncertainty*,

$$(2.1) \qquad\qquad f(l,\theta) = \theta g(l),$$

where g is an increasing concave function, and θ is a positive random variable with a positive continuous density over an interval. The firm is assumed to be risk-neutral, and therefore maximizing the mathematical expectation of $\theta g(l) - lw(l)$ is its objective.

Workers' utility is an increasing function of earnings $lw(l)$ and a decreasing function of the level of employment. Because workers are risk-averse, we write their objective as

$$(2.2) \qquad\qquad Eu(lw(l),l),$$

where u is a concave function. The expectation in (2.2) is taken with respect to the distribution of l. However, l is chosen by firms. Its distribution will therefore depend on the form of the entire contract and on $p(\theta)$, the probability density of θ.

Under any contract $w(l)$ in any state θ, the firm chooses the level of employment $l(\theta)$ and pays the associated wage $w(l(\theta))$. It is notationally simpler to work with total compensation than with the wage rate; thus we define

$$(2.3) \qquad\qquad r(\theta) = l(\theta)w(l(\theta)).$$

The problem is to choose $w(\cdot)$ so as to maximize

$$(2.4) \qquad\qquad Eu(r(\theta),l(\theta)),$$

subject to

$$(2.5) \qquad\qquad E\theta g(l(\theta)) - r(\theta) \geqq c,$$

where $l(\theta)$ is defined by the solution to

(2.6) $$\max_{l} f(l,\theta) - lw(l),$$

and $r(\theta)$ is given by (2.3). By varying c parametrically, the family of efficient contracts will be delineated.

We shall examine the characteristics of solutions to this problem and show that overemployment is the typical outcome. By comparing our solution with solutions to related problems, we shall ascertain some of the qualitative implications of informational asymmetry and differential attitudes toward risk. Specifically we ask whether and to what extent profits, employment, and labor compensation are more stable in this problem than when these features are absent.

Before proceeding farther, let us look at three simpler versions of this problem that will be useful as benchmarks.

First, consider the maximization of (2.4) subject to (2.5), but where $l(\theta)$ can be chosen arbitrarily. This corresponds to that part of the implicit contracts literature in which the realization of uncertainties can be verified by both parties and therefore can be used explicitly to condition the outcomes.

In this case the solution can be characterized by the two equations,

(2.7) $$-\theta g'(l(\theta)) = u_l(r(\theta),l(\theta))/u_r(r(\theta),l(\theta))$$

(2.8) $$u_r(r(\theta),l(\theta)) = K, \quad \text{a constant.}$$

The former is the condition for productive efficiency. That is, in all states θ, marginal productivity of an extra unit of labor is equal to the marginal disutility of that unit. The latter equation is the condition for efficiency in risk-bearing (Borch's equation where one of the two parties is risk-neutral).

Next, we can consider the original problem in the case when utility takes the particular form,

(2.9) $$u(r,l) = v(r - h(l)),$$

where h is an increasing function describing the marginal disutility of labor and v is an arbitrary increasing concave function. The utility functions (2.9) are precisely those in which the income elasticity of leisure demanded (or labor supplied) is zero.

Hall and Lilien [1979] studied implicit contracting under (2.9) in the case when v is linear. The solution they found applies to the case of concave v is linear. The solution they found applies to the case of

WAGE-EMPLOYMENT CONTRACTS 177

concave v as well. It is to set $w(\ )$ and thus $r(\ )$ so as to implicitly describe an indifference curve; that is,

$$(2.10) \qquad\qquad r(l) - h(l) = \bar{u}.$$

It is easy to see why the firm's solution to its problem automatically satisfies (2.8). Regardless of the choice of l, (2.10) guarantees that (2.8) will hold because the argument of $v(\cdot)$ is fixed.

The firm's choices in each state will also automatically satisfy the productive efficiency condition. For this particular utility function, condition (2.7) becomes

$$(2.11) \qquad\qquad \theta g'(l) = h'(l).$$

In each state the firm chooses the point of $r(l)$ such that the marginal cost of hiring labor is just equal to the marginal revenue product. Thus,

$$(2.12) \qquad\qquad \theta g'(l) = r'(l).$$

And from (2.10), since $\bar{u}$ is constant along the contract, we have

$$(2.13) \qquad\qquad r'(l) = h'(l).$$

Combining (2.12) and (2.13), we see that the profit-maximizing choice is invariably the productively efficient choice.

This same argument can be shown graphically. Figures Ia and Ib show the firm's isoprofit curves for two different values of θ and specify a particular contract $r(l)$. Profits increase to the southeast. Points A, A' are the profit-maximizing points, satisfying condition (2.12). For a profit-maximizing firm to choose the productively efficient points, this requires that the slope of the contract always be equal to the worker's marginal rate of substitution. In other words,

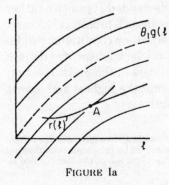

FIGURE Ia

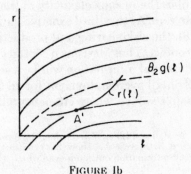

FIGURE Ib

178   QUARTERLY JOURNAL OF ECONOMICS

$\bar{u}$ should be constant along $r(l)$. Efficiency in risk-bearing requires that u_r should be constant along $r(l)$. For utility functions of the form (2.9), there is no conflict between productive efficiency and risk-sharing, and thus, no loss due to the private nature of observation of θ. With constant u_r no further income smoothing is desirable; thus there is nothing to be gained from further insurance by the firm. With efficient production in all periods, there is no Pareto-improvement to be had from recontracting.[2]

For the first-best contract to be incentive-compatible, utility functions must be of the form (2.9). Our final example is a simple instance of what can go wrong when (2.9) does not hold.

Suppose that the worker's utility function is additively separable:

$$(2.14) \qquad\qquad u(r,l) = m(r) - n(l),$$

with $m(\cdot)$ concave and $n(\cdot)$ convex. Now condition (2.8) becomes

$$(2.15) \qquad\qquad m'(r) = K.$$

In other words, in this case the optimal contract would involve paying the worker a fixed amount in all states of the world. The labor required should vary smoothly according to

$$(2.16) \qquad\qquad K/n'(l) = \theta g'(l),$$

which is the version of condition (2.7) for this particular utility function. It is easy to see that this contract could not be enforced under differential information. Because the contract does not provide for any variation in salary with respect to working time, the firm would always require the maximal amount of labor.

In subsequent sections of the paper we shall examine the general solution to the problem when (2.9) does not hold and when, in particular, the income elasticity of leisure demanded is positive rather than zero. As this third example indicates, in such problems (2.7) and (2.8), the risk-sharing and productive efficiency conditions, will be in conflict. Thus, devising a contract that can be implemented despite differential information will be a second-best problem. Its solution will entail overemployment for all θ (except the highest and lowest possible values, where efficiency will hold).

---

2. Hall and Lilien also consider the consequences of random effects in the utility function. In this case they show that a contract administered by firms cannot implement the full-information optimum even when utility functions are of the form shown in equation (2.9).

III. SOLUTION

The method of solution to be used below is novel in models of implicit contracting, drawing heavily on some techniques first developed in the literature on incentive compatibility and optimal auction design.[3]

The idea is to regard the problem as the choice of two functions of θ, $r(\theta)$ and $l(\theta)$, instead of the single relation $w(l)$. Thus, we have

$$(3.1) \qquad \max Eu(r(\theta), l(\theta))$$

subject to

$$(3.2) \qquad E\theta g(l(\theta)) - r(\theta) \geqq c$$

and that, for each θ,

$$(3.3) \qquad \max_{\tilde{\theta}} \theta g(l(\tilde{\theta})) - r(\tilde{\theta}) \text{ occurs at } \tilde{\theta} = \theta.$$

The second set of constraints corresponds to (2.6).

It is clear that given any solution of the original problem, we can define $r(\theta)$ and $l(\theta)$ by the values these variables actually take on for each value of θ, and then $r(\theta), l(\theta)$ will solve (3.1)–(3.3). Conversely, if we can arrange for a "truthtelling" solution $r(\theta), l(\theta)$ to (3.1)–(3.3), then the implicit relation,

$$(3.4) \qquad r(l) \equiv r(l^{-1}(l)),$$

where $l^{-1}(l)$ is the value of θ such that $l(\theta) = l$, gives us a solution to the original problem. It must only be insured that this inverse is well defined. We shall see below that this is not a problem because any solution to (3.1)–(3.3) will satisfy

$$(3.5) \qquad l'(\theta) > 0$$

by virtue of the second-order conditions necessary for (3.3) to hold.[4]

---

3. See Wilson [1977] and Riley and Samuelson [1979], for an introduction to the auction design problem. Stochastic auction designs have been treated by Maskin, Riley, and Weitzman [1979]. On incentive compatibility see Green and Laffont [1979] and Laffont and Maskin [1980], where the treatment of the continuous-parameter problem is closest to what will be used here.

4. There is no a priori reason to restrict contracts $w(l)$ to functions; for some problems correspondence might work better. Furthermore, two contracts $w_1(l)$ and $w_2(l)$ that differ only on portions which are never chosen in any state are to all intents and purposes equivalent. Thus, in cases (unlike the present one) where there is not an exact equivalence between the $w(l)$ formulation and the $(w(\theta), l(\theta))$ formulation, it would seem that it is the latter that is the more fundamental specification.

The next step is to replace (3.3) by the statement that the first- and second-order conditions for that problem hold as identities in θ at $\bar{\theta} = \theta$. These are

(3.6) $$\theta g'(l(\theta))l'(\theta) - r'(\theta) = 0$$

and

(3.7) $$\theta g''(l(\theta))\,(l'(\theta))^2 + \theta g'(l(\theta))l''(\theta) - r''(\theta) < 0.$$

Since (3.6) is an identity in θ, we can differentiate it to obtain an expression for $r''(\theta)$. Substituting this in (3.7), we can rewrite the second-order conditions as

$$g'(l(\theta))l'(\theta) > 0$$

or simply $l'(\theta) > 0$ by the monotonicity of g. In this way we see that (3.5) is automatically satisfied, and can be dropped as an explicit constraint in the maximization.

The problem we solve is to maximize (3.1) subject to (3.2) and (3.6).[5] To simplify subsequent calculations, we let

(3.8) $$y(\theta) = g(l(\theta))$$

and

(3.9) $$v(r,y) = u(r,g^{-1}(y)).$$

In this notation the problem is.

(3.10) $$\max Ev(r,y)$$

subject to

(3.11) $$E\{\theta y - r\} \geqq c$$

(3.12) $$\theta y' - r' = 0 \quad \text{for all } \theta.$$

Because v is concave and because the restrictions are linear, the first-order conditions and the transversality conditions are sufficient for a maximum (see Ewing [1969], pp. 129–31).

---

5. For the purposes of this exposition, we are simply *assuming* that the constraint (3.5) is nowhere binding. A complete solution, taking this constraint into account is considerably messier. Such a solution will be composed of two types of subportions. In regions of θ over which (3.5) is not binding, the contract will continue to satisfy equations of the form of (3.14)–(3.16). In regions in which (3.5) is binding, both l and r will be constant. The resultant contract curves will be similar to those described in the text, but they will be kinked at certain points. The conclusions we derive will not be affected. We are also ignoring the possibility of discontinuous contract curves. It turns out that having income a normal good is sufficient for a continuous contract to be optimal. These issues will be discussed more fully in a subsequent paper.

WAGE-EMPLOYMENT CONTRACTS   181

Writing the Lagrangian expression,

$$(3.13) \quad \int_a^b p(\theta)v(r(\theta),y(\theta)) + f(\theta)(r'(\theta) - \theta y'(\theta))$$

$$+ p(\theta)k(\theta y(\theta) - r(\theta) - c)\, d\theta,$$

we obtain the first-order conditions,

$$(3.14) \quad p(\theta)(v_r - k) = \frac{d}{d\theta}f(\theta) = f'$$

$$(3.15) \quad p(\theta)(v_y + k\theta) = \frac{d}{d\theta}(-f\cdot\theta) = -\theta f' - f$$

$$(3.16) \quad r' - \theta y' = 0;$$

and the transversality conditions,

$$(3.17) \quad f(a) = f(b) = 0$$

$$(3.18) \quad -f(a)a = -f(b)b = 0,$$

where a and b are the endpoints of the support of the distribution of $p(\theta)$. Under reasonable smoothness assumptions (including differentiability of p), these equations will yield unique continuous, smooth solutions $f(\ )$, $g(\ )$, $r(\ )$. Expressions (3.14) and (3.15) can be combined to yield

$$(3.19) \quad v_y + v_r\theta + f/p = 0.$$

As efficiency requires that $v_y + v_r\theta = 0$, the bias of employment away from the efficient level depends solely on the sign of the function f. If $f > 0$, we have overemployment: the value of the marginal product of labor $\theta g'$ falls short of the rate at which labor must be compensated on the margin $-u_l/u_r$. By definition, $u_l/u_r \equiv v_y g'/v_r$ and thus $f > 0$ implies that $v_y + v_r\theta < 0$, or,

$$\theta g' < -u_l/u_r.$$

We now turn to a proof of this main result—that indeed $f > 0$, except at a and b where $f = 0$, and thus that overemployment always obtains.

Differentiating (3.14) with respect to θ, we have

$$f'' = [v_{rr}r' + v_{ry}y']p + p'[v_r - k];$$

using (3.16) and (3.14),

$$f'' = [(v_{rr}\theta + v_{ry})y']p + p'(f'/p);$$

using (3.19),

$$(3.20) \quad f'' = \left[v_{rr} \left(\frac{-f - pv_y}{pv_r} \right) + v_{ry} \right] y' p + p' \frac{f'}{p}$$

$$= \left[pv_{rr} \left(\frac{-v_y}{v_r} \right) + pv_{ry} - \frac{v_{rr}}{v_r} f \right] y' + \frac{p'f'}{p}.$$

The condition that leisure demand be a normal good is just

$$(3.21) \qquad (u_{rr}(-u_l/u_r) + u_{rl}) < 0.$$

Since $u_{rr} \equiv v_{rr}$, $u_l = v_y g'$, $u_{rl} = v_{ry} g'$, and $g' > 0$, the first two bracketed terms above can be signed by this assumption:

$$(3.22) \qquad p(v_{rr}(-v_y/v_r) + v_{ry}) < 0.$$

If $f \leq 0$, the third term in the brackets and thus the entire bracketed expression is negative. Moreover, $y' > 0$. Thus, we know that if $f \leq 0$,

$$(3.23) \qquad f'' < p'f'/p.$$

We now prove that assuming $f \leq 0$ in the interior of $[a,b]$ leads to a contradiction. Suppose that $f \leq 0$ for some value in (a,b). Then f must attain a local minimum at some point x^* in the interior, with $f(x^*) \leq 0$. At that point $f'(x^*) = 0$ and $f''(x^*) \geq 0$. But this contradicts (3.23). Thus, $f \geq 0$, and in particular, $f > 0$ for all θ in the interior of $[a,b]$. A corollary is that u decreases as θ increases along the contract.

The function f can also be used to derive information about u_r along the contract. From (3.14) we know that $v_r = f' + \kappa$, and we can show that $\kappa = Ev_r$. Since we know from the above theorem that $f'(a) > 0$ and $f'(b) < 0$, these relations are sufficient to show that for θ near a u_r is greater than its average value and for θ near b u_r is less than its average value.[6]

IV. INTUITION AND COMPARISON WITH OTHER RESULTS

The discussion above has been quite abstract, yet the intuition behind the overemployment result is actually very clear. Figure II represents the utility function of workers, increasing to the northwest. The curve $\bar{u}$ is an indifference curve, and $\bar{u}_r$ is a constant marginal utility of income locus. When leisure is a normal good, $\bar{u}_r$ must have

6. If we knew that f'' were less than zero everywhere, we could easily show that u_r declines along the entire length of the contract. But this need not hold in general, and so the claim can only be made near the endpoints.

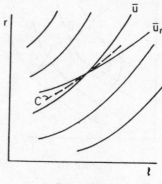

FIGURE II

a smaller slope (algebraically) than $\bar{u}$. Moving northeastward along $\bar{u}$, the marginal utility of income declines.

If $\bar{u}$ were implemented as the contract, we would always have productive efficiency, but u_r would not be constant. The first-best contract would lie along u_r; but if we left it to a profit-maximizing firm to implement $\bar{u}_r$ as a contract, we would have efficiency in risk bearing, but not in production. The firm would profit maximize by setting marginal product equal to the slope of the contract not of the indifference curve. Because of the relationship between these two slopes, the level of employment is too high under the $\bar{u}_r$ contract.

The solution to our problem C will produce a compromise between $\bar{u}$ and $\bar{u}_r$.[7] But, as this will still be less than $\bar{u}$, it will still be characterized by overemployment for all θ.

We can now justify claims (1) and (2) of the introduction. First, let us compare the optimal contract C with any constant utility contract whose path it crosses, as shown in Figure III. Let A and B be the locus of points (r,l) such that $u_r/u_l = a$ and b, respectively. As long as leisure is a normal good, these curves move leftward with increases in utility. We know from the transversality conditions that under contract C the endpoints are on these loci. Similarly, in a constant utility contract, since productive efficiency is achieved at all times, the firm's choices at $\theta = a$ and $\theta = b$ also lie on these loci. Thus, when leisure is a normal good, the spread between $l(b)$ and $l(a)$ is greater in the optimal contract than in the constant utility contract.

When income is a normal good (so that A and B move upward with increases in u, as they do in Figure III), then a similar argument

7. If f'' is always negative, then the slope of the optimal contract at any point lies between the slopes of the $\bar{u}$ curve and of the $\bar{u}_r$ curve through that point.

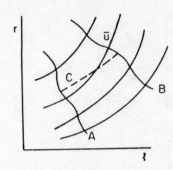

FIGURE III

demonstrates that $r(b) - r(a)$ is *smaller* in the optimal contract than in the constant utility contract.

Because u_r is not necessarily monotonic, we cannot make quite as general a claim for arbitrary u_r crossed by the optimal contract, but we can make an analogous argument if we stick to the locus of constant u_r at a value equal to Eu_r along the contract curve.

Compare the second-best optimal contract and its associated Eu_r level with a first-best contract at which u_r is identically equal to this Eu_r. Efficiency once again guarantees that the endpoints of the contract lie on A and B. And from the conclusions of the previous section, we know that the contract C must start with a higher u_r at a and end with a lower u_r at b. Thus, if leisure is a normal good, the variation of employment is greater along the first-best than along the second-best contract. If income is a normal good, the variation of income is less along the first-best than along the second-best. (See Figure IV.)

In the papers by Grossman and Hart [1981] and Azariadis [1983], underemployment is shown to be the rule. These papers use the no-

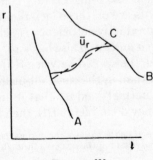

FIGURE IV

WAGE-EMPLOYMENT CONTRACTS 185

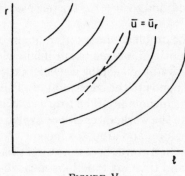

FIGURE V

income-effect utility function but introduce risk aversion on the part of firms. The same diagram, reproduced here as Figure V, is useful to explain these results. Now $\bar{u}$ and $\bar{u}_r$ coincide. But efficiency in risk-bearing requires u_r/ϕ' to be constant, where ϕ' is the marginal utility of profit. Profit is increasing in θ, and $l'(\theta) > 0$, so we know that ϕ' will be decreasing as we move northeastward along the contract. To keep u_r/ϕ' constant, u_r must decrease with l as well. This means that the locus where u_r/ϕ' is constant must cut $\bar{u}_r$ from below. A contract with u_r/ϕ' constant is thus one with underemployment. Combining both goals in the second-best problem will still produce underemployment.

This seems to be the appropriate point at which to relate this model to the principal-agent literature and to the problem of optimal income taxation. In our problem the "agent" is the firm who has proprietary information. With a risk-neutral agent we expect full efficiency to be feasible. But here, the "effort" of the agent, choosing l, enters directly into the principal's welfare and not only indirectly through its influence on "output," which here is total revenue to be shared $(\theta g(l(\theta)))$. It is this composition of an externality problem with an incentive problem that gives the model its second-best character.

Comparison with the optimal income tax literature is more difficult.[8] There are, indeed, many more similarities than differences. If we think of θ as distinguishing various types of individuals according to their productivity, then the optimal tax problem is to find a schedule of taxes to maximize

$$\int u(r,l) \, d\theta \quad \text{such that} \quad E\{\theta l - r\} \geq C.$$

8. Mirrlees [1971, 1979]. Our use of the transversality condition mirrors the investigation by Seade [1977].

Here r is net income, and so $\theta l - r$ is tax received from individuals of type θ.

The firm in our problem under different circumstances θ is like the workers in an optimal income tax problem with different levels of ability. The constraint of keeping workers' expected utility above a fixed level corresponds to the constraint of raising a fixed amount of revenue from the income tax. The firm's choice of l along a fixed (r,l) schedule is like the workers' choice of l when faced with a fixed relation between before- and after-tax income.

In the taxation literature there is no direct way of observing the individual's type, and thus tax functions must rely on charging according to observable characteristics. This creates an incentive problem analogous to the one we have discussed. We must allow the firm to choose its preferred combination of w and l in each state along the contract given it; the government presents a tax schedule to its citizens and then must allow the individuals each to choose the level of work and net income they prefer along it.

Thus, the problems are extremely close formally. Where then are the differences? What is the special structure of our problem that causes overemployment to result? Why is this result sensitive to the income elasticity of leisure demand; whereas it is the price elasticity that determines the departure of optimal income taxation from the first-best of lump-sum taxation of ability?

The details of the optimal tax problem differ because the parameters that are controlled by the schedule are different: In the tax system the schedule specifies net income not as a function of hours worked l, but as a function of gross income wl. This single difference is sufficient to make the tax problem sensitive not to the income elasticity of leisure, but to the price elasticity of leisure.

V. Conclusion

Since its beginnings, the implicit contracts literature has had the explanation of unemployment and wage rigidity as its goal. The intention was to offer a structure under which wage rigidity is optimal, and in which unemployment follows as a result. To some extent, these goals were achieved, but, it is safe to say, always by introducing some special features in the contracting process that were not obviously an essential part of the model. For example, a common device is a two-period structure in which the contract operates somewhat differently in the second period than in the first.

WAGE-EMPLOYMENT CONTRACTS 187

In this paper we have given what we believe to be the first results using the implicit contracts theme that does not rely on any of these structural conditions. Paradoxically, the interaction of differential risk aversion and incomplete information is precisely the opposite of the original intention. Long-term relationships between employers and workers increase employment variability, resulting in more employment that would be ex post efficient when profitability conditions are adverse. Thus, the implicit contracts theory may not yield the underpinnings for a theory of macroeconomic fluctuations.

HARVARD UNIVERSITY AND NATIONAL BUREAU OF ECONOMIC RESEARCH
UNIVERSITY OF CHICAGO

REFERENCES

Azariadis, C., "Implicit Contracts and Related Topics: A Survey," CARESS Working Paper, No. 79-17, 1979.
——, "Employment with Asymmetric Information," this *Journal, Supplement,* XCVIII (1983), 157–72.
Ewing, G. M., *Calculus of Variations with Applications* (N.Y.: Norton, 1969).
Green, J., and J.-J. Laffont, *Incentives in Public Decision-Making* (Amsterdam: North-Holland, 1979).
Grossman, S., and O. Hart, "Implicit Contracts, Moral Hazard, and Unemployment," *American Economic Review,* LXXI (1981), 301–07.
Hall, R., and D. M. Lilien, "Efficient Wage Bargains Under Uncertain Supply and Demand," *American Economic Review,* LXIX (1979), 868–79.
Intriligator, M., *Mathematical Optimization and Economic Theory* (Englewood Cliffs, NJ: Prentice-Hall, 1971).
Laffont, J.-J., and E. Maskin, "A Differential Approach to Dominant Strategy Mechanisms," *Econometrica,* XLVIII (1980), 1507–20.
Maskin, E., J. Riley, and M. Weitzman, "Optimal Stochastic Auctions," mimeographed, M.I.T., 1979.
Mirrlees, J. A., "An Exploration in the Theory of Optimum Income Taxation," *Review of Economic Studies,* XXXVIII (1971), 175–208.
——, "The Theory of Optimum Taxation," in *Handbook of Mathematical Economics,* K. Arrow and M. D. Intriligator, eds. (Amsterdam: North-Holland, 1979).
Phelps, E. S., and G. Calvo, Appendix to "Indexation Issues," in *Stabilization of the Domestic and International Economy,* K. Brunner and A. H. Meltzer, eds., Carnegie-Rochester Conference Series #5 (Amsterdam: North-Holland, 1977).
Riley, J., and W. Samuelson, "Optimal Auctions," mimeographed, M.I.T., 1979.
Seade, J., "On the Shape of Optimal Tax Schedules," *Journal of Public Economics,* VII (1977), 203–36.
Wilson, R. W., "A Bidding Model of Perfect Competition," *Review of Economic Studies,* XLIV (1977), 511–18.

[18]

IMPLICIT CONTRACTS UNDER ASYMMETRIC INFORMATION

SANFORD J. GROSSMAN AND OLIVER D. HART

A model is analyzed where the firm knows more about its own profit opportunities than do its workers. It is shown that because of this asymmetric information, shifts in the productivity of labor can lead to large variations in employment even when labor supply is very inelastic. This is because the employment level chosen by the firm reveals information about its own profitability. This information is useful in making insurance contracts incentive-compatible. Comparative statics results are derived that show the extent to which firm or worker risk aversion, and the probability distribution of labor productivity affect the optimal employment contract and the equilibrium degree of employment variability.

I. INTRODUCTION

In a Walrasian economy where labor supply is very inelastic, variations in labor demand will lead to variations in the real wage with little or no variation in employment. However, cyclical fluctuations in output seem to be associated with large amounts of employment variability and only small amounts of wage variability (see Hall [1980]). The implicit contract model of employment attempts to explain the low variability of wages in the context of variable labor demand in terms of optimal risk-sharing arrangements between firms and workers (for a survey of this literature see Azariadis [1979]). Unfortunately, when the employer and employees are assumed to share common information, the theory can explain only half of the above phenomenon; the ability to share risk will lead less risk-averse firms to offer more risk-averse workers low wage variability contracts; but if workers' labor supply is inelastic, the optimal contract will also involve low variability in employment (see Akerlof and Miyazaki [1980] and Bryant [1978]). Once we drop the assumption that workers can observe the increase in profit associated with hiring additional labor $\bar{s}$, however, then this last conclusion is no longer true; the optimal contract may involve high variability of employment, even though the workers' labor supply is inelastic. In this paper we explore in detail the amount of unemployment that is generated due to workers having less information than firms. We analyze the effect on unemployment of risk aversion and the probability distribution of $\bar{s}$.

It is not difficult to see why under common (symmetric) information, the implicit contract model cannot explain employment fluctuations in excess of those predicted by the Walrasian model. The

© 1983 by the President and Fellows of Harvard College. Published by John Wiley & Sons, Inc.
The Quarterly Journal of Economics, Vol. 98, Supplement, 1983
CCC 0033-5533/83/030123-34$04.40

firm and workers agree on a wage-employment contract which is ex ante Pareto optimal. That is, if $\tilde{s}$ is the random variable that determines the workers' marginal product, *and it can be observed by all parties*, then the firm and workers agree on a wage rule $w(s)$ and employment rule $l(s)$ with the property that there are no other rules that can make them all better off. The ex ante optimal rule $w(s),l(s)$ must be ex post optimal in each state s. For if in any state s both the firm and workers could be made better off by deviating from $w(s),l(s)$, then $w(s),l(s)$ would be the wrong rule to choose ex ante. Consequently, the employment rule will call for employment of a worker if and only if his marginal product is above his reservation wage. Since the optimal ex ante employment rule leads to all gains from ex post trade being exploited, the actual employment outcomes with implicit contracts are identical to those that would arise if there was a spot market for labor for each realization of $\tilde{s}$.[1] Consequently, if the supply of labor is very inelastic, then variations in the marginal revenue product will not lead to variations in employment.

Recently, models have been developed in which firms and workers have asymmetric information about the state—in particular, where firms have better information than workers.[2] Such models, which incorporate certain types of moral hazard or adverse selection, can be shown to provide a considerably richer theory of employment than the symmetric information models. In particular, Grossman and Hart [1981] have shown that the presence of asymmetric information will, under certain assumptions, cause unemployment to be greater than in the symmetric information case or than in the Walrasian model, and unemployment can occur when the marginal revenue product of labor *exceeds* the reservation wage.[3]

Our earlier result is based upon the idea that insurance creates moral hazard when the underlying source of risk is not observed by both parties to the insurance contract. In particular, if the net payments made by one party (the firm) must fluctuate in order to achieve insurance and that party is more informed than the other party (the workers), then moral hazard will disrupt the insurance. More importantly, both parties, being cognizant of moral hazard, may decide

---

1. The conclusion that the employment outcomes are the same as in a spot market depends on the assumption that the worker's reservation wage is independent of his income. We assume this in what follows.

2. See, e.g., Azariadis [1983], Calvo and Phelps [1977], Chari [1983], Green and Kahn [1983], Grossman and Hart [1981], and Hall and Lilien [1979] for some models of asymmetric information and unemployment.

3. The possible importance of asymmetric information has been recognized by a number of authors. See, e.g., Gordon [1976].

to change the employment rule to be ex post inefficient as a method of generating an ex ante optimal contract.

To understand the basic issue, assume that the firm is risk-averse with respect to its profit stream (In Section VI we provide a justification for this.) This implies that it is never optimal for the firm to bear all the risk of the variations in profit caused by $\tilde{s}$. This means that its wage bill must vary with $\tilde{s}$. In particular, its wage bill must be low when $\tilde{s}$ is low. Consider two different contracts that the firm might offer its workers. In one (the "variable wage-fixed employment" contract), workers are guaranteed employment, but agree to take a wage rate cut in bad states of the world. In the other ("fixed wage-variable employment"), workers are guaranteed a particular wage rate but may be laid off (or made redundant) in bad states. Each of these contracts permits the wage bill to vary with $\tilde{s}$ and shifts some of the risk from the firm to the workers. In a world where both the firm and the workers observe the state ex post, there is no clear reason for the workers to prefer one type of contract to the other. Matters change considerably, however, if only the firm can observe the state. For then the workers must rely on the firm to tell them which state has occurred. In general, however, the firm may wish to misreport the state. In particular, given the "variable wage-fixed employment" contract, it is always in the firm's interest to claim that a bad state has occurred, since this allows the firm to reduce wages without sacrificing employment. Thus, even though the contract may specify that wages should be high in good states and low in bad states, *actual* wages will always be low, and so the "variable wage-fixed employment" contract becomes a "fixed (low) wage-fixed employment" contract.[4]

In contrast, the "fixed wage-variable employment" contract is

---

4. This problem will be less serious if workers can observe variables that are correlated with the state in this firm, e.g., the state in the industry as a whole. The moral hazard problem will also be reduced if the firm and workers have a very long relationship with each other and (1) the shocks (states of the world) that the firm is subject to are independent over time and (2) there is no discounting. For then workers need only check that the firm is telling the truth on average. See Radner [1981]. In this paper we shall study a "one-shot" situation, where average truthtelling cannot be verified over a long period. Our results should, however, generalize to "many-shot" situations in which the firm's shocks are serially correlated or the time horizon is relatively short or there is discounting.

It might be thought that, since the implicit contract model is based upon the idea that firms establish reputations, in the long run workers will be able to verify the truthfulness of the firm's announcements. However, this requires stronger assumptions than are necessary for the firm to establish a reputation about layoffs. Workers can observe immediately whether the firm deviates from an announced wage-employment schedule $w(l)$ to be defined below. This is because its wage-employment implicit contract is defined in terms of quantities that are immediately observable. Thus, even if $\tilde{s}$ is correlated over time or the discount rate is positive (so Radner's result would not hold), firms can develop a reputation for their wage-employment policy.

less obviously open to abuse, for this contract specifies that layoffs should occur in bad states, but that wage rates should remain constant. Thus, by claiming that the state is bad (respectively, good) when in fact it is good (respectively, bad), all the firm achieves is a loss (respectively, gain) of labor at a time when this labor is relatively productive (respectively, unproductive). This possibility does not seem very attractive. We may conclude that the "fixed wage-variable employment" contract may be implementable in a way that the "variable wage-fixed employment" contract is not.

In general, there will be a set of variable wage-variable employment contracts that are implementable $(w(s),l(s))$, where w is the total wage bill and l is labor supply. For the reason given above, w can vary with s only if it is accompanied by l varying with s. Therefore, the implementable policies can be thought of as $w(l),l(s)$, where the wage bill is taken to be a predetermined function of the labor utilization. Furthermore, since only the firm observes s, it has effective control over employment and so for a policy to be implementable $l(s)$ must maximize the firm's ex post profit $f(s,l) - w(l)$ for each s, where f is the revenue function. The firm and the workers agree ex ante on a Pareto optimal member of this class. The main result of Grossman and Hart [1981] is that a Pareto optimal contract will generally involve some unemployment in states of nature where a worker's marginal product is above his reservation wage.[5] Though Grossman and Hart [1981] show that there will be ex post inefficient unemployment, they do not analyze the determinants of its magnitude. Here we shall be interested in how the amount of employment explained by the implicit contract-asymmetric information theory—over and above that explained by Walrasian theory—depends on such exogenous variables

5. Our argument assumes that the reservation wage is a constant R and is motivated as follows. Suppose that contrary to what we claim, workers are always employed to the point where their marginal product equals the reservation wage. This must mean that $w'(l) = R$ for all l, or else the firm would not be choosing l to maximize profit. This implies that the workers' wage bill is given by $w(0) + Rl$. This means that the net income of the workers (net of disutility of effort) is $w(l) - Rl = w(0)$ which is a constant independent of the state $\bar{s}$. As a consequence, the workers bear no risk, and the firm bears all the risk. This is clearly suboptimal when the firm is risk-averse.

Suppose instead that the firm and the workers agree on a new contract $\hat{w}(l)$ with $\hat{w}'(l) > R$ and $\hat{w}(0) < w(0)$. This twisting of the wage schedule means that in bad states of nature, i.e., when $\bar{s}$ is low, the firm has a lower wage bill than under the contract $w(l)$. Thus, under $\hat{w}(l)$, the firm has a less risky profit stream than under $w(l)$. For a small twist in the schedule, the efficiency losses due to $\hat{w}'(l) > R$ are of second order, since at $w'(l) = R$ the net marginal benefit (or loss) involved in a small deviation in employment from the optimum is zero. Hence, given a wage schedule that has ex post efficient employment (i.e., $w'(l) = R$), a wage schedule $\hat{w}(l)$ always exists that can make the firm and the workers better off and has the property that $\hat{w}'(l) > R$. With $\hat{w}'(l) > R$, there will be states of nature where the workers' marginal product is larger than their reservation wage and hence there is underemployment.

IMPLICIT CONTRACTS UNDER ASYMMETRIC INFORMATION 127

as the firm's risk aversion, the workers' risk aversion, the productivity of labor, the workers' reservation wage, etc. Getting some idea of the importance of these factors would seem to be an essential step toward assessing the empirical significance of the implicit contract-asymmetric information theory of employment. The comparative statics results that we obtain may also provide a way of distinguishing at the empirical level between the implicit contract-asymmetric information theory and other theories of unemployment (see also Section VI).

Analyzing the effect of risk aversion and productivity on unemployment in a general model in which each firm makes a contract with many workers is difficult. We shall therefore simplify matters considerably by confining our attention to the case where a representative firm makes a contract with, and employs, a single worker. This is obviously a very special case, but it should be noted that our results generalize to the case of a firm which makes a contract with many workers under the assumption that each worker can observe only whether or not he is employed, but not how many other workers are employed by his firm. It is to be hoped also that our results will be a useful starting point for the analysis of the many-worker case when total employment within the firm, and perhaps other variables too, are observed by the workers.

The paper is organized as follows. In Section II the model is described. In Section III we analyze how unemployment is affected by changes in the risk aversion of the firm and worker. In Sections IV and V we consider how unemployment is affected by changes in the probability distribution of the marginal product of labor. Finally, concluding remarks appear in Section VI.

II. THE MODEL

The model is based on that of Grossman and Hart [1981]. Consider a (representative) firm that can employ at most one worker. If employed, the output or revenue (we shall not distinguish between the two) of the worker is given by the random variable $\tilde{s}$. Let G be the distribution function of $\tilde{s}$. We assume that $G(\underline{s}) = 0$, $G(\bar{s}) = 1$ for some $\underline{s} < \bar{s}$. We assume that G has a continuous density function $g(s)$, which is positive for $\underline{s} \leq s \leq \bar{s}$.

All potential workers are assumed identical. Each worker has a von Neumann-Morgenstern utility function U. If the worker is employed, his utility is $U(W - R)$, and if he is unemployed, his utility is $U(W')$, where W (respectively, W') is the worker's wealth when employed, (respectively, unemployed). Here R represents the worker's disutility of effort; it is the amount that he must be paid to compensate him for working. We shall call R the worker's reservation wage.[6] We shall assume that $\bar{s} > R$; i.e., the marginal product of labor exceeds the reservation wage with positive probability. We shall suppose that the attitudes to risk of the firm's owners can be represented by a von Neumann-Morgenstern utility function of profit $V(\pi)$.

The model is a two-period one. At date 0, the firm decides whether to sign a contract with a worker. No actual production or employment occurs at this date, however. At date 1, if we assume that a contract has been signed, production and employment can occur. The contract will specify under what conditions they will occur. If production does occur at date 1, i.e., the worker is employed, the firm's output is $\tilde{s}$, as described above. If production does not occur, i.e., the worker is unemployed, the firm's output is zero. It is also assumed that if the worker signs a contract with this firm, he cannot work anywhere else at date 1, or to put it another way, his productivity elsewhere is zero. This is an extreme assumption, which could be relaxed. What we are trying to model is the idea that the worker is generally less productive in other firms at date 1 than in the firm with which he has signed the contract—that is, we have in mind that the period between date 0 and date 1 is a training period during which the worker acquires skills that are useful for this firm, but that cannot readily be transferred to other firms.[7]

We suppose that at date 0, when the contract is signed, G is known to both parties, but that the realization of $\tilde{s}$ is known to neither. (We also assume that U, V, and R are known to both parties at date 0.) Thus, at date 0, the firm and worker have *symmetric* information. We shall suppose, however, that at date 1, before any employment decisions have to be made, the firm learns the realization of $\tilde{s}$. The worker, in contrast, is assumed not to observe s.[8] Thus, there is *asymmetric* information at date 1. Finally, we suppose that there is a minimum level of expected utility $\overline{U}$ that the worker must be offered by the firm if it wishes the worker to sign a contract at date 0. One can

6. We shall assume that the worker's reservation wage is independent of his wealth W. For models in which the reservation wage is allowed to depend on wealth, see Chari [1983] and Green and Kahn [1983].

7. There is no difficulty in generalizing the model to the case where at date 1 the worker can earn a certain amount $R' > 0$ elsewhere if he is laid off by this firm. The only effect this has is to increase the effective opportunity cost of labor or reservation wage from R to $(R + R')$. Matters become complicated (and more interesting) if R' is a random variable, particularly if workers have better information about the realization of R' than does the firm.

8. See Section VI and footnote 4 for a motivation for the asymmetric information assumption.

imagine that there are many identical firms and workers trying to find partners at date 0, and that $\overline{U}$ is the market-clearing "wage" (in expected utility terms) in the market for contracts.[9]

The Optimal Contract

We wish to study the form of the optimal contract between the firm and worker at date 0. In order to proceed, we make the following assumptions about U and V.

A1. U is defined and twice differentiable on an interval $\mathcal{I} = (a, \infty)$ of the real line and $\lim_{x \to a}, U(x) = -\infty$. In addition, $U' > 0, U'' \leq 0$ on $\mathcal{I}$.

A2. V is defined and twice differentiable on an interval $\mathcal{I}' = (a', \infty)$ of the real line and $\lim_{x \to a'} V(x) = -\infty$. In addition, $V' > 0, V'' \leq 0$ on $\mathcal{I}'$.

In (A1) and (A2) we allow for the possibility that a or $a' = -\infty$.

It is helpful to begin by considering the case where, in contrast to our above asymmetric information assumption, $\tilde{s}$ is observed by both parties at date 1; i.e., it is common knowledge. Then a contract can make both wages and employment at date 1 conditional on the realization of $\tilde{s}$. Thus, a contract under symmetric information is a pair of functions $(w(s), L(s); \underline{s} \leq s \leq \overline{s})$, where $L(s) = 0$ or 1 for each s, indicating for each state (1) whether the worker is employed ($L(s) = 1$) or unemployed ($L(s) = 0$); (2) his wage $w(s)$. Note that we allow $w(s) > 0$ when $L(s) = 0$; i.e., we permit layoff (or redundancy) pay.[10]

When $\tilde{s}$ is common knowledge, it is easy to characterize an optimal contract, i.e., a contract that maximizes the firm's expected utility subject to the constraint that the worker's expected utility is at least $\overline{U}$. Note first that any contract which is ex ante optimal at date 0 before s is known must be ex post optimal at date 1 for each realization of s (for if both the firm and the worker can be made better off in some

9. The market for contracts at date 0 is taken to be a standard Walrasian one. Thus, our model does not explain (involuntary or non-Walrasian) unemployment at date 0. It is important to emphasize the different assumptions that we make about the mobility of labor at dates 0 and 1. At date 0 it is assumed that workers have not yet acquired firm-specific skills and therefore could work in a large number of different firms; i.e., labor is highly mobile. In contrast, by the time firm-specific skills have been acquired at date 1, mobility is assumed to be much reduced (in the extreme case considered here it is taken to be zero).

10. This is in contrast to much of the implicit contract literature; see Azariadis [1979]. Allowing layoff-redundancy pay changes the form of the optimal employment rule both when s is common knowledge and when it is observed only by the firm. See Grossman and Hart [1981]. Unless other considerations are introduced, there seems no reason to rule out layoff-redundancy pay in the present model.

state s and no worse off in any other state, then their expected utilities at date 0 can be increased). Now a necessary condition for ex post Pareto optimality is that production should occur if and only if $s > R$. For if production does not occur in some state $s > R$, then both parties can be made better off by letting production occur and increasing the wage from $w(s)$ to $w(s) + R + \epsilon$, where $\epsilon > 0$ is small; conversely, if production occurs when $s < R$, both parties can be made better off by stopping production and reducing the wage from $w(s)$ to $w(s) - R + \epsilon$. It follows that any ex ante optimal contract must specify the employment rule: employ if and only if $s > R$.[11]

The remaining part of the optimal contract when s is common knowledge at date 1 concerns the wage function $w(s)$. This will be chosen to ensure optimal risk sharing between the firm and the worker. Under (A1)–(A2), this involves choosing the wage function $w(s)$ such that $w(s) = w_u$, a constant, over the states s, which satisfy $L(s) = 0$, and

$$(2.1) \qquad \frac{V'(s - w(s))}{V'(-w_u)} = \frac{U'(w(s) - R)}{U'(w_u)}$$

over states s, where $L(s) = 1$. Equation (2.1) is the condition that the marginal rate of substitution between income in employment and unemployment states should be the same for the firm and worker. The reason $w(s)$ is constant over unemployment states is that social output is constant (equal to zero) over such states. Finally, w_u will be chosen so that the worker's expected utility equals $\overline{U}$.

We turn now to the more interesting case where, at date 1, s is observed only by the firm. We suppose, however, that the worker does observe whether he is employed at date 1; i.e., whether $L(s) = 0$ or 1. We analyze the optimal contract in terms of the following revelation game. We suppose that, at date 1, the firm is asked to announce the realization of $\tilde{s}$ it has observed. The contract then specifies a wage $w(\hat{s})$ and an employment level $L(\hat{s})$ (equal to zero or one), conditional on the announcement $s = \hat{s}$.

Matters can be simplified considerably by appealing to results from the incentive-compatibility literature. There it is shown that in studying the optimal contract attention can be confined to the case where truthtelling is an optimal strategy for all agents (see, e.g.,

---

11. There is an obvious and unimportant ambiguity when $s = R$. This argument depends on the possibility of layoff-redundancy pay. If layoff-redundancy pay is ruled out, it is no longer the case that ex ante optimality implies ex post efficiency. In fact, it can be shown that without layoff-redundancy pay the ex ante optimal employment rule is employ if and only if $s > k$, where k is a number less than R. See Azariadis [1979].

IMPLICIT, CONTRACTS UNDER ASYMMETRIC INFORMATION 131

Dasgupta, Hammond, and Maskin [1979], and Myerson [1978]). In other words, we may assume without loss of generality that the contract is such that the firm always wishes to report the true state. Let $E = \{s \,|\, L(s) = 1\}$ be the set of employment states and $U = \{s \,|\, L(s) = 0\}$ be the set of unemployment states designated by the contract. Then the condition that truthtelling is optimal implies that $w(s)$ equals a constant w_e on E and that $w(s)$ equals a (possibly different) constant w_u on U. For, if $w(s_1) > w(s_2)$, where $s_1, s_2 \in E$, the firm will pretend that $s = s_2$ when $s = s_1$, since by doing this, it can reduce wages without sacrificing employment; similarly, if $w(s_1) > w(s_2)$ where $s_1, s_2 \in U$.

Thus, under asymmetric information, a contract in effect specifies two wages: wage w_e when the worker is employed at date 1, and wage w_u when he is not employed at date 1. Let $k = (w_e - w_u)$. Then the condition that truthtelling is an optimal strategy tells us that $E \equiv \{s \,|\, L(s) = 1\} = \{s \,|\, s > k\}$ and $U \equiv \{s \,|\, L(s) = 0\} = \{s \,|\, s < k\}$.[12] For whenever $s > k$, the firm gains more from employing the worker than it has to pay for this employment, and vice versa when $s < k$. Thus, if $s \notin E, s > k$, the firm will pretend that the state which has occurred lies in E, and if $s \notin U, s < k$, the firm will pretend that the state which has occurred lies in U. Neither of these possibilities is consistent with truthtelling.[13]

We see then that in the case where only the firm observes the state at date 1, a contract can be characterized by two numbers: w_u, the wage when the worker is unemployed at date 1, and k, the extra amount the firm has to pay to employ him at date 1. From this, we can deduce the wage when employed, $w_e = w_u + k$, and the employment rule: employ if and only if $s > k$. Note that in the case where there is full employment always (respectively, unemployment always), there is an indeterminacy in k: any $k \leq \underline{s}$ (respectively, $\geq \bar{s}$) will do. We rule out this indeterminacy by adopting the convention that $\underline{s} \leq k \leq \bar{s}$. Note also that, given the form of the optimal contract, there is no need for the firm actually to report s at date 1. Instead we can imagine that given the wages w_u and $(w_u + k)$, the firm simply chooses whether or not to employ the worker at date 1.

---

12. The state $s = k$ can lie either in E or in U. We do not bother about this state, since it occurs with probability zero (however, see Remark 1 below and Section V).

13. This argument assumes that E and U are nonempty. However, if U is empty, we can always set $w_u = w_e - \underline{s}$ and $k = \underline{s}$ without changing anything; and if E is empty, we can set $w_e = w_u + \bar{s}, k = \bar{s}$. In both cases $E = \{s \,|\, s > k\}$, and $U = \{s \,|\, s < k\}$.

132   *QUARTERLY JOURNAL OF ECONOMICS*

DEFINITION. A contract when only the firm observes the state at date
    1 is a pair (w_u, k) satisfying $\underline{s} \leq k \leq \bar{s}$.[14]

An optimal contract is one that maximizes the firm's expected
utility subject to the worker's expected utility being at least $\overline{U}$.

DEFINITION. An optimal contract under asymmetric information is
    a pair (w_u, k), $s \leq k\ \bar{s}$, which maximizes

(2.2) $$\int_k^{\bar{s}} V(s - w_u - k)g(s)\ ds + \int_{\underline{s}}^k V(-w_u)g(s)\ ds$$

subject to

(2.3) $$U(w_u + k - R)(1 - G(k)) + U(w_u)G(k) \geq \overline{U}$$

and

(2.4) $$w_u \epsilon \mathcal{J}, \quad (w_u + k - R)\epsilon \mathcal{J}, \quad -w_u \epsilon \mathcal{J}.$$

Expression (2.2) is the firm's expected utility, since when $s > k$
the worker is employed and paid $(k + w_u)$, while when $s \leq k$ the
worker is unemployed and paid w_u.[15] The left-hand side of (2.3) gives
the worker's expected utility; the worker receives a net income of $(w_u
+ k - R)$ when employed and w_u when unemployed.

Under (A1)–(A2), (2.3) will hold with equality, since, if not, the
firm can always increase profit by reducing w_u. (A1)–(A2) also ensure
that as long as the constraint set is nonempty; i.e. there are k, w_u sat-

14. In the above, we have confined our attention to deterministic contracts; that
is, we have assumed that the contract specifies a certain wage $w(s)$ and employment
level $L(s)$ for each s announced by the firm. Recently, Maskin [1981] has shown that
it may be desirable to make the contract stochastic; that is, to specify a random wage
$\tilde{w}(s)$ and employment level $\tilde{L}(s)$ conditional on the announcement s, where the realization of $\tilde{w}(s)$ and $\tilde{L}(s)$ is determined by an objective lottery. Such schemes make the
firm's profit $sL(s) - \tilde{w}(s)$ a stochastic function of s. However, note that it may be difficult to implement a random contract. In particular, having signed such a contract,
the firm will always wish to go to a (risk-neutral) insurance company and arrange that,
if at date 1 the firm announces that the state is s, the insurance company will guarantee
the firm a certain income of $E[sL(s) - \tilde{w}(s)]$ in exchange for the firm giving the insurance company $sL(s) - w(s)$, where $w(s)$, $L(s)$ is the outcome of the lottery. Note
that there is no moral hazard in such an arrangement, since the insurance is conditional
on the announcement s and, once this announcement is made, the realization of $\tilde{L}(s)$
and $\tilde{w}(s)$ are determined by an objective lottery over which the firm has no control.
Thus, if the worker cannot monitor (and hence prevent) such insurance, the firm's
actual profit will be a deterministic function of s. Under such conditions, it can be shown
that stochastic contracts have no advantage over deterministic contracts, when the
set of feasible employment and output levels is convex. In the situation given in the
text, L is discrete, so there is some benefit from randomization that will disappear when
L is a continuous choice variable and the production function is concave.
    15. We assume that V is defined for some levels of negative income (if $w_u \geq 0$).
Alternatively, one can imagine that the firm earns profit π_0 elsewhere which is sufficient
to cover its wage bill; i.e., $V(-w_u) = W(\pi_0 - w_u)$ for some function W, where $\pi_0 \geq
w_u$.

IMPLICIT CONTRACTS UNDER ASYMMETRIC INFORMATION 133

isfying (2.3)–(2.4), an optimal contract exists. The nonemptiness of the constraint set is guaranteed by

(A3). There exists $\overline{w}$ satisfying $\overline{w} \epsilon \mathcal{J}$, $-\overline{w} \epsilon \mathcal{J}'$, $U(\overline{w}) = \overline{U}$.

In general, there may be more than one optimal contract. This is because the maximization problem in (2.2)–(2.4) is nonconvex. (In contrast, when s is common knowledge, the optimal contract is unique, unless both the firm and the worker are risk-neutral.) The proposition below, which was also proved in Grossman and Hart [1981], provides some information about the form of an optimal contract.

PROPOSITION 1. Assume (A1)–(A3). Let (w_u, k) be an optimal contract. Then (1) $\bar{s} > k \geq R$; (2) if the firm is risk-neutral, i.e., $V''(\pi) = 0$ for all $\pi \epsilon \mathcal{J}'$, $k = \max(\underline{s}, R)$; (3) if $R > \underline{s}$ and the firm is risk-averse, i.e., $V''(\pi) < 0$ for all $\pi \epsilon \mathcal{J}'$, then $k > R$.

Proposition 1(1) tells us that the probability of unemployment at date 1 will never be lower under asymmetric information than under symmetric information or than in the usual Walrasian model of the labor market (in the latter two cases, ex post efficiency is always achieved and so unemployment occurs if and only if $s < R$; i.e., the probability of unemployment is $G(R)$).[16] Proposition 1(2) says that the probability of unemployment will still be $G(R)$ under asymmetric information if the firm is risk-neutral. Proposition 1(3) says that the probability of unemployment will be greater than $G(R)$ under asymmetric information if (a) the firm is risk-averse, and (b) $R > \underline{s}$; i.e., if the probability of unemployment is positive under symmetric information. If $R \leq \underline{s}$, i.e., there is full employment under symmetric information, Proposition 1 says that the optimal k may exceed $\underline{s}$ or it may equal $\underline{s}$; that is, depending on the exact form of U, V, G, there may or may not be unemployment under asymmetric information. We will consider this case further in Section V. Note finally that Proposition 1(1) also tells us that, in an optimal contract, unemployment will not occur in states close to $\bar{s}$.

Proof of Proposition 1. If the firm is risk-neutral, the optimal contract under symmetric information can be implemented even when there is asymmetric information. For when $V' = $ constant, the solution of (2.1) is $w(s) = w_u + R$ for s satisfying $L(s) = 1$. However, this wage path can be realized under asymmetric information by setting $k = R$, and this yields efficient employment. Since the firm's expected utility

---

16. When we speak of the Walrasian model, we are referring to the standard model in which there are no training costs or locking-in effects, and where there is simply a spot market for labor at date 1.

can clearly be no higher under asymmetric information than under symmetric information (any contract that is feasible under asymmetric information is feasible under symmetric information), this proves part (2).

Note that part (1) clearly holds if $R \leq \underline{s}$, since $k \geq \underline{s}$. We prove part (1) for the case $R > \underline{s}$. Consider the first-order conditions for the problem (2.2)–(2.4), with equality in (2.3). These yield

$$
(2.5) \quad \frac{\displaystyle\int_k^{\bar{s}} V'(s - w_u - k)\, dG}{\displaystyle\int_k^{\bar{s}} V'(s - w_u - k)\, dG + \int_{\underline{s}}^k V'(-w_u)\, dG}
$$

$$
= \frac{U'(w_u + k - R)(1 - G(k)) + (U(w_u) - U(w_u + k - R))g(k)}{U'(w_u + k - R)(1 - G(k)) + U'(w_u)G(k)}
$$

if $\underline{s} < k < \bar{s}$. (If $k = \underline{s}$, we must replace the equality by $\geq$; if $k = \bar{s}$, by $\leq$.) Since $V'(s - w_u - k) \leq V'(-w_u)$ when $s > k$, the left-hand side (LHS) of (2.5) $\leq (1 - G(k))$. However, if $k < R$, the right-hand side (RHS) of (2.5) $> (1 - G(k))$, since $U'(w_u + k - R) \geq U'(w_u)$ and $U(w_u) > U(w_u + k - R)$. Hence (2.5) cannot hold when $\underline{s} < k < R < \bar{s}$. On the other hand, the first-order conditions are also not satisfied if $\underline{s} = k < R$.

This proves that $k \geq R$. Note also that the first-order conditions are not satisfied at $k = \bar{s}$. Hence part (1) is true. If $V'' < 0$, the above argument shows that $k = R$ also does not satisfy (2.5). For when $k = R$, the right-hand side of (2.5) $= (1 - G(k))$, while the left-hand side $< (1 - G(k))$, since $V'(s - w_u - k) < V'(-w_u)$ for $s > k$. This establishes part (3).

Q.E.D.

Remark 1. Proposition 1 holds for the case where G has a density function g. If G is discrete, it can be shown that parts (1) and (2) still hold, although part (3) may not (i.e., we may have $k = R$). Note that when G is discrete, it matters whether $s = k$ is an employment state or an unemployment state. Since the firm is indifferent between employment and unemployment when $s = k$, it is clearly optimal to make $s = k$ an employment state if $k > R$ (since then $w_e = w_u + k - R > w_u$ and so the worker prefers to be employed) and an unemployment state if $k < R$ (since then $w_e = w_u + k - R < w_u$ and so the worker prefers to be unemployed).

Proposition 1 supports the intuition given in the introduction. If the worker cannot observe s, wages cannot be conditioned on s directly, but only on observed variables determined by s, such as em-

IMPLICIT CONTRACTS UNDER ASYMMETRIC INFORMATION 135

ployment. As a result, in order to get the right degree of risk sharing, it may be necessary for employment to vary more than is desirable from an efficiency standpoint. In particular, it may be desirable at date 0 to agree to let unemployment occur in states where the marginal product of labor exceeds the reservation wage, in particular in states satisfying $k > s > R$. This is because this is the only way that the (risk-averse) firm can reduce its wage bill in times when s is low (the firm would like to reduce wages without sacrificing employment, but because of moral hazard this is not possible).

One may ask whether the unemployment that occurs at date 1 is voluntary or involuntary. It is involuntary in the sense that the worker is better off in employment states than in unemployment states (for $k > R \Rightarrow w_e = w_u + k - R > w_u$) and hence the worker regrets the fact that he is unemployed. It is voluntary in the sense that the worker is a willing party to the contract at date 0.

Remark 2. There is a close formal relationship between the model presented here and optimal income tax theory (see Mirrlees [1971]). In our model the firm has information that the worker does not. The firm would like to make wages depend on this information directly, but instead must base wages on the consequences of this information, i.e., employment levels. In the taxation problem, the consumer-worker has information about his ability that the government does not. The government would like taxes to depend on ability directly, but instead must base taxes on the observed consequences of ability, i.e., labor supply or income. Thus, the worker (the uninformed agent) in our model corresponds to the government (the uninformed agent) in the tax model and the firm to the consumer-worker.

Note that in the implicit contract model one considers a contract between a worker and one firm which may end up in one of a large number of states, whereas in the tax model one thinks of the government taxing a large number of different people in different states. For this reason, the government in the tax model needs to balance demands and supplies only in average or expected terms; i.e., in terms of this paper, the government is risk-neutral. In contrast, in the contract model one is interested in the case where the worker may be risk-averse. Note also that our result that $k > R$ is exactly analogous to the result that the optimal marginal tax rate is positive—both results imply that the utility of the uninformed agent (the utility of the worker or the revenue received by the government) is higher the better is the state or ability of the informed agent (the firm or the consumer-worker). Finally, our result that unemployment will not occur in states close to $\bar{s}$, i.e., that the level of employment under asymmetric

136   *QUARTERLY JOURNAL OF ECONOMICS*

information is equal to the Walrasian level in the best state of nature, is analogous to the result that the marginal tax rate should be zero for the most able (see Sadka [1977]). Proposition 1 is generalized to the case of a firm that employs many workers in Grossman and Hart [1981].[17]

III. How the Risk Aversion of the Firm and Worker Affects the Level of Employment

In the last section we saw that an optimal contract under asymmetric information is generally characterized by unemployment in excess of the spot market level or of the unemployment under symmetric information. In this section we consider how this excess unemployment depends on the degree of risk aversion of the worker and firm. For the remainder of the paper we shall assume that the firm does find it in its interest to make a contract with a worker at date 0.

Proposition 1 tells us that the probability of unemployment will exceed the Walrasian level only if the firm is risk-averse. It is therefore natural to ask whether the probability of unemployment increases as the firm becomes more risk-averse. In order to answer this and other comparative statics questions, it is useful to investigate the constraint (2.3) when there is equality. The left-hand side of (2.3) is increasing in w_u, but may be increasing or decreasing in k (an increase in k raises the wage when employed but reduces the probability of employment). We therefore use (2.3) to write w_u as a function of k: $w_u = w_u(k)$; that is,

$$(3.1) \quad U(w_u(k) + k - R)(1 - G(k)) + U(w_u(k))G(k) = \overline{U}.$$

Clearly $w_u(R) = w_u(\bar{s}) = \overline{w}$, where $U(\overline{w}) = \overline{U}$ (the existence of $\overline{w}$ is guaranteed by (A3)). Also, for $\bar{s} > k > R$, the left-hand side of (3.1) exceeds $\overline{U}$ when $w_u = \overline{w}$, and therefore $w_u(k) < \overline{w}$. Finally, w_u is differentiable for $\bar{s} > k > \max(\underline{s}, R)$. Hence $w_u(k)$, for $\max(\underline{s}, R) < k \leq \bar{s}$, is as in Figure I.

The firm's expected utility EV, given by (2.2), is also a function of w_u, k. (Note that EV is decreasing in w_u and in k.) Thus, we can draw indifference curves for the firm in Figure 1. We know from the proof of Proposition 1 that, if $R > \underline{s}$,

---

17. The model presented here is also an example of the principal-agent problem. A paper that adopts a somewhat similar approach to that taken here, and that obtains comparative statics results for some special cases, is Weitzman [1980].

IMPLICIT CONTRACTS UNDER ASYMMETRIC INFORMATION 137

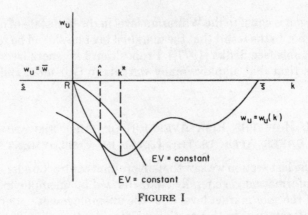

FIGURE I

$$\left.\frac{dw_u}{dk_*}\right|_{EV=\text{constant}} = -\text{LHS of (2.5)} > -\text{RHS of (2.5)}$$

$$= \left.\frac{dw_u}{dk}\right|_{EU=\text{constant}}$$

at $k = R$. In other words, the firm's indifference curves are less steep than the worker's at $k = R$. It is thus clear from the diagram that if $R > \underline{s}$, every optimal contract will satisfy $k > R$, which restates Proposition 1. The optimal contract is at $k = \hat{k}$ in Figure I.

Suppose now that the firm becomes more risk-averse. This will change the slope of the firm's indifference curves. We now show that this will have the effect of increasing the optimal k and thus increasing the probability of unemployment $G(k)$. Note that to prove this proposition, it is not sufficient to differentiate the first-order conditions (2.5), since (1) these are necessary but not generally sufficient and (2) there may be more than one optimal contract.

PROPOSITION 2. Let the firm's utility function V be replaced by $H(V)$, where H is a differentiable, increasing, strictly concave function defined on the range of $V(\pi)$. Assume that (A1)–(A3) hold before and after the change. Then, if $(\hat{w}_u, \hat{k})$ is an optimal contract before the change and $(\hat{w}'_u, \hat{k}')$ is an optimal contract after the change, $\hat{k}' \geq \hat{k}$. Furthermore, if $\underline{s} < R, \hat{k}' > \hat{k}$.

Proof. See Appendix.

The intuition behind Proposition 2 is the following. An increase in k increases the wage that the worker is paid in employment states, and this enables the firm to reduce $w_u(k)$. As á result, the firm's profits become less risky in a well-defined sense—they rise in bad unem-

138   QUARTERLY JOURNAL OF ECONOMICS

ployment states and fall in good employment states (expected profit may, however, fall). This opportunity to reduce risk is more attractive, the more risk-averse is the firm.

Proposition 2 says that k increases as the firm becomes more risk-averse. Is there an upper limit to the optimal k as the firm becomes more and more risk-averse? To answer this question, it is helpful to look at Figure I. Let k^* be the value of k that minimizes $w_u(k)$ (if there is more than one k that minimizes $w_u(k)$, let k^* be the smallest of these). It is clear that no firm, whatever its attitudes to risk, would ever select $k > k^*$. For if it did so, it would be paying a higher wage both when the worker is unemployed and employed, and realizing fewer employment states, than if it selected $k = k^*, w_u = w_u(k^*)$. Hence if (w_u,k) is an optimal contract, we must have $k \leq k^*$. The next proposition shows that as the firm becomes more and more risk-averse, k will converge to k^*.

PROPOSITION 3. Assume (A1)–(A3). Let k^* be the smallest k that minimizes $w_u(k)$, where $w_u(k)$ satisfies (3.1). Then (1) if (w_u,k) is an optimal contract, $k < k^*$; (2) given $\epsilon > 0$, there exists α such that, if $(-V''(\pi)/V'(\pi)) \geq \alpha$ for all π, any optimal contract has the property that $|k - k^*| < \epsilon$.

Proof. See Appendix.

Proposition 3 is easy to understand. A very risk-averse firm wishes approximately to maximize income in the worst state, i.e., to "maximin." Profit in unemployment states $-w_u(k)$ is less than profit in employment states $s - k - w_u(k)$. Hence the firm wants to maximize $-w_u(k)$. This is done by setting $k = k^*$.

Propositions 2 and 3 tell us how the probability of unemployment depends on the firm's risk aversion. We now consider the influence of the worker's risk aversion. We have argued that an increase in k makes the firm's profit stream less risky (in some sense). The opposite is true of the worker; an increase in k causes wages when employed to rise but when unemployed to fall, which makes the worker's net income riskier. This suggests that an increase in the worker's risk aversion may reduce the optimal k. The next proposition establishes this for the case where the worker's and firm's utility functions exhibit constant absolute risk aversion.

It should be noted that when the worker's risk aversion changes, this will also generally lead to a change in $\overline{U}$, the worker's opportunity cost of labor at date 0. We shall write $\overline{U} = U(\overline{w})$ as in (A3) and assume that the worker can continue to get the certain income $\overline{w}$ if he goes elsewhere at date 0, so that if the utility function U is replaced by $\hat{U}$, then $\overline{U}$ is replaced by $\hat{U}(\overline{w})$.

PROPOSITION 4. Let the firm's utility function be given by $V(\pi) = -e^{-b\pi}$ and the worker's utility function by $U(w) = -e^{-aw}$, where $a,b > 0$. Also let $\overline{U} = -e^{-a\overline{w}}$. Then, if $(\hat{w}_u, \hat{k})$ is an optimal contract when $a = a_0$ and $(\hat{w}'_u, \hat{k}')$ is an optimal contract when $a = a_1 > a_0$, $\hat{k}' \leq \hat{k}$. Furthermore, if $\underline{s} < R$, then $\hat{k}' < \hat{k}$.

Proof. See Appendix.

It is worth noting that the proof of Proposition 4 establishes that the optimal k (or k's if there is more than one) is independent of $\overline{U}$ in the exponential case; i.e., there are no wealth effects. Proposition 4 does not appear to hold for general utility functions.

As in the case of the firm, we can ask what happens to the optimal k as the worker's risk aversion becomes very large. The next proposition tells us that k will be very close to $\max(\underline{s}, R)$ under these conditions.

PROPOSITION 5. Assume (A1)–(A3). Then, given $\epsilon > 0$, there exists α such that if $(-U''(w)/U'(w)) \geq \alpha$ for all w, any optimal contract has the property that $|k - \max(\underline{s}, R)| < \epsilon$.

Proof. See Appendix.

The intuition behind Proposition 5 is that if the worker is very risk-averse, it is optimal for the firm to offer the worker something close to complete net income insurance. This it does by setting k close to R if $R > \underline{s}$, since then $w_u(k) + k - R \simeq w_u(k)$.

We may summarize the results of this section as follows. The probability of unemployment will be higher the more risk-averse the firm is, ranging from $G(R)$, the Walrasian level, when the firm is risk-neutral (see Proposition 1), to $G(k^*)$, when the firm is infinitely risk-averse, where k^* is defined in Proposition 3. In the exponential case the probability of unemployment will also be higher the less risk-averse the worker is, reaching its minimum level $G(R)$ when the worker is infinitely risk-averse (the last statement is also true in the general non-exponential case). It follows from these results that, in the exponential case, if we regard as variable both the firm's and the worker's utility functions, the probability of unemployment is at its greatest when the firm is infinitely risk-averse and the worker is risk-neutral. In fact, this last result is true in the general non-exponential case, as the next proposition shows.

Note that when the worker is risk-neutral, $w_u(k) = \overline{U} - (k - R)(1 - G(k))$, and so k^* is the smallest value of k that maximizes $(k - R)(1 - G(k))$. Call this $\overline{k}$.

PROPOSITION 6. Assume (A1)–(A3). Let $\overline{k}$ be the smallest value of k that maximizes $(k - R)(1 - G(k))$. Then (1) if (w_u, k) is an optimal contract, $k < \bar{k}$; (2) given $\epsilon > 0$, there exist $\alpha, \beta > 0$ such that if $(-V''(\pi)/V'(\pi)) \geq \alpha$ for all π and $(-U''(x)/U'(x)) \leq \beta$ for all x, any optimal contract has the property that $|k - \bar{k}| < \epsilon$.

Proof. See Appendix.

Proposition 6 is useful if we know the distribution function G but do not know the form of the utility functions U and V. It tells us that, depending on how risk-averse the firm and worker are, the probability of unemployment can lie anywhere between $G(R)$ and $G(\bar{k})$. In particular, given G, the maximum increase in the probability of unemployment relative to the Walrasian case, which can be explained by the implicit contract-asymmetric information theory, is $G(\bar{k}) - G(R)$.

IV. How Changes in the Distribution Function G Affect the Probability of Unemployment

In the last section we considered comparative statics with respect to a change in the firm's and worker's attitudes to risk. We now analyze the effect of changes in the distribution function G.

Consider first what happens if there is a uniform shift to the right in the distribution of $\tilde{s}$, and R increases by the same amount; i.e., $\tilde{s}$ is replaced by $(\tilde{s} + \alpha)$ and R by $(R + \alpha)$, where $\alpha > 0$. In the case of symmetric information the probability of unemployment = prob($\tilde{s} \leq R$) is unchanged by this. Proposition 7 says that the same is true under asymmetric information.

PROPOSITION 7. Assume (A1)–(A3). Let the random variable $\tilde{s}$ be replaced by $(\tilde{s} + \alpha)$ and R by $(R + \alpha)$, where $\alpha > 0$. Then, if (w_u, k) is an optimal contract initially, $(w_u, k + \alpha)$ will be an optimal contract after the change. In particular, the probability of unemployment = prob($\tilde{s} \leq k$) will not change.

Proof. If we substitute $R' = R + \alpha$, $\tilde{s}' = \tilde{s} + \alpha$, $w'_u = w_u$, $k' = k + \alpha$ in (2.2)–(2.4), problem (2.2)–(2.4) remains the same.

Q.E.D.

We consider now what happens if there is an increase in R, but s stays the same. Under symmetric information this will lead to a lower probability of employment. Under asymmetric information, it appears difficult to say what will happen in general. However, if U and V are exponential, we have

PROPOSITION 8. Let the firm's utility function be given by $V(\pi) = -e^{b\pi}$ and the worker's by $U(w) = -e^{-aw}$, where $a, b > 0$. Let R

IMPLICIT CONTRACTS UNDER ASYMMETRIC INFORMATION 141

be replaced by $(R + \alpha)$, where $\alpha > 0$. Then, if $(\hat{w}_u, \hat{k})$, $(\hat{w}'_u, \hat{k}')$ are optimal contracts, respectively, before and after the change, we must have $\hat{k}' \geq \hat{k}$. Furthermore, if $\underline{s} < R$, $\hat{k}' > \hat{k}$; i.e., the probability of unemployment rises.

Proof. See Appendix.

If we combine Propositions 7 and 8, we get immediately the following corollary.

COROLLARY. Let the firm's utility function be given by $V(\pi) = -e^{-b\pi}$ and the worker's by $U(w) = -e^{-aw}$, where $a, b > 0$. Let s be replaced by the random variable $(\tilde{s} + \alpha)$, where $\alpha > 0$. Then, if $(\hat{w}_u, \hat{k})$, $(\hat{w}'_u, \hat{k}')$ are optimal contracts, respectively, before and after the change, we must have $\hat{k}' \leq (\hat{k} + \alpha)$. Furthermore, if $\underline{s} < R$, $\hat{k}' < \hat{k} + \alpha$; i.e., the probability of unemployment falls.

Proof. Suppose that $\tilde{s}$ and R both increase by α. Then we know by Proposition 7 that k increases by α. Now reduce R by α. Then, by Proposition 8, k falls.

Q.E.D.

Propositions 7 and 8 are concerned with additive shifts in s and R. We next consider the case of a multiplicative shift; i.e., we suppose that $\tilde{s}$ and R are multiplied by $\lambda > 0$, and that $\overline{w}$, given by (A3), is also multiplied by λ. This means that all production activities (including the opportunity cost of labor at date 0) are scaled up or down by the same amount. Under symmetric information, the probability of employment is unchanged by this. Proposition 9 says that the same is true under asymmetric information in the case where U exhibits constant relative risk aversion and $V(\pi) \equiv W(\pi_0 + \pi)$, where W exhibits constant relative risk aversion, as long as π_0 is also subject to the scaling effect.

PROPOSITION 9. Suppose that $U(w)$ exhibits constant relative risk aversion and that $V(\pi)$ can be written as $W(\pi_0 + \pi)$ for all π for some $\pi_0 > 0$, where W also exhibits constant relative risk aversion. Let s, R, $\overline{w}$, and π_0 be replaced by λs, λR, $\lambda\overline{w}$, and $\lambda\pi_0$, where $\lambda > 0$. Assume that (A1)–(A3) hold before and after the change. Then if $(\hat{w}_u, \hat{k})$ is an optimal contract initially, $(\lambda\hat{w}_u, \lambda\hat{k})$ is an optimal contract after the change. In particular, the probability of unemployment stays the same.

Proof. Consider the problem, maximize (2.2) subject to (2.3). Under constant relative risk aversion, either $W(\lambda\pi_0 + \lambda\pi) = \phi(\lambda)W(\pi_0 + \pi)$, or $W(\lambda\pi_0 + \lambda\pi) = \phi(\lambda) + W(\pi_0 + \pi)$ (the former holds if $W(\pi_0 + \pi)$ is a power function, the latter if it is the logarithm

142   *QUARTERLY JOURNAL OF ECONOMICS*

function). The same is true for U. It follows that if we substitute R' $= \lambda R, \tilde{s}' = \lambda \tilde{s}, w'_u = \lambda w_u, k' = \lambda k, \overline{w}' = \lambda \overline{w}$, problem (2.2)–(2.4) remains the same.

Q.E.D.

The reason for introducing π_0 is that constant relative risk aversion utility functions are defined only for nonnegative wealth. Therefore, if $\pi_0 = 0$, the firm cannot pay the worker a positive wage when it does not employ him. The best way to think of π_0 is as the output (revenue) of the firm coming from sources other than the worker's production. It is then quite natural to scale π_0 by λ too.

In general, it appears difficult to establish further results about the behavior of k as a function of the distribution function G. In the next section, however, we shall show that some results can be obtained for the case where the firm is extremely risk-averse and the worker is approximately risk-neutral.

V. THE CASE WHERE THE FIRM IS EXTREMELY RISK-AVERSE AND THE WORKER IS APPROXIMATELY RISK-NEUTRAL

In the last section we obtained some results about how the probability of unemployment is affected by changes in the distribution function G. In this section we obtain some further results for the case where the firm is extremely risk-averse and the worker is approximately risk-neutral. In this case, as we noted in Proposition 6 of Section III, the optimal k will be close to $\overline{k}$, where

(5.1) $\overline{k}$ is the smallest value of k that maximizes

$$(k - R)(1 - G(k)).$$

An illuminating special case is where $\tilde{s}$ can take on only two values, s_L with probability π_L and s_H with probability π_H, where $\pi_L + \pi_H = 1, \pi_L \geq 0$, and $\pi_H \geq 0$. This case violates our assumption that G has a density function, but this will not matter for what follows. In particular, parts (1) and (2) of Proposition 1 continue to hold (see Remark 1 of Section II).

If $s_L \leq R < s_H$, then Proposition 1(1) tells us that employment will occur if and only if $s = s_H$; i.e., $k \geq s_L$. Since this employment rule is also optimal under symmetric information, we see that there is no difference between symmetric and asymmetric information. It follows that when $\tilde{s}$ can take on only two values, the only interesting case is where $R < s_L < s_H$. Then under symmetric information we get employment in both states, whereas under asymmetric information we *may* get unemployment when $s = s_L$ (note that we shall always have employment when $s = s_H$—see Proposition 1).

If $R < s_L < s_H$, $w_u(k)$, as defined in (3.1), is given as follows for $s_H \geq k \geq s_L = \max(s_L, R)$:

(5.2)
$$U(w_u(k) + k - R) = \overline{U} \equiv U(\overline{w}) \qquad \text{if } k = s_L$$
$$U(w_u(k) + k - R)\pi_H + U(w_u(k))\pi_L = \overline{U} \quad \text{if } s_H \geq k > s_L.$$

As noted in Remark 1 of Section II, in the discrete case, $s = k$ is always considered an employment state when $k > R$. Note that there is a discontinuity in $w_u(k)$ at the point $k = s_L$, $(\lim_{k + s_L} w_u(\overline{k}) > w_u(s_L))$. Except for the discontinuity, $w_u(k)$ is decreasing in k. It is possible to have either $w_u(s_H) > w_u(s_L) = (\overline{w} + R - s_L)$ or $w_u(s_H) < w_u(s_L)$.

It is easy to show that Proposition 6 continues to hold in the discrete case (where $(1 - G(k))$ is replaced by $\text{prob}[\tilde{s} > k]$). Consider an infinitely risk-averse firm and a risk-neutral worker. The optimal contract involves either employment in both states or unemployment when $s = s_L$. In the first case $k = s_L$ and the worker's wage when employed is $\overline{w} + R$ (see (5.2)). Thus, the firm's profits in the worst state are $s_L - \overline{w} - R$. In the second case the worker's wage when unemployed $= w_u = \overline{w} - \pi_H(k - R)$. If the firm is infinitely risk-averse, it is obviously optimal to maximize k, i.e., to set $k = s_H$. Thus, the two cases yield profit for the firm in the worst state of $(s_L - \overline{w} - R)$ and $(-\overline{w} + \pi_H(s_H - R))$, respectively, from which it follows that the optimal contract will involve unemployment when the firm is infinitely risk-averse and the worker is risk-neutral if

(5.3) $s_L - R < \pi_H(s_H - R).$

As in Proposition 6 this is also a necessary and sufficient condition for unemployment to occur in the bad state for *some* utility function U, V. We therefore have as a special case of Proposition 6:

PROPOSITION 10. Suppose that $\tilde{s}$ takes on just two values—s_L, s_H; that is, $G(s) = 0$ for $0 \leq s < s_L$, $G(s) = \pi_L$ for $s_L \leq s < s_H$, $G(s) = 1$ for $s \geq s_H$, where $R < s_L < s_H$. Then a necessary and sufficient condition for there to be some U, V satisfying (A1)–(A3) for which there is an optimal contract (w_u, k) with $k > s_L$ is that (5.3) holds. ($k > s_L$ means that unemployment occurs in the bad state $s = s_L$.) Furthermore, if (5.3) holds, there exist $\alpha, \beta > 0$ such that if U, V satisfy (A1)–(A3) and $(-V''(\pi)/V'(\pi)) \geq \alpha$ for all π, $(-U''(w)/U'(w)) \leq \beta$ for all w, then every optimal contract satisfies $k > s_L$. That is, if (5.3) holds and the firm is sufficiently risk-averse and the worker is approximately risk-neutral, unemployment will occur when $s = s_L$.

Condition (5.3) tells us that unemployment is more likely to occur in the bad state (A) the lower is the probability of the bad state; (B) the lower is the net social return in the bad state relative to that in the good state. (A) and (B) are fairly intuitive. If π_L or $(s_L - R)$ is small, the expected efficiency loss that results from making $s = s_L$ an unemployment state is small. In contrast, if the firm is extremely risk-averse, the gain from improved risk sharing may be large. This is because by making $s = s_L$ an unemployment state the firm is able to reduce wages in this state, and this is very important to a highly risk-averse firm even if the probability of $s = s_L$ is low.

It is clear from Proposition 10 that in the two-state case Propositions 8 and 9 generalize to the case where the firm is extremely risk-averse and the worker is approximately risk-neutral. For if (5.3) holds initially, then it will continue to hold if R increases. Similarly, if s_H, s_L and R are all increased by the same proportion, then (5.3) is unaffected. In fact, approximate versions of Propositions 8 and 9 can be established for the many-state case when the firm is extremely risk-averse and the worker is approximately risk-neutral. In particular, if $\bar{k}$ satisfies (5.1), then an increase in R can be shown to reduce $\bar{k}$, while a proportionate change in $\tilde{s}$ and R will lead to the same proportionate change in $\bar{k}$.

Proposition 10 also enables us to determine for what two-point distribution the probability of unemployment will be highest. Suppose that we keep $(s_H - R)$, $(s_L - R)$ constant and vary π_L. Then we know from Proposition 10 that, if (5.3) holds, unemployment will occur for some U, V. The *probability* of unemployment will then be π_L. Condition (5.3) will hold for all $\pi_L < (s_H - s_L)/(s_H - R)$. Thus, given an extremely risk-averse firm and an approximately risk-neutral worker, we have a relationship between the probability of unemployment and π_L, the probability of the bad state, as shown in Figure II. Clearly, the relationship is not monotonic. In particular, after a certain point, an increase in π_L reduces the probability of unemployment, since we switch from the regime in which $s = s_L$ is an unemployment state to the regime in which there is employment in both states.

The probability of unemployment reaches its supremum as $\pi_L \to ((s_H - s_L)/(s_H - R))$. Note that in the limit when $\pi_L = ((s_H - s_L)/(s_H - R))$, $(k - R)(1 - G(k))^+$ (see Proposition 6) is maximized at both $k = s_L$ and $k = s_H$.[18] That $(k - R)(1 - G(k))^+$ has two maxi-

---

18. $(1 - G(k))^+$ denotes the probability that $\tilde{s} \geq k$.

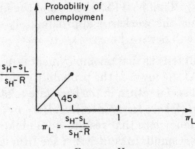

FIGURE II

mizers is no coincidence. Let $G(x)^-$ be the probability that $s < x$. The next proposition shows the following: if $\bar{s}$ can take on n values $s_1 < \cdots < s_n$, with probabilities $\pi_1, \ldots, \pi_n$, respectively, with each $s_i > R$, then, if we regard the π_i's as variables, the probability of unemployment, $G(\bar{k})^-$, where $\bar{k}$ is given by (5.1), has a supremum equal to $(s_n - s_1)/(s_n - R)$ and in the limit $\pi_1^0, \ldots, \pi_n^0$ satisfy

$$(5.4) \quad (s_1 - R) = (s_2 - R)(1 - \pi_1^0)$$
$$= (s_3 - R)(1 - \pi_1^0 - \pi_2^0) = \cdots = (s_n - R)\pi_n^0.$$

In other words, the limiting distribution in which $G(\bar{k})^-$ "achieves" the supremum has the property that $(k - R)(1 - G(k))^+$ is constant for k equal to the mass points of $\bar{s}$.

PROPOSITION 11. Suppose that $\bar{s}$ can take on n fixed values $s_1 < s_2 < \cdots < s_n$, where each $s_i > R$. For each vector of probabilities $\pi = (\pi_1, \ldots, \pi_n) \in \Delta_n = \{\pi \epsilon R^n \mid \sum_{i=1}^n \pi_i = 1, \pi \geq 0\}$, let $\bar{k}(\pi)$ maximize $(k - R)(1 - G(k))^+ \equiv (k - R)^\epsilon \sum_{s_i \geq k} \pi_i$. Then $\sup_{\pi \epsilon \Delta} G(\bar{k}(\pi))^- = (s_n - s_1)/(s_n - R)$.

Proof. See Appendix.

Thus, under the conditions of Proposition 11, the maximum probability of unemployment when both π and the risk aversion of the worker and firm are variable is $(s_n - s_1)/(s_n - R)$.

Note that by regarding $s_1, \ldots, s_n$ as well as $\pi_1, \ldots, \pi_n$ as variable, we can make $(s_n - s_1)/(s_n - R)$ as close to one as we like (simply let $s_1 \downarrow R$). This shows that, if the distribution function G can be chosen arbitrarily, there is no limit to the amount of unemployment which can be explained by the implicit contract-asymmetric information model relative to the implicit contract-symmetric information model. For as $s_1 \downarrow R$, the probability of unemployment tends to one in the former case, while it equals zero in the latter case.

If we return to the case where $\bar{s}$ takes on two values, we can also use Proposition 10 to obtain some negative results. We have seen that increases in k allow the firm to transfer some of the risk it is bearing to the worker. Ceteris paribus, the desire to shed risk will be greater for the firm the riskier is profit when $k = R$; for when $k = R$, the firm is bearing all the risk and the worker none (the wage in employment states $= w_u + k - R = w_u =$ the wage in unemployment states). This suggests that an increase in the riskiness (in the sense of Rothschild-Stiglitz [1970]) of "first-best" profit or net social return $\max(\bar{s} - R, 0)$ may lead to an increase in k and possibly to an increase in unemployment. This is not true in general, however. To see this, suppose that $s_H = 10, s_L = 4, R = 0$, and $\pi_H = \pi_L = \frac{1}{2}$. Then $\pi_H(s_H - R) > s_L - R$, and so if the firm is sufficiently risk-averse and the worker is approximately risk-neutral, there is unemployment when $s = s_L$. Now let $\hat{s}_H = (7 - 3\frac{3}{4}\hat{\pi}_L)/(1 - \hat{\pi}_L), \hat{s}_L = 3\frac{3}{4}$, where $\hat{\pi}_L$ is close to one. Then $\hat{s}_H > s_H, \hat{s}_L < s_L, \hat{\pi}_H\hat{s}_H + \hat{\pi}_L\hat{s}_L = 7 = \pi_H s_H + \pi_L s_L$, and so this corresponds to a mean preserving spread in the sense of Rothschild-Stiglitz. However, $\hat{\pi}_H(\hat{s}_H - R) < \hat{s}_L - R$ when $\hat{\pi}_L$ is close to one, and so now there will be full employment for all utility functions U, V.

For similar reasons, it is not true that an improvement in the worker's information about s necessarily leads to an increase in the probability of employment. Suppose again that $s = s_H$ or s_L with probability π_H, π_L, respectively. Assume now that at date 1 the worker receives a signal ρ about s. In particular, assume that $\rho = \rho_0$ or ρ_1, and that the conditional probability that $\rho = \rho_i$ given $s = s_H$ is π_{iH} and that $\rho = \rho_i$ given $s = s_L$ is π_{iL}, where $\pi_{0H} + \pi_{1H} = \pi_{0L} + \pi_{1L} = 1$. A contract now is a vector $(w_u(\rho_0), k(\rho_0), w_u(\rho_1), k(\rho_1))$, since wages can be made to depend on ρ, which is common knowledge. An optimal contract is defined in the obvious way, where now, for each ρ, one uses the posterior probabilities $\text{prob}[s = s_H | \rho = \rho_i] = (\pi_{iH}\pi_H)/\lambda_i$, $\text{prob}[s = s_L | \rho = \rho_i] = (\pi_{iL}\pi_L)/\lambda_i$, where $\lambda_i = \text{prob}[\rho = \rho_i] = \pi_{iH}\pi_H + \pi_{iL}\pi_L$, to compute expected utility.

Using Proposition 10, we may easily construct examples in which the probability of unemployment rises as a result of the signal ρ being observed. In particular, let $R = 0, s_H = 10, s_L = 6, \pi_H = \frac{1}{2}$, and $\pi_L = \frac{1}{2}$. Then $\pi_H(s_H - R) < s_L - R$ and so if ρ is not observed, the probability of unemployment is zero if the firm is sufficiently risk-averse and the worker is approximately risk-neutral. Now suppose that ρ is observed and $\pi_{0H} = \frac{3}{4}, \pi_{1H} = \frac{1}{4}, \pi_{0L} = \frac{1}{4}, \pi_{1L} = \frac{3}{4}$, and $\lambda_0 = \lambda_1 = \frac{1}{2}$. Then $\pi_{0H}(s_H - R) > s_L - R$. It follows that if the firm is sufficiently risk-averse and the worker is approximately risk-neutral, there will now be unemployment when $\rho = \rho_0$ in the state $s = s_L$.

Of course, the above cannot happen if the signal ρ gives perfect information about s. For then we move from the case of asymmetric information to the case of symmetric information and the probability of unemployment must fall (or stay the same).

Further insight into why increases in risk or improvements in information do not have unambiguous effects on unemployment can be obtained by returning to the general case where there are many states. Then $\bar{k}$ maximizes $(k - R)(1 - G(k))$, which yields the first-order conditions,

$$(5.5) \qquad \bar{k} - R = (1 - G(\bar{k}))/G'(\bar{k}).$$

The right-hand side of (5.5) is the reciprocal of the *hazard rate* of the distribution G. Equation (5.5) will have a unique solution if the hazard rate is increasing. This is true for a number of well-known distributions such as the normal (see Barlow and Proschan [1975]). Clearly how a change in the distribution function G affects the probability of unemployment will depend, among other things, on how it affects the hazard rate $G'/(1 - G)$. Unfortunately, increases in riskiness and improvements in informativeness do not generally affect the hazard rate in a simple way.

VI. Conclusions

This paper has been concerned with analyzing the implications of the assumption that a worker's marginal revenue product $\tilde{s}$ is observed by the firm but not its workers. If the firm's owners are risk-averse, optimal risk sharing requires a fall in the firm's wage bill when $\tilde{s}$ is low. In a world where $\tilde{s}$ is common knowledge, this need have no implication regarding employment (especially if labor supply is inelastic). When $\tilde{s}$ is not observed by workers, the wage bill cannot be made an arbitrary function of the true $\tilde{s}$, since workers cannot determine $\tilde{s}$. However a contract which specifies that the wage bill is an appropriately increasing function of total employment can induce the firm to cut wages only when $\tilde{s}$ is low. This is because a drop in employment makes the firm bear a cost of decreasing the wage bill that is high in states where $\tilde{s}$ is high and low in states where $\tilde{s}$ is low. Thus, employment is a good instrument for inducing incentive-compatible risk sharing.

We have been concerned with analyzing what determines how much unemployment the asymmetry of information between firms and workers can cause in situations where labor supply is inelastic (over the region where wages exceed the reservation wage). The benefit of unemployment is that the firm is able to reduce the wage bill in bad states and hence to bear less risk (the worker correspondingly bears more risk). The cost of unemployment is that it is ex post inefficient. As we showed in Section III, benefits from risk sharing will be higher, and thus unemployment will be higher, the more risk-averse is the firm and the less risk-averse is the worker. By "unemployment will be higher," we mean that even though labor supply is inelastic under symmetric information (over the region where wages are larger than the reservation wage R), variations in productivity $\tilde{s}$ (in the region where $\tilde{s} > R$) will lead to variations in employment under asymmetric information.

It is intuitively clear that the cost of introducing ex post inefficient unemployment in state s is smaller the closer the state is to R. Since the benefits in terms of risk-sharing are unaffected by the magnitude of $(s - R)$, this suggests that the optimal amount of unemployment will be lower the smaller is the probability mass of states close to R. This was made precise in the Corollary to Proposition 8 in Section IV, which showed that a shift in each s from s to $s + \alpha$, where $\alpha > 0$, reduces the probability of unemployment.

In this paper we have concentrated on the case where $L = 0$ or $L = 1$. In Grossman and Hart [1981], however, we showed that if L can take on any finite number of values, then our implicit contracts model implies that there will be *less* (or the same) employment in each state than there would be in a spot market model (with employment being equal in both models in the best state of nature).[19]

Our analysis makes two important assumptions: (1) that the owners or managers of the firm are unwilling to bear all of the profit risk associated with variations in $\tilde{s}$, i.e., they are risk-averse; and (2) that the only variable which is common knowledge is employment; in particular, gross profit $\tilde{s}$ is not common knowledge. If $\tilde{s}$ could be observed by the market, then the owners of the firm could condition income transfers directly on the realization of $\tilde{s}$. Note that once $\tilde{s}$ is unobservable, employment is a useful screening device for *any* party that the firm wishes to share risk with. Even if the firm uses an insurance company to achieve risk sharing, the insurance company unable to observe $\tilde{s}$ would find it in its interest to condition income transfers on the level of employment.

---

19. The difficulty in generalizing the comparative statics results of this paper to the case of many workers stems from the fact that, if workers can observe the employment level in the firm, wages can be conditioned on this variable. As a result, the wage function can no longer be represented by just two numbers—a wage when employed and a wage when unemployed—as in the one-worker model. Note that all our results generalize to the many-worker case if each worker can observe only whether or not he is employed, but not the employment level in the firm as a whole.

IMPLICIT CONTRACTS UNDER ASYMMETRIC INFORMATION 149

The assumption that owners are risk-averse and profits are not observed does not seem unreasonable for the case of small owner-managed firms. It is less reasonable as a description of public corporations that publish profit statements and pay dividends, and where owners can diversify away risk through the stock market. We wish to argue, however, that our model, with some modifications, applies to this case too. Consider a corporation that is run by a manager who takes actions which the owners cannot observe; i.e., the owners and the manager are in a principal-agent relationship. Then in order to induce the manager to take the right actions, the owners will give the manager an incentive scheme that makes the manager's utility depend positively on the firm's performance (e.g., profit)—such an incentive scheme may, for example, involve the manager holding a significant fraction of the firm's shares. Obviously if the manager can then diversify away risk by selling off these shares, the manager will have no incentive to manage the corporation well and the incentive scheme will be self-defeating. Thus, the owners will prevent the manager from diversifying (assuming they can monitor this), which means that the manager will be *risk-averse* with respect to the firm's profit stream. Under this interpretation, V refers to the risk aversion of the manager.

Note that under these conditions, ex post profit, even if observed, will not be a perfect signal about the firm's performance, since profit depends on unobserved actions of the manager; i.e., it is an endogenous variable like employment. As a result, while it can be shown that in an optimal contract wages will now be conditioned on profits as well as on employment, the moral hazard problems discussed in this paper remain. In particular, it will still be the case that the firm will have to create too much unemployment (from an efficiency standpoint) in bad states in order to show workers that times really are bad. Thus, under certain assumptions our underemployment result can be shown to generalize. A formal model along these lines is developed in Hart [1983].

An essential feature of our theory is that there is an asymmetric response to productivity shocks. When $\tilde{s}$ is low, optimal risk sharing implies that there should be a cut in the wage bill, and this can be achieved in an incentive compatible manner only if it is accompanied by a decrease in employment. However, when $\tilde{s}$ is high, the firm can always increase wages to get more employment and better risk sharing. To put it differently, a moral hazard arises with respect to the bad states of nature because it is there that the firm asks workers to take a wage cut (the firm would *always* claim the state is bad if there was no accompanying employment reduction). There is no moral hazard

150   *QUARTERLY JOURNAL OF ECONOMICS*

with respect to the best state of nature because the firm would never claim that times are very good and give workers an increase in pay if this were not truly the case. As a consequence of this, we were able to show that the level of employment under asymmetric information equals the Walrasian level in the best state of nature.

The fact that in our model bad states create non-Walrasian unemployment but good states do not create non-Walrasian employment suggests a method for distinguishing our theory from some other asymmetric information theories of employment. In particular, Lucas [1972] proposed a model where short-run labor supply depends on the expected interest rate (which in his model is the real return to holding money—the only asset in the model). Workers in a particular submarket have incomplete information about the real interest rate. Workers in all submarkets make correlated errors in forecasting interest rates because they all condition their forecasts on the observed price level in their submarket which is in turn affected by the *economy-wide* money supply. In linearized versions of Lucas' [1972] model such as Barro [1976], labor supply is a linear function of the difference between the expected economy-wide price level and the actual price level: $L(E[P|\text{Info}] - P)$. In all of these Lucas-like models, the driving variable that converts long-run inelastic labor supply into a short-run elastic labor supply is a variable like $x - E[x|\text{Info}]$.[20] In all of these models this is a symmetric variable. Further, there is no reason (or emphasis in the logic of the theory) for $L(\cdot)$ to respond in an asymmetric way: agents make "up side" and "down side" forecast errors, and this leads to labor supply fluctuations. In our model this is not the case. It is at the very essence of the model that labor supply response is asymmetric. Good states lead to *Walrasian* levels of unemployment, while bad states lead to *non-Walrasian* levels of unemployment.

Grossman, Hart, and Maskin [1982] develop a general equilibrium model of implicit contracts in order to explore the above asymmetric effect. In a model of relative demand shocks across industries, the above asymmetry implies that relative demand shocks decrease employment by more than they would under complete information. A model where the relative demand shocks are caused by wealth re-

___

20. Though Lucas [1972] and Barro [1976] consider models where "inefficient" unemployment occurs because of monetary nonneutrality, there are versions of Lucas' model where the driving shocks are real (not nominal) and the inefficiency in output also depends on expectational errors. For example, Grossman and Weiss [1982] considered a model where there are real productivity shocks and employment is a linear function of the difference between the observed productivity r and the anticipated real opportunity cost of investment: $L(r - E[r|\text{info}])$.

distributions associated with unanticipated movements in the price level leads to implications that are very different from those of Lucas-like models of the same phenomenon.

APPENDIX

Proof of Proposition 2: Step 1. Our proof will involve the use of the following lemma. Let $X_1(s)$, $X_2(s)$ be real-valued functions of s. The distribution function of $\tilde{s}$ induces distribution functions on $\tilde{X}_1$ and $\tilde{X}_2$, say $F_1(\cdot)$ and $F_2(\cdot)$, respectively. For convenience, define $F_1(\cdot)$ on the whole real line. We say that F_2 satisfies the single crossing property with respect to F_1 (written "F_2 scp F_1") if there exists an x^0 such that

$$F_1(x) - F_2(x) \leq 0 \quad \text{for } x \leq x^0$$
$$F_1(x) - F_2(x) \geq 0 \quad \text{for } x > x^0.$$

We do *not* require that $E\tilde{X}_1 = E\tilde{X}_2$. We shall sometimes say that $\tilde{X}_1$ is less risky than $\tilde{X}_2$ in the above case.

LEMMA 1. Suppose that $X_1(s)$ and $X_2(s)$ are functions of s, and that a risk-averse person with $U'(x) > 0$ weakly prefers $\tilde{X}_1$ to $\tilde{X}_2$; i.e., $EU(\tilde{X}_1) \geq EU(\tilde{X}_2)$. Let F_2 satisfy the single crossing property with respect to F_1, and assume that $F_2(x) \neq F_1(x)$ for some x. Consider a person more risk-averse than person U in the sense that the new person's utility function is $g(U(x))$, where $g(\cdot)$ is a strictly increasing, strictly concave function. Then $Eg(U(\tilde{X}_1)) > Eg(U(\tilde{X}_2))$.

Proof. Suppose that $Eg(U(\tilde{X}_1)) \leq Eg(U(\tilde{X}_2))$. Consider the class of concave transforms $g_\lambda(\cdot)$, $0 \leq \lambda \leq 1$, defined by $g_\lambda(U) = \lambda g(U) + (1 - \lambda)U$ for all U. Since $Eg_1(U(\tilde{X})) \leq Eg_1(U(\tilde{X}_2))$ and $Eg_0(U(\tilde{X}_1)) \geq Eg_0(U(\tilde{X}_2))$, by continuity there exists λ such that $Eg_{\bar{\lambda}}(U(\tilde{X}_1)) = Eg_{\bar{\lambda}}(U(\tilde{X}_2))$. That is, the individual with utility function $g_{\bar{\lambda}}(U)$ is indifferent between $\tilde{X}_1$ and $\tilde{X}_2$. However, in view of the single crossing property, $\tilde{X}_2$ is riskier than $\tilde{X}_1$ in the sense of Diamond-Stiglitz [1974]. It follows that, since an individual with utility function $g_1(U)$ is more risk-averse than an individual with utility function $g_{\bar{\lambda}}(U)$, the individual with utility function $g_1(U)$ must prefer $\tilde{X}_1$ to $\tilde{X}_2$; that is, $Eg(U(\tilde{X}_1)) > Eg(U(\tilde{X}_2))$. Contradiction.

Q.E.D.

Proof of Proposition 2: Step 2. Suppose that $\hat{k}' < \hat{k}$, and hence there are more employment states under $\hat{k}'$. Note first that it is impossible to have $\hat{w}'_u \leq \hat{w}_u$, since then $\hat{w}'_u + \hat{k}' < \hat{w}_u + \hat{k}$, which means that under $(\hat{w}'_u, \hat{k}')$ the firm pays less both when the worker is employed and when he is unemployed. But this means that whatever V is the firm will prefer $(\hat{w}'_u, \hat{k}')$ to $(\hat{w}_u, \hat{k})$; i.e., $(\hat{w}_u, \hat{k})$ is never chosen. Hence $\hat{w}'_u > \hat{w}_u$. A similar argument shows that $\hat{w}'_u + \hat{k}' < \hat{w}_u + \hat{k}$. Therefore, $\hat{w}_u < \hat{w}'_u < \hat{w}'_u + \hat{k}' < \hat{w}_u + \hat{k}$. But this means that the firm's net profit $\max(s - w_u - k, -w_u)$ is lower for small s and higher for large s under $(\hat{w}'_u, \hat{k}')$ than under $(\hat{w}_u, \hat{k})$; i.e.,

$$u(s) \equiv \max(s - \hat{w}'_u - \hat{k}', -\hat{w}'_u) - \max(s - \hat{w}_u - \hat{k}, -\hat{w}_u)$$

is negative for $s <$ some s^* and positive for $s > s^*$. It follows that the distribution of $\max(s - \hat{w}'_u - \hat{k}', -\hat{w}'_u)$ satisfies the single crossing property with respect to the distribution of $\max(s - \hat{w}_u - \hat{k}, -\hat{w}_u)$. By Lemma 1, this contradicts the fact that a more risk-averse firm (weakly) prefers $(\hat{w}'_u, \hat{k}')$ to $(\hat{w}_u, \hat{k})$ and a less risk-averse firm (weakly) prefers $(\hat{w}_u, \hat{k})$ to $(\hat{w}'_u, \hat{k}')$.

This proves that $\hat{k}' \geq \hat{k}$. To establish the last part of the proposition, one shows that $\hat{k}' = \hat{k}$ violates the first-order conditions (2.5).

Q.E.D.

Proof of Proposition 3: Step 1. We shall need the following lemma. Let I_1 and I_2 be two functions of s that are bounded above by a number b. We show that if a person has constant absolute risk aversion of a sufficiently large size, then he will always choose the gamble with the higher minimum value.

LEMMA 2. Suppose that $V(x) = -e^{-\alpha x}$. Let $\mathbf{I}_i \equiv \inf\{x \mid \text{prob}(\tilde{I}_i \leq x) > 0\}$ for $i = 1,2$. Suppose that $\mathbf{I}_1 < \mathbf{I}_2$. Then, if α is sufficiently large, $EV(\tilde{I}_1) < EV(\tilde{I}_2)$.

Proof.

$$\{EV(\tilde{I}_2) - EV(\tilde{I}_1)\}e^{+\alpha \mathbf{I}_2} = -E\left[e^{-\alpha(\tilde{I}_2 \mathbf{I}_2)} - e^{-\alpha(\tilde{I}_1 - \mathbf{I}_2)}\right]$$

$$= -Ee^{-\alpha(\tilde{I}_2 - \tilde{I}_2)} + \int_{\mathbf{I}_2}^{b} e^{-\alpha(\tilde{I}_1 - \mathbf{I}_2)}\, dF + \int_{\mathbf{I}_1}^{\mathbf{I}_2} e^{-\alpha(\tilde{I}_1 - \mathbf{I}_2)}\, dF.$$

As α goes to infinity, the first two terms are bounded, while the third term goes to positive infinity. Therefore, for α sufficiently large, the left-hand side of the expression is positive.

Q.E.D.

Proof of Proposition 3: Step 2. We have shown in Section II that $k \leq k^*$. Now $dw_u/dk = -\text{RHS of } (2.5) = 0$ at $k = k^*$. But LHS of (2.5) > 0, and so $k = k^*$ does not satisfy the first-order conditions for problem (2.2)–(2.4). Hence $k < k^*$.

To prove (2), suppose that it is false. Then we can find a sequence of optimal $k(\alpha)$ converging to $\hat{k} < k^*$ as $\alpha \to \infty$. Using the argument of the proof of Proposition 2, we may conclude that $w_u(k^*) < w_u(k(\alpha)) < w_u(k(\alpha)) + k(\alpha) < w_u(k^*) + k^*$, since otherwise $k(\alpha)$ would not be preferred to k^*. Hence, again by the proof of Proposition 2, the firm's profit stream when $k = k(\alpha)$ will satisfy the single crossing property relative to the profit stream when $k = k^*$. By definition, a firm with utility function V prefers $k = k(\alpha)$ to k^*. It follows from Lemma 1 that a firm with utility function $-e^{-\alpha \pi}$ will prefer $k = k(\alpha)$ to $k = k^*$. Note that as $\alpha \to \infty$, $w_u(k(\alpha)) \to w_u(\hat{k}) > w_u(k^*)$. But this contradicts Lemma 2, which says that, for α large, a firm with utility function $-e^{-\alpha \pi}$ prefers the profit stream with the higher value in the worst state.

Q.E.D.

IMPLICIT CONTRACTS UNDER ASYMMETRIC INFORMATION 153

Proof of Proposition 4. Consider (2.3). In the exponential case, this can be written as $e^{-aw_\mu}\phi(k) = \overline{U}$, where ϕ is a function of k. Substituting in (2.2) yields an objective function for the firm of the form $\overline{U}^{(-b/a)}\psi(k)$. It follows that the optimal k is independent of $\overline{U}$ in the exponential case.

The next point to notice is that we can equally well think of an optimal contract as maximizing the worker's expected utility subject to the firm's expected utility being equal to some $\overline{V}$ ($\overline{V}$ of course depends on $\overline{U}$). The above argument shows that in the exponential case the optimal k will be independent of $\overline{V}$. Hence fix $\overline{V}$ and let the worker become more risk-averse; i.e., increase a. Assume that $\hat{k}' > \hat{k}$. Use the equation,

$$(A.1) \qquad \int_k^{\overline{s}} V(s - k - w_u)\, dG + \int_{\underline{s}}^k V(-w_u)\, dG = \overline{V},$$

to express w_u as a function of k: $w_u = \tilde{w}_u(k)$. It is easy to see that w_u is decreasing in k and $(w_u + k)$ is increasing in k. Hence $\hat{k}' > \hat{k}$ implies that $\tilde{w}_u(\hat{k}') < \tilde{w}_u(\hat{k}) < \tilde{w}_u(\hat{k}) + \hat{k} < \tilde{w}_u(\hat{k}') + \hat{k}'$. Therefore, the worker's net income (w_u when unemployed, $w_u + k - R$ when employed) is riskier in the sense of the single crossing property when $k = \hat{k}'$ than when $k = \hat{k}$. This contradicts the fact that the worker prefers $\hat{k}$ to $\hat{k}'$ when $a = a_0$ and $\hat{k}'$ to $\hat{k}$ when $a = a_1$, by Lemma 1.

It follows that $\hat{k}' \leq \hat{k}$. That $\hat{k}' < \hat{k}$ if $\underline{s} < R$ follows from the fact that $\hat{k}' = \hat{k}$ is not consistent with the first-order conditions (2.5).

Q.E.D.

Proposition 4 does not appear to hold for general utility functions. The proof breaks down because $\overline{V}$ changes when the worker becomes more risk-averse and the optimal k is not independent of $\overline{V}$.

Proof of Proposition 5. One proceeds as in the proof of Proposition 3. If $k = R$, then $w_u = \overline{w}$ satisfies (2.3) for all utility functions U. If $k = \underline{s} > R$, then $w_u = \overline{w} - \underline{s} + R$ satisfies (2.3) for all utility functions U. In both cases the worker's net income is $\overline{w}$ with probability 1. Take $k > \max(\underline{s}, R)$. Then the worker's net income is $w_u(k) < \overline{w}$ if unemployed and $w_u(k) + k - R$ if employed. When α is large, i.e., the worker is very risk-averse, $w_u(k)$ must be close to $\overline{w}$ for the worker to be indifferent between the lottery ($w_u(k)$ with probability $G(k)$; $w_u(k) + k - R$ with probability $(1 - G(k))$) and $\overline{w}$ with certainty (see Lemma 2). In particular, $w_u(k,\alpha) \to \overline{w}$ as $\alpha \to \infty$. But this means that if k is bounded away from $\max(\underline{s}, R)$, the firm pays in the limit $\overline{w}$ when the worker is unemployed and more than $(\overline{w} + R)$ when the worker is employed. Clearly the firm could do better by setting $k = \max(\underline{s}, R)$. This proves that $k(\alpha) \to \max(\underline{s}, R)$ as $\alpha \to \infty$.

Q.E.D.

Proof of Proposition 6. Note first that $\overline{k}$ is by construction the smallest value of k that minimizes $w_u(k)$, defined in (3.1), for the case where U is linear; i.e., the worker is risk-neutral. In view of Proposition 3, to prove part (1), it is enough to establish that $k^* \leq \overline{k}$ when U is nonlinear, where k^* is defined in Proposition 3. Suppose that $k^* > \overline{k}$. Then $w_u(k^*) < w_u(\overline{k})$, where w_u refers to the nonlinear utility

154   *QUARTERLY JOURNAL OF ECONOMICS*

function U. But this means that a risk-averse worker with utility function U is indifferent between the lottery $L_1 = (w_u(k^*)$ with probability $G(k^*)$; $w_u(k^*) + k^* - R$ with probability $(1 - G(k^*)))$ and the lottery $L_2 = (w_u(\bar{k})$ with probability $G(\bar{k})$; $w_u(\bar{k}) + \bar{k} - R$ with probability $(1 - G(\bar{k})))$. Since the probability of employment is lower under L_1, it follows that $w_u(k^*) + k^* - R > w_u(\bar{k}) + \bar{k} - R$. But this means that L_1 is riskier in the sense of Diamond-Stiglitz [1974] than L_2, and so a risk-neutral worker will prefer L_1 to L_2; i.e.,

$$w_u(k^*)G(k^*) + (w_u(k^*) + k^* - R)(1 - G(k^*))$$
$$\geq w_u(\bar{k})G(\bar{k}) + (w_u(\bar{k}) + \bar{k} - R)(1 - G(\bar{k})),$$

which implies that $(k^* - R)(1 - G(k^*)) > (\bar{k} - R)(1 - G(\bar{k}))$, since $w_u(k^*) < w_u(\bar{k})$. This contradicts the definition of $\bar{k}$.

To prove (2), note that if the worker is risk-neutral, Proposition 3(2) tells us that there exists α such that $(-V''(\pi)/V'(\pi)) \geq \alpha \Rightarrow |k - \hat{k}| < \epsilon$. That the same is true if the worker is approximately risk-neutral follows from a continuity argument.

Q.E.D.

Proof of Proposition 8. Suppose that $\hat{k}' < \hat{k}$. As in the proof of Proposition 4, we may think of the optimal contract as maximizing the worker's expected utility subject to the firm's expected utility being at least $\bar{V}$. The latter constraint may be used to solve for $w_u = \tilde{w}_u(k)$, where $\tilde{w}_u(k)$ is decreasing in k and $(\tilde{w}_u(k) + k)$ is increasing in k. Hence we may write the worker's expected utility as

(A.2) $EU(R,k) = U(\tilde{w}_u(k))G(k) + U(\tilde{w}_u(k) + k - R)(1 - G(k))$.

Differentiate (A.2) with respect to R. This yields

(A.3) $\dfrac{\partial EU}{\partial R}(R,k) = -U'(\tilde{w}_u(k) + k - R)(1 - G(k))$.

From this, it follows that $\partial EU/\partial R$ is larger the larger is k (since $(\tilde{w}_u(k) + k)$ is increasing in k). Since we know that $EU(R,\hat{k}) \geq EU(R,\hat{k}')$ ($\hat{k}$ is initially optimal), it follows that $EU(R + \alpha,\hat{k}) > EU(R + \alpha,\hat{k}')$ given that $\hat{k} > \hat{k}'$. But this contradicts the fact that $\hat{k}'$ is optimal under $(R + \alpha)$.

This proves that $\hat{k}' \geq \hat{k}$. Finally, $\hat{k}' = \hat{k}$ violates the first-order conditions (2.5).

Proof of Proposition 11. By choosing π close to the π, which solves (5.4), we can ensure that $(k - R)(1 - G(k))^+$ is maximized at $k = s_n$. Thus, the probability of unemployment can be made arbitrarily close to $(1 - \pi_n^0) = (s_n - s_1)/(s_n - R)$. To show that the probability of unemployment cannot exceed $(s_n - s_1)/(s_n - R)$, suppose that it does. Note that by Proposition 1(1) we always have employment when $s = s_n$. Thus, for the probability of unemployment to exceed $(s_n - s_1)/(s_n - R)$, we must have $\pi_n < (s_1 - R)/(s_n - R)$. But then $(k - R)(1 - G(k))$ is greater at $k = s_1$ than at $k = s_n$. Hence $\bar{k} < s_n$. Therefore, $\bar{k} \leq s_{n-1}$, since $(k - R)(1 - G(k))$ cannot reach a maximum except at a mass point. This shows that employment will

IMPLICIT CONTRACTS UNDER ASYMMETRIC INFORMATION 155

occur when $s = s_{n-1}$ as well as when $s = s_n$. Thus, for the probability of unemployment to exceed $(s_n - s_1)/(s_n - R)$, we must have $\pi_{n-1} + \pi_n < (s_1 - R)/(s_n - R) < (s_1 - R)/(s_{n-1} - R)$. But this means that $(k - R)(1 - G(k))$ is greater at $k = s_1$ than at $k = s_{n-1}$. Hence $\bar{k} < s_{n-1}$, and so $\bar{k} \le s_{n-2}$. Continuing this argument yields $\bar{k} = s_1$. But this means that employment occurs in all states, i.e., the probability of unemployment is zero, which is a contradiction.

Q.E.D.

UNIVERSITY OF CHICAGO
LONDON SCHOOL OF ECONOMICS

REFERENCES

Akerlof, G., and H. Miyazaki, "The Implicit Contract Theory of Unemployment Meets the Wage Bill Argument," *Review of Economic Studies*, XLVII (Jan. 1980), 321–38.
Azariadis, C., "Implicit Contracts and Related Topics: A Survey," Working Paper #79-17, University of Pennsylvania, 1979.
——, "Employment with Asymmetric Information," this *Journal*, *Supplement*, XCVIII (1983), 157–72.
Barlow, R., and F. Proschan, *Statistical Theory of Reliability and Life Testing* (New York: Holt, Rinehart, and Winston, Inc., 1975).
Barro, R., "Rational Expectations and the Role of Monetary Policy," *Journal of Monetary Economics*, III (1976), 1–32.
Bryant, J., "An Annotation of 'Implicit Contracts and Underemployment,' " *Journal of Political Economy*, LXXXVI (1978), 1159–60.
Calvo, G., and E. Phelps, "Employment Contingent Wage Contracts," *Journal of Monetary Economics*, Supplement, V (1977), 160–68.
Chari, V., "Involuntary Unemployment and Implicit Contracts," this *Journal*, *Supplement*, XCVIII (1983), 107–22.
Dasgupta, P., P. Hammond, and E. Maskin, "The Implementation of Social Choice Rules: Some General Results on Incentive Compatibility," *Review of Economic Studies*, XLVI (April, 1979), 185–216.
Diamond, P., and J. Stiglitz, "Increases in Risk and Risk Aversion," *Journal of Economic Theory*, VIII (1974), 337–60.
Gordon, R., "Recent Developments in the Theory of Inflation and Unemployment," *Journal of Monetary Economics*, II (1976), 185–219.
Green, J., and C. Kahn, "Wage Employment Contracts," this *Journal*, *Supplement*, XCVIII (1983), 173–87.
Grossman, S., and O. Hart, "Implicit Contracts, Moral Hazard, and Unemployment," *American Economic Review*, LXXI (1981), 301–07.
Grossman, S., O. Hart, and E. Maskin, "Unemployment with Observable Aggregate Shocks," mimeo, 1982.
Grossman, S., and L. Weiss, "Heterogeneous Information and the Theory of the Business Cycle, *Journal of Political Economy*, XC (1982), 696–727.
Hall, R., "Employment Fluctuations and Wage Rigidity," *Brookings Papers of Economic Activity* (1980), 91–124.
——, and D. Lilien, "Efficient Wage Bargains Under Uncertain Supply and Demand," *American Economic Review*, LXIX (Dec. 1979), 868–79.
Hart, O., "Optimal Labour Contracts Under Asymmetric Information: An Introduction," *Review of Economic Studies*, L (Jan. 1983), 3–36.
Lucas, R., "Expectations and the Neutrality of Money," *Journal of Economic Theory*, IV (1972), 13–34.
Maskin, E., "Randomization in the Principal-Agent Problem," mimeo, 1981.

156   *QUARTERLY JOURNAL OF ECONOMICS*

Mirrlees, J., "An Exploration in the Theory of Optimum Income Taxation," *Review of Economic Studies*, XXXVIII (April 1971), 175–208.
Myerson, R., "Incentive Compatibility and the Bargaining Problem," *Econometrica*, XLVII (Jan. 1978), 61–74.
Radner, R., "Monitoring Cooperative Agreements in a Repeated Principal-Agent Relationship," *Econometrica*, II (1981), 1127–48.
Rothschild, M., and J. Stiglitz, "Increasing Risk," *Journal of Economic Theory*, II (1970), 225–43.
Sadka, E., "On Income Distribution, Incentive Effects, and Optimal Income Taxation," *Review of Economic Studies*, XLIII (1976), 261–67.
Weitzman, M., "Efficient Incentive Contracts," this *Journal*, XCIV (June 1980), 719–730.

Part VII
Integration and Assessments

[19]

Review of Economic Studies (1983) L, 3–35
© 1983 The Society for Economic Analysis Limited

0034-6527/83/00010003$00.50

Optimal Labour Contracts under Asymmetric Information: An Introduction

OLIVER D. HART
London School of Economics

The Review of Economic Studies has instituted a new series of lectures to be given annually by a "younger" British economist at the Association of University Teachers of Economics Meetings. The choice of lecturer is determined by a panel whose members are currently Professors Hahn, Mirrlees and Nobay. This paper is a revised version of the first lecture in the series. It was presented at the AUTE Meeting held at the University of Surrey in April 1982, and was refereed in the usual way.—MAK.

1. INTRODUCTION

The theory of implicit contracts (see Azariadis (1975), Baily (1974), and Gordon (1974)) was developed in order to explain the observation that cyclical fluctuations in output are associated with large amounts of employment variability and only small amounts of (real) wage variability. The theory is based on the idea that it is optimal for less risk-averse firms to insure more risk-averse workers against fluctuations in the marginal (revenue) product of labour by offering them a sticky (real) wage. Recently it has become clear that although such optimal risk-sharing arrangements may be able to explain the low variability of wages, they cannot, by themselves, explain greater fluctuations in employment than those predicted by the usual Walrasian model (see, e.g., Akerlof and Miyazaki (1980)). In fact, under the assumption made by Azariadis *et al.* that firms and workers have symmetric information about the state of the world, it can be shown that in simple cases the implicit contract model predicts exactly the same employment level in each state of the world as the Walrasian model, i.e. any unemployment is "Walrasian".[1]

In the last two years or so, a number of authors have shown that a contract model *can* explain "non-Walrasian" unemployment if instead it is assumed that firms and workers have asymmetric information; in particular, if firms have better information about the state of the world than workers (see, e.g., Grossman and Hart (1981) and the papers by Azariadis, Chari, Green and Kahn, and Grossman and Hart in the forthcoming QJE symposium).[2] Specifically, Azariadis (1982) and Grossman and Hart (1981, 1982) have shown that under asymmetric information, if firms are risk-averse, unemployment will be greater than in the Walrasian model.

The reason is the following. If a firm is risk-averse, it would like its workers to take a wage cut in bad states. However, if only the firm and not the workers can observe the state, wages cannot be made to depend on the state directly. For if the contract says that wages should fall in bad times, then it is in the interest of the firm always to claim that times are bad. Instead wages can only depend on variables such as employment within the firm, which are observable to both the firm and the workers. Thus the contract will specify that the firm can reduce total wages, but only if it reduces employment. As a consequence, in bad states, employment will fall by more than it should from an efficiency point of view, simply because this is the only way the firm can get wages down.

3

4   REVIEW OF ECONOMIC STUDIES

The purpose of the present paper is to survey and extend some of the recent work on optimal labour contracts under asymmetric information. Since it is much too early for a full-blown survey of this area, however, this paper should be thought of more as an introduction to the field than anything else. Our particular interest will be whether this theory provides a solid foundation for the idea that a low marginal revenue product of labour in a firm will lead to an excessively (in Walrasian terms) low level of employment—we call this the underemployment result.

We begin in Section 2 by describing the model of Azariadis (1982) and Grossman and Hart (1981, 1982). In Section 3, we discuss how the model of Chari (1982) and Green and Kahn (1982) differs from this model. We also extend the model of Section 2 to the case where workers observe new information about the state of the world at the time when employment decisions are made, and we consider indexed contracts. In Section 4, we consider the case where workers can observe other endogenous variables in addition to employment, such as capital. In Section 5, we discuss what happens if workers can observe the firm's (ex-post) profit. We also consider further extensions, including the case of multiperiod contracts, and uncertain reservation wages. Finally Section 6 contains some conclusions.

Throughout we will be concerned with a partial equilibrium analysis of one firm making a contract with a number of workers. A general equilibrium, macroeconomic model of contracts under asymmetric information is presented in Grossman, Hart and Maskin (1982).

Before we start, it should be pointed out that the tools used to analyse optimal labour contracts under asymmetric information are very similar to those found in a number of other areas of "information economics". In particular, there is a considerable overlap with the theories of optimal income taxation; non-linear pricing; signalling and screening; incentive compatibility; the principal-agent problem; price versus quantity instruments in planning problems; and optimal auctions. We will not spell out the connections, but we feel that it is appropriate to mention the paper to which our analysis perhaps owes most: Mirrlees (1971).

2. THE BASIC MODEL

The model is a two period one. We will consider a single firm which makes a contract with a group of m workers (we will take this contract to be explicit—see Section 6 for some comments on the relationship between explicit and implicit contracts). We will suppose that there is an initial date before any real economic activity occurs, called date 0, at which the contract is signed. Production and employment do not occur until a later date, called date 1. The date 0 contract specifies what will happen at this later date.

In order to motivate the idea of a contract, imagine that workers go through a training period during which they acquire skills, some of which are specific to the firm they work for. This training takes place, say, between date 0 and date 1. Then at date 1, each worker is generally more productive in the firm where he has been trained than elsewhere,[3] and hence a separation at this date is costly both to the workers who must find jobs elsewhere and to the firm which must find new recruits. For this reason, it is in the interest of all parties to make arrangements about wage and employment conditions at date 1 in advance, i.e. at date 0.

A similar justification for contracts can be given in the absence of firm-specific skills if the workers have to incur mobility costs to work in the firm, e.g. they have to move nearby. A separation at date 1 will again be costly since it means that further mobility costs must be incurred.

A (long-term) contract signed at date 0 can be interpreted as a way of insuring that the right benefit-cost calculations are made concerning employment at date 1.[4]

For simplicity, the m workers are assumed to be identical. Each worker is assumed to have a von Neumann–Morgenstern utility function $U(w - Rl)$, where w is the wage payment at date 1 from the firm and $l \geqq 0$ is the worker's labour supply at date 1 (l is assumed to be a continuous variable). Here R stands for the opportunity cost or reservation wage of labour at date 1, which is taken to be constant. R can be interpreted as the disutility of effort or as the wage that can be earned by the worker in some alternative non-contract occupation at date 1. (In the latter case, the worker's utility is $\hat{U}(w + R(\bar{l} - l))$, where $\bar{l}$ is endowment of labour, and $(\bar{l} - l)$ is his supply of non-contract labour. This can be rewritten as $U(w - Rl)$, where U is a translation of $\hat{U}$.)[5]
We will assume:

Assumption 1. U is defined and twice differentiable on an interval $\mathcal{I} = (a, \infty)$ of the real line and $\lim_{x \to a} U(x) = -\infty$ (we allow for the possibility $a = -\infty$). In addition $U' > 0$, $U'' \leqq 0$ on $\mathcal{I}$.

The firm is assumed to have a gross revenue function $f(\tilde{s}, L)$, where L is total labour supply at date 1, and $\tilde{s}$ is a random variable reflecting the fact that the firm's revenue is uncertain. Here a particular realization $\tilde{s} = s$ may correspond to a demand shock, e.g. a low price for the firm's output, or a supply shock, e.g. a technological innovation. To simplify matters we will assume that the firm cannot hire any new labour at date 1, so that $L = \sum_{i=1}^{m} l_i$, the supply of labour by the m workers under contract.[6] It will be convenient to assume that $\tilde{s}$ can take on a finite number of values $s_1, \ldots, s_n$ lying in some set S of possible states of the world, with associated probabilities $\pi_1, \ldots, \pi_n > 0, \sum_{i=1}^{n} \pi_i = 1$. We assume that the revenue function f has standard properties as a function of L:

Assumption 2. $f(\tilde{s}, L)$ is a twice differentiable function defined for all $L \geqq 0$, with

$$f(\tilde{s}, 0) \geqq 0, \quad \frac{\partial f}{\partial L}(\tilde{s}, L) > 0, \quad \frac{\partial^2 f}{\partial L^2}(\tilde{s}, L) < 0, \quad \frac{\partial f}{\partial L}(\tilde{s}, 0) > R, \quad \lim_{L \to \infty} \frac{\partial f}{\partial L}(\tilde{s}, L) = 0.$$

The firm's profit is given by $f(\tilde{s}, L) - W$, where W represents total wage payments. We will assume that the firm has a single owner/manager who has a von Neumann–Morgenstern utility function $V(f(\tilde{s}, L) - W)$. We will assume:

Assumption 3. V is defined and twice differentiable on an interval $\mathcal{I}' = (b, \infty)$ of the real line and $\lim_{x \to b} V(x) = -\infty$ (we allow for the possibility $b = -\infty$). In addition $V' > 0$, $V'' \leqq 0$ on $\mathcal{I}'$.[7]

Finally, we assume that each worker must be guaranteed an expected utility of at least $\bar{U}$ if he is to be induced to sign a contract at date 0. What we have in mind is that at date 0 there are many firms and workers, similar to the ones described, looking for partners with whom to sign contracts. Since no training or mobility costs have yet been incurred, workers and firms can move freely. It is then quite natural to suppose that there is a competitive market for contracts at date 0. One can interpret $\bar{U}$ as the equilibrium wage in utility terms in this market.
In what follows we will assume that workers and firms at date 0 know the probabilities $\pi_1, \ldots, \pi_n$; the revenue function $f(\tilde{s}, L)$; the utility functions U, V; and $\bar{U}$. It is assumed that nobody knows the state of the world s_i at date 0. Thus there is *symmetric* information at date 0. At date 1, the realization of $\tilde{s}, \tilde{s} = s_i$, becomes known to the firm. We will distinguish between two cases: in the first $\tilde{s}$ is observed also by the workers at date 1 (we call this the case of symmetric information), while in the second the workers do not observe s (we call this the case of asymmetric information).

6   REVIEW OF ECONOMIC STUDIES

The optimal contract under symmetric information

In this case, since s is public information at date 1, wages and employment can be made conditional on s. Thus a contract can be represented by a vector $(w_k(s_i), l_k(s_i))_{k=1,...,m, i=1,...,n}$ indicating the wage and labour supply of each worker $k = 1, \ldots, m$ in each state $s_i, i = 1, \ldots n$. An optimal contract maximizes the firm's expected utility of profit subject to the constraint that each worker's expected utility is no less than $\bar{U}$, i.e. it solves:

$$\text{Maximize} \sum_{i=1}^{n} \pi_i V(f(s_i, \sum_{k=1}^{m} l_k(s_i)) - \sum_{k=1}^{m} w_k(s_i)) \tag{1}$$

subject to

$$\sum_{i=1}^{n} \pi_i U(w_k(s_i) - Rl_k(s_i)) \geqq \bar{U} \quad \text{for each } k = 1, \ldots, m, \tag{2}$$

$$w_k(s_i) - Rl_k(s_i) \in \mathscr{I} \quad \text{for each } k = 1, \ldots, m \text{ and } i = 1, \ldots, n, \tag{3}$$

$$f(s_i, \sum_{k=1}^{m} l_k(s_i)) - \sum_{i=1}^{m} w_k(s_i) \in \mathscr{I}' \quad \text{for each } i = 1, \ldots, n.$$

This is a simple risk-sharing problem with production (see, e.g. Wilson (1968)), and it is easy to characterize the solution. We make a further assumption.

Assumption 4. There exist $\bar{w}$ and $\bar{l}$ such that $\bar{w} - R\bar{l} \in \mathscr{I}$, $U(\bar{w} - R\bar{l}) \geqq \bar{U}$, and $f(s_i, m\bar{l}) - m\bar{w} \in \mathscr{I}'$ for all $i = 1, \ldots, n$.

Assumption 4 guarantees that the set of contracts satisfying (2)–(3) is nonempty. Problem (1)–(3) is convex. It follows that given a solution $(w_k(s_i), l_k(s_i))$,

$$w'_k(s_i) = \frac{1}{m} \sum_{j=1}^{m} w_j(s_i), \quad l'_k(s_i) = \frac{1}{m} \sum_{j=1}^{m} l_j(s_i) \quad \text{for all } k \tag{4}$$

is also a solution. Thus we can confine our attention to symmetric solutions where $l_k(s_i), w_k(s_i)$ are independent of k.

Proposition 1. *Given Assumptions 1 to 4 there is a unique symmetric optimal contract. Furthermore this contract satisfies*

$$\frac{\partial f}{\partial L}(s_i, ml(s_i)) = R \quad \text{for all } i = 1, \ldots, n; \tag{5}$$

$$V'(f(s_i, ml(s_i)) - mw(s_i)) = \lambda U'(w(s_i) - Rl(s_i)) \tag{6}$$

for some $\lambda > 0$ and all $i = 1, \ldots, n$;

$$\sum_{i=1}^{n} \pi_i U(w(s_i) - Rl(s_i)) = \bar{U}. \tag{7}$$

The idea behind the proposition is straightforward. When s is publicly observed at date 1, efficient production and optimal risk sharing are complementary rather than conflicting goals. The former is achieved by choosing the employment level in each state so that the marginal product of labour equals its opportunity cost ((5)), while the latter is achieved by choosing wages so as to equalize marginal rates of substitution between incomes in different states for the firm and workers ((6)). (7) says that each worker will obtain an expected utility equal to $\bar{U}$.

The proof of Proposition 1 is straightforward and is therefore omitted. Note, however, that (5) follows directly from the fact that if $ml(s_i)$ does not maximize $f(s_i, L) - RL$, then an ex-post Pareto improvement can be realized in state s_i by setting $\hat{l}_k(s_i) = (1/m)\hat{L}(s_i)$, $\hat{w}_k(s_i) = w(s_i) + R(\hat{l}_k(s_i) - l(s_i))$ for each $k = 1, \ldots, m$, where $\hat{L}(s_i)$ is the maximizer of $f(s_i, L) - RL$. This in turn yields an ex-ante Pareto improvement at date 0.[8]

HART   CONTRACTS UNDER ASYMMETRIC INFORMATION   7

Remark 1.   Proposition 1 implies that, if the firm is risk neutral and workers are risk-averse, i.e. $V'' \equiv 0$ and $U'' < 0$, $w(s_i) - Rl(s_i)$ equals some constant μ, independent of s_i. Thus in this case each worker receives complete insurance concerning his net income or utility. This provides a possible explanation of *sticky* (real) *wages* (or net incomes) in the face of exogenous uncertainty (see Azariadis (1975), Baily (1974), Gordon (1974)). If the firm is risk-averse, however, i.e. $V'' < 0$, $(w(s_i) - Rl(s_i))$ will vary with s_i and in fact (6) implies that it will be high in states where $f(s_i, ml(s_i)) - mw(s_i)$ is high (coinsurance). Note, however, that *within* a particular state workers receive complete insurance, even if the firm is risk-averse, i.e. all workers are treated equally (this is also true in non-symmetric solutions of (1)–(3) if $U'' < 0$, i.e. $w_k(s_i) - Rl_k(s_i)$ is independent of k). Given our assumption that labour supply is continuous, this is achieved by work-sharing. However, even in the absence of this assumption, there would be equal treatment. For example, suppose $l_k(s_i)$ can only take the values 0 or 1. Then (6) would be achieved by letting some workers work in state s_i and others not and paying those who work R more than those who don't (this is the model of Grossman and Hart (1981)). Thus, even if worksharing is impossible, this model does not predict involuntary unemployment, in the sense of unequal treatment between laid-off and retained workers.

Remark 2.   Everything we have said generalizes to the case where the worker's utility function is $U(w - G(l))$, where G is some convex, increasing function of l. If we assume that U is a more general function of w and l, $U(w, l)$, things become somewhat more complicated, although not fundamentally different. Now (5) must be replaced by a condition of the form that the marginal product of labour equals the marginal rate of substitution between income and labour. This has the implication that the simple feature of the model above, that the optimal employment level in each state is determined by efficiency considerations alone and is independent of attitudes to risk, is lost (for more on this, see Section 3A). The risk-sharing condition (6) remains basically unchanged but, if work-sharing is not feasible, it no longer implies that unemployed workers and employed workers receive equal treatment.[9]

The model can also be generalized to the case of non-identical workers (under the assumption that any differences are objectively discernible), to the case where L is a vector of labour inputs, and to the case where the reservation wage is a random variable, whose realization at date 1 is publically observed (the wage-employment contract is now made conditional on s and R). Finally, m, the number of workers on contract, can be made endogenous, i.e. we can assume that m is a choice variable in problem (1)–(3).

We now turn to the case where workers do not observe s at date 1.

The optimal contract under asymmetric information

Many of the contracts which were previously feasible are no longer so once s cannot be observed by the workers. For example, suppose the contract calls for a lower wage in state s_2 than in state s_1 for each worker but the same level of employment: $l(s_1) = l(s_2)$. If the workers cannot distinguish between s_1 and s_2 they will not know whether it is appropriate for them to take a wage cut. Furthermore, if they rely on the firm to tell them, then it is in the firm's interest to claim that state s_2 has occurred rather than s_1, since the firm thereby pays lower wages while employing the same amount of labour.

Drawing on the results from the by now large incentive compatibility literature, we may represent a contract for the case where the workers do not observe s at date 1 as follows. We imagine that the firm is asked to *report* at date 1 the state s which has occurred to the workers. Given this reported state s_r, the contract then specifies a wage $w_k(s_r)$ and labour supply $l_k(s_r)$ for each worker $k = 1, \ldots, m$, appropriate for this state. In general, as we have seen, the firm will have an incentive to lie, i.e. it will report $s_r \neq s$. An *incentive-compatible* (or feasible) contract is one such that the firm is always prepared

Implicit Contract Theory

to tell the truth, i.e.

$$s_r = s \text{ maximizes } f(s, \sum_{k=1}^{m} l_k(s_r)) - \sum_{k=1}^{m} w_k(s_r) \quad \text{for all } s. \tag{8}$$

In writing the truth-telling constraints in this way, we are assuming that the firm makes a single report $s = s_r$ to all m workers as a group.

We will restrict our attention to incentive-compatible contracts. It turns out, however, that there is no loss of generality in doing this. In particular, any contract in which firms have an incentive to lie is, given that workers recognize this, equivalent to another contract in which firms tell the truth (see, e.g. Dasgupta, Hammond and Maskin (1979)). Thus condition (8) characterizes the true set of feasible contracts.

This describes the set of feasible contracts. An optimal contract is a feasible contract which maximizes the firm's expected utility of profit subject to the constraint that each worker's expected utility is no less than $\bar{U}$. Formally, an optimal contract is a vector $(w_k(s_i), l_k(s_i))_{k=1,\dots,m, i=1,\dots,n}$, indicating the wage and labour of each worker in each state, which solves:

$$\text{Maximize } \sum_i \pi_i V(f(s_i, \sum_{k=1}^{m} l_k(s_i)) - \sum_{k=1}^{m} w_k(s_i)) \tag{9}$$

subject to

$$f(s_i, \sum_{k=1}^{m} l_k(s_i)) - \sum_{k=1}^{m} w_k(s_i) \geqq f(s_i, \sum_{k=1}^{m} l_k(s_j)) - \sum_{k=1}^{m} w_k(s_j) \tag{10}$$

for all $i = 1, \dots, n, j = 1, \dots, n$,

$$\sum_i \pi_i U(w_k(s_i) - Rl_k(s_i)) \geqq \bar{U} \quad \text{for each } k = 1, \dots, m, \tag{11}$$

$$w_k(s_i) - Rl_k(s_i) \in \mathscr{I} \quad \text{for each } k = 1, \dots, m, i = 1, \dots, n, \tag{12}$$

$$f(s_i, \sum_{k=1}^{m} l_k(s_i)) - \sum_{k=1}^{m} w_k(s_i) \in \mathscr{I}' \quad \text{for each } i = 1, \dots, n.$$

Comparing this problem to that in (1)–(3), we see that the only difference is the presence of the $n(n-1)$ constraints (10). These are the truth-telling or incentive compatibility constraints, which ensure that, for all i, j, the firm does not find it in its interest to report that $s = s_j$ has occurred when the true state is $s = s_i$ (i.e. (10) is equivalent to (8)). Given the presence of these constraints, the feasible set is generally smaller than before, and so we may conclude that the firm is worse off under asymmetric information than under symmetric information.[10]

Note that an implication of (10) is that total wages $W(s_i) = \sum_{k=1}^{m} w_k(s_i)$ can vary with s_i only to the extent that total employment $L(s_i) = \sum_{k=1}^{m} l_k(s_i)$ does, i.e. W can be written as a function of L: $W = W(L)$. For if $L(s_1) = L(s_2)$ and $W(s_1) > W(s_2)$, then the firm will report that state s_2 has occurred when the true state is s_1, violating truth-telling. In view of this, the constraints (10) can be re-expressed as:

$$L = L(s_i) \text{ solves: } \text{Max}_L f(s_i, L) - W(L) \quad \text{for each } s_i. \tag{13}$$

That is, another way of thinking about the contract is that it specifies how total wages vary with total employment L, and the firm in each state then chooses L to maximize profit, $f(s, L) - W(L)$. If one thinks of the contract this way, then there is no need for any direct reporting of the state by the firm.[11]

Two conclusions about problem (9)–(12) can be drawn immediately. First, since taking a convex combination of the $w_k(s_i)$ and $l_k(s_i)$ does not affect the constraints, we may, as in the symmetric information case, concentrate on symmetric solutions satisfying

$$l_k(s_i) = l(s_i) \text{ independent of } k,$$

$$w_k(s_i) = w(s_i) \text{ independent of } k, \quad \text{for all } i = 1, \cdots, n. \tag{14}$$

Secondly, if the firm is risk-neutral, i.e. $V'' \equiv 0$, the incentive compatibility constraints (10) can be ignored. For in this case, the solution to (5)–(7) satisfies $w(s_i) - Rl(s_i) = \mu$,

HART   CONTRACTS UNDER ASYMMETRIC INFORMATION   9

independent of s_i, which means that (10) is automatically satisfied. Thus if the firm is risk-neutral the optimal contract under asymmetric information is the same as that under symmetric information. (In such cases, we will say that the second-best (asymmetric information) equals the first-best (symmetric information).)

In order to proceed beyond this to the risk-averse case, it is necessary to identify which of the truth-telling constraints (10) is binding (the assumption of firm risk-aversion is motivated in Section 5). This requires some further assumptions.

Suppose that the states $s_1, \ldots, s_n$ can be ranked according to their marginal product of labour, i.e. possibly after renumbering,

Assumption 5

$$\frac{\partial f}{\partial L}(s_n, L) > \frac{\partial f}{\partial L}(s_{n-1}, L) > \cdots > \frac{\partial f}{\partial L}(s_1, L) \quad \text{for all } L.$$

Assume also

Assumption 6. $f(s_n, L) \geqq f(s_{n-1}, L) \geqq \cdots \geqq f(s_1, L)$ for all L, with strict inequality for $L > 0$.

This, together with Assumption 5, says that high marginal products of labour go together with high total products of labour. Note that Assumption 6 is implied by Assumption 5 if $f(s_i, 0) = 0$ for all i.

Result 1. *Assume $V'' < 0$ and Assumptions 1–6 hold. Then, in problem (9)–(12), we can replace the set of constraints (10) by the following:*

(a) $f(s_i, \sum_{k=1}^{m} l_k(s_i)) - \sum_{k=1}^{m} w_k(s_i) \geqq f(s_i, \sum_{k=1}^{m} l_k(s_{i-1})) - \sum_{k=1}^{m} w_k(s_{i-1})$

for all $i = 2, \ldots, n$,   (10')

(b) $\sum_{k=1}^{m} l_k(s_i) \geqq \sum_{k=1}^{m} l_k(s_{i-1})$ *for all $i = 2, \ldots, n$.*

Proof. See Appendix 3.

(10')(a) is a strict subset of (10) corresponding to the case $j = (i - 1)$, while (10')(b) says that total employment should be monotonically increasing in i.

Given Result 1 we can now establish

Proposition 2. *Assume $V'' < 0$ and Assumptions 1–6 hold. Then a solution to (9)–(12) exists. Furthermore any symmetric solution satisfies*

$$\frac{\partial f}{\partial L}(s_n, ml(s_n)) = R; \tag{15}$$

$$\frac{\partial f}{\partial L}(s_i, ml(s_i)) \geqq R \quad \text{for all } i < n; \tag{16}$$

$$f(s_i, ml(s_i)) - mw(s_i) \geqq f(s_{i-1}, ml(s_{i-1})) - mw(s_{i-1}) \quad \text{for all } i = 2, \ldots, n; \tag{17}$$

$$w(s_i) - Rl(s_i) \geqq w(s_{i-1}) - Rl(s_{i-1}) \quad \text{for all } i = 2, \ldots, n; \tag{18}$$

$$\sum_i \pi_i U(w(s_i) - Rl(s_i)) = \bar{U}. \tag{19}$$

In addition, if $(w(s_i), l(s_i))$ is not also a solution of (1)–(3), (16) holds with strict inequality for some $i < n$. Finally, if $U'' \equiv 0$, there will be strict inequality in (16) for all $i < n$.

The most interesting result from our point of view is (15)–(16), which says that there will be the same level of employment as in the symmetric information case in the best state s_n and *underemployment* (or the same level of employment) in all other states. The penultimate part of the proposition says that we will get strict underemployment in at least one state unless the second-best equals the first-best. Given $V'' < 0$, it is very unlikely that the second-best equals the first-best, especially if there are "many" states (we have seen that the second-best equals the first-best if $V'' \equiv 0$). In particular, if there is a continuum of states $[\underline{s}, \bar{s}]$, the truth-telling constraints are always binding and it can be shown that we get strict underemployment with probability 1 for $s < \bar{s}$. The final part of the proposition tells us that the truth telling constraints will be binding also with a finite number of states if the workers are risk-neutral (more generally, not too risk-averse).[12] Moreover, in this case there will be strict underemployment for all $i < n$ (see Guesnerie–Seade (1982) for a similar result).[13,14]

To see why we get underemployment, suppose that we do not, i.e. $\partial f(s_i, ml(s_i))/\partial L < R$ for some i. Reduce $l(s_i)$ and $w(s_i)$ a little, so that $f(s_i, ml(s_i)) - mw(s_i)$ remains constant. If $l(s_i) > l(s_{i-1})$, this does not affect (10')(b). On the other hand, since $f(s_i, ml(s_i)) - mw(s_i)$ stays constant and $l(s_i)$ falls, $f(s_{i+1}, ml(s_i)) - mw(s_i)$ must fall since the marginal product of labour is higher in s_{i+1} than in s_i by Assumption 5. Thus (10')(a) continues to hold. However, workers' net incomes in state s_i must increase since

$$m[dw(s_i) - Rdl(s_i)] = m\left[\frac{\partial f}{\partial L}(s_i, ml(s_i)) - R\right] dl(s_i) > 0.$$

Thus by reducing $l(s_i)$ we have achieved an ex-post Pareto improvement in state s_i. This in turn leads to an ex-ante Pareto improvement at date 0, which contradicts the optimality of the contract. This proves (16) for the case $l(s_i) > l(s_{i-1})$.

If $l(s_i) = l(s_{i-1})$, we cannot reduce $l(s_{i-1})$ in this way. Suppose, however, that $l(s_i) = l(s_{i-1}) > l(s_{i-2})$. Then we can apply the above argument to $l(s_{i-1})$ to obtain.

$$\frac{\partial f}{\partial L}(s_{i-1}, ml(s_{i-1})) \geqq R. \tag{20}$$

But this implies, in view of Assumption 5, that

$$\frac{\partial f}{\partial L}(s_i, ml(s_i)) = \frac{\partial f}{\partial L}(s_i, ml(s_{i-1})) > \frac{\partial f}{\partial L}(s_{i-1}, ml(s_{i-1})) \geqq R. \tag{21}$$

Thus (16) is again established (a similar argument can be given if $l(s_i) = l(s_{i-1}) = l(s_{i-2}) > l(s_{i-3})$, etc.).

That we get an efficient level of employment in the top state s_n follows from the fact that, if $\partial f(s_n, ml(s_n))/\partial L > R$, a small increase in $l(s_n)$ and $w(s_n)$ which keeps $f(s_n, ml(s_n)) - mw(s_n)$ constant will lead to a Pareto improvement without violating (10').

The proof of the remainder of Proposition 2 is given in the Appendix.[15] Note that (17)–(18) is a coinsurance result. It says that in better states, i.e. when i is higher (see Assumption 6), both the firm and workers will be better off. Note also that all workers are treated equally in each state, so that in this sense, as in the symmetric information case, there is no involuntary unemployment (this conclusion remains true even if work-sharing is infeasible—see Grossman and Hart (1981)). On the other hand, (18) (which generally holds with strict inequality) and (10')(b) together imply that all workers are worse off in low employment states than in high employment ones. It follows that if workers could choose the level of employment subject to the wage function $W(L)$ (see (13)), they would choose $l = l(s_n)$. In this sense workers are involuntarily underemployed in bad states.

Remark 3. Assumption 5 is important for the underemployment result. In its absence, Result 1 no longer holds and neither does our argument establishing underemployment. Specifically, a reduction in $l(s_i)$ and $w(s_i)$ which keeps $f(s_i, ml(s_i)) - mw(s_i)$ constant may cause $f(s_j, ml(s_i)) - mw(s_i)$ to increase for some j in such a way that the constraints (10) are violated. As a result, an optimal contract may involve overemployment in some states.

Assumption 6 is also important for the underemployment result. If, say, $f(s, L) = sg(L) + 1/s$, where $g(L) < 1$ for all L and $0 < s < 1$, then the marginal product and total product of labour are negatively related. In this case one gets the opposite of Proposition 2: in an optimal contract the marginal product of labour will be equal to R in the worst state (i.e. the one where total product is lowest) and will be less than or equal to R in all other states (see, e.g. Cooper (1981)). Thus the model now predicts (uniform) overemployment.[16] On the other hand, if the marginal product and total product of labour are not uniformly positively or negatively related, we may get overemployment in some states and underemployment in others (it follows from results in Guesnerie and Seade (1982) that there will always be some state where the marginal product of labour equals R).

While the assumption that the marginal products of labour can be compared uniformly across states and the assumption that total and marginal products move together are both important, in the present context the former seems the stronger one. This assumption will be satisfied in simple cases, such as $f(s, L) = sg(L)$, where, say, $g(L)$ represents the quantity of output and s is the market price, but in general it obviously will not be. At the same time, because it is not unreasonable and yields great simplification, Assumption 5 seems to provide a natural starting point for the analysis of optimal contracts.

Remark 4. A small generalization of Assumptions 5 and 6 can be made. Define equivalence classes for the states, $E(s_1), \ldots, E(s_n)$, where $s \in E(s_i)$ if and only if $\partial f(s, L)/\partial L = \partial f(s_i, L)/\partial L$ for all $L \geqq 0$. Under Assumption 5, these equivalence classes are degenerate. A slight generalization of Assumptions 5 and 6 is:

Assumption 5'.   If $s \in E(s_i)$, $s' \in E(s_j)$, $i > j$, then $\partial f(s, L)/\partial L > \partial f(s', L)/\partial L$ for all L.

Assumption 6'.   For each L and $i = 2, \ldots, n$, the conditional distribution of $f(\tilde{s}, L)$ given that $\tilde{s} \in E(s_i)$ dominates in the sense of first degree stochastic dominance the conditional distribution of $f(\tilde{s}, L)$ given that $\tilde{s} \in E(s_{i-1})$.

Assumptions 5' and 6' hold if, for example, $s_i = (s_{i1}, s_{i2})$ and $f(s_1, L) = s_1 g(L) + s_2$ where s_1 and s_2 are independent (s and s' are then in the same equivalence class if and only if $s_1 = s_1'$). With Assumptions 5' and 6' replacing Assumptions 5 and 6, Proposition 2 continues to hold with appropriate modifications (now (15) holds for all $s \in E(s_n)$ and (16) holds for all $s \in E(s_i)$, $i < n$).

Remark 5.   The maximization problem (9)–(12) is not generally convex, and so the solution may not be unique. One case where convexity and uniqueness are guaranteed is when s is a scalar and $f(s, L) = sg(L)$ (see Green and Kahn (1982)). Then, if one defines the new variable $q = g(L)$, the constraints (10) are linear in the q's, while (11) is convex in the q's.

Remark 6.   We have assumed that the contract specifies that the firm reports the state $s_r = s$ to the workers and this results in a deterministic labour supply $l(s)$ and wage $w(s)$ for each worker. One may ask, however, whether it might not be better to make the selection of l and w uncertain. That is, we could replace $l(s)$ and $w(s)$ by a lottery

12   REVIEW OF ECONOMIC STUDIES

$(\tilde{l}(s), \tilde{w}(s))$, where the random variables $\tilde{l}$ and $\tilde{w}$ are drawn from some joint probability distribution $F(w, l; s_r)$ which depends on the reported s (one can imagine that l and w are drawn from an urn, and there is a different urn for each reported state). At first sight, the idea of introducing randomness seems curious. Since both parties are risk averse, it seems that this could only make things worse. This is not the case, however. For this is a second-best world, and the firm and workers are concerned not only with optimal risk-sharing, but also with the truth-telling constraints (10). It turns out that lotteries may be useful in allowing these constraints to be met at lower cost. An example illustrating this, together with some discussion of why it may be difficult to implement lotteries, is provided in Appendix 2.[17]

3. EXTENSIONS OF THE BASIC MODEL

In this and the next two sections we consider some extensions of the basic model with asymmetric information. For the rest of the paper we will simplify matters by assuming that the firm makes a contract with a single worker, i.e. $m = 1$. All our results generalize to the case of many workers, however. In the case $m = 1$, there is no distinction between l and L or w and W.

A. *More general utility functions for workers*

In order to establish Proposition 2, we assumed that the worker's utility function was $U(w - Rl)$. There is no difficulty in generalizing Proposition 2 to the case $U(w - G(l))$ where G is some convex, increasing function of l. However, with general utility functions $U(w, l)$, new problems arise (these are the focus of the studies of Chari (1982), and Green and Kahn (1982)).

Consider first the case of symmetric information. For the one worker case, we obtain, in place of (5)–(7),

$$\frac{\partial f}{\partial L}(s_i, l(s_i)) = -\left[\frac{\partial U}{\partial l}(w(s_i), l(s_i))\Big/\frac{\partial U}{\partial w}(w(s_i), l(s_i))\right], \qquad (22)$$

$$V'(f(s_i, l(s_i)) - w(s_i)) = \lambda \frac{\partial U}{\partial w}(w(s_i), l(s_i)) \quad \text{for some } \lambda > 0 \quad \text{and all } i = 1, \ldots, n, \quad (23)$$

$$\sum_i \pi_i U(w(s_i), l(s_i)) = \bar{U}. \qquad (24)$$

Now suppose we have asymmetric information. Then, in general, *even if the firm is risk neutral*, (22)–(24) are not consistent with the truth telling constraints (10) (see Chari (1982), Green and Kahn (1982)). (In contrast, in the model of Section 2, the first-best equals the second-best under risk neutrality.)

This can be seen from the following example. Suppose $U(w, l) = \alpha(w) - l$, where α is strictly concave. Then if $V'' = 0$, (23) implies that $w(s_i)$ is constant. This means that in the first-best the worker's utility is lower the higher l is, i.e. in good (high marginal product) states, where l is high, the worker is badly off. We no longer get coinsurance.

It should now be clear why this scheme cannot be implemented under asymmetric information. For if $w(s_i)$ is constant, then it is in the firm's interest always to report $s = s_n$ since, by doing this, it obtains more labour and pays no higher wages.

In this example, there is a tendency for the firm to overemploy the worker. Chari and Green–Kahn analyse the form of an optimal second-best contract when the firm is risk neutral and the worker's utility function takes the general form $U(w, l)$ (see also Worrall (1982)). They show that the contract will involve overemployment in the sense that

$$\frac{\partial f}{\partial L}(s_i, l(s_i)) \leq -\left[\frac{\partial U}{\partial l}(w(s_i), l(s_i))\Big/\frac{\partial U}{\partial w}(w(s_i), l(s_i))\right] \qquad (25)$$

HART   CONTRACTS UNDER ASYMMETRIC INFORMATION   13

if leisure is a normal good.[18] The inequality in (25) is reversed and one gets underemployment if leisure is an inferior good. (The borderline case is where the demand for leisure is independent of income. This is the case $U = U(w - g(L))$.) Chari and Green–Kahn do not consider the case where the firm is risk-averse.

It turns out, however, that this inefficiency or distortion can be overcome if a third party is included in the contractural negotiations.[19] In particular, suppose that the firm and worker have access to a risk-neutral insurance company at date 0. Let $U(w, l)$ be a twice differentiable concave function defined on $R \times R_+$, with $\partial U/\partial w > 0$, $\partial U/\partial l < 0$. Then an optimal contract under asymmetric information solves:

$$\text{Maximize} \sum_i \pi_i V(f(s_i, l(s_i)) - \hat{w}(s_i)) \tag{26}$$

subject to

$$f(s_i, l(s_i)) - \hat{w}(s_i) \geqq f(s_i, l(s_j)) - \hat{w}(s_j) \quad \text{for all } i, j, \tag{27}$$

$$\sum_i \pi_i U(w(s_i), l(s_i)) \geqq \bar{U}, \tag{28}$$

$$\sum_i \pi_i(\hat{w}(s_i) - w(s_i)) = 0. \tag{29}$$

The only difference between this and (9)–(12) is that the wage paid by the firm $\hat{w}(s_i)$ may now not equal the wage received by the worker, $w(s_i)$. The difference is made up by the insurance company and must satisfy (29).

We will show that, if the firm is risk-neutral, the first-best contract can be implemented under asymmetric information. Let $w(s_i)$, $l(s_i)$ be the first-best contract. Choose $\hat{w}(s_i)$ so that

$$f(s_i, l(s_i)) - \hat{w}(s_i) = f(s_i, l(s_{i-1})) - \hat{w}(s_{i-1}) \quad \text{for all } i \geqq 2, \tag{30}$$

and so that (29) is satisfied. Then by the proof of Result 1 in the Appendix, all of the constraints in (27) are satisfied. (Note that (22) and (23) imply that $l(s_i)$ is increasing in i.) Since the firm is risk-neutral, however, it is no worse off paying $\hat{w}(s_i)$ than $w(s_i)$ in view of (29). Thus we have shown that, with a risk-neutral third party, the first-best and second-best are the same for the case where the firm is risk-neutral.

Suppose the firm is risk-averse. Now the first-best and second-best are no longer the same, even with a risk-neutral third party. In Appendix 3 we prove

Proposition 3. *Assume $V'' < 0$ and Assumptions 1–6 hold. Assume also that $U(w, l)$ is a twice differentiable concave function defined on $R \times R_+$, with $\partial U/\partial w > 0$, $\partial U/\partial l < 0$, and $\partial f(s_1, 0)/\partial L > -\partial U(w, 0)/\partial l/\partial U(w, 0)/\partial w$ for all w. Then any solution $(w(s_i), \hat{w}(s_i), l(s_i))$ to (26)–(29) satisfies*

$$\frac{\partial f}{\partial L}(s_n, l(s_n)) = -\left[\frac{\partial U}{\partial l}(w(s_n), l(s_n)) \Big/ \frac{\partial U}{\partial w}(w(s_n), l(s_n))\right], \tag{31}$$

$$\frac{\partial f}{\partial L}(s_i, l(s_i)) > -\left[\frac{\partial U}{\partial l}(w(s_i), l(s_i)) \Big/ \frac{\partial U}{\partial w}(w(s_i), l(s_i))\right] \quad \text{for all } i < n. \tag{32}$$

Thus the (strict) underemployment result for risk-averse firms holds for general utility functions $U(w, l)$ if a risk-neutral third party is added.[20]

Remark 7. In the model of Section 2, adding a risk-neutral third party changes nothing if the worker is risk-neutral. For in this case the worker is indifferent between receiving $w(s_i)$ from the third party and $\hat{w}(s_i)$ directly from the firm if (29) holds. More generally, in the model of Section 2, the presence of the third party makes the worker behave as if he was risk-neutral even if he isn't, i.e. it is optimal for the third party to give the worker complete insurance by setting $w(s_i) - Rl(s_i) = w^*$ for all i, where $U(w^*) = \bar{U}$.

14   REVIEW OF ECONOMIC STUDIES

B. *Additional public information at date* 1

In Section 2 we assumed that the worker observes nothing at date 1 except wages and employment. In general, however, the worker may also receive directly some information about the state s_i. This can be modelled as follows. Let $\tilde{I}$ be a random variable, correlated with s, which takes the values $I_1, \ldots, I_Q$ with associated probabilities $\alpha_1, \ldots, \alpha_Q > 0$. We assume that both the worker and firm observe the realization of $\tilde{I}$, I_q, at date 1 before any reports or employment decisions are made. Let the conditional probability that $s = s_i$, given that $I = I_q$, be $\beta_{iq} > 0$, where $\sum_i \beta_{iq} = 1$ for all q and

$$\text{Prob}\,[s = s_i] = \pi_i = \sum_{q=1}^{Q} \beta_{iq}\alpha_q \quad \text{for all } i. \tag{33}$$

A contract is now a vector $(w(s_i, I_q), l(s_i, I_q))_{i=1,\ldots,n,\,q=1,\ldots,Q}$ indicating the wage and employment when the realization I_q is observed and the firm reports s_i. An optimal contract solves:

$$\text{Maximize} \sum_i \sum_q \alpha_q \beta_{iq} V(f(s_i, l(s_i, I_q)) - w(s_i, I_q)) \tag{34}$$

subject to

$$f(s_i, l(s_i, I_q)) - w(s_i, I_q) \geqq f(s_i, l(s_j, I_q)) - w(s_j, I_q) \quad \text{for all } i, j, q, \tag{35}$$

$$\sum_i \sum_q \alpha_q \beta_{iq} U(w(s_i, I_q) - Rl(s_i, I_q)) \geqq \bar{U}, \tag{36}$$

$$w(s_i, I_q) - Rl(s_i, I_q) \in \mathcal{I} \quad \text{for each } i, q, \tag{37}$$
$$f(s_i, l(s_i, I_q)) - w(s_i, I_q) \in \mathcal{I}' \quad \text{for each } i, q.$$

Now this problem is only slightly more complicated than (9)–(12). (The truth telling constraints now imply that w must be a function of l and I_q; cf (13).) In particular, let

$$\bar{U}(q) = \sum_i \beta_{iq} U(w(s_i, I_q) - Rl(s_i, I_q)). \tag{38}$$

Here $\bar{U}(q)$ is the expected utility of the worker conditional on I_q being observed at date 1. Then it is easy to see that a *necessary* condition for a contract $(w(s_i, I_q), l(s_i, I_q))$ to solve (34)–(37) is that for *each* q it solves:

$$\text{Maximize} \sum_i \beta_{iq} V(f(s_i, l(s_i, I_q)) - w(s_i, I_q)) \tag{39}$$

subject to

$$f(s_i, l(s_i, I_q)) - w(s_i, I_q) \geqq f(s_i, l(s_j, I_q)) - w(s_j, I_q) \quad \text{for all } i, j, \tag{40}$$

$$\sum_i \beta_{iq} U(w(s_i, I_q) - Rl(s_i, I_q)) \geqq \bar{U}(q), \tag{41}$$

$$w(s_i, I_q) - Rl(s_i, I_q) \in \mathcal{I} \quad \text{for each } i, \tag{42}$$
$$f(s_i, l(s_i, I_q)) - w(s_i, I_q) \in \mathcal{I}' \quad \text{for each } i.$$

For if not, an ex-post Pareto improvement can be achieved in the event $I = I_q$. But this means that an ex-ante Pareto improvement can be achieved at date 0, contradicting the optimality of the contract.

We see then that we can now think of the contract in two stages. First the $\bar{U}(q)$'s are determined to satisfy $\bar{U} \leqq \sum_q \alpha_q \bar{U}(q)$ and so that risks are shared optimally across the events $q = 1, \ldots, Q$. Secondly, for each q, problem (39)–(42) is solved. This problem, however, is identical to that of Section 2. Therefore we can apply Proposition 2 to conclude that

$$\frac{\partial f}{\partial L}(s_n, l(s_n, I_q)) = R \quad \text{for all } q, \tag{43}$$

$$\frac{\partial f}{\partial L}(s_i, l(s_i, I_q)) \geqq R \quad \text{for all } q \text{ and } i < n. \tag{44}$$

Thus the underemployment result generalizes to the case of additional public information at date 1 (as in Section 2, there will generally be strict inequality for some q, i in (44)).

Allowing for the possibility of public information is particularly important if one wishes to model macroeconomic disturbances. Then aggregate unemployment, prices, etc. will be important (publicly observed) signals about the state s_i. For an analysis of macroeconomic shocks which uses the above approach, see Grossman, Hart and Maskin (1982).[21]

C. *Indexation*

So far, we have expressed everything in money terms (or we have assumed that there is a single good in the economy). In reality, of course, firms and workers are interested in the goods money can buy. In order to allow for this, assume that there are G consumption goods. We noted in Section 2 that the reservation wage R has two interpretations: it may be the disutility of effort or the amount that the worker can earn elsewhere at date 1 in a non-contract occupation.

Consider the second interpretation first. Let the prices of the G consumption goods at date 1 be given by the vector $\tilde{p}$. We allow $\tilde{p}$ to be a random variable, since there may be uncertainty at date 0 about prices (we also allow $\tilde{p}$ to be correlated with $\tilde{s}$). Assume that at date 1 the realization p_q of $\tilde{p}$ is observable to both the firm and workers, so that contracts can be indexed. Write the indirect utility function of the firm and worker at date 1 as

$$V(f(s, l) - w; p_q),\tag{45}$$

$$U(w - Rl; p_q).\tag{46}$$

Then, since p_q is publicly observable, it is just like the additional public information I_q in Section B above. The only new feature is that the utility functions V and U depend on p_q directly as well as through the conditional distribution of s given p. (Note that V, U are still concave in income, given p_q.) This, however, does not affect the argument that a necessary condition for (34)–(37) to be solved is that (39)–(42) is solved. Thus we may conclude that we will again get underemployment in an optimal indexed contract.[22]

Consider now the case where R represents the disutility of labour. This case is somewhat more difficult. Suppose that the worker's utility function of goods and labour $W(x, l)$ satisfies

$$W(x, l) = H(T(x) - Rl),\tag{47}$$

where H is concave and T is homogeneous of degree one in the G-dimensional vector x. Here H represents attitudes to risk and $T(x) - Rl$ represents ordinal preferences. Then the worker's indirect utility function is

$$H(\hat{T}(p)w - Rl).\tag{48}$$

For each p, this is like the utility function $U(w - Rl)$ of Section 2. The only difference is that the effective reservation wage is $(R/\hat{T}(p))$, which varies with p. This is unimportant, however, and we can again apply the argument of Section B above to show that we will get underemployment for each p. Thus we will get underemployment in an optimal indexed contract.

The formulation (47) is used in Grossman, Hart and Maskin (1982). With more general functions $W(x, L)$, we lose the property that the marginal rate of substitution between income and labour is independent of income (constant "marginal utility of money"). The considerations discussed in Section A above now therefore become relevant.

4. THE CASE OF MORE THAN ONE INPUT

We have assumed that labour is the only input in production. In general, of course, the firm will use other inputs, such as capital, raw materials, etc. To the extent that workers can observe the quantities of these other inputs, they will want to condition wages on them.

Suppose that revenue net of input costs other than labour is given by

$$y = f(s, l) - \sum_{q=2}^{Q} R_q l_q, \tag{49}$$

where $R_q > 0$ is the cost per unit of l_q, $l = (l_1, \ldots, l_Q)$, and l_1 stands for labour. We assume that

Assumption 2'. $f(\tilde{s}, l)$ is a twice differentiable concave function defined for all $l \geqq 0$, with $f(\tilde{s}, 0) \geqq 0$, $\partial f(\tilde{s}, l)/\partial L_q > 0$, $\partial f(\tilde{s}, l)/\partial L_q > R_q$ if $l_q = 0$, $\lim_{L_q \to \infty} \partial f(\tilde{s}, l)/\partial L_q = 0$.

The worker's utility is $U(w - R_1 l_1)$ as before.

We assume that the worker can observe l. Thus now wages, w, can vary with l: $w = w(l)$. An optimal contract under asymmetric information is a solution $w(s_i)$, $l(s_i)$ to (9)–(12), where we replace l by the vector l except in the worker's utility function where l_1 appears (we continue to set $m = 1$). Unfortunately when l is a vector, the analysis of this problem is considerably more complicated since it is not clear which of the constraints (10) will be binding. In particular, there is no obvious generalization of Result 1 (what corresponds to monotonicity when l is a vector?). Nor is there a natural generalization of Assumptions 5 and 6. The following is a very strong generalization of Assumptions 5 and 6—it requires that marginal products can be ranked uniformly across states for all inputs:

$$\frac{\partial f}{\partial L_q}(s_n, l) > \frac{\partial f}{\partial L_q}(s_{n-1}, l) > \cdots > \frac{\partial f}{\partial L_q}(s_1, l) \quad \text{for all } q \text{ and } l; \tag{50}$$

$$f(s_n, l) \geqq f(s_{n-1}, l) \geqq \cdots \geqq f(s_1, l) \quad \text{for all } l. \tag{51}$$

Even under (50)–(51), however, I have only been able to prove that there is *some* state in which the marginal product of each input exceeds its opportunity cost.

We now consider two cases where more can be said. Assume:

Assumption 2''. $f(\tilde{s}, l) = g(\tilde{s}, \phi(l))$, where ϕ is a non-negative concave, function defined on $l \geqq 0$, with $\phi(0) = 0$ and range $\{\phi(l)\} = [0, \infty)$, and g is a twice differentiable concave function defined for all $\phi \geqq 0$, with $\partial g(\tilde{s}, \phi)/\partial \phi > 0$, $\lim_{\phi \to \infty} \partial g(\tilde{s}, \phi)/\partial \phi = 0$.

An example is where ϕ is the production function and s represents output price: $f = s\phi(l)$. Assume further that

Assumption 5'

$$\frac{\partial g}{\partial \phi}(s_n, \phi) > \frac{\partial g}{\partial \phi}(s_{n-1}, \phi) > \cdots > \frac{\partial g}{\partial \phi}(s_1, \phi) \quad \text{for all } \phi \geqq 0.$$

Assumption 6'. $g(s_n, \phi) \geqq g(s_{n-1}, \phi) \geqq \cdots \geqq g(s_1, \phi)$ for all $\phi \geqq 0$, with strict inequality if $\phi > 0$.

Under these conditions ϕ has the same role as l in Section 2, and we can apply the same analysis. Specifically, let $\hat{w} = $ total input costs for the firm $= w(s_i) + \sum_{q>1} R_q l_q$. Then the firm's utility $= V(g(s_i, \phi(l)) - \hat{w})$, while the worker's is $U(\hat{w} - \sum_{q=1}^{Q} R_q l_q)$. As in (13) the truth telling constraints can be expressed as the two conditions: $\hat{w}$ can be written as

$\hat{w}(\phi)$ and $l(s_i)$ maximizes $g(s_i, \phi(l)) - \hat{w}(\phi)$ for each i. Define

$$C(\phi) = \min \{\textstyle\sum_{q=1} R_q l_q | \phi(l) \geqq \phi\}. \tag{52}$$

It is clear that an optimal contract will be efficient in the sense that

$$\textstyle\sum_{q=1}^{Q} R_q l_q(s_i) = C(\phi(l(s_i))) \quad \text{for all } s_i. \tag{53}$$

Otherwise a Pareto improvement could be achieved. Thus the worker's utility can be written as $U(\hat{w} - C(\phi(l(s_i))))$.

Since we have now expressed the firm's utility $V(g(s_i, \phi) - \hat{w})$ and the worker's utility $U(\hat{w} - C(\phi))$ in terms of ϕ, we can apply the analysis of Section 2 with ϕ replacing l (the fact that C is nonlinear in ϕ is unimportant). Assume

Assumption 4'. There exist $\bar{w}$ and $\bar{\phi}$ such that $\bar{w} - C(\bar{\phi}) \in \mathcal{I}$, $U(\bar{w} - C(\bar{\phi})) \geqq \bar{U}$ and $g(s_i, \bar{\phi}) - \bar{w} \in \mathcal{I}'$ for all i.

Then we have

Proposition 4. *Assume Assumptions 1, 2″, 3, 4', 5' and 6' hold, that C is twice differentiable, and $\partial g(s_1, 0)/\partial\phi > C'(0)$. Then an optimal contract $(w(s_i), l(s_i))$ satisfies*

$$\frac{\partial g}{\partial \phi}(s_n, \phi(l(s_n))) = C'(\phi(l(s_n))); \tag{54}$$

$$\frac{\partial g}{\partial \phi}(s_i, \phi(l(s_i))) \geqq C'(\phi(l(s_i))) \quad \text{for all } i < n; \tag{55}$$

and there is strict inequality for some i in (55) *if* $(w(s_i), l(s_i))$ *is not also a solution to* (1)–(3) *(with $m = 1$, g replacing f, ϕ replacing l and $C(\phi)$ replacing Rl).*

This proposition tells us that in the second-best ϕ will be too low. It follows that there will be underemployment of every input that is "normal", i.e. of every input for which the cost minimizing solution l_q of (52) is increasing in ϕ.

We now consider a second case where the underemployment result generalizes. Suppose that

$$f(s, l) = \textstyle\sum_{q=1}^{Q} s_q f_q(l_q) \tag{56}$$

where the s_q are independent positive random variables, the f_q are non-negative real-valued functions, and $s = (s_1, \ldots, s_Q)$. In this case it is as if there were Q distinct activities, each one corresponding to a different input. One is led to consider the possibility that the worker's wage—which we know from (10) is a function of l—can be written as a separable function of the inputs: $w(l) = \sum_{q=1}^{Q} w_q(l_q)$ for some real-valued functions w_q. If $w(l)$ is separable in this way, then the analysis of Section 2 can be applied. For in state s the firm chooses l to maximize $\sum s_q f_q(l_q) - \sum w_q(l_q)$, i.e. to maximize $s_q f_q(l_q) - w_q(l_q)$ for each q. For each q, this problem is similar to that considered in Section 2. In particular, the underemployment result will generalize for each input (note that Assumptions 5 and 6 automatically hold under (56)).

Unfortunately, in general, $w(l)$ cannot be written as $\sum w_q(l_q)$. This was first observed by Adams and Yellen (1976) in the price discrimination literature, where the phenomenon is known as "bundling".[23] It turns out, however, that $w(l)$ does equal $\sum w_q(l_q)$ for the special case where V is quadratic and U is linear (this violates Assumption 3). In this case, therefore, we have underemployment of each input.

Proposition 5. *Assume Assumption 2' and that (56) holds where the s_q are independent. Assume also that*

$$U(x) \equiv x, \quad V(y) \equiv cy + dy^2, \quad d < 0.$$

Let $(w(s_i), l(s_i))$ be an optimal contract. Write $s_i = (s_{1i_1}, s_{2i_2}, \ldots, s_{Qi_Q})$. Then there exist functions $w_1, \ldots, w_Q, l_1, \ldots, l_Q$ such that

$$l(s_i) = (l_1(s_{1i_1}), l_2(s_{2i_2}), \ldots, l_Q(s_{Qi_Q})) \quad \text{for all } i = 1, \ldots, n, \tag{57}$$

$$w(s_i) = \sum_{q=1}^{Q} w_q(l_q(s_{qi_q})) \quad \text{for all } i = 1, \ldots, n. \tag{58}$$

Furthermore,

$$s_{qn_q} f_q'(l_q(s_{qn_q})) = R \quad \text{for all } q = 1, \ldots, Q, \tag{59}$$

$$s_{qi_q} f_q'(l_q(s_{qi_q})) > R \quad \text{for all } q = 1, \ldots, Q \text{ and } i < n. \tag{60}$$

Proof. See Appendix 3.

5. FURTHER EXTENSIONS

In this section, we consider some further extensions of the model of Section 2.

A. *The case where profits are observed*

In the model of Section 2, we assumed that the workers could observe employment, but not the firm's gross profit (or revenue) $f(s, l)$. This is important because, if $f(s, l)$ is observed, the first-best can be achieved under asymmetric information. To see this (for the case $m = 1$), note that optimal risk-sharing, i.e. (6), implies that both the worker's net income $w(s_i) - Rl(s_i)$ and the firm's net profit $f(s_i, l(s_i)) - w(s_i)$ will depend only on the net social surplus $f(s_i, l(s_i)) - Rl(s_i)$. Thus we can write

$$f(s_i, l(s_i)) - w(s_i) = h(f(s_i, l(s_i)) - Rl(s_i))$$

and

$$w(s_i) - Rl(s_i) = k(f(s_i, l(s_i)) - Rl(s_i))$$

for some functions h, k. In the second-best, if $f(s, l)$ and l are observed so is net social surplus, and so we can ensure that the same wages are paid in each state as in the first-best. Now if we let the firm choose l, it will select l to maximize $h(f(s_i, l) - Rl)$, and so we will also get the same employment rule as in the first-best.

Thus the model of Section 2, as it stands, is reasonable as a model of a small owner-managed company, the profits of which are not observable, but does not seem reasonable as a model of a public company or corporation where profit statements are published and dividend payments can be observed. We now argue that, with some modifications, it is also relevant for a public company or corporation. Suppose that the firm is run by a manager and that the firm's profits depend on how hard this manager works. In particular, let gross revenue be given by

$$\pi = f(l, s, a) \tag{61}$$

where $a \geq 0$ is managerial effort. We will assume that the worker and owners can observe l and π, but not s or a. Thus in order to induce the manager to work hard, the owners reward him according to the observed performance of the firm, that is, his salary is some function $I(l, \pi)$ (the owners and manager are thus in a principal-agent relationship). The manager is assumed to observe s before choosing a and l. We assume that the owners are risk-neutral.

We suppose that the manager, ceteris paribus, dislikes working hard. Specifically, we assume that the manager's utility is given by

$$V(I(l, \pi) - C(a)) \qquad (62)$$

where $C(a)$, which is increasing and convex, represents the cost of effort. Here V represents the attitudes to risk of the manager. The worker's utility function is $U(w - Rl)$ as before.

Since the worker is risk-averse, it is clearly optimal for the risk-neutral owners to offer him complete insurance, i.e. to set $w(s_i) - Rl(s_i) = w^*$, where $U(w^*) = \bar{U}$ (there is no moral hazard on the worker's side). That is, we can imagine that the owners pay the worker $w^* + Rl(s_i)$ directly, pay the manager $I(l, \pi)$ and that in return the manager hands over to them the gross revenue π. The owners' expected profits are then given by

$$E(\pi - I(l, \pi) - Rl(s_i) - w^*). \qquad (63)$$

Note that this is the same arrangement as discussed in Section 3, Remark 7.

It is helpful to think of the manager's choice variables as being l and π rather than l and a. That is, we write the manager's expected utility as

$$EV(I(l, \pi) - C(a(l, \pi, s))), \qquad (64)$$

where $a = a(l, \pi, s)$ is the inverse of (61), i.e.

$$\pi = f(l, s, a(l, \pi, s)). \qquad (65)$$

Incentive compatibility tells us that in state s the manager will choose $l(s)$, $\pi(s)$ such that

$$l(s), \pi(s) \text{ maximizes } I(l, \pi) - C(a(l, \pi, s)). \qquad (66)$$

An optimal contract consists of a salary schedule $I(l, \pi)$, and employment and profit functions $l(s)$, $\pi(s)$, which maximize (64) subject to (66) and the condition that $(63) \geq \bar{R}$. This last constraint reflects the fact that owners require a minimum expected profit to invest in the firm.

This problem is formally equivalent to that considered in Section 4. The variables l, π are like different inputs, $\pi - C(a(l, \pi, s))$ corresponds to the firm's revenue function $f(s, l) - \sum_{q>1} R_q l_q$, and $I(l, \pi)$ corresponds to $\pi - w(l, \pi)$. Thus Proposition 4 provides conditions under which l and π will be lower in the second-best than in the first-best. In Appendix 1, we present an example to illustrate this.

The intuition underlying the example is as follows. When times are bad, the manager would like the owners and workers to accept a lower total payment, $(\pi - I)$. If s is not publically observable, however, the only way to do this is to gear owners' and workers' payments to l and π. l and π are useful signals about the state s, but both are imperfect in view of the extra input, managerial effort. Therefore, in order to "prove" that things are really bad, the manager will have to set both l and π too low from an efficiency point of view.

The introduction of a manager who takes an action a also justifies the assumption made throughout that the firm is risk-averse. The risk-aversion of the firm simply reflects the risk-aversion of the manager. Furthermore, the manager is risk-averse because the owners, in order to make him work hard, give him an incentive scheme $I(l, \pi)$ which makes him bear a lot of risk. That is, in contrast to an ordinary shareholder, the manager is not allowed (by the owners) to diversify away risk, since this would give him no incentive to work.

B. *Multiperiod contracts*

Suppose that productive activity takes place at dates $1, \ldots, T$, rather than just at date 1. The contract at date 0 will now specify how wages and employment will be determined at each date and in each event. In general the analysis becomes much more complicated. We consider here two cases where the analysis generalizes fairly directly. In these cases, R is to be interpreted as the wage which can be earned in a non-contract occupation. To make this clear, we will write $U = U(w + R(\bar{l} - l))$ (see Section 2).

Suppose that there is a perfect bond market which both the firm and worker have access to. Consider first the case where the firm learns the state of the world, i.e. the full history of the environment from date 1 to date T, at date 1 before it makes any employment decisions. The firm will report this state to the worker at date 1 and the contract will specify a wage and employment path from date 1 to date T. Since both parties will therefore know the complete employment and wage path at date 1, the firm's utility at date 1 will depend only on the net present value of profits, and the worker's utility at date 1 will depend only on the net present value of wages. Thus at date 0 the firm's *expected* utility can be written as

$$EV(f(s, l) - w) \tag{67}$$

and the worker's expected utility as

$$EU(w + \sum_{t=1}^{T} R_t(\bar{l} - l_t)) \tag{68}$$

where l_t is labour supply at date t, $l = (l_1, \ldots, l_T)$, $f(s, l)$ is the present value of profits from date 1 to date T in state s, w is the present value of wages from date 1 to date T, and R_t is the (discounted) reservation wage of a unit of labour at date t.

It should be clear that this model is similar to that of the last section. In particular, $(l_1, \ldots, l_T)$ correspond to different inputs. Define $w' = w - \sum_{t>1} R_t l_t$. Then the firm's expected utility is $EV(f(s, l) - w' - \sum_{t>1} R_t l_t)$ and the worker's is $EU(w' - R_1 l_1 + \sum_t R_t \bar{l})$. The formulation is now identical to that of the last section. Thus Propositions 4 and 5 provide conditions under which the underemployment result generalizes to a multiperiod setting.

The assumption that the firm learns the whole state of the world at date 1 is very strong. It is more realistic to suppose that the firm obtains new information at each date t. Consider the case where the firm's gross revenue at each date $t = 1, \ldots, T$ is given by

$$f_t(\tilde{s}_t, l_t) \tag{69}$$

where the $\tilde{s}_t$ are random variables, $s = (s_1, \ldots, s_T)$, and l_t is labour supply at each date. Assume that the firm learns the realization s_t of $\tilde{s}_t$ at date t before l_t is chosen (the worker never learns s_t). For simplicity, take $T = 2$. Then the contract can be thought of as follows. At date 1, the firm reports s_1, and corresponding wages $w_1(s_1)$ and employment $l_1(s_1)$ at date 1 are determined. At date 2, the firm reports s_2, and this, together with the previous report s_1, determines wages $w_2(s_1, s_2)$ at date 2.

Assume that the firm and worker have access to a perfect bond market between date 1 and date 2, and suppose for simplicity that the rate of interest is zero. Assume also that all consumption takes place at date 2 (labour, however, is supplied at dates 1 and 2). Then we can assume that all wages are paid at date 2, i.e. we do not have to distinguish between $w_1(s_1)$ and $w_2(s_1, s_2)$. Write total wages as $w(s_1, s_2)$. Let s_1 take on n_1 possible values and s_2 n_2 possible values. Suppose finally that s_1, s_2 are independent, and that Prob $[s_1 = s_{1i}] = \pi_i$, Prob $[s_2 = s_{2k}] = \hat{\pi}_k$. Then an optimal contract is a vector $(l_1(s_{1i}), w(s_{1i}, s_{2k}), l_2(s_{1i}, s_{2k}))_{i=1,\ldots,n_1, k=1,\ldots,n_2}$, which solves:

$$\text{Maximize } \sum_{i=1}^{n_1} \sum_{k=1}^{n_2} \pi_i \hat{\pi}_k V[f_1(s_{1i}, l_1(s_{1i})) + f_2(s_{2k}, l_2(s_{1i}, s_{2k})) - w(s_{1i}, s_{2k})] \tag{70}$$

subject to

$$f_2(s_{2k}, l_2(s_{1i}, s_{2k})) - w(s_{1i}, s_{2k}) \geqq f_2(s_{2k}, l_2(s_{1i}, s_{2j})) - w(s_{1i}, s_{2j}) \tag{71}$$

for all $j = 1, \ldots, n_2, k = 1, \ldots, n_2, i = 1, \ldots, n_1,$

$$\sum_{k=1}^{n_2} \hat{\pi}_k V[f_1(s_{1i}, l_1(s_{1i})) + f_2(s_{2k}, l_2(s_{1i}, s_{2k})) - w(s_{1i}, s_{2k})]$$

$$\geq \sum_{k=1}^{n_2} \hat{\pi}_k V[f_1(s_{1i}, l_1(s_{1i})) + f_2(s_{2k}, l_2(s_{1j}, s_{2k})) - w(s_{1j}, s_{2k})] \tag{72}$$

for all $i = 1, \ldots, n_1, j = 1, \ldots, n_1,$

$$\sum_{i=1}^{n_1} \sum_{k=1}^{n_2} \pi_i \hat{\pi}_k U(w(s_{1i}, s_{2k}) + R_1(\bar{l} - l_1(s_{1i})) + R_2(\bar{l} - l_2(s_{1i}, s_{2k}))) \geq \bar{U}. \tag{73}$$

We ignore (12), i.e. we assume $\mathcal{I} = \mathcal{I}' = (-\infty, \infty)$.

(71)–(72) are the truth telling constraints. (71) says that, whatever is reported at date 1, it must pay the firm to tell the truth at date 2. (72) says that it is in the firm's interest to tell the truth at date 1.

In general this problem is considerably more complicated than that of Section 2 since (72) involves the firm's attitudes to risk. One case where we can simplify matters is where V is exponential ($V(y) = -e^{-by}$, $b > 0$), and U is linear.[24] If V is exponential, $V(x + y) = -V(x)V(y)$ and so the right-hand side of (72) can be rewritten as

$$-V(f_1(s_{1i}, l_1(s_{1j})))[\sum_k \hat{\pi}_k V(f_2(s_{2k}, l_2(s_{1j}, s_{2k})) - w(s_{1j}, s_{2k}))]. \tag{74}$$

Now let γ_j satisfy

$$V(\gamma_j) = \sum_k \hat{\pi}_k V(f_2(s_{2k}, l_2(s_{1j}, s_{2k})) - w(s_{1j}, s_{2k})). \tag{75}$$

Then (74) can be rewritten as

$$-V(f_1(s_{1i}, l_1(s_{1j})))[V(\gamma_j)] = V(f_1(s_{1i}, l_1(s_{1j})) + \gamma_j). \tag{76}$$

Thus the constraints (72) become

$$f_1(s_{1i}, l_1(s_{1i})) + \gamma_i \geq f_1(s_{1i}, l_1(s_{1j})) + \gamma_j \quad \text{for all } i = 1, \ldots, n_1, j = 1, \ldots, n_1. \tag{77}$$

These conditions do not involve attitudes to risk and are very similar in form to (10). It thus should not be surprising that a version of Result 1 can be established as long as for $t = 1, 2$:

$$\frac{\partial f_t}{\partial l}(s_{ti}, l) > \frac{\partial f_t}{\partial l}(s_{t,i-1}, l) \quad \text{for all } l \text{ and } i = 2, \ldots, n_t, \tag{78}$$

$$f_t(s_{ti}, l) \geq f_t(s_{t,i-1}, l) \quad \text{for all } l \text{ and } i = 2, \ldots, n_t, \tag{79}$$

with strict inequality if $l > 0$.

In particular, we may replace the condition that (71) holds for all k, j and i by the condition that (71) holds for all $k, j = k - 1$ and i, and $l_2(s_{1i}, s_{2k})$ is increasing in k for each i; and we may replace the condition that (77) holds for all i and j by the condition that (77) holds for all i and $j = i - 1$ and $l_1(s_{1i})$ is increasing in i.

We may now apply the same argument as in Proposition 2 to conclude that we will have underemployment at each date. In particular, the following is established in Appendix 3.

Proposition 6. *Assume that Assumption 2 holds for $f_1, f_2, V(y) \equiv -e^{-by}, b > 0$, $U(x) \equiv x, s_1, s_2$ are independent, and that (78)–(79) hold for $t = 1, 2$. Let $(l_1(s_{1i}), w(s_{1i}, s_{2k}), l_2(s_{1i}, s_{2k}))_{i=1,\ldots,n_1, k=1,\ldots,n_2}$ solve (70)–(73). Then*

$$\frac{\partial f_2}{\partial l}(s_{2k}, l_2(s_{1i}, s_{2k})) \geq R_2 \text{ for all } i, k, \text{ with equality if and only if } k = n_2; \tag{80}$$

$$\frac{\partial f_1}{\partial l}(s_{1i}, l_1(s_{1i})) \geq R_1 \text{ for all } i, \text{ with equality if and only if } i = n_1.[25] \tag{81}$$

22   REVIEW OF ECONOMIC STUDIES

C. *Uncertainty about the reservation wage R*

We have assumed that the reservation wage R is a known constant. As we noted in Section 2, there is no difficulty in generalizing our analysis to the case where $\tilde{R}$ is a random variable as long as its realization is observed by all parties (the contract will now simply make wages and employment conditional on R). New problems arise, however, if there is asymmetric information about R.

Suppose, for example, that the worker observes the realization of $\tilde{R}$ but the firm does not. Consider first the case where both the firm and worker observe $\tilde{s}$. Then the model is essentially the same as that of Section 2, but with the roles of the firm and worker reversed. In particular, if the worker's utility is $U(w - \tilde{R}l)$, the corresponding versions of Assumptions 5 and 6 hold, i.e. the marginal "product" of labour $(-R)$ and the total "product" $(w - Rl)$ are positively related, and so, by the argument of Proposition 2, we will get *underemployment*. The idea here is that, in the first-best, high $\tilde{R}$'s would call for high w's, with possibly little variation in l. In the second-best, there is therefore an incentive for the worker to overstate R. In order to make this unattractive, a high R will be accompanied by a low l rather than a high w.

In the formulation just described, $\tilde{R}$ is the disutility of effort. We noted, however, in Section 2 that $\tilde{R}$ can also be thought of as earnings elsewhere. In this case, the worker's utility is $U(w + \tilde{R}(\bar{l} - l))$, where $\bar{l} \geqq l \geqq 0$. Now the marginal "product" of labour $(-R)$, and the total "product" $w + R(\bar{l} - l)$ are negatively related. Thus we will now get *overemployment* (see Cooper (1981) and Moore (1982)). The reason is that in this situation, in the first-best, low R's call for high wages. Thus the worker has an incentive to understate R. He is discouraged from doing this in the second-best by making l high when R is low.[26]

Let us consider now briefly the case where the worker observes R (but the firm doesn't) and the firm observes s (but the worker doesn't), i.e. there is asymmetric information on both sides. This is much more complicated, as one might expect. The contract will now specify that at date 1 the firm will report s and the worker will report R, and that, given these reports, there will be a corresponding wage $w(s, R)$ and employment $l(s, R)$.

The incentive compatibility constraints are now more complicated since the firm's optimal report depends on the worker's reporting strategy, and vice versa. Under truth telling, however, the worker's (resp. firm's) report has the same probability distribution as the underlying reservation wage R (resp. underlying s). Assume $\tilde{s}$ and $\tilde{R}$ are independent and that their probability distributions are common knowledge. Then we may write the firm's truth telling constraints as

$$s_r = s \text{ maximizes } E_R V[f(s, l(s_r, R)) - w(s_r, R)] \quad \text{for all } s, \tag{82}$$

where the expectation is with respect to R. Similarly the worker's truth telling constraint can be written as

$$R_r = R \text{ maximizes } E_s[U(w(s, R_r) - Rl(s, R_r))] \quad \text{for all } R, \tag{83}$$

where the expectation is with respect to s.

In the incentive compatibility literature, (82)–(83) describe what is known as a Bayesian equilibrium (in the sense of Harsanyi). An optimal contract is one which maximizes the firm's expected utility subject to (82)–(83) and the constraint that the worker's expected utility is no less than $\bar{U}$. Little is known in general about the properties of an optimal contract. One interesting result, which is due to d'Aspremont and Gerard-Varet (1979), is that if the firm and worker are risk neutral, the optimal contract under symmetric information can be sustained under asymmetric information, i.e. the second-best equals the first-best (this result depends on the assumption that s and R are independent; see Laffont and Maskin (1979)). Thus there is no productive inefficiency under risk neutrality. Whether when U and V are strictly concave, the optimal contract will lead to underemployment is not known.

It should be noted that Hall and Lillien (1979) (who effectively consider the case of risk neutrality) *do* find productive inefficiency in an optimal contract. The reason is that they restrict their attention to a smaller class of feasible contracts than those in (82)–(83); in particular, they do not allow joint reporting by the firm and the worker.

6. CONCLUSIONS

In this paper, we have tried to summarize and extend recent work on optimal labour contracts under asymmetric information. Our particular interest has been whether this work provides a rationale for the idea that when a firm's marginal revenue product of labour is low, there will be underemployment (in Walrasian terms). In the basic model of Azariadis (1982) and Grossman and Hart (1981, 1982), there is underemployment. Once one gets beyond this model, we have seen that the analysis of optimal contracts quickly becomes intractable. We have, however, been able to generalize the underemployment result in certain directions.

At this point, it is appropriate to mention a number of weaknesses and qualifications of our analysis. The most important concerns the interpretation of a contract. In reality, there exist few contracts between firms and workers containing the amount of detail which this paper suggests is appropriate. Furthermore contracts tend to be in force for limited periods of time, and are then renegotiated. It is for these reasons that people have appealed to the idea of implicit, rather than explicit, contracts. Presumably one important reason that we do not see explicit, long-term contracts in reality is bounded rationality: individuals simply cannot conceive of all the possible eventualities that may occur, and so prefer to adopt a "wait and see" approach.

However, if one appeals to the idea of an implicit contract, one has to say how it is enforced. Consider the model of Section 2. What is to stop a firm at date 1 from announcing a wage-employment function which is different from that of the implicit contract? If no precommitment is possible, one might even argue that the only stable (or perfect) outcomes at date 1 are those that exhaust all gains from trade ex-post. In this case, of course, employment will be at the Walrasian level.

Presumably, one thing which may keep a firm to an unwritten wage-employment function is reputation. A firm that, contrary to its implicit contract, tries to force its workers to take a wage cut may find it difficult to recruit other workers in the future. While this argument is suggestive, a formal analysis which uses reputation effects to justify implicit contracts has yet to be provided.[27,28]

We have noted that the firm is always made worse off by the asymmetry of information. It follows that it is in the interest of the owners or managers to agree in advance to reveal the state s to the workers if this is at all possible, e.g. by showing workers the accounts or putting some workers on the board of directors. It is a basic hypothesis of the approach taken in this paper that there are significant obstacles to doing this in practice. One problem is that it is not clear what the appropriate indicators of a firm's long-run performance are; current accounting profits may be quite a poor signal (see the model of Section 5A). Also it does not follow that simply by being present at board meetings workers will receive the same information about the company as management does (some of the most important discussions may take place off the board, particularly once workers are made board members). The basic point is that, to the extent that managers and workers have different functions in the firm, they will have access to different information and, for moral hazard reasons, it may be very difficult to share this information.

In order to motivate the idea of a contract between a firm and workers, we have appealed to the existence of firm-specific training and mobility costs. These, however, are not essential for our underemployment result. Suppose, for example, that there are no lock-in effects, and that the firm cannot sign a risk-sharing agreement with the workers (the firm, say, hires all its labour in a spot market at date 1). The firm might still sign a risk-sharing agreement with another party, e.g. an insurance company or the firm's shareholders (if we think of the firm as being run by a manager). In this case, employment (if observable) will still be a useful signal about profitability, and we may apply our analysis to show that an optimal risk-sharing agreement will entail underemployment (see Section 5A).

We have noted in Section 2 that our analysis does not explain "involuntary" unemployment, in the sense of workers with identical characteristics being treated differently at the lay-off date. Nor does it explain "involuntary" unemployment at the contract date.[29] What the model *does* explain is inefficient and excessive unemployment after the contract has been signed.[30] How important this inefficient employment will be in explaining the observations about aggregate fluctuations referred to in the introduction remains to be seen. A starting point in using the theory of labour contracts under asymmetric information to build a model of macroeconomic shocks has been made by Grossman, Hart and Maskin (1982).

APPENDIX 1

Example Illustrating Section 5A

Suppose that $\pi = f(l, s, a) = sh(l)a$, where $s \geqq 0$ and h is a well-behaved production function with $h(0) > 0$. In the first-best, l and a are chosen to maximize net profit

$$sh(l)a - C(a) - Rl. \tag{A.1}$$

Let $x = (\pi/h(l)) = sa$. Then we can rewrite (A.1) as

$$xh(l) - Rl - C\left(\frac{x}{s}\right). \tag{A.2}$$

A necessary condition for (A.2) to be maximized is that l maximizes

$$xh(l) - Rl. \tag{A.3}$$

Let $\gamma(x) = \max_l [xh(l) - Rl]$. Then in the first-best, x is chosen to maximize

$$\gamma(x) - C\left(\frac{x}{s}\right). \tag{A.4}$$

The first term in (A.4) is convex in x while the second is concave. We will assume that h and C are such that the difference is concave.

In the second-best, the manager maximizes (66). As in the first-best, it is convenient to regard l and x as the manager's choice variables. (66) then becomes

$$\text{Maximize}_{x,l} \hat{I}(l, x) - C\left(\frac{x}{s}\right), \tag{A.5}$$

where $\hat{I}(l, x) \equiv I(l, xh(l))$. From (A.5) it is clear that without loss of generality we can write $\hat{I}(l, x)$ as some function of x only: $\hat{I}(l, x) = \beta(x)$ (for if $\hat{I}(l_1, \hat{x}) > \hat{I}(l_2, \hat{x})$, the manager will never choose $l = l_2$ when $x = \hat{x}$ and so we might as well set $\hat{I}(l_1, \hat{x}) = \hat{I}(l_2, \hat{x})$). So the manager in state s solves:

$$\text{Maximize}_x \, \beta(x) - C\left(\frac{x}{s}\right) \tag{A.6}$$

and his expected utility is

$$EV\left(\beta(x)-C\left(\frac{x}{s}\right)\right). \tag{A.7}$$

The owners' expected profit is

$$E(xh(l)-Rl-\beta(x)-w^*). \tag{A.8}$$

It follows from (A.8) that, since (A.7) does not depend on l directly, l will be chosen to maximize (A.3) in an optimal contract (as in the first-best). Thus we may rewrite (A.8) as

$$E(\gamma(x)-\beta(x)-w^*). \tag{A.9}$$

An optimal contract consists of functions $\beta(x)$ and $x(s)$ which maximize (A.7) subject to the constraint that $x(s)$ solves (A.6) for each s and that $(A.9) \geq \bar{R}$. This problem is formally the same as that considered in Section 2. Here x corresponds to l, $-C(x/s)$ to $f(s, l)$, $\beta(x)$ to $-w(l)$, and $\gamma(x)$ to $-Rl$. Note that Assumptions 5 and 6 are satisfied since the marginal product of x, $-(1/s)C'(x/s)$, and the total product, $-C(x/s)$, are positively related. Thus we may apply Proposition 2 to conclude that x will be lower in the second-best than in the first-best. Now in both the second-best and first-best, l is chosen to maximize (A.3). It follows that if x is lower in the second-best, so is l. Hence there will be underemployment.

APPENDIX 2

In this appendix we elaborate on Remark 6 of Section 2 on the use of random contracts.

A striking example of this is the following. Consider the model of Section 2 with $m = 1$. Suppose that the firm is extremely risk-averse, i.e. $-V''/V'$ is very large, and the worker is risk-neutral. In fact consider the limiting case where $-V''/V'$ is infinite, so that the firm is (lexicographic) "maximin". This case is considered in Grossman and Hart (1982), where it is shown that (for the case where l can only take on the values 0 and 1), if only deterministic schemes are considered, underemployment will be at its highest, i.e. the difference between the first-best and second-best is in some sense greatest. We now show that if the firm is infinitely risk-averse, and lotteries are allowed, the first-best can be achieved under asymmetric information!

Since the firm is infinitely risk-averse, in the first-best the worker will provide complete insurance, i.e. $\hat{l}(s_i)$ will satisfy (5) and $\hat{w}(s_i)$ will be such that

$$f(s_i, \hat{l}(s_i)) - \hat{w}(s_i) = \text{a constant } k, \text{ independent of } s_i. \tag{A.10}$$

Now if this deterministic contract is tried in the second-best, (10) will obviously be violated since, by Assumption 6,

$$f(s_i, \hat{l}(s_{i-1})) - \hat{w}(s_{i-1}) > f(s_{i-1}, \hat{l}(s_{i-1})) - \hat{w}(s_{i-1})$$
$$= f(s_i, \hat{l}(s_i)) - \hat{w}(s_i). \tag{A.11}$$

However, consider the following random contract: if the firm reports $s = s_i$, then with probability $(1 - \varepsilon)$ it obtains labour supply $\hat{l}(s_i)$ and pays wage $\hat{w}(s_i)$, and with probability ε it obtains labour supply equal to zero and pays the worker $-k + \eta(s_i)$. Here ε and $\eta(s_i)$ are small positive numbers satisfying

$$\eta(s_1) > \eta(s_2) > \cdots > \eta(s_n). \tag{A.12}$$

We will assume that $f(s_i, 0) = 0$ for all s_i.

Note first that if the firm reports truthfully the worker does almost as well out of this contract as out of the first-best one, since the contracts are the same with probability

$(1-\varepsilon)$. On the other hand, the firm also does approximately as well, since if it reports s_i, the worst that can happen is that $l = 0$, $w = -k + \eta(s_i)$, in which case profit is only slightly less than k (in this case, the worker's wage is negative if $k > 0$; we ignore the possibility of worker bankruptcy).

Will the firm tell the truth? The answer is yes. For suppose $s = s_i$ and the firm announces s_j. Since the firm is maximin, it is pessimistic and puts all the weight on the worst outcome. If $j > i$, the worst outcome is that $l = \hat{l}(s_j)$ and $w = \hat{w}(s_j)$, in which case the firm's profit is

$$f(s_i, \hat{l}(s_j)) - \hat{w}(s_j) < f(s_j, \hat{l}(s_j)) - \hat{w}(s_j) = k, \tag{A.13}$$

by Assumption 6. Hence for $\eta(s_i)$ small enough,

$$f(s_i, \hat{l}(s_j)) - \hat{w}(s_j) < k - \eta(s_i), \tag{A.14}$$

which means that the firm does worse by reporting s_j if $j > i$, than if it tells the truth.

On the other hand, if $j < i$, the worst outcome is that $l = 0$ and $w = -k + \eta(s_j)$, in which case the firm's profits are $k - \eta(s_j)$. In view of (A.12) truth telling would again have been better.

We see then that this random contract satisfies the truth-telling constraints. Furthermore, by letting $\eta \to 0$, $\varepsilon \to 0$, we can asymptotically approach the first-best.

This example shows that random contracts may provide considerable gains over deterministic contracts in particular cases. It is important to realize, however, that the example above where one can use random contracts to obtain the first-best is very special, and depends critically on the firm being extremely risk-averse. In general, the second-best will be worse than the first-best, even with random-contracts.

It would obviously be very nice if we could extend the analysis of Section 2 to deal with the possibility of random contracts. Unfortunately, this seems very difficult. The problem is that now the truth telling constraints (10) take the form

$$\int V(f(s_i, l) - w) dF(w, l; s_i) \geqq \int V(f(s_i, l) - w) dF(w, l; s_j). \tag{A.15}$$

These are more complicated than the constraints (10) since they involve the firm's attitudes to risk. It now seems much harder to say which of the truth telling constraints are binding. There seems in particular no obvious generalization of Result 1. Because of this, it is not clear whether the underemployment result generalizes to the case of lotteries.

A small amount is known, however. First if there are only two states s_1 and s_2, it can be shown that Proposition 2 holds, i.e. we get efficient employment in state s_2 (with probability 1), and underemployment in state s_1 (with probability 1). More generally, for the case of n states, there will be underemployment in the worst state s_1 (given Assumption 5 and 6, the argument establishing underemployment in Section 2 continues to hold for state j as long as there is equality in (10) only for states $i > j$; this must be true for the worst state). Also for the case where U is linear and either $f(s, l) = sl$, or there is one worker and l can only take the values 0 and 1, underemployment has been established by Moore (1982).

A possible justification for *not* considering lotteries has been given by Grossman and Hart (1982). Suppose that the contract specifies that, given the reported $s = s_r$, l and w are to be drawn from the joint distribution $F(w, l; s_r)$. Then the firm could arrange in advance with a (risk-neutral) insurance company that, if it reports s_r, it will pay the insurance company

$$f(s_r, \hat{l}) - \hat{w} - \int (f(s_r, l) - w) dF(w, l; s_r)$$

HART   CONTRACTS UNDER ASYMMETRIC INFORMATION   27

if the outcome of the draw is $l = \hat{l}, w = \hat{w}$. As long as the insurance company can observe the firm's report and the outcome of the lottery, it will be prepared to accept this arrangement (as no moral hazard is involved). On the other hand, the firm is better off since it has transformed a random return stream into a non-random one with the same mean. By doing this, the firm effectively subverts the use of random contracts.

This story only makes sense, of course, if the worker cannot observe this side-arrangement with the insurance company. If he could, he would prohibit it. Once we assume that the worker cannot observe side-arrangements, however, we must also consider the possibility that the firm will try to make contracts with other parties, e.g. insurance companies, even when the original contract with the worker is deterministic, as in Section 2 (such side-arrangements, in contrast to the above, will involve moral hazard). The analysis of optimal contracts when side-contracts cannot be observed is relatively unexplored territory, although some progress has been made in a related context by Arnott and Stiglitz (1982).

APPENDIX 3

In this appendix, we provide proofs of a number of results.

Proof of Result 1 *and Proposition* 2.   Note first that (10) implies (10')(a). Also setting $i = i_0, j = (i_0 - 1)$ and $i = (i_0 - 1), j = i_0$ in (10) and adding yields

$$f(s_i, \textstyle\sum_k l_k(s_i)) - f(s_i, \textstyle\sum_k l_k(s_{i-1})) \geqq f(s_{i-1}, \textstyle\sum_k l_k(s_i)) - f(s_{i-1}, \textstyle\sum_k l_k(s_{i-1})) \qquad \text{(A.16)}$$

which implies, by Assumption 5, (10')(b). Thus (10) implies (10'). Hence, if we can show that the solution to (9), (10'), (11), (12) satisfies (10), we will have established that $(10) \Rightarrow (10') \Rightarrow (10)$, i.e. we will have proved Result 1.

Consider the problem: maximize (9) subject to (10'), (11), (12). Existence of a solution follows from standard arguments. (15)–(16) have been proved in the text. Also (19) must hold, since otherwise wages could be reduced in all states by the same constant amount, and the firm would be better off.

Lemma 1.   *Suppose* $f(s_i, ml(s_i)) - mw(s_i) > f(s_i, ml(s_{i-1})) - mw(s_{i-1})$ *for some i at a solution to* (9), (10'), (11), (12). *Then* $l(s_{i-1}) = l^*(s_{i-1})$, *the first-best employment level, and* $w(s_i) - Rl(s_i) > w(s_{i-1}) - Rl(s_{i-1})$.

Proof.   The assumption of the lemma is that (10')(a) is not binding at the optimum. Hence, by Assumption 6,

$$\begin{aligned} f(s_i, ml(s_i)) - mw(s_i) &> f(s_i, ml(s_{i-1})) - mw(s_{i-1}) \\ &\geqq f(s_{i-1}, ml(s_{i-1})) - mw(s_{i-1}) \end{aligned} \qquad \text{(A.17)}$$

and so firm i's net profit is higher in state i than in state $(i-1)$. Suppose that

$$w(s_i) - Rl(s_i) \leqq w(s_{i-1}) - Rl(s_{i-1}),$$

i.e. workers do at least as well in state $(i-1)$ as in state i. We show that this is inconsistent with optimal risk-sharing. For the marginal rate of substitution between income in states s_i and s_{i-1} for the firm is given by

$$\frac{\pi_i V'(f(s_i, ml(s_i)) - mw(s_i))}{\pi_{i-1} V'(f(s_{i-1}, ml(s_{i-1})) - mw(s_{i-1}))} < \frac{\pi_i}{\pi_{i-1}} \leqq \frac{\pi_i U'(w(s_i) - Rl(s_i))}{\pi_{i-1} U'(w(s_{i-1}) - Rl(s_{i-1}))}, \qquad \text{(A.18)}$$

the latter being the marginal rate of substitution between income in states s_i and s_{i-1} for workers. Thus $w(s_i)$ can be raised a little and $w(s_{i-1})$ lowered a little to make both the firm and workers better off. Furthermore (10') will continue to hold if this is done since

28   REVIEW OF ECONOMIC STUDIES

$(10')(a)$ is not binding at i. This contradicts the fact that we are at an optimum. We have therefore proved that

$$w(s_i) - Rl(s_i) > w(s_{i-1}) - Rl(s_{i-1}).$$

This, together with (A.17), implies that $l(s_i) \neq l(s_{i-1})$. It follows that neither $(10')(a)$ nor $(10')(b)$ is binding at i. We already know from the text that $l(s_{i-1}) \leq l^*(s_{i-1})$. Suppose that we have strict inequality. Then raise $l(s_{i-1})$ a little, and raise also $w(s_{i-1})$ so that $f(s_{i-1}, ml(s_{i-1})) - mw(s_{i-1})$ stays constant. The firm is indifferent to such a change, while the workers are better off since $\partial f(s_{i-1}, ml(s_{i-1}))/\partial L > R$. Furthermore, $(10')$ still holds. Thus we have obtained a Pareto improvement, which contradicts the fact that we are at an optimum. This shows that $l(s_i) = l^*(s_i)$. (This is the same argument which we used to establish (15) in the text.) This proves Lemma 1. ‖

We now apply Lemma 1 to show that (10) must hold at a solution to (9), $(10')$, (11), (12). We show first that (10) holds for adjacent i and j, i.e. $j = (i+1)$ or $(i-1)$. Consider $(10')(a)$. Either this is binding at i or it is not. If it is, then by Assumption 5 and $(10')(b)$,

$$[f(s_{i-1}, ml(s_{i-1})) - mw(s_{i-1})] - [f(s_{i-1}, ml(s_i)) - mw(s_i)]$$

$$= f(s_{i-1}, ml(s_{i-1})) - f(s_{i-1}, ml(s_i)) - mw(s_{i-1}) + mw(s_i)$$

$$\geq f(s_i, ml(s_{i-1})) - f(s_i, ml(s_i)) - mw(s_{i-1}) + mw(s_i)$$

$$= 0. \tag{A.19}$$

Therefore, if $(10')(a)$ is binding at i, (10) holds at $i' = (i-1), j' = i$. On the other hand, suppose $(10')(a)$ is not binding at i. Then, by Lemma 1,

$$[f(s_{i-1}, ml(s_{i-1})) - mw(s_{i-1})] - [f(s_{i-1}, ml(s_i)) - mw(s_i)]$$

$$> [f(s_{i-1}, ml(s_{i-1})) - mRl(s_{i-1})] - [f(s_{i-1}, ml(s_i)) - mRl(s_i)]$$

$$\geq 0 \tag{A.20}$$

since $l(s_{i-1}) = l^*(s_{i-1})$, the maximizer of $f(s_{i-1}, L) - RL$. Thus (10) again holds at $i' = (i-1), j' = i$.

We have shown that, whether or not $(10')(a)$ is binding at i, (10) holds at $i' = i - 1, j' = i$ (and at $i' = i, j' = (i-1)$). Applying this for all i, we may conclude that $(10')$ implies that (10) holds for all adjacent i, j. The final step is to show that $(10') \Rightarrow (10)$ for all i, j. Note that

$$\begin{cases} f(s_{i-1}, ml(s_{i-1})) - mw(s_{i-1}) \geq f(s_{i-1}, ml(s_{i-2})) - mw(s_{i-2}), \\ l(s_{i-1}) \geq l(s_{i-2}) \end{cases} \tag{A.21}$$

implies, by Assumption 5, that

$$f(s_i, ml(s_{i-1})) - mw(s_{i-1}) \geq f(s_i, ml(s_{i-2})) - mw(s_{i-2}), \tag{A.22}$$

which, together with $(10')(a)$, implies that

$$f(s_i, ml(s_i)) - mw(s_i) \geq f(s_i, ml(s_{i-2})) - mw(s_{i-2}). \tag{A.23}$$

Arguing in this way yields (10) for all $i > j$. A similar argument yields (10) for all $i < j$.

We have therefore shown that the solution to (9), $(10')$, (11), (12) satisfies (10). This establishes Result 1. We have also proved (15)–(16) and (19) of Proposition 2. It remains to establish (17)–(18). However (17) follows from $(10'')(a)$ and Assumption 6.

HART   CONTRACTS UNDER ASYMMETRIC INFORMATION   29

Also, if (10″)(a) is not binding at i, (18) follows from Lemma 1, while if it is binding

$$m[w(s_{i-1}) - Rl(s_{i-1})] = f(s_i, ml(s_{i-1})) - f(s_i, ml(s_i)) + mw(s_i) - Rml(s_{i-1})$$

$$\leq m[w(s_i) - Rl(s_i)] + [f(s_i, ml(s_{i-1})) - Rml(s_{i-1})]$$

$$- [f(s_i, ml(s_i)) - Rml(s_i)]$$

$$\leq m[w(s_i) - Rl(s_i)] \tag{A.24}$$

since $l(s_{i-1}) \leq l(s_i) \leq l^*(s_i)$ and f is concave. Thus (18) is established.

Next we prove that, if $(w_k(s_i), l_k(s_i))$ is not also a solution of (1)–(3), (16) holds with strict inequality for some $i < n$. To do this, we use the first order conditions for problem (9), (10′), (11), (12). These are:

$$-\pi_i V'(f(s_i, ml(s_i)) - mw(s_i)) - \lambda_i + \lambda_{i+1} = -v\pi_i U'(w(s_i) - Rl(s_i)), \tag{A.25}$$

$$\pi_i V'(f(s_i, ml(s_i)) - mw(s_i)) \frac{\partial f}{\partial L}(s_i, ml(s_i)) - \frac{\partial f}{\partial L}(s_{i+1}, ml(s_i))\lambda_{i+1}$$

$$+ \lambda_i \frac{\partial f}{\partial L}(s_i, ml(s_i)) + \mu_i - \mu_{i+1} \leq v\pi_i RU'(w(s_i) - Rl(s_i)), \tag{A.26}$$

for all i, where λ_i, μ_i, v are non-negative Lagrange multipliers corresponding to the constraints (10′)(a), (10′)(b) and (11), respectively, and there is equality in (A.26) if $l(s_i) > 0$. We also have the complementary slackness conditions and

$$\lambda_1 = \lambda_{n+1} = \mu_1 = \mu_{n+1} = 0. \tag{A.27}$$

Suppose that (16) holds with equality for all i. Then $l(s_i) > 0$ for all i and (A.25)–(A.26) simplify to

$$\mu_i - \mu_{i+1} = \left\{ \frac{\partial f}{\partial L}(s_{i+1}, ml(s_i)) - R \right\} \lambda_{i+1} \quad \text{for all } i = 1, \ldots, n. \tag{A.28}$$

Since $\partial f(s_i, ml(s_i))/\partial L = R$, it follows from Assumption 5 that $\mu_i \geq \mu_{i+1}$ for all i. Since $\mu_{n+1} = \mu_1 = 0$, however, this means that $\mu_i = 0$ for all i. Therefore, from (A.28), $\lambda_{i+1} = 0$ for all i. If we set $\lambda_i \equiv \mu_i \equiv 0$ in (A.25)–(A.26), however, we obtain (5)–(6), which are the necessary and sufficient conditions for the solution to (1)–(3). This establishes that, if $(w_k(s_i), l_k(s_i))$ is not a solution of (1)–(3), (16) holds with strict inequality for some $i < n$.

Finally, we show that if workers are risk-neutral (16) holds with strict inequality for all $i < n$. For suppose (16) holds with equality for some i. Then from the argument above, $\mu_i \geq \mu_{i+1}$. Suppose $\mu_i > 0$. Then $l(s_i) = l(s_{i-1})$. Therefore, by Assumption 5,

$$\frac{\partial f}{\partial L}(s_{i-1}, l(s_{i-1})) < \frac{\partial f}{\partial L}(s_i, l(s_{i-1})) = \frac{\partial f}{\partial L}(s_i, l(s_i)) = R,$$

which contradicts (16). It follows that $0 = \mu_i \geq \mu_{i+1}$, i.e. $\mu_{i+1} = 0$. Hence from (A.28) $\lambda_{i+1} = 0$. Applying (A.25) at $i, (i + 1)$, we may conclude that

$$V'(f(s_i, ml(s_i)) - mw(s_i)) \leq v \leq V'(f(s_{i+1}, ml(s_{i+1})) - mw(s_{i+1})). \tag{A.29}$$

But (10′)(a) and Assumption 6 imply that $f(s_{i+1}, ml(s_{i+1})) - mw(s_{i+1}) > f(s_i, ml(s_i)) - mw(s_i)$ (the strict inequality holds since $l(s_i) = l^*(s_i) > 0$), which contradicts (A.29). ∥

Proof of Proposition 3. As in Proposition 2, we replace (27) by (10′) (with $m = 1$ and $\hat{w}$ replacing w). That is, we consider the problem: maximize (26) subject to (10′), (28) and (29). To prove (31)–(32), where the latter has a weak inequality, we use exactly the same argument as in Proposition 2. Suppose (32) is violated. Suppose also that

$l(s_i) > l(s_{i-1})$. Then reduce $l(s_i)$ and $\hat{w}(s_i)$ a little so as to keep $f(s_i, l(s_i)) - \hat{w}(s_i)$ constant. Reduce $w(s_i)$ by the same amount. (10′) will continue to hold, the worker is better off, and the firm and third party are no worse off. This Pareto improvement contradicts the optimality of the contract. Thus (32) holds. On the other hand, if $l(s_i) = l(s_{i-1}) > l(s_{i-2})$, say, then we prove (32) for $(i-1)$, and then conclude that it must also hold for i (note that $l(s_i) = l(s_{i-1}) \Rightarrow w(s_i) = w(s_{i-1})$ by optimal risk-sharing with the third party). A similar argument shows that (31) holds.

Next we prove that a solution of (26), (10′), (28), (29) satisfies (27). (The existence of a third party is crucial for this step.) We show that (10′)(a) will be binding for all i. Suppose not. Then, by (A.17), the firm's profit will be strictly higher in state i than in state $(i-1)$. But suppose we increase $\hat{w}(s_i)$ a little and reduce $\hat{w}(s_{i-1})$ a little so that

$$\pi_i \Delta \hat{w}(s_i) + \pi_{i-1} \Delta \hat{w}(s_{i-1}) = 0. \qquad (A.30)$$

The risk-neutral third party and worker are indifferent to this change, while the firm is made better off since profits become less risky while staying the same in expected terms. Since (10′) continues to hold, this Pareto improvement contradicts the optimality of the contract.

Hence (10′)(a) is binding for all i. But now by the argument of (A.19), (27) holds for all adjacent constraints. Hence, by the argument of (A.21)–(A.23), (27) holds for all i, j.

This establishes (31)–(32) (with weak inequality). To show that (32) holds strictly for all i, one applies the first-order conditions for problem (26), (10′), (28), (29). We omit this since the argument parallels that of the proof of Proposition 2. $\cdot \|$

Proof of Proposition 5. We prove the proposition for the case $Q = 2$. The more general case follows similarly. It will be convenient to change notation: denote s_1 by s, s_2 by t, l_1 by l, l_2 by k, f_1 by f, f_2 by g. Let s take on the values $s_1, \ldots, s_X$ and t the values $t_1, \ldots, t_Y$. We know that s, t are independent. To simplify matters we assume that s, t are uniformly distributed (nothing depends on this). The optimal contract solves:

$$\text{Maximize} \sum_{x,y} \frac{1}{XY} V[s_x f(l_{xy}) + t_y g(k_{xy}) - W_{xy}] \qquad (A.31)$$

subject to

$$s_x f(l_{xy}) + t_y g(k_{xy}) - W_{xy} \geq s_x f(l_{x'y'}) + t_y g(k_{x'y'}) - W_{x'y'} \quad \text{for all } x, y, x', y', \quad (A.32)$$

$$\sum_{x,y} \frac{1}{XY} [W_{xy} - R_1 l_{xy} - R_2 k_{xy}] \geq \bar{U}. \qquad (A.33)$$

Here we are using the notation $l_{xy} = l(s_x, t_y)$, etc., and $W_{xy} = w_{xy} + R_2 k_{xy}$ refers to total input costs for the firm. Call (A.31)–(A.33) problem A.

We now replace (A.32) by the following constraints:

$$s_x f(l_{xy} + t_y g(k_{xy}) - W_{xy} \geq s_x f(l_{(x-1)y}) + t_y g(k_{(x-1)y}) - W_{(x-1)y} \quad \text{for all } y \text{ and } x = 2, \ldots, X,$$
$$(A.34a)$$

$$l_{xy} \geq l_{(x-1)y} \quad \text{for all } y \text{ and } x = 2, \ldots, X, \qquad (A.34b)$$

$$s_x f(l_{xy}) + t_y g(k_{xy}) - W_{xy} \geq s_x f(l_{x(y-1)}) + t_y g(k_{x(y-1)}) - W_{x(y-1)} \quad \text{for all } x \text{ and } y = 2, \ldots, Y,$$
$$(A.35a)$$

$$k_{xy} \geq k_{x(y-1)} \quad \text{for all } x \text{ and } y = 2, \ldots, Y. \qquad (A.35b)$$

These constraints are analogous to (10′). (A.34a), (A.35a) say that a firm in state (s_x, t_y) does not want to report (s_{x-1}, t_y) or $(s_x, t_{(y-1)})$ and (A.34b), (A35b) are monotonicity conditions. Note that (A.34)–(A.35) are implied by (A.32), i.e. they are *necessary*. We will show that they are also *sufficient*, i.e. the solution of (A.31), (A.33), (A.34), (A.35) satisfies (A.32). Call (A.31), (A.33), (A.34), (A.35) problem B.

Consider the first-order conditions for problem B. These yield for all x, y:

$$-\frac{1}{XY} V'_{xy} - \lambda_{xy} + \lambda_{(x+1)y} - \rho_{xy} + \rho_{x(y+1)} = \frac{-\nu}{XY}, \tag{A.36}$$

$$\frac{1}{XY} V'_{xy} s_x f'(l_{xy}) + \lambda_{xy} s_x f'(l_{xy}) - \lambda_{(x+1)y} s_{x+1} f'(l_{xy})$$

$$+ \mu_{xy} - \mu_{(x+1)y} + \rho_{xy} s_x f'(l_{xy}) - \rho_{x(y+1)} s_x f'(l_{xy}) \leqq \frac{\nu}{XY} R_1, \tag{A.37}$$

$$\frac{1}{XY} V'_{xy} t_y g'(k_{xy}) + \lambda_{xy} t_y g'(k_{xy}) - \lambda_{(x+1)y} t_y g'(k_{xy})$$

$$+ \sigma_{xy} - \sigma_{x(y+1)} + \rho_{xy} t_y g'(k_{xy}) - \rho_{x(y+1)} t_{y+1} g'(k_{xy}) \leqq \frac{\nu}{XY} R_2, \tag{A.38}$$

with equality in (A.37) (resp. (A.38)) if l_{xy} (resp. k_{xy}) > 0. Here λ, μ, ρ, σ, ν are non-negative Lagrange multipliers corresponding to the constraints (A.34a), (A.34b), (A.35a), (A.35b), (A.33) respectively and

$$V_{xy} = V[s_x f(l_{xy}) + t_y g(k_{xy}) - W_{xy}].$$

We also have the complementary slackness conditions and

$$\lambda_{1y} = \lambda_{(X+1)y} = \mu_{1y} = \mu_{(X+1)y} = 0 \quad \text{for all } y, \tag{A.39}$$

$$\rho_{x1} = \rho_{x(Y+1)} = \sigma_{x1} = \sigma_{x(Y+1)} = 0 \quad \text{for all } x. \tag{A.40}$$

Proposition 5 says that the solution to this problem has the property that $W_{xy} \equiv (\alpha_x + \beta_y)$ for some α_x, β_y and that $l_{xy} = l_x$, independent of y, $k_{xy} = k_y$, independent of x. If this is the case, the constraints (A.34)–(A.35) simplify to

$$s_x f(l_x) - \alpha_x \geqq s_x f(l_{x-1}) - \alpha_{x-1} \quad \text{for all } x > 1, \tag{A.41a}$$

$$l_x \geqq l_{x-1} \quad \text{for all } x > 1, \tag{A.41b}$$

$$t_y g(k_y) - \beta_y \geqq t_y g(k_{y-1}) - \beta_{y-1} \quad \text{for all } y > 1, \tag{A.42a}$$

$$k_y \geqq k_{y-1} \quad \text{for all } y > 1. \tag{A.42b}$$

Consider now the solution to the problem: maximize (A.31) subject to (A.33) and (A.41)–(A.42), where the choice variables are $\alpha_x, \beta_y, l_x, k_y$. Call this problem C. The first-order conditions for C are:

$$-\frac{1}{XY} \sum_y V'_{xy} - \hat{\lambda}_x + \hat{\lambda}_{x+1} = \frac{-\nu}{X}, \tag{A.43}$$

$$\frac{1}{XY} \sum_y V'_{xy} s_x f'(l_x) + \hat{\lambda}_x s_x f'(l_x) - \hat{\lambda}_{x+1} s_{x+1} f'(l_x) + \hat{\mu}_x - \hat{\mu}_{x+1} \leqq \frac{\nu R_1}{X}, \tag{A.44}$$

$$-\frac{1}{XY} \sum_x V'_{xy} - \hat{\rho}_y + \hat{\rho}_{y+1} = \frac{-\nu}{Y}, \tag{A.45}$$

$$\frac{1}{XY} \sum_x V'_{xy} t_y g'(k_y) + \hat{\rho}_y t_y g'(k_y) - \hat{\rho}_{y+1} t_{y+1} g'(k_y) + \hat{\sigma}_y - \hat{\sigma}_{y+1} \leqq \frac{\nu R_2}{Y}, \tag{A.46}$$

where $\hat{\lambda}$, $\hat{\mu}$ etc, are Lagrange multipliers, and there is equality in (A.44) (resp. (A.46)) if $l_x(\text{resp. } k_y) > 0$. We also have the complementary slackness conditions and

$$\hat{\lambda}_1 = \hat{\lambda}_{X+1} = \hat{\mu}_1 = \hat{\mu}_{X+1} = 0, \tag{A.47}$$

$$\hat{\rho}_1 = \hat{\rho}_{Y+1} = \hat{\sigma}_1 = \hat{\sigma}_{Y+1} = 0. \tag{A.48}$$

We will show that any solution of (A.43)–(A.48) is also a solution of (A.36)–(A.40). Since problems B and C are convex (see Remark 5 of Section 2), this proves that any solution of problem C is also a solution of problem B. Since the solutions of the two problems are unique (again by convexity), the converse is also true: any solution of B is also a solution of C.

Consider the solution of (A.43)–(A.48). Since $V = cy + dy^2$,

$$V'_{xy} = V'(s_x f(l_x) + t_y g(k_y) - \alpha_x - \beta_y) = V'(s_x f(l_x) - \alpha_x) + V'(t_y g(k_y) - \beta_y) - c. \tag{A.49}$$

From this it follows that

$$V'_{xy} = \frac{1}{Y}\sum_y V'_{xy} + \frac{1}{X}\sum_x V'_{xy} - \frac{1}{XY}\sum_x\sum_y V'_{xy}. \tag{A.50}$$

Therefore, using (A.43) and (A.45) and the fact that $\sum_{x=1}^{X}(\hat{\lambda}_{x+1} - \hat{\lambda}_x) = 0$ by (A.47), we obtain

$$-\frac{1}{XY}V'_{xy} - \frac{\hat{\lambda}_x}{Y} + \frac{\hat{\lambda}_{x+1}}{Y} - \frac{\hat{\rho}_y}{X} + \frac{\hat{\rho}_{y+1}}{X} = \frac{-\nu}{XY}. \tag{A.51}$$

This is the same as (A.36) with $\lambda_{xy} = \hat{\lambda}_x/Y, \rho_{xy} = \hat{\rho}_y/X$. Also if we set $\mu_{xy} = \hat{\mu}_x/Y$, $\sigma_{xy} = \hat{\sigma}_y/X, l_{xy} = l_x, k_{xy} = k_y$, it is straightforward to show that, since (A.43), (A.45) and (A.51) hold, (A.37) and (A.38) hold if (A.44) and (A.46) do. This proves that any solution of the first-order conditions of C is also a solution of the first-order conditions of B.

We have therefore shown that every solution of B is a solution of C and vice versa. Therefore problems B and C have the same value. Problem A's value can be no higher since B has fewer constraints. However, by the proof of Proposition 2, any solution of C satisfies all of the truth-telling constraints

$$s_x f(l_x) - \alpha_x \geq s_x f(l_{x'}) - \alpha_{x'}$$

for all x, x' and

$$t_y g(k_y) - \beta_y \geq t_y g(k_{y'}) - \beta_{y'}$$

for all y, y' (Assumptions 5 and 6 are automatically satisfied under (56)). Hence any solution of C satisfies (A.32). Therefore A has the same value as B and C. It follows that since A, B, C are convex problems with unique solutions, they have the same solution. But, by the argument of Section 2, the solution of C satisfies (59)–(60). Therefore, so does the solution of A. ‖

Proof of Proposition 6. Consider the problem: maximize (70) subject to (73) and

$$f_2(s_{2k}, l_2(s_{1i}, s_{2k})) - w(s_{1i}, s_{2k}) \geq f_2(s_{2k}, l_2(s_{1i}, s_{2(k-1)}))$$

$$- w(s_{1i}, s_{2(k-1)}) \quad \text{for all } i \text{ and } k > 1, \tag{A.52a}$$

$$l_2(s_{1i}, s_{2k}) \geq l_2(s_{1i}, s_{2(k-1)}) \quad \text{for all } i \text{ and } k > 1, \tag{A.52b}$$

$$f_1(s_{1i}, l_1(s_{1i})) + \gamma_i \geq f_1(s_{1i}, l_1(s_{1(i-1)})) + \gamma_{i-1} \quad \text{for all } i > 1, \tag{A.53a}$$

$$l_1(s_{1i}) \geq l_1(s_{1(i-1)}) \quad \text{for all } i > 1, \tag{A.53b}$$

$$V(\gamma_i) = \sum_{k=1}^{n_2} \hat{\pi}_k V(f_2(s_{2k}, l_2(s_{1i}, s_{2k})) - w(s_{1i}, s_{2k})) \quad \text{for all } i. \tag{A.54}$$

HART   CONTRACTS UNDER ASYMMETRIC INFORMATION   33

We show first that (A.52a) and (A.53a) will be binding at a solution. Suppose (A.52a) is not binding for some i, k. Then, by the argument of Lemma 1 (see the proof of Proposition 2), the firm's profits are higher in state (s_{1i}, s_{2k}) than in state $(s_{1i}, s_{2(k-1)})$. Now raise $w(s_{1i}, s_{2k})$ a little and lower $w(s_{1i}, s_{2(k-1)})$ so as to keep γ_i constant in (A.54). Such a change will make the risk-neutral worker better off and will not disrupt any of the constraints (A.52)–(A.54). Since the firm's expected utility $= \sum_i \pi_i V[f_1(s_{1i}, l_1(s_{1i})) + \gamma_i]$ the firm is indifferent to this change. This contradicts the optimality of the contract.

On the other hand, suppose (A.53a) is not binding for some i. Now raise $w(s_{1i}, s_{2k})$ by ε for all k and lower $w(s_{1i-1}, s_{2k})$ by η for all k. This lowers γ_i and raises γ_{i-1} without affecting (A.52a). Since the firm's "profits" in state i, $f_1(s_{1i}, l_1(s_{1i})) + \gamma_i$, are greater than "profits" in state $(i-1)$, $f_1(s_{1(i-1)}, l_1(s_{1(i-1)})) + \gamma_{i-1}$, ε and η can be chosen so that both the firm and worker are better off. (In proving this, one uses the fact that with exponential utility, higher expected utility implies lower expected marginal utility.) Since (A.53a) still holds after the change, optimality of the contract is again contradicted.

Given that (A.52a), (A.53a) are both binding at a solution, the argument of Proposition 2 shows that (71) and (77) hold. This proves that an optimal contract is a solution to (70), (73), (A.52)–(A.54). Underemployment follows immediately from this, as noted in the text. Finally, inspection of the first order conditions of (70), (73) (A.52)–(A.54) shows that there will be strict inequality in (80) and (81) for $k < n_2, i < n_1$. ‖

First version received April 1982, final version accepted October 1982 (Eds.).

The ideas presented here are an outgrowth of joint work with Sandy Grossman, and many of them are as much his as mine. I have also benefited from discussions with Frank Hahn, Eric Maskin, Martin Hellwig and John Moore. Finally, I would like to thank two anonymous referees and Mervyn King for useful suggestions.

NOTES

1. This is as long as lay off or redundancy pay is permitted. See Grossman and Hart (1981). For a survey of the literature on implicit contracts under symmetric information, see Azariadis (1979).

2. One of the first papers to point out the importance of asymmetric information was Calvo and Phelps (1977). See also Hall and Lilien (1979).

3. He should be understood to mean he or she throughout.

4. Evidence that a sizeable proportion of firm–worker relationships are long-term is contained in Hall (1980).

5. R can also be interpreted as unemployment (or underemployment) benefits. Since the non-contract occupation will not involve firm-specific skills, we imagine that at least sometimes R will be significantly lower than the worker's productivity in the firm where he has a contract.

6. This is not an unreasonable assumption if labour must be trained to work in the firm. A more general model would allow for the possibility that the firm can hire new (untrained) labour at date 1. One might imagine that, in addition to the market for contract labour at date 0, there is a spot market for non-contract labour at date 1. In such a model, the reservation wage R might reflect the wage in the date 1 spot market.

7. Here b can be thought of as the bankruptcy point for the firm. Since we wish to use the calculus, it is convenient to assume that bankruptcy is approached smoothly, i.e. $\mathcal{I}'$ is an open set, but our results would not change significantly if $\mathcal{I}' = [b, \infty)$.

8. The original implicit contract models of Azariadis (1975), Baily (1974), Gordon (1974) and others assumed that s is observed by both parties at date 1, and so Proposition 1 is relevant for these models. These authors, however, found that the marginal product of labour should be less than the reservation wage (i.e. there should be overemployment). The reason is that Azariadis et. al. assumed that a worker could only be paid by the firm at date 1 if his labour supply was positive (since in these models $l_k(s_i) = 0$ or 1, this means that $w_k(s_i) > 0$ only if $l_k(s_i) = 1$). To put it another way, Azariadis et. al. ruled out lay off or redundancy pay. This, however, seems arbitrary. If one allows lay off pay, as we have done here, then equality between the marginal product of labour and its reservation wage is guaranteed.

9. Depending on the form of the utility function, unemployed workers may be better or worse off than employed workers.

10. This is with $\bar{U}$ fixed. In a general equilibrium model with many firms, a shift from symmetric to asymmetric information in all firms would be likely to reduce the demand for labour and hence $\bar{U}$.

11. If workers can observe only their own wages and employment and not those in the firm as a whole, a contract will specify each worker's wage as a function of his employment, $w_k = w_k(l)$, rather than $W = W(L)$. This corresponds to the case where the firm can make different reports of the state to different workers.

12. The assumption that workers are risk-neutral while the firm is risk-averse may seem far fetched. For a justification, see Section 3, Remark 7 and Section 5A.

13. In this respect the discrete state model differs from the continuous state one. For in the latter model, in some cases there will be efficient employment in the worst state when workers are risk-neutral. See, e.g., Seade (1977) in the context of optimal income taxation. Note, however, that the conditions for efficiency in the worst state are by no means innocuous.

14. A similar analysis to the one above is given by Spence (1980) in the context of non-linear pricing.

15. Another way of understanding the underemployment result is the following. Consider (13). If s is a continuous variable, it is clear that efficient employment levels can only be sustained by having $W(L) = W(0) + RL$. But this means that the net income of the workers $W(L) - RL$ is constant. Thus all risk is borne by the firm. This is clearly suboptimal when the firm is risk-averse. Suppose instead that the firm and the workers agree on a new contract $\hat{W}(L)$ with $\hat{W}'(L) > R$ and $\hat{W}(0) < W(0)$. This twisting of the schedule means that in bad states, i.e. when s is low, the firm has a lower wage bill than under the contract $W(L)$. Thus, under $\hat{W}(L)$, the firm has a less risky profit stream than under $W(L)$. For a small twist in the schedule, the efficiency losses due to $\hat{W}'(L) > R$ are of second order since at $W'(L) = R$ the net marginal cost involved in a small deviation of employment from the optimum is zero. Hence, given a wage schedule which has ex post efficient employment (i.e. $W'(L) = R$), a wage schedule $\hat{W}(L)$ with $\hat{W}'(L) > R$ always exists which can make the firm and workers better off. Since $\hat{W}'(L) > R$, the marginal product of labour is larger than the reservation wage.

16. The reason for this can be seen easily from the argument in Footnote 15. Now optimal risk sharing tells us that $\hat{W}'(L)$ should be made less than R, since then wages are reduced in high s-high employment states, which is when the firm is badly off.

17. The usefulness of lotteries has also been noted in other contexts. See, e.g., Maskin and Riley's (1982) analysis of auctions.

18. This is a weaker notion of overemployment than used previously. With a general utility function $U(w, l)$, the $l(s_i)$ which solves (22) depends on $w(s_i)$, attitudes to risk, etc. (25) does not therefore imply that $l(s_i)$ is higher in the second-best than the first-best. It simply says that the second-best has the property that the marginal product of labour is less than the marginal rate of substitution between income and labour.

19. This surprising observation is due to Sandy Grossman.

20. If we think of a firm as consisting of owners, managers and workers, then owners may be the risk-neutral third party while V may represent the attitudes to risk of management. Such an interpretation is provided in Section 5A.

21. It should be noted that matters become considerably more complicated if the additional public information I_q is observed after employment decisions are taken but before wages are paid. Then the firm's profits are a random variable when it reports s since, although employment will be a deterministic function of s, wages will be stochastic as they depend on the realization of I. Thus the truth telling constraints now involve the firm's attitudes to risk. Whether the underemployment result generalizes in this case is not known.

22. It should be noted that some new difficulties arise when we allow for indexation. In particular, the risk-sharing conditions are more complicated. If, for example, firms and worker are both risk-neutral (i.e. their indirect utility functions are homogeneous of degree one in income), but have different tastes, then an optimal contract may not exist under either symmetric or asymmetric information if $a = b = -\infty$.

23. In that context, the conclusion is that it is not profit-maximizing for a multi-product firm to price its different products separately, i.e. it should offer discounts for bundles of products purchased, even if the demands for the various products are independent.

24. The exponential class has a number of nice properties with regard to optimal contracts. For example, if U and V are exponential, then the optimal employment rule $l(s_i)$ in Proposition 2 is independent of $\bar{U}$.

25. Proposition 6 generalizes to the case $T > 2$. However, if the firm's expected profit is kept constant, the amount of underemployment becomes small when T is large, as long as the shocks hitting the firm are independent. This is because the variance of profit tends to zero and so the moral hazard problem disappears in the limit. See Radner (1981) for a general analysis of this phenomenon.

26. In the above, we have considered the case of one worker. When there are many workers, matters become more complicated. In particular, one must now specify whether the R's of different workers are independent, positively correlated, etc. For more on this, see Moore (1982).

27. The approach adopted by Kreps, Milgrom, Roberts and Wilson (1982) may be useful here.

28. In practice, it may also be difficult to keep workers to their part of the contract. For example, suppose the workers' reservation wage is uncertain and is positively correlated with the marginal product of labour in this firm. If the firm is risk-neutral, say, it will offer the workers a sticky wage related to the average marginal product of labour. This means that in high marginal product states the reservation wage may be higher than the wage in the firm. But in the absence of a binding contract, what is there to stop the workers leaving? The consequences of this problem for the case of implicit contracts under symmetric information have been investigated by Holmstrom (1982). (Note that the more important firm-specific training and mobility costs are, i.e. the lower R is relative to the marginal product of labour within the firm, the less important this problem will be.)

29. More generally, the model cannot explain unequal treatment within a (uniform) cohort of workers. It can, however, explain unequal treatment *across* cohorts; older workers might, for example, have higher wages than younger workers because they signed their contracts when the firm's prospects seemed better.

HART   CONTRACTS UNDER ASYMMETRIC INFORMATION   35

30. In some cases this unemployment will take the form of layoffs (see Section 2, Remark 1). These layoffs may be temporary or permanent (redundancies). In the two period model we have focussed on, there is obviously no distinction between the two, but the distinction becomes interesting in a multiperiod context. For some evidence suggesting that a sizeable proportion of actual layoffs are temporary, see Feldstein (1975).

REFERENCES

ADAMS, W. and YELLEN, J. (1976), "Commodity Bundling and the Burden of Monopoly", *Quarterly Journal of Economics*, 475–498.

AKERLOF, G. and MIYAZAKI, H. (1980), "The Implicit Contract Theory of Unemployment Meets the Wage Bill Argument", *Review of Economic Studies*, **47** (2), 321–338.

ARNOTT, R. and STIGLITZ, J. (1982), "Equilibrium in Competitive Insurance Markets: The Welfare Economics of Moral Hazard" (mimeo).

AZARIADIS, C. (1975), "Implicit Contracts and Underemployment Equilibria", *Journal of Political Economy*, 1183–1202.

AZARIADIS, C. (1979), "Implicit Contracts and Related Topics: A Survey" (Department of Economics, University of Pennsylvania).

AZARIADIS, C. (1982), "Employment With Asymmetric Information", *Quarterly Journal of Economics* (forthcoming).

BAILY, M. N. (1974), "Wages and Employment Under Uncertain Demand", *Review of Economic Studies*, **41**, 37–50.

CALVO, G. and PHELPS, E. (1977), "Employment Contingent Wage Contracts", *Journal of Monetary Economics*, Supplement, 160–168.

CHARI, V. (1982), "Involuntary Unemployment and Implicit Contracts", *Quarterly Journal of Economics* (forthcoming).

COOPER, R. (1981), "Optimal Labour Contracts With Bilateral Asymmetric Information" (mimeo, University of Pennsylvania).

DASGUPTA, P., HAMMOND, P. and MASKIN, E. (1979), "The Implementation of Social Choice Rules: Some General Results on Incentive Compatibility", *Review of Economic Studies*, **46**, 185–216.

D'ASPREMONT, C. and GERARD-VARET, L. (1979), "Incentives and Incomplete Information", *Journal of Public Economics*, **11**, 25–45.

FELDSTEIN, M. (1975), "The Importance of Temporary Layoffs: An Empirical Analysis", *Brookings Papers*, **3**, 725–44.

GORDON, D. F. (1974), "A Neo-Classical Theory of Keynesian Unemployment", *Economic Inquiry*, **12**, 431–459.

GREEN, J. and KAHN, C. (1982), "Wage-Employment Contracts", *Quarterly Journal of Economics* (forthcoming).

GROSSMAN, S. and HART, O. (1981), "Implicit Contracts, Moral Hazard, and Unemployment", *American Economic Review*, **71**, 301–307.

GROSSMAN, S. and HART, O. (1982), "Implicit Contracts Under Asymmetric Information", *Quarterly Journal of Economics* (forthcoming).

GROSSMAN, S., HART, O. and MASKIN, E. (1982), "Unemployment with Observable Aggregate Shocks" (mimeo).

GUESNERIE, R. and SEADE, J. (1982), "Nonlinear Pricing in a Finite Economy", *Journal of Public Economics*, 157–180.

HALL, R. and LILIEN, D. (1979), "Efficient Wage Bargains Under Uncertain Supply and Demand", *American Economic Review*, **69**, 868–879.

HALL, R. (1980), "Employment Fluctuations and Wage Rigidity", *Brookings Papers*, 91–123.

HOLMSTROM, B. (1982), "Equilibrium Long-term Labor Contracts", *Quarterly Journal of Economics* (forthcoming).

KREPS, D., MILGROM, P., ROBERTS, J. and WILSON, R. (1982), "Rational Cooperation in the Finitely Repeated Prisoners' Dilemma", *Journal of Economic Theory*, **27** (2).

LAFFONT, J.-J. and MASKIN, E. (1979), "A Differential Approach to Expected Utility Maximising Mechanisms", in Laffont, J.-J. (ed.) *Aggregation and Revelation of Preferences* (North-Holland) 289–308.

MASKIN, E. and RILEY, J. (1982), "Optimal Auctions with Risk Aversion", *Econometrica* (forthcoming).

MIRRLEES, J. (1971), "An Exploration in the Theory of Optimum Income Taxation", *Review of Economic Studies*, **38**, 175–208.

MOORE, J. (1982), "Optimal Labour Contracts when Workers have a Variety of Privately Observed Reservation Wages" (mimeo, Birkbeck College).

RADNER, R. (1981), "Monitoring Cooperative Agreements in a Repeated Principal Agent Relationship", *Econometrica*, 1129–1148.

SEADE, J. (1977), "On the Shape of Optimal Tax Schedules", *Journal of Public Economics*, 203–236.

SPENCE, M. (1980), "Multi-product, Quantity-dependent Prices and Profitability Constraints", *Review of Economic Studies*, 821–841.

WILSON, R. (1968), "The Theory of Syndicates", *Econometrica*, **36**, 119–132.

WORRALL, T. (1982), "Implicit Contracts and Asymmetric Information" (mimeo, University of Liverpool).

[20]

Journal of Economic Literature
Vol. XXIII (September 1985), pp. 1144–1175

Implicit Contracts: A Survey

By SHERWIN ROSEN

University of Chicago

I am indebted to Oliver Hart, Charles Kahn, Robert Lucas, Robert Topel and Yoram Weiss for comments and criticism. They do not necessarily concur with my interpretations. The National Science Foundation provided financial support.

I. Introduction

IDEAS associated with implicit contracts originate in the work of Martin Baily (1974), Costas Azariadis (1975)—who apparently coined the term—and Donald F. Gordon (1974) though certain pre-Keynesian views of the labor market such as the remarkably enduring work of John R. Hicks (1932) and later analyses by Armen Alchian (1969) and others are important predecessors. This line of research has been extremely active in the past decade and is notable for bringing microeconomic theory to bear on the problem of unemployment and employment fluctuations. Forty years ago Franco Modigliani (1944) identified the workings of the labor market as the weak link in understanding macroeconomic fluctuations. The promise of implicit contract theory lies in taking a step toward repairing that deficiency. Practical interest in this theory also has been promoted by a search for alternatives to the Phillips' Curve approach to labor market equilibrium, which was criticized for its inconsistencies with microtheory by Milton Friedman (1968) and Robert Lucas (1973), and which failed empirically in the inflationary environment of the 1970s.

The speed with which the term *implicit contracts* has entered the economics vocabulary is slightly astonishing, but perusal of the literature reveals considerable controversy and strongly held differences of opinion on the meaning of the term and its implications. It is natural enough that passions tend to be aroused by any model purporting to analyze employment security and stability, and professional disagreements in this area undoubtedly are not made less intense by intellectual tensions in the field of macroeconomics today. These debates will not be joined here. My goal is limited to presenting some elementary versions of the theory with sufficient clarity to reveal its main content and its relationship with more conventional ways of thinking about labor markets. For these reasons as well as the fact that research in this area is proceeding at a rapid pace, it is inevitable that this survey is incomplete. Additional material may be found in the surveys by Azariadis (1979), Azariadis and Joseph Stiglitz (1983), Oliver Hart (1983), Takatoshi Ito (1982) and Aba Schwartz (1983), which differ in style and perspective from what is presented here. The following serves as a summary and overview.

(1) Viewing labor market exchange in terms of contracts represents an interesting and novel methodological departure from conventional models in which market wage rates decentralize impersonal and unilateral labor demand decisions by firms on the one hand and labor supply decisions by workers on the other. In contrast, contracts are inherently bilateral negotiations between partners that are disciplined by external opportunities, making analysis of the labor market more akin to the marriage market than to the bourse. Contract markets are supported by frictions and specificity of employment relationships that tend to insulate contracting parties from short-run external shocks and which take current wage rates "out of competition" in allocating labor resources.

(2) A contract is a voluntary ex-ante agreement that resolves the distribution of uncertainty about the value and utilization of shared investments between contracting parties. The contract specifies precisely the amount of labor to be utilized and the wages to be paid in each state of nature, that is, conditional on information (random variables) observed by both parties. Wage payments in a contract reflect both allocative production decisions and risk-sharing and income transfer decisions jointly determined by both parties.

(3) Contract theory neither resolves nor illuminates questions of Keynesian unemployment based on nominal wage and price rigidities, money illusion and non-market clearing. Explanations for "sticky" wages and prices that impede efficient labor utilization must be sought in other quarters. Contracts allocate resources through a subtle and "flexible" nonlinear pricing mechanism, which sometimes gives the outward appearance of rigidities

in observed real wages and prices. But these observed rigidities signal little about market failure.

(4) The most important empirical implications of contract theory follow from the hypothesis that contract wages embody implicit payments of insurance premiums by workers in favorable states of nature and receipt of indemnities in unfavorable states. Contractual income transfers smooth consumption, which interacts with labor utilization by eliminating income effects. The prominence of substitution effects promotes an elastic labor utilization response to socially diversifiable external shocks. *Contracts tend to increase the volatility of employment,* but these effects are difficult to detect in structural econometric models because observed wages reflect more than production/labor supply efficiency margins in contract markets.

(5) Only socially diversifiable risks are contracturally insurable. Complete contracts and full risk-shifting imply that all ex post aspects of contracts, including possible layoffs and unemployment, are "voluntary": laid-off workers in a firm are no worse off than those remaining employed, distinctly non-Keynesian. Nondiversifiable and uninsurable risks, risk aversion of firms, information asymmetries and other costs that make contracts incomplete are needed to create ex post involuntary aspects into contract terms. Incomplete risk shifting qualifies the main empirical implications of contracts because income effects play a more prominent role under those circumstances: Consumption varies more and labor utilization varies less in response to demand shocks than when contracts are complete, similar to conventional theory.

The paper is organized as follows: The next section presents some background and contextual discussion of labor market contracts. An elementary contract is analyzed in Section III, where employment is modeled as an all-or-nothing affair. This model has some simple properties, but its special features obscure the relations between contract theory and conventional theories of labor markets. Section IV presents a more familiar model which clarifies these relationships. Section V takes up the distinction between layoffs and worksharing viewed as choices at the extensive and intensive margins. Section VI sketches some extensions to intertemporal problems and the relation between contract theory and intertemporal substitution theory. The models in Section II–VII are based on common information assumptions. Much research in this area has investigated asymmetric information models as sources of market failure. Discussion of that work necessarily requires more advanced methods and appears in Section VII. Conclusions are found in Section VIII.

II. *Background*

The first substantial treatment of the effects of unemployment on a labor market is Adam Smith's discussion of equalizing wage differences on unemployment risk. Smith recognized that workers exposed to such risks, e.g., bricklayers, would require higher wages while employed to compensate for less regular work patterns and to sustain consumption during periods of slack demand. An extra premium might be needed to compensate risk averse workers for bearing earnings risk.

Refined development of this idea has occurred only in recent years, beginning with the work of Michael Todaro (1969), John Harris and Todaro (1970), Arnold Harberger (1971) and Jacob Mincer (1976), which is notable for analyzing the effects of market controls and minimum wages on unemployment, viewed as an equilibrium phenomenon. Workers array their search activities across markets to equate expected earnings in each. If

wages are constrained as a clearing mechanism, something else must do the job and that is the probability of finding employment. In equilibrium workers queue up for high wage jobs in the regulated sector: greater unemployment and smaller job finding probabilities are observed in those markets where wages are highest to enforce the equilibrium supply condition. These models have had some success in explaining urban unemployment in less developed economies.

Robert Hall (1970) incorporated some novel inventory theoretic ideas into models of this type to account for persistent spatial differences in unemployment. Cities with greater equilibrium unemployment rates must pay wage premiums to attract workers. Higher wages support longer unemployment spells and more frequent transitions between jobs, and represent the implicit prices that firms must pay for the privilege of drawing on an inventory of ready labor. The advantage of this reserve army of the unemployed, as it were, lies in greater flexibility and quicker responses of employment decisions by firms facing shifting and uncertain demands. Robert Topel (forthcoming) extended the argument to incorporate intermarket mobility and found evidence of equalizing differences on local unemployment rates when unemployment insurance is properly accounted for. A full market equilibrium analysis in this vein was attempted, but incompletely realized by Hall (1979).

So far, the most complete micro-analysis of equalizing differences in the Smithian mode is by John Abowd and Orley Ashenfelter (1981, 1984), based on utility theory and rationing constraints on hours availability. This and related work by Robert Hutchens (1983) and Stephen Bronars (1983) find small, but persistent equalizing wage rate differences among jobs, but insignificant, if not perverse effects on the variability or risk elements. Small effects for mean differences might be expected when the value of leisure is taken into account, but the unsubstantial effects of risk are not consistent with this theory.

The literature reviewed here concentrates much more on the contractural features of labor market exchange than on implicit risk attributes of jobs. However, an important link between the two is provided in an unpublished paper by H. Gregg Lewis (1969) and more recently by Tomio Kinoshita (1985). Lewis analyzed a deterministic market in which both employers and employees care about hours worked per employee. The equilibrium that emerges out of this analysis looks much different than that of a traditional market: a single wage does not clear the market. Instead, each firm offers fixed wage-hours packages, insisting that its employees work a fixed number of hours in exchange for a fixed income or seek employment elsewhere. A nonlinear equalizing wage-hours locus across firms serves as the equilibrium concept. There is an important sense in which implicit contract theory extends these ideas to incorporate uncertainty, since a contract specifies wage-work package deals for each state of nature.

Professional interest in contract theory has been stimulated by a number of recent empirical observations on labor market institutions. Many features of labor markets bear little resemblance to impersonal Walrasian auction markets. Chief among them is the remarkable degree of observed worker-firm attachment. Martin Feldstein's (1975) surprising finding that over 70 percent of layoffs are temporary, with most laid-off workers ultimately returning to their original employers, was confirmed on similar aggregate data by David Lilien (1980) and by much different methods on micro-panel data in a recent study by Lawrence Katz (1984). The typical adult male worker spends twenty years or more on a single job (Hall 1982) and the proba-

bility of job turnover is a sharply declining function of job tenure (e.g., Mincer and Boyan Jovanovic 1981; William Randolph 1983). Most job changes in a worker's life occur at younger ages, and a person who has persisted in the same job for a few years is likely to continue employment in it for a long time to come. If tenure is de jure in academia, it is de facto in much of the labor market at large. These findings can be explained by search theory through "job shopping" (William Johnson 1978) or searching for the best "match" between a worker and a firm (Jovanovic 1979).

The rationale for observed employment continuity ultimately rests on Gary Becker's (1964) concept of firm-specific human capital, which formed the basis of the earlier quasi-fixed cost theory of employment fluctuations originated by Walter Oi (1962). Robert Hart (1984) presents an up-to-date discussion and prior references. Quasi-fixed cost theory and implicit contract theory share many of the same features and assumptions, as demonstrated in the recent book by Arthur Okun (1981), who attempted an integration of the two. Charles Schultze (1985) pursues this line. Fixed costs, firm-specific investments or match-specific capital create the equivalent of market frictions that render significant value to enduring employment relationships. Maintenance of existing employment attachments creates shared rents which introduce a wedge between the value of a current job and outside opportunities. Rents relax momentary arbitrage constraints between current wages, current fortunes of the firm, and general labor maket conditions, as in the economics of marriage (Becker 1973). Under these circumstances it is expected present values of wages that matter to firms and workers, not necessarily the current wage. Wage income is in part an installment payment on specific-investments: Hall (1980); James R. Millar (1971) presents an inter-

1148   *Journal of Economic Literature, Vol. XXIII (September 1985)*

esting early model along these lines which deserves to be pursued.

Fixed cost theory focuses on quantity adjustments of labor inputs to changing demand conditions. Implicit contract theory potentially provides a more complete description of wage adjustments as well. For if firm-specific investments are an important component of labor market exchange, employment specificity implies that the worker is effectively a partner in his enterprise. But the return on specific capital embodied in workers is inherently stochastic and its joint ownership raises deep questions of how this capital is utilized and how its risks are shared. An ex ante agreement, or contract, resolves these issues of utilization and risk-sharing.

Theoretical research on contracts has been propelled by recent developments in the economics of uncertainty and information. Feldstein's (1976) and Baily's (1977) analyses of the U.S. unemployment insurance system showed the practical relevance of applying insurance principles to certain labor market activities. Economists' increasing understanding of state-contingent claims theory (Kenneth Arrow 1964; Gerard Debreu 1959) has played its part as well.

However, the idea of implicit contracts goes back to Frank Knight's (1921) views of the entrepreneur as a residual income recipient and bearer of risk. Knight's entrepreneur makes contractual commitments to input suppliers and earns a risky return on the difference between stochastic receipts and fixed contractual and other costs (Friedman 1962). Contracts with workers are supported by human capital specificity. Occupational selection suggests that entrepreneurs are less risk averse than the average person (Richard Kihlstrom and Jean-Jacques Laffont 1979, 1983). Modern analysis also shows that entrepreneurs shift some of these risks to the capital market. Nonetheless, a firm's owners may have comparative advantage

at risk management through portfolio diversification, whereas a worker's main wealth is nonmarketable human capital. Specialized human capital, and firm-specific human capital in particular, is not diversifiable and does not collateralize consumption loans in modern economies. Furthermore, there are practical limitations, from moral hazard and adverse selection, on private unemployment insurance markets, because workers and employers share employment and wage decisions in any state of nature. The insurance features of contracts therefore manifest the gains from trade between effectively more and less risk averse agents, and, since employment and earnings decisions are internalized at the firm level, partially avoid direct monitoring by third parties. It is these risk-shifting gains from trade that intermingles insurance and productive efficiency considerations in observed contract wages, and which determines how risks on shared investments are allocated.

Casting employment arrangements in contractual terms leads to a fundamentally different analysis, conceptually, from that of a standard competitive market. In traditional theory the worker is presented with a market-determined wage and decides how much labor to supply to the market at large at that wage. The firm decides how much impersonal labor services to buy. A contract specifies, up front, exactly how much labor the worker must supply and exactly what the wage will be in various circumstances at some particular firm. When the state of nature is actually realized there is no further scope for free choice at some external, market-determined wage rate. Instead, the worker supplies precisely the agreed upon quantity of labor (possibly none) at the previously agreed-upon wage payment, even though he might ex post prefer something different. Sometimes the agreement even transfers the rights of employment and hours determination to the complete discretion of a specific employer. These aspects of ex ante bilateral negotiation and agreement inherent in a contract system have no counterpart in an idealized decentralized competitive market in which all decisions are impersonal and unilateral. This difference is well expressed by Okun's (1981) felicitous characterization of a contract market as the "invisible handshake" rather than the invisible hand.

An employment relationship represents a complex interaction of authority, delegation, personal interactions and monitoring, so complex that remakably few provisions are actually written down.[1] Yet the economic analysis of implicit contracts amounts to working out the details of an explicit contract concerning wages and employment under uncertainty. Hence an implicit contract must be intepreted in the "as if" sense of an explicit one, as a mutual understanding between worker and employer that the invisible handshake implies, as in commercial contracts. At one level applying this as-if principle is no different from most theorizing in economics. At another, we know that contracts do not contain all contingencies because many of them cannot be foreseen and there are so many possibilities that contracting costs are prohibitive. The extent to which formal consideration of these costs and benefits affects any as-if model which ignores them is an open question that can be answered only by the empirical usefulness of the simpler theory.

III. *Contracts with Layoffs*

The literature on implicit contracts has introduced some new language and tech-

---

[1] The common law doctrine of at-will governs employment contracts (Clive Bull 1983; Richard Epstein 1984) and allows termination without fault at the will of either party at any time. Union contracts and certain Equal Opportunity legislation are major exceptions to at-will contracts. Both stipulate for-cause provisions and extensive adjudication procedures.

nical paraphernalia that sometimes makes the fundamental ideas difficult to grasp. This section sets out a simple one-period model aimed at clarifying the essential concepts. Models of this timeless type were first introduced by Azariadis (1975) and much of the subsequent literature has followed in this vein.

The basic set-up is this: the firm contracts with a group of workers. For simplicity, they are assumed to be identical in talents and preferences. The firm produces an output with a production function that depends on the utilized labor of its contract employees. This production function has conventional properties, except that it is shocked by a random variable θ. The stochastic disturbance θ is meant to reflect demand uncertainty and shocks to technology or other input supplies that are produced by external forces not controlled by contracting parties. The term "common knowledge" refers to the assumption that all relevant information is available to all parties. The probability distribution function of θ and the actual ex post realization of θ is costlessly observed and agreed upon by all contracting parties. This assumption carries great force, for it implies that the contract can be conditioned on the realization, that is, on the "state of nature" that actually materializes ex post.

The contract is a set of conditions such as: "if θ turns out to have the value θ_1 then the worker agrees to supply exactly xxxx units of labor in exchange for exactly xxxx dollars." Statements of this form cover every possible realization of θ. This, and the fact that information is complete means that there is no economic rationale for any ex post renegotiation of terms (no "new" information comes in). Of course, nature is random, so contracting parties might well regret certain ex post realizations, similar to the way a poker player might have ex post regret, though there is nothing to be done about it then. These informational assumptions seem severe, to be sure, but they are exactly the same as the Arrow-Debreu contingent claims market model. Much work has been and continues to be done on models in which information is not common in this sense. However, the basic ideas are most easily seen in the simpler common information models.

The key simplifying assumption in Azariadis' model is specifying worker preferences in the form $u = U(C + mL)$, where C is consumption, L is the fraction of time devoted to leisure, and m is a constant. Normalize L so that $0 \leq L \leq 1$. The worker is assumed to be risk averse: $U' > 0$ and $U'' < 0$. This utility function has linear indifference curves: C and L are perfect substitutes, with constant marginal rate of substitution m. Alternatively, imagine the worker dividing his available unit of time between market work and the production of an equivalent but nonmarketable good with production function mL. Here, m is the marginal product of time in producing nonmarket goods. In either case, m is the unique reservation price of time supplied to market work. The conventional labor supply problem has a very simple solution in this case: either the worker supplies his entire endowment of time to the market or to leisure. This feature carries over to a contract as well. It is natural to identify a contractual provision which stipulates $L = 1$ in some state of the world as a layoff in that state.

The firm's production function is assumed to be of the form $x = \theta f(N)$, where N is utilized labor services and $f'(N) > 0$ and $f''(N) < 0$—positive and decreasing marginal product of labor. Capital is ignored. The random variable θ is distributed with known distribution function $G(\theta)$ and density function $G'(\theta) = g(\theta)$. Its mean is $E\theta = \mu$, known at the time the contract is struck (alternatively, μ may be random, but the contract is conditioned on it). Because the contract will specify either $L = 0$ or $L = 1$, for workers

with preferences such as these, write $N = \rho n$, where n is the fixed number of workers under contract, ρ is the proportion of them who work, and $1 - \rho$ is the proportion who don't work or the layoff rate. Furthermore, $0 \leq \rho \leq 1$. Given some realization of θ, the contract specifies a wage payment C_1 to those employees instructed to work and possibly a layoff payment C_2 to those who are laid off. Work or nonwork assignments are drawn by lot, represented by the employment probability, ρ. Thus, the contract specifies a set of three numbers (C_1, C_2, ρ) for each possible outcome θ. Another way to describe it is by three functions of the outcomes: $C_1(\theta)$, $C_2(\theta)$ and $\rho(\theta)$.

An employed worker $(L = 0)$ receives no nonmarket goods and obtains utility $U(C_1(\theta))$ under the contract. This occurs with probability $\rho(\theta)$. A laid off worker $(L = 1)$ produces m units of the nonmarket good and has contracted for $C_2(\theta)$ of market goods, so utility is $U(C_2(\theta) + m)$. This occurs with probability $(1 - \rho(\theta))$. Therefore the ex ante, expected utility of a worker in this firm is

$$Eu = \int [U(C_1(\theta))\rho(\theta) \\ + U(C_2(\theta) + m)(1 - \rho(\theta))] dG(\theta). \quad (1)$$

The contract $\{C_1(\theta), C_2(\theta), \rho(\theta)\}$ maximizes the worker's expected utility (1) subject to an expected profit or utility constraint for the firm. It is Pareto optimal by construction.[2] In state θ the firm produces output of value $\theta f(\rho(\theta)n)$ and incurs contractual costs of $n\rho(\theta)C_1(\theta)$ paid to employed workers and costs of $n(1 - \rho(\theta))C_2(\theta)$ paid to laid-off workers. The

---

[2] The origins of this problem lie in Wassilly Leonteif (1946). Contract curve approaches to trade union bargaining have been developed recently by Ian McDonald and Robert Solow (1981), Thomas MaCurdy and John Pencavel (forthcoming) and Orley Ashenfelter and James Brown (forthcoming). Implicit contract theory substantially differs from these in resolving the uncertainty in the distribution of utility among parties using the theory of optimal risk sharing.

Rosen: Implicit Contracts—A Survey 1151

managers of the firm have utility function $v(\cdot)$ defined over profits, so the expected utility of the firm is

$$Ev = \int v(\pi(\theta))dG$$
$$= \int v(\theta f(\rho(\theta)n) - n\rho(\theta)C_1(\theta) \qquad (2)$$
$$-n(1 - \rho(\theta))C_2(\theta))dG(\theta).$$

The equilibrium contract maximizes (1) subject to $Ev = \bar{v}$ and corresponds to one point on the Pareto frontier between Eu and Ev.

Think of an economy composed of many such firms with the disturbance θ independently distributed among them, so many in fact that the mean $E\theta = \mu$ is realized with probability 1 (the entire distribution $G(\theta)$ is realized across firms ex post—otherwise feasibility requires the contract to be conditioned on the sample mean). To justify the solution of the constrained maximum problem as a description of the observed contract, think of firms competing for contract workers and making their joint investments (not modeled in this literature) at the beginning of the period. Firms compete for workers by offering favorable contract terms, given investments, and, in devising these terms, manager/owners diversify their risks by trading residual profit claims on an asset market. Possible risk aversion of firms is justified by some incompleteness in risk markets. For example, there may be bankruptcy possibilities or agency problems between owners and managers that make complete managerial diversification undesirable. If managers' reservation utility level is $\bar{v}$ and they are supplied elastically, then the equilibrium contract transfers rents to workers and the proposed solution follows as a competitive market equilibrium.

Associating a negative-valued multiplier λ (from Pareto optimality) with constraint (2), setting up the Lagrangian function and differentiating, yields the first order conditions for C_1, C_2, and ρ, respectively:[3]

$$U'(C_1) = -\lambda n v'(\pi)$$
$$U'(C_2 + m) = -\lambda n v'(\pi) \qquad (3)$$
$$\rho(1 - \rho)[U(C_1) - U(C_2 + m)$$
$$-\lambda n v'(\pi)(\theta f'(\rho n) - C_1 + C_2)] = 0.$$

The arguments C_1, C_2, ρ and π (profits) in (3) should be understood as functions of θ, but this functional notation is suppressed to save space. The term in $\rho(1 - \rho)$ in the third condition takes care of the constraint $0 \leq \rho \leq 1$.[4]

The first two conditions determine optimal risk sharing among risk averse agents as in Karl Borch (1962), Arrow (1971), and Robert Wilson (1968): marginal utilities between agents are proportional in all possible realizations; or, $U'(C_1(\theta)) = U'(C_2(\theta) + m)$, which in turn implies $C_1(\theta) = C_2(\theta) + m$ and $U(C_1(\theta)) = U(C_2(\theta) + m)$. Therefore, when the firm provides layoff pay (C_2) contracts make no ex post utility distinctions between employed and unemployed workers for any given value of θ. Of course workers attached to firms with favorable realizations of θ are better off ex post than workers attached to firms with unfavorable realizations of θ (if the

---

[3] The method may be unfamiliar. Think of the integrals in (1) and (2) as the limits of sums across a large number T of discrete possible realizations of θ (the relation between a histogram and a continuous density). The discrete formulation is a gigantic multivariate optimization problem which, by the logic of the contracts, associates specific values of the C's and ρ with each possible realization. These $3T$ marginal conditions are compactly written as (3) in the limit. For the first equation in (3), note that a ρ is associated with each value of θ and that is why there are no integrals in these conditions. Some of the literature works with the dual problem, but the solution is equivalent by Pareto optimality.

[4] Something equivalent to U-shaped average cost curves is required to determine n. Contract theory adds no insights to the determination of firm size and this issue is ignored here. Hájime Miyazaki and Hugh Neary (1983) determine n as in a worker-managed firm. Rosen (1983) does it by a local public goods argument. These papers and one by Dale Mortensen (1983a) further elaborate models of this type.

firm is risk averse and not all risk is shifted), but all workers in the same firm get the same ex post utility independent of employment status. Layoffs are voluntary in this sense, though workers attached to a low θ firm may envy those in a larger θ firm ex post.

The third condition in (3) determines $\rho(\theta)$ according to

$$\rho(\theta)(1 - \rho(\theta))[\theta f\,'(\rho(\theta)n) - m] = 0 \quad (4)$$

because $U(C_1) - U(C_2 + m) = 0$ and $C_1 - C_2 = m$ from the first two conditions. If θ is such that $0 < \rho < 1$, then $\rho(\theta)$ is determined so that the marginal product of a unit of labor equals its social opportunity cost: $\theta f\,'(\rho n) = m$. However, this marginal condition does not hold with equality at the corners. When θ turns out to be very large, the firm would like to employ a great deal of labor, but has contracted with only n workers. In this case $\rho = 1$ and $\theta f\,'(n) > m$. Similarly, when θ is small enough, the marginal value product of labor falls short of its opportunity cost, in which case the firm shuts down its operations and $\theta f\,'(0) < m$. This is illustrated in Figure 1. The elbow shaped curve is the firm's internal supply curve of contract labor. Labor utilization decisions have a reservation property: for $\theta \geq \theta^*$, ρ is set equal to 1, and all of the firm's workers are fully employed. θ^* is defined by $\theta^* f\,'(n) = m$. For $\theta \leq \theta^{**}$, the firm shuts down, and all workers are laid off. The condition $\theta^{**} f\,'(0) = m$ defines θ^{**}. For $\theta^{**} < \theta < \theta^*$, some of the firm's workers are fully employed and others are laid off. In this region the employment rate $\rho(\theta)$ is increasing in θ, and the firm's layoff rate is decreasing in θ.

Notice that the ex post marginal product of labor is not equated across all firms in a contract market. It is equated only for the fraction $G(\theta^*) - G(\theta^{**})$ which have a common shadow price of labor m. The marginal product of labor exceeds m for those firms experiencing outcomes

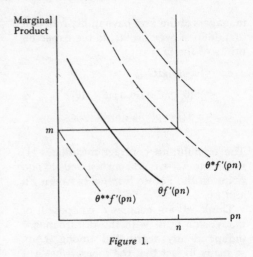

Figure 1.

more favorable than θ^*. This is not a sign of social inefficiency because employment specificity makes it too costly to move workers from one firm to another.

Nonetheless, those firms for which $\theta > \theta^*$ have ex post demands for temporary labor, and one might envision certain labor market institutions arising to take advantage of the situation. One possibility is a subcontract market of temporary workers (Melvin Reder 1962). The personal productivity of such workers would not be as large as that of contract workers due to less specific human capital, though movements across firms would help arbitrage differences in marginal values of labor across firms. It has been claimed that the Japanese labor market makes heavy reliance on this type of system, and perhaps guest workers in European economies (and use of illegal immigrants in the U.S.) can be partially explained in these terms. A temporary labor maket for laid off workers would also serve these purposes. Further, if workers differ in their reserve price of labor m, it is straightforward to show that the firm rationally contracts with several different classes of workers. Those with larger values of m are used as reserves, and are called to work only in the most favorable realizations, similar to the way a power pool brings relatively inefficient generators on line only in periods of peak demand (Azariadis 1976; Rosen 1983). Finally, there may be incentives for firm mergers or product diversification that more easily accommodate worker transfers between operating units. The limits of the firm would then be determined by balancing the gains of internal reassignments of workers against the usual diseconomies of scale and lesser overall productivity of the firm's work force due to lesser labor specialization among divisions. This point is related to the gains to flexibility and adaptability in an uncertain environment (George Stigler 1939).

The implications of this model can be seen in an especially striking manner when firms are risk neutral [$v'(\pi) = 1$]. Then (3) implies complete consumption insurance for all workers in all firms. In this case the first two marginal conditions in (3) are independent of θ because the term in $v'(\pi(\theta))$ equals unity. Therefore $C_1(\theta)$ and $C_2(\theta)$ are constants for all value of θ, given μ. All employed workers in *all* firms receive the same incomes and so do all unemployed workers. Furthermore, the ex post utility levels $U(C_1) = U(C_2 + m)$ are independent of θ and the same for all workers. The labor utilization condition in (4) remains unchanged. This case is, in fact, equivalent to complete and costless contingent claims markets in which all socially insurable risks are diversified away, and is identical to the standard insurance result that risk averse people are completely insured when premiums are actually fair. It is as if firms contracted with an actuarially fair insurance company, turned over their entire output to the common fund and contracted to withdraw pro-rata shares.

To further clarify this strong result, write $\theta = \mu\epsilon$ where ϵ is an idiosyncratic, independent and identically distributed firm-specific random variable with distri-

bution function $Z(\epsilon)$ where $E\epsilon = 1$ and μ is a common economy-wide aggregate shock which strikes all firms equally. In a one-period model μ is an undiversifiable risk. (This is not necessarily true in a multiperiod dynamic model. See Section VI.) Given the information assumptions, all ex ante contracts must be conditioned on μ as well as on ϵ because of social budget constraints: feasible contracts cannot redistribute more market income than is actually produced.

A larger value of μ shifts the marginal value product curves to the right in Figure 1 for every possible value of ϵ and a smaller μ value shifts these curves down and to the left. Substituting $\theta = \mu\epsilon$ into (4), we see that given some realization μ, firms for which $\epsilon \geq . \epsilon^* = m/\mu f'(n)$ fully utilize their work force. The value of ρ for firms on the interior of (4) is also increasing in μ. Consequently the utilization rate of labor in the work force as a whole is increasing in μ and the aggregate unemployment rate is decreasing in μ. Finally, when $v(\pi)$ is linear, (2) defines the social budget constraint for feasible contracts, given μ, as

$$\mu\!\int\!\epsilon f(\rho(\epsilon/\mu)n)dZ(\epsilon)$$

$$= n\!\int\![C_1\rho(\epsilon/\mu) + C_2(1 - \rho(\epsilon/\mu))]dZ(\epsilon) \quad (5)$$

$$= n\,[C_2 + m\!\int\!\rho(\epsilon/\mu)dZ(\epsilon)].$$

National income per head (the left-hand side of (5) divided by n) is increasing in μ through its direct multiplicative effect and its indirect effect of increasing ρ. Therefore $C_1(\mu)$ and $C_2(\mu)$ are increasing in μ.

Diversifiable risk ϵ is shifted completely in this complete contracts case: consumption and utility are independent of local demand ϵ, suggestive of a form of "real wage rigidity" for these types of demand shocks. Laid off workers are no worse off than employed workers, and layoffs are voluntary. However, a contract market does not at all imply real wage rigidity for uninsurable risks: the consumption and utility levels of workers, be they employed or not, are strictly increasing functions of "aggregate demand" μ. Everyone is better off ex post when μ is larger and worse off when μ is smaller.[5]

The model sketched above has the undesirable prediction that laid off workers fare no worse than employed workers. It is the assumption that consumption and employment risk can be shifted without transactions costs that accounts for much of this result. By analogy, a person who can buy actuarial no-load insurance buys enough to be indifferent to whether his house burns down or not. But that is just a consequence of a simplifying assumption. Most people are worse off if their house burns because they are not fully insured. Incomplete insurance is rational when premiums are nonactuarial and when full insurance implies moral hazard. This is also true of the insurance in an implicit contract. The point gains greater force in this context because workers and firms jointly control layoff decisions, precisely the type of situation where coinsurance is known to be desirable. Therefore, incomplete insurance, or more generally some incompleteness in state contingent claims markets, is necessary to get involuntary layoffs into these models. John Bryant (1978) was the first to point this out; see also, Thomas Sargent (1979), Sanford Grossman and Hart (1981), and Bengt Holstrom (1981). While the point has created much controversy on the usefulness of common knowledge contract models, it seems to me that considerable insight is gained by analyzing actuarial cases, as in more conventional insurance problems.

It is by no means obvious how to incorporate nonactuarial elements into a formal model. The most straightforward way is to interpret the contract as a pooling arrangement with a risk-neutral, mutual insurance company and add an unemployment claims processing cost to the company's budget constraint, similar to the way load factors are calculated in conventional insurance premiums. Space limitations preclude extended development here. Consider, instead, an extreme case in which costs of providing private insurance to the unemployed are so large that none is provided at all. This adds the constraint $C_2(\theta) = 0$ to the problem above and is exactly Azariadis' (1975) original formulation.

The absence of indemnities to unemployed persons means that unemployed workers receive incomes of m alone, and the second marginal condition in (3) is irrelevant. But the first one remains. All employed workers receive the same wage C_1 if the firm is risk neutral ($v' = 1$) and their consumption is fully insured. The wage C_1 paid to employed persons must exceed m or else no one would be inclined to work. Therefore $U(C_1) > U(m)$ and employed persons in the same firm are better off ex post than the unemployed. Laid off workers have drawn the losing hand and definitely prefer employment.[6]

One might expect incomplete insurance to affect production efficiency. The third condition in (3) verifies this intuition. Substituting for $\lambda n v'$ from the first condi-

---

[6] Perceptive readers may have noticed that the complete contract could have been equivalently implemented by having all employees work ρ percent of the time and consume leisure $(1 - \rho)$ percent of the time rather than having a fraction ρ fully employed and a fraction $(1 - \rho)$ completely unemployed. These same possibilities arise in the incomplete contract, but are definitely not equivalent. The virtue of worksharing does not seem to have been noticed in this connection. Some factor that gives value to the continuity of a worker's employment time over the period is necessary to avoid pure worksharing solutions. See below.

tion in (3) and noting that $C_2 = 0$ by assumption, we have, for $\rho > 0$

$$\theta f'(\rho n) \geq$$
$$C_1 - [U(C_1) - U(m)]/U'(C_1). \tag{6}$$

This condition holds with equality on the interior $(0 < \rho < 1)$, and with inequality for almost all firms whose workers are fully employed. It follows directly from risk aversion $(U'' < 0)$ that the bracketed term on the right hand side of (6) exceeds $C_1 - m$, the difference in incomes between employed and unemployed workers. The shadow price of labor is the entire expression on the right hand and therefore falls short of m when insurance is incomplete. The horizontal portion of the internal supply curve in Figure 1 now lies below m. $\theta f'(\rho n)$ is compared with a smaller supply price in determining ρ, and the firm utilizes *more* of its contract labor compared with complete contracts. m is the social opportunity cost for firms with $0 < \rho < 1$. There is socially excessive employment in the incomplete contract equilibrium and social output would be greater if more people were unemployed!

This surprising result is part of a more general proposition in the economics of insurance. Availability of insurance promotes the undertaking of socially beneficial risks by separating the average benefits of actions from fear of risk. Risk averse persons act too cautiously and do not take enough good risks when insurance is unavailable. The only way a risk averse worker can partially insure against the utility loss of layoff and unemployment in this problem is by working in circumstances when it is socially inefficient to do so.

One more comparison must be made before concluding this section, and that is to a situation where employment relationships provide no insurance at all. This state of affairs is sometimes called an "auction market." George Akerlof and Miya-

zaki (1980) showed that an auction market can imply more unemployment than a contract market. The point is easy to see in this model when employers are risk neutral. Then workers in the firm must go it alone. Any incomes they receive must be distributed out of own firm's output, because claims on other firms' outputs are unavailable by assumption. In making its collective employment decisions, the firm could then do no better than to compare the marginal productivity of its own labor with the opportunity cost of its workers' time, which is m. Therefore, m again becomes the effective shadow price of labor as in Figure 1, employment decisions are socially efficient and identical to the full contract model. However, these workers are bearing consumption and wage risks, depending on their own realized value of θ, and some of these are socially diversifiable. Though efficient in production decisions, this solution is inefficient on risk sharing grounds. Clearly it is inefficient in the latter respect relative to a complete contract. However, it is not obviously less efficient than the incomplete contract, which is inefficient on the productivity account but possibly more efficient on the risk-sharing account. Therefore, no contracts at all may dominate an incomplete contract, depending on the extent of worker risk aversion.

IV. *Contracts and Labor Supply*

The unusual and unattractive assumptions about worker preferences in the model above conceals an intimate relationship between contract theory and the familiar theory of labor supply. Contracts embody an implicit nonlinear pricing mechanism that eliminates the income effects of insurable risks in the traditional consumption-leisure choice problem. They thereby smooth consumption which interacts with labor utilization and promotes elastic labor supply responses to external stimuli. Contracts suggest much more volatility of employment to insurable risks than conventional models do.

To illustrate these important points in the most straightforward way, worker preferences in Section III are generalized, and the technology is simplified. Assume neoclassical worker preferences $u = U(C,L)$. The indifference curves of $U(C,L)$ are strictly convex and the worker is risk averse. As in the conventional labor supply problem, the quantity $(1 - L)$ is identified with time worked, and remaining time L is associated with nonmarket production (partial layoffs if one wishes). Assume that the firm consists of one worker $(n = 1)$ with production function $x = \theta f(1 - L)$ where θ is the productivity shock. To simplify even more, assume $f(1 - L)$ is linear. Then the production function is $x = \theta(1 - L)$ and θ has the ready interpretation of the marginal product of the worker's labor, similar to a wage rate. Everything to be said here applies to a concave function $f(\cdot)$, a refinement that only adds expository noise to the main point.

Consider, first, the conventional problem of labor supply under uncertainty. Nature draws a ball out of the θ urn, the worker observes θ and makes the optimal labor-consumption decision. If an external market does not allow risks to be spread, the worker is constrained to consume out of own production (the "auction market" of Section III) and any source of non-earned income, say y. So given θ, the budget constraint is the standard one, $C = \theta(1 - L) + y$. The solution is described by the budget constraint and the first order condition $\theta = U_L/U_C$, which define demand functions $C = C(\theta, y)$ and $L = L(\theta, y)$. Assume that both C and L are normal goods and compare two alternative realizations of θ. A larger value of θ increases C, but has ambiguous effects on L. The substitution effect tends to induce greater labor supply $(1 - L)$ but the in-

come effect works in the other direction and may cause labor supply to fall. Substituting the demand functions into the utility function yields the indirect utility function $u(\theta, y)$. Indirect utility is increasing in θ (and y) irrespective of the labor supply response because full income is increasing in θ.[7]

An economy with many persons opens possibilities for mutually advantageous social arrangements that allow risk pooling. The conventional problem strictly ties a worker's consumption to current production, but a contract allows current consumption to be disassociated from current production for any given person if risks are diversifiable. The simplest way to model this is to replace the personal budget constraint with its expectation (over all workers), precisely what an actuarially fair insurance policy would do. Yet this is not standard insurance: the contract specifies exactly how much the person has to work for each possible realization of θ in order to eliminate adverse effects on work incentives that consumption insurance implies.

Assuming common knowledge, the contract specifies that the worker puts forth $(1 - L(\theta))$ hours of work in state θ and that the wage payment or consumption is $C(\theta)$ in state θ. Expected profitability of the firm is the difference between expected output and expected wage (consumption) payments

$$\int [x(\theta) - C(\theta)]dG(\theta)$$
$$= \int [\theta(1 - L(\theta)) - C(\theta)]dG. \tag{7}$$

---

[7] Increasing the spread of the distribution function $G(\theta)$ does not necessarily make the worker worse off, and Smithian risk compensation is more complex than would appear on the surface. Riskier distributions decrease welfare on risk aversion grounds, but have benefits in allowing workers to choose labor supply most advantageously in more probable high productivity states. John Hey (1979) summarizes this approach to uncertainty. Nonearned income is ignored in what follows because those issues are better treated in an intertemporal context.

Complete contracts (given μ) are analyzed in what follows, assuming risk-neutral firms, to bring out the connections between conventional theory and contract theory in the clearest possibly way. Competition in the market for contracts implies that the equilibrium contract solves:

$$\max_{L(\theta),C(\theta)} \int U(C(\theta), L(\theta))dG(\theta) \quad (8)$$

subject to

$$\int [\theta(1 - L(\theta)) - C(\theta)]dG(\theta) = 0. \quad (9)$$

The Lagrangian for this problem is

$$\int [U(C,L) - \lambda[\theta(1 - L) - C]]dG. \quad (10)$$

The first order conditions for $L(\theta)$ and $C(\theta)$ given θ equivalent to (3) above are

$$\cdot U_C(C(\theta), L(\theta)) = -\lambda \quad (11)$$

$$U_L(C(\theta), L(\theta)) = -\theta\lambda \quad (12)$$

where $\lambda < 0$ as before. C and L are solved as functions of θ and λ from equations (11) and (12). Then the expected income constraint is used to solve for λ and hence the optimum contract $L(\theta)$ and $C(\theta)$. Notice that the conventional problem is completely nested in this one. It is feasible that $C(\theta) = x(\theta)$, but the contract surely will not specify equality of consumption and output for every realization of θ. True, (11) and (12) imply $U_L/U_C = \theta$—the marginal rate of substitution between leisure and consumption is equated with the marginal product of labor for any θ in a complete contract. However, now there is an extra degree of freedom: the expected income constraint allows the marginal utility of consumption to be equated in all states of the world: condition (11) is the Borch-Arrow-Wilson risk-sharing condition when one of the agents is risk neutral, equivalent to optimal choice of insurance in the actuarial, no-load case.

The properties of $L(\theta)$ and $C(\theta)$ in the contract are implicit in the first order conditions (11) and (12). Since λ does not depend on θ, comparative statics on (11) and (12) show directly how C and L respond to θ in the contract. Equations (11) and (12) define marginal-utility-constant demand functions (Ragnar Frisch 1932), which prove useful when preferences are additively separable, as they are across states-of-the-world here. Martin Browning, et al. (forthcoming) contains an elegant statement of the method and gives prior references. Differentiating with respect to θ yields

$$U_{CC}C'(\theta) + U_{CL}L'(\theta) = 0$$

$$U_{CL}C'(\theta) + U_{LL}L'(\theta) = -\lambda$$

with solutions

$$L'(\theta) = -\lambda U_{CC}/\Delta \quad (13)$$

$$C'(\theta) = \lambda U_{CL}/\Delta \quad (14)$$

where $\Delta = [U_{CC}U_{LL} - U_{CL}^2] > 0$, by risk aversion.

From (13) we have $L'(\theta) < 0$, since $U_{CC} < 0$ by concavity and $\lambda < 0$. $d(1 - L(\theta))/d\theta = 1 - L'(\theta) > 0$. *The implicit contract always specifies that the employee works more hours in favorable states* (larger values of θ) *and works less in less favorable states.* There is no ambiguity due to opposing income and substitution effects in the optimal contract. Negativity of $L'(\theta)$ is basically a result of substitution effects. The worker is constrained by the expectation of output, not by realized output itself. A favorable or unfavorable drawing of θ carries no income effects because the good fortunes of one firm are counterbalanced by bad fortunes of another for diversifiable risks. Therefore, it is always efficient for the worker to work more when the marginal product of labor is larger (to make hay when the sun shines) and to redistribute consumption by insurance. If leisure is a normal good, contracts result in greater variance in hours worked than standard models and intuition based on them suggest.

Equation (14) shows that the total wage payments—identified with consumption under the contract—are rising, constant, or falling in θ as $U_{CL} \lessgtr 0$. Only when preferences are *strongly* separable in C and L it is true that $C'(\theta) = 0$ and consumption is completely smoothed, as in the permanent income hypothesis (Friedman 1957). Nonzero cross derivatives U_{CL} strongly link consumption behavior with labor supply.[8]

That a contract with full insurance does not necessarily imply full consumption smoothing suggests that the connection between complete insurance and income effects is more subtle than usual. Full insurance does not stabilize consumption except when preferences are strongly separable. More surprising, it does not stabilize ex post utility when leisure is a normal good. In this bivariate problem full insurance is completely described by condition (11) that the *marginal* utility of consumption is equalized in all states of the world, not necessarily equalization of total utility. Define $u(\theta)$ as ex post, indirect utility given θ in the optimal contract. Then

$$
\begin{aligned}
u'(\theta) &= U_C C' + U_L L' \\
&= -(U_C/U_{CC})[U_{CL} - (U_L/U_C)U_{CC}]L'(\theta).
\end{aligned}
\tag{15}
$$

The second equality follows from (13) and (14). The bracketed term in (15) is familiar.

It determines the sign of the income effect in a conventional labor supply problem. Ex post utility is completely assured by the contract only if $u' = 0$, and this happens only when the income effect is zero, or when $U(C, L) = U(C + \psi(L))$ of which Section III is a special case. But if utility is completely assured, consumption $C(\theta)$ cannot be assured for it must compensate for the variation in L. The contract does not assure utility if the income effect is nonzero. $u'(\theta)$ is negative when the income effect is positive.[9]

A complete insurance contract makes a worker who has "suffered" an adverse draw of an insurable risk better off ex post than a worker who draws a more favorable value except when income effects are negative. Contracts underinsure ex post utility levels only when leisure is an inferior good. This strong result is a result of strong assumptions. It is not necessarily true when the firm is risk averse (then $v'(\cdot)$ multiplies the right hand side of (11) and (12)) so that risks are shared and insurance is incomplete. Nor is it necessarily true when information is private or when the shock is not diversifiable. A nondiversifiable risk affects μ, and has a powerful effect on the total amount of consumption produced and redistributed. It changes the marginal utility of consumption λ. Ex post utility necessarily increases in μ, as it did in Section III.

The consumption smoothing and insurance aspects of contracts have profound implications on the meaning of wage data in a contract market. Observed wages do two things in a contract: they allocate la-

---

[8] Notice that consumption is positively correlated with labor supply only when $U_{CL} < 0$ from (14). The sign of U_{CL} is determined by the degree of risk aversion as well as by the usual curvature restrictions in demand theory. A richer specification of nonmarket production yields more interesting implications. For example, those on short work schedules would substitute nonmarket goods production for market goods (Gilbert Ghez and Becker 1975). Michael Grossman (1973) and Daniel Hamermesh (1982) find these types of predictable differences in consumption (e.g., food prepared away from home) between the employed and the unemployed.

[9] This result is formally identical to a paradox found by James Mirrlees (1972) in an optimum spatial equilibrium problem. Mirrlees' paradox arises because of the nonconvexity that a person can occupy only one location (Richard Arnott and John Riley 1977). The "nonconvexity" here is that nonmarket production must be self-consumed. If it were possible to trade leisure on a competitive market then $u(\theta)$ is nondecreasing.

bor and shift risks.[10] These roles are best described by thinking of the observed wage as the outcome of a two-part variable tariff. The insurance aspect determines the equivalent of nonearned income in a conventional labor supply problem, conditional on the realized state θ. For risk pooling and insurance to have meaning, it must be that workers experiencing favorable realizations of θ subsidize those with unfavorable realizations. Given these "lump sum" taxes and subsidies, the contract allows workers to "choose" their optimal labor supply at the correct "marginal wage" θ, the marginal product of labor.

Define $s(\theta)$ as the worker's net debit position with the firm: $s(\theta) = C(\theta) - \theta(1 - L(\theta))$ is the difference between the wage payment and output in state θ. This equation is of the conventional budget form except that $s(\theta)$ has replaced the usual nonearned income term. A worker for whom $s(\theta) > 0$ is effectively subsidized by the contract ex post and one for whom $s(\theta) < 0$ is effectively taxed. Substituting $s(\theta)$ into the budget constraint (9) reveals that these subsidies and taxes balance each other, on average, across all workers in an actuarial system. Differentiate $s(\theta)$ with respect to θ and substitute from (13) and (14)

$$s'(\theta) = -(1 - L)$$
$$- (L'/U_{CC})[U_{CL} - (U_L/U_C)U_{CC}] \qquad (16)$$

---

[10] The emerging literature on efficiency wages (Stiglitz' 1984 survey) also rests on the proposition that the wage performs more than one economic function. Multi-part pricing would allocate resources efficiently in these models (e.g., a lump-sum bond as well as a marginal wage rate in Carl Shapiro and Stiglitz' 1984 shirking problem), but two-part pricing is ruled out by assumption. Involuntary unemployment results because some margin is not satisfied when there are not enough prices available to perform all functions. Involuntary layoffs in contracts result from imperfections in state-claims markets, which is a different way of saying that there are not enough prices.

so $s(\theta)$ is decreasing in θ if leisure is noninferior.

The two-part tariff interpretation of contracts is shown in Figure 2. The first panel shows the solution to the conventional problem (assuming zero nonearned income). Two budget lines are shown. The realized marginal product θ_1 is assumed to be larger than θ_2, and comparison of equilibrium points involves the usual income and substitution effects. The second panel shows the effects of a contract, assuming $U_{CL} < 0$. For θ_1 above the mean we know from (16) that the worker is taxed and $s(\theta_1) < 0$. For θ_2 below the mean the worker is subsidized and $s(\theta_2) > 0$. The contract acts as if it puts the θ_1 worker "in the hole" by amount $s(\theta_1)$ and lets him work out of it by choosing L at (marginal) wage rate θ_1 along the altered budget constraint. The contract acts as if it gives the θ_2 worker a subsidy of $s(\theta_2)$ and then allows him to choose hours worked at marginal wage rate θ_2. The heavy curve labeled $C(L)$ is the locus of (C,L) pairs satisfying marginal condition (11), and $C'(L) < 0$ when $U_{CL} < 0$. The familiar marginal condition $U_L/U_C = \theta$ implied by (11) and (12) jointly is shown by the tangencies with the contract budget constraints. It is these adjustments in the "lump sum" portions of the two part tariff that ameliorate income effects, that promote consumption smoothing and elastic labor supply responses to diversifiable risks.

Figure 2 is useful for studying the observable wage consequences of contracts. The observed "average hourly wage rate" is measured by dividing total earnings (equals $C(\theta)$ in contracts) by hours worked:

$$W(\theta) = C(\theta)/(1 - L(\theta)). \qquad (17)$$

This is how wage rates are measured in virtually all available data. Differentiating (17) and substituting from above yields

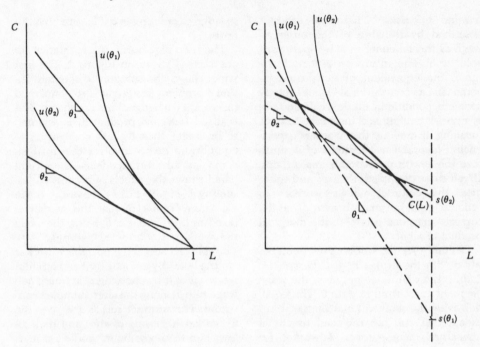

Figure 2.

$$W'(\theta)/W(\theta)$$
$$= [-(U_{CL}/CU_{CC}) + (1/(1-L))]L'(\theta). \tag{18}$$

The sign of this expression is unambiguous only when $U_{CL} \geq 0$, in which case $W(\theta)$ is actually decreasing in θ, given μ. The sign of $W'(\theta)$ is ambiguous when $U_{CL} < 0$ as in Figure 2. Figure 3 illustrates the construction of $W(\theta)$ for preferences without income effects. Here $C(L)$ coincides with an indifference curve because utility is constant in the contract, from (15). The points marked A and B correspond to large and small values of θ respectively. The measured average hourly wage rate is given by the slope of the line connecting either point with $L = 1$ and $C = 0$, from (17). The two values of θ have been chosen so that the wage rate is the same, illustrating nonmonotonicity of $W(\theta)$. In this case $W(\theta)$ is U-shaped. It is decreasing for θ sufficiently small and is increasing for θ sufficiently large. Two points follow from this.

First, there is no presumption that the measured average wage in a contract is positively correlated with the state θ, as the U-shaped pattern in Figure 3 shows, a possibility that could be confused with wage rigidity. This statement refers to real, average wage rates and to the diversifiable component of the state. If the economy experienced an adverse aggregate shock μ, the contract would have to be recalibrated. The equilibrium indifference curve in Figure 3 would be shifted down and the average hourly wage at each level of hours worked would be smaller than indicated. Average hourly wage rates should be positively correlated with noninsurable disturbances in a contract market.

The behavior of average real wages over the business cycle has been studied for many years. Manufacturing hourly wage rates show no obvious relationship with aggregate output (Salih Neftci 1978). Joseph Altonji and Ashenfelter (1980) suggest that the manufacturing real-wage rate resembles a random walk. However, panel and personal survey data indicate significant responses of measured personal wage rates to local labor market conditions (John Raisian 1983; Mark Bils, forthcoming; and Topel, forthcoming). James Heckman and Guilerme Sedlacek (1984) show that BLS manufacturing numbers may contain selection bias, because less productive workers are less likely to be employed in manufacturing during business cycle troughs, making measured wages fall less than a properly weighted index.

Second, using measured wage rates may lead to misleading inferences regarding unemployment or overemployment in personal surveys. Optimality of the contract means that ex post Pareto-improving recontracts are not possible. There is also no possibility of choosing hours worked ex post at some exogenously determined wage. In Figure 3 the worker is instructed to work $(1 - L_1)$ hours in the θ_1 state. Total earnings of C_1 go along with this, so the average hourly wage is $C_1/(1 - L_1)$ $= W$. If the worker could freely choose hours at an hourly wage rate W he would work up to point D rather than stay at A. In the θ_2 state, the contract specifies point B. Here the worker would choose to work more hours (point D) than the contract specifies if hours could be freely chosen at wage rate W. A survey respondent might indicate constraints on hours worked under these circumstances. The person who drew θ_2 might say that he would like more work than he is getting at the "going" wage rate and that he is involuntarily underemployed. The worker who drew θ_1 might respond that work hours are excessive and that he is involuntarily overemployed.

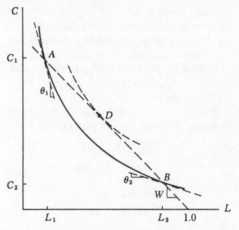

Figure 3. Measured Wage Rates

All this points out a significant problem for empirical analysis. Virtually all work on labor supply uses a model that assumes point D, that the worker is free to unilaterally choose hours at the *measured* wage rate W, whereas the insurance features of contracts disassociate the measured average wage rate from both the marginal product of labor and from the marginal rate of substitution. This point is conceptual and applies even if average wages were perfectly measured, so econometric techniques for dealing with measurement error does not dispose of it. This is not trivial because virtually all econometric work (in this field and elsewhere) lives or dies by the assumption that measured prices indicate efficiency margins. Contracts require that the data be adjusted for the lump sum components $s(\theta)$ to impute marginal wage rates. Some recent studies have attempted to include information on survey responses pertaining to whether or not the worker is constrained in the choice of hours, but this is generally viewed as a ration, not as an equilibrium phenomenon along contract lines (Shelly Lundberg, 1984, gives references and a related discussion).

This section concludes with an interesting and surprising comparative static experiment. Complete contracts imply that an *increase* in diversifiable risk increases expected utility of risk averse workers.

Following Michael Rothschild and Stiglitz (1970), parameterize the density function as $g(\theta) = \xi(\theta) + ar(\theta)$, where $\xi(\theta)$ is a density, a is a positive number, and $r(\theta)$ is a step function with properties:

$$R(\theta) = \int_0^\theta r(z)dz$$
$$R(0) = R(\infty) = 0 \qquad (19)$$
$$\int_0^\infty R(\theta)d\theta = 0$$
$$\int_0^\theta R(z)dz \geq 0.$$

Some reflection reveals that $r(\theta)$ is positive for large and small values of θ and is negative for intermediate values. Therefore an increase in a puts more weight in the tails of $g(\theta)$ and increases the spread of the distribution.

Differentiating the Lagrangian of the maximum problem in (8) with respect to a and using the envelope property gives

$$\partial Eu/\partial a = \int u(\theta)r(\theta)d\theta$$
$$- \lambda \int [\theta(1 - L) - C]r(\theta)d\theta.$$

This expression may be signed by integrating by parts (twice) and exploiting the properties of (19): Peter Diamond and Rothschild (1978). Assuming $g(\theta)$ has bounded support, integration by parts gives

$$\partial Eu/\partial a = -\int [u'(\theta) + \lambda[\theta L'(\theta)$$
$$+ C'(\theta)]]R(\theta)d(\theta) + \lambda \int (1 - L(\theta))R(\theta)d\theta$$
$$= \lambda \int (1 - L(\theta))R(\theta)d\theta$$

since the first integral vanishes from first order conditions and (15). Integrating by parts again gives

$$\partial Eu/\partial a = -\lambda \int_0^\infty \int_0^\theta -L'(\theta)R(\tau)d\tau d\theta. \quad (20)$$

The sign of (20) is unambiguously positive because $\lambda < 0$, $L'(\theta) < 0$, from (13), and $\int_0^\theta R(z)dz > 0$, from (19). Greater diversifiable risk makes the worker better off.

This result is unexpected in light of the Smithian equalizing differences logic, but it is easily explained. Full insurance eliminates the adverse, direct consequences of risk aversion on expected utility. Increasing spread affords the worker superior opportunities of allocating work to the most favorable states and limiting losses of unfavorable outcomes by consuming more leisure. The opportune substitution of work effort toward more productive states has a value similar to that of an option: that less work is called for in the less favorable states serves to truncate the lower tail of the θ distribution.

V. *Layoffs or Worksharing?*

Misconceptions about the nature of the price mechanism in contracts has led to the impression that contracts somehow rationalize layoffs through "sticky" wages and prices, and nonmarket clearing. This impression is wide of the mark because it confuses ex post contractual wages and prices with conventional "auction" market prices. Section IV clearly demonstrates that resources in contracts are really allocated by a sophisticated nonlinear price system. This nonlinear scheme is as flexible as one ordinarily supposes in competitive market theory and allocates resources as efficiently as the completeness of contingent claims markets permits. The true fact is that contracts per se have little to say about the split between changes in hours per head and layoffs. Contract outcomes fundamentally depend on preferences and technology, so the question of layoffs must rest on these same primitives. Section III produced layoffs by a peculiar assumption about preferences, that market and nonmarket goods are perfect substitutes. The conventional formulation in Section IV is not detailed enough to decide these issues.

Basically, there are two ways of introducing layoffs in contract (or any other) models. One links layoffs to capital utilization decisions based on capital heterogeneity and limited ex post substitution between labor and capital (Leif Johansen 1972). The idea is related to the "marginal firm." Marginal mines shut down completely when the price of ore falls because their quasi-rents are driven to zero. Production in marginal operations might begin when demand increases. Restricted ex post, capital-labor substitution and fixed operating costs create nonconvexities that make it advantageous to shut down inefficient facilities rather than operate them at excess capacity. These ideas could be extended to various divisions of a multiproduct or multiplant firm. The contract model must be extended to incorporate productivity differences among firms, perhaps based on vintage capital ideas (Solow 1960), differences in site-specific factors or in entrepreneurial capacities. This line has not been pursued much, and will not be developed here.

The other possibility is to directly introduce hours and employees (bodies) into the firm's technology (Feldstein 1967; Rosen 1968; Ray Fair 1969; M. Ishaq Nadiri and Rosen 1969; Ben Bernanke 1983), which serves to link the models of Sections III and IV above. Miyazaki and Neary (1983) and Murray Brown and Elmar Wolfstetter (1984) have constructed contract models along these lines.

Extend the production function of Section III to $x = \theta f(\rho n, h)$, where h is the intensity of work per employed person and $f(\cdot)$ is concave. Think of ρ as the fraction of contract labor who are employed. Then $1 - \rho$ is the layoff rate. Alternatively, maintain a timing convention in which the "period" is a year. Then h can be regarded as the length of the work week when employed and ρ as the fraction of the year (number of weeks) of employment. $h = 0$ during nonworking weeks spent on layoff. To simplify the presentation, I again assume complete contracts

(of course conditional on the mean μ of θ) and risk neutral employers.

Writing the utility function in terms of h rather than L, an employed worker receives contractual wage payment $C_1(\theta)$ and works $h(\theta)$ in state θ, receiving utility $U(C_1(\theta), h(\theta))$. A laid off worker receives payment $C_2(\theta)$ and h is zero, so utility is $U(C_2(\theta), 0)$. The probability of these events is ρ and $1 - \rho$ respectively, so

$$Eu = \int [U(C_1, h)\rho + U(C_2, 0)(1 - \rho)] dG(\theta). \quad (21)$$

The budget constraint is

$$\int [\theta f(\rho n, h) - n(C_1\rho + C_2(1 - \rho))] dG(\theta) = 0. \quad (22)$$

The equilibrium contract $\{C_1(\theta), C_2(\theta), h(\theta), \rho(\theta)\}$ maximizes (21) subject to (22). First order conditions for C_1 and C_2 are familiar by now

$$U_C(C_1(\theta), h(\theta)) = U_C(C_2(\theta), 0) = -\lambda n \quad (23)$$

and imply that C_2 is independent of θ (because λn is independent of θ). C_1 depends on θ (unless $U_{CH} = 0$) only if h does. The intensive margin h is (note that $U_h < 0$)

$$-\rho(\theta) U_h(C_1(\theta), h(\theta)) = -\lambda \theta f_2(\rho(\theta)n, h(\theta)) \quad (24)$$

or, substituting from (23) and rearranging, $\theta f_2 = (\rho n)(-U_h/U_C)$: the marginal product of h in state θ equals its marginal cost, which is the shadow price $(-U_n/U_c)$ per employed worker times the number employed. The extensive margin ρ is, assuming $\rho > 0$ (the firm never closes)

$$U(C_1, h) - U(C_2, 0) - \lambda n [\theta f_1(\rho n, h) - (C_1 - C_2)] \geq 0 \quad (25)$$

so the shadow price of labor utilization ρ is

$$(C_1 - C_2) - [U(C_1, h) - U(C_2, 0)]/U_C(C_1, h).$$

Further analysis of these conditions is neither elementary nor illuminating. At this level of generality about all that can be said is that $d\rho/d\theta \geq 0$ and $dh/d\theta \geq 0$. Yet time-series data on employment and hours follow systematic patterns. Aggregate hours and employment variations are positively correlated with output growth rates (deviations about trend), and hours per week show variation of less than two hours peak to trough. Employment fluctuations account for the bulk of total labor utilization adjustments even in deep recessions. Indivisibilities appear necessary to account for this (Mortensen 1978; Kenneth Burdett and Mortensen 1980).

Consider an example: Assume $U(C, h) = U(C - \phi(h))$ where $U'' < 0$ and $\phi(h)$ is an increasing convex function. Then (23) implies equal utility in all states—there are no income effects—and $C_1(\theta) - C_2 = \phi(h(\theta)) - \phi(0)$. For production assume $f(\rho n, h) = F(\rho n \gamma(h))$, where $\gamma(h)$ has the interpretation of efficiency units of work hours. A long tradition of labor market research suggests that $\gamma(h)$ may have an ogive shape, due to set-up costs (Sidney Chapman 1909; Arthur C. Pigou 1920): productivity of a worker's time is small at small values of h, rises rapidly after some threshold is passed, and finally shows diminishing returns when h is very large. Indivisibilities due to fixed costs of market participation (John Cogan 1980, Giora Hanoch 1980) have similar implications. Hanoch includes both hours worked and weeks worked as arguments of utility functions, which generalizes (21). Then (24) and (25) become

$$\theta\gamma'(h)F'(\cdot) = \phi'(h) \qquad (26)$$
$$\theta F'(\cdot) \geq [\phi(h) - \phi(0)]/\gamma(h).$$

When $0 < \rho < 1$, the second condition in (26) holds with equality. Dividing the two expressions yields

$$\gamma'(h)/\gamma(h) = \phi'(h)/[\phi(h) - \phi(0)] \quad (27)$$

which gives a unique solution for h, say h^*. At $h = h^*$ we must have diminishing returns, or $\gamma''(h^*) < 0$. Equation (27) is independent of both ρ and θ, so $h(\theta) = h^*$, a constant whenever *any* layoffs occur. Furthermore we have in this region

$$\theta F'(\rho n \gamma(h^*)) = \phi'(h^*)/\gamma'(h^*)$$
$$= [\phi(h^*) - \phi(0)]/\gamma(h^*), \qquad (28)$$

so the shadow price of labor is $[\phi(h^*) - \phi(0)]/\gamma(h^*)$, a constant independent of θ. (28) defines $\rho(\theta)$ when layoffs are positive, and implies that $\rho(\theta)$ is increasing in θ. Fewer workers are laid off in more favorable states. Furthermore, wages $C_1(\theta)$ paid to employed workers are rigid and independent of θ whenever layoffs are positive.

Since $\rho(\theta)$ is increasing, there must be some critical value θ^* beyond which $\rho = 1$. The firm would like to hire more workers than it has contracted with in states more favorable than this. Therefore, for $\theta > \theta^*$ it is h that does all the adjusting. In this range $h(\theta)$ is defined by the first condition in (26) with ρ set equal to one. The firm's shadow price of labor is $\phi'(h)/\gamma'(h)$ here and is increasing in h on the assumptions above. Therefore $h(\theta)$ is increasing for $\theta \geq \theta^*$. $C_1(\theta)$ is increasing here as well.

The overall solution is pieced together in Figure 4. The employment rate does all the adjusting when θ falls short of θ^*. h is rigidly set at h^* here and the shadow price of labor to the firm is constant. For $\theta > \theta^*$, the shadow price of labor is rising, $\rho = 1$, and hours do all the adjusting. Furthermore, the wage paid to employed persons is "rigid" downward: C_1 is constant for $\theta \leq \theta^*$. The internal supply price of labor would be smaller than shown if contracts did not fully indemnify laid-off workers, and layoffs would be involuntary, as above. In either case the layoff rate is

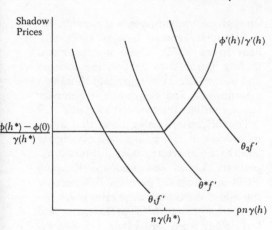

Figure 4.

decreasing in μ (the undiversifiable risk) because θ^* is decreasing in μ.

This example suggests the following interpretation of hours and employment data. In normal times (the mean of θ exceeds θ^*) hours per worker account for most total manhours variation (hours are a leading indicator). Workers are not laid off until conditions get sufficiently bad to pass beyond the threshold θ^*, at which point hours per head show downward rigidity that puts distinct limits on the use of worksharing.

This type of model can account for some of the broader features of the data, but recent international comparisons present interesting and important challenges. Robert J. Gordon (1982) compared the U.S. with Japan. Both countries exhibit about equal variance in total hours worked, but hours per worker varies more in Japan than in the U.S. and employment varies more in the U.S. The widespread use of bonuses makes for greater wage variability in Japan as well. Models of this type account for these differences on the basis of differences in preferences and technology and surely leave much unexplained. It appears as if some consideration of differences in firm-specific human

capital, labor mobility, and quasi-fixed factor ideas are required to fully account for these differences (Masanori Hashimoto 1979).

VI. Intertemporal Contracts

This survey follows the literature in expositing timeless single period models. There is a parallel intertemporal formulation, following Baily (1974) who suggested that contracts might exploit gains from trade due to capital market imperfections. The firm's greater access to capital markets allows it to save and dissave on the worker's behalf, and eliminates intertemporal uncertainty in consumption (James N. Brown 1982) that the worker cannot accomplish on his own. The contract again specifies consumption (wage payments) and labor utilization in each state and each time period, conditional on information available in that period. It mimics the solution to an intertemporal, expected utility maximization problem. Now the observed wage payments intermingle elements of intertemporal savings and dissavings as well as the usual productive efficiency considerations. Nonetheless, the formal analysis has many features in common with the one-period model. Under complete information the contract specifies (C_t, L_t) pairs conditional on the history of state realizations θ_t up to the present time t. In the leading model the worker has an intertemporally separable utility function of the form $E\Sigma U(C_t, L_t)D^t$, where D is the rate of time preference, similar to (8), and the firm is risk neutral. The budget constraint at time t equates the expected present value of future consumption to the expected present value of future production, conditional on the observed sequence $\{\theta_r\}$ at t, similar to (9).

The precise solution depends on the properties of $\{\theta_t\}$ and the extent to which capital consumption allows intertemporal

1166   *Journal of Economic Literature, Vol. XXIII (September 1985)*

diversification of aggregate disturbances (Richard Cantor 1983). Consider the simplest case in which θ is independently distributed over agents with a constant mean (Sanford Grossman and Laurence Weiss 1984). Then the insurance of Section IV is achieved by a consumption loan market, subordinated through firms. Those with adverse realizations borrow on their worker's behalf and those with favorable realizations are lenders. The loan market is cleared at a rate of interest equal to the rate of time preference (to satisfy intertemporal marginal conditions) and the analysis of Section IV carries through intact. Here the $s(\theta)$ terms of Figure 2 are the savings and dissavings components of observed earnings of workers, personal consumption is smoothed and personal labor supply is accentuated by substitution effects. "Capital market imperfections" introduce, ex post, involuntary elements in contract terms, as above.

More generally, write $\theta_{it} = \mu_t \epsilon_{it}$. Then the contract is conditioned on the history of the aggregate shock as well as on local disturbances. These aggregate shocks are undiversifiable if there are no stores of nonhuman wealth. An unanticipated adverse aggregate disturbance increases the demand for consumption loans. The rate of interest rises to ration reduced supply. Smaller aggregate consumption is redistributed out of the diversifiable risks, as before, but observed consumption and employment contain elements of Keynesian income effects. The optimal program embodies forecasts of permanent wealth to the extent that the μ-process is serially correlated and persistent. These redistribute planned consumption and labor supply over time through direct wealth effects and indirectly through their anticipated effects on interest rates. In the most general formulation, capital allows the aggregate disturbance to be partially diversified through capital accumulation in favorable aggregate conditions and

through decumulation in unfavorable circumstances (Truman Bewley 1980; William Brock 1982). These intertemporal trading possibilities reduce the income and wealth effects of aggregate shocks on consumption and employment behavior and accentuate pure substitution effects.[11]

This discussion makes clear that intertemporal contract models are closely related to the intertemporal substitution hypothesis (Lucas and Leonard Rapping 1970). A substantial practical difference is the role of measured wage rates in uncovering the structure of preferences and technology from actual data, because average wage rates do not index the true marginal product of labor or the marginal rate of substitution between C and L in contracts (Section IV). This point is important because almost all empirical studies of intertemporal substitution assume that measured wage rates fully reflect both margins in the data. Two notable exceptions are James N. Brown (1982), who attempted to estimate the optimal program directly on functional form restrictions, and Abowd and David Card (1983), who attempt to estimate the fraction of workers for whom wage rates reflect marginal conditions. The methods of Finn Kydland and Edward Prescott (1982) also rest heavily on functional forms and avoid the use of market price and wage data. But, on the conventional assumption, most recent estimates of intertemporal substitution on microdata are negligible for prime-age males (MaCurdy 1981; Joseph Altonji 1982); but they are much larger for those classes of workers, such as married women, who exhibit regular labor force transitions (Heckman and MaCurdy 1980). It is worth pointing out that in light of

---

[11] This general framework strongly links consumption and labor supply behavior unless one period preferences are strongly separable. Recent research has found excess volatility of consumption relative to permanent income and interest rates, but the extent to which this volatility can be explained by interactions with labor supply has not been studied.

the greater labor force and (contractual) job attachments traditionally exhibited by men, the maintained assumption that observed wage rates index marginal conditions is less likely to apply to them.

Studies by Finn Kydland and Edward Prescott (1982), Robert Barro and Robert King (1982), Kydland (1984), and Jisoon Lee (1984) conclude that the conventional intertemporal model cannot explain certain comovements in aggregate time-series data. The preferred specification is controversial and may require nonseparable preferences and technology. However, contract theory does not depend on these special assumptions. A contract can be written for any preferences and technology, but it always divorces measured wage rates from the production efficiency conditions of the optimum program that it embodies.

VII. *Contracts with Private Information*

As noted above, it is difficult to incorporate transactions costs and incomplete insurance in contract models. Interest in asymmetric information models has been sustained by their potential for doing this in an analytically tractable manner. The problem investigated most thoroughly so far is identical to that of Section IV with one bit of information removed: the firm is assumed to observe the realization of θ but the worker doesn't observe it (Guillermo Calvo and Edmund Phelps 1977; Hall and Lilien 1979). Recent work by Russell Cooper (1981) and John Moore (1984) consider two-sided private information models and cannot be reviewed here. Readers are forewarned that this section is more technically demanding than the rest of the survey. However, it may be skipped without significant loss of continuity.

The contract cannot be conditioned on θ because the worker cannot observe it, and since any rational employment decision must depend on the marginal product of labor, that decision must be delegated to the agent with the information, namely the firm. The contract takes the following form (Jerry Green and Charles Kahn 1983): the worker and firm agree ex ante on a compensation schedule $C(L)$ (equivalently $C(1 - L)$). The firm observes θ and instructs the employee to work $(1 - L)$ units of time in exchange for contractual compensation $C(L)$. Market competition takes the form of offering attractive compensation schedules $C(L)$, so the competitive contract maximizes expected utility of the worker subject to expected firm utility (or profit) and information constraints. The nonlinear contract pricing schedule $C(L)$ is closely related to the multipart-tariffs of Section IV. In fact the solution of the problem is formally identical to the theory of nonlinear pricing (Michael Mussa and Rosen 1978; Eric Maskin and Riley 1984).

Given any schedule $C(L)$, the firm observes θ and chooses L to maximize profit. The firm's ex post profit is $\pi(\theta, L) = \theta(1 - L) - C(L)$ so given $C(L)$ and θ, L is chosen to satisfy

$$\frac{\partial \pi}{\partial L} = -\theta - C'(L) = 0 \qquad (29)$$

so long as

$$\frac{\partial^2 \pi}{\partial L^2} = -C''(L) < 0.$$

The firm chooses L in (29) so that the marginal product of labor equals its marginal cost to the firm. Write the solution to (29) as $L(\theta)$. Comparative statics reveals

$$L'(\theta) = -1/C'' < 0.$$

The worker is always instructed to work more in favorable states and less in unfavorable states. Define $C(\theta) = C(L(\theta))$. Then $C'(\theta) = -\theta L'(\theta) > 0$, and compensation unambiguously increases in θ independently of worker preferences.

The method of solution follows an idea of Mirrlees (1971). Given $C(L)$, the firm exploits its information through (29), which holds for every possible realization of θ. Therefore (29) may be regarded as a differential equation $dC/dL = -\theta$, or $dC = -\theta dL$. Integrating by parts will yield

$$C(\theta) - C(0) = -\theta L + \int_0^\theta L(\nu)d\nu \quad (30)$$

which is a convenient way of representing the information constraint (29).

The competitive equilibrium contract maximizes the worker's expected utility subject to the firm's expected utility, as before, and to the firm's exploitation of its information (30). Define the transformation $z(\theta) = \int_0^\theta L(\nu)d\nu$. Then $z'(\theta) = L(\theta)$ and (30) becomes

$$C(\theta) = C(0) - \theta z'(\theta) + z(\theta). \quad (31)$$

Furthermore, (assuming $f(1 - L) = 1 - L$ simplifies the presentation without affecting essentials):

$$\pi(\theta) = \max_L \pi(\theta, L)$$
$$= \max_L \theta(1 - L(\theta)) - C(\theta)$$
$$= \theta - \theta z' - C(0) + \theta z' - z$$
$$= \theta - C(0) - z(\theta).$$

Now the contract can be described as a variational problem in z and z'. Recalling that $Eu = \int U(C, L)dG$, and substituting for C from (31), we seek a function $z(\theta)$ and real numbers λ and $C(0)$ that maximize

$$\int U(C(0) - \theta z' + z, z')dG$$
$$+ \lambda[\bar{v} - \int v(\theta - z - C(0))dG] \quad (32)$$

where $v(\cdot)$ is the utility function of the firm. Once $z'(\theta) = L(\theta)$ has been found, (3) is used to calculate $C(\theta)$. Eliminating θ from these two expressions implies $C(L)$.

Two marginal conditions and a boundary condition characterize the solution.

Differentiating (32) with respect to $C(0)$, yields:

$$\int_0^\infty U_C dG = -\lambda \int_0^\infty v'dG. \quad (33)$$

The *average* marginal utility of consumption for the worker is proportional to *average* marginal utility of the firm. Marginal utilities are not necessarily equated state-by-state. An Euler equation gives the margin for z:

$$(U_C + \lambda v')g(\theta) = \frac{d}{d\theta}(U_L - \theta U_C)g(\theta). \quad (34)$$

Denote the upper and lower limits of θ in $G(\theta)$ by $\hat{\theta}$ and $\underline{\theta}$ respectively. Then multiplying (34) through by $d\theta$ integrating and exploiting (33) yields

$$U_L(\hat{\theta}) - \hat{\theta}U_C(\hat{\theta}) = U_L(\underline{\theta}) - \underline{\theta}U_C(\underline{\theta}). \quad (35)$$

The boundary condition sets (35) to zero, so the contract is production efficient ($\theta = U_L/U_C$) in the best and worst states (Cooper, 1983 gives an intuitive explanation in terms of the revelation principle: the firm cannot overstate the most extreme realizations to the worker if the distribution $G(\theta)$ is bounded and the bounds are common knowledge). Using this fact and integrating (34) yields the fundamental condition

$$\int_0^\theta(U_C + \lambda v')g(\theta)d\theta = (U_L - \theta U_C)g(\theta). \quad (36)$$

Equation (36) nicely illustrates the tension between insurance and efficiency under private information. The contract cannot be production efficient for $\underline{\theta} < \theta < \hat{\theta}$ unless there is efficient sharing of risks in the Borch-Arrow sense for each state. In addition the solution generally depends on $G(\theta)$. For example, it can be shown (Mussa and Rosen 1978; Kahn and Jose Scheinkman, forthcoming) that the firm may choose the same work hours $1 - L$ for a closed interval of states. The contract certainly doesn't achieve first-best efficiency in these regions.

Much effort has gone into analyzing the sign of the inefficiency implied by (36).

Rosen: Implicit Contracts—A Survey   1169

The interpretation plays heavily on a notion of contractual commitment and enforcement that does not arise in the common information case. For suppose the contract implies production inefficiency in some state. The worker and the firm have agreed to contractual terms $C(L)$ ex ante. When this state materializes, the worker generally can infer the realized value of θ by his implicit knowledge of (29): the production function and utility function are common knowledge in this formulation; Schwartz (1983), questions how this knowledge becomes common. At that point there are unexploited gains from trade and both parties could benefit by recalibrating L so that $\theta = U_L/U_C$ ex post. However, if recontracting is allowed, the contract must unravel, because it is written under the assumption that both parties bind themselves to its ex ante terms. The extent to which private information models produce "involuntary" unemployment and overemployment depends on how these ex ante commitments can be enforced ex post. While some authors are careful to recognize this important point (especially Oliver Hart 1983), a convincing description of labor market institutions that embody this enforcement mechanism in *implicit* contracts has not been forthcoming.

Three special cases of (36) have been analyzed. The method of proof is established by Green and Kahn (1983), to which the reader is referred for details. Denote the left hand side of (36) as a function of θ, say $\zeta(\theta)$. The sign of $\zeta(\theta)$ is established by calculating its derivatives and ascertaining whether it achieves a local maximum or minimum for some interior value of θ, using boundary condition (35). The results are sensitive to the nature of risk aversion and to income effects in worker preferences.

Case 1 (Hall and Lilien 1979). Assume firms are risk neutral, workers are risk averse and have preferences of the form

$u = U(C + \psi(L))$—no income effects. Then the left hand side of (36) turns out to be identically zero, and the contract specifies $\theta = U_L/U_C$ for every θ. There is, furthermore, complete and optimal risk shifting: $u(\theta)$ is constant and the firms eats all risks. Here the $C(L)$ schedule coincides with an indifference curve, as in Figure 3 Section IV. Private and common knowledge contracts are identical in this case.

Case 2 (Grossman and Hart 1983; Azariadis 1983). Maintain the same assumptions about workers as Case 1, but let the firm be risk averse. Here Green and Kahn's proof may be extended to show that the left hand side of (36) is negative for almost all θ. Therefore, $U_L/U_C < \theta$ and the marginal social cost of labor is less than its ex post marginal product. The worker would like to recontract for more employment, ex post, in practically every state, and there is involuntary underemployment in the sense qualified above. Furthermore, the worker bears consumption risk and $u(\theta)$ is increasing in θ.

Case 3 (Green and Kahn 1983; V. V. Chari 1983). The firm is risk neutral, the worker is risk averse and has a positive income elasticity of demand for leisure (as in Section IV). Now the integral in (36) is positive for almost all θ. Therefore $U_L/U_C > \theta$, and the marginal cost of labor exceeds its marginal product. The contract leads to "involuntary overemployment" and the worker would like to recontract ex post for less work than the firm chooses. Here $u(\theta)$ is decreasing in θ and the worker is worse off in the more favorable states, as in Section IV.

The nature of these contracts is altered if workers have means to disassociate current consumption decisions from current earnings. Thus, consider the third case and assume that the worker can self-insure (Topel and Finis Welch 1983), for example, by borrowing and lending in a perfect capital market in the intertemporal context. Then the worker's self-insurance ac-

1170   *Journal of Economic Literature, Vol. XXIII (September 1985)*

tivities imply $U_C = -\lambda$ for each θ. Since the firm is risk neutral, the left side of (36) vanishes and the asymmetric information contract is perfectly efficient. Its employment and consumption properties duplicate that of Section IV. Oliver Hart (1983) adds the assumption that the firm is risk averse and gives an ingenious argument for the relevance of Case 2. Risk neutral stockholders would be reluctant to provide full insurance to the firm's management on moral hazard grounds. However, they would not be so reluctant to contract for consumption insurance with workers, because workers' labor supply is delegated through the manager in private information contracts and there are no direct moral hazards. Hence, these third parties could conceivably enforce the $U_C = -\lambda$ condition for workers. But then, risk aversion of managers ($v'' < 0$) implies that the left side of (36) must be negative for bad realizations, or involuntary underemployment. This argument is a delicate one, for it implies that the effect of third party insurance to workers is partially subverted by workers intermediating it and providing partial insurance to managers (because workers become, effectively, risk neutral). Income risks to managers are reduced by making the contractual $C(L)$ function steeper than when third party insurance is available. In favorable states the marginal cost of labor to the firm is increasing too rapidly in $(1 - L)$ and the firm does not employ as much labor as is socially desirable. In unfavorable states the marginal cost of labor is falling too fast and too much labor is released.

VIII. *Conclusion*

Not all marriages are made in heaven. Firms go bankrupt, demand shifts to other locations, supply shifts to other countries, products become obsolete and relative demands for goods have been known to change over time. Contracts call for permanent dissolutions when quasi-rents on firm specific human capital fall to zero. Serious critics of contract theory have built their case on the observation that quits rise noticeably during business cycle expansions (Herschel Grossman 1977, 1978). Contracts break down if workers accept insurance payments opportunistically in bad times and renege on premium payments by skipping out in good times. How much of observed, voluntary turnover reflects opportunism and how much of it is the rational outcome of moving workers from lower to higher valued uses?

These issues occupy much attention in current research, which is proceeding in a number of different directions too disparate to be usefully reviewed here. However, these problems are important for delimiting the scope for self-enforcing contracts that the at-will labor market, contracting institution requires, and for pointing out potential reasons why contracts might be incomplete. The common knowledge framework illustrates some of these ideas. Under these circumstances the contract would specify the conditions and terms of its dissolution up front.

A suitable reinterpretation of the model in Section III clarifies the point. Think of θ as a disturbance that permanently affects the fortunes of the firm, and interpret mL as the value of the worker's time in an alternative job in another market.[12] Then ρ has the interpretation of the probability of a permanent separation. The solution is exactly the same as shown above. The complete contract stipulates a severance payment C_2 to those workers who depart when θ falls short of θ^*. Turnover

---

[12] Holmstrom (1983) analyzes an offer-matching equilibrium when the outside opportunity is stochastic. Hall and Edward Lazear (1984) discuss two-sided uncertainty in which the bargaining costs preclude ex post renegotiation. Turnover is socially excessive in this case.

Rosen: Implicit Contracts—A Survey 1171

is efficient if the severance payment offers complete insurance, but is inefficient if severance payments are constrained and workers are not fully protected against permanent separations. For the same reasons as before, there is insufficient turnover in these latter circumstances. (See, especially, Ito 1984, also Herakles Polemarchakis and Laurence Weiss 1978; Arnott, Arthur Hosios and Stiglitz 1983; John Geanakoplos and Ito 1982; Barry Nalebuff and Richard Zeckhauser 1984.)

The need for interfirm mobility in a well functioning labor market suggests important reasons why contracts might be incomplete. A worker's knowledge and perception of outside opportunities do not materialize out of the blue. Information gathering and job search activities are costly and cannot be a matter of common knowledge by the idiosyncratic nature of job-worker matches. A worker must bear some residual job finding risks because of the moral hazard effects of personal actions on success probabilities (Steven Shavell and Laurence Weiss 1979). Furthermore, the nature of searchers' interactions gives rise to externalities that have only recently begun to be understood (Diamond 1982; Christopher Pissarides 1984). A contract must embody a delicate balance of encouraging mobility in response to permanent changes in demands and discouraging it for temporary shocks. Full insurance discourages mobility by subsidizing leisure and reducing job search intensity (Bronars 1983; Mortensen 1983b; Ito 1984). This is undesirable when severance is economically warranted, but not when demand and supply disturbances have a more transient character. Since inferences on the permanent-temporary decomposition of disturbances is itself uncertain, it appears as if contracts cannot provide complete insurance. We are driven back to conventional models to the extent that this is true.

REFERENCES

ABOWD, JOHN AND ASHENFELTER, ORLEY. "Anticipated Unemployment and Compensating Wage Differentials," in *Studies in labor markets.* Ed.: SHERWIN ROSEN. Chicago: U. of Chicago Press for NBER, 1981, pp. 141–70.

——. "Compensating Wage and Earnings Differentials for Employer Determined Hours of Work." U. of Chicago, 1984.

ABOWD, JOHN AND CARD, DAVID. "Intertemporal Substitution in the Presence of Long-Term Contracts." Working Paper 166, Industrial Relations Section, Princeton U., 1983.

AKERLOF, GEORGE AND MIYAZAKI, HAJIME. "The Implicit Contract Theory of Unemployment Meets the Wage Bill Argument," *Rev. Econ. Stud.,* Jan. 1980, 47(2), pp. 321–38.

ALCHIAN, ARMEN. "Information Costs, Pricing and Resource Unemployment," *Western Econ. J.,* June 1969, 7(2), pp. 109–28.

ALTONJI, JOSEPH G. "The Intertemporal Substitution Model of Labour Market Fluctuations: An Empirical Analysis," *Rev. Econ. Stud.,* Special Issue, 1982, 49(5), pp. 783–824.

—— AND ASHENFELTER, ORLEY. "Wage Movements and the Labour Market Equilibrium Hypothesis," *Economica,* Aug. 1980, 47(187), pp. 217–45.

ARNOTT, RICHARD AND RILEY, JOHN G. "Asymmetrical Production Possibilities, the Social Gains from Inequality and the Optimal Town," *Scand. J. Econ.,* 1977, 79(3), pp. 301–11.

——; HOSIOS, ARTHUR AND STIGLITZ, JOSEPH E. "Implicit Contracts, Labor Mobility and Unemployment," Princeton U., 1983.

ARROW, KENNETH J. "The Role of Securities in the Optimal Allocation of Risk-Bearing," *Rev. Econ. Stud.,* Apr. 1964, 31, pp. 91–96.

——. *Essays in the theory of risk bearing.* Chicago: Markham, 1971.

ASHENFELTER, ORLEY AND BROWN, JAMES. "Testing the Efficiency of Employment Contracts," *J. Polit. Econ.,* forthcoming.

AZARIADIS, COSTAS. "Implicit Contracts and Underemployment Equilibria," *J. Polit. Econ.,* Dec. 1975, 83(6), pp. 1183–1202.

——. "On the Incidence of Unemployment," *Rev. Econ. Stud.,* Feb. 1976, 43(1), pp. 115–25.

——. "Implicit Contracts and Related Topics: A Survey," in *The economics of the labour market.* Eds.: ZMIRA HORNSTEIN, et al. London: HMSO, 1979, 221–48.

——. "Employment with Asymmetric Information," *Quart. J. Econ.* Supplement 1983, 98(3), pp. 157–72.

—— AND STIGLITZ, JOSEPH E. "Implicit Contracts and Fixed Price Equilibria," *Quart. J. Econ.* Supplement 1983, 98(3), pp. 1–22.

BAILY, MARTIN N. "Wages and Employment under Uncertain Demand," *Rev. Econ. Stud.,* Jan. 1974, 41(1), pp. 37–50.

——. "On the Theory of Layoffs and Unemployment," *Econometrica*, July 1977, *45*(5), pp. 1043–64.

BARRO, ROBERT AND KING, ROBERT G. "Time-Separable Preferences and Intertemporal-Substitution Models of Business Cycles." U. of Rochester, 1982.

BECKER, GARY S. *Human capital.* NY: Columbia U. Press for NBER, 1964.

———. "A Theory of Marriage, Part I," *J. Polit. Econ.*, July/Aug. 1973, *81*(4), pp. 813–46.

BERNANKE, BEN. "An Equilibrium Model of Industrial Employment, Hours and Earnings, 1923–39." Grad. School of Bus., Stanford U., 1983.

BEWLEY, TRUMAN F. "The Permanent Income Hypothesis and Long-Run Economic Stability," *J. Econ. Theory*, June 1980, *22*(3), pp. 377–94.

BILS, MARK. "Real Wages over the Business Cycle: Evidence from Panel Data," *J. Polit. Econ.*, forthcoming.

BORCH, KARL. "Equilibrium in a Reinsurance Market," *Econometrica*, July 1962, *30*(3), pp. 424–44.

BROCK, WILLIAM A. "Asset Prices in a Production Economy," *Economics of information and uncertainty.* Ed.: JOHN JOSEPH McCALL. Chicago: U. of Chicago Press, 1982, pp. 1–47.

BRONARS, STEPHEN. "Compensating Wage Differentials and Layoff Risk in U.S. Manufacturing Industries." Ph.D. diss., U. of Chicago, 1983.

BROWN, JAMES N. "How Close to an Auction Is the Labor Market?" *Res. Lab. Econ.*, 1982, *5*, pp. 182–235.

BROWN, MURRAY AND WOLFSTETTER, ELMAR. "Underemployment and Normal Leisure," *Econ. Letters*, 1984, *15*(1–2), pp. 157–63.

BROWNING, MARTIN; DEATON, ANGUS AND IRISH, MARGARET. "A Profitable Approach to Labor Supply and Commodity Demands Over the Life-Cycle," *Econometrica*, forthcoming.

BRYANT, JOHN. "An Annotation of 'Implicit Contracts and Underemployment Equilibria,'" *J. Polit. Econ.*, Dec. 1978, *86*(6), pp. 1159–60.

BULL, CLIVE. "The Existence of Self-Enforcing Implicit Contracts." C. V. Starr Center, NYU, 1983.

BURDETT, KENNETH AND MORTENSEN, DALE T. "Search, Layoffs and Labor Market Equilibrium," *J. Polit. Econ.*, Aug. 1980, *88*(4), pp. 652–72.

CALVO, GUILLERMO A. AND PHELPS, EDMUND S. "Indexation Issues: Appendix," *J. Monet. Econ.*, Supplementary Series 1977, *5*, pp. 160–68.

CANTOR, RICHARD. "Long-Term Labor Contracts, Consumption Smoothing and Aggregate Wage Dynamics." Ohio State U., 1983.

CHAPMAN, SIDNEY J. "Hours of Labour," *Econ. J.*, Sept. 1909, *19*(3), pp. 354–79.

CHARI, V. V. "Involuntary Unemployment and Implicit Contracts," *Quart. J. Econ.*, Supplement, 1983, *98*(3), pp. 107–22.

COGAN, JOHN. "Labor Supply With Costs of Market Entry," in *Female labor supply.* Ed.: JAMES P. SMITH. Princeton, NJ: Princeton U. Press, 1980, pp. 327–64.

COOPER, RUSSELL. "Risk-Sharing and Productive Efficiency in Labor Contracts Under Bilateral Asymmetric Information." U. of Pennsylvania, 1981.

———. "A Note on Overemployment/Underemployment in Labor Contracts Under Asymmetric Information," *Econ. Letters*, 1983, *12*(1), pp. 81–87.

DEBREU, GERARD. *The theory of value.* Cowles Foundation Monograph 17. New Haven: Yale U. Press, 1959.

DIAMOND, PETER. "Aggregate Demand Management in Search Equilibrium," *J. Polit. Econ.*, Oct. 1982, *90*(5), pp. 881–94.

——— AND ROTHSCHILD, MICHAEL. *Uncertainty in economics.* NY: Academic Press, 1978.

EPSTEIN, RICHARD A. "In Praise of the Contract at Will," *Univ. Chicago Law Rev.*, Fall 1984, *51*(4), pp. 956–82.

FAIR, RAY C. *The short-run demand for workers and hours.* Amsterdam: North-Holland Pub. Co., 1969.

FELDSTEIN, MARTIN. "Specification of the Labour Input in the Aggregate Production Function," *Rev. Econ. Stud.*, Oct. 1967, *34*, pp. 375–86.

———. "The Importance of Temporary Layoffs: An Empirical Analysis," *Brookings Pap. Econ. Act.*, 1975, *3*, pp. 725–44.

———. "Temporary Layoffs in the Theory of Unemployment," *J. Polit. Econ.*, Oct. 1976, *84*(5), pp. 937–57.

FISCHER, STANLEY. "Long-Term Contracts, Rational Expectations and the Optimum Money Supply Rule," *J. Polit. Econ.*, Feb. 1977, *85*(1), pp. 191–205.

FRIEDMAN, MILTON. "The Role of Monetary Policy," *Amer. Econ. Rev.*, Mar. 1968, *58*(1), pp. 1–17.

———. *Price theory: A provisional text.* Chicago: Aldine Pub. Co., 1962.

———. *A theory of the consumption function.* Princeton, NJ: Princeton U. Press, 1957.

FRISCH, RAGNAR. *New methods of measuring marginal utility.* Tübingen: J.C.B. Mohr, 1932.

GEANAKOPLOS, JOHN AND ITO, TAKATOSHI. "On Implicit Contracts and Involuntary Unemployment." Cowles Foundation Discussion Paper No. 640, 1982.

GHEZ, GILBERT AND BECKER, GARY S. *The allocation of time and goods over the life cycle.* NY: Columbia U. Press for NBER, 1975.

GORDON, DONALD F. "A Neo-Classical Theory of Keynesian Unemployment," *Econ. Inquiry*, Dec. 1974, *12*(4), pp. 431–59.

GORDON, ROBERT J. "Why U.S. Wage and Employment Behavior Differs from That in Britain and Japan," *Econ. J.*, Mar. 1982, *92*(365), pp. 13–44.

GRAY, JO ANNA. "Wage Indexation: A Macroeconomic Approach," *J. Monet. Econ.*, Apr. 1976, *2*(2), pp. 221–36.

GREEN, JERRY AND KAHN, CHARLES M. "Wage Employment Contracts," *Quart. J. Econ.*, Supplement 1983, *98*(3), pp. 173–87.

GROSSMAN, HERSCHEL. "Risk Shifting, Layoffs and Seniority," *J. Monet. Econ.*, Nov. 1978, *4*(4), pp. 661–86.

———. "Risk Shifting and Reliability in Labor Markets," *Scand. J. Econ.*, 1977, *79*(2), pp. 187–209.

GROSSMAN, MICHAEL. "Unemployment and Con-

Rosen: Implicit Contracts—A Survey 1173

sumption: Note" *Amer. Econ. Rev.*, Mar. 1973, *63*(1), pp. 208–13.

GROSSMAN, SANFORD J. AND HART, OLIVER D. "Implicit Contracts, Moral Hazard and Unemployment," *Amer. Econ. Rev.*, May 1981, *71*(2), pp. 301–07.

———. "Implicit Contracts under Asymmetrical Information," *Quart. J. Econ.* Supplement 1983, *98*(3), pp. 123–56.

GROSSMAN, SANFORD J. AND WEISS, LAURENCE. "Saving and Insurance," in *Bayesian models in economic theory.* Eds.: M. BOYER AND R. E. KIHLSTROM. NY: Elsevier, 1984, pp. 303–11.

HALL, ROBERT E. "Why is the Unemployment Rate So High at Full Employment?" *Brookings Pap. Econ. Act.*, 1970, *3*, pp. 369–410.

———. "A Theory of the Natural Unemployment Rate and the Duration of Employment," *J. Monet. Econ.*, Apr. 1979, *5*(2), pp. 153–69.

———. "Employment Fluctuations and Wage Rigidity." *Brookings Pap. Econ. Act.*, 1980a, *1*, pp. 91–123.

———. "Labor Supply and Aggregate Fluctuations," *Carnegie-Rochester Conference Series on Public Policy*, *12*, 1980b, pp. 7–33.

———. "The Importance of Lifetime Jobs in the U.S. Economy," *Amer. Econ. Rev.*, Sept. 1982, *72*(4), pp. 716–24.

——— AND LAZEAR, EDWARD P. "The Excess Sensitivity of Layoffs and Quits to Demand," *J. Lab. Econ.*, 1984, *2*(2), pp. 253–58.

——— AND LILIEN, DAVID M. "Efficient Wage Bargains Under Uncertain Supply and Demand," *Amer. Econ. Rev.*, Dec. 1979, *69*(5), pp. 868–79.

HAMERMESH, DANIEL. "Social Insurance and Consumption," *Amer. Econ. Rev.*, Mar. 1982, *72*(1), pp. 101–13.

HANOCH, GIORA. "A Multivariate Model of Labor Supply: Methodology and Estimation," in *Female labor supply.* Ed.: JAMES P. SMITH. Princeton, NJ: Princeton U. Press, 1980, pp. 249–326.

HARBERGER, ARNOLD C. "On Measuring the Social Opportunity Cost of Labor," *Int. Lab. Rev.*, June 1971, *103*(6), pp. 559–79.

HARRIS, JOHN R. AND TODARO, MICHAEL P. "Migration, Unemployment and Development: A Two-Sector Analysis," *Amer. Econ. Rev.*, Mar. 1970, *60*(1), pp. 126–42.

HART, OLIVER D. "Optimal Labour Contracts Under Assymmetric Information: An Introduction," *Rev. Econ. Stud.*, Jan. 1983, *50*(1), pp. 3–35.

HART, ROBERT A. *The economics of non-wage labour costs.* London: George Allen & Unwin, 1984.

HASHIMOTO, MASANORI. "Bonus Payments, On-the-Job Training and Lifetime Employment in Japan," *J. Polit. Econ.*, Part 1, Oct. 1979, *87*(5), pp. 1086–1104.

HECKMAN, JAMES J. AND MACURDY, THOMAS. "A Life Cycle Model of Female Labor Supply," *Rev. Econ. Stud.*, Jan. 1980, *47*(1), pp. 47–74.

——— AND SEDLACEK, GUILERMO. "An Equilibrium Model of the Industrial Distribution of Workers and Wages." U. of Chicago, 1984.

HEY, JOHN D. *Uncertainty in microeconomics.* NY: NYU Press, 1979.

HICKS, JOHN R. *The theory of wages.* London: Macmillan, 1932.

HOLMSTROM, BENGT. "Contractual Models of the Labor Market," *Amer. Econ. Rev.*, May 1981, *71*(2), pp. 308–13.

———. "Equilibrium Long Term Contracts," *Quart. J. Econ.*, Supplement 1983, *98*(3), pp. 23–54.

HUTCHENS, ROBERT M. "Layoffs and Labor Supply," *Int. Econ. Rev.*, Feb. 1983, *24*(1), pp. 37–55.

ITO, TAKATOSHI. "Implicit Contract Theory: A Critical Survey." U. of Minnesota, 1982.

———. "Labor Contracts With Voluntary Quits." U. of Minnesota, 1984.

JOHANSEN, LEIF. *Production functions.* Amsterdam: North-Holland Pub. Co., 1972.

JOHNSON, WILLIAM R. "A Theory of Job Shopping," *Quart. J. Econ.*, May 1978, *92*(2), pp. 261–78.

JOVANOVIC, BOYAN. "Job Matching and the Theory of Turnover," *J. Polit. Econ.*, Oct. 1979, *87*(5), pp. 972–90.

KAHN, CHARLES M. AND SCHEINKMAN, JOSE. "Optimal Employment Contracts With Bankruptcy Constraints," *J. Econ. Theory*, forthcoming.

KATZ, LAWRENCE. "Layoffs, Uncertain Recall and the Duration of Unemployment." MIT, 1984.

KIHLSTROM, RICHARD E. AND LAFFONT, JEAN-Jacques. "A General Equilibrium Enterpreneurial Theory of Firm Formation Based on Risk Aversion," *J. Polit. Econ.*, Aug. 1979, *87*(4), pp. 719–48.

———. "Implicit Contracts and Free Entry," *Quart. J. Econ.*, Supplement 1983, *98*(3), pp. 55–106.

KINOSHITA, TOMIO. "Working Hours and Hedonic Wages in the Market Equilibrium." Musachi U., 1985.

KNIGHT, FRANK H. *Risk, uncertainty and profit.* Boston: Houghton Mifflin & Co., 1921.

KYDLAND, FINN E. "Labor Force Heterogeneity and the Business Cycle," *Carnegie-Rochester Conference Series on Public Policy*, Autumn 1984, *20*.

——— AND PRESCOTT, EDWARD C. "Time To Build and Aggregate Fluctuations," *Econometrica*, Nov. 1982, *50*(6), pp. 1345–70.

LEE, JISOON. "A Rational Expectations Model of Labor Supply." Ph.D. diss., U. of Chicago, 1984.

LEONTIEF, WASSILY. "The Pure Theory of the Guaranteed Annual Wage Contract," *J. Polit. Econ.*, Feb. 1946, *54*(1), pp. 76–79.

LEWIS, H. GREGG. "Employer Interests in Employee Hours of Work." U. of Chicago, 1969.

LILIEN, DAVID. "The Cyclical Pattern of Temporary Layoffs in United States Manufacturing," *Rev. Econ. Statist.*, Feb. 1980, *62*(1), pp. 24–31.

LUCAS, ROBERT E., JR. "Some International Evidence of Output-Inflation Trade Offs," *Amer. Econ. Rev.*, June 1973, *63*(2), pp. 326–34.

——— AND RAPPING, LEONARD A. "Real Wages, Employment and Inflation," in *Microeconomic foundations of employment and inflation theory.* Eds.: EDMUND PHELPS, et al. NY: W. W. Norton, 1970.

LUNDBERG, SHELLY. "Tied Wage Hours Offers and

the Endogeneity of Wages." NBER Working Paper no. 1431, 1984.

MACURDY, THOMAS E. "An Empirical Model of Labor Supply in a Life-Cycle Setting," *J. Polit. Econ.*, Dec. 1981, *89*(6), pp. 1059–86.

——— AND PENCAVEL, JOHN. "Testing Between Competing Models of Wage and Employment Determination in Unionized Markets," *J. Polit. Econ.*, forthcoming.

MCDONALD, IAN M. AND SOLOW, ROBERT M. "Wage Bargaining and Employment," *Amer. Econ. Rev.*, Dec. 1981, *71*(5), pp. 896–908.

MASKIN, ERIC AND RILEY, JOHN. "Monopoly With Incomplete Information," *Rand J. Econ.*, Summer 1984, *15*(2), pp. 171–96.

MILLAR, JAMES R. "A Theory of On-the-Job Training." U. of Toronto, 1971.

MINCER, JACOB. "Unemployment Effects of Minimum Wages," *J. Polit. Econ.*, Aug. 1976, *84*(4, Part 2), pp. S87–S104.

——— AND JOVANOVIC, BOYAN. "Labor Mobility and Wages," in *Studies in labor markets*. Ed.: SHERWIN ROSEN. Chicago: U. of Chicago Press for NBER, 1981, pp. 21–64.

MIRRLEES, JAMES. "An Exploration in the Theory of Optimum Income Taxation," *Rev. Econ. Stud.*, Apr. 1971, *38*(114), pp. 175–208.

——— "The Optimum Town," *Swedish J. Econ.*, Mar. 1972, *74*(1), pp. 114–35.

MIYAZAKI, HAJIME AND NEARY, HUGH M. "The Illyrian Firm Revisited," *Bell J. Econ.*, 1983, *14*(1), pp. 259–70.

——— "Output, Work Hours and Employment in the Short-Run of a Labor-Managed Firm." Stanford U., 1983.

MODIGLIANI, FRANCO. "Liquidity Preference and the Theory of Interest and Money," *Econometrica*, Jan. 1944, *12*(1), pp. 45–88.

MOORE, JOHN. "Contracting Between Two Parties with Private Information." London School of Econ., 1984.

MORTENSEN, DALE T. "On the Theory of Layoffs." Northwestern U., 1978.

——— "A Welfare Analysis of Unemployment Insurance: Variations on Second Best Themes," *Carnegie-Rochester Series on Public Policy*, Autumn 1983a, *19*, pp. 67–98.

——— "Labor Contract Equilibria in an 'Island' Economy." Northwestern U., 1983b.

MUSSA, MICHAEL AND ROSEN, SHERWIN. "Monopoly and Product Quality," *J. Econ. Theory*, Aug. 1978, *18*(2), pp. 301–07.

NADIRI, M. ISHAQ AND ROSEN, SHERWIN. "Interrelated Factor Demand Functions," *Amer. Econ. Rev.*, Sept. 1969, *59*(4, Part 1), pp. 457–71.

NALEBUFF, BARRY AND ZECKHAUSER, RICHARD. "Involuntary Unemployment Reconsidered: Second-Best Contracting with Heterogeneous Firms and Workers." Harvard U., 1984.

NEFTCI, SALIH N. "A Time-Series Analysis of the Real Wages-Employment Relationship," *J. Polit. Econ.*, Apr. 1978, *86*(2), pp. 281–91.

OI, WALTER Y. "Labor as a Quasi-Fixed Factor," *J. Polit. Econ.*, Dec. 1962, *70*(6), pp. 538–55.

OKUN, ARTHUR. *Prices and quantities*. Wash., DC: The Brookings Institution, 1981.

PIGOU, ARTHUR C. *The economics of welfare*. London: Macmillan, 1920.

PISSARIDES, CHRISTOPHER A. "Search Intensity, Job Advertising and Efficiency," *J. Lab. Econ.*, Jan. 1984, *2*(1), pp. 128–43.

POLEMARCHAKIS, HERAKLES M. AND WEISS, LAURENCE. "Fixed Wages, Layoffs, Unemployment Compensation and Welfare," *Amer. Econ. Rev.*, Dec. 1978, *68*(5), pp. 909–17.

RAISIAN, JOHN. "Contracts, Job Experience and Cyclical Labor Market Adjustments," *J. Lab. Econ.*, Apr. 1983, *1*(2), pp. 152–70.

RANDOLPH, WILLIAM C. "Employment Relationships: Till Death Do Us Part?" Ph.D. diss., SUNY, Stony Brook, 1983.

REDER, MELVIN W. "Wage Structure Theory and Measurement," in *Aspects of Labor economics: A conference of the Universities-National Bureau Committee for Economic Research*. Princeton, NJ: Princeton U. Press, 1962, pp. 257–318.

ROSEN, SHERWIN. "Short-Run Employment Variation on Class-I Railroads in the U.S., 1947–1963," *Econometrica*, July–Oct. 1968, *36*(3), pp. 511–29.

——— "Unemployment and Insurance," *Carnegie-Rochester Conference Series on Public Policy*, Autumn 1983, *20*, pp. 5–49.

ROTHSCHILD, MICHAEL AND STIGLITZ, JOSEPH E. "Increasing Risk: I. A Definition," *J. Econ. Theory*, Sept. 1970, *2*(3), pp. 225–43.

SARGENT, THOMAS J. *Macroeconomic theory*. NY: Academic Press, 1979.

SCHULTZE, CHARLES. "Microeconomic Efficiency and Nominal Wage Stickiness," *Amer. Econ. Rev.*, Mar. 1985, *75*(1), pp. 1–15.

SHAPIRO, CARL AND STIGLITZ, JOSEPH E. "Equilibrium Unemployment as a Worker Discipline Device," *Amer. Econ. Rev.*, June 1984, *74*(3), pp. 433–44.

SHAVELL, STEPHEN AND WEISS, LAURENCE. "The Optimal Payment of Unemployment Insurance Benefits Over Time," *J. Polit. Econ.*, Dec. 1979, *87*(6), pp. 1347–62.

SMITH, ADAM. *The wealth of nations*. Modern Library Edition. NY: Random House, [1776] 1947.

SOLOW, ROBERT M. "Investment and Technical Progress," in *Stanford symposium on mathematical models in the social sciences*. Eds.: KENNETH J. ARROW, SAMUEL KARLIN AND PATRICK SUPPES. Stanford: Stanford U. Press, 1960, pp. 89–104.

STIGLER, GEORGE J. "Production and Distribution in the Short Run," *J. Polit. Econ.*, June 1939, *47*(3), pp. 305–27.

STIGLITZ, JOSEPH E. "Theories of Wage Rigidity." Princeton U., 1984.

SCHWARTZ, ABA. "The Implicit Contract Model and Labor Markets: A Critique." Tel Aviv U., 1983.

TAYLOR, JOHN. "Aggregate Dynamics and Staggered Contracts," *J. Polit. Econ.*, Feb. 1980, *88*(1), pp. 1–23.

TODARO, MICHAEL P. "A Model for Labor Migration and Urban Unemployment In Less-Developed

Rosen: Implicit Contracts—A Survey 1175

Countries," *Amer. Econ. Rev.*, Mar. 1969, *59*(1), pp. 138–48.

TOPEL, ROBERT E. "On Layoffs and Unemployment Insurance," *Amer. Econ. Rev.*, Sept. 1983, *83*(4), pp. 541–59.

———. "Local Labor Markets," *J. Polit. Econ.*, forthcoming.

——— AND WELCH, FINIS. "Self-Insurance and Efficient Employment Contracts." U. of Chicago, 1983.

WILSON, ROBERT. "The Theory of Syndicates," *Econometrica*, Jan. 1968, *36*, pp. 119–32.

Part VIII
Related Approaches

[21]

Wage Bargaining and Employment

By IAN M. MCDONALD AND ROBERT M. SOLOW*

One of the perennial problems of business cycle theory has been the search for a convincing empirical description and theoretical explanation of the behavior of wage rates during fluctuations in output and employment. Even the empirical question is hardly settled, although the most recent careful study (see P. T. Geary and John Kennan) confirms the prevailing view that real-wage movements are more or less independent of the business cycle. There are really two subquestions here. The first presumes that nominal wage stickiness is the main route by which nominal disturbances have real macroeconomic effects, and asks why nominal wages should be sticky. The second focuses on real wages, and asks why fluctuations in the demand for labor should so often lead to large changes in employment and small, unsystematic, changes in the real wage.

We address only the second of these subquestions. We do so in the context of explicit bargaining over wages and employment by a trade union and a firm or group of firms, though one could hope that the results might apply loosely even where an informally organized labor pool bargains implicitly with one or more long-time employers. We do not harbor the illusion that trade unions are the only important source of wage stickiness. There are other plausible (and implausible) stories. Some, like this one, rest partially on optimizing decisions; others do not.

The impulse to this study was macroeconomic, but our focus is on a single employer and a single labor pool. Our methods, and therefore our conclusions, are entirely partial equilibrium. If the short-run mobility of labor is slight, and if fluctuations in real aggregate demand affect many sectors synchronously, then perhaps the mechanism we uncover here could be important in the business cycle

*University of Melbourne and Massachusetts Institute of Technology, respectively.

context. But the work of embedding it in a complete macroeconomic model remains to be done.

We begin with a model in which the union is a simple monopolist, setting the wage rate unilaterally to maximize the expected or total utility of its members, and allowing the employer complete discretion over employment. We then consider a more complex institutional setup in which the union and the firm are supposed to bargain over both wage and employment and reach an outcome efficient for them both. (The monopoly outcome is not efficient, for the traditional reason.) There is, of course, a whole range of efficient bargains. A complete theory must single out one of them, but there is unlikely ever to be universal agreement on the right way to do so. Our approach is simply to try out several simple conventions and several formal solutions to the bargaining problem. We provide a framework within which they are all seen to bear a family resemblance to one another. Moreover, there is a certain assumption which makes all the proposed solutions share an important characteristic: the effects of a downswing or upswing in final demand on the negotiated outcome can be decomposed into two steps which reinforce each other with respect to employment and offset each other with respect to the wage. So it would not be surprising to find large fluctuations in employment and small unsystematic fluctuations in real wages during business cycles.

The key assumption is that product-market conditions are more sensitive to the business cycle than the reservation wage is. This would be the case, for instance, if (a) nonmarket opportunities including unemployment insurance benefits, which are not cyclically vulnerable, play an important role in the determination of the reservation wage, and/or (b) interemployer mobility is so limited that outside market opportunities figure only slightly in workers' calculations.

to different degrees by aggregate fluctuations. For this reason alone—as a referee has pointed out—one might expect the relevant reservation wage, and even its average across industries, to vary systematically during business cycles. Nevertheless, to the extent that industrial and occupational mobility is limited in the time span relevant to business cycles, we believe our story retains plausibility.

The best developed analytical approach to this problem is the theory of implicit contracts (surveyed by Costas Azariadis). In that literature, a contract is a long-term agreement in the sense that the economic environment will change in an only probabilistically known way during the life of the contract. On the reasonable assumption that the firm is less risk averse than its employees, the typical outcome is that an efficient contract will be wage stabilizing and (unless special features are introduced) employment stabilizing as well. In our approach, by contrast, the wage-employment bargain is struck after economic conditions in the firm's product market and in the surrounding labor market are known. It is a short-term or one-shot contract. Risk enters only in a trivial sense: if the contract calls for a fraction of the union's homogeneous membership to be unemployed, the unlucky ones are chosen at random.

In real life, negotiated contracts are usually long term. But they do not specify employment, which typically is left to the discretion of the employer; in consequence, employment fluctuates a lot. Our reconciliation of the stylized facts, the theory of implicit contracts, and our own theory goes like this: if a series of short contracts would lead as our model suggests to wide variation in employment and fairly stable wages, then the same outcome might reasonably well be achieved by a long-term contract in which a stable wage is specified but the level of employment is chosen at will by the firm. (We do need a general restraint on employers of a sort that could be accomplished by "featherbedding" work rules.)

I. A Simple Monopoly Union

The simplest interesting noncompetitive institutional setup is that of a monopoly union which can set the wage unilaterally. The employer (or employers) then chooses the volume of employment. Most collective bargaining agreements do give the employer discretion over the volume of employment. Why this should be so is an interesting question (see Robert Hall and David Lilien). But it is a rare trade union that literally controls the wage and we take up more complicated bargaining arrangements later. The simple monopoly case has been analyzed before, of course (see, for example, Allan Cartter), and we have only a few novelties to add. We use this analysis mainly as a vehicle to introduce concepts, establish notation, and draw some diagrams.

The firm is characterized by a revenue function $R(L)$ giving sales proceeds as a function of employment. If the firm were a price taker in its product market, $R(L)$ would be simply $pF(L)$ where p is the parametric product price and $F(L)$ is the production function relating employment to output. We assume, as usual, that $R(0)=0$ and $R(L)$ is concave, with marginal revenue eventually becoming very small or even negative. Profit is then $R(L)-wL$.[1] If the firm is a profit maximizer, it is indifferent among (w, L) combinations that leave $R(L)-wL$ constant. These isoprofit curves in the (w, L) plane serve as indifference curves for the firm. The slope of an isoprofit curve through (w, L) is $dw/dL=(R'(L)-w)/L$. For any L, isoprofit curves have positive slope until w reaches $R'(L)$, then negative. For higher L, the switch occurs at a lower w, so the firm's indifference map is as shown in Figure 1. For any L, a smaller w creates a bigger profit, so lower isoprofit curves are better for the firm.

Let the union quote a wage w_1. The firm then seeks the lowest indifference curve that touches the horizontal line at height w_1. That is to say, it solves $R'(L_1)-w_1=0$: marginal

---

[1]Product price and wage rate are to be thought of as deflated by a general price index.

898   *THE AMERICAN ECONOMIC REVIEW*   *DECEMBER 1981*

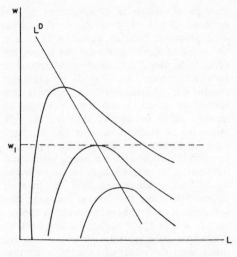

FIGURE 1

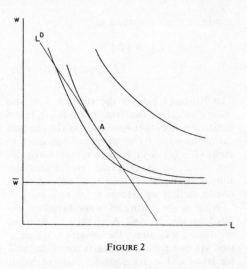

FIGURE 2

revenue product of labor equals the wage. In other words, the firm's demand curve for labor is the locus of maximum points of the indifference curves in the (w, L) plane. It is downward sloping, by virtue of the concavity of $R(L)$.

The union can achieve any point along the firm's demand curve. What is the union's objective? That is an old question in labor economics. We choose a particular answer and use it throughout. Suppose the union has N members, all alike. If L of them are employed, each member has probability L/N of having a job and achieving a level of utility $U(w) - D$ and probability $1 - (L/N)$ of not being employed by the firm, where D is the fixed additive disutility of holding a job.[2] If not employed by the firm a worker achieves a level of utility $U(w_u)$, where w_u can be thought of, for short, as an unemployment compensation benefit, but should really include all the other contributions to the standard of living that would not be received if the worker were employed by the bargaining firm. $U(x)$ is the standard sort of concave utility function.

[2] We ignore—by choice—the possibility that workers are free to choose the hours and intensity of work.

The expected utility of a union member is therefore $N^{-1}\{L(U(w) - D) + (N - L)U(w_u)\}$, which can be written as $U(w_u) + N^{-1}L\{U(w) - D - U(w_u)\}$. Since w_u and N are treated as data for the purpose of union wage setting, we can set $D + U(w_u) = \bar{U}$ and summarize by saying that the union wishes to maximize $L(U(w) - \bar{U})$. The logic of this is that $L(U - \bar{U})$ is the membership's aggregate gain from employment, over and above the income w_u that every member starts with. The union's indifference map is derived from $L(U(w) - \bar{U}) = $ constant; the indifference curves have the usual downward-sloping convex shape in the (L, w) plane. They have the special property that they are all asymptotic to the horizontal at $w = \bar{w}$, where $\bar{w}$ is derived from $U(\bar{w}) = \bar{U}$. This is shown in Figure 2.

The best wage for the union to set is determined in the obvious way by the tangency of an indifference curve with the employer's labor-demand curve as shown in Figure 2. Mathematically, this amounts to finding the maximum of $L(U(w) - \bar{U})$ with respect to L and w, subject to the constraint $R'(L) - w = 0$. We can write down the first-order condition directly by equating the slope of the indifference curve through (w, L) (i.e., $-(U - \bar{U})/LU'$) to the slope of the (inverse) demand function (i.e., $R''(L)$). Since $w = R'(L)$ at any eligible point, the first-order condition can be written as

$$(1) \quad -LR''(L)/R'(L)$$
$$= \left(U(w)-\overline{U}\right)/wU'(w).$$

The left-hand side is the reciprocal of the wage elasticity of the demand for labor, taken positively; the right-hand side is the reciprocal of the elasticity of the gain from employment $(U-\overline{U})$ with respect to the wage. So the condition is that the two elasticities should be equal. (There is a second-order condition that we assume to be satisfied.)

What is the nature of wage behavior implied by this model? A change in demand conditions will affect the union's wage decision via two routes, the elasticity of demand for labor and $\overline{w}$. We consider them in order.

Solve $w = R'(L)$ to give the demand function in direct form, and insert a parameter B (for business cycle), with the convention that an increase in B increases the demand for labor at any wage. Thus the demand for labor is $L = G(w, B)$. As B rises and falls, how is the effect divided between changes in w and changes in L? Consider the first-order condition (1) written as

$$(2) \quad wG_w(w, B)/G(w, B)$$
$$= wU'(w)/\left(U(w)-\overline{U}\right).$$

The cyclical sensitivity of the wage clearly depends on the extent to which changes in B affect the elasticity of demand for labor at any given wage. For instance, if the demand function shifts isoelastically—that is, the demand for labor falls in a recession, but with its elasticity unchanged at each wage—then we can always write $G(w, B) = BG(w)$, and it is obvious that (2) does not depend on B at all. In that case, the wage will be rigid during business cycles and fluctuations will fall entirely on employment. One can easily imagine cases in which the monopoly wage will move countercyclically, or procyclically for that matter, thus diminishing or magnifying the accompanying fluctuations in employment.

The other way in which the level of aggregate activity can affect the desired wage is through $\overline{w}$, which is composed of several elements. Some of these elements, such as unemployment benefits, the value of leisure, the value of working around the house, net gains from illegal activities, would appear to be affected very little, if at all, by aggregate conditions. (Unemployment benefits are sometimes raised in recession, imparting an upward effect on $\overline{w}$ and thus w.) But the other major element in $\overline{w}$ is the expected value of alternative employment opportunities and this should have a strong procyclical fluctuation through changes in the probability of finding alternative jobs and in their wages. The effect this has on the wage rate will depend on just how important a component of $\overline{w}$ it is. If job mobility is low, and/or if changes in wage rates in other jobs are small, then the effect of changes in alternative job opportunities will be slight.

We conclude this section with a canonical example. Let f be a constant elasticity of demand for labor, however generated. Take $U(w) = w^b/b$, where b is less than one, but may be negative. Then (1) yields $w/\overline{w} = (1 - b/f)^{-1/b}$. Thus the monopoly wage depends negatively on the elasticity of labor demand and negatively on the risk-aversion parameter $(1-b)$. Intuitively this is how it should be. For example, if $f = \frac{1}{2}$ and $(1-b) = 3$, then the monopoly wage is $(5)^{1/2}$ times the "minimum supply price" $\overline{w}$. If f is as low as $\frac{1}{4}$, $w = 3\overline{w}$. If $f = \frac{1}{2}$ and $(1-b) = 2$, $w = 3\overline{w}$. If $f = \frac{1}{4}$, $(1-b) = 2$ then $w = 5\overline{w}$. These low values of f are in accord with econometric results. Notice that if they are combined with positive values of $(1-b)$ less than 1 the outcome is much less "realistic": thus $f = \frac{1}{2}$ and $1-b = 2/3$ implies $w = 27\overline{w}$.

II. Efficient Bargains

The model of wage determination just described is even more like simple product-market monopoly than it looks. The difference in appearance arises because the monopolist, in this case the union, maximizes a utility function and not profits. It is not surprising, then, that the wage-employment outcome shown at point A in Figure 2 is not efficient. There are wage-employment points at which both parties are better off. This is

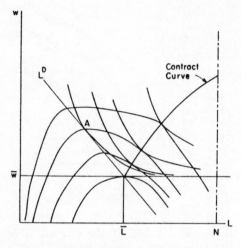

FIGURE 3

easily seen in Figure 3. The constant-profit curve passing through A is by construction horizontal at A. Therefore it cuts the downward-sloping indifference curve through A. The region to the southeast of A, between the isoprofit curve and the indifference curve, is the set of outcomes Pareto superior to A. The monopoly wage is too high and employment too low. Obviously efficient bargains are points of tangency between an isoprofit curve and an indifference curve. We call the locus of such points the contract curve; in this context that is the *mot juste*. An example is shown in Figure 3.

More complicated institutional arrangements are necessary for the achievement of efficient bargains. In particular, the union has to exercise some sort of influence over the level of employment, in contrast to the simple case where the level of employment is set unilaterally by the employer. Since the objective is to increase employment beyond the level given by the labor demand schedule, manning agreements or "featherbedding" are likely to be adopted. If it is impractical to specify the level of employment in the contract, an efficient outcome may be approximately achievable if the contract specifies the number of workers per machine, or some other similar rule, and leaves the overall aggregate to the discretion of the employer.

The contract curve is characterized by equality of the slopes of a union indifference curve and an isoprofit curve. This condition yields the equation

$$(3) \quad (U(w) - U(\bar{w}))/U'(w) = w - R'(L).$$

The first thing to notice is that the contract curve intersects the firm's labor demand curve at $w = \bar{w}$, because the right-hand side of (3) vanishes along the demand curve, and the left-hand side[3] is zero only at $\bar{w}$. The point $(\bar{w}, \bar{L})$ is actually the competitive outcome for this model. If there were no union and $\bar{U}$ were the level of utility attainable elsewhere in the economy,[4] then $\bar{w}$ would be the given supply price of labor to the employer, who would maximize profits at $\bar{L}$.

The slope of the contract curve is, by differentiation of (3),

$$dw/dL = -U'(w)R''(L)$$
$$/(U''(w)(R'(L) - w)).$$

Thus the contract curve is momentarily vertical at $(\bar{w}, \bar{L})$, and positively sloped elsewhere (because, from (3) $w \gtreqless \bar{w}$ implies $w \gtreqless R'(L)$).[5] No bargain can be struck with $w < \bar{w}$ so the contract curve does not extend below $\bar{w}$. If we take the total membership of the union as a given number N, then the contract curve rises to the northeast until it reaches the vertical at N, where it ends. The effective part of the contract curve might end earlier if there is an $L < N$ at which the firm's operating profit becomes small enough to induce it to shut down.

Everywhere along the contract curve, except at $(\bar{w}, \bar{L})$, the wage exceeds the marginal revenue product of employment. The firm is

---

[3] The expression on the left comes up frequently in the theory of contracts. If expected utility is $pU(w) + (1-p)U(\bar{w})$, then the left-hand side of (3) is the marginal rate of substitution between p and w evaluated at $p = 1$ (full employment).

[4] That would be the case, for instance, if there were no unemployment compensation, but a large supply of jobs at wage $\bar{w}$.

[5] If the marginal utility of income were constant then the contract curve would be vertical, as in Hall and Lilien.

thus being induced, presumably by an all-or-none offer, to employ more workers than it would like at the agreed-upon wage. This is the insight that led to Wassily Leontief's pioneering paper. An even stronger statement is true: all along the contract curve, except at $(\bar{w}, \bar{L})$, the marginal revenue product of employment falls short of $\bar{w}$. If one thinks of $\bar{w}$ as the true supply price of labor to the employer or industry, then this is a strong reminder that the bargains along the contract curve are efficient only from the point of view of the employer and the fixed membership of the union.

To see how the contract curve is affected by changes in the economic environment, we rewrite the revenue function as $R(L, B)$, and assume that R_B and R_{LB} are both positive: prosperity increases total revenue and the marginal revenue product of labor at any level of employment. Then (3) becomes

$$(3') \quad (U(w) - U(\bar{w}))/U'(w)$$

$$= w - R_L(L, B).$$

If we now differentiate (3') with respect to B, holding L constant, we find

$$\partial w/\partial B = R_{LB}(L, B)U'(w)^2$$

$$/((U(w) - U(\bar{w}))U''(w)) < 0,$$

and similarly

$$\partial w/\partial \bar{w} = -U'(w)U'(\bar{w})$$

$$/((U(w) - U(\bar{w}))U''(w)) > 0.$$

Thus an increase in B (an improvement in the firm's product market) shifts the contract curve to the right. It starts at $\bar{w}$ on the new demand curve; the negotiated level of employment is higher at any wage in an efficient bargain. An increase in $\bar{w}$ (an improvement in the economy-wide alternatives open to workers) has a different effect. If the new value is $\bar{w}$, the new contract curve begins at $(\bar{w}, \bar{L})$, where $\bar{L}$ comes from the labor-demand curve. Hence the starting point of the new contract curve is shifted to the NW, and the new contract curve lies everywhere

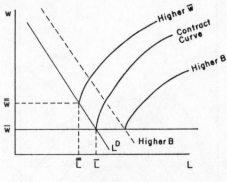

FIGURE 4

above the old one. If the external labor market improves, efficient bargains have a higher wage at any level of employment. (See Figure 4.)

Generally speaking, simultaneous improvements in the labor market and the product market produce offsetting effects on the contract curve. Since B and $\bar{w}$ are not easily commensurable, it is hard to know how to model a generalized upswing or downswing in the economy. When we need to do so, we will tentatively assume that the B response outweighs the $\bar{w}$ response. For a "typical" labor pool, therefore, the contract curve shifts to the SE when economic conditions improve and to the NW when they deteriorate.

The contract curve probably has some approximate descriptive value. Even so, there is no generally acceptable solution concept that singles out a point on it as a likely outcome. Before we analyze some of the simpler possibilities, we digress to consider a slightly different institutional setup, as a useful conceptual exercise.

III. The Union as a Commune: A Digression

Everywhere along a positively sloped contract curve, the marginal revenue product of labor is less than $\bar{w}$, the supply price of labor. Efficiency implies starkly excessive employment. Why? The answer appears to lie in the fact that it is *ex post* more attractive to be employed than to be unemployed. To see this, let us change the rules and imagine the union acting as a family or commune, pooling all earnings and redistributing income from its employed to its unemployed members, so that they all have equal utility. Specifically, suppose the union pays out y_e to each of its employed members and y_u to each of its unemployed members. These payments are connected by

$$(4) \qquad U(y_u) = U(y_e) - D;$$

the employed worker is compensated for the disutility of work. (For any old-timers who remember the Art Young cartoon: "Me slaving over this hot stove and you working in a nice cool sewer," it is perfectly all right to think of D as negative.) The union can only pay out what its members pay in, so there is a second constraint

$$(5) \quad Ly_e + (N-L)y_u = Lw + (N-L)w_u;$$

the employed contribute the negotiated wage and the others their unemployment benefits. Since everyone is equally well off *ex post*, the aggregate utility function is simply $NU(y_u)$. Here (4) and (5) can be solved for y_e and y_u as functions of w and L, so that the collective utility function can be thought of as a function of the negotiated outcome as before.

Straightforward differentiation of (4) and (5) leads to the slope of the union's indifference curve through (w, L):

$$dw/dL = -L^{-1}\big[(w-w_u) - (y_e - y_u)\big].$$

This expression is negative because the union actually redistributes cash income from the employed to the unemployed.

The locus of tangencies between the indifference curves and the isoprofit curves defines a new contract curve. Its equation is

$$R'(L) = y_e - y_u + w_u,$$

where y_e and y_u are functions of w and L. We omit the details but record that this contract curve is *downward* sloping, passes through $(\bar{w}, \bar{L})$, and lies to the right of the demand curve for labor. The picture is thus as in Figure 5.

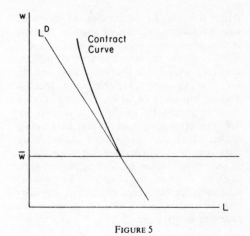

FIGURE 5

It remains true that the wage exceeds the marginal revenue product of employment in efficient bargains. The employer would prefer to reduce employment at the negotiated wage if that were permitted. But employment at a given wage is smaller in the setup of Figure 5 than it is at the same wage in the setup of Figure 3. The reason is that the *ex post* equalization of Figure 5 diminishes the incentive of the individual member to be among the employed. One important consequence is that in Figure 5 the marginal revenue product of employment exceeds the supply price of labor at every efficient bargain.

IV. Some Simple Conventions

Most formal theories of bargaining assume that the negotiated outcome will lie on the contract curve, except perhaps for the occasional conflict—a strike, say—when bargaining breaks down. We have some doubts about the empirical relevance of this assumption. But it is hard to see how one could proceed without it; so we will use it tentatively, with an eye out for its compatibility with common observation. Even so, as we have said, there is no generally accepted rule for selecting a point or other small subset of the contract curve as an especially likely candidate for the actual negotiated outcome. (The book by George de Menil contains an excellent, fairly recent, summary of the state of the theory of wage bargaining. Models of auction markets or sealed bid procedures hardly seem to apply in this context.) In this section, we consider a few very simple conventions, any one of which might seem plausible in a specific context, but none of which has any serious claim to generality. In the next section we will take up a couple of formal bargaining models which do make such a claim. After that, we turn to conventions that might apply to the renegotiation of an original bargain when the environment changes. Throughout, we emphasize the "business cycle" implications of each solution, not its place in the theory of bargaining.

A. *A Dominant Union and "Fair Shares"*

Points to the northeast along the contract curve are successively less profitable for the employer and more favorable to the workers. A powerful union might be able to force the firm to accept zero profits, if we take zero somewhat arbitrarily as the level of profit below which the firm would leave the industry or shut down. That suggests adjoining to the equation of the contract curve (3′) the zero-profit condition $R(L, B) = wL$. Geometrically speaking, this hypothesis singles out the point at which the contract curve intersects the zero-isoprofit curve.

The hypothesis of a zero level of profits can easily be generalized and made less extreme. Suppose that history has led to the notion that there is a "fair" division of net revenue between the workers and the employer. If the normal share of wages is $100k$ percent, we can write

(6) $wL = k R(L, B).$

The case of zero profits is simply $k = 1$. Now (3′) and (6) are the two equations defining the negotiated wage and employment. (Except when $k = 1$, (6) does not coincide with a particular isoprofit locus.)

The contract curve (3), as we know, is upward sloping in the (w, L) plane; (6), on the other hand, represents w as a fraction k of the average revenue product of labor and slopes downward by our assumptions on R.

This pattern will repeat itself: the negotiated outcome is at the intersection of an upward-sloping *efficiency* locus and a downward-sloping locus that can be interpreted as reflecting *equity* (or power) considerations.

Suppose the economic environment deteriorates in a recession. If the product-market effect dominates the labor-market effect, we can concentrate on a reduction in B. The contract curve shifts to the left, as shown earlier. The locus (6) shifts down. From the crude geometry it is clear that employment must fall, but the negotiated wage can go either way. That is a promising beginning for a wage-stickiness story, so we work out the result exactly.

Differentiation of (3′) and (6) leads in the conventional way to:

$$\begin{pmatrix} z & -R_{LL} \\ L & w - kR_L \end{pmatrix} \begin{pmatrix} dw/dB \\ dL/dB \end{pmatrix} = \begin{pmatrix} R_{LB} \\ kR_B \end{pmatrix}$$

where z stands for $d/dw[w - (U(w) - U(\bar{w})) / U'(w)] = ((U(w) - U(\bar{w}))U''(w)) / U'(w)^2$. The determinant has sign pattern $\begin{pmatrix} - & + \\ + & + \end{pmatrix}$ and is therefore negative. Calculation, and substitution of the value of k from (6) shows that

(7) $\operatorname{sgn} dw/dB = -\operatorname{sgn}\{ R_{LB}(1 - LR_L/R)$
$$+ LR_{LL}R_B/R\}$$

This does not depend explicitly on the utility function, except as it helps determine the point at which R is evaluated. The first term is positive and the second negative, confirming the indeterminacy of the sign of dw/dB.

Two special cases are worth noting. First of all, suppose $R(L, B)$ can be written in the form $BS(L/B)$; this gives rise to the isoelastically shifting labor-demand curve discussed earlier in connection with (2). Then $dw/dB = 0$, always. So whenever the elasticity of demand for labor at the going wage is approximately invariant to the business cycle, the wage will be sticky.

The second special case puts $R(L, B) = BS(L)$; this makes the inverse demand curve for labor shift isoelastically in the business cycle so that the demand elasticity at the going level of employment is invariant. Then dw/dB is opposite in sign to $d/dL(LR_L/R)$, which again suggests the lack of any strong directionality in the business cycle.

If it were the case that firms typically become sales constrained in recessions, so that revenue elasticity falls, the model would indicate a countercyclical rise in the wage. That seems extreme; but perhaps one might conclude that efficient bargaining will make employment, more than the wage, bear the brunt of cyclical adjustment.

We do not explore dL/dB in detail, because it is obvious from the geometry that this model makes employment strongly cyclical.

B. *A Dominant Employer*

If the union calls the tune, it is limited in its demands by the possibility that the firm will shut down. If the employer calls the tune, there is (usually) some similar limit to complete freedom of action. It may come from the possibility of a strike or other disruption, or it may come from the need of the employer to preserve a labor pool when there are opportunities for employment elsewhere in the economy. Even a dominant employer will push only so far to the SW along the contract curve. We can imagine that there is an indifference curve below which the firm will not wish to push its labor pool. There is a conceptual choice here: we could take such an indifference curve to be given by $L(U(w) - U(\overline{w}))$ = constant, that is, by the *gain* to the workers from membership in the firm's labor pool. The significance of this choice is that if $\overline{w}$ falls, the firm can lower its wage at given employment to keep the workers' gain constant. On the other hand if we had fixed the limiting indifference curve by $LU(w) + (N-L)U(\overline{w}) = NU(\overline{w}) + L(U(w) - U(\overline{w})) = $ constant, the firm would have to increase its wage offer to make up for a reduction in $\overline{w}$. That seems rather too paternalistic for real life.

In this excessively paternalistic case, in fact, a simultaneous reduction in $\overline{w}$ and B must always lead to a *higher* negotiated wage along the new contract curve. Under the alternative assumption, as usual, there are

forces working in both directions. The reduction in B pushes the negotiated wage upward; the contract curve shifts to the NW and so does its intersection with the unchanged limiting indifference curve. A reduction in $\overline{w}$ lowers the limiting indifference curve at given employment (more than one for one, in fact) and thus pushes the outcome to the SW. Generalized recession thus reduces the employment side of the bargain unambiguously, but the wage can go either way.

V. Formal Bargaining Theory

Most formal theories of the bargaining process proceed axiomatically. Usually one of the axioms is that the bargained outcome is efficient. But then, instead of arguing that this or that outcome on the contract curve is more "natural" than others, the bargaining theorist proposes desirable properties for a rule that would permit a referee equipped with it to go from one bargaining problem to another in some broad class, and produce a solution to each one by application of the rule. (One of the desirable properties, of course, is that the rule should always choose a point on the contract curve.) The goal of the theorist is to find a set of plausible or acceptable properties and show that there is only one rule with those properties. Raiffa argued early on that such solutions of the bargaining problem might best be thought of as Arbitration Rules; they might not have much descriptive validity in predicting the outcome of raw bargaining, but they provide a defensible handbook for an arbitrator whose job is precisely to settle a stream of bargaining conflicts. From our point of view, Raiffa's interpretation is perfectly acceptable.

Formal theories usually operate not in terms of the contract curve but in the "bargaining set" and its efficient frontier. The bargaining set is related to the contract curve in exactly the way that a production possibility set is related to the contract curve in a production box or a utility possibility set is related to the contract curve in an Edgeworth exchange box. To begin with, we need to construct the bargaining set for our model

426   *Implicit Contract Theory*

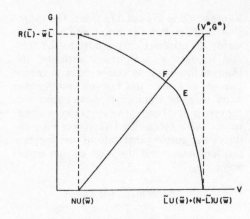

FIGURE 6

of wage bargaining. Each possible outcome (w, L) corresponds to a payoff to each party. In the case of the employer, the payoff is $G = R(L) - wL$; to the union, the payoff is $V = LU(w) + (N-L)U(\bar{w})$. The set of (G, V) swept out as (w, L) ranges over its possibilities is the bargaining set. If no bargain is struck, we take it that $G = 0$[6] and $V = NU(\bar{w})$. As (w, L) traverses the contract curve, (G, V) traverses the undominated efficient subset of the bargaining set, by construction.

Axiomatic bargaining theories require that the bargaining set be convex so that, in the usual way, the efficient payoff-possibility curve is a decreasing concave function in the (G, V) plane. They justify an assumption of convexity by the possibility of randomization. That would hardly do in the wage-bargaining context, but fortunately the assumptions we have made on $R(.)$ and $U(.)$ guarantee, as tedious calculation will show, that the frontier of the bargaining set is well behaved. The picture, therefore, is as in Figure 6. (Here $\bar{w}$ is the highest wage the employer can pay and still break even at a point on the contract curve; see Figure 3.) Selection of a point on the contract curve is equivalent to selection of a point on the efficiency locus.

The best-known formal solution to the bargaining problem is Nash's. It selects the

efficient point that maximizes the *product* of the parties' gains over and above the no-contract outcome. In this case, it maximizes $G \cdot (V - NU(\bar{w}))$ or $(R(L) - wL)(U(w) - U(\bar{w}))L$ over the bargaining set. In principle, one might think of maximizing that product subject to the equation of the contract curve; but on reflection, the constraint can be omitted. Unconstrained maximization of the product by choice of (w, L) will certainly try to maximize $R(L) - wL$ for any given value of $L(U(w) - U(\bar{w}))$, so the equation of the contract curve will reappear as one of the first-order conditions of the unconstrained problem. It does. The other first-order condition turns out to imply, rather oddly,

$$(8) \qquad w = (R/L + R'(L))/2.$$

At the Nash solution, the wage is equal to the arithmetic mean of the average and marginal revenue products of labor!

The Nash solution is thus defined by (3) and (8). Under our assumptions about $R(.)$, both the average and marginal revenue products are decreasing. So (8) defines a negatively sloped "equity" locus that intersects the contract curve once, at the Nash solution to the bargaining problem. Once again, we can replace R by $R(L, B)$ and ask how variation in B affects the wage coordinate of the solution. Upon calculation, it turns out that the criterion (7) holds here too, and so do the paragraphs of text immediately following (7).

One of the axioms leading to the Nash solution of the bargaining problem requires the rule to be "independent of irrelevant alternatives." Suppose that E is the solution to the bargaining problem pictured in Figure 6; now define a new bargaining problem by deleting part of the bargaining set, any part so long as the point E remains. The axiom requires that E be the solution of the new bargaining problem. Since the deleted outcomes were not chosen by the rule when they were available, they are "irrelevant" and their absence should make no difference to the outcome. This axiom has been much complained about, and justly. Intuitions about "bargaining power" and "fairness" might include the notion that if A *could* win a lot in a bargaining situation, he or she is "entitled"

---

[6]It would not be hard to allow for fixed costs F, so that $G = -F$ if no agreement is reached.

to more than if he or she could only, in the best of circumstances, win a little. Anyone who shares that intuition does not believe that "irrelevant" alternatives are irrelevant.

Dissatisfaction with this axiom has led to other definitions of the solution to a bargaining problem. Ehud Kalai and Meir Smorodinsky propose replacing the unsatisfactory axiom with another. Start again with Figure 6 and suppose again that E is the solution chosen by the rule. Now alter the bargaining set in the following way: leave the "best possible" outcomes for the vertical and horizontal parties unchanged, but fix things so that for each possible benefit to the horizontal party the largest possible gain to the vertical party is bigger than it was before. Then the axiom of monotonicity requires that the rule assign to this new bargaining set a solution that gives the vertical party more than at E. If the environment becomes more favorable for the vertical party in this strong sense, the vertical party must profit from the change. (Of course the environment can become more favorable for both parties; then they must both gain.)

Kalai and Smorodinsky show that replacing the axiom of irrelevance of independent alternatives with the axiom of monotonicity leads to a unique solution different from Nash's. It is easily described. Let G^* be the best that the vertical party could hope for, $R(\bar{L})-\bar{w}\bar{L}$ in Figure 6. Let V^* be the best the horizontal party could hope for. Find the point (G^*, V^*) and draw a line connecting it with the no-bargain point, whose coordinates in Figure 6 are $(0, NU(\bar{w}))$. The solution is the unique point at which that line intersects the efficiency frontier. It is shown in Figure 6 as F.

Although the geometry is simple, the arithmetic of the Kalai-Smorodinsky solution is not. The equation to be adjoined to that of the contract curve is

$$(9) \quad (R(L)-wL)/(L(U(w)-U(\bar{w})))$$

$$= (R(\bar{L})-\bar{w}\bar{L})/(\bar{L}(U(\check{w})-U(\bar{w}))),$$

where $(\bar{w}, \bar{L})$ and $(\check{w}, \check{L})$ are the left- and

right-hand end position of the contract curve. Thus $R'(\bar{L})=\bar{w}$ and $R(\check{L})=\check{w}\check{L}$. (We are assuming here that $\check{L}\leq N$; otherwise $\check{L}$ has to be replaced by N and $\check{w}$ by the wage at which the contract curve generates employment of N workers.)

The comparative statics of the solution is messy, mainly because one must keep track of changes in $\bar{w}$, $\check{w}$, $\bar{L}$, and $\check{L}$, so we hold our comments to a minimum. If we set $R(L, B) = BR(L)$ and calculate dw/dB by total differentiation, the familiar quantity $d/dL[LR'/R]=RR'/L+RR''-(R')^2$ appears; positive (negative) values are associated with $dw/dB<0(>0)$. But this time there is an additional negative term, so that even if $R(L)$ has constant elasticity, $dw/dB<0$. So the Kalai-Smorodinsky solution is more likely than the Nash solution to yield "perverse" countercyclical wage flexibility. There is not much else to be said. Even the effects of changes in $\bar{w}$ are complicated.

VI. Sales Constraints and Incremental Bargaining

This brief section serves three purposes. We make an initial stab at the potentially important case of a fix-price firm which experiences a progressively more binding sales constraint as a recession proceeds. Then we use this sketch as a vehicle to introduce another idea: that bargaining conventions may apply to the sharing of gains and losses when a change in the environment makes an initial situation untenable. The initial situation could even be arbitrary; this is an entry point for historical happenstance. Finally, the same sketch helps to clarify the underlying reason why efficient bargaining holds the potential for countercyclical movement of wage rates.

We can model a sales-constrained firm by assuming that every isoprofit curve simply ends when it reaches the value of L corresponding to maximal sales, as illustrated in Figure 7. This assumption is a bit too strong, because it ignores possible substitution among variable factors with constant output. But we shall use it for illustration.

When the firm experiences a sales constraint, the contract curve cannot extend to the right of its intersection with the vertical

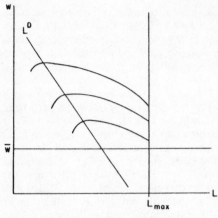

FIGURE 7

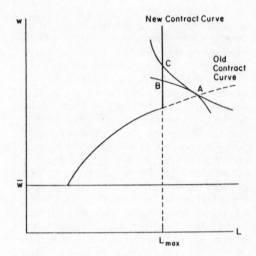

FIGURE 8

at L_{max}, because such points are inaccessible. In fact, the contract curve coincides with the vertical *above* the intersection point, as in Figure 8. (Below the intersection, points on the vertical are dominated by points on the contract curve to the left of L_{max}.)

A simple recession story might go as follows. To begin, the sales constraint is not binding and the wage-employment bargain is somewhere on the contract curve. It remains there in the early stages of the recession as L_{max} moves to the left but is not yet binding. Eventually, the constraint just binds, and then moves still further to the left. The initial bargain is no longer tenable. (We ignore labor hoarding only in order to concentrate on the logic of bargaining.) What happens now?

Given an accepted equity rule (which might also be shifting systematically as the recession proceeds) a new wage-employment bargain might be struck at the intersection of the recession-shifted equity and contract curves. But suppose the initial bargain A had arisen mostly by historical accident. It might not even be efficient. A natural incremental equity rule might be that both parties should gain, or both lose, by the change, but not one gain and the other lose. In the recession case, both must lose. This suggests that the new bargain would have $L=L_{max}$ and a wage somewhere in the interval BC between the isoprofit curve and the indifference curve

associated with the initial bargain. This is shown in Figure 8.

Any point on BC has a wage higher than A; the wage would rise as employment falls. This is too sharp to be taken literally. The logic of this result provides, however, a clear insight into the mechanism through which efficient bargaining can generate countercyclical wage variation. At any point on the contract curve, the firm would prefer a lower volume of employment at the bargained wage. We have already suggested that contractual work rules and manning agreements might serve the purpose of enforcing this extra employment on the firm. A binding sales constraint thus benefits the employer by necessitating, or providing the excuse for, a reduction in employment. At the old wage, the firm would be better off and the union worse off. If the incremental equity rule forbids such an outcome, the wage must rise to transfer some of the loss from union to firm. This shows up with great clarity here because the recession is assumed to leave the revenue function unchanged except by imposing a barrier at L_{max}.

VII. Conclusion

We set out to understand why real wages might be sticky, why fluctuations in aggregate demand might have their major effect on employment and little or none on the wage. Our partial-equilibrium bargaining models can hardly be expected to do that. But they do quite generally confirm a tendency for fluctuations in real product demand at the firm or industry level to be accompanied by large correlated fluctuations in employment and small changes in real wage rates that could go in either direction. What is the source of that tendency?

Geometrically speaking, it is because both our efficiency locus and our "equity" or "power" locus shifts to the left in recession and to the right in upswings, provided cyclical changes in product markets dominate those in the effective reservation wage. The shifts operate in the same direction on employment, but in opposite directions on the negotiated wage, so there is a clear possibility that the two will be statistically independent, as empirical investigation suggests.

A deeper, less mechanical, answer might go something like this. Efficient bargaining pushes the firm to hire more workers than it would like at the negotiated wage. The outcome is thus on the falling part of the iso-profit curve. The contract curve slopes upward. Higher employment and higher wages favor the workers; lower employment and lower wages favor the firm. When circumstances enforce a reduction in employment, the employer gains and the workers lose. Equity and bargaining power are likely to seek an adjustment that will transfer some of the employer's gain to the union or shift some of the union's loss back to the firm. The part of this adjustment that falls (efficiently) on wages will involve an increase in the wage. This tendency can, in principle, offset the normal cyclical deterioration of the demand for labor, in part, wholly, or not at all.

Most of the paper represents variations on this theme. If short-term contracting would lead to cyclical fluctuation in employment at a more or less stable wage, then convenience could easily lead the parties to contract for a long-term steady wage, with current employment decisions made by the firm. The union would need protection against excessive (i.e., profitable but "inefficient") reduction in the average level of employment; this could be provided by work rules or manning agreements.

Our main result is in sharp contrast to the outcome of standard models of implicit contracting with symmetric information. There, long-run contracts tend to be employment stabilizing as compared with spot-competitive labor markets. The crucial difference appears to be that implicit-contract models are closed by a utility constraint. We replace this condition by the sort of equity convention that arises naturally in the bargaining context and is less dominated by opportunities available elsewhere in the economy.

REFERENCES

C. Azariadis, "Implicit Contracts and Related Topics: A Survey," unpublished working paper, 1979.

A. M. Cartter, *Theory of Wages and Employment*, Homewood: Irwin, 1959.

George de Menil, *Bargaining: Monopoly Power versus Union Power*, Cambridge, Mass. 1971.

P. T. Geary and J. Kennan, "The Employment-Real Wage Relationship: An International Study," *J. Polit. Econ.*, forthcoming.

R. E. Hall and D. M. Lilien, "Efficient Wage Bargains under Uncertain Supply and Demand," *Amer. Econ. Rev.*, Dec. 1979, *69*, 868–79.

E. Kalai and M. Smorodinsky, "Other Solutions to Nash's Bargaining Problem," *Econometrica*, May 1975, *43*, 513–18.

W. Leontief, "The Pure Theory of the Guaranteed Annual Wage Contract," *J. Polit. Econ.*, Feb. 1946, *54*, 76–79.

H. Raiffa, "Arbitration Schemes for Generalized Two-Person Games," in H. W. Kuhn and A. W. Tucker, *Contributions To The Theory of Games*, II, Princeton 1953, 361–87.

[22]

Cooperation, Harassment, and Involuntary Unemployment: An Insider-Outsider Approach

By Assar Lindbeck and Dennis J. Snower*

We present a theory of involuntary unemployment which explains why the unemployed workers ("outsiders") are unable or unwilling to find jobs even though they are prepared to work for less than the prevailing wages of incumbent workers ("insiders"). The outsiders do not underbid the insiders since, were they to do so, the insiders would withdraw cooperation from them and make their work unpleasant (that is, "harass" them), thereby reducing the productivity and increasing the reservation wages of the underbidders. The resulting labor turnover costs create economic rent which the insiders tap in wage setting and, as a result, involuntary unemployment may arise.

In order to understand how free-market economies may suffer from protracted spells of involuntary unemployment, it is important to explain why underbidding is not a preponderant feature of labor markets. In this context, we take "underbidding" to mean an agreement between a worker and a firm that a particular job be performed at less than the prevailing wage. (Whether the low-wage offer is made by the worker, the firm, or both, is immaterial in this regard.) If underbidding would occur whenever unemployed workers were willing to work for less than the prevailing wages (normalized for any productivity differences), then involuntary unemployment would either disappear or be accompanied by the empirically unobserved phenomenon of persistent wage deflation.

In the absence of government intervention, underbidding failures can be rationalized by showing (a) why firms have no incentive to agree on low-wage bids in the presence of involuntary unemployment, or

*Institute for International Economic Studies, University of Stockholm, S-106 91 Stockholm, Sweden, and Birkbeck College, Department of Economics, 7/15 Gresse Street, London W1P 1PA, England, respectively. We are deeply indebted to Alan Manning, Torsten Persson, Lars Svensson, and two anonymous referees for their valuable comments and suggestions.

(b) why workers lack this incentive. The recent theoretical literature on unemployment has pursued both of these routes. The efficiency wage theories (for example, George Akerlof, 1982; Jeremy Bulow and Lawrence Summers, 1986; Jim Malcomson, 1981; Carl Shapiro and Joseph Stiglitz, 1984; and Andrew Weiss, 1980) have focused on route (a), and much of the labor union literature which has bearing on unemployment and layoffs (for example, Ian McDonald and Robert Solow, 1981; Andrew Oswald, 1982) takes route (b).

This paper attempts to provide a rationale for what many people regard as a well-established social norm, namely, that workers should not "steal" jobs from their fellow workers by agreeing to work for lower wages, and that employers should not permit such "job theft."

Our analysis pursues the two routes above in the following way: Route (a): Firms may refuse to replace incumbent employees with workers who wish to underbid because they realistically expect that, if they would do so, the remaining incumbents would withdraw cooperation from the underbidders in the process of production. Route (b): Unemployed workers may not agree to underbid because they realistically expect that, if they thereby succeeded in replacing some incumbents, their personal relations with the remaining incumbents would be unpleasant (i.e., they would be "harassed" by the incumbents).

In the standard literature on the theory of labor markets, harassment has received little attention, while the theory of teams (for example, Armen Alchian and H. Demsetz, 1972; Jacob Marshak and Roy Radner, 1972), recognizes employees' productivities to be interdependent. However, the crucial, distinctive feature of our analysis is that *cooperation and harassment activities do not occur automatically; rather, they lie within the control of the employees, especially the incumbents.*

In describing the causes and consequences of incumbents' cooperation and harassment activities, we adopt an "insider-outsider" approach to the labor market. The basic idea underlying this general approach is that there are labor turnover costs that generate economic rent which incumbent workers ("insiders") manipulate and exploit in the process of wage determination. In doing so, the insiders primarily take account of their own interests. The unemployed workers are disenfranchized in the process of wage negotiation and, as shown below, involuntary unemployment may occur. It is worth emphasizing that the distinction between "insiders and outsiders" is not merely one between employed and unemployed workers, but rather between groups of workers with different employment opportunities: the insiders face more favorable opportunities than the outsiders due to the insiders' ability and willingness to use turnover costs to drive up their wages.

The insider-outsider approach has been outlined in general terms in Assar Lindbeck and Dennis Snower (1984a, 1985b, 1986a, c). Avner Shaked and John Sutton (1984) provide a bargaining rationale (one of many conceivable ones) for insider market power. The approach has been extended to a two-period framework by Robert Solow (1985) and its implications for time dependence of unemployment (i.e., dependence of current unemployment on past unemployment) were developed by Olivier Blanchard and Lawrence Summers, 1986; Niels Gottfries and Henrik Horn, 1986; and Lindbeck and Snower, 1986b. Robert Gregory (1986) has given some preliminary empirical support (from Australia) for the notion that wages are influenced more by firms' internal conditions than by external conditions in the labor market.

In this paper, the insiders are assumed to create a special, potentially important, variety of labor turnover cost by withdrawing cooperation from, and by harassing the entrants who attempt to underbid. As a result, the insiders are able to raise their wages above the market-clearing level without inducing underbidding.

At these wages, the unemployed workers ("outsiders") would prefer to trade places with the insiders (i.e., they would prefer to be employed for insider wages under insider conditions of work rather than to be unemployed), but they do not have this option. They are victims of *discrimination*, because whenever they gain employment through underbidding, they receive less cooperation and more harassment than the insiders do. In fact, the outsiders may be willing to work for sufficiently less than the insider wages so as to compensate the firms for their more limited cooperation skills, but they may nevertheless be unable to find jobs. Given that the outsiders find themselves with lower productivity and higher disutility of work than the insiders, there may exist no wage that *both* induces firms to hire outsiders *and* induces outsiders to work. This is the sense in which involuntary unemployment can arise in our analysis.

In the literature on unemployment theory, the "insider-outsider" approach may be regarded as an alternative (though complementary rather than mutually exclusive) to the "efficiency wage" approach. Whereas the former explains unemployment through insiders' market power which is used to exploit the rent from labor turnover costs in the process of wage determination, the latter approach explains unemployment through asymmetric information and firms' market power in wage determination (see Lindbeck and Snower, 1986c) for a comparison of the two approaches). In the insider-outsider world, the unemployed workers do not engage in underbidding because the insiders prevent them from doing so; in the efficiency-wage world, underbidding does not occur because it is not in the firms' interests. Among the contributions to the efficiency wage literature, George Akerlof's (1982) "gift exchange model" is closest in spirit to our approach here, in that his analysis describes how employers' wage offers may be used to promote their workers' cooperation and effort.

Section I deals with the microeconomic behavior of workers and firms in our model. Section II describes the equilibrium of a single firm and its employees. In Section III, we incorporate this equilibrium in an aggregate analysis of the labor market and examine how involuntary unemployment can occur in this context. Section IV deals with potential objections to our analysis. Finally, Section V contains concluding remarks.

I. The Behavior of Economic Agents

A. *The Underlying Setup*

Though our explanation of involuntary unemployment rests on two distinct, logically independent arguments (one of which focuses on cooperation, the other on harassment), for brevity, the formal model in Sections II and III deals with these arguments simultaneously.

The cooperation and harassment activities, which the insiders use to protect themselves against underbidding, may be defined as follows. "Cooperation" refers to all those activities in which workers help one another in the process of production and thereby raise their productivity. "Harassment" stands for all those activities whereby workers make one another's jobs more disagreeable (primarily by damaging their personal relations) and thereby raise their disutility of work.

In practice, those workers who have spent a long time at their jobs are often more capable of cooperation and harassment than their newly arrived counterparts. We capture this observation roughly by supposing that when workers first enter their firms, they are unable to cooperate with or harass other workers, but after a fixed period of time— call it the "initiation period"—they all gain identical access to these abilities.

Within this context, we identify three homogeneous groups of workers: (*i*) *insiders*, the "experienced" employees who are able to engage in the full range of cooperation and harassment activities; (*ii*) *entrants*, the "inexperienced" employees who have no access to these activities; and (*iii*) *outsiders*, the unemployed workers.

In this section, we build a simple model that captures the role of insiders' cooperation and harassment activities in the formulation of wage and employment decisions within a firm. Our model is based on the following salient structural assumptions:

1. *Wage Decisions*. Each employee's wage is negotiated for one period at a time, where (for simplicity) the length of the period is assumed equal to the initiation period.[1]

2. *Outsiders Are Perfect Competitors for Jobs*. Thus, when an outsider is hired (and thereby turns into an entrant), the person's entrant wage is equal to his reservation wage (for the duration of the initiation period).

3. *Insiders Have Some Market Power*. Each insider sets his wage "individualistically" (taking the strategies of all other agents as given).[2]

4. *Monitoring*. An insider's wage cannot be made contingent on his cooperation and harassment activities, since the firm is unable to monitor these activities directly. (All that the firm can observe is its output and the number of insiders and entrants it employs.[3])

---

[1] In other words, there are no "long-term" wage contracts (extending over the employees' lifetimes). If such contracts were possible and if employees lacked market power on entering the firms, then involuntary unemployment could not exist.

[2] The assumption of unilateral wage setting by insiders is made only for expositional simplicity, as noted in Section II, Part B.

[3] Our conclusions would not be substantively affected if we would make the more general assumption that the firm (through supervision of its employees) monitors the cooperation and harassment activities imperfectly.

5. *Employment Decisions*. These are made unilaterally by the firms.

6. *Sequence of Decisions*. In the first stage of the decision-making process, the insider wage and the cooperation and harassment levels are set, taking into account how these decisions affect employment. The entrant wage is determined as well. In the second stage, the firms make the employment decisions, taking the insider and entrant wages, as well as the cooperation and harassment levels, as given.

B. *The Firm*

Consider a firm that has two variable factors of production: insiders (L_I) and entrants (L_E). Let a_I represent the level of cooperation among insiders (measured as the actual number of insiders divided into the number that would be required to produce the same output in the absence of cooperation among insiders), and let a_E stand for the level of cooperation between insiders and entrants (measured as the actual number of entrants divided into the number that would be required to produce the same output in the absence of cooperation from insiders). We will call a_I and a_E the "labor endowments" of the insiders and entrants, respectively. The firm is assumed to know the levels of these endowments but it cannot observe the cooperation activities of individual workers. We write the firm's production function as $Q = f(a_I \cdot L_I + a_E \cdot L_E)$, $f' > 0$, $f'' < 0$, where Q is the level of output.

Let W be the insider wage and R_E be the entrant wage (which is equal to the entrants' reservation wage). All insiders are identical and receive the same wage, and similarly for entrants. The firm can observe W and R_E, but it cannot observe the harassment activities which are reflected in the level of R_E.

Within the two-stage, decision-making process specified in Section I (with wages, cooperation, and harassment decisions made in the first stage and employment decisions made in the second), the firm's problem is to maximize its profit with respect to L_I and L_E, taking the insider and entrant wages, the overall cooperation and harassment levels, as well as the production function f as given.

To present our analysis in the simplest possible way, we assume that the firm has a one-period time horizon.[4]

Let m be the firm's "incumbent work force," that is, it is the stock of insiders carried forward from the past. Since we assume that cooperation and harassment skills are firm-specific and that entrants acquire them only after they go through the initiation period, it is clear that $L_I \leq m$.

Thus, the firm's profit-maximization problem is

$$(1) \quad \text{Maximize} \quad \pi = f(a_I \cdot L_I + a_E \cdot L_E)$$
$$- W \cdot L_I - R_E \cdot L_E$$

subject to $H_I \leq m$; $L_I, L_E \leq 0$.

Let $\lambda = a_I \cdot L_I + a_E \cdot L_E$ be the firm's effective work force (i.e., its work force in efficiency units of labor). Then the first-order conditions may be expressed as follows:

$$(2a) \quad \frac{\partial \pi}{\partial L_I} = a_I \cdot f'(\lambda) - W \geq 0,$$

$$\frac{\partial \pi}{\partial L_I} \cdot (m - L_I) = 0;$$

$$(2b) \quad \frac{\partial \pi}{\partial L_E} = a_E \cdot f'(\lambda) - R_E \leq 0,$$

$$\frac{\partial \pi}{\partial L_E} \cdot L_E = 0,$$

where we ignore the nonnegativity constraint on L_I and we assume that the firm is able to hire all the entrants it demands at the wage R_E.[5]

---

[4] With regard to our analytical conclusions, this turns out not to be a restrictive assumption. Naturally, if the firm has a multiperiod time horizon, it faces an inherently intertemporal problem, since the entrants hired in one period become insiders in the next. Lindbeck and Snower (1985a) extend our model to a two-period, overlapping-generations setting.

[5] Since $L_I \leq m$, the marginal incumbent may generate positive profit, as shown by the inequality in (2a).

C. The Workers

Insider i has the following decision variables:

1) The level of his harassing activity directed at entrants: h^i_E (implicitly assuming that the insider harasses all entrants in equal measure). We assume that the insider does not harass other insiders.[6]

2) The levels of his cooperative activities directed at other insiders and entrants: a^i_I and a^i_E, respectively, defined analogously to a_I and a_E above. (We assume implicitly that he cooperates with all the other insiders in equal measure, and similarly for all the entrants.)

3) The insider i's wage: W^i.

The insider makes these decisions "individualistically," that is, he takes the optimal cooperation, harassment, wage setting, and employment strategies of all other agents as given. Let us examine the role of each of these decision variables in the context of the insider's decision-making problem.

Since we are primarily concerned with the effect of insiders' cooperation and harassment activities on their wages and employment, it is natural to make the simplifying assumption that the insider i's cooperation and harassment activities do not affect his own utility directly, but only indirectly via the wage he is able to achieve.[7] In other

words, the insider is assumed to regard the activities h^i_E, a^i_I, and a^i_E as neither desirable nor undesirable per se and therefore (as shown below) he uses them only to support his wage claims.

We specify insider i's utility function quite simply as $\Omega^i = C^i - l^i$, where C_i is his consumption and l^i is his labor (in units of time). Labor is taken to be a discrete activity, with $l = 1$ for an employed worker and $l = 0$ for an unemployed one. We assume that each worker consumes his entire income in each period. For insider i, this means that $C^i = W^i$.

The insider's reservation wage, R^i_I, is defined as that wage (W^i) which makes him indifferent between employment (yielding utility $W^i - 1$) and unemployment (yielding utility 0):

$$(3a) \qquad R^i_I = R_I = 1, \qquad \text{for all } i.$$

Let entrant j's utility be $\Omega^j = C^j - l^j - H_E$, where H_E stands for his disutility from being harassed by the insiders.[8] Naturally, we assume that

$$(3b) \qquad (\partial H_E / \partial h^i_E) > 0 \quad \text{for any insider } i.$$

Thus the entrant's reservation wage is

$$(3c) \qquad R^j_E = R_E = 1 + H_E, \qquad \text{for all } j.$$

We assume that each insider's harassing activity (h^i_E) is bounded from above and below, so that each entrant's disutility from being harassed (H_E) is also bounded as

$$(3d) \qquad 0 \leq H_E \leq H,$$

Since $L_E \geq 0$, the marginal potential entrant may generate negative profit, as shown by the inequality in (2b). Finally, we assume that $A \cdot f'(0) > 1$, where A is the upper bound on a_I, as given in (4c), so that it is always profitable to the firm to employ some insiders: $L^*_I > 0$.

[6] This assumption could be derived from more basic postulates. For example, we could assume that each insider finds it disagreeable to harass the other insiders and then show that, in the Nash equilibrium (described below), no insider is able to achieve a higher wage by harassing other insiders. Thus, each insider chooses not to harass the other insiders.

[7] Allowing the insider's cooperation and harassment activities to affect his utility directly has self-evident implications for our results. In practice, of course, this direct utility effect might be positive or negative. Whereas it is usually safe to assume that harassment activities are disagreeable to the harassers, the same cannot be said of cooperation activities. For example, there are direct utility gains from cooperation when an

---

insider prefers to work in cooperation with entrants or other insiders than to work in isolation. On the other hand, direct utility losses from cooperation are conceivable as well, since an insider who cooperates may expend more "effort" than one who does not.

[8] Recall that the entrants, unlike the insiders, are unable to perform harassment activities. Furthermore, note that H_E is the same for every entrant (since we have assumed that each insider harasses all entrants in equal measure).

where H is a nonnegative constant (described in fn. 17, below).

We now turn to the insider i's cooperation activities and specify how they affect the productivities of the other insiders and the entrants. We wish to ensure, quite plausibly, that an insider is able to raise the marginal products of workers by cooperating with them. For this purpose, we make the following two assumptions:

$$(4a) \qquad \partial a_I / \partial a_I^i, \ \partial a_E / \partial a_E^i > 0,$$

and

$$(4b) \qquad 0 < \eta_I, \ \eta_E < 1,$$

where $\eta_I = -(f''/f') \cdot a_I \cdot L_I$ and $\eta_E = -(f''/f') \cdot a_E \cdot L_E$ are the elasticities of the marginal product of labor with respect to the insider and entrant work forces. Thus, when an insider increases his cooperative activity with other insiders and entrants, the marginal products of the insider and entrant work forces rise:

$$\frac{\partial(a_I \cdot f')}{\partial a_I^i} = \frac{\partial a_I}{\partial a_I^i} \cdot \frac{1}{f'} \cdot (1 + \eta) > 0,$$

$$\frac{\partial(a_E \cdot f')}{\partial a_E^i} = \frac{\partial a_E}{\partial a_E^i} \frac{1}{f'} \cdot (1 + \eta) > 0.$$

Assumption (4a) means that the jobs within the firm are sufficiently interdependent so that an individual insider's cooperation with other insiders or entrants has a significant, positive effect on their labor endowments. This assumption is unnecessary to our analysis whenever insiders can influence a_I and a_E through coordinated (rather than individualistic) activity. Indeed this suggests that, in large plants with little job interdependence, insiders may have a special incentive to form a union. An insider-outsider explanation for the emergence of unions is to be found here.

We let each insider's cooperating activities $(a_I^i$ and $a_E^i)$ be bounded from above and below, so that the labor endowments of insiders and entrants $(a_I$ and $a_E)$ are bounded

as follows:

$$(4c) \qquad 1 \le a_I, \ a_E \le A,$$

where A is a constant greater than unity.[9]

Finally, we turn to the insider's influence over his wage W^i. To reach our qualitative conclusions, we only need to assume that (a) each insider's wage captures at least some of the economic rent generated through his cooperation and harassment activities, and (b) the greater this rent, the higher his wage. These properties hold in a variety of well-known bargaining games (for example, Shaked and Sutton, 1984) and are in accord with commonsense ideas on wage-setting processes. However, to make our exposition as simple as possible, we consider only the extreme case in which each insider sets his own wage unilaterally and individualistically (as noted in Section I). This means that each insider takes the wages and employment of all other insiders as given. Consequently, if he wishes to retain his job, he must set his wage so that the firm has an incentive to employ him in addition to all the other insiders it is employing. In other words, each insider regards himself as the marginal worker in the firm's employment decisions.

The insider i faces two wage-setting options: (i) he may set his wage at some level V^i, which is sufficiently low to ensure his continued employment, or (ii) he may achieve his reservation wage R_I^i by choosing not to be employed. Clearly, the insider will choose the first option only if the maximum achievable wage V^i, denoted by V_{max}^i, is at least as great as the reservation wage; other-

---

[9] The assumption that A is a constant is merely an expositional simplification. Our analysis could be easily extended to cover the possibility that A is an increasing function of L_I (i.e., the more insiders there are, the greater the potential for cooperative activity). In that case, we would require that the marginal product of insiders (in the Nash equilibrium described below) diminishes as more insiders are hired.

$$\partial(a \cdot f')/\partial L_I = A \cdot f'' + A' \cdot f' < 0.$$

(This implies that the demand curve for insider labor is downward sloping.)

wise, the second option is preferable:

(5a) $W^i = \max[R_I, V^i_{max}]$.

V^i_{max} may be inferred from the firm's employment behavior as described by the first-order condition (2a) and (2b). If entrants are not employed, then only (2a) is relevant for determining the maximum achievable wage: $W \le a_I \cdot f'(\lambda)$ and thus V^i_{max} is the maximum of $[a_I \cdot f'(\lambda)]$ with respect to a^i_I and a^i_E. On the other hand, if entrants are employed (in addition to insiders), then both (2a) and (2b) are relevant and the first parts of (2a) and (2b) hold as equalities:

$$f'(\lambda) = f'(a_I \cdot m + a_E \cdot L_E)$$

$$= V^i/a_I = R_E/a_E,$$

and thus V^i_{max} is the maximum of $[(a_I/a_E) \cdot R_E]$ with respect to a^i_I, a^i_E, and h^i_E.

In short, V^i_{max} may be expressed as follows:

(5b) $V^i_{max} = \max_{a^i_I, a^i_E, h^i_E} [\min\{a_I \cdot f'(a_I \cdot L_I),$

$$(a_I/a_E) \cdot R_E\}].$$

Substituting (5b) into (5a), and recalling that $R_I = 1$ and $R_E = 1 + H_E$, we obtain insider i's wage:

(5c) $W^i = \max_{a^i_I, a^i_E, h^i_E} [1, \min\{a_I \cdot f'(a_I \cdot L_I),$

$$(a_I/a_E) \cdot (1 + H_E)\}].$$

II. The Microeconomic Equilibrium: The Firm and Its Employees

We now show how the equilibrium levels of wages, employment, and cooperation and harassment activities are determined through the interaction of a firm and its employees. Our concept of equilibrium (for the two-stage, decision-making process described above) may be specified as follows:

Definition: In the Nash equilibrium of the firm and its employees, (a) each insider i maximizes his utility with respect to his decision variables W^i, a^i_I, a^i_E, and h^i_E, taking the strategies of the firm and the other employees as given, and (b) the firm maximizes its profit with respect to its decision variables L_I and L_E, taking the strategies of its employees as given.

Let us now turn to the characteristics of this equilibrium.

A. Cooperation

Under equilibrium conditions, each insider cooperates fully with other insiders, but does not cooperate with entrants.

Intuitively, the reason is that (a) by cooperating with the other insiders, the insider raises the marginal product of the firm's incumbent work force and is thereby able to achieve a higher wage, and (b) by refusing to cooperate with entrants, the insider reduces the marginal product of the entrant work force, and consequently reduces the number of entrants hired, thereby raising the marginal product of the incumbent work force and achieving a higher wage.

This can be shown formally by deriving the cooperation activities a^i_I and a^i_E, which permit the insider i to earn his maximum achievable wage V^i_{max}. By the V^i_{max} equation (5b), the insider's optimal (equilibrium) levels of cooperation are $(a^i_I)^* = \max(a^i_I)$ and $(a^i_E)^* = \min(a^i_E)$, so that

(6a) $a^*_I = A$ and $a^*_E = 1$.

B. Harassment

Under equilibrium conditions, each insider harasses maximally all workers who enter the firm.

Intuitively, we see that by doing so, the insider maximizes the entrants' reservation wage and thereby discourages them from entering the firm, so that a minimal number of entrants are hired. Thus, the marginal product of the incumbent work force is maximized, so that the insider achieves the highest possible wage.

Formally, the V_{max}^i equation (5b) implies that the insider's equilibrium level of harassment (which permits him to earn his maximum achievable wage) is $(h_E^i)^* = \max(h_E^i)$, so that

$$(6b) \qquad H_E^* = H$$

(recalling that, by (3d), H is the upper bound of H_E).

C. Wage Determination

Substituting the optimal cooperation levels (6a) and the optimal harassment level (6b) into the W^i equation (5c), we obtain the following wage equation:

$$(7) \quad (W^i)^* = W^*$$

$$= \max\big[1, \min\{A \cdot f'(A \cdot L_I),$$

$$A \cdot (1+H)\}\big] \quad \text{for all } i.$$

This equation has a straightforward interpretation. If the insider's reservation wage (R_I = 1) falls short of his maximum wage achievable through employment, ($\min\{A \cdot f'(A \cdot L_I), A \cdot (1+H)\}$), then the insider sets his wage with two independent considerations in mind: W^i must be sufficiently low so that (a) the insider does not become unprofitable to the firm, that is,

$$(8a) \qquad W^i \le A \cdot f'(A \cdot L_I),$$

(for otherwise he would be dismissed) and (b) the insider remains at least as profitable as the marginal entrant, that is,

$$(8b) \qquad W^i \le A \cdot (1+H),$$

(for otherwise he would be replaced by the entrant). We call (8a) the "absolute profitability constraint" (APC) and (8b) the "relative profitability constraint" (RPC) on the insider wage.

D. Employment Determination

Whether the insider wage is given by the reservation wage, the APC or the RPC depends on the size of the firm's incumbent work force m. Recall that the firm faces diminishing returns to labor (i.e., $f'' < 0$) and thus the larger the incumbent work force, the lower the incumbent's marginal product. There are three possible scenarios:

(i) A "large" incumbent work force: Here the incumbent work force is so large that its marginal product is less than the insiders' reservation wage (R_I). In particular, $m > \bar{m}$, where $\bar{m}$ is the "maximum sustainable incumbent work force" (i.e., the largest possible number of incumbents which the firm may have an incentive to employ) and $\bar{m}$ is given by[10]

$$(9) \qquad A \cdot f'(A \cdot \bar{m}) = 1.$$

When the incumbent work force is greater than its maximum sustainable level ($m > \bar{m}$), it is clear that the firm finds it worthwhile to reduce employment. What remains to be examined is how large the new work force will be and whether some insiders will be replaced by entrants.

To this end, note that in this scenario *the insider wage will be set equal to the reservation wage*:

$$(10a) \quad W^* = R_I = 1, \qquad \text{for } m > \bar{m}.$$

The reason is that if W were set beneath this level, then some insiders would have an incentive to quit; whereas, if W were above this level, then some insiders would be dismissed even though they prefer employment to unemployment and these insiders would consequently have an incentive to opt for a lower wage.

---

[10] *Proof.* If the firm is not constrained by $L_I \le m$ in its maximization problem (1), then (by the first-order condition (2a)) its demand for insiders (L_I^*) rises with a_i and falls with W. By (3a) and (4c), $\max(a_I) = A$ and $\min(W) = R_I = 1$. Substituting these values into the insider demand function (2a), as equality, yields (9).

Given that the insider wage is at its minimum level $W = 1$, then (by (2a) and (9)) *the firm employs the maximum sustainable incumbent work force*:

(10b) $\qquad L_I^* = \overline{m}, \qquad$ for $m > \overline{m}$.

Since the insiders' marginal product is equal to their reservation wage $(A \cdot f'(A \cdot L_I) = 1)$, the marginal product of an entrant (hired in addition to the insiders) must be less than his reservation wage $(f'(A \cdot L_I^*) < 1 + H)$. Thus, *the firm hires no entrants*:[11,12]

(10c) $\qquad L_E^* = 0, \qquad$ for $m > \overline{m}$.

(*ii*) *An "intermediate" incumbent work force*: Here the incumbent work force is (a) small enough so that its marginal product exceeds the insiders' reservation wage, but (b) large enough so that the marginal product of entrants (hired in addition to incumbents) falls short of the entrants' reservation wage. In particular, $\underline{m} \le m \le \overline{m}$, where m is the "minimum sustainable incumbent work force" (i.e., the smallest possible number of incumbents that the firm could employ without having an incentive to hire entrants).

m is given by[13]

(11) $\qquad f'(A \cdot \underline{m}) = 1 + H$.

Under these circumstances, *the firm hires no entrants*:

(12a) $\qquad L_E^* = 0, \qquad$ for $\underline{m} \le m \le \overline{m}$,

since (by (11)) the marginal product of an entrant is less than the entrant's reservation wage $(f'(A \cdot m) < 1 + H = R_E^*)$.

Consequently, in setting his wage, each insider is constrained not by the need to remain at least as profitable as the entrants (since entrants are never profitable in this scenario), but only by the need to keep his absolute profitability from falling below zero. In other words, the binding constraint on the insider wage (given by the wage equation (7)) is the APC (Constraint (8a)), whereas the RPC (Constraint (8b)) is redundant.[14] This means that *each insider sets his wage equal to the marginal product of the incumbent work force*:

(12b) $\quad W^* = A \cdot f'(A \cdot m) \qquad$ for $\underline{m} \le m \le \overline{m}$.

At this wage, *the firm retains all its incumbents*:[15]

(12c) $\qquad L_I^* = m, \qquad$ for $\underline{m} \le m \le \overline{m}$.

---

[11] The firm has no incentive to replace some (but not all) of its insiders by entrants, since the profit contribution from replacing one insider by one entrant is

$$\Phi = (\partial \pi / \partial L_E) - (\partial \pi / \partial L_I)$$
$$= (W - R_E) - (A - 1) \cdot f'(\lambda) < 0,$$

by (2a) and (2b), and

$$(d\Phi / dL_E)|_{dL_E = -dL_I} = (A-1)^2 \cdot f'' < 0.$$

Clearly, this applies to all three scenarios.

[12] The firm has no incentive to replace all of its insides by entrants for the following reason. In the equilibrium for scenario I, the firms's profit is $\pi^*(I) = f[A \cdot g(1/A)] - g(1/A)$, where $g = (f')^{-1}$. If the firm replaced all its insiders by entrants, its profits would be $\hat{\pi} = f[g(1)] - g(1)$ (since entrants do not harass one another and thus $R_E = 1$). $\pi^*(I)$ (which is described by the area under the insider demand curve and above the $W^* = 1$ line in Figure 2A below) is greater than $\hat{\pi}$ (which is described by the area under the entrant demand curve and above the $W^* = 1$ line in the same figure).

[13] *Proof*. If $m = \underline{m}$, then $L_E^* = 0$, provided that $a_E = 1$ and $R_E = 1 + H$. (The reason is that, by (2b), $(\partial \pi / \partial L_E) = f'(A \cdot \underline{m}) - (1 + H) = 0$.) If $m < \underline{m}$, then $L_E^* > 0$, for any feasible a_E and R_E. (The reason is that $(\partial \pi / \partial L_E) = a_E \cdot f'(A \cdot \underline{m}) - R_E > 0$ for any feasible a_E and R_E.)

[14] Formally, this may be shown as follows. Since $m \ge \underline{m}$ then (by 11) $f'(A \cdot m) \le 1 + H$. Since $m \le \overline{m}$, then (by (9)) $A \cdot f'(A \cdot m) \ge 1$. Therefore, $1 \le A \cdot f'(A \cdot m) \le A \cdot (1 + H)$. By the wage equation (7), we obtain (12b).

[15] The firm has no incentive to replace all of its insiders by entrants, for the following reason. In the equilibrium for scenario II, the firm's profit is $\pi^*(II) = f(A \cdot m) - A \cdot f'(A \cdot m) \cdot m$. In the equilibrium for scenario III, the firm's profit is $\pi^*(III) = f[g(1 + H)] - A \cdot (1 + H) \cdot m - (1 + H) \cdot A \cdot \{(1/A) \cdot g(1 + H) - m\}$. Observe that in Figures 2A and 2B below, $\pi^*(II)$ and $\pi^*(III)$, respectively, are described by the areas under the insider demand curve, above the $W^* = 1$ line, and to the left of the incumbent work force m (where $\underline{m} \le m \le \overline{m}$ for $\pi^*(II)$ and $m < \underline{m}$ for $\pi^*(III)$). Clearly, $\pi^*(II) > \pi^*(III)$. The upper bound on H, given in fn. 17, implies that $\pi^*(III) > \hat{\pi}$ (where $\hat{\pi}$ is defined in fn. 12). Consequently, $\pi^*(II) > \hat{\pi}$.

(*iii*) *A "small" incumbent work force*: Here the incumbent work force is sufficiently small so that the marginal products of both the incumbents and some entrants (hired in addition to the incumbents) exceed their respective reservation wages. In particular, $m \leq \underline{m}$.

Under this scenario, the insiders cannot completely exclude the outsiders from getting jobs (regardless of their cooperation and harassment activities). Thus, each insider must set his wage with a view to his profitability vis-à-vis the entrants, that is, the binding constraint on the insider wage is the RPC (Constraint (8b)).[16] By the wage equation (7), this means that *the insider wage is a markup* (*by the factor A*) *over the entrants' equilibrium reservation wage* ($R_E^* = 1 + H$):

(13a)
$$W^* = A \cdot (1 + H), \quad \text{for } m \leq \underline{m}.$$

At this wage, the marginal incumbent is just as profitable as the first entrant (hired in addition to the incumbent work force): $(\partial \pi / \partial L_I^*) = A f'(A \cdot m) - W^* = (\partial \pi / \partial L_I) = f'(A \cdot m) - (1 + H)$. Since the incumbent work force is "small," the first entrant generates positive profit; thus, the marginal incumbent does so, too. Consequently, *the firm retains all its incumbents*:

(13b) $\quad L_I^* = m, \quad \text{for } m < \underline{m},$

provided (as shown below) that the firm lacks the incentive to replace all its incumbents by entrants.

Moreover, *entrants are hired until their marginal product is brought into equality with their reservation wage*: $A \cdot L_I^* + L_E^* = A \cdot \underline{m}$ (by (11)) and thus

(13c) $\quad L_E^* = A \cdot (\underline{m} - m).$

We now inquire under what conditions the firm has no incentive to replace all its incumbents by entrants. If the firm were to

pursue this replacement strategy, it would encounter a loss and a gain: the loss would arise because the entrants (unlike the incumbents) could not cooperate with one another, and the gain would emerge because the entrants (in the absence of incumbents) would not be subject to harassment. For the loss to exceed the gain, the harassment level *H* must fall beneath an upper bound, which is easily derived.[17]

E. *The Microeconomic Equilibrium*

Our results above are summarized in the following proposition:

PROPOSITION 1: *For the Nash equilibrium, the insiders' cooperation and harassment activity levels are* $a_I^* = A$, $a_E^* = 1$, *and* $h_E^* = H$, *whenever* $L_E^* > 0$. *Let the firm's incumbent work force* (*m*) *be exogenously given. Then the equilibrium wage and employment levels may be characterized as follows:*

(I) $\quad$ *If* $m > \bar{m}$, *then* $W^* = 1$,
$$L_I^* = \bar{m}, \quad L_E^* = 0.$$

Thus, if the incumbent work force (*m*) *is "large," then the insiders receive their reservation wage* ($W^* = 1$) *and, in response, the firm employs the maximum sustainable incumbent work force* ($\bar{m}$) *and does not hire any entrants.*

(II) $\quad$ *If* $\underline{m} < m < \bar{m}$, *then* $W^* = A \cdot f'(A \cdot m)$,
$$L_I^* = m, \quad L_E^* = 0.$$

Thus, if the incumbent work force is "intermediate," then the insiders are paid the marginal product of the incumbent work force (W^*

---

[16] Formally, it follows from $m < \underline{m}$ that $f'(A \cdot m) > 1 + H$. Thus, $A \cdot f'(A \cdot m) > A \cdot (1 + H) > 1$. By the wage equation (7), we obtain (13a).

[17] Thus, we assume that $0 \leq H \leq H^c$, where H^c is the harassment level at which the profit from retaining all the incumbents and additionally hiring the profit-maximizing number of entrants (π^*(III), defined in fn. 15) is equal to the profit from firing all the incumbents and hiring the profit-maximizing number of entrants instead ($\hat{\pi}$, defined in fn. 12). In particular, H^c is a constant implicitly given by $f[g(1 + H^c)] - A \cdot (1 + H^c) \cdot m - (1 + H^c) \cdot A \cdot \{[g(1 + H^c)/A] - m\} = f[g(1)] - g(1)$.

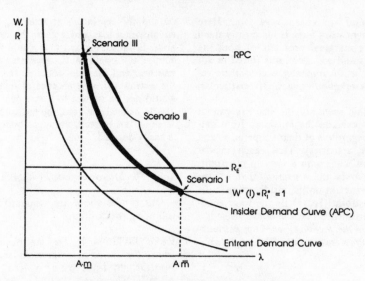

FIGURE 1. THE MICROECONOMIC EQUILIBRIUM; RPC:
$W^*(\text{III}) = A \cdot R_E^* = A(1 + H)$; INSIDER DEMAND CURVE: $A \cdot f'(\lambda) = W^*$;
ENTRANT DEMAND CURVE: $f'(\lambda) = R_E$

$= A - f'(A \cdot m))$ and the firm retains all its incumbents and hires no entrants.

(III)   *If* $m < \underline{m}$, *then* $W^* = A \cdot (1 + H)$,

$$R_E^* = 1 + H, \ L_I^* = m, \ L_E^* = A \cdot (\underline{m} - m).$$

In other words, if the incumbent work force is "small," then the insider wage is a markup over the reservation wage (with the size of the markup depending on the insider-entrant cooperation differential A) and the firm retains all its incumbents and hires some entrants. The entrants receive the reservation wage, which is raised by the insiders' harassment activity.

Proposition 1 is illustrated in Figure 1. The figure contains two demand curves: an *insider demand curve*, along which the insiders' marginal product is equal to the insider wage, assuming that only insiders are employed: $A \cdot f'(A \cdot L_I) = 0$, and an *entrant demand curve*, along which the entrants' marginal product is equal to the entrant wage (R_E), assuming that only entrants are employed: $f'(L_E) = R_E$. (Thus $f'(A \cdot L_I +$

$L_E) = R_E$ is the demand curve for entrants hired in addition to a given insider work force L_I.)

Observe that the insider demand curve lies above the entrant demand curve (by a factor of A), because the insiders cooperate with one another but are not prepared to cooperate with entrants. The point at which the $R_I^* = 1$ line crosses the insider demand curve yields (by (9)) the maximum sustainable incumbent work force ($A \cdot \overline{m}$, in efficiency units). Similarly, the intersection of the $R_E^* = 1 + H$ line and the entrant demand curve yields (by (11)) the minimum sustainable incumbent work force ($A \cdot \underline{m}$, in efficiency units).

The RPC is denoted by the uppermost horizontal line in the figures. The APC coincides with the insider demand curve (since the APC is the locus of wage-employment points at which the absolute profitability of the marginal insider is zero).

In Figure 1, scenario II is depicted by the thick segment along the insider demand curve. In other words, there is a continuum of equilibrium points, each corresponding to a different incumbent work force:

(14a) $[W^*(\text{II}), \lambda^*(\text{II})]$

$= [A \cdot f'(A \cdot L_I^*),$

$(A \cdot L_I^* + L_E^*)] = [A \cdot f'(A \cdot m), A \cdot m].$

Here the insiders prevent all entry into the firm through their cooperation and harassment activities and set their wage so as to exploit all their marginal rent ($W^*(\text{II}) = A \cdot f'(A \cdot m)$) and retain their jobs.

Scenario I is pictured by the lowest point on the thick line segment:

(14b) $[W^*(I), \lambda^*(I)]$

$= [R_I^*(A \cdot L_I^* + L_E^*)] = [1, A \cdot \overline{m}].$

Here the incumbent work force is sufficiently large so that the insider wage is reduced to the reservation wage, and, in response, the firm employs only the maximum sustainable incumbent work force.

Finally, scenario III is illustrated by the highest point on the thick line segment:

(14c) $[W^*(\text{III}), \lambda^*(\text{III})]$

$= [A \cdot (1 + H), (A \cdot L_I^* + L_E^*)]$

$= [A \cdot (1 + H), A \cdot \underline{m}].$

Here the incumbent work force is sufficiently small for some entrants to be profitable at their reservation wage. Thus, the insider wage is set so that the marginal incumbent is just as profitable as the marginal entrant ($W^*(\text{III}) = A \cdot (1 + H)$). In response, the firm retains all its incumbents and hires entrants until their marginal product (given by the entrant demand curve in the figure) is equal to their reservation wage (given by the line $R_E^* = 1 + H$ in the figure). Thus the firm's total work force, in efficiency units, is equal to what it would be if the minimum sustainable incumbent work force were employed ($\lambda^*(\text{III}) = A \cdot \underline{m}$).

Figure 1 shows quite simply what the insiders' cooperation and harassment activities are meant to achieve. By cooperating with other insiders, each insider raises the insider demand curve (in the figure) and is thereby able to achieve a higher wage than would otherwise have been possible. This is true for one of two reasons: (i) when entrants are not profitable (in scenario II) so that the insider wage is equal to the marginal product of the incumbent work force ($W^*(\text{II}) = A \cdot f'(A \cdot m)$), then cooperation among insiders raises this marginal product; and (ii) when entrants are profitable (in scenario III) so that the insider wage is a markup over the entrant wage ($W^*(\text{III}) = A \cdot (1 + H)$), then cooperation among insiders raises the firm's cost of replacing an insider by an entrant and thereby increases the markup between the insider wage (W) and the entrant wage (R_E).

When the insider withdraws cooperation from potential entrants, he lowers the potential entrant demand curve (in the figure) and, once again, raises the cost of replacing insiders by entrants.

Finally, when the insider increases his harassment of potential entrants, he raises the entrants' reservation wage, which is the basis on which the insider wage is marked up.

Observe that the insiders' threats to withdraw cooperation and to harass entrants are credible. Given that the firm has already hired a fixed amount, L_E, of entrants, it remains in the insiders' interest to fulfill their threats. For in withdrawing cooperation, each insider causes a reduction in a_E and thereby also reduces the firm's effective work force ($\lambda = a_I^* \cdot L_I^* + a_E \cdot L_E$); as a result, he is able to raise his marginal product and his wage (i.e., for given L_E, $(\partial W_E^i / \partial a_E^i)$ $= a_I \cdot f'' \cdot (\partial a_E / \partial a_E^i) < 0$ for any insider i). Furthermore, each insider still has an incentive to fulfill his harassment threat because, in doing so, he raises the entrants' reservation wage and is thereby able to achieve a higher wage for himself.

III. The Aggregate Labor Market: Involuntary Unemployment

We now shift the focus of our attention from the microeconomic equilibrium within a firm to unemployment in the labor market.

Consider an economy that contains a fixed number n of identical firms and a fixed number s of workers. The wage and employment decisions are made in a decentralized fashion within each firm, along the lines indicated in the previous section.

Aggregate labor market activity may be described in terms of three building blocks:

(*i*) *The aggregate labor demand curve*, denoted by N^D (the thick downward-sloping curve) in Figures 2A–C. (These figures picture the labor market under scenarios I–III, respectively.) When aggregate labor demand (N^D, in efficiency units) is less than or equal to the aggregate incumbent work force ($A \cdot m \cdot n$, also in efficiency units), employment decisions are made along the aggregate insider demand curve:

(15a) $N^D = n \cdot g(W^*/A)$,

                 for $0 \le N^D \le A \cdot m \cdot n$,

(by equation (2a), with $a_I = A$), where $g = (f')^{-1}$. Yet when aggregate labor demand exceeds the aggregate incumbent work force, employment decisions are given by the aggregate entrant demand curve:

(15b) $N^D = n \cdot g(R_E^*)$,   for $N^D > A \cdot m \cdot n$

(by equation (2b), when $a_E = 1$).

(*ii*) The *aggregate labor supply curve*, denoted by N^S (the dashed step function) in Figures 2A–C:

(16a) $W = R_I^*$,   for $0 \le N^S \le A \cdot m$,

(16b) $W = R_E^*$,   for $A \cdot m < N^S \le \tilde{S}$,

where N^S is measured in terms of efficiency units of labor and $\tilde{s}$ is the total labor force in efficiency units ($\tilde{s} = A \cdot m + (s - m)$).

(iii) The *wage-setting curve*, denoted by W^* (the dotted horizontal lines) in Figures 2A–C. When the aggregate incumbent work force is "large" (Figure 2A), insiders receive their reservation wage:

(17a) $W^* = 1$,   for $N^D > A \cdot \bar{m} \cdot n$.

When this work force is "intermediate" (Figure 2B), workers receive their marginal product:

(17b) $W^* = A \cdot f'(A \cdot m)$,

             for $A \cdot \underline{m} \cdot n \le N^D \le A \cdot \bar{m} \cdot n$.

When it is "small" (Figure 2C), workers receive a markup over the entrant wage (which is equal to the entrants' reservation wage):

(17c) $W^* = A \cdot R_E^* = A \cdot (1 + H)$,

             for $0 \le N^D < A \cdot \underline{m} \cdot n$.

Figures 2A–C are drawn so that the labor force $\tilde{s}$ exceeds the demand for labor at the equilibrium insider wage W^*; thus, some workers remain unemployed. The question to which we now turn is whether this unemployment is *involuntary*.

Clearly, it is not involuntary in scenario I, Figure 2A. Here the wage-setting curve (W^*) passes through the intersection of the aggregate labor demand curve (N^D) and supply curve (N^S). Employment (in efficiency units) curve (N^S) is $A \cdot \bar{m} \cdot n$, leaving ($\tilde{s} - A \cdot \bar{m} \cdot n$) workers unemployed—voluntarily so, since the incumbents who lose their jobs (($m - \bar{m}$) in number) prefer to be unemployed than to work for their marginal product ($W^* = R_I^* > A \cdot f(A \cdot m)$) and the outsiders (($s - m$) in number) would be unwilling to work at the prevailing wage even if they were not harassed ($R_E^* > R_I^* = W_I^*$).

In scenarios II and III, the nature of unemployment is a more complex matter. The reason is that insiders and outsiders in our labor market have different employment opportunities. The difference is twofold:

a) They do not face "identical conditions of employment" (ICE), that is, job attributes lying outside the workers' control. Insiders are able to work under full cooperation and without harassment from the other

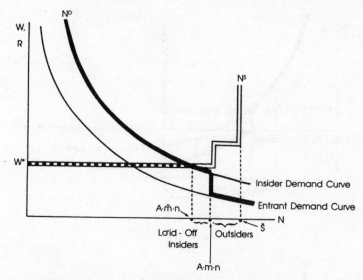

FIGURE 2A. SCENARIO I; N^D: AGGREGATE LABOR DEMAND CURVE (—); N^S:
AGGREGATE LABOR SUPPLY CURVE (=); W_* WAGE-SETTING
CURVE (●●●●)

insiders, whereas outsiders do not have this option.

b) Even under ICE, insiders and outsiders are not equally productive. Even if insiders and outsiders would receive equal cooperation from their colleagues, the outsiders would still be less productive since they (unlike the insiders) are unable to engage in cooperative activities with others.

These differences suggest that, in order for unemployment to be involuntary, it is not sufficient for workers to be unsuccessful in finding jobs at less than the prevailing wage. Differences in ability should be included in our conception of involuntary unemployment, but differences in conditions of employment (lying beyond the workers' control) should be excluded.

Let the prevailing "efficiency wage" be defined as the prevailing wage normalized for differences in productivity. Then, we propose the following definition of involuntary unemployment:

Definition: A worker is involuntarily unemployed over a particular period of time if he

does not have a job during that period, even though he would wish to work at an efficiency wage which is less than the efficiency wage of a current employee, provided that he had the opportunity to be employed under identical conditions of employment (ICE) as that employee.

This definition is easily extended to a multiperiod context.[18] The definition is meant to

---

[18] For our analysis, the relevant period is the single period over which the firm and the workers optimize their objectives. In a multiperiod context, our definition may be restated in terms of present values: a worker is involuntarily unemployed if he unsuccessfully seeks work (under ICE) for a discounted stream of efficiency wages which is less than the corresponding discounted stream of a current employee, over the same set of time periods. In other words, an outsider is involuntarily unemployed if he has less favorable opportunities than a current employee to earn a present value of wage income for a given stream of productive services. Under our simplifying assumption that outsiders turn into insiders after a single period of work (the initiation period), our intertemporal definition of involuntary un-

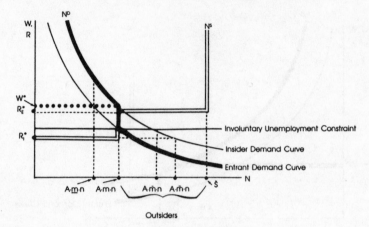

FIGURE 2B. SCENARIO II

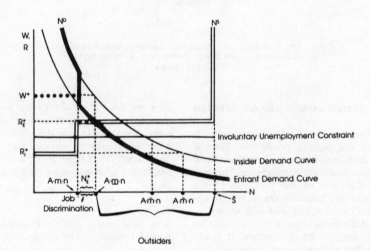

FIGURE 2C. SCENARIO III

employment reduces to the condition that the outsider has less favorable opportunities than a current employee *during the initiation period*. Observe that our definition involves a comparison of the wage-labor service opportunities of an outsider and a current employee over a *unique* set of time periods. It is *not* concerned with a comparison of those opportunities over an outsider's future working lifetime with those over an insider's past, present, and future working lifetime. We believe that the notions of unemployment commonly adopted by the news media, politicians, and compilers of unemployment statistics are more readily captured by the former comparison than the latter.

capture the idea that outsiders are out of work because they have a smaller choice set —in terms of wages received per efficiency unit of labor—than the insiders. In our model, an insider's efficiency wage is (W/a_I). Under ICE, an outsider's efficiency wage is (R_E^{ICE}/a_E^{ICE}). If outsiders are involuntarily unemployed, then their choice set is smaller than that of the insiders in the sense that

$$(18a) \qquad \left(R_E^{ICE}/a_E^{ICE} \right) < (W/a_I).$$

Defining $x \equiv (a_E^{ICE}/a_I)$ as the ratio of an entrant and insider's labor endowments under identical conditions of work,[19] our condition for involuntary unemployment becomes

$$(18b) \qquad W > x \cdot R_E^{ICE} = x \cdot R_I^* = x.$$

This means that, under identical conditions of employment, an outsider would be cheaper (in terms of efficiency wages) than an insider. (An outsider's labor costs, normalized for productivity differences is $x \cdot R_E^{ICE}$, whereas an insider's labor cost is W.) The reason why the firms in our analysis nevertheless do not replace insiders by outsiders is that these workers do *not* in fact face identical conditions of employment. Under *actual* conditions of employment (in which insiders receive cooperation and no harassment, whereas potential entrants receive harassment and no cooperation), an outsider is more expensive (in terms of efficiency wages) than an entrant. There is no underbidding because insiders rob their firms of the incentive to employ outsiders.

Our definition of involuntary employment sheds light on the nature of unemployment in scenarios II and III, as shown in Figures 2B and 2C, respectively. Observe that, in both figures, the wage-setting curve (shown by the dotted horizontal line W^*) crosses the N^D curve to the left of the intersection of the N^D and N^s curves. This implies that the outsiders $(\bar{s} - A \cdot m \cdot n)$ are willing to work for less than the prevailing insider wage (W^*), but are unable to do so. In order for this unemployment to be involuntary, we require that condition (18b) be satisfied, so that the insider wage lies above the "involuntary unemployment constraint," $W^* = x$, in Figures 2B and 2C.[20]

The wage $W = x$ corresponds to a particular size ($\tilde{m}$) of the firm's incumbent work force:

$$(19) \qquad x \equiv A \cdot f'(A \cdot \tilde{m}).$$

Thus, we see that the outsiders $(s - A \cdot m \cdot n)$ are involuntarily unemployed only if the aggregate incumbent work force is less than $n \cdot \tilde{m}$. It is easy to show that

$$(20) \qquad \underline{m} < \tilde{m} < \overline{m}.^{21}$$

This means that when the aggregate incumbent work force is "small" (scenario I), all the unemployment is involuntary. However, when the aggregate incumbent work force is "intermediate" (scenario II) the unemployment is involuntary when $m < \tilde{m}$ and voluntary when $m \geq \tilde{m}$. (As Figure 2B is drawn, it is involuntary.)

The workers who enter the firm in scenario III face a similar form of discrimination as the outsiders, in that they have a smaller choice set (in wage/efficiency-labor space) than the insiders. In particular, if the entrants and insiders faced identical conditions of employment, then each entrant's compensation per efficiency unit of labor would be less than that of each insider $(R_E^{ICE}/a_E^{ICE}) < (W/a_I)$. Hence, in Figure 2C the distance $(A \cdot n \cdot (\overline{m} - m))$ may be called "job discrimination."

Our conclusions concerning the existence of involuntary unemployment are summarized in the following proposition:

PROPOSITION 2: *Consider a labor market described by the aggregate labor demand curve* (15a) *and* (15b), *the aggregate labor supply curve* (16b) *and* (16c), *and the wage-setting curve* (17a) *and* (17b). *Let aggregate incumbent work force, $m \cdot n$, be historically given* (where n is the number of firms and m is the size of each firm's incumbent work force). If this work force happens to fall short of a

[19] The ratio of the insiders and entrants' marginal products under identical conditions of employment is $[(a_I \cdot f'(\lambda))/(a_E^{ICE} \cdot f'(\lambda))] = a_I/a_E^{ICE}$.
[20] Clearly, $1 < x < A$, because the insider is able to engage in cooperative activity whereas the entrant is not. (If insiders and entrants had equal cooperative abilities, then $x = 1$; when insiders cooperate fully with one another but not at all with potential entrants, then $(a_E/a_I) = A$.)

[21] *Proof.* $\tilde{m} < \overline{m}$, since $x > 1$ (by fn. 20) and given the definition of $\tilde{m}$ (in (19)) and $\overline{m}$ (in (9)). Furthermore, $\tilde{m} > \underline{m}$, since $x < A$ (by fn. 20) and given the definitions of $\tilde{m}$ and $\underline{m}$ (in (11)).

particular critical level, $\bar{m} \cdot n$ *(by* (19)), *then there is involuntary unemployment.*

Although our model deals with the simultaneous performance of cooperation and harassment activities, our explanation of involuntary unemployment may rest on each of these activities alone. If insiders engage in cooperation but no harassment activities, then the equilibrium within the firm is given by Proposition 1 with $H = 0$ and involuntary unemployment arises under the conditions in Proposition 2. When harassment but no cooperation activities are performed, we must not only set $A = 1$ in Proposition 1, but we must also assume that the firm faces some costs of replacing insiders by outsiders. The reason is that, in the absence of such costs, the firm would always find it worthwhile to fire all its harassing insiders and hire entrants who (by assumption) are incapable of harassing.[22]

IV. Some Potential Objections

We now turn to some potential objections to our explanation of wages, employment, and unemployment.

A. *Labor Turnover*

If incumbent workers are able to restrict labor turnover of their firms, why do firms often have large labor turnover rates in practice? Is our analysis inapplicable whenever a firm's work force has large simultaneous inflows and outflows?

When our model is extended to include quits and retirements of employees, it is able to account for simultaneous inflows and outflows. In particular, suppose that $r \cdot m$ randomly chosen[23] incumbents in each firm quit

or retire at the end of each time period (where $0 < r < 1$). If the incumbent work force initially exceeds its minimum sustainable level ($m > \underline{m}$), then the separations cause this work force to shrink. As it does so, the insider wage (W) and the marginal product of the insiders and potential entrants rise. However, once the incumbent work force falls beneath $\underline{m}$, the marginal product of potential entrants is so high that the insiders are no longer able to prevent all outsiders from being hired. Consequently, work force inflows and outflows occur simultaneously. In the stationary equilibrium, they are of equal magnitude. It can be shown[24] that these flows are $r \cdot L_I^* = L_E^* = (r \cdot A \cdot n \cdot \underline{m})/(r + A)$, and the associated level of unemployment is $u = s - L_I^* - L_E^* = s - (1 + r) \cdot (A \cdot n \cdot \underline{m})/(r + A)$.

Another reason why insiders' discriminatory activities do not preclude labor turnover in the real world is the following. Suppose that a firm employs "teams" of heterogeneous workers who are complementary to one another in the production process. In this context, insiders have no incentive to prevent the replacement of workers who have quit or retired. On the contrary, since all members of a team are complementary, it is in the insiders' interest to cooperate with and avoid harassing new entrants who fill vacancies on the team. In this light, it becomes clear that our analysis, in the case of heterogeneous labor, applies not to labor turnover within teams, but rather to turnover of teams (namely, the replacement of a team of insiders by a team of entrants).

---

[22] Formally, by the definition of H^c given in fn. 17, if $A = 1$, then $H^c = 0$ and thus, $H = 0$. This implies that the insiders would be unable to erect entry barriers against the outsiders and thus there could be no involuntary unemployment.

[23] The assumption of random choice is made only for expository simplicity, guaranteeing that all workers have the same reservation wage. Had we assumed that workers

retire after reaching a particular age, then (a) the reservation wage would rise with age; (b) the firm would hire the youngest entrants available; and (c) it is the reservation wage of these entrants that is relevant to insider wage determination.

[24] Suppose that the incumbent work force is $\hat{m}$ ($< \underline{m}$) when it first falls short of m. In that period of time, the firm hires $L_E^* = A \cdot (m - \hat{m})$. Then, in the next period, the incumbent work force becomes $(1 - r) \cdot \hat{m} + A \cdot (\underline{m} - \hat{m})$. In general, $m_t = (1 - r) \cdot m_{t-1} + A \cdot (\underline{m} - m_{t-1})$. Assuming that $r + A < 1$, the incumbent work force rises monotonically to its stationary level $(A \cdot n \cdot \underline{m})/(r + A)$.

B. *Creation of Firms*

Does our explanation of involuntary unemployment hinge on an assumption that the number of firms in the economy is fixed? Would free entry of firms lead to the elimination of this unemployment?

Our analysis suggests that when insider market power is widespread, entry of new firms (which have no insiders) may be a potentially important route to reducing unemployment. However, it is worth noting that, in practice, the creation of firms is often a lengthy process. Thus, even if free entry would eventually permit full employment to be achieved, the involuntary unemployment may nevertheless last a long time.

Moreover, the existence of involuntary unemployment does not necessarily generate an incentive to create new firms. The mere fact that insiders keep outsiders from being hired by the existing firms does not mean that new firms would find it profitable to hire these outsiders. Observe that new firms, in our analysis, are at a disadvantage vis-à-vis the existing firms, since new firms can employ only entrants (who are unable to cooperate with one another) whereas existing firms also employ insiders (who do cooperate with one another). There are of course many other reasons why new firms may be unprofitable even when existing firms are not, for example, setup costs, capital market imperfections, scarcity of entrepreneurial skills, reduction of product prices due to entry of firms. Hence, the involuntary unemployment of Section IV may persist even after all profitable opportunities for entry of firms have been exhausted.

C. *Output-Related Wage Contracts*

Does our explanation of involuntary unemployment hinge on our assumption that time-rate wages are the only form of labor remuneration? Could output-related wage contracts be used to bribe the insiders not to discriminate against entrants, thereby making the employed and unemployed workers as well as the firms better off and eliminating the unemployment?

Although Pareto-superior alternatives to time-rate wages may exist under some circumstances, they may not be available in others. In fact, they are never available for unemployment generated through differential harassment activities. The reason is that the firm is unable to infer the performance of these activities from the variables it can observe—namely, its total output, its employment of insiders and entrants, and its wages[25]—and thus it has no opportunity to reward insiders for foregoing harassment of entrants.

The matter is not quite so simple for cooperation activities. Although the firm cannot observe these activities directly, it is able to observe its total output. Thus, it may reward its insiders for cooperating with entrants by sharing the proceeds of its output with these insiders. This could take the form of profit or revenue sharing.

Yet, there are a variety of obstacles to designing and implementing such output-related wage contracts. Consider the following three significant ones, which are analyzed formally in Lindbeck and Snower (1985a):

Monitoring-Cost Difficulty. Since profit and revenue-sharing schemes are generally costly for workers to monitor,[26] managers may have an incentive to use their superior position in composing profit or revenue figures to their own advantage. In response, the employees may have an incentive to implement monitoring procedures (and possibly also to engage in litigation). The gains from profit or revenue sharing may not fully compensate the firm and its employees for these monitoring costs.

---

[25]We assume that firms do not know what the outsiders' reservation wages would be in the absence of harassment (for example, they do not know whether these reservation wages are the same as those of the insiders). Thus they cannot infer the presence of harassment by observing the entrant wages (in the event that scenario III obtains).

[26]For instance, managers often have considerable latitude in their choice of profit and revenue accounting practices (for example, how to price intermediate goods and inventories, how to evaluate the firm's debt in real terms, how to treat depreciation and obsolescence).

Risk-Aversion Difficulty. Profit and revenue sharing schemes inevitably involve the imposition of risk on employees. If these employees are risk averse, then they thereby suffer a utility loss. The firm may be unable to compensate them for this loss without robbing itself of the incentive to implement such schemes.

Market-Power Difficulty. When an insider decides to cooperate with entrants, he loses something and gains something: (*i*) he loses market power vis-à-vis the entrants and thus his time-rate wage sinks toward the reservation wage; and (*ii*) he gains some of the profit or revenue which accrues as a result of his cooperation with the entrants. In order for the output-related wage contract to induce insider-outsider cooperation, the second effect must outweight the first. However, that will happen only if the firm relinquishes at least a certain amount of its gross profit. Yet if the firm does so, it may find that its net profit is lower than in the noncooperative equilibrium, and then it has no incentive to implement the contract.

These difficulties, and perhaps others, help explain why output-related wage contracts do not play a particularly prominent role in today's labor markets. However, there is no reason to believe that the difficulties are necessarily insuperable; indeed, the model of differential cooperation activities surely suggests that there is a real-world case to be made for seeking alternatives to time-rate contracts. Be that as it may, time-rate wages are in fact the predominant form of labor remuneration and our analysis indicates how involuntary unemployment may arise when they are used.

D. *Economic Recovery*

Given that insiders can prevent outsiders from getting jobs, does our analysis imply that they can prevent employment from recovering after a recession? In particular, suppose that there has been an upswing in business conditions, shifting the insider and entrant demand curves in Figure 1 to the right. Does our analysis lead to the counterfactual implication that insiders invariably

take advantage of such an upswing by raising their wages so that employment remains unchanged?

To see why this potential objection does not hold, let us consider how our macroeconomy responds to an upswing in each of the three scenarios. (Lindbeck and Snower, 1985a, contains a formal analysis of the repercussions of business variations.) To begin with, note that the minimum and maximum sustainable incumbent work force ($\underline{m}$ and $\overline{m}$, respectively) rise in an upswing, so that the dividing lines between the three scenarios in Figure 1 shift to the right. If the incumbent work force is "large" (before and after the upswing), then the insider wage remains at $W^*(I)) = R_I^* = 1$ and more insiders are retained on account of the upswing. If the incumbent work force is "intermediate" (before and after the upswing), the insiders raise their wage ($W^*(II)$) by the full amount of the upward shift of the insider demand curve (without thereby encouraging entry of new employees), and as a result, employment remains unchanged. Finally, if the incumbent work force is "small" (before and after the upswing), the insiders are unable to raise their wage, for otherwise they would induce the firm to replace them by entrants. Consequently, the insider wage remains at $W^*(III) = A \cdot (1 + H)$ and the firm hires more entrants on account of the upswing.

In short, under scenarios I and III, insiders do *not* prevent employment from rising in an upswing, but they do have this effect under Scenario II. In this connection, it is important to mention that if insider wages are assumed to be the outcome of a bargaining process that splits the marginal rent between the insiders and their employers, then an upswing will lead to a rise in employment even under scenario II.

The degree to which an upswing leads to higher wages versus higher employment may depend on the size of this upswing. Consider, for example, a labor market suffering from unemployment and stuck in scenario II. If the upswing is "small," so that the labor market remains in this scenario, then employment will continue to stagnate while insider wages rise. Yet if the upswing is "large," so that the labor market moves into scenario III, then insider wages rise to a particular markup over entrants' reservation wages and employment expands (the larger the upswing, the greater the expansion). Here we observe that a large business stimulus reduces the level of unemployment whereas a small stimulus is unable to do so.

As another example of how the magnitude of the upswing matters to the wage-employment response, consider a labor market in scenario I. Here a "small" upswing (which maintains the existence of scenario I) keeps wages stable and induces firms to fire fewer incumbents than they would have done in the absence of the upswing. Yet if the upswing is large enough to put the labor market into scenario II, then all incumbents are retained and wages rise.

V. Concluding Remarks

This article outlines how insiders' cooperation and harassment activities may give rise to unemployment. The central idea is that firms find it costly to substitute outsiders for insiders, and that insiders manage to capture at least some of the associated economic rent in the process of wage determination. Consequently, insiders raise their wages above the level at which outsiders would be willing to work, but firms nevertheless lack the incentive to replace insiders by outsiders or to add outsiders to their work forces.

In general, the insider-outsider turnover cost can come in many guises, for example, hiring, training, and firing costs (Lindbeck and Snower, 1984a), morale effects of labor turnover (Lindbeck and Snower, 1984b), and this paper explores another one: the insiders' ability and incentive to cooperate with and harass some workers but not others. This ability enables them to create rent and thereby drive up their wages.

In this context involuntary unemployment can arise in the sense that outsiders are unable to find work even though they would be just as profitable to the firm as the insiders, provided that they faced identical conditions of employment. It is the insiders'

cooperation and harassment activities which ensure that these conditions are not the same for insiders and outsiders.

Our analysis has a variety of empirical implications. On the whole, these do not square with those of the natural rate hypothesis, since employment within our framework is not uniquely determined by preferences, endowments, and production technologies. Rather, our analysis suggests that the size of the incumbent work force may be an important determinant of employment, since insiders may have market power over wages whereas outsiders do not. As we have seen (in Section II, Part E), past employment (by virtue of its influence on the current incumbent work force) may affect current employment. In particular, over an "intermediate" range of incumbent employment levels ($\underline{m} \leq m \leq \overline{m}$), there is inertia in employment; but this inertia disappears at "low" incumbent employment levels ($m < \underline{m}$) and at "high" ones ($m > \overline{m}$).

Our model also includes the size of the incumbent work force as an argument in the insider wage equation. In particular, over an "intermediate" range of incumbent employment levels, the insider wage is determined in the traditional way, namely, from the relevant marginal productivity condition associated with an estimated labor demand curve (for insiders); yet at "high" and "low" incumbent employment levels, the insider wage is given by the reservation wage (proxied, for example, by unemployment pay, Social Security benefits, etc.) and a markup over the reservation wage, respectively. The reservation wage itself depends on the size of the incumbent work force in our model (since insiders have an incentive to harass other workers only when the incumbent work force is sufficiently small).

Of course, when conducting empirical studies, it is important to take heed of the production technologies under consideration. To the extent that these differ from the diminishing returns to labor assumed in our model, our predictions (regarding the effect of the incumbent work force on employment and wage formation) must be altered accordingly.

Furthermore, our analysis suggests that business upswings will tend to generate fewer jobs in countries with large insider power (due, for example, to unions' ability to exploit cooperation and harassment opportunities) than in countries where insiders are weak. Moreover (as shown in Section IV, Part D), whether a business upswing leads primarily to higher wages or higher employment may depend on the magnitude of this upswing relative to the size of the incumbent work force.

Our model also has implications for cyclical variations in labor market activity. As shown in Lindbeck and Snower (1985a), the movement of wages and employment in an upswing and a downswing may not be symmetric. In particular, a downswing may be characterized by stable insider wages and a contraction of the incumbent work force through retirements and layoffs, while an upswing (as in Section IV, Part D) may take the form of rising insider wages and only modest (if any) increases in employment.

In these and other respects, our insider-outsider approach yields an interrelated set of predictions about labor market activity.

REFERENCES

Akerlof, George A., "Labour Contracts and Partial Gift Exchange," *Quarterly Journal of Economics*, November 1982, *98*, 543–69.

Alchian, Armen A. and Demsetz, H., "Production, Information Costs, and Economic Organization," *American Economic Review*, December 1972, *62*, 777–95.

Blanchard, Olivier and Summers, Lawrence, "Hysteresis and the European Unemployment Problem," *NBER Macroeconomics Annual*, Vol. I, Cambridge: MIT Press, 1986, 15–77.

Bulow, Jeremy I. and Summers, Lawrence H., "A Theory of Dual Labor Markets with Application to Industrial Policy, Discrimination, and Keynesian Unemployment," *Journal of Labor Economics*, September 1986, *4*, 377–414.

Corden, W. Max, "Taxation, Real Wage Rigidity, and Employment," *Economic Journal*, June 1981, *91*, 309–33.

Gottfries, Niels and Horn, Henrik, "Wage Formation and the Persistency of Unemployment," Seminar Paper No. 347, Institute for International Economic Studies, University of Stockholm, April 1986.

Gregory, Robert, "Wages Policy and Unemployment in Australia," *Economica*, 1986, *53*, 553–74.

Lindbeck, Assar and Snower, Dennis, J., (1984a) "Involuntary Unemployment as an Insider-Outsider Dilemma," Seminar Paper No. 282, Institute for International Economics Studies, University of Stockholm; rev. version, "Wage Rigidity, Union Activity, and Unemployment," in W. Beckerman, ed., *Wage Rigidity and Unemployment*, London: Duckworth, 1986, 97–125.

_____ and _____, (1984b) "Labor Turnover, Insider Morale, and Involuntary Unemployment," Seminar Paper No. 310, Institute for International Economic Studies, University of Stockholm, 1984.

_____ and _____, (1985a) "Cooperation, Harassment, and Involuntary Unemployment," Seminar Paper No. 321, Institute for International Economic Studies, University of Stockholm; rev. version as Discussion paper No. DRD257, Washington, DC: World Bank, 1987.

_____ and _____, (1985b) "Explanations of Unemployment," *Oxford Review of Economic Policy*, Spring 1985, No. 2, *1*, 34–69.

_____ and _____, (1985a) "Wage Setting, Unemployment, and Insider-Outsider Relations," *American Economic Review Proceedings*, May 1986, *76*, 235–39.

_____ and _____, (1986b) "Union Activity and Wage-Employment Movements," *European Economic Review Proceedings*, 1986, *31*, 157–67.

_____ and _____, (1986c) "Efficiency Wages versus Insiders and Outsiders," *European Economic Review Proceedings*, 1986, *31*, 407–16.

Malcomson, Jim M., "Unemployment and the Efficiency Wage Hypothesis," *Economic Journal*, December 1981, *91*, 848–66.

Marshak, Jacob and Radner, Roy, *Economic Theory of Teams*, New Haven: Yale University Press, 1972.

McDonald, Ian M. and Solow, Robert M. "Wage Bargaining and Employment," *American Economic Review*, December 1981, *71*, 896–908.

Oswald, Andrew J., "The Microeconomic Theory of the Trade Union," *Economic Journal*, September 1982, *92*, 576–95.

Shaked, Avner and Sutton, John, "Involuntary Unemployment as a Perfect Equilibrium in a Bargaining Model," *Econometrica*, November 1984, *52*, 1351–64.

Shapiro, Carl and Stiglitz, Joseph E., "Equilibrium Unemployment as a Worker Discipline Device," *American Economic Review*, June 1984, *74*, 433–44.

Solow, Robert M., "Insiders and Outsiders in Wage Determination," *Scandinavian Journal of Economics*, No. 2, 1985, *87*, 711–28.

Weiss, Andrew, "Job Queues and Layoffs in Labor Markets with Flexible Wages," *Journal of Political Economy*, June 1980, *88*, 526–38.

[23]

Equilibrium Unemployment as a Worker Discipline Device

By Carl Shapiro and Joseph E. Stiglitz*

Involuntary unemployment appears to be a persistent feature of many modern labor markets. The presence of such unemployment raises the question of why wages do not fall to clear labor markets. In this paper we show how the information structure of employer-employee relationships, in particular the inability of employers to costlessly observe workers' on-the-job effort, can explain involuntary unemployment[1] as an equilibrium phenomenon. Indeed, we show that imperfect monitoring necessitates unemployment in equilibrium.

The intuition behind our result is simple. Under the conventional competitive paradigm, in which all workers receive the market wage and there is no unemployment, the worst that can happen to a worker who shirks on the job is that he is fired. Since he can immediately be rehired, however, he pays no penalty for his misdemeanor. With imperfect monitoring and full employment, therefore, workers will choose to shirk.

To induce its workers not to shirk, the firm attempts to pay more than the "going wage"; then, if a worker is caught shirking and is fired, he will pay a penalty. If it pays one firm to raise its wage, however, it will pay all firms to raise their wages. When they all raise their wages, the incentive not to shirk again disappears. But as all firms raise their wages, their demand for labor decreases, and unemployment results. With unemployment, even if all firms pay the same wages, a worker has an incentive not to shirk. For, if he is fired,

an individual will not immediately obtain another job. The equilibrium unemployment rate must be sufficiently large that it pays workers to work rather than to take the risk of being caught shirking.

The idea that the threat of firing a worker is a method of discipline is not novel. Guillermo Calvo (1981) studied a static model which involves equilibrium unemployment.[2] No previous studies have treated general market equilibrium with dynamics, however, or studied the welfare properties of such unemployment equilibria. One key contribution of this paper is that the punishment associated with being fired is endogenous, as it depends on the equilibrium rate of unemployment. Our analysis thus goes beyond studies of information and incentives within organizations (such as Armen Alchian and Harold Demsetz, 1972, and the more recent and growing literature on worker-firm relations as a principal-agent problem) to inquire about the equilibrium conditions in markets with these informational features.

The paper closest in spirit to ours is Steven Salop (1979) in which firms reduce turnover costs when they raise wages; here the savings from higher wages are on monitoring costs (or, at the same level of monitoring, from increased output due to increased effort). As in the Salop paper, the unemployment in this paper is definitely involuntary, and not of the standard search theory type (Peter Diamond, 1981, for example). Workers have perfect information about all job opportunities in our model, and unemployed workers strictly prefer to work at wages less than the prevailing market wage (rather than to remain unemployed); there are no vacancies.

*Woodrow Wilson School of Public and International Affairs, and Department of Economics, respectively, Princeton University, Princeton, NJ 08540. We thank Peter Diamond, Gene Grossman, Ed Lazear, Steve Salop, and Mike Veall for helpful comments. Financial support from the National Science Foundation is appreciated.

[1] By involuntary unemployment we mean a situation where an unemployed worker is willing to work for less than the wage received by an equally skilled employed worker, yet no job offers are forthcoming.

[2] In his 1979 paper, Calvo surveyed a variety of models of unemployment, including his hierarchical firm model (also with Stanislaw Wellisz, 1979). There are a number of important differences between that work and this paper, including the specification of the monitoring technology.

The theory we develop has several important implications. First, we show that unemployment benefits (and other welfare benefits) increase the equilibrium unemployment rate, but for a reason quite different from that commonly put forth (i.e., that individuals will have insufficient incentives to search for jobs). In our model, the existence of unemployment benefits reduces the "penalty" associated with being fired. Therefore, to induce workers not to shirk, firms must pay higher wages. These higher wages reduce the demand for labor.

Second, the model explains why wages adjust slowly in the face of aggregate shocks. A decrease in the demand for labor will ultimately cause a lower wage and a higher level of unemployment. In the transition, however, the wage decrease will match the growth in the unemployment pool, which may be a sluggish process.

Third, we show that the market equilibrium which emerges is not, in general, Pareto optimal, where we have taken explicitly into account the costs associated with monitoring. There exist, in other words, interventions in the market that make everyone better off. In particular, we show that there are circumstances in which wage subsidies are desirable. There are also circumstances where the government should intervene in the market by supplying unemployment insurance, even if all firms (rationally) do not. A (small) turnover tax is desirable, because high turnover increases the flow of job vacancies, and hence the flow out of the unemployment pool, making the threat of firing less severe.

Additionally, our theory provides predictions about the characteristics of labor markets which cause the natural rate (i.e., equilibrium level) of unemployment to be relatively high: high rates of labor turnover, high monitoring costs, high discount rates for workers, significant possibilities for workers to vary their effort inputs, or high costs to employers (such as broken machinery) from shirking.

Finally, our theory shows how wage distributions (for identical workers) can persist in equilibrium. Firms which find shirking particularly costly will offer higher wages than

other firms do. The dual role wages play by allocating labor and providing incentives for employee effort allows wage dispersion to persist.

Although we have focused our analysis on the labor market, it should be clear that a similar analysis could apply to other markets (for example, product or credit markets) as well. This paper can be viewed as an analysis of a simplified general equilibrium model of an economy in which there are important principal-agent (incentive) problems, and in which the equilibrium entails *quantity constraints* (job rationing). As in all such problems, it is important to identify what is observable, and, based on what is observable, what are the set of feasible contractual arrangements between the parties to the contract. Under certain circumstances, for instance, workers might issue performance bonds and this might alleviate the problems with which we are concerned in this paper. In Section III we discuss the role of alternative incentive devices.

In the highly simplified model upon which we focus here, all workers are identical, all firms are identical, and thus, in equilibrium, all pay the same wage. The assumption that all workers are the same is important, because it implies that being fired carries no stigma (the next potential employer knows that the worker is no more immoral than any other worker; he only infers that the firm for which the worker worked must have paid a wage sufficiently low that it paid the worker to shirk). We have made this assumption because we wished to construct the simplest possible model focussing simply on incentive effects, in which adverse selection considerations play no role. In a sequel, we hope to explore the important interactions between the two fundamental information problems of adverse selection and moral hazard.[3]

The assumption that all firms are the same is not critical for the existence of equilibrium unemployment. Firm heterogeneity will, however, lead to a wage distribution. If the

---

[3] Other studies have focused on quantity constraints (rationing) with adverse-selection problems. See Stiglitz (1976), Charles Wilson (1980), Andrew Weiss (1980), and Stiglitz and Weiss (1981).

damage that a particular firm incurs as a result of a worker not performing up to standard is larger, the firm will have an incentive to pay the worker a higher wage. Similarly, if the cost of monitoring (detecting shirking) for a firm is large, that firm will also pay a higher wage. Thus, even though workers are all identical, workers for different firms will receive different wages. There is considerable evidence that, in fact, different firms do pay different wages to workers who appear to be quite similar (for example, more capital intensive firms pay higher wages). The theory we develop here may provide part of the explanation of this phenomenon.

In Section I, we present the basic model in which workers are risk neutral. Quit rates and monitoring intensities are exogenous. A welfare analysis of the unemployment equilibrium is provided. In Section II, we comment on extensions of the analysis to situations where monitoring intensities and quit rates are endogenous, and where workers are risk averse. Section III compares the role of unemployment as an incentive device with other methods of enforcing discipline on the labor force.

I. The Basic Model

In this section we formulate a simple model which captures the incentive role of unemployment as described above. Extensions and modifications of this basic model are considered in subsequent sections.

A. Workers

There are a fixed number, N, of identical workers, all of whom dislike putting forth effort, but enjoy consuming goods. We write an individual's instantaneous utility function as $U(w, e)$, where w is the wage received and e is the level of effort on the job. For simplicity, we shall assume the utility function is separable; initially, we shall also assume that workers are risk neutral. With suitable normalizations, we can therefore rewrite utility as $U = w - e$. Again, for simplicity, we assume that workers can provide either minimal effort ($e = 0$), or some fixed positive level of

$e > 0$.[4] When a worker is unemployed, he receives unemployment benefits of $\overline{w}$ (and $e = 0$).

Each worker is in one of two states at any point in time: employed or unemployed. There is a probability b per unit time that a worker will be separated from his job due to relocation, etc., which will be taken as exogenous. Exogenous separations cause a worker to enter the unemployment pool. Workers maximize the expected present discounted value of utility with a discount rate $r > 0$.[5] The model is set in continuous time.

B. The Effort Decision of a Worker

The only choice workers make is the selection of an effort level, which is a discrete choice by assumption. If a worker performs at the customary level of effort for his job, that is, if he does not shirk, he receives a wage of w and will retain his job until exogenous factors cause a separation to occur. If he shirks, there is some probability q (discussed below), per unit time, that he will be caught.[6] If he is caught shirking he will be fired,[7] and forced to enter the unemployment pool. The probability per unit time of acquiring a job while in the unemployment pool (which we call the job acquisition rate, an endogenous variable calculated below) determines the expected length of the unemployment spell he must face. While unemployed he receives unemployment compensation of $\overline{w}$ (also discussed below).

---

[4] Including effort as a continuous variable would not change the qualitative results.

[5] That is, we assume individuals are infinitely lived, and have a pure rate of time preference of r. They maximize

$$W = E \int_0^\infty u(w(t), e(t)) \exp(-rt)\, dt,$$

where we have implicitly assumed that individuals can neither borrow nor lend. Allowing an exponential death rate would not alter the structure of the model; neither would borrowing in the risk-neutral case.

[6] For now we take q as exogenous; later it will be endogenous. The assumption of a Poisson detection technology, like a number of the other assumptions employed in the analysis, is made to ensure that the model has a simple stationary structure.

[7] This will be firm's optimal policy in equilibrium.

The worker selects an effort level to maximize his discounted utility stream. This involves comparison of the utility from shirking with the utility from not shirking, to which we now turn. We define V_E^S as the expected lifetime utility of an employed shirker, V_E^N as the expected lifetime utility of an employed nonshirker, and V_u as the expected lifetime utility of an unemployed individual. The fundamental asset equation for a shirker is given by

$$(1) \quad rV_E^S = w + (b+q)(V_u - V_E^S),$$

while for a nonshirker, it is

$$(2) \quad rV_E^N = w - e + b(V_u - V_E^N).$$

Each of these equations is of the form "interest rate times asset value equals flow benefits (dividends) plus expected capital gains (or losses)."[8] Equations (1) and (2) can be solved for V_E^S and V_E^N:

$$(3) \quad V_E^S = \frac{w + (b+q)V_u}{r + b + q};$$

$$(4) \quad V_E^N = \frac{(w-e) + bV_u}{r + b}.$$

The worker will choose not to shirk if and only if $V_E^N \geq V_E^S$. We call this the *no-shirking condition* (*NSC*), which, using (3) and (4), can be written as

$$(5) \quad w \geq rV_u + (r + b + q)e/q \equiv \hat{w}.$$

Alternatively, the *NSC* also takes the form $q(V_E^S - V_u) \geq e$. This highlights the basic im-

plication of the *NSC*: unless there is a penalty associated with being unemployed, everyone will shirk. In other words, if an individual could immediately obtain employment after being fired, $V_u = V_E^S$, and the *NSC* could never be satisfied.

Equation (5) has several natural implications. If the firm pays a sufficiently high wage, then the workers will not shirk. The critical wage, $\hat{w}$, is higher

    (a) the higher the required effort (e),
    (b) the higher the expected utility associated with being unemployed (V_u),
    (c) the lower the probability of being detected shirking (q),
    (d) the higher the rate of interest (i.e., the relatively more weight is attached to the short-run gains from shirking (until one is caught) compared to the losses incurred when one is eventually caught),
    (e) the higher the exogenous quit rate b (if one is going to have to leave the firm anyway, one might as well cheat on the firm).

C. Employers

There are M identical firms, $i = 1, ..., M$. Each firm has a production function $Q_i = f(L_i)$, generating an aggregate production function of $Q = F(L)$.[9] Here L_i is firm i's effective labor force; we assume a worker contributes one unit of effective labor if he does not shirk. Otherwise he contributes nothing (this is merely for simplicity). Therefore firms compete in offering wage packages, subject to the constraint that their workers choose not to shirk. We assume that $F'(N) > e$, that is, full employment is efficient.

The monitoring technology (q) is exogenous. Monitoring choices by employers are analyzed in the following section. We assume

---

[8] A derivation follows: taking V_u as given and looking at a short time interval $[0, t]$ we have

$$V_E = wt + (1 - rt)[btV_u + (1 - bt)V_E],$$

since there is probability bt of leaving the job during the interval $[0, t]$ and since $e^{-rt} \approx 1 - rt$. Solving for V_E, we have

$$V_E = [wt + (1 - rt)btV_u]/[1 - (1 - rt)(1 - bt)].$$

Taking limits as $t \to 0$ gives (1). Equation (2) can be derived similarly.

[9] That is,

$$F(L) \equiv \max_{\{L_i\}} \sum f_i(L_i)$$

such that $\sum L_i = L$. This assumes that in market equilibrium, labor is efficiently allocated, as it will be in the basic model of this section. The modifications required for more general cases, when different firms face different critical no-shirking wages, $\hat{w}_i$, or have different technologies, are straightforward.

that other factors (for example, exogenous noise or the absence of employee specific output measures) prevent monitoring of effort via observing output.

A firm's wage package consists of a wage, w, and a level of unemployment benefits, $\bar{w}$.[10] Each firm finds it optimal to fire shirkers, since the only other punishment, a wage reduction, would simply induce the disciplined worker to shirk again.

It is not difficult to establish that all firms offer the smallest unemployment benefits allowed (say, by law).[11] This follows directly from the *NSC*, equation (5). An individual firm has no incentive to set $\bar{w}$ any higher than necessary. An increase in $\bar{w}$ raises V_u and hence requires a higher w to meet the *NSC*. Therefore, increases in $\bar{w}$ cost the firm both directly (higher unemployment benefits) and indirectly (higher wages). Since the firm has no difficulty attracting labor (in equilibrium), it sets $\bar{w}$ as small as possible. Hence we can interpret $\bar{w}$ in what follows as the minimum legal level, which is offered consistently by all firms.

Having offered the minimum allowable $\bar{w}$, an individual firm pays wages sufficient to induce employee effort, that is, $w = \hat{w}$ to meet the *NSC*. The firm's labor demand is given by equating the marginal product of labor to the cost of hiring an additional employee. This cost consists of wages and future unemployment benefits. For $\bar{w} = 0$,[12] the labor demand is given simply by $f'(L_i) = \hat{w}$, with aggregate labor demand of $F'(L) = \hat{w}$.

D. *Market Equilibrium*

We now turn to the determination of the equilibrium wage and employment levels. Let us first indicate heuristically the factors which determine the equilibrium wage level.

If wages are very high, workers will value their jobs for two reasons: (a) the high wages themselves, and (b) the correspondingly low level of employment (due to low demand for labor at high wages) which implies long spells of unemployment in the event of losing one's job. In such a situation employers will find they can reduce wages without tempting workers to shirk.

Conversely, if the wage is quite low, workers will be tempted to shirk for two reasons: (a) low wages imply that working is only moderately preferred to unemployment, and (b) high employment levels (at low wages there is a large demand for labor) imply unemployment spells due to being fired will be brief. In such a situation firms will raise their wages to satisfy the *NSC*.

Equilibrium occurs when each firm, taking as given the wages and employment levels at other firms, finds it optimal to offer the going wage rather than a different wage. The key market variable which determines individual firm behavior is V_u, the expected utility of an unemployed worker. We turn now to the calculation of the equilibrium V_u.[13]

The asset equation for V_u, analogous to (1) and (2), is given by

$$(6) \qquad rV_u = \bar{w} + a(V_E - V_u),$$

where a is the job acquisition rate and V_E is the expected utility of an employed worker (which equals V_E^N in equilibrium). We can now solve (4) and (6) simultaneously for V_E and V_u to yield

$$(7) \qquad rV_E = \frac{(w-e)(a+r) + \bar{w}b}{a+b+r};$$

$$(8) \qquad rV_u = \frac{(w-e)a + \bar{w}(b+r)}{a+b+r}.$$

---

[10] More complex employment contracts, for example, wages rising with seniority, are discussed in Section III. With our assumptions of stationarity and identical workers, employers cannot improve on the simple employment provisions considered here.

[11] We are implicitly assuming that the firm cannot offer $\bar{w}$ only to workers who quit. This is so because the firm can always fire a worker who wishes to quit, and it would be optimal for the firm to do so.

[12] For $\bar{w} > 0$ the expected cost of a worker is the wage cost for the expected employment period of $1/b$, followed by $\bar{w}$ for the expected period of unemployment, $1/a$. This generates labor demand given by

$$f'(L_i) = w + \bar{w}b/(a+r).$$

[13] We have already shown that all firms offer the same employment benefits $\bar{w}$, so V_u is indeed a single number, i.e., an unemployed person's utility is independent of his previous employer.

Substituting the expression for V_u (i.e., (8)) into the *NSC* (5) yields the *aggregate NSC*

$$(9) \quad w \geq \bar{w} + e + e(a+b+r)/q.$$

Notice that the critical wage for nonshirking is greater: (a) the smaller the detection probability q; (b) the larger the effort e; (c) the higher the quit rate b; (d) the higher the interest rate r; (e) the higher the unemployment benefit $(\bar{w})$; and (f) the higher the flows out of unemployment a.

We commented above on the first four properties; the last two are also unsurprising. If the unemployment benefit is high, the expected utility of an unemployed individual is high, and therefore the punishment associated with being unemployed is low. To induce individuals not to shirk, a higher wage must be paid. If a is the probability of obtaining a job per unit of time, $1/a$ is the expected duration of being unemployed. The longer the duration, the greater the punishment associated with being unemployed, and hence the smaller the wage that is required to induce nonshirking.

The rate a itself can be related to more fundamental parameters of the model, in a steady-state equilibrium. In steady state the flow *into* the unemployment pool is bL where L is aggregate employment. The flow *out* is $a(N-L)$ (per unit time) where N is the total labor supply. These must be equal, so $bL = a(N-L)$, or

$$(10) \quad a = bL/(N-L).$$

Substituting for a into (9), the aggregate *NSC*, we have

$$(11) \quad w \geq e + \bar{w} + \frac{e}{q}\left(\frac{bN}{(N-L)} + r\right)$$

$$= e + \bar{w} + (e/q)(b/u + r) \equiv \hat{w},$$

where $u = (N-L)/N$, the unemployment rate. This constraint, the aggregate *NSC*, is graphed in Figure 1. It is immediately evident that *no shirking is inconsistent with full employment*. If $L = N$, $a = +\infty$, so any shirking worker would immediately be re-

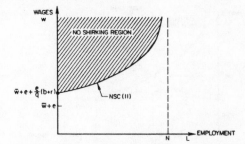

FIGURE 1. THE AGGREGATE NO-SHIRKING CONSTRAINT

hired. Knowing this, workers will choose to shirk.

The equilibrium wage and employment level are now easy to identify. Each (small) firm, taking the aggregate job acquisition rate a as given, finds that it must offer at least the wage $\hat{w}$. The firm's demand for labor then determines how many workers are hired at the wage. Equilibrium occurs where the aggregate demand for labor intersects the aggregate *NSC*. For $\bar{w} = 0$, equilibrium occurs when

$$F'(L) = e + (e/q)(bN/(N-L)+r).$$

The equilibrium is depicted in Figure 2.[14] It is important to understand the forces which cause E to be an equilibrium. From the firm's point of view, there is no point in raising wages since workers are providing effort and the firm can get all the labor it wants at w^*. Lowering wages, on the other hand, would induce shirking and be a losing idea.[15]

From the worker's point of view, *unemployment is involuntary*: those without jobs would be happy to work at w^* or lower, but cannot make a credible promise not to shirk at such wages.

---

[14]Aggregate labor demand is $F'(L)$ only when $\bar{w} = 0$ (see fn. 12).

[15]We have assumed that output is zero when an individual shirks, but we need only assume that a shirker's output is sufficiently low that hiring shirking workers is unprofitable.

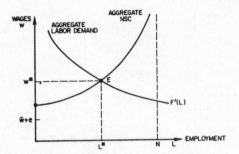

FIGURE 2. EQUILIBRIUM UNEMPLOYMENT

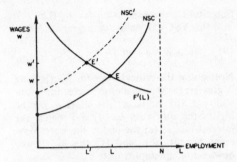

FIGURE 3. COMPARATIVE STATICS

Note: A decrease in the monitoring intensity q, or an increase in the quit rate b, leads to higher wages and more unemployment

Notice that the type of unemployment we have characterized here is very different from search unemployment. Here, all workers and all firms are identical. There is perfect information about job availability. There is a different information problem: firms are assumed (quite reasonably, in our view) not to be able to monitor the activities of their employees costlessly and perfectly.

E. *Simple Comparative Statics*

The effect of changing various parameters of the problem may easily be determined. As noted above, increasing the quit rate b, or decreasing the monitoring intensity q, decreases incentives to exert effort. Therefore, these changes require an increase in the wage necessary (at each level of employment) to induce individuals to work, that is, they shift the *NSC* curve upwards (see Figure 3). On the other hand, they leave the demand curve for labor unchanged, and hence the equilibrium level of unemployment and the equilibrium wage are both increased. Increases in unemployment benefits have the same impact on the *NSC* curve, but they also reduce labor demand as workers become more expensive, so they cause unemployment to rise for two reasons.

Inward shifts in the labor demand schedule create more unemployment. Due to the *NSC*, wages cannot fall enough to compensate for the decreased labor demand. The transition to the higher unemployment equilibrium will not be immediate: wage decreases by individual firms will only become

attractive as the unemployment pool grows. This provides an explanation of wage sluggishness.

F. *Welfare Analysis*

In this section we study the welfare properties of the unemployment equilibrium. We demonstrate that the equilibrium is not in general Pareto optimal, when information costs are explicitly accounted for.

We begin with the case where the owners of the firms are the same individuals as the workers, and ownership is equally distributed among N workers. The central planning problem is to maximize the expected utility of the representative worker subject to the *NSC* and the resource constraint:

$$(12) \quad \max_{w, \bar{w}, L} (w - e)L + \bar{w}(N - L)$$

subject to $w \geq e + \bar{w} + (e/q)((bN$

$$/(N - L)) + r) \quad (NSC)$$

subject to $wL + \bar{w}(N - L) \leq F(L)$

(Feasibility)

subject to $\bar{w} \geq 0$.

Since workers are risk neutral it is easy to check[16] that the optimum involves $\bar{w}$ at the minimum allowable level, which is assumed to be 0. The reason is that increases in $\bar{w}$ tighten the *NSC*, so all payments should be made in the form of w rather $\bar{w}$.

Setting $\bar{w} = 0$, the problem simplifies to

$$(12') \quad \max_{w, L} (w - e) L$$

subject to $w \geq e + (e/q)((bN/(N-L)) + r)$;

and $\quad wL \leq F(L)$.

The set of points which satisfy the constraints is shaded in Figure 4. Iso-utility curves are rectangular hyperboles. So long as $F'(L) > e$, these are steeper than the average product locus, so the optimum occurs at point A where the *NSC* intersects the curve $w = F(L)/L$, that is, where wages equal the average product of labor. In contrast, the market equilibrium occurs at E where the marginal product of labor curve, $w = F'(L)$, intersects the *NSC* (Figure 2). Observe that in the case of constant returns to scale, $F'(L)L = F(L)$, so the equilibrium is optimal.

Wages should be subsidized, using whatever (pure) profits can be taxed away. An equivalent way to view the social optimum is a tax on unemployment to reduce shirking incentives; the wealth constraint on the un-

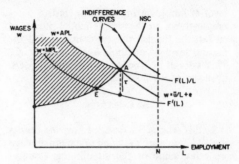

FIGURE 4. SOCIAL OPTIMUM AT A

employed requires that $\bar{w} \geq 0$, or equivalently that profits after taxes be nonnegative.[17] The optimum can be achieved by taxing away all profits and financing a wage subsidy of τ, shown in Figure 4. *The "natural" unemployment rate is too high.*

In the case where the workers and the owners are distinct individuals, the tax policy described above would reduce profits, increase wages, and increase employment levels. While it would increase aggregate output (net of effort costs), such a tax policy would *not* constitute a Pareto improvement, since profits would fall. For this reason, the equilibrium is Pareto optimal in this case, even though it fails to maximize net national product. We thus have the unusual result that the Pareto optimality of the equilibrium depends upon the distribution of wealth. The standard separation between efficiency and income distribution does not carry over to this model.

It should not be surprising that the equilibrium level of unemployment is in general inefficient. Each firm tends to employ too few workers, since it sees the private cost of an additional worker as w, while the social cost is only e, which is lower. On the other hand, when a firm hires one more worker, it fails to take account of the effect this has on V_u (by reducing the size of the unemployment pool). This effect, a negative externality imposed by one firm on others as it raises its

---

[16]Formally,

$$\mathcal{L} = (w - e)L + \bar{w}(N - L)$$

$$+ \lambda[w - e - \bar{w} - (e/q)(bN/(N-l) + r)]$$

$$+ \mu[F(L) - wL - \bar{w}(N - L)].$$

Differentiating with respect to w and $\bar{w}$ yields

$\mathcal{L}_w = L + \lambda - \mu L \leq 0$ and $= 0$ if $w > 0$.

$\mathcal{L}_{\bar{w}} = (N - L) - \lambda - \mu(N - L) \leq 0$ and $= 0$ if $\bar{w} > 0$.

We know $w > 0$ by the *NSC*, so $\mathcal{L}_w = 0$, i.e., $L(1 - \mu) + \lambda = 0$. Therefore, since $\lambda > 0$, $\mu > 1$. But then $\mathcal{L}_{\bar{w}} = (N - L)(1 - \mu) - \lambda < 0$. This implies that $\bar{w} = 0$.

[17]The constraint $\bar{w} \geq 0$ can be rewritten, using the resource constraint, as $F(L) - wL \geq 0$, i.e., $\pi \geq 0$.

level of employment, tends to lead to over-employment. In the simple model presented so far, the former effect dominates, and the natural level of unemployment is too high. This will not be true in more general models, however, as we shall see below.

II. Extensions

In this section we describe how the results derived above are modified or extended when we relax some of the simplifying assumptions. We discuss three extensions in turn: endogenous monitoring, risk aversion, and endogenous turnover. Detailed derivations of the claims made below are available in our earlier working paper.

A. *Endogenous Monitoring*

When employees can select the monitoring intensity q, they can trade off stricter monitoring (at a cost) with higher wages as methods of worker discipline. In general, firms' monitoring intensities will not be optimal, due to the externalities between firms described above. In general, it is not possible to ascertain whether the equilibrium entails too much or too little employment. In the case of constant returns to scale ($F(L) = L$), however (which led to efficiency with exogenous monitoring), the competitive equilibrium involves too much monitoring and too much employment.

The result is not as unintuitive as it first seems: each firm believes that the only instrument at its control for reducing shirking is to increase monitoring. There is, however, a second instrument: by reducing employment, workers are induced not to shirk. This enables society to save resources on monitoring (supervision). These gains more than offset the loss from the reduced employment.

It is straightforward to see how this policy may be implemented. If firms can be induced to reduce their monitoring, welfare will be increased. Hence a tax on monitoring, with the proceeds distributed, say, as a lump sum transfer to firms, will leave the no-shirking constraint/national-resource constraint unaffected, but will reduce monitoring.

B. *Risk Aversion*

With risk neutrality, the optimum and the market both involve $\bar{w} = 0$. Clearly $\bar{w} = 0$ cannot be optimal if workers are highly risk averse and may be separated from their jobs for exogenous reasons. Yet the market always provides $\bar{w} = 0$ (or the legal minimum). The proof above that $\bar{w} = 0$ carries over to the case of risk-averse workers.

When equilibrium involves unemployment, firms have no difficulty attracting workers and hence offer $\bar{w} = 0$, since $\bar{w} > 0$ merely reduces the penalty of being fired. When *other* firms offer $\bar{w} = 0$, this argument is only strengthened: unemployed workers are even easier to attract. It is striking that the market provides no unemployment benefits even when workers are highly risk averse. Clearly the social optimum involves $\bar{w} > 0$ if risk aversion is great enough. This may provide a justification for mandatory minimum benefit levels.

C. *Endogenous Turnover*

In general a firm's employment package will influence the turnover rate it experiences among its employees. Since the turnover rate b affects the rate of hiring out of the unemployment pool, and hence V_u, it affects other firms' no-shirking constraints. Because of this externality, firms' choices of employment packages will not in general be optimal. This type of externality is similar to search externalities in which, for example, one searcher's expected utility depends on the number or mix of searchers remaining in the market. In the current model, policies which discourage labor turnover are attractive as they make unemployment more costly to shirkers.

III. Alternative Methods for the Enforcement of Discipline

This paper has explored a particular mechanism for the enforcement of discipline: individuals who are detected shirking are fired, and in equilibrium the level of unemployment is sufficiently large that this threat serves as an effective deterrent to shirking. The question naturally arises whether there are alternative, less costly, or more effective discipline mechanisms.

A. *Performance Bonds*

The most direct mechanism by which discipline might be enforced is through the posting by workers of performance bonds. Under this arrangement the worker would forfeit the bond if the firm detected him shirking. One problem with this solution is that workers may not have the wealth to post bond.[18] A more fundamental problem with this mechanism is that the firm would have an incentive to *claim* that the worker shirked so that it could appropriate the bond. Assuming, quite realistically, that third parties cannot easily observe workers' effort (indeed, it is usually more costly for outsiders to observe worker inputs than for the employer to do so), there is no simple way to discipline the *firm* from this type of opportunism.

Having recognized this basic point, it is easy to see that a number of other plausible solutions face the same difficulty. For example, consider an employment package which rewards effort by raising wages over time for workers who have not been found shirking. This is in fact equivalent to giving the worker a level wage stream, but taking back part of his earlier payments as a bond, which is returned to him later. Therefore, by the above argument, the firm will have an incentive to fire the worker when he is about to enter the "payoff" period in which he recovers his bond. This is the equivalent to the firm's simply appropriating the bond. It is optimal for the firm to replace expensive senior workers by inexpensive junior ones.[19]

Clearly the firm's reputation as an honest employer can partially solve this problem; the employer is implicitly penalized for firing a worker if this renders him less attractive to prospective employees. Yet this reputation mechanism may not work especially well, since prospective employees often do not know the employer's record, and previous dismissals may have been legitimate (it is not possible for prospective employees to distinguish legitimate from unfair earlier dismissals, if they are aware of them at all). If the reputation mechanism is less than perfect, it will be augmented by the unemployment mechanism.

B. *Other Costs of Dismissal*

Unemployment in the model above serves the role of imposing costs on dismissed workers. If other costs of dismissal are sufficiently high, workers may have an incentive to exert effort even under conditions of full employment. Examples of such costs are search costs, moving expenses, loss of job-specific human capital, etc. In markets where these costs are substantial, the role of equilibrium unemployment is substantially diminished. The effect we have identified above will still be present, however, when effort levels are continuous variables: each firm will still find that employee effort is increasing with wages, so wages will be bid up somewhat above their full-employment level. The theory predicts that involuntary (as well as frictional) unemployment rates will be higher for classes of workers who have lower job switching costs.

---

[18] This is especially true if detection is difficult (low q) so that an effective bond must be quite large. Even if workers could borrow to post the bond, so long as bankruptcy is possible, the incentives for avoiding defaulting on the bond are not different from the incentives to avoid being caught shirking by the firm in the absence of a bond. Note once again the importance of the wealth distribution in determining the nature of the equilibrium. If all individuals inherit a large amount of wealth, then they could post bonds.

[19] In competitive equilibrium, the average (discounted) value of the wage must be equal to the average (discounted) value of the marginal product of the worker. If there is a bonus for not shirking, *initially* the wage must be below the value of the marginal product. It is as if the worker were posting a bond (the difference between his marginal product and the wage), and as such this scheme is susceptible to precisely the same objections raised against posting performance bondings. The employer has an incentive to appropriate the bond. Since workers know this, this is not a viable incentive scheme. For a fine study in which firms' reputations are assumed to function so as to make this scheme viable, see Edward Lazear (1981).

C. Heterogeneous Workers

The strongest assumption we have made is that of identical workers. This assumption ruled out the possibility that firing a worker would carry any stigma. Such a stigma could serve as a discipline device, even with full employment.[20] In reality, of course, employers *do* make wage offers which are contingent on employment history. Such policies make sense when firms face problems of adverse selection.

We recognize that workers' concern about protecting their reputations as effective, diligent workers may provide an effective incentive for a disciplined labor force.[21] Shapiro's earlier (1983) analysis of reputation in product markets showed, however, that for reputations to be an effective incentive device, there must be a cost to the loss of reputation. It is our conjecture that, under plausible conditions, even when reputations are important, equilibrium will entail some use of unemployment as a discipline device for the labor force, at least for lower-quality workers. An important line of research is the study of labor markets in which adverse selection as well as moral hazard problems are present. In this context, our model should provide a useful complement to the more common studies of adverse selection in labor markets.

IV. Conclusions

This paper has explored the role of unemployment, or job rationing, as an incentive device. We have argued that when it is costly to monitor individuals, competitive equilibrium will be characterized by unemployment, but that the natural rate of unemployment so engendered will not in general be optimal. We have identified several forces at

---

[20] See Bruce Greenwald (1979) for a simple model in which those who are in the "used labor market" are in fact a lower quality than those in the "new" labor market.

[21] This suggests once again that our results may be most significant in labor markets for lower-quality workers: in such markets employment histories are utilized less and workers already labeled as below average in quality have less to lose from being labeled as such.

work, some which tend to make the market equilibrium unemployment rate too high, and others which tend to make it too small. Each firm fails to take into account the consequences of its actions on the level of monitoring and wages which other firms must undertake in order to avoid shirking by workers. Although these externalities are much like pecuniary externalities, they are important, even in economies with a large number of firms.[22] As a result, we have argued that there is scope for government interventions, both with respect to unemployment benefits and taxes or subsidies on monitoring and labor turnover, which can (if appropriately designed) lead to Pareto improvements.

The type of unemployment studied here is not the only or even the most important source of unemployment in practice. We believe it is, however, a significant factor in the observed level of unemployment, especially in lower-paid, lower-skilled, blue-collar occupations. It may well be more important than frictional or search unemployment in many labor markets.

---

[22] For a more general discussion of pecuniary, or more general market mediated externalities, with applications to economies with important adverse selection and moral hazard problems, see Greenwald and Stiglitz (1982).

REFERENCES

Alchian, Armen A. and Demsetz, Harold, "Production, Information Costs, and Economic Organization," *American Economic Review*, December 1972, *62*, 777–95.

Calvo, Guillermo A., "Quasi-Walrasian Theories of Unemployment," *American Economic Review Proceedings*, May 1979, *69*, 102–06.

_____, "On the Inefficiency of Unemployment," Columbia University, October 1981.

_____ and Wellisz, Stanislaw, "Hierarchy, Ability and Income Distribution," *Journal of Political Economy*, October 1979, *87*, 991–1010.

Diamond, Peter, "Mobility Costs, Frictional Unemployment, and Efficiency," *Journal* of *Political Economy*, August 1981, *89*, 798–812.

Greenwald, Bruce, C. N., *Adverse Selection in the Labor Market*, New York; London: Garland, 1979.

_____ and Stiglitz, Joseph E., "Pecuniary Externalities," unpublished, Princeton University, 1982.

Lazear, Edward P., "Agency, Earnings Profiles, Productivity, and Hours Restrictions," *American Economic Review*, September 1981, *71*, 606–20.

Salop, Steven C., "A Model of the Natural Rate of Unemployment," *American Economic Review*, March 1979, *69*, 117–25.

Shapiro, Carl, "Premiums for High Quality Products as Returns to Reputations," *Quarterly Journal of Economics*, November 1983, *98*, 658–79.

_____ and Stiglitz, Joseph E., "Equilibrium Unemployment as a Worker Discipline Device," Discussion Papers in Economics, No. 28, Woodrow Wilson School, Princeton University, April 1982.

Stiglitz, Joseph E., "Prices and Queues as Screening Devices in Competitive Markets," IMSSS Technical Report No. 212, Stanford University, 1976.

_____ and Weiss, Andrew, "Credit Rationing in Markets with Imperfect Information," *American Economic Review*, June 1981, *71*, 393–410.

Weiss, Andrew, "Job Queues and Layoffs in Labor Markets with Flexible Wages," *Journal of Political Economy*, June 1980, *88*, 526–38.

Wilson, Charles, "The Nature of Equilibrium in Markets with Adverse Selection," *Bell Journal of Economics*, Spring 1980, *11*, 108–30.

Name Index

The International Library of Critical Writings in Economics

34. The Economics of Transport (Volumes I and II)
   Herbert Mohring

35. Implicit Contract Theory
   Sherwin Rosen

36. Foundations of Analytical Marxism (Volumes I and II)
   John E. Roemer

37. The Economics of Product Differentiation (Volumes I and II)
   Jacques-François Thisse and George Norman

Future titles will include:

Recent Developments in the Economics of Education
Geraint Johnes and Elchanan Cohn

Markets and Socialism
Alec Nove and Ian Thatcher

Economics and Discrimination
William A. Darity, Jr

Economic Growth in Theory and Practice: A Kaldorian Perspective
John E. King

The Theory of Inflation
Michael Parkin

The Economics of Information
David K. Levine and Steven A. Lippman

Financial Intermediaries
M.K. Lewis

The Political Economy of Privatization and Deregulation
Elizabeth E. Bailey and Janet Rothenberg Pack

Gender and Economics
Jane Humphries

The Economics of Location
Melvin L. Greenhut and George Norman

The Economics of Altruism
Stephano Zamagni

Economics and Biology
Geoffrey M. Hodgson

Fiscal and Monetary Policy
Thomas Mayer and Stephen Sheffrin

General Equilibrium Theory
Gerard Debreu

International Trade
J. Peter Neary

The Foundations of Public Finance
Peter Jackson

Labor Economics
Orley C. Ashenfelter and Kevin F. Hallock

International Finance
Robert Z. Aliber

Welfare Economics
William J. Baumol and Janusz A. Ordover

Agricultural Economics
G.H. Peters

The Theory of the Firm
Mark Casson

The Economics of Inequality and Poverty
A.B. Atkinson

Business Cycle Theory
Finn E. Kydland

The Economics of Housing
John M. Quigley

Population Economics
Julian L. Simon

The Economics of Crime
Isaac Ehrlich

The Economics of Integration
Willem Molle

The Rhetoric of Economics
Donald McCloskey

Ethics and Economics
Amitai Etzioni

Migration
Oded Stark

The Economics of Ageing
John Creedy

Economic Forecasting
Paul Ormerod

Macroeconomics and Imperfect Competition
Jean-Pascal Benassy

The Economics of Training
Robert J. LaLonde

The Economics of Defence
Keith Hartley and Nicholas Hooper

Transaction Cost Economics
Oliver Williamson

Long Wave Theory
Christopher Freeman

Consumer Theory
Kelvin Lancaster

Law and Economics
Judge Richard A. Posner

The Economics of Business Policy
John Kay

International Debt
Graham Bird and P.N. Snowdon

Rent Seeking
Robert D. Tollison

The Role of Money in the Economy
Marco Musella and Carlo Panico

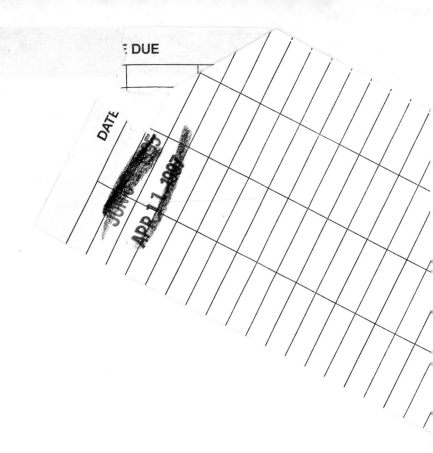